T0192021

Lecture Notes in Computer Science 13641

More information about this series at https://link.springer.com/bookseries/558

Alastair R. Beresford · Arpita Patra ·
Emanuele Bellini (Eds.)

Cryptology and Network Security

21st International Conference, CANS 2022
Abu Dhabi, United Arab Emirates, November 13–16, 2022
Proceedings

Editors
Alastair R. Beresford
University of Cambridge
Cambridge, UK

Arpita Patra
Indian Institute of Science
Bangalore, India

Emanuele Bellini
Cryptography Research Center
Technology Innovation Institute
Abu Dhabi, United Arab Emirates

ISSN 0302-9743 ISSN 1611-3349 (electronic)
Lecture Notes in Computer Science
ISBN 978-3-031-20973-4 ISBN 978-3-031-20974-1 (eBook)
https://doi.org/10.1007/978-3-031-20974-1

This Springer imprint is published by the registered company Springer Nature Switzerland AG
The registered company address is: Gewerbestrasse 11, 6330 Cham, Switzerland

Preface

The 21st International Conference on Cryptology and Network Security (CANS 2022) was held in Abu Dhabi during November 13–16, 2022.

CANS is an established annual conference presenting novel research work on cryptology, computer and network security, data security and privacy. Previous editions of CANS were held in Taipei (2001), San Francisco (2002), Miami (2003), Xiamen (2005), Suzhou (2006), Singapore (2007), Hong Kong (2008), Kanazawa (2009), Kuala Lumpur (2010), Sanya (2011), Darmstadt (2012), Parary (2013), Crete (2014), Marrakesh (2015), Milan (2016), Hong Kong (2017), Naples (2018), Fuzhou (2019) and virtually due to COVID-19 (2020, 2021).

In 2022 we received 54 submissions, out of which 18 full papers and two short papers were accepted for publication. We used a double-blind review process with three reviews per submission. The Program Committee chairs handled conflicts and used written reviews as well as online discussion with the reviewers to select the papers included in these proceedings. All authors were given the opportunity to revise their papers in response to reviewer feedback; a few papers were assigned a member of the Program Committee as a shepherd to support this process.

We would like to thank the Technology Innovation Institute (TII) for their support during the planning and running of the conference as well as Springer for their assistance in the production of the proceedings. We are extremely grateful to all the authors of the submitted papers as well as the 45 Program Committee members and 23 external reviewers for their care and dedication. Finally, we would like to thank the steering committee and organizing committee for their support and encouragement.

September 2022

Alastair R. Beresford
Arpita Patra
Emanuele Bellini

Organization

General Chair

Emanuele Bellini	Technology Innovation Institute, UAE

Program Committee Chairs

Alastair R. Beresford	University of Cambridge, UK
Arpita Patra	Indian Institute of Science Bangalore, India

Steering Committee

Yvo G. Desmedt (Chair)	University of Texas at Dallas, USA
Juan A. Garay	Texas A&M University, USA
Yi Mu	Fujian Normal University, China
Panos Papadimitratos	KTH Royal Institute of Technology, Sweden
David Pointcheval	CNRS and ENS Paris, France
Huaxiong Wang	Nanyang Technological University, Singapore

Organizing Committee

Emanuele Bellini	Technology Innovation Institute, UAE
Ana Castillo	Technology Innovation Institute, UAE

Program Committee

Cristina Alcaraz	University of Malaga, Spain
Subhadeep Banik	École Polytechnique Fédérale de Lausanne (EPFL), Switzerland
Emanuele Bellini	Technology Innovation Institute, UAE
Arka Rai Choudhury	University of California, Berkeley, USA
Sherman Chow	Chinese University of Hong Kong, Hong Kong
Sandro Coretti-Drayton	Input Output Hong Kong (IOHK), Switzerland
Bernardo David	IT University of Copenhagen (ITU), Denmark
F. Betül Durak	Microsoft Research, USA
Pooya Farshim	Durham University, UK
Chaya Ganesh	Indian Institute of Science Bangalore, India
Satrajit Ghosh	IIT Kharagpur, India

Ariel Hamlin	MIT Lincoln Laboratory, USA
Panagiotis Ilia	University of Illinois, USA
Tetsu Iwata	Nagoya University, Japan
Ashwin Jha	CISPA Helmholtz Center for Information Security, Germany
Martin Kleppmann	University of Cambridge, UK
Ivan Martionvic	University of Oxford, UK
René Mayrhofer	Johannes Kepler University Linz, Austria
Veelasha Moonsamy	Ruhr University Bochum, Germany
Mridul Nandi	Indian Statistical Institute, India
Guevara Noubir	Northeastern University, USA
Emmanuela Orsini	Katholieke Universiteit (KU) Leuven, Belgium
Sergio Pastrana	Universidad Carlos III de Madrid, Spain
Sikhar Patranabis	IBM Research India, India
Constantinos Patsakis	University of Piraeus, Greece
Somitra Sanadhya	IIT Jodhpur, India
Dominique Schroder	University of Erlangen-Nuremberg, Germany
Mridula Singh	CISPA Helmholtz Center for Information Security, Germany
Alberto Sonnino	Mysten Labs, UK
Angelo Spognardi	Sapienza Università di Roma, Italy
Christoph Striecks	AIT Austrian Institute of Technology, Austria
Ajith Suresh	Technische Universität Darmstadt, Germany
Willy Susilo	University of Wollongong, Australia
Daniel Tschudi	Concordium, Switzerland
Giorgos Vasiliadis	FORTH and Hellenic Mediterranean University, Greece
Damien Vergnaud	LIP6, Sorbonne Université, France
João Vilela	University of Porto, Portugal
Corrado Aaron Visaggio	University of Sannio, Italy
Isabel Wagner	De Montfort University, UK
Huaxiong Wang	Nanyang Technological University, Singapore
Edgar Weippl	University of Vienna, Austria
Xingliang Yuan	Monash University, Australia
Zhenfei Zhang	Ethereum Foundation, USA

Additional Reviewers

Navid Alamati
Khashayar Barooti
Suvradip Chakraborty
Gwangbae Choi
Daniel Collins
Mariana Cunha
Avijit Dutta
Loïs Huguenin-Dumittan
Amit Jana
Matthias J. Kannwischer

Shangqi Lai
Benjamin Lipp
Omid Mir
Munkenyi Mukhandi
Rahul Rachuri
Gerald Schoiber
Karl Southern
Erkan Tairi
Serge Vaudenay
Dabao Wang
Harry W. H. Wong
Bang Wu
Huangting Wu

Contents

Zero-Knowledge and MPC

Efficient NIZK Arguments with Straight-Line Simulation and Extraction 3
Michele Ciampi and Ivan Visconti

Updatable NIZKs from Non-Interactive Zaps 23
Karim Baghery and Navid Ghaedi Bardeh

Through the Looking-Glass: Benchmarking Secure Multi-party Computation Comparisons for ReLU 's 44
Abdelrahaman Aly, Kashif Nawaz, Eugenio Salazar, and Victor Sucasas

Public-Key Infrastructure

Oh SSH-it, What's My Fingerprint? A Large-Scale Analysis of SSH Host Key Fingerprint Verification Records in the DNS 71
Sebastian Neef and Nils Wisiol

Attribute-Based Anonymous Credential: Optimization for Single-Use and Multi-Use 89
Kwan Yin Chan and Tsz Hon Yuen

Auditable Asymmetric Password Authenticated Public Key Establishment 122
Antonio Faonio, Maria Isabel Gonzalez Vasco, Claudio Soriente, and Hien Thi Thu Truong

(Augmented) Broadcast Encryption from Identity Based Encryption with Wildcard 143
Anaïs Barthoulot, Olivier Blazy, and Sébastien Canard

Attacks and Countermeasures

Passive Triangulation Attack on ORide 167
Shyam Murthy and Srinivas Vivek

HyperDetector: Detecting, Isolating, and Mitigating Timing Attacks in Virtualized Environments 188
Musa Sadik Unal, Arsalan Javeed, Cemal Yilmaz, and Erkay Savas

Cryptanalysis and Provable Security

The Construction and Application of (Related-Key) Conditional Differential Neural Distinguishers on KATAN 203
Dongdong Lin, Shaozhen Chen, Manman Li, and Zezhou Hou

How to Design Authenticated Key Exchange for Wearable Devices: Cryptanalysis of AKE for Health Monitoring and Countermeasures via Distinct SMs with Key Split and Refresh 225
Łukasz Krzywiecki and Hannes Salin

Cryptanalysis of the Multi-Power RSA Cryptosystem Variant 245
Didier Alquié, Guy Chassé, and Abderrahmane Nitaj

Provable Security of HADES Structure 258
Yuan Gao and Chun Guo

Cryptographic Protocols

Practical Single-Pass Oblivious Aggregation and Billing Computation Protocols for Smart Meters 279
Kalikinkar Mandal

Anonymous Random Allocation and Its Applications 292
Azam Soleimanian

ACDC: Anonymous Crowdsourcing Using Digital Cash 314
Luis A. Saavedra and Alastair R. Beresford

Blockchain and Payment Systems

Analyzing Price Deviations in DeFi Oracles 329
Ankit Gangwal, Rahul Valluri, and Mauro Conti

Redacting Blockchain Without Exposing Chameleon Hash Collisions 339
Thiago Leucz Astrizi and Ricardo Custódio

Codes and Post-quantum Cryptography

Efficient Proofs of Retrievability Using Expander Codes 361
Françoise Levy-dit-Vehel and Maxime Roméas

Post-Quantum Electronic Identity: Adapting OpenID Connect and OAuth 2.0 to the Post-Quantum Era 371
Frederico Schardong, Alexandre Augusto Giron, Fernanda Larisa Müller, and Ricardo Custódio

Author Index 391

Zero-Knowledge and MPC

Efficient NIZK Arguments with Straight-Line Simulation and Extraction

Michele Ciampi[1(✉)] and Ivan Visconti[2]

[1] The University of Edinburgh, Edinburgh, UK
michele.ciampi@ed.ac.uk
[2] University of Salerno, Salerno, Italy
visconti@unisa.it

Abstract. Non-interactive zero-knowledge (NIZK) arguments allow a prover to convince a verifier about the truthfulness of an $\mathcal{NP}$-statement by sending just one message, without disclosing any additional information. In several practical scenarios, the Fiat-Shamir transform is used to convert an *efficient* constant-round public-coin honest-verifier zero-knowledge proof system into an efficient NIZK argument system. This approach is provably secure in the random oracle model, crucially requires the programmability of the random oracle and extraction works through rewinds. The works of Lindell [TCC 2015] and Ciampi et al. [TCC 2016] proposed efficient NIZK arguments with non-programmable random oracles along with a programmable common reference string.

In this work we show an efficient NIZK argument with straight-line simulation and extraction that relies on features that alone are insufficient to construct NIZK arguments (regardless of efficiency). More specifically we consider the notion of quasi-polynomial time simulation proposed by Pass in [EUROCRYPT 2003] and combine it with simulation and extraction with non-programmable random oracles thus obtaining a NIZK argument of knowledge where neither the zero-knowledge simulator, nor the argument of knowledge extractor needs to program the random oracle. Still, both the simulator and the extractor are straight-line. Our construction uses as a building block a modification of the Fischlin's transform [CRYPTO 2005] and combines it with the concept of dense puzzles introduced by Baldimtsi et al. [ASIACRYPT 2016]. We also argue that our NIZK argument system inherits the efficiency features of Fischlin's transform, which represents the main advantage of Fischlin's protocol over existing schemes.

Research partly supported by H2020 project PRIVILEDGE #780477.

A. R. Beresford et al. (Eds.): CANS 2022, LNCS 13641, pp. 3–22, 2022.
https://doi.org/10.1007/978-3-031-20974-1_1

1 Introduction

A proof system allows an entity, called prover, to convince another entity, called verifier, about the truthfulness of a claim. Informally, a proof[1] system is *zero-knowledge* (ZK) [17] if the prover holds a secret that is required to successfully convince the verifier and moreover the proof does not disclose any information about the secret. In the *non-interactive* scenario only the prover can speak and sends just one message. This kind of proofs, introduced in [6], are called *Non-Interactive Zero-Knowledge (NIZK)* proofs. Since it is impossible to construct a NIZK proof for non-trivial languages without setup assumptions, Blum et al. [6] proposed the *Common Reference String* (CRS) model. In the CRS model there exists a trusted string (the exact shape of the CRS depends on the specific NIZK proof instantiation) that is given as input to both the prover and the verifier.

In [13] the authors show NIZK proofs in the CRS model for any $\mathcal{NP}$-language in a setting where the same CRS can be reused to generate multiple proofs. Even though NIZK proofs exist for all $\mathcal{NP}$, the candidate constructions are rather inefficient due to the $\mathcal{NP}$-reduction that needs to be performed before computing the actual NIZK proof. One of the most used approaches to obtain efficient NIZK proofs consists in starting with an efficient interactive constant-round public-coin honest-verifier zero-knowledge (HVZK) proof system and making it non-interactive by replacing the role of the verifier with a hash function modelled as a random oracle [5] (RO). In particular, the hash function takes as input the transcript computed so far and returns the message on the behalf of a verifier. This approach is the so-called *Fiat-Shamir (FS) transform* [14]. To prove the security of such a transform, the ZK simulator needs to program the RO (i.e., the simulator decides how the RO answers the queries). Similarly, the argument of knowledge property requires an extractor that programs the random oracle. Exploiting the programmability of the random oracle makes it difficult to prove the composability of the argument system in a setting where multiple instantiations of it are run in concurrency. The work of Canetti et al. [8], for example, considers the natural scenario where multiple instantiations of different cryptographic protocols use the same random oracle without programming it. In general, in order to avoid such issues it is preferrable to avoid simulators that need to program the random oracle.

Lindell in [20] provides a NIZK argument that can be proven secure assuming the existence of a non-programmable random-oracle (NPRO) and a programmable CRS. In more detail, the ZK of Lindell's protocol is proved without relying on the RO at all (though, the CRS needs to be programmed), and the soundness is proved *without* programming the RO. In a follow-up work [10], the authors improve the construction of Lindell in terms of efficiency and generality under the same setup considered in [20]. A different approach towards round-efficient ZK arguments consists in allowing the simulator to run in quasi-

[1] When discussing informally we will use the word proof to refer to both unconditionally and computationally sound proofs. Only in the more formal part of the paper we will make a distinction between arguments and proofs.

polynomial time instead of expected polynomial time [23]. This notion implies that a malicious verifier can learn from the prover anything that can be learned by a quasi-polynomial time algorithm. As observed in [3], the simulator is usually not run by parties running the NIZK argument, and thus quasi-polynomial simulation can still be useful in various applications. In [25] it is shown that two rounds are necessary and sufficient for quasi-polynomial time simulatable arguments. Therefore, even though the notion of ZK with quasi-polynomial time simulation allows to overcome some of the impossibility results of standard ZK, the impossibility of constructing NIZK arguments holds also in this less demanding model.

Given the impossibility shown in [25] of obtaining NIZK arguments with quasi-polynomial simulation, and the obvious impossibility of obtaining NIZK arguments without setup assumptions in the non-programmable RO (NPRO) model, we focus on the following relevant question:

> *Is it possible to construct an efficient NIZK argument of knowledge with quasi-polynomial time simulation where neither the zero-knowledge simulator nor the argument of knowledge extractor needs to program the random oracle?*

In this work we answer affirmatively to this question assuming that dense cryptographic puzzles exist. In more detail, our protocol is proved to enjoy *perfect* concurrent zero knowledge (ZK) via quasi-polynomial simulation and is moreover an argument of knowledge (AoK) with online extraction (i.e., the extraction process does not rewind the prover). Interestingly, even though we prove the ZK property using quasi-polynomial simulation, the security of our NIZK argument does not rely on any complexity-leveraging-type assumptions (i.e., we do not require hardness assumptions to hold against superpolynomial-time adversaries).

Our Techniques. We start with the work of Fischlin [15] that presents a NIZK AoK with an online extractor starting with a Σ-protocol (i.e., a 3-round public-coin proof system enjoying a special notion of soundness and a special notion of HVZK). In more detail, Fischlin's protocol is proved ZK by exploiting the programmability of the random oracle (RO), whereas the soundness is proved by relying just on the *observability* of the RO (i.e., the online extractor has only access to the queries made by the adversary to the RO). The aim of our work is to circumvent the need to program the RO by using quasi-polynomial time simulation (i.e., we allow the ZK simulator to run in quasi-polynomial time).

We present our construction in an incremental way. We first show that the modified version of Fischlin's protocol proposed in [19] is witness indistinguishable (WI) with an on-line extractor that does not need to program the RO, therefore relying on a non-programmable RO (NPRO). Then we use it as the main building block together with dense cryptographic puzzles. Roughly speaking, a cryptographic puzzle is defined together with a hardness parameter g. So, if a randomly sampled puzzle is given to an adversary then she should not be able to find a solution with non-negligible probability in less than a number of steps that is function of g. We consider the notion of puzzle system proposed in [2], where the hardness of a puzzle holds as long as the puzzle is sampled from a uniformly random distribution. Baldimtsi et al. [2] also show how to instantiate such a puzzle from standard number-theoretic assumptions (e.g., the discrete logarithm (DL) problem) and from NPROs. In a nutshell, our NIZK argument combines a dense puzzle system PuzSys with a non-interactive WI argument of knowledge $\Pi^{\mathcal{WI}}$ as follows. The prover queries the random oracle with the statement x that he wants to prove, thus obtaining a puzzle puz. Then the prover computes a non-interactive WI (NIWI) proof where he proves knowledge of either the witness corresponding to the instance x or the solution of the puzzle. We observe that a malicious prover could fool the verifier by finding a solution to the puzzle and using it as a witness for the WI proof. To avoid this we just need to carefully choose the hardness factor of the puzzle in such a way that a malicious probabilistic polynomial-time prover cannot solve it, but a quasi-polynomial time simulator can. As discussed above, one of the main building blocks of our construction is $\Pi^{\mathcal{WI}}$. More precisely, $\Pi^{\mathcal{WI}}$ is an argument of knowledge with an online extractor in which the WI property holds against *all-powerful* adversaries. Equipped with this tool we can prove the security of our NIZK argument of knowledge without using complexity leveraging arguments. We show how to obtain $\Pi^{\mathcal{WI}}$ starting from any Σ-protocol Π, this yields to the following theorem.

Theorem (informal). *Let Π be a Σ-protocol for the $\mathcal{NP}$ relation* Rel. *Assuming the hardness of the discrete logarithm problem then there exists an efficient NIZK AoK with online extraction and straight-line (perfect) quasi-polynomial time simulation for* Rel *where neither the simulator nor the AoK extractor needs to program the RO.*

We stress that our construction has a ZK straight-line simulator and an online AoK simulator. This yields a protocol that can be more easily composed concurrently with other cryptographic protocols[2]. Moreover, the construction that we propose is almost as efficient as Fischlin's construction and can be instantiated from a large class of Σ-protocols (even larger than the class considered in [15]) and cryptographic puzzles. Indeed, in [15], in order to prove the zero-knowledge property it is required that the first round of the underlying Σ-protocol has min-entropy that is superlogarithmic in the security parameter. In our approach, we do not need to rely on this additional requirement.

Related Work. As observed by Fischlin in [15], in the prior work of Pass [22] the author showed a NIZK AoK where the argument of knowledge extractor does not need to rewind the adversary. These are exactly the same security properties offered by the protocol of [15]. Moreover, in [22] the author shows

[2] Since our simulator does not run in expected polynomial time, it is not possible to prove results related to the Universal Composable (UC) setting [7]. We observe that the property of our protocol of being concurrently composable is still meaningful as showed in [4] where general concurrent composition with superpolynomial-time computation is considered.

that the WI property can be obtained without the simulator programming the RO. The main improvement of Fischlin's construction (and ours) over Pass' protocol is in the size of the proof. Indeed, in [15] the author argues that even considering a modified[3] version Pass' protocol, for reasonable parameters the size of a single proof, requires between 10000 and 25000 bits. Therefore, with the goal of obtaining shorter proofs, in our work we study a variant of Fischlin's construction, instead of simply taking out from the box the NIWI protocol of [22]. For more details on the efficiency of our protocol, we refer the reader to Sect. 5.

We have already mentioned the recent work of Kondi et al. [19]. In this, the authors propose a modified version of Fischlin's construction (that we rely on). We extend the results of [19] showing that this modified version of Fischlin's protocol preserves WI and online extraction with a NPRO. The work of Kondi et al. [19] proposes also other results, based on Fischlin's paradigm, that improve the efficiency of Schnorr/EdDSA signature aggregation schemes.

2 Definitions and Tools

Preliminaries. We denote the security parameter by λ and for a finite set Q, $x \leftarrow Q$ the sampling of x from Q with uniform distribution. We use the abbreviation PPT that stays for probabilistic polynomial time. We use $\mathbb{N}$ to denote the set of natural numbers and $\mathsf{poly}(\cdot)$ to indicate a generic polynomial function. A *polynomial-time $\mathcal{NP}$-relation* Rel (or *$\mathcal{NP}$-relation*, in short) is a subset of $\{0,1\}^* \times \{0,1\}^*$ such that membership of (x, w) in Rel can be decided in time polynomial in $|x|$. For $(x, w) \in \mathsf{Rel}$, we call x the *instance* and w a *witness* for x. For a polynomial-time relation Rel, we define the $\mathcal{NP}$-language L_{Rel} as $L_{\mathsf{Rel}} = \{x | \exists\ w : (x, w) \in \mathsf{Rel}\}$. Analogously, unless otherwise specified, for an $\mathcal{NP}$-language L we denote by $\mathsf{Rel}_{\mathsf{L}}$ the corresponding polynomial-time relation (that is, $\mathsf{Rel}_{\mathsf{L}}$ is such that $L = L_{\mathsf{Rel}_{\mathsf{L}}}$). We define $\hat{L}$ to be the input language that includes both the NP-language L and all well-formed instances that do not have a witness. Let A and B be two interactive probabilistic algorithms. We denote by $\langle A(\alpha), B(\beta)\rangle(\gamma)$ the distribution of B's output after running on private input β with A using private input α, both running on common input γ. A *transcript* of $\langle A(\alpha), B(\beta)\rangle(\gamma)$ consists of the messages exchanged during an execution where A receives a private input α, B receives a private input β and both A and B receive a common input γ. Moreover, we will refer to the *view* of A (resp. B) as the messages it received during the execution of $\langle A(\alpha), B(\beta)\rangle(\gamma)$, along with its randomness and its input. A function $\nu(\cdot)$ from non-negative integers to reals is called negligible, if for every constant $c > 0$ and all sufficiently large $\lambda \in \mathbb{N}$ we have $\nu(\lambda) < \lambda^{-c}$.

[3] The original Pass' protocol is particularly inefficient due to the number of parallel repetitions required to amplify the soundness. In [15] the author considers an improved version, that uses Merkle trees to reduce the size of the proof. We refer to the introductory section of [15] for more details.

2.1 Argument Systems

Here we recall the notions of completeness and online extraction provided in [15]. A pair $\Pi = (\mathcal{P}, \mathcal{V})$ of probabilistic polynomial-time algorithms is called a non-interactive argument of knowledge for the $\mathcal{NP}$-relation $\mathsf{Rel_L}$ with an online extractor (in the non-programmable random oracle model) if the following holds.

Completeness. For any non-programmable random oracle $\mathcal{O}$, any $(x, w) \in \mathsf{Rel_L}$ and any $\pi \leftarrow \mathcal{P}^{\mathcal{O}}(x, w)$ we have $\text{Prob}\left[\ \mathcal{V}^{\mathcal{O}}(x, \pi) = 1\ \right] = 1 - \nu(|x|)$, for some negligible function ν.

Argument of Knowledge with Online Extractor. There exist a probabilistic polynomial-time algorithm Ext called *AoK online extractor* such that for any PPT adversary $\mathcal{A}^{\mathcal{O}}$ there exists a negligible function ν such that the following holds: $\text{Prob}\left[\ (x, w) \notin \mathsf{Rel} \text{ and } \mathcal{V}^{\mathcal{O}}(x, \pi) = 1\ \right] \leq \nu(\lambda)$, where $(x, \pi) \leftarrow \mathcal{A}^{\mathcal{O}}(\lambda)$ (where x is the theorem and π is the proof generated by the adversary), $w \leftarrow \mathsf{Ext}(x, \pi, \mathcal{Q}_{\mathcal{O}}(\mathcal{A}))$ and $\mathcal{Q}_{\mathcal{O}}(\mathcal{A})$ represents the sequence of queries/answers for the oracle $\mathcal{O}$. Not to overburden the descriptions of protocols and simulators, we omit to specify that the parties have access to the NPRO $\mathcal{O}$ whenever it is clear from the context.

Quasi-polynomial Time Simulation. Since the verifier in an interactive argument is often modeled as a PPT machine, the classical zero-knowledge definition requires that the simulator runs also in (expected) polynomial time. In [23], the simulator is allowed to run in time $\lambda^{\mathtt{poly}(\mathtt{log}(\lambda))}$. Loosely speaking, we say that an interactive argument is $\lambda^{\mathtt{poly}(\mathtt{log}(\lambda))}$-perfectly simulatable if for any adversarial verifier there exists a simulator running in time $\lambda^{\mathtt{poly}(\mathtt{log}(\lambda))}$, where λ is the size of the statement being proved, whose output is identically distributed to the output of the adversarial verifier.

Definition 1 (straight-line $T(\lambda)$ simulatability, Def. 31 of [24]). *Let $T(\lambda)$ be a class of functions that is closed under composition with any polynomial. We say that an interactive argument $(\mathcal{P}, \mathcal{V})$ for the language $L \in \mathcal{NP}$, with the witness relation* $\mathsf{Rel_L}$, *is* straight-line $T(\lambda)$-simulatable *if for every* PPT *machine $\mathcal{V}^\star$ there exists a probabilistic simulator S with running time bounded by $T(\lambda)$ such that the following two ensembles are computationally indistinguishable*

- $\{(\langle \mathcal{P}(w), \mathcal{V}^\star(z) \rangle (x))\}_{z \in \{0,1\}^*, x \in L}$ *for arbitrary w s.t.* $(x, w) \in \mathsf{Rel_L}$
- $\{(\langle S, \mathcal{V}^\star(z) \rangle (x))\}_{z \in \{0,1\}^*, x \in L}$

The following theorem shows the power of straight-line $\lambda^{\mathtt{poly}(\mathtt{log}(\lambda))}$-perfect simulatability by connecting it to concurrent composition of arguments.

Theorem 1 ([24]). *If an argument system $\Pi = (\mathcal{P}, \mathcal{V})$ is straight-line $\lambda^{\mathtt{poly}(\mathtt{log}(\lambda))}$-simulatable then it is also straight-line concurrent $\lambda^{\mathtt{poly}(\mathtt{log}(\lambda))}$-simulatable.*

We also consider the notion of *perfect straight-line simulation.* This is equal to the Definition 1 with the difference that the malicious distinguisher can be unbounded instead of being PPT and that the two ensembles (the simulated execution and the real execution) are identically distributed (see Definition 30 of [24]).

2.2 Cryptographic Puzzles

In [2] the authors introduce a new class of protocols with prover and verifier called Proof of Work or Knowledge (PoWorK). To formalize PoWorK, the authors give the notion of *puzzle system.* A puzzle system PuzSys is a tuple of algorithms $\mathsf{PuzSys} = (\mathsf{Sample}, \mathsf{Solve}, \mathsf{Verify})$ that are defined in the following way. Sample on input the security parameter 1^λ and the hardness factor h outputs a puzzle puz; Solve on input the security parameter 1^λ, a hardness factor h and a puzzle instance puz outputs a potential solution $\mathtt{sol}$; Verify on input the security parameter 1^λ, a hardness factor h, a puzzle instance puz, and a potential solution $\mathtt{sol}$ outputs 0 or 1. Moreover, while the algorithms Sample and Verify are efficient, it is difficult to compute a solution for a sampled puzzle. More precisely, a puzzle system is g-hard if no adversary can solve the puzzle in less than $g(\cdot)$ steps with more than negligible probability. The authors of [2] propose also a stronger notion of puzzles that enjoys the property of *dense samplability.* That is, the puzzles can be sampled by just generating random strings (i.e., the puzzle instances should be dense over $\{0,1\}^{\ell(h,\lambda)}$) for a polynomial ℓ. We consider the same notion of puzzle system with dense samplability of [2]. We remark that the notion of dense samplable puzzles considered in [2] is equipped with an additional efficient algorithm that generates a puzzle together with its solution, but we do not need this additional requirement in our work. We denote the puzzle space as $\mathcal{PS}_\lambda$, the solution space as $\mathcal{SS}_\lambda$, and the hardness space as $\mathcal{HS}_\lambda$.

Definition 2. *A Dense Samplable Puzzle (DSP) system* $\mathsf{PuzSys} = (\mathsf{Sample}, \mathsf{Solve}, \mathsf{Verify})$ *enjoys the following properties, denoting with* ν *a negligible function.*

Completeness. *A puzzle system* PuzSys *is complete, if for every* h *in the hardness space* $\mathcal{HS}_\lambda$*:*

$\text{Prob}\left[\,\mathsf{puz} \leftarrow \mathsf{Sample}(1^\lambda, h), \mathtt{sol} \leftarrow \mathsf{Solve}(1^\lambda, h, \mathsf{puz}) : \mathsf{Verify}(1^\lambda, h, \mathsf{puz}, \mathtt{sol}) = 0\,\right] \le \nu(\lambda)$.

The number of steps that Solve *takes to run is monotonically increasing in the hardness factor* h *and may exponentially depend on* λ*, while* Verify *and* Sample *run in time polynomial in* λ.

g-Hardness. *Let* $\mathsf{Steps}_B(\cdot)$ *be the number of steps (i.e., machine/operation cycles) executed by algorithm* B*. We say that a puzzle system* PuzSys *is* g*-hard for some function* g*, if for every adversary* $\mathcal{A}$ *there exists a negligible function* ν *such that for every auxiliary tape* $z \in \{0,1\}^*$ *and for every* $h \in \mathcal{HS}_\lambda$ *the following holds:*

$$\begin{aligned}\text{Prob}[&\mathsf{puz} \leftarrow \mathsf{Sample}(1^\lambda, h), \mathtt{sol} \leftarrow \mathcal{A}(1^\lambda, z, \mathsf{puz}) : \mathsf{Verify}(1^\lambda, h, \mathsf{puz}, \mathtt{sol}) = 1 \,\wedge \\ &\mathsf{Steps}_\mathcal{A}(1^\lambda, z, h, \mathsf{puz}) \le g(\mathsf{Steps}_{\mathsf{Solve}}(1^\lambda, h, \mathsf{puz}))] \le \nu(\lambda).\end{aligned}$$

Dense Puzzles. *Given* $\lambda, h \in \mathbb{Z}^+$ *and a polynomial function* ℓ*, there exists a negligible function* ν *such that* $\Delta[\mathsf{Sample}(1^\lambda, h), \mathsf{U}_{\ell(\lambda,h)})] \le \nu(\lambda)$ *where* $\mathsf{U}_{\ell(\lambda,h)}$ *stands for the uniform distribution over* $\{0,1\}^{\ell(\lambda,h)}$.

We observe that the properties of density and g-hardness imply that for every adversary $\mathcal{A}$, there exists a negligible function ν such that for every auxiliary tape $z \in \{0,1\}^\star$ and for every $h \in \mathcal{HS}_\lambda$ the following holds:

$$\text{Prob}[\texttt{sol} \leftarrow \mathcal{A}(1^\lambda, z, \eta) : \eta \leftarrow \{0,1\}^{\ell(\lambda,h)} \wedge \mathsf{Verify}(1^\lambda, h, \eta, \texttt{sol}) = 1 \wedge \mathsf{Steps}_{\mathcal{A}}(1^\lambda, z, h, \eta) \leq g(\mathsf{Steps}_{\mathsf{Solve}}(1^\lambda, h, \eta))] \leq \nu(\lambda).$$

Puzzles from the DL Assumption. In [1,2] the authors show how to construct puzzles assuming the hardness of the discrete logarithm (DL) problem. In particular, at the end of [1, p. 37] the authors argue that it is possible to obtain a puzzle by randomly sampling an instance of the DL problem. The solution to this puzzle is simply the DL of the instance. This puzzle moreover has the following properties. For every hardness factor $h \in \mathcal{HS}_\lambda$ there exists a negligible function ν such:

1. $\text{Prob}\left[\, \mathsf{puz} \leftarrow \mathsf{Sample}(1^\lambda, h) : g(\mathsf{Steps}_{\mathsf{Solve}}(1^\lambda, h, \mathsf{puz})) \leq \lambda^{\log \lambda} \,\right] \leq \nu(\lambda)$;
2. the worst-case running time of $\mathsf{Solve}(1^\lambda, h, \cdot)$ is $\lambda^{\mathsf{poly}(\log \lambda)}$.

For our NIZK argument of knowledge we need a puzzle that has exactly these hardness parameters. The nice feature of the construction based on DL proposed in [1, p. 37] is that it admits an efficient Σ-protocol. That is, a prover can prove the knowledge of the solution of a puzzle y by simply running the Schnorr protocol. When providing an efficiency analysis of our protocol we will use this puzzle instantiation.

Witness Indistinguishability. To formalize the notion of WI we consider a game $\mathsf{ExpAWI}^b_{\Pi,\mathcal{A}}$ between a challenger $\mathcal{C}$ and an adversary $\mathcal{A}$ in which the instance x and two witnesses w_0 and w_1 for x are chosen by $\mathcal{A}$. The challenger, upon receiving (x, w_0, w_1) starts interacting with $\mathcal{A}$ accordingly to the prover procedure of Π using w_b as a witness. The adversary wins the game if she can guess which of the two witnesses was used by the challenger. We now formally define the WI experiment $\mathsf{ExpAWI}^b_{\Pi,\mathcal{A}}(\lambda, \zeta)$ that is parameterized by a protocol $\Pi = (\mathcal{P}, \mathcal{V})$ for an $\mathcal{NP}$-relation Rel and by a PPT adversary $\mathcal{A}$. We denote with $\mathcal{A}^b_{\mathsf{ExpAWI}}$ the view of $\mathcal{A}$ in the experiment $\mathsf{ExpAWI}^b_{\Pi,\mathcal{A}}(\lambda, \zeta)$. The experiment has as input the security parameter λ and auxiliary information ζ for $\mathcal{A}$.

$\mathsf{ExpAWI}^b_{\Pi,\mathcal{A}}(\lambda, \zeta)$:

1. $\mathcal{A}$ picks an instance x, witnesses w_0 and w_1 such that $(x, w_0), (x, w_1) \in \mathsf{Rel}$, and sends (x, w_0, w_1) to a challenger $\mathcal{C}$.
2. $\mathcal{C}$ interacts with $\mathcal{A}$ as $\mathcal{P}$ would do using the witness w_b.

Definition 3 (Witness Indistinguishability). *An argument system Π is* WI *if for every distinguisher $\mathcal{D}$, there exists a negligible function ν such that for any $\zeta \in \{0,1\}^*$ it holds that*

$$\left|\text{Prob}\left[\, \mathcal{D}(\lambda, \zeta, \mathcal{A}^0_{\mathsf{ExpAWI}}) = 1 \,\right] - \text{Prob}\left[\, \mathcal{D}(\lambda, \zeta, \mathcal{A}^1_{\mathsf{ExpAWI}}) = 1 \,\right]\right| \leq \nu(\lambda).$$

We also consider the notion of *perfect* WI where $\mathcal{A}$ it is not restricted to be PPT and $\nu(\lambda) = 0$.

Σ-Protocols A Σ-protocol $\Pi = (\mathcal{P}, \mathcal{V})$ is a 3-round public-coin protocol. An execution of Π proceeds with the following 3 moves:

1. $\mathcal{P}$ computes the first message using as input the instance to be proved x with the corresponding witness w, and outputs the first message a with an auxiliary information aux (we denote this action with $(a, \mathsf{aux}) \leftarrow \mathcal{P}(x, w)$).
2. $\mathcal{V}$ upon receiving a, computes and sends a random $c \leftarrow \{0,1\}^l$ with $l \in \mathbb{N}$.
3. $\mathcal{P}$ on input c and aux computes and sends z to $\mathcal{V}$ (we denote this action with $z \leftarrow \mathcal{P}(\mathsf{aux}, c)$).
4. $\mathcal{V}$, on input (x, a, c, z) outputs 1 to accept, 0 to reject (we denote this action with $\mathcal{V}(x, a, c, z) = b$ where $b \in \{0,1\}$ denotes whether $\mathcal{V}$ accepts or not).

Definition 4 (Σ-protocols [12]). *A 3-move protocol Π with challenge length $l \in \mathbb{N}$ is a* Σ-protocol *for a relation* Rel *if it enjoys the following properties:*

1. ***Completeness.*** *If $(x, w) \in \mathsf{Rel}$ then all honest 3-move transcripts for (x, w) are accepting.*
2. ***Special Soundness.*** *There exists an efficient algorithm* $\mathsf{Extract}$ *that, on input two accepting transcripts for x (a, c, z) and (a, c', z') with $c' \neq c$ outputs a witness w such that $(x, w) \in \mathsf{Rel}$.*
3. ***Special Honest-Verifier Zero Knowledge (SHVZK).*** *There exists a* PPT *simulator algorithm* Sim *that takes as input $x \in L_{\mathsf{Rel}}$, security parameter 1^λ and $c \in \{0,1\}^l$ and outputs an accepting transcript for x where c is the challenge (we denote this action with $(a, z) \leftarrow \mathsf{Sim}(x, c)$). Moreover, for all l-bit strings c, the distribution of the output of the simulator on input (x, c) is identical to the distribution of the 3-move honest transcript obtained when $\mathcal{V}$ sends c as challenge and $\mathcal{P}$ runs on common input x and any private input w such that $(x, w) \in \mathsf{Rel}$.*

Following [15] we require the Σ-protocols to have a *quasi-unique* third round, i.e., it should be infeasible to find another valid third round to a proof (a, c, z), even if one knows the witness. As noted in [15], this property holds for example if the third round z is uniquely determined by x, a, and c as for the protocols by Guillou-Quisquater [18] and Schnorr [26]. More in general, this property holds for the class of Σ-protocol for proving the knowledge of a preimage of a group homomorphism defined in [11,21]. A formalization of this property follows.

Definition 5. *A Σ-protocol $\Pi = (\mathcal{P}, \mathcal{V})$ has* quasi-unique third round *if there exists a negligible function ν such that for any (x, a, c, z, z')*

$$\text{Prob}\left[\ \mathcal{V}(x, a, c, z) = \mathcal{V}(x, a, c, z') = 1 \text{ and } z \neq z'\ \right] \leq \nu(\lambda).$$

2.3 Or-Composition of Σ-Protocols

In this section we recall the or-composition of Σ-protocols proposed in [12]. Let $\Pi_0 = (\mathcal{P}_0, \mathcal{V}_0)$ be a Σ-protocol for the $\mathcal{NP}$-relation Rel_0 and $\Pi_1 = (\mathcal{P}_1, \mathcal{V}_1)$ be a

Σ-protocol for the $\mathcal{NP}$-relation Rel_1. Moreover, let Sim_0 be the Special HVZK simulator for Π_0 and Sim_1 be the Special HVZK simulator for Π_1. We consider the following 3-round public coin protocol $\Pi^{\mathtt{OR}} = (\mathcal{P}^{\mathtt{OR}}, \mathcal{V}^{\mathtt{OR}})$ where $\mathcal{P}^{\mathtt{OR}}$ and $\mathcal{V}^{\mathtt{OR}}$ has a common input (x_0, x_1) where $x_0 \in \hat{L}_0$ and $x_1 \in \hat{L}_1$. $\mathcal{P}^{\mathtt{OR}}$ has a private input w_b with $b \in \{0,1\}$ and $(x_b, w_b) \in \mathsf{Rel}_b$.

1. $\mathcal{P}^{\mathtt{OR}}$ picks $c_{1-b} \leftarrow \{0,1\}^l$, computes $(a_{1-b}, z_{1-b}) \leftarrow \mathsf{Sim}_{1-b}(x_{1-b}, c_{1-b})$ with $l \in \mathbb{N}$, computes $(\mathsf{aux}, a_b) \leftarrow \mathcal{P}_b(x_b, w_b)$ and sends (a_0, a_1) to $\mathcal{V}^{\mathtt{OR}}$.
2. $\mathcal{V}^{\mathtt{OR}}$ upon receiving (a_0, a_1), computes and sends a random string $c \leftarrow \{0,1\}^l$.
3. $\mathcal{P}^{\mathtt{OR}}$, upon receiving c computes $c_b = c \oplus c_{1-b}$ and $z_b \leftarrow \mathcal{P}_b(\mathsf{aux}, c_b)$ and sends (c_0, z_0, c_1, z_1) to $\mathcal{V}^{\mathtt{OR}}$.
4. $\mathcal{V}^{\mathtt{OR}}$, upon receiving (z_0, z_1) checks if $\mathcal{V}_0(x_0, a_0, c_0, z_0) = 1$ and $\mathcal{V}_1(x_1, a_1, c_1, z_1) = 1$ and $c = c_0 \oplus c_1$. If it is, then $\mathcal{V}^{\mathtt{OR}}$ outputs 1, 0 otherwise.

Theorem 2 ([12,16])**.** *Let Π_0 be a Σ-protocol for the $\mathcal{NP}$-relation Rel_0 and Π_1 be a Σ-protocol for the $\mathcal{NP}$-relation Rel_1 then $\Pi^{\mathtt{OR}}$ is a Σ-protocol that is perfect WI for relation $\mathsf{Rel}_{\mathtt{OR}} = \{((x_0, x_1), w) : ((x_0, w) \in \mathsf{Rel}_{L_0}) \vee ((x_1, w) \in \mathsf{Rel}_{L_1})\}$.*

We recall the above theorem just for completeness even though in this work we use $\Pi^{\mathtt{OR}}$ in a non-blackbox way and we do not rely on its WI property directly. We just find convenient to use the prover and the verifier of $\Pi^{\mathtt{OR}}$ to shorten and make more clear the description of the protocols proposed in this work. Only in the security proof we make non-black box use of $\Pi^{\mathtt{OR}}$ in order to rely on the security of the underling Σ-protocols Π_0 and Π_1.

3 Fischlin's NIZK Argument and Its Randomized Version

In [15] the author provides a NIZK AoK, where the AoK extractor relies only on the *observability* of the RO[4]. The main advantage of Fischlin's construction, other than its efficiency, is that the AoK extractor does not need to rewind the malicious prover in order to extract the witness. Following [15], we refer to such an extractor as *online extractor.* As remarked in [15], the arguments of knowledge with online extractors are especially suitable for settings with concurrent executions. Indeed, Fischlin shows an example in which a NIZK argument with *standard* knowledge extractors cannot be used due to the rewinds made by the extractor. As we mentioned, Fischlin's construction works only if the input Σ-protocol has a quasi-unique third round. As recently observed in [19] this excludes some interesting Σ-protocols, like for example the output protocols of the OR-transform of [12]. Indeed, in [19] the authors prove that Fischlin's NIZK argument is not even witness indistinguishable if compiled with a protocol

[4] We observe that even though the author of [15] talks about Proof of Knowledge, they still need to polynomially bound the number of queries that an adversary can make to the random oracle. To avoid any ambiguity, in this work we consider only the notion of AoK since the malicious prover is implicitly bounded by the number of queries that can be made to the RO.

obtained from the OR composition of [12]. Interestingly, [19] shows how to solve this problem by proposing a modification of Fischlin's protocol that works for a more general class of Σ-protocols that, in particular, includes the Σ-protocols output of the transform of [12]. Our starting point is the modified version of Fischlin's protocol, which following [19] we refer to as the *randomized* version of Fischlin's protocol. In this section we denote this randomized version of Fischlin's protocol with $\Pi^{\mathsf{Rand-F}}$, and then we show how to bootstrap $\Pi^{\mathsf{Rand-F}}$ to a NIZK AoK with quasi-polynomial time straight-line simulation and online extraction where simulator and extractor do not program the RO. We refer the reader to Fig. 1 for the formal description of $\Pi^{\mathsf{Rand-F}}$.

Let $\Pi = (\mathcal{P}, \mathcal{V})$ be a Σ-protocol with quasi-unique third round and challenge length $\ell = O(\log \lambda)$ for the $\mathcal{NP}$-relation $\mathsf{Rel_L}$. Define the parameters b, r, S, t (as functions of λ) such that $br = \omega(\log \lambda)$, $2^{t-b} = \omega(\log \lambda)$, b, r, $t = O(\log \lambda)$, $S = O(r)$ and $b \leq t \leq \ell$. Define the following non-interactive argument system $\Pi^{\mathsf{Rand-F}} = (\mathcal{P}^{\mathsf{Fischlin}}, \mathcal{V}^{\mathsf{Fischlin}})$ for relation $\mathsf{Rel_L}$. The RO $\mathcal{O}$ maps to b bits.
Common input: security parameter λ, $\mathcal{NP}$-statement $x \in L$, the parameters b, r, S, t as defined above.
Input to $\mathcal{P}^{\mathsf{Fischlin}}$: w s.t. $(x, w) \in \mathsf{Rel_L}$.
Proof. The prover $\mathcal{P}^{\mathsf{Fischlin}}$ executes the following steps.

1. Run r times $\mathcal{P}$ (each time using fresh randomness) on input (x, w) thus obtaining $((\mathtt{aux}_1, a_1), (\mathtt{aux}_2, a_2), \ldots, (\mathtt{aux}_r, a_r))$. Let $A = (a_1, a_2, \ldots, a_r)$.
2. For $i = 1, \ldots, r$
   (a) Set $\mathcal{E}_i = \emptyset$.
   (b) Sample $c_i \leftarrow \{0,1\}^t \backslash \mathcal{E}_i$, compute $z \leftarrow \mathcal{P}(\mathtt{aux}_i, c_i)$.
   (c) If $\mathcal{O}(x, A, i, c_i, z_i) \neq 0^b$, update $\mathcal{E}_i = \mathcal{E}_i \cup \{c_i\}$ and go to Step 2.b.
3. Output $\pi = (\{a_i, c_i, z_i\}_{i=1,\ldots,r})$.

Verification. The verifier $\mathcal{V}^{\mathsf{Fischlin}}$ on input x and $\pi = (\{a_i, c_i, z_i\}_{i=1,\ldots,r})$ accepts if and only if for $i = 1, \ldots, r$, $\mathcal{V}(x, a_i, c_i, z_i) = 1$ and $\Sigma_{i=1}^{r} \mathcal{O}(x, A, i, c_i, z_i) \leq S$.

Fig. 1. $\Pi^{\mathsf{Rand-F}}$: Randomized version of Fischlin's protocol proposed in [19].

As remarked in [15], this protocol has a small completeness error. For deterministic verifiers this error can be removed by standard techniques, namely, by letting the prover check on behalf of the verifier that the proof is valid before outputting it; if not, the prover simply sends the witness to the verifier.

Efficiency. As in [15], we set $b = 9$, $t = 12$, $r = 10$ and $S = 10$. With these parameters our online-extractor fails with probability at most $Q2^{-72}$ where Q is the maximal number of hash queries (assuming that finding distinct responses is infeasible). Then the total number of hash function evaluations is roughly $2^9 r$ and the number of executions of Π is 10.[5]

[5] We used the same parameters as in [15] to provide a fair efficiency measurement of our protocol. However, it should be noted that the security parameters can be made larger with a minimal effect on the size of the NIZK proof.

4 On the WI of Protocol in Fig. 1

In this section we show how to use the randomized Fischlin protocol to obtain an efficient NIWI argument of knowledge with a straight-line extractor that does not program the RO. To do that, we construct a Σ-protocol $\Pi^{\mathtt{OR}}$ for a relation Rel_0 OR Rel_1 using the compiler of Sect. 2.3 by combining a Σ-protocol Π_0 for Rel_0 with a Σ-protocol Π_1 for Rel_1. For completeness, we formally prove that the randomized Fischlin protocol is an AoK with online extraction even though $\Pi^{\mathtt{OR}}$ does not have a quasi-unique third round. A similar proof can be also found in [19]. Then we prove that if $\Pi^{\mathtt{OR}}$ is perfect HVZK, then the randomized Fischlin protocol applied on $\Pi^{\mathtt{OR}}$ is perfect WI. For more details on our proof approach, we refer the reader to the proof of Theorem 3. We denote the instantiation of the randomized Fischlin protocol that uses $\Pi^{\mathtt{OR}}$ as input with $\Pi^{\mathcal{WI}} = (\mathcal{P}^{\mathcal{WI}}, \mathcal{V}^{\mathcal{WI}})$ and propose it in Fig. 2. $\Pi^{\mathcal{WI}}$ is similar to the protocol proposed in Fig. 1, with the exception that it takes as input two Σ-protocols Π_0 and Π_1 and combines them using the compiler of [12].

Let $\Pi_0 = (\mathcal{P}_0, \mathcal{V}_0)$ and $\Pi_1 = (\mathcal{P}_1, \mathcal{V}_1)$ be the Σ-protocols described above with challenge length $\ell = O(\log \lambda)$. Define the parameters b, r, S, t (as functions of λ) such that $br = \omega(\log \lambda)$, $2^{t-b} = \omega(\log \lambda)$, b, r, $t = O(\log \lambda)$, $S = O(r)$ and $b \leq t \leq \ell$. Define the following non-interactive argument system $\Pi^{\mathcal{WI}} = (\mathcal{P}^{\mathcal{WI}}, \mathcal{V}^{\mathcal{WI}})$ for relation $\mathsf{Rel}_{\mathtt{OR}}$. The RO $\mathcal{O}$ maps to b bits.

Common input: security parameter λ, $\mathcal{NP}$-statement $x_0 \in L_0 \vee x_1 \in L_1$, the parameters b, r, S, t as defined above.

Input to $\mathcal{P}^{\mathcal{WI}}$: w_b s.t. $(x_b, w_b) \in \mathsf{Rel}_b$.

Proof. The prover $\mathcal{P}^{\mathcal{WI}}$ executes the following steps.

1. On input (x_b, w_b) run r times $\mathcal{P}_b$ (each time using fresh randomness) on input (x_b, w_b) thus obtaining $((\mathtt{aux}_1^b, a_1^b), (\mathtt{aux}_2^b, a_2^b), \ldots, (\mathtt{aux}_r^b, \ldots, a_r^b))$.
2. For $i = 1, \ldots, r$, pick $c_i^{1-b} \leftarrow \{0,1\}^t$ and compute $(a_i^{1-b}, z_i^{1-b}) \leftarrow \mathsf{Sim}(x_{1-b}, c_i^{1-b})$.
   Let $A = ((a_1^0, a_1^1), (a_2^0, a_2^1), \ldots, (a_r^0, a_r^1))$.
3. For $i = 1, \ldots, r$:
   (a) Set $\mathcal{E}_i = \emptyset$.
   (b) Sample $c_i \leftarrow \{0,1\}^t \backslash \mathcal{E}_i$, compute $z_i^b \leftarrow \mathcal{P}_b(\mathtt{aux}_i, c_i^b)$.
   (c) If $\mathcal{O}(x_0, x_1, A, i, c_i, c_i^0, c_i^1, z_i^0, z_i^1) \neq 0^b$ where $c_i = c_i^0 \oplus c_i^1$, update $\mathcal{E}_i = \mathcal{E}_i \cup \{c_i\}$ and go to Step 3.b
4. Output $\pi = (\{a_i^0, a_i^1, c_i^0, c_i^1, z_i^0, z_i^1\}_{i=1,\ldots,r})$.

Verification. The verifier $\mathcal{V}^{\mathcal{WI}}$ accepts if and only if for $i = 1, \ldots, r$: $\mathcal{V}_0(x_0, a_i^0, c_i^0, z_i^0) = 1$, $\mathcal{V}_1(x_1, a_i^1, c_i^1, z_i^1) = 1$, $c_i = c_i^0 \oplus c_i^1$ and $\Sigma_{i=1}^r \mathcal{O}(x_0, x_1, A, i, c_i, c_i^0, c_i^1, z_i^0, z_i^1) \leq S$.

Fig. 2. $\Pi^{\mathcal{WI}}$: Our NIWI AoK with an on-line extractor that does not program the RO.

Theorem 3. *Let Π_0 be a Σ-protocol for the $\mathcal{NP}$-relation* Rel_0 *and Π_1 be a Σ-protocol for the $\mathcal{NP}$-relation* Rel_1 *such that both Π_0 and Π_1 have a quasi-unique third round, then $\Pi^{\mathcal{WI}}$ is perfect WI for the $\mathcal{NP}$-relation* $\mathsf{Rel}_{\mathtt{OR}}$ *and is an AoK with an online extractor that does not program the RO.*

Proof. **Completeness.** It follows exactly the completeness of Theorem 6.2 of [19].
Witness Indistinguishability. We prove that if the transform of [12] showed in Sect. 2.3 on input Π_0 and Π_1 outputs a new Σ-protocol that is perfect WI for the $\mathcal{NP}$-relation $\mathsf{Rel}_{\mathtt{OR}}$ then $\Pi^{\mathcal{WI}}$ is WI for $\mathsf{Rel}_{\mathtt{OR}}$ as well.

We assume by contradiction that $\Pi^{\mathcal{WI}}$ is not WI and then we construct an adversary $\mathcal{A}^{\mathsf{SHVZK}}$ that breaks the Special HVZK of either Π_0 or Π_1. More formally, let $\mathcal{A}^b_{\mathsf{ExpAWI}}$ be the view of the adversary in the experiment $\mathsf{ExpAWI}^b_{\Pi^{\mathcal{WI}},\mathcal{A}}(\lambda,\zeta)$. By contradiction, we have that there exists a distinguisher $\mathcal{D}$, and a non-negligible function δ such that

$$\left|\mathrm{Prob}\left[\ \mathcal{D}(\lambda,\zeta,\mathcal{A}^0_{\mathsf{ExpAWI}})=1\ \right]-\mathrm{Prob}\left[\ \mathcal{D}(\lambda,\zeta,\mathcal{A}^1_{\mathsf{ExpAWI}})=1\ \right]\right|=\delta(\lambda).$$

Let b, r, S, t be the parameters defined in the description of $\Pi^{\mathcal{WI}}$ in Fig. 2, we now define the hybrid experiment $\mathcal{H}_i$ and we denote with $\mathcal{A}_{\mathcal{H}_i}$ the view of the adversary in the experiment $\mathcal{H}_i$ with $i \in \{1,\ldots,r\}$.

The hybrid experiment $\mathcal{H}_i$ is formally described in Fig. 3 and takes as input the security parameter λ, the auxiliary information ζ for $\mathcal{A}$ and contains b, r, S and t.

Upon receiving (x, w_0, w_1) from $\mathcal{A}$ execute the following steps.

1. Run i times $\mathcal{P}^{\mathtt{OR}}$ (each time using fresh randomness) on input (x_0, x_1, w_1) thus obtaining $((\mathbf{aux}^1_1, a^1_1),\ldots,(\mathbf{aux}^1_i, a^1_i))$ and $((a^0_1, z^0_1),\ldots,(a^0_i, z^0_i))$.
2. Run $r-i$ times $\mathcal{P}^{\mathtt{OR}}$ (each time using fresh randomness) on input (x_0, x_1, w_0) thus obtaining $((\mathbf{aux}^0_{i+1}, a^0_{i+1}),\ldots,(\mathbf{aux}^0_r, a^0_r))$ and $((a^1_{i+1}, z^1_{i+1}),\ldots,(a^1_r, z^1_r))$. Let $A = ((a^0_1, a^1_1),\ldots,(a^0_r, a^1_r))$.
3. For $j = 1,\ldots,i$;
   Pick a random $c_j \in \{0,1\}^t$ such that $\mathcal{O}(x_0, x_1, A, j, c_j, c^0_j, c^1_j, z^0_j, z^1_j) = 0^b$ where $c_j = c^0_j \oplus c^1_j$ and $z^1_j \leftarrow \mathcal{P}_1(\mathbf{aux}^1_j, c^1_j)$.
   If such a c_j does not exist, then pick the first one for which the hash value is minimal among all 2^t hash values.
4. For $j = i+1,\ldots,r$:
   Pick a random $c_j \in \{0,1\}^t$ such that $\mathcal{O}(x_0, x_1, A, j, c_j, c^0_j, c^1_j, z^0_j, z^1_j) = 0^b$ where $c_j = c^0_j \oplus c^1_j$ and $z^0_j \leftarrow \mathcal{P}_0(\mathbf{aux}^0_j, c^0_j)$.
   If such a c_j does not exist, then pick the first one for which the hash value is minimal among all 2^t hash values.
5. Send $\pi = (\{a^0_i, a^1_i, c^0_i, c^1_i, z^0_i, z^1_i\}_{i=1,\ldots,r})$ to $\mathcal{A}$.

Fig. 3. Hybrid experiment $\mathcal{H}_i$, with $i \in \{1,\ldots,r\}$.

We observe that $\mathsf{ExpAWI}^0_{\Pi^{\mathcal{WI}},\mathcal{A}}(\lambda,\zeta) = \mathcal{H}_0(\lambda,\zeta)$ and that $\mathsf{ExpAWI}^1_{\Pi^{\mathcal{WI}},\mathcal{A}}(\lambda,\zeta) = \mathcal{H}_r(\lambda,\zeta)$. Therefore, by contradiction, there must be a value $i \in \{1,\ldots r\}$ such that $|\text{Prob}[\,\mathcal{D}(\lambda,\zeta,\mathcal{A}_{\mathcal{H}_{i-1}})=1\,]-\text{Prob}[\,\mathcal{D}(\lambda,\zeta,\mathcal{A}_{\mathcal{H}_i})=1\,]|=\delta(\lambda)$. In order to reach a contradiction we consider the additional intermediate hybrid experiment $\mathcal{H}_{\mathsf{int}}$ of Fig. 4. Informally, the difference between $\mathcal{H}_{i-1}$ and $\mathcal{H}_{\mathsf{int}}$ is that the honest prover procedure $\mathcal{P}_1$ is used in $\mathcal{H}_{\mathsf{int}}$ to compute (a_i^1, z_i^1) instead of the simulated one. Instead, the difference between $\mathcal{H}_{\mathsf{int}}$ and $\mathcal{H}_i$ is that in $\mathcal{H}_i$ the messages (a_i^0, z_i^0) are computed using the Special HVZK simulator of Π_0 instead of the honest prover procedure. The following lemma completes the proof of the theorem.

Upon receiving (x, w_0, w_1) from $\mathcal{A}$ execute the following steps.

1. Run $i-1$ times $\mathcal{P}_1$ (each time using fresh randomness) on input (x_1, w_1) thus obtaining $((\mathsf{aux}_1^1, a_1^1), \dots, (\mathsf{aux}_{i-1}^1, a_{i-1}^1))$.
2. For $j = 1, \dots, i-1$ pick $c_j^0 \leftarrow \{0,1\}^t$ and compute $(a_j^0, z_j^0) \leftarrow \mathsf{Sim}_0(x_0, c_j^0)$.
3. Run $\mathcal{P}_1$ in input (x_1, w_1) thus obtaining $(a_i^1, \mathsf{aux}_i^1)$ and run $\mathcal{P}_0$ in input (x_0, w_0) thus obtaining $(a_i^0, \mathsf{aux}_i^0)$.
4. Run $r-i$ times $\mathcal{P}_0$ (each time using fresh randomness) on input (x_0, w_0) thus obtaining $((\mathsf{aux}_{i+1}^0, a_{i+1}^0), \dots, (\mathsf{aux}_r^0, a_r^0))$.
5. For $j = i+1, \dots, r$ pick $c_j^1 \leftarrow \{0,1\}^t$ and compute $(a_j^1, z_j^1) \leftarrow \mathsf{Sim}_1(x_1, c_j^1)$. Let $A = ((a_1^0, a_1^1), (a_2^0, a_2^1), \dots, (a_r^0, a_r^1))$.
6. For $j = 1, \dots, i-1$: pick a random $c_j \in \{0,1\}^t$ such that $\mathcal{O}(x_0, x_1, A, j, c_j, c_j^0, c_j^1, z_j^0, z_j^1) = 0^b$ where $c_j = c_j^0 \oplus c_j^1$ and $z_j^1 \leftarrow \mathcal{P}_1(\mathsf{aux}_j^1, c_j^1)$; if such a c_j does not exist, then pick the first one for which the hash value is minimal among all 2^t hash values.
7. Pick a random $c_i \in \{0,1\}^t$ such that $\mathcal{O}(x_0, x_1, A, i, c_i, c_i^0, c_i^1, z_i^0, z_i^1) = 0^b$ where $c_i^0 \leftarrow \{0,1\}^t$, $c_i = c_i^0 \oplus c_i^1$, $z_i^1 \leftarrow \mathcal{P}_1(\mathsf{aux}_i^1, c_i^1)$ and $z_i^0 \leftarrow \mathcal{P}_0(\mathsf{aux}_i^0, c_i^0)$ If such a c_i does not exist, then pick the first one for which the hash value is minimal among all 2^t hash values.
8. For $j = i+1, \dots, r$: pick a random $c_j \in \{0,1\}^t$ such that $\mathcal{O}(x_0, x_1, A, j, c_j, c_j^0, c_j^1, z_j^0, z_j^1) = 0^b$ where $c_j = c_j^0 \oplus c_j^1$ and $z_j^0 \leftarrow \mathcal{P}_0(\mathsf{aux}_j^0, c_j^0)$; if such a c_j does not exist, then pick the first one for which the hash value is minimal among all 2^t hash values.
9. Send $\pi = (\{a_i^0, a_i^1, c_i^0, c_i^1, z_i^0, z_i^1\}_{i=1,\dots,r})$ to $\mathcal{A}$.

Fig. 4. Hybrid experiment $\mathcal{H}_{\mathsf{int}}$.

Lemma 1. *There exists a negligible function ν such that for every distinguisher $\mathcal{D}$*

$$|\text{Prob}[\,\mathcal{D}(\lambda,\zeta,\mathcal{A}_{\mathcal{H}_{i-1}})=1\,]-\text{Prob}[\,\mathcal{D}(\lambda,\zeta,\mathcal{A}_{\mathcal{H}_{\mathsf{int}}})=1\,]|\le\nu(\lambda)\ \textit{and}$$
$$|\text{Prob}[\,\mathcal{D}(\lambda,\zeta,\mathcal{A}_{\mathcal{H}_{\mathsf{int}}}=1\,]-\text{Prob}[\,\mathcal{D}(\lambda,\zeta,\mathcal{A}_{\mathcal{H}_i})=1\,]|\le\nu(\lambda)$$

Proof. Assume by contradiction that one of the above two conditions does not hold. Therefore there exists a non-negligible function δ such that[6]

[6] The proof for the other case follows using exactly the same arguments but in that case we break the Special HVZK of Π_0 instead of Π_1.

$|\text{Prob}[\mathcal{D}(\lambda, \zeta, \mathcal{A}_{\mathcal{H}_{i-1}}) = 1] - \text{Prob}[\mathcal{D}(\lambda, \zeta, \mathcal{A}_{\mathcal{H}_{\text{int}}}) = 1]| = \delta(\lambda)$ In this case we can construct an adversary $\mathcal{A}^{\mathsf{SHVZK}}$ that breaks the Special HVZK of Π_1. Let $\mathcal{C}^{\mathsf{SHVZK}}$ be the challenger of the Special HVZK security game, $\mathcal{A}^{\mathsf{SHVZK}}$ internally runs $\mathcal{A}$ and executes the following steps.

1. Upon receiving (x_0, x_1, w_0, w_1) from $\mathcal{A}$, pick $\mathsf{c} \leftarrow \{0,1\}^t$ and send (x_1, w_1, c) to $\mathcal{C}^{\mathsf{SHVZK}}$.
2. Upon receiving (a, z) from $\mathcal{C}^{\mathsf{SHVZK}}$, run $i-1$ times $\mathcal{P}_1$ (each time using fresh randomness) on input (x_1, w_1) thus obtaining $((\mathbf{aux}_1^1, a_1^1), \ldots, (\mathbf{aux}_{i-1}^1, a_{i-1}^1))$. For $j = 1, \ldots, i-1$ pick $c_j^0 \leftarrow \{0,1\}^t$ and compute $(a_j^0, z_j^0) \leftarrow \mathsf{Sim}_0(x_0, c_j^0)$.
3. Run $\mathcal{P}_0$ in input (x_0, w_0) thus obtaining $(a_i^0, \mathbf{aux}_i^0)$, set $a_i^1 = \mathsf{a}$.
4. Run $r-i$ times $\mathcal{P}_0$ (each time using fresh randomness) on input (x_0, w_0) thus obtaining $((\mathbf{aux}_{i+1}^0, a_{i+1}^0), \ldots, (\mathbf{aux}_r^0, a_r^0))$.
5. For $j = i+1, \ldots, r$ pick $c_j^1 \leftarrow \{0,1\}^t$ and compute $(a_j^1, z_j^1) \leftarrow \mathsf{Sim}_1(x_1, c_j^1)$.
6. Define $A = ((a_1^0, a_1^1), (a_2^0, a_2^1), \ldots, (a_r^0, a_r^1))$.
7. For $j = 1, \ldots, i-1$:
   Pick a random $c_j \in \{0,1\}^t$ such that $\mathcal{O}(x_0, x_1, A, j, c_j, c_j^0, c_j^1, z_j^0, z_j^1) = 0^b$ where $c_j = c_j^0 \oplus c_j^1$ and $z_j^1 \leftarrow \mathcal{P}_1(\mathbf{aux}_j^1, c_j^1)$.
   If such a c_j does not exist, then pick the first one for which the hash value is minimal among all 2^t hash values.
8. Pick a random $c_i \in \{0,1\}^t$ such that $\mathcal{O}(x_0, x_1, A, i, c_i, c_i^0, c_i^1, z_i^0, z_i^1) = 0^b$ where $c_i = \mathsf{c} \oplus c_i^0$, $z_i^0 \leftarrow \mathcal{P}_0(\mathbf{aux}_i^0, c_i^0)$ and $z_i^1 = \mathsf{z}$.
   If such a c_i does not exist, then pick the first one for which the hash value is minimal among all 2^t hash values[7].
9. For $j = i+1, \ldots, r$:
   Pick a random $c_j \in \{0,1\}^t$ such that $\mathcal{O}(x_0, x_1, A, j, c_j, c_j^0, c_j^1, z_j^0, z_j^1) = 0^b$ where $c_j = c_j^0 \oplus c_j^1$ and $z_j^0 \leftarrow \mathcal{P}_0(\mathbf{aux}_j^0, c_j^0)$.
   If such a c_j does not exist, then pick the first one for which the hash value is minimal among all 2^t hash values.
10. Send $\pi = (\{a_i^0, a_i^1, c_i^0, c_i^1, z_i^0, z_i^1\}_{i=1,\ldots,r})$ to $\mathcal{A}$.
11. Output what $\mathcal{A}$ outputs.

It is easy to see that if the messages (a, z) have been computed by $\mathcal{C}^{\mathsf{SHVZK}}$ using the Special HVZK simulator Sim_1 then the output of $\mathcal{A}^{\mathsf{SHVZK}}$ corresponds to the output of $\mathcal{A}$ in $\mathcal{H}_{i-1}$, and to the output of $\mathcal{A}$ in $\mathcal{H}_{\text{int}}$ if (a, z) are computed using $\mathcal{P}_1$ on input the witness w_1 for x_1. Therefore $\mathcal{A}^{\mathsf{SHVZK}}$ breaks the security of the Special HVZK of Π_1 thus reaching a contradiction. □

Argument of Knowledge. Here we follow in large part the proof of Theorem 2 of [15]. We show a knowledge extractor $\mathsf{Ext}(x, \pi, \mathcal{Q}_{\mathcal{O}}(\mathcal{A}))$ that except with negligible probability over the choice of $\mathcal{O}$, outputs a witness w_b such that $(x_b, w_b) \in \mathsf{Rel}_b$ for an accepted proof $\pi = (\{a_i^0, a_i^1, c_i^0, c_i^1, z_i^0, z_i^1\}_{i=1,\ldots,r})$ with respect to (x_0, x_1). Since Π^{OR} is special-sound, then the algorithm Ext just needs

[7] $\mathcal{A}^{\mathsf{SHVZK}}$ can iterate on all possible c_j since she can pick any possible c_j^0.

to look into $\mathcal{Q}_{\mathcal{O}}(\mathcal{A})$ for a query $\mathcal{O}(x_0, x_1, A, i, c_i, c_i^0, c_i^1, z_i^0, z_i^1)$ and for another query $\mathcal{O}(x_0, x_1, A, i, \tilde{c}_i, \tilde{c}_i^0, \tilde{c}_i^1, \tilde{z}_i^0, \tilde{z}_i^1)$ such that $\mathcal{V}^{\mathsf{OR}}(x_0, x_1, a_i^0, a_i^1, \tilde{c}_i^0, \tilde{c}_i^1, \tilde{z}_i^0, \tilde{z}_i^1) = 1$ and $c_i \neq \tilde{c}_i$. Indeed, from the special soundness of Π^{OR}, this yields an efficient extraction procedure of either the witness for x_0 or x_1. If there are no such queries then Ext simply outputs $\bot$. We now need to bound the probability that such two queries do not exist, but still, $\mathcal{V}^{\mathcal{WI}}$ accepts π with non-negligible probability. Consider the set of tuples (x_0, x_1, A) such that $\mathcal{A}$ queries $\mathcal{O}$ about $(x_0, x_1, A, i, c_i^0, c_i^1, z_i^0, z_i^1)$ for some $i, c_i^0, c_i^1, z_i^0, z_i^1$ and such that $\mathcal{V}^{\mathsf{OR}}(x_0, x_1, a_i^0, a_i^1, c_i^0, c_i^1, z_i^0, z_i^1) = 1$ (we can neglect tuples with invalid proofs since they are not useful to the prover to compute an accepting proof for the protocol). Let $Q = |\mathcal{Q}_{\mathcal{O}}(\mathcal{A})|$, then there are at most $Q+1$ of these tuples (x_0, x_1, A). Fix one of the tuples for the moment, say, (x_0, x_1, A). By contradiction, for this tuple and any i, $\mathcal{A}$ never queries $\mathcal{O}$ about two values $(x_0, x_1, A, i, c_i, c_i^0, c_i^1, z_i^0, z_i^1)$, $(x_0, x_1, a_i^0, a_i^1, \tilde{c}_i^0, \tilde{c}_i^1, \tilde{z}_i^0, \tilde{z}_i^1)$ with $c_i \neq \tilde{c}_i$ which $\mathcal{V}^{\mathsf{OR}}$ would accept (we note that if $c_i \neq \tilde{c}_i$ then either $c_i^0 \neq \tilde{c}_i^1$ or $c_i^1 \neq \tilde{c}_i^1$). Similarly, we can assume that $\mathcal{A}$ never queries about $(x_0, x_1, A, i, c_i, c_i^0, c_i^1, z_i^0, z_i^1)$, $(x_0, x_1, a_i^0, a_i^1, \tilde{c}_i^0, \tilde{c}_i^1, \tilde{z}_i^0, \tilde{z}_i^1)$ with either $z_i^0 \neq \tilde{z}_i^0$ or $z_i^1 \neq \tilde{z}_i^1$, otherwise this would contradict the property of unique responses of either Π_0 or Π_1. This allows us to assign a set of unique values $s_1, \ldots, s_r$ to (x_0, x_1, A) such that s_i equals $\mathcal{O}(x_0, x_1, A, i, c_i, c_i^0, c_i^1, z_i^0, z_i^1)$ if $\mathcal{A}$ queries about any such tuple[8]. Conclusively, the values $s_1, \ldots, s_r$ assigned to (x_0, x_1, A) are all random and independent. Given such an assignment we calculate the probability that the sum does not exceed the threshold value S. We consider $\binom{T+r-1}{r-1}$ combinations to represent a sum $T \leq S$ with r values $s_1, \ldots, s_r \geq 0$. There are $\sum_{T=0}^{S} \binom{T+r-1}{r-1} \leq (S+1) \cdot \binom{S+r-1}{r-1} \leq (S+1) \cdot \frac{e(S+r)}{r-1}^{r-1}$ possibilities. Since $S = O(r)$ we have $S + r \leq c(r-1)$ for some constant c, and the number of combinations is bounded above by $(S+1) \cdot 2^{\log{(ec)r}}$, which is polynomial in λ. Since $s_1, \ldots, s_r$ are random, the probability of obtaining such a sum $T \leq S$ is this number of combinations divided by 2^{br}. By the choice of parameters, this is negligible. Finally, we extend the analysis from a fixed query to the set of the $Q+1$ possibilities (x_0, x_1, A). Since Q is polynomial the probability of finding a valid proof among this set for which the extractor also fails is bounded by $(Q+1)(S+1) \cdot 2^{(\log(ec)-b)r}$. This remains negligible.

Theorem 3 claims that Π_0 and Π_1 can be instantiated with any Σ-protocol such as Schnorr's protocol for discrete logarithm, the protocol for Diffie-Hellman (DH) tuples and all Σ-protocols in the well-known class proposed by Cramer in [11] and Maurer in [21].

5 Our Efficient NIZK Argument of Knowledge

In order to construct our NIZK argument of knowledge with quasi-polynomial simulation and online extraction (still without requiring simulator and extractor to program the RO) for the $\mathcal{NP}$ relation $\mathsf{Rel_L}$ $\Pi^{\mathsf{NIZK}} = (\mathcal{P}^{\mathsf{NIZK}}, \mathcal{V}^{\mathsf{NIZK}})$, we make use of the following tools.

---

[8] From this point forward the proof follows exactly the same steps proposed in [15], but for completeness we propose the complete proof.

- A dense samplable puzzle system $\mathsf{PuzSys} = (\mathsf{Sample}, \mathsf{Solve}, \mathsf{Verify})$ such that for every hardness factor $h \in \mathcal{HS}_\lambda$ there exists a negligible function ν such that the following holds:
  1. $\text{Prob}\left[\ \mathsf{puz} \leftarrow \mathsf{Sample}(1^\lambda, h) : g(\mathsf{Steps}_{\mathsf{Solve}}(1^\lambda, h, \mathsf{puz})) \leq \lambda^{\log \lambda}\ \right] \leq \nu(\lambda)$;
  2. the worst-case running time of $\mathsf{Solve}(1^\lambda, h, \cdot)$ is $\lambda^{\mathsf{poly}(\log \lambda)}$.[9]
- $\Pi^{\mathcal{WI}} = (\mathcal{P}^{\mathcal{WI}}, \mathcal{V}^{\mathcal{WI}})$: a perfect NIWI AoK with online extractor for the $\mathcal{NP}$-relation $\mathsf{Rel}_{\mathcal{WI}} = \{((x, \mathsf{puz}), w) : (x, w) \in \mathsf{Rel}_\mathsf{L} \text{ or } \mathsf{Verify}(1^\lambda, h, \mathsf{puz}, w) = 1\}$.

$\mathcal{P}^{\mathsf{NIZK}}$ and $\mathcal{V}^{\mathsf{NIZK}}$ have also access to a RO (that will not be programmed by the simulator and by the extractor) $\mathcal{O} : \{0,1\}^* \rightarrow \{0,1\}^{\ell(\lambda,h)}$ where $\ell(\lambda, h)$ is a function of the security and the hardness parameters of PuzSys. We need to relate the output length of the random oracle to the parameters of PuzSys because $\mathcal{O}$ is used to generate a puzzle in our construction. More details are given in the security proof.

Common input: security parameter λ, $\mathcal{NP}$-statement $x \in L$.
Input to $\mathcal{P}^{\mathsf{NIZK}}$: w s.t. $(x, w) \in \mathsf{Rel}_\mathsf{L}$.

Proof. $\mathcal{P}^{\mathsf{NIZK}}$ computes the puzzle puz for PuzSys by querying the random oracle $\mathcal{O}$ on input x: $\mathsf{puz} \leftarrow \mathcal{O}(x)$. $\mathcal{P}^{\mathsf{NIZK}}$ defines $x_{\mathcal{WI}} = (x, \mathsf{puz})$, $w_{\mathcal{WI}} = w$ and runs $\mathcal{P}^{\mathcal{WI}}$ on input $(x_{\mathcal{WI}}, w_{\mathcal{WI}})$ thus obtaining $\pi_{\mathcal{WI}}$ which is sent to $\mathcal{V}^{\mathsf{NIZK}}$.
Verification. $\mathcal{V}^{\mathsf{NIZK}}$ queries $\mathcal{O}$ with x thus obtaining puz and defines $x_{\mathcal{WI}} = (x, \mathsf{puz})$. $\mathcal{V}^{\mathsf{NIZK}}$ now outputs what $\mathcal{V}^{\mathcal{WI}}$ outputs on input $(x_{\mathcal{WI}}, \pi_{\mathcal{WI}})$.

Fig. 5. Our NIZK AoK with straight-line simulator and online extractor.

Theorem 4. *If $\Pi^{\mathcal{WI}} = (\mathcal{P}^{\mathcal{WI}}, \mathcal{V}^{\mathcal{WI}})$ is a non-interactive perfect WI AoK with online extractor for the $\mathcal{NP}$-relation $\mathsf{Rel}_{\mathcal{WI}}$ that does not program the RO and* PuzSys *is a dense samplable puzzle system according to Definition 2, then Π^{NIZK} is a straight-line concurrent perfectly $\lambda^{\mathsf{poly}(\log \lambda)}$-simulatable argument of knowledge with online extraction where neither the zero-knowledge simulator nor the AoK extractor needs to program the RO.*

Proof. **Completeness.** It follows from the completeness of $\Pi^{\mathcal{WI}}$ and PuzSys.
Quasi-polynomial time perfect simulation. Let $\mathcal{V}^{\mathsf{NIZK}}$ be an arbitrary verifier. We construct a simulator Sim that runs in $\lambda^{\mathsf{poly}(\log \lambda)}$ time, such that the distributions $\left\{(\langle \mathcal{P}^{\mathsf{NIZK}}(w), \mathcal{V}^{\mathsf{NIZK}\star}(z)\rangle(x))\right\}_{z\in\{0,1\}^*, x\in L}$ for arbitrary w s.t. $(x, w) \in \mathsf{Rel}_\mathsf{L}$ and $\left\{(\langle \mathsf{Sim}, \mathcal{V}^{\mathsf{NIZK}\star}(z)\rangle(x))\right\}_{z\in\{0,1\}^*, x\in L}$ are perfectly indistinguishable. The simulator Sim works as follows

- Compute the puzzle puz for PuzSys by querying the random oracle $\mathcal{O}$ on input x: $\mathsf{puz} \leftarrow \mathcal{O}(x)$ and compute $\mathtt{sol} \leftarrow \mathsf{Solve}(1^\lambda, h, \mathsf{puz})$.

[9] This is the same puzzle used in Theorem 7 of [2].

- Define $x_{\mathcal{WI}} = (x, \mathsf{puz})$, $w_{\mathcal{WI}} = \mathtt{sol}$ and run $\mathcal{P}^{\mathcal{WI}}$ on input $(x_{\mathcal{WI}}, w_{\mathcal{WI}})$ thus obtaining $\pi_{\mathcal{WI}}$.
- Send $\pi_{\mathcal{WI}}$ to $\mathcal{V}^{\mathsf{NIZK}^\star}$ and output what $\mathcal{V}^{\mathsf{NIZK}^\star}$ outputs.

Note that Sim can compute the solution of the puzzle puz in time $\lambda^{\mathsf{poly}(\log \lambda)}$ and $\Pi^{\mathcal{WI}}$ is perfect WI. **Argument of knowledge.** By assumption there exist a PPT AoK online extractor Ext for $\Pi^{\mathcal{WI}}$ such that the following holds for any *ppt* algorithm $\mathcal{P}^{\mathcal{WI}^\star}$. Let $\mathcal{O}$ be a random oracle, $(x_{\mathcal{WI}}, \pi_{\mathcal{WI}}) \leftarrow \mathcal{P}^{\mathcal{WI}^\star}(\lambda)$ and $\mathcal{Q}_{\mathcal{O}}(\mathcal{P}^{\mathcal{WI}^\star})$ be the sequence of queries of $\mathcal{P}^{\mathcal{WI}^\star}$ to $\mathcal{O}$ and $\mathcal{O}$'s answers. Let $w_{\mathcal{WI}} \leftarrow \mathsf{Ext}(x, \pi, \mathcal{Q}_{\mathcal{O}}(\mathcal{P}^{\mathcal{WI}^\star}))$. Then there exists a negligible function ν such that

$\mathrm{Prob}\left[\, (x_{\mathcal{WI}}, w_{\mathcal{WI}}) \notin \mathsf{Rel}_{\mathcal{WI}} \text{ and } \mathcal{V}^{\mathcal{WI}}(x_{\mathcal{WI}}, \pi_{\mathcal{WI}}) = 1 \,\right] \leq \nu(\lambda)$.

The AoK PPT extractor $\mathsf{E}^{\mathsf{NIZK}}$ for Π^{NIZK} simply internally runs Ext and outputs what Ext would output. We now observe that $\mathsf{E}^{\mathsf{NIZK}}$ could fail only because the output of the internal extractor Ext is a solution $\mathtt{sol}$ for $\mathsf{puz} = \mathcal{O}(x)$. Let us assume by contradiction that this happens. That is, let $\mathcal{O}$ be a random oracle, $(x, \pi_{\mathsf{NIZK}}) \leftarrow \mathcal{P}^{\mathsf{NIZK}^\star}(\lambda)$, $\mathcal{Q}_{\mathcal{O}}(\mathcal{P}^{\mathsf{NIZK}^\star})$ be the sequence of queries of $\mathcal{P}^{\mathsf{NIZK}^\star}$ to $\mathcal{O}$ and $\mathcal{O}$'s answers and let $\eta \leftarrow \mathsf{Ext}(x, \pi, \mathcal{Q}_{\mathcal{O}}(\mathcal{P}^{\mathsf{NIZK}^\star}))$, then

$\mathrm{Prob}\left[\, \mathsf{Verify}(1^\lambda, h, \mathcal{O}(x), \eta) = 1 \text{ and } \mathcal{V}^{\mathsf{NIZK}}(x, \pi_{\mathsf{NIZK}}) = 1 \,\right] = \delta(\lambda)$.

But this would contradict the fact that PuzSys cannot be solved in less than $\lambda^{\log \lambda}$ steps. Indeed the extractor $\mathsf{E}^{\mathsf{NIZK}}$ outputs in PPT a solution to a puzzle sampled from an uniform distribution (since $\mathcal{O}$ is modelled as a random oracle). We observe that even though in the above proof the ZK simulator needs to run in quasi-polynomial time we can still rely on the WI property of $\Pi^{\mathcal{WI}}$ since the WI of $\Pi^{\mathcal{WI}}$ holds against all-powerful adversary.

Complexity Analysis. Our construction consists of one execution of $\Pi^{\mathcal{WI}}$ and one evaluation of $\mathcal{O}$ on input x. Therefore, to give a concrete idea of the efficiency of our protocol we need to define the two Σ-protocols used as input of $\Pi^{\mathcal{WI}}$ (see Fig. 2). Thus, we need a Σ-protocol Π^{puz} for the $\mathcal{NP}$-relation $\mathsf{Rel}_{\mathsf{puz}} = \{(\mathsf{puz}, \mathtt{sol}) : \mathsf{Verify}(1^\lambda, h, \mathsf{puz}, w) = 1)\}$ and a Σ-protocol Π^{L} for the $\mathcal{NP}$-relation $\mathsf{Rel}_{\mathsf{L}}$. We need to use a dense samplable puzzle system that admits a Σ-protocol. As discussed in Sect. 2.2, in [1] the authors propose a dense samplable puzzle system where the puzzle is an instance of the DL problem. So we can instantiate Π^{puz} with the well known protocol of Schnorr [26]. Following the analysis of Sect. 3, we obtain an online-extractor that fails with probability at most $\mathcal{Q}2^{-72}$ where the total number of hash function evaluations is at most $2^9 r + 1$ and the number of executions of $\Pi^{\mathtt{OR}}$ is $r = 10$, where $\Pi^{\mathtt{OR}}$ denotes the output of the or-composition proposed in Sect. 2.3 using Π^{puz} and Π^{L} as input. To give a practical example, let us consider the complexity of Π^{NIZK} when $\mathsf{Rel}_{\mathsf{L}}$ is the discrete log $\mathcal{NP}$ relation $\{((\mathcal{G}, q, g, Y), y) : g^y = Y\}$ where $\mathcal{G}$ is a group of prime-order q. We construct $\Pi_{\mathcal{WI}}$ using two instantiations of the Schnorr protocol thus obtaining a Σ-protocol that requires 3 exponentiations to be executed (cf. [9]). So our protocol Π^{NIZK} requires 30 exponentiations and $2^9 r + 1 = 5121$ hash evaluations.

References

1. Baldimtsi, F., Kiayias, A., Zacharias, T., Zhang, B.: Indistinguishable proofs of work or knowledge. Cryptology ePrint Archive, Paper 2015/1230 (2015), https://eprint.iacr.org/2015/1230
2. Baldimtsi, F., Kiayias, A., Zacharias, T., Zhang, B.: Indistinguishable proofs of work or knowledge. In: Cheon, J.H., Takagi, T. (eds.) ASIACRYPT 2016. LNCS, vol. 10032, pp. 902–933. Springer, Heidelberg (2016). https://doi.org/10.1007/978-3-662-53890-6_30
3. Barak, B., Pass, R.: On the possibility of one-message weak zero-knowledge. In: Theory of Cryptography, First Theory of Cryptography Conference, TCC 2004, Cambridge, MA, USA, 19–21 February 2004, Proceedings.,pp. 121–132 (2004)
4. Barak, B., Sahai, A.: How to play almost any mental game over the net - concurrent composition via super-polynomial simulation. In: 46th Annual IEEE Symposium on Foundations of Computer Science (FOCS 2005), 23–25 October 2005, Pittsburgh, PA, USA, Proceedings, pp. 543–552. IEEE Computer Society (2005)
5. Bellare, M., Rogaway, P.: Random oracles are practical: a paradigm for designing efficient protocols. In: CCS 1993, Proceedings of the 1st ACM Conference on Computer and Communications Security, Fairfax, Virginia, USA, 3–5 November 1993, pp. 62–73 (1993)
6. Blum, M., Feldman, P., Micali, S.: Non-interactive zero-knowledge and its applications (extended abstract). In: Proceedings of the 20th Annual ACM Symposium on Theory of Computing, 2–4 May 1988, Chicago, Illinois, USA, pp. 103–112 (1988)
7. Canetti, R.: Universally composable security: a new paradigm for cryptographic protocols. In: 42nd Annual Symposium on Foundations of Computer Science, FOCS 2001, 14–17 October 2001, Las Vegas, Nevada, USA, pp. 136–145 (2001)
8. Canetti, R., Jain, A., Scafuro, A.: Practical UC security with a global random oracle. In: Proceedings of the 2014 ACM SIGSAC Conference on Computer and Communications Security, Scottsdale, AZ, USA, 3–7 November 2014, pp. 597–608 (2014)
9. Ciampi, M., Persiano, G., Scafuro, A., Siniscalchi, L., Visconti, I.: Improved OR-composition of sigma-protocols. In: Kushilevitz, E., Malkin, T. (eds.) TCC 2016. LNCS, vol. 9563, pp. 112–141. Springer, Heidelberg (2016). https://doi.org/10.1007/978-3-662-49099-0_5
10. Ciampi, M., Persiano, G., Siniscalchi, L., Visconti, I.: A transform for NIZK almost as efficient and general as the fiat-Shamir transform without programmable random oracles. In: Theory of Cryptography - 13th International Conference, TCC 2016-A, Tel Aviv, Israel, 10–13 January 2016, Proceedings, Part II, pp. 83–111 (2016)
11. Cramer, R., Damgård, I.: Zero-knowledge proofs for finite field arithmetic, or: can zero-knowledge be for free? In: Krawczyk, H. (ed.) CRYPTO 1998. LNCS, vol. 1462, pp. 424–441. Springer, Heidelberg (1998). https://doi.org/10.1007/BFb0055745
12. Cramer, R., Damgård, I., Schoenmakers, B.: Proofs of partial knowledge and simplified design of witness hiding protocols. In: Advances in Cryptology - CRYPTO '94, 14th Annual International Cryptology Conference, Santa Barbara, California, USA, 21–25 August 1994, Proceedings, pp. 174–187 (1994)
13. Feige, U., Lapidot, D., Shamir, A.: Multiple non-interactive zero knowledge proofs based on a single random string (extended abstract). In: 31st Annual Symposium on Foundations of Computer Science, St. Louis, Missouri, USA, 22–24 October 1990, vol. I, pp. 308–317. IEEE Computer Society (1990)

14. Fiat, A., Shamir, A.: How to prove yourself: practical solutions to identification and signature problems. In: Proceedings of Advances in Cryptology - CRYPTO 1986, Santa Barbara, California, USA, 1986, pp. 186–194 (1986)
15. Fischlin, M.: Communication-efficient non-interactive proofs of knowledge with online extractors. In: Shoup, V. (ed.) CRYPTO 2005. LNCS, vol. 3621, pp. 152–168. Springer, Heidelberg (2005). https://doi.org/10.1007/11535218_10
16. Garay, J.A., MacKenzie, P., Yang, K.: Strengthening zero-knowledge protocols using signatures. J. Cryptol. **19**(2), 169–209 (2006)
17. Goldwasser, S., Micali, S., Rackoff, C.: The knowledge complexity of interactive proof systems. SIAM J. Comput. **18**(1), 186–208 (1989)
18. Guillou, L.C., Quisquater, J.-J.: A Practical zero-knowledge protocol fitted to security microprocessor minimizing both transmission and memory. In: Barstow, D., et al. (eds.) EUROCRYPT 1988. LNCS, vol. 330, pp. 123–128. Springer, Heidelberg (1988). https://doi.org/10.1007/3-540-45961-8_11
19. Kondi, Y., Abhi Shelat: Improved straight-line extraction in the random oracle model with applications to signature aggregation. Cryptology ePrint Archive, Paper 2022/393 (2022). https://eprint.iacr.org/2022/393
20. Lindell, Y.: An efficient transform from sigma protocols to NIZK with a CRS and non-programmable random oracle. In: Theory of Cryptography - 12th Theory of Cryptography Conference, TCC 2015, Warsaw, Poland, 23–25 March 2015, Proceedings, Part I, pp. 93–109 (2015)
21. Maurer, U.: Zero-knowledge proofs of knowledge for group homomorphisms, Des. Codes Cryptogr. **77**, 663–676 (2015)
22. Pass, R.: On Deniability in the common reference string and random oracle model. In: Boneh, D. (ed.) CRYPTO 2003. LNCS, vol. 2729, pp. 316–337. Springer, Heidelberg (2003). https://doi.org/10.1007/978-3-540-45146-4_19
23. Pass, R.: Simulation in quasi-polynomial time, and its application to protocol composition. In: Biham, E. (ed.) EUROCRYPT 2003. LNCS, vol. 2656, pp. 160–176. Springer, Heidelberg (2003). https://doi.org/10.1007/3-540-39200-9_10
24. Pass, R.: Alternative variants of zero-knowledge proofs. Master's thesis, Kungliga Tekniska Högskolan, Licentiate Thesis Stockholm, Sweden (2004)
25. Pass, R.: Bounded-concurrent secure multi-party computation with a dishonest majority. In: Babai, L. (ed.) Proceedings of the 36th Annual ACM Symposium on Theory of Computing, Chicago, IL, USA, 3–16, June 12004, pp. 232–241. ACM (2004)
26. Schnorr, C.P.: Efficient Identification and Signatures for Smart Cards. In: Brassard, G. (ed.) CRYPTO 1989. LNCS, vol. 435, pp. 239–252. Springer, New York (1990). https://doi.org/10.1007/0-387-34805-0_22

Updatable NIZKs from Non-Interactive Zaps

Karim Baghery[1(✉)] and Navid Ghaedi Bardeh[2]

[1] imec-COSIC, KU Leuven, Leuven, Belgium
karim.baghery@kuleuven.be
[2] Norwegian University of Science and Technology, Trondheim, Norway

Abstract. In ASIACRYPT 2016, Bellare, Fuchsbauer, and Scafuro studied the security of NIZK arguments under subverted Structured Reference String (SRS) and presented some positive and negative results. In their best positive result, they showed that by defining an SRS as a tuple of knowledge assumption in bilinear groups (e.g. g^a, g^b, g^{ab}), and then using a Non-Interactive (NI) zap to prove that either there is a witness for the statement x or one knows the trapdoor of SRS (e.g. a or b), one can build NIZK arguments that can achieve soundness and *subversion zero-knowledge* (zero-knowledge without trusting a third party; Sub-ZK). In this paper, we expand their idea and use NI zaps (of knowledge) to build NIZK arguments (of knowledge) with *updatable*, *universal*, and *succinct* SRS. To this end, we first show that their proposed sound and Sub-ZK NIZK argument can also achieve *updatable* soundness, which is a more desired notion than the plain soundness. Updatable soundness allows the verifier to update the SRS one time and bypass the need for a trusted third party. Then, we show that using a similar OR language, given a NI zap (of knowledge) and a *key-updatable* signature scheme, one can build NIZK arguments that can achieve Sub-ZK and *updatable* simulation soundness (resp. *updatable* simulation extractability). The proposed constructions are the first NIZK arguments that have updatable and succinct SRS, and do not require a random oracle. Our instantiations show that in the resulting NIZK arguments the computational cost for the parties to verify/update the SRS is negligible, namely, a few exponentiations and pairing checks. The run times of the prover and verifier, as well as the size of the proof, are asymptotically the same as those of the underlying NI zap.

Keywords: Non-interactive zaps · Non-interactive zap of knowledge · NIZK · Subversion ZK · Updatable soundness · Updatable SRS Model

1 Introduction

Let $\mathbf{R_L}$ be an NP relation which defines the language $\mathbf{L}$ of all statements x for which there exists a witness w s.t. $(\mathsf{x}, \mathsf{w}) \in \mathbf{R_L}$. A Non-Interactive Zero-Knowledge (NIZK) argument [11,25] for $\mathbf{R_L}$ allows a party P (called prover),

A. R. Beresford et al. (Eds.): CANS 2022, LNCS 13641, pp. 23–43, 2022.
https://doi.org/10.1007/978-3-031-20974-1_2

knowing w, to non-interactively prove the truth of a statement x without leaking extra information about the witness w. As the basic requirements, a NIZK argument is expected to satisfy, (i) *Completeness*, guaranteeing that an honest P will convince an honest V with probability 1. (ii) *Soundness* (SND), ensuring that no malicious P can convince (honest) V of a false statement, except with negligible probability. (iii) *Zero-Knowledge* (ZK), guaranteeing that the verifier V learns nothing beyond the truth of statement x from the proof. In [19], Feige and Shamir proposed (vi) *Witness Indistinguishability* (WI), as a relaxation of ZK, which only guarantees that V cannot distinguish which witness was used by the prover to generate the proof.

To achieve SND and ZK at the same time, NIZK arguments [11] rely on the existence of a common reference string. The later and more efficient constructions need a Structured Reference String (SRS) which is supposed to be generated by a Trusted Third Party (TTP) and shared with P and V. Finding a TTP to generate the SRS can be a serious concern in practical applications where parties mutually distrust each other. In [18], Dwork and Naor presented a two-round proof system for NP, so called zap, that *does not require* a TTP while achieves WI and SND. A zap is a two-round protocol which starts by sending a message from V to the P, and finishes by sending the proof from P to V. Later in [29], Groth, Ostrovsky and Sahai presented a Non-Interactive (NI) zap under standard assumptions, where P sends the proof in one round to V. In comparison with NIZK arguments, NI zaps come with a weaker security guarantee, namely WI and SND, while they do not need a trusted setup phase. Recently, in [21], Fuchsbauer and Orru showed that under knowledge of exponent assumption [8,15], the NI zap of Groth, Ostrovsky and Sahai, can be extended to achieve WI and (v) *Knowledge Soundness* (KS), which guarantees that no malicious P can convince (honest) V, unless he *knows* a witness w for the statement x, s.t. $(\mathsf{x}, \mathsf{w}) \in \mathbf{R_L}$. Their construction is the first NI Zap of Knowledge (NI-ZoK). Zaps and NI zaps for NP are shown to be extremely useful in the design of various cryptographic primitives.

Subversion-Resistant and Updatable NIZK Arguments. In 2016, Bellare, Fuchsbauer and Scafuro [8] studied achievable security in NIZK arguments in the face of a subverted SRS. They first presented a stronger variation of standard notions, so called Subversion-SND (Sub-SND), Subversion-WI (Sub-WI), Subversion-ZK (Sub-ZK), that respectively imply SND, WI, ZK even if the SRS is generated by an adversary $\mathcal{A}$. For instance, (vi) Sub-ZK implies that the NIZK argument guarantees ZK even if $\mathcal{A}$ sets up the SRS. Given the new definitions, they presented some negative and positive results for building subversion-resistant NIZK arguments. As the best positive result, they showed that using an OR-based language one can use a NI zap (e.g. [29]) along with an SRS (e.g. a tuple of a knowledge assumption in bilinear groups [8,15], which can be verified publicly) and build a NIZK argument that satisfies SND and Sub-ZK. The resulting NIZK argument will have a *universal* and *succinct* SRS. A universal and succinct SRS allows one to prove knowledge of a witness for different languages, and it additionally enables more efficient SRS verification to achieve Sub-ZK. Two follow-up works [1,20] studied achieving Sub-ZK in zero-knowledge

Succinct Non-interactive ARguments of Knowledge (zk-SNARKs) [10,27,31]. In Sub-ZK NIZK arguments (of knowledge), the prover does not need to trust a third party, while the verifier still has to trust the SRS generator. In 2018, Groth et al. [28] introduced *updatable* SRS model that allows both P and V to update a *universal* SRS and bypass the need for a TTP. Unlike a language-dependent SRS, a universal SRS can be used for various languages. They defined new notions (vii) *Updatable KS*, (U-KS), (viii) *Updatable SND*, (U-SND), and (ix) *Updatable ZK*, (U-ZK), which each implies the standard notion, as long as the initial SRS generation or one of (the follow up) SRS updates is done by an honest party. Then, Groth et al. [28] presented the first zk-SNARK that can achieve Sub-ZK and U-KS. In such zk-SNARKs, the prover verifies the final SRS, and the verifier one-time updates the SRS and they avoid trusting a third party. The follow-up works in this direction [13,14,33] are more efficient. In 2019, Baghery [4] showed that Sub-ZK and KS SNARKs can be lifted to achieve Sub-ZK and (x) *Simulation Extractability* (SE) (a.k.a. *Simulation Knowledge Soundness*), which implies an $\mathcal{A}$ cannot convince (honest) V, even if he has seen polynomially many simulated proofs, unless he *knows* a witness w for the statement x. Recent studies achieve Sub-ZK and SE in quasi-adaptive NIZK arguments [3] and ad-hoc construction of zk-SNARKs [6]. A follow-up work [2] showed that Sub-ZK and U-KS zk-SNARKs can be lifted to achieve Sub-ZK and (xi) *Updatable SE* (U-SE) which ensures that the protocol satisfy SE as long as the initial SRS generation or one of the SRS updates is done honestly. A recent study [23], shows that some of the zk-SNARKs with updatable SRS, can also achieve U-SE [14,22,30]. TIRAMISU allows one to lift such constructions to achieve *black-box* extractability [7], in the updatable SRS model.

Our Contribution. The core of our contribution is to show that the technique used by Bellare et al. [8] for building a Sub-ZK and NIZK argument, can also be expanded to build NIZK arguments with updatable SRS. Namely, one can use NI zap (resp. NI-ZoK) arguments along with an OR language and build Sub-ZK NIZK arguments (resp. of knowledge) with an updatable SRS, that can satisfy U-X, where $X \in \{\text{SND}, \text{KS}, \text{Simulation Soundness}, \text{SE}\}$.

To this end, we first propose an *SRS updating* and an *SRS verification* algorithms for the Sub-ZK and SND NIZK argument of Bellare et al. [8], and then show that under the same assumptions used in the security proof of their scheme, namely, the Diffie-Hellman Knowledge-of-Exponent (DH-KE) [8], the Computational Diffie-Hellman (CDH), and the Decision Linear (DLin) [12] assumptions, their scheme can also achieve U-SND. This results in the first NIZK argument with *updatable*, *universal*, and *succinct* SRS that does not exploit a random oracle. By instantiating Bellare et al.'s [8] construction with Fuchsbauer and Orru's NI-ZoK [21], our results lead to a universal and updatable NIZK argument of knowledge that can satisfy Sub-ZK and U-KS.

After that, we generalize Bellare et al.'s idea and show that given a NI zap argument (resp. NI-ZoK) and a *key-updatable* signature scheme [2], one can define an OR language, namely,

$$((\mathsf{x}, \mathsf{w}) \in \mathbf{R_L}) \cup \text{(I know the } \mathsf{sk} \text{ associated with the signature's updatable } \mathsf{pk}),$$

where $(\mathsf{sk}, \mathsf{pk})$ are a pair of secret and public keys, and build NIZK arguments that can achieve Sub-ZK and *Updatable* Simulation Soundness, U-SS, (resp. U-SE). Our resulting Sub-ZK and U-SS NIZK arguments are the first constructions that can achieve these notions. But, Abdolmaleki et al. [2] also built Sub-ZK and U-SE zk-SNARKs using a similar OR language. However, as stated in [[2], theorems 2, and 3], they require a NIZK argument that satisfies Sub-ZK and (U-)KS, which are stronger security requirements than what a NI zap (or NI-ZoK) achieves. In nutshell, we require weaker security guarantees from the input proof system, but, on the other side, we obtain Sub-ZK and U-SE NIZK arguments with succinct SRS and linear proofs.

Key Insights. Our key insights to generalize the OR-based technique of Bellare et al. that uses NI zaps have been the following: First, since NI zap (or NI-ZoK) arguments do not have an SRS, therefore once we define an OR-based language based on them, the SRS of the resulting NIZK argument only contains the elements that are added from the second clause in the OR language. Consequently, to simulate the proofs in the resulting NIZK argument, one uses the trapdoors of the SRS that come from the second clause of the OR relation. The second key point is that by using an *updatable* SRS in the second clause, one can construct NIZK arguments with *universal* and *updatable* SRS. This allows us to build the first NIZK arguments with succinct (constant group elements), updatable and universal SRS. The third insight is that if the updatable SRS in the second clause of the OR language be the public key of a (key-updatable) signature scheme [2], then we can construct Sub-ZK NIZK arguments that can achieve U-SS or U-SE.

It is worth mentioning that we mainly used the NI zap of Groth, Ostrovsky and Sahai [29], and the NI-ZoK of Fuchsbauer and Orru [21]. However, our constructions and techniques can be instantiated and adapted with other NI zaps, e.g. [32]. As we discuss later, in all the resulting NIZK arguments, to bypass the need for a TTP, the computational cost for the prover/verifier is a few numbers of exponentiation and pairing operations.

The rest of the paper is organized as follows; Sect. 2 presents necessary preliminaries for the paper. In Sect. 3, we show that the Sub-ZK and SND NIZK argument of Bellare, Fuchsbauer and Scafuro [8], can also achieve U-SND. In Sect. 4, we show how one can build NIZK arguments with updatable, universal, and succinct SRS using NI zaps and key-updatable signature schemes. Finally, we conclude the paper in Sect. 5.

2 Preliminaries

Let λ be the security parameter and $\mathsf{negl}(\lambda)$ denotes a negligible function. We use $x \leftarrow\!\!\$\ X$ to denote x sampled uniformly according to the distribution X. PPT stands for probabilistic polynomial-time. All adversaries are assumed to be state-full. For an algorithm $\mathcal{A}$, let $\mathrm{im}(\mathcal{A})$ be the image of $\mathcal{A}$, i.e., the set of valid outputs of $\mathcal{A}$. Moreover, assume $\mathsf{RND}(\mathcal{A})$ denotes the random tape of $\mathcal{A}$, and $r \leftarrow\!\!\$\ \mathsf{RND}(\mathcal{A})$ denotes sampling of a randomizer r of sufficient length for

$\mathcal{A}$'s needs. By $y \leftarrow \mathcal{A}(x;r)$ we mean given an input x and a randomizer r, $\mathcal{A}$ outputs y. For algorithms $\mathcal{A}$ and $\mathsf{Ext}_\mathcal{A}$, we write $(y \,\|\, y') \leftarrow (\mathcal{A} \,\|\, \mathsf{Ext}_\mathcal{A})(x;r)$ as a shorthand for "$y \leftarrow \mathcal{A}(x;r)$, $y' \leftarrow \mathsf{Ext}_\mathcal{A}(x;r)$".

In pairing-based groups, we use additive notation together with the bracket notation, i.e., in group $\mathbb{G}_\mu$, $[a]_\mu = a\,[1]_\mu$, where $[1]_\mu$ is a fixed generator of $\mathbb{G}_\mu$. A *bilinear group generator* $\mathsf{BGgen}(1^\lambda)$ returns $(p, \mathbb{G}_1, \mathbb{G}_2, \mathbb{G}_T, \hat{e}, [1]_1, [1]_2)$, where p (a large prime) is the order of cyclic abelian groups $\mathbb{G}_1$, $\mathbb{G}_2$, and $\mathbb{G}_T$. Finally, $\hat{e} : \mathbb{G}_1 \times \mathbb{G}_2 \rightarrow \mathbb{G}_T$ is an efficient non-degenerate bilinear pairing, s.t. $\hat{e}([a]_1, [b]_2) = [ab]_T$. Denote $[a]_1 \bullet [b]_2 = \hat{e}([a]_1, [b]_2)$.

We adopt the definition of NI zap and NI-ZoK arguments from [21,29], and the definition of standard, subversion-resistant and updatable NIZK arguments from [1,2,8,27,28], and in few cases we define a natural extension of current definitions that we achieve in our proposed schemes. Let $\mathcal{R}$ be a relation generator, such that $\mathcal{R}(1^\lambda)$ returns a polynomial-time decidable binary relation $\mathbf{R} = \{(\mathsf{x}, \mathsf{w})\}$, where x is the statement and w is the corresponding witness. Let $\mathbf{L}_\mathbf{R} = \{\mathsf{x} : \exists\, \mathsf{w} \mid (\mathsf{x}, \mathsf{w}) \in \mathbf{R}\}$ be an **NP**-language including all the statements which there exist corresponding witnesses in relation $\mathbf{R}$.

2.1 NI Zap and NI-ZoK Arguments

Definition 1 (NI Zap). *A pair of PPT algorithms* (P, V) *is a non-interactive zap (a.k.a. NIWI) for an* **NP** *relation* $\mathbf{R}$ *if it satisfies,*

1. Completeness*: For all* $(\mathsf{x}, \mathsf{w}) \in \mathbf{R}$, $\Pr[\pi \leftarrow \mathsf{P}(\mathbf{R}, \mathsf{x}, \mathsf{w}) : \mathsf{V}(\mathbf{R}, \mathsf{x}, \pi) = 1] = 1$.
2. Soundness*: there exists a negligible function* $\mathsf{negl}(\lambda)$*, such that for every* $\mathsf{x} \notin \mathbf{L}_\mathbf{R}$ *and* $\pi \in \{0,1\}^\star$*:* $\Pr[\mathsf{V}(\mathbf{R}, \mathsf{x}, \pi) = 1] \leq \mathsf{negl}(\lambda)$.
3. Witness Indistinguishable (WI)*: for any sequence* $I = \{(\mathsf{x}, \mathsf{w}_1, \mathsf{w}_2) : (\mathsf{x}, \mathsf{w}_1) \in \mathbf{R} \wedge (\mathsf{x}, \mathsf{w}_2) \in \mathbf{R}\}$*:*

$$\{\pi_1 \leftarrow \mathsf{P}(\mathbf{R}, \mathsf{x}, \mathsf{w}_1) : \pi_1\}_{(\mathsf{x}, \mathsf{w}_1, \mathsf{w}_2) \in I} \approx_c \{\pi_2 \leftarrow \mathsf{P}(\mathbf{R}, \mathsf{x}, \mathsf{w}_2) : \pi_2\}_{(\mathsf{x}, \mathsf{w}_1, \mathsf{w}_2) \in I}.$$

NI-ZoK arguments are NI zaps that additionally satisfy KS, defined as bellow:

Definition 2 (Knowledge Soundness (KS)). *A NI argument* Ψ_{NIZK} *is* KS *for* $\mathcal{R}$*, if for any PPT* $\mathcal{A}$*, there exists a PPT* $\mathsf{Ext}_\mathcal{A}$ *s.t. for all* λ*,*

$$\Pr\left[\begin{array}{l}\mathbf{R} \leftarrow \mathcal{R}(1^\lambda), \mathsf{srs} \leftarrow \mathsf{K}_{\mathsf{srs}}(\mathbf{R}), r \leftarrow\$\ \mathsf{RND}(\mathcal{A}), ((\mathsf{x}, \pi) \,\|\, \mathsf{w}) \leftarrow ... \\ ...(\mathcal{A} \,\|\, \mathsf{Ext}_\mathcal{A})(\mathbf{R}, \mathsf{srs}; r) : (\mathsf{x}, \mathsf{w}) \notin \mathbf{R} \wedge \mathsf{V}(\mathbf{R}, \mathsf{srs}, \mathsf{x}, \pi) = 1\end{array}\right] = \mathsf{negl}(\lambda),$$

2.2 NIZKs with Trusted, Subverted, and Updatable SRS

A *NIZK argument* Ψ_{NIZK} with updatable SRS for $\mathcal{R}$ consists of PPT algorithms $(\mathsf{K}_{\mathsf{srs}}, \mathsf{SU}, \mathsf{SV}, \mathsf{P}, \mathsf{V}, \mathsf{Sim})$, such that:

- $(\mathsf{srs}_0, \Pi_{\mathsf{srs}_0}) \leftarrow \mathsf{K}_{\mathsf{srs}}(\mathbf{R})$: Given $\mathbf{R}$, $\mathsf{K}_{\mathsf{srs}}$ sample the trapdoor ts and then use it to generate srs_0 along with Π_{srs_0} as a proof of its well-formedness.

- $(\mathsf{srs}_i, \Pi_{\mathsf{srs}_i}) \leftarrow \mathsf{SU}(\mathbf{R}, \mathsf{srs}_{i-1}, \{\Pi_{\mathsf{srs}_j}\}_{j=0}^{i-1})$: SU return the pair of $(\mathsf{srs}_i, \Pi_{\mathsf{srs}_i})$, where srs_i is the updated SRS and Π_{srs_i} is a proof for correct updating.
- $(\bot/1) \leftarrow \mathsf{SV}(\mathbf{R}, \mathsf{srs}_i, \{\Pi_{\mathsf{srs}_j}\}_{j=0}^{i})$: Given a potentially updated srs_i, and $\{\Pi_{\mathsf{srs}_j}\}_{j=0}^{i}$, SV return either $\bot$ (if srs_i is incorrectly formed or updated) or 1.
- $(\pi/\bot) \leftarrow \mathsf{P}(\mathbf{R}, \mathsf{srs}_i, \mathsf{x}, \mathsf{w})$: Given the tuple of $(\mathbf{R}, \mathsf{srs}_i, \mathsf{x}, \mathsf{w})$, such that $(\mathsf{x}, \mathsf{w}) \in \mathbf{R}$, P output an argument π. Otherwise, it returns $\bot$.
- $(0/1) \leftarrow \mathsf{V}(\mathbf{R}, \mathsf{srs}_i, \mathsf{x}, \pi)$: Given $(\mathbf{R}, \mathsf{srs}_i, \mathsf{x}, \pi)$, V verify the proof π and return either 0 (reject) or 1 (accept).
- $\pi \leftarrow \mathsf{Sim}(\mathbf{R}, \mathsf{srs}_i, \mathsf{ts}_i, \mathsf{x})$: Given $(\mathbf{R}, \mathsf{srs}_i, \mathsf{ts}_i, \mathsf{x})$, where ts_i is the (simulation) trapdoor of the updated SRS, namely srs_i, Sim output a simulated π.

In the standard SRS model, a NIZK argument for $\mathcal{R}$ has a tuple of algorithms $(\mathsf{K}_{\mathsf{srs}}, \mathsf{P}, \mathsf{V}, \mathsf{Sim})$ (and $\mathsf{K}_{\mathsf{srs}}$ does not return the Π_{srs_0}), while subversion-resistant constructions [1,8] additionally have an SV algorithm which is used to verify the well-formedness of the SRS elements to achieve Sub-ZK [8]. But as listed above, in the *updatable* SRS model, a NIZK argument additionally has an SU algorithm that allows the parties to update the SRS and add their own private shares to the SRS generation. Note that in the latest case, the algorithms $\mathsf{K}_{\mathsf{srs}}$, SU and SV do not necessarily need $\mathbf{R}$, and they just deduce 1^λ and the length of the SRS from it. In the standard case, Ψ_{NIZK} is expected to satisfy *completeness*, *ZK* and *soundness*, while in the case of subverted setup, Ψ_{NIZK} is expected to achieve *Sub-WI*, *Sub-ZK* and *Sub-SND*. Finally, in the *updatable* SRS model, Ψ_{NIZK} can achieve *updatable completeness*, *U-ZK*, *U-SND*, *U-SE*, *U-SS*, and *U-SE*.

Next, we recall the security definitions of Sub-WI, Sub-ZK, U-SND, U-SS and U-SE used or achieved by our presented constructions, and refer to the full version of paper [5] for the definitions of NIZK arguments in the SRS model.

Definition 3 (Sub-WI). *A NI argument Ψ is* Sub-WI *for $\mathcal{R}$, if for any PPT* Sub*, for all λ, all $\mathbf{R} \in \operatorname{im}(\mathcal{R}(1^\lambda))$, and for any PPT $\mathcal{A}$, one has $\varepsilon_0 \approx_\lambda \varepsilon_1$, where*

$$\varepsilon_b = \Pr\left[\begin{array}{l} r \leftarrow\!\!\$\ \mathsf{RND}(\mathsf{Sub}), (\mathsf{srs}, \xi_{\mathsf{Sub}}) \leftarrow \mathsf{Sub}(\mathbf{R}; r) : \\ \mathcal{A}^{\mathsf{O}_b(\cdot,\cdot)}(\mathbf{R}, \mathsf{srs}, \xi_{\mathsf{Sub}}) = 1 \end{array}\right].$$

Here, ξ_{Sub} is auxiliary information generated by subvertor Sub*, and the oracle $\mathsf{O}_b(\mathsf{x}, \mathsf{w}_b)$ returns $\bot$ (reject) if $(\mathsf{x}, \mathsf{w}_b) \notin \mathbf{R}$, and otherwise it returns $\mathsf{P}(\mathbf{R}, \mathsf{srs}, \mathsf{x}, \mathsf{w}_b)$.*

Definition 4 (Sub-ZK). *A NI argument Ψ is* computationally Sub-ZK *for $\mathcal{R}$, if for any PPT subvertor* Sub *there exists a PPT extractor $\mathsf{Ext}_{\mathsf{Sub}}$, s.t. for all λ, all $\mathbf{R} \in \operatorname{im}(\mathcal{R}(1^\lambda))$, and for any PPT $\mathcal{A}$, one has $\varepsilon_0 \approx_\lambda \varepsilon_1$, where*

$$\varepsilon_b = \Pr\left[\begin{array}{l} r \leftarrow\!\!\$\ \mathsf{RND}(\mathsf{Sub}), ((\mathsf{srs}, \Pi_{\mathsf{srs}}, \xi_{\mathsf{Sub}}) \parallel \mathsf{ts}) \leftarrow (\mathsf{Sub} \parallel \mathsf{Ext}_{\mathsf{Sub}})(\mathbf{R}; r) : \\ \mathsf{SV}(\mathbf{R}, \mathsf{srs}, \Pi_{\mathsf{srs}}) = 1 \wedge \mathcal{A}^{\mathsf{O}_b(\cdot,\cdot)}(\mathbf{R}, \mathsf{srs}, \mathsf{ts}, \xi_{\mathsf{Sub}}) = 1 \end{array}\right].$$

Here, ξ_{Sub} is auxiliary information generated by subvertor Sub*, and the oracle $\mathsf{O}_0(\mathsf{x}, \mathsf{w})$ returns $\bot$ (reject) if $(\mathsf{x}, \mathsf{w}) \notin \mathbf{R}$, and otherwise it returns $\mathsf{P}(\mathbf{R}, \mathsf{srs}, \mathsf{x}, \mathsf{w})$. Similarly, $\mathsf{O}_1(\mathsf{x}, \mathsf{w})$ returns $\bot$ (reject) if $(\mathsf{x}, \mathsf{w}) \notin \mathbf{R}$, and otherwise it returns $\mathsf{Sim}(\mathbf{R}, \mathsf{srs}, \mathsf{ts}, \mathsf{x})$. Ψ is* perfectly Sub-ZK *for $\mathcal{R}$ if one requires that $\varepsilon_0 = \varepsilon_1$.*

Definition 5 (U-SND). *A NI argument* Ψ_{NIZK} *is* updatable sound for $\mathcal{R}$, *if for every PPT* $\mathcal{A}$, *any PPT* Sub, *for all* $\mathbf{R} \in \mathrm{im}(\mathcal{R}(1^\lambda))$, *and for all* λ,

$$\Pr\left[\begin{array}{l}(\mathsf{srs}_0, \Pi_{\mathsf{srs}_0}) \leftarrow \mathsf{K}_{\mathsf{srs}}(\mathbf{R}), (\{\mathsf{srs}_j, \Pi_{\mathsf{srs}_j}\}_{j=1}^{i}, \xi_{\mathsf{Sub}}) \leftarrow \mathsf{Sub}(\mathsf{srs}_0, \Pi_{\mathsf{srs}_0}),\\ \mathsf{SV}(\mathsf{srs}_i, \{\Pi_{\mathsf{srs}_j}\}_{j=0}^{i}) = 1, (\mathsf{x}, \pi) \leftarrow \mathcal{A}(\mathbf{R}, \mathsf{srs}_i, \xi_{\mathsf{Sub}}) : \mathsf{x} \notin \mathbf{L} \wedge \mathsf{V}(\mathbf{R}, \mathsf{srs}_i, \mathsf{x}, \pi) = 1\end{array}\right] \approx_\lambda 0 .$$

Here $\mathsf{RND}(\mathcal{A}) = \mathsf{RND}(\mathsf{Sub})$, *and* Π_{srs} *is a proof for correctness of SRS generation or updating process. In the definition,* ξ_{Sub} *can be seen as an auxiliary information provided by* Sub *to* $\mathcal{A}$.

Definition 6 (U-SS). *A NI argument* Ψ_{NIZK} *is* updatable simulation soundness for $\mathcal{R}$, *if for all* $\mathbf{R} \in \mathrm{im}(\mathcal{R}(1^\lambda))$, *for any PPT* Sub, *and every PPT* $\mathcal{A}$, *for all* λ,

$$\Pr\left[\begin{array}{l}((\mathsf{srs}_0, \Pi_{\mathsf{srs}_0}) \,\|\, \mathsf{ts}_0 := \mathsf{ts}'_0) \leftarrow \mathsf{K}_{\mathsf{srs}}(\mathbf{R}), r_s \leftarrow\!\$\ \mathsf{RND}(\mathsf{Sub}),\\ ((\{\mathsf{srs}_j, \Pi_{\mathsf{srs}_j}\}_{j=1}^{i}, \xi_{\mathsf{Sub}}) \,\|\, \{\mathsf{ts}'_j\}_{j=1}^{i}) \leftarrow (\mathsf{Sub} \,\|\, \mathsf{Ext}_{\mathsf{Sub}})(\mathsf{srs}_0, \Pi_{\mathsf{srs}_0}, r_s),\\ \mathsf{SV}(\mathsf{srs}_i, \{\Pi_{\mathsf{srs}_j}\}_{j=0}^{i}) = 1, (\mathsf{x}, \pi) \leftarrow \mathcal{A}^{\mathsf{O}(\mathsf{ts}_i, \ldots)}(\mathbf{R}, \mathsf{srs}_i, \xi_{\mathsf{Sub}}) :\\ (\mathsf{x}, \pi) \notin Q \wedge \mathsf{x} \notin \mathbf{L} \wedge \mathsf{V}(\mathbf{R}, \mathsf{srs}_i, \mathsf{x}, \pi) = 1\end{array}\right] = \mathsf{negl}(\lambda),$$

where Π_{srs} *is a proof for correctness of SRS generation/updating,* ts_i *is the simulation trapdoor associated with the final SRS that can be computed using* $\{\mathsf{ts}'_j\}_{j=0}^{i}$, *and* Q *is the set of simulated statement-proof pairs returned by* $\mathsf{O}(.)$.

Definition 7 (U-SE). *A NI argument* Ψ_{NIZK} *is* updatable simulation-extractable (with non-black-box extraction) for $\mathcal{R}$, *if for every PPT* $\mathcal{A}$ *and* Sub, *for all* $\mathbf{R} \in \mathrm{im}(\mathcal{R}(1^\lambda))$, *the following probability is* $\mathsf{negl}(\lambda)$,

$$\Pr\left[\begin{array}{l}((\mathsf{srs}_0, \Pi_{\mathsf{srs}_0}) \,\|\, \mathsf{ts}_0 := \mathsf{ts}'_0) \leftarrow \mathsf{K}_{\mathsf{srs}}(\mathbf{R}), r_s \leftarrow\!\$\ \mathsf{RND}(\mathsf{Sub}),\\ ((\{\mathsf{srs}_j, \Pi_{\mathsf{srs}_j}\}_{j=1}^{i}, \xi_{\mathsf{Sub}}) \,\|\, \{\mathsf{ts}'_j\}_{j=1}^{i}) \leftarrow (\mathsf{Sub} \,\|\, \mathsf{Ext}_{\mathsf{Sub}})(\mathsf{srs}_0, \Pi_{\mathsf{srs}_0}, r_s),\\ \mathsf{SV}(\mathsf{srs}_i, \{\Pi_{\mathsf{srs}_j}\}_{j=0}^{i}) = 1, r_{\mathcal{A}} \leftarrow\!\$\ \mathsf{RND}(\mathcal{A}), (\mathsf{x}, \pi) \leftarrow \mathcal{A}^{\mathsf{O}(\mathsf{ts}_i, \ldots)}(\mathbf{R}, \mathsf{srs}_i, \xi_{\mathsf{Sub}}; r_{\mathcal{A}}),\\ \mathsf{w} \leftarrow \mathsf{Ext}_{\mathcal{A}}(\mathbf{R}, \mathsf{srs}_i, \mathsf{Ext}_{\mathsf{Sub}}, \pi) : (\mathsf{x}, \pi) \notin Q \wedge (\mathsf{x}, \mathsf{w}) \notin \mathbf{R} \wedge \mathsf{V}(\mathbf{R}, \mathsf{srs}_i, \mathsf{x}, \pi) = 1\end{array}\right],$$

where $\mathsf{Ext}_{\mathsf{Sub}}$ *in a PPT extractor,* Π_{srs} *is a proof for correctness of SRS generation/updating, and* ts_i *is the simulation trapdoor associated with the final SRS that can be computed using* $\{\mathsf{ts}'_j\}_{j=0}^{i}$. *Here,* $\mathsf{RND}(\mathcal{A}) = \mathsf{RND}(\mathsf{Sub})$ *and* Q *is the set of the statement and simulated proofs returned by* $\mathsf{O}(.)$.

2.3 Assumptions

Definition 8 (Diffie-Hellman Knowledge of Exponent Assumption (DH-KEA) [8]). *We say that a bilinear group generator* BGGen *is* DH-KE secure *for relation set* $\mathcal{R}$ *if for any* λ, $\mathbf{R} \in \mathrm{im}(\mathcal{R}(1^\lambda))$, *and PPT adversary* $\mathcal{A}$ *there exists a PPT extractor* $\mathsf{Ext}_{\mathcal{A}}$, *such that, the following probability is* $\mathsf{negl}(\lambda)$,

$$\Pr\left[\begin{array}{l}(p, \mathbb{G}, \mathbb{G}_T, \hat{e}, [1]_1) \leftarrow \mathsf{BGGen}(1^\lambda), r \leftarrow\!\$\ \mathsf{RND}(\mathcal{A}), ([k]_1, [l]_1) \leftarrow \mathbb{G}, ([s]_1, [t]_1, [st]_1\\ \,\|\, x, y) \leftarrow (\mathcal{A} \,\|\, \mathsf{Ext}_{\mathcal{A}})(\mathbf{R}, [k]_1, [l]_1; r) : [s]_1 \bullet [t]_1 = [1]_1 \bullet [st]_1 \wedge x \neq s \wedge y \neq t\end{array}\right].$$

Definition 9 (Computational Diffie-Hellman (CDH) Assumption). *We say that the decisional Diffie-Hellman assumption holds for a group generator* GGen *if for any PPT adversary* $\mathcal{A}$ *the following probability is* $\mathsf{negl}(\lambda)$,

$$\Pr\left[(p, \mathbb{G}, g) \leftarrow \mathsf{GGen}(1^\lambda), x, y \leftarrow \mathbb{Z}_p, h \leftarrow \mathcal{A}(\lambda, g^x, g^y) : h = g^{xy}\right].$$

Definition 10 (Decisional Linear (dLin) Assumption [12]**).** *We say that the decisional linear assumption holds for a group generator* GGen *if for any PPT adversary* $\mathcal{A}$ *the following probability is* $\mathsf{negl}(\lambda)$,

$$\Pr\left[\begin{array}{l}(p, \mathbb{G}, g) \leftarrow \mathsf{GGen}(1^\lambda), u, v, s, t, \xi \leftarrow \mathbb{Z}_p, b \leftarrow \{0,1\} \\ b' \leftarrow \mathcal{A}(1^\lambda, g^u, g^v, g^{us}, g^{vt}, g^{s+t+b\xi}) : b = b'\end{array}\right].$$

Definition 11 (Bilinear Diffie-Hellman Knowledge of Exponent (BDH-KE) Assumption [1]**).** *We say* BGgen *is* BDH-KE secure *for relation set* $\mathcal{R}$ *if for any* λ, $\mathbf{R} \in \mathrm{im}(\mathcal{R}(1^\lambda))$, *and PPT adversary* $\mathcal{A}$, *there exists a PPT extractor* $\mathsf{Ext}_\mathcal{A}$, *such that, the following probability is* $\mathsf{negl}(\lambda)$,

$$\Pr\left[\begin{array}{l}(p, \mathbb{G}_1, \mathbb{G}_2, \mathbb{G}_T, \hat{e}, [1]_1, [1]_2) \leftarrow \mathsf{BGgen}(1^\lambda), r \leftarrow\!\!\$\ \mathsf{RND}(\mathcal{A}), ([\alpha_1]_1, [\alpha_2]_2 \\ \parallel a) \leftarrow (\mathcal{A} \parallel \mathsf{Ext}_\mathcal{A})(\mathbf{R}, r) : [\alpha_1]_1 \bullet [1]_2 = [1]_1 \bullet [\alpha_2]_2 \wedge a \neq \alpha_1\end{array}\right].$$

2.4 Key Updatable, One-time, and Key Homomorphic Signatures

Some of our constructions exploit key-updatable signature schemes that allow parties to update the secret and public keys and inject their shares into the keys. We adopt their definition from [2], which we review next.

An updatable signature scheme Σ is a tuple $\Sigma = (\mathsf{KG}, \mathsf{Upk}, \mathsf{Vpk}, \mathsf{Sign}, \mathsf{SigVerify})$ of PPT algorithms, which are defined as follows.

- $\mathsf{KG}(1^\lambda)$: Given 1^λ, return a signing key sk and a verification key pk with associated message space $\mathcal{M}$.
- $\mathsf{Upk}(\mathsf{pk}_{i-1})$: Given a pk_{i-1}, output an updated verification key pk_i with the associated secret updating key $\bar{\mathsf{sk}}_i$, and a proof Π_i.
- $\mathsf{Vpk}(\mathsf{pk}_i, \mathsf{pk}_{i-1}, \Pi_i)$: Given a verification key pk_{i-1}, an updated verification key pk_i, and the proof Π_i, check if pk_i has been updated correctly.
- $\mathsf{Sign}(\mathsf{sk}_i, m)$: Given sk_i and a message $m \in \mathcal{M}$, output a signature σ_i.
- $\mathsf{SigVerify}(\mathsf{pk}_i, m, \sigma_i)$: Given a verification key pk_i, a message $m \in \mathcal{M}$, and a signature σ_i, output a bit $b \in \{0,1\}$.

Definition 12 (Updatable Correctness). *An updatable signature scheme* Σ *is correct, if*

$$\Pr\left[\begin{array}{l}(\mathsf{sk}_{i-1}, \mathsf{pk}_{i-1}, \Pi_{i-1}) \leftarrow \mathsf{KG}(1^\lambda), (\bar{\mathsf{sk}}_i, \mathsf{pk}_i, \Pi_i) \leftarrow \mathsf{Upk}(\mathsf{pk}_{i-1}), \\ \mathsf{Vpk}(\mathsf{pk}_i, \mathsf{pk}_{i-1}, \Pi_i) = 1 : \mathsf{SigVerify}(\mathsf{pk}_{i-1}, m, \mathsf{Sign}(\mathsf{sk}_{i-1}, m)) = 1 \\ \wedge\, \mathsf{SigVerify}(\mathsf{pk}_i, m, \mathsf{Sign}(\mathsf{sk}_{i-1} + \bar{\mathsf{sk}}_i, m)) = 1\end{array}\right] = 1.$$

Definition 13 (Updatable EUF-CMA). *A signature scheme Σ is updatable EUF-CMA secure, if for all PPT subverter* Sub, *there exists a PPT extractor* $\mathsf{Ext}_{\mathsf{Sub}}$ *such that for all λ, and all PPT adversaries $\mathcal{A}$*

$$\Pr\left[\begin{array}{l}(\mathsf{sk}_{i-1}, \mathsf{pk}_{i-1}, \Pi_{i-1}) \leftarrow \mathsf{KG}(1^\lambda), w_{\mathsf{Sub}} \leftarrow\!\!\$\ \mathsf{RND}(\mathsf{Sub}),\\ (\mathsf{pk}_i, \Pi_i, \xi_{\mathsf{Sub}}) \leftarrow \mathsf{Sub}(pk_{i-1}; w_{\mathsf{Sub}}), \bar{\mathsf{sk}}_i \leftarrow \mathsf{Ext}_{\mathsf{Sub}}(\mathsf{pk}_{i-1}; w_{\mathsf{Sub}})\\ (m^*, \sigma^*) \leftarrow \mathcal{A}^{\mathsf{Sign}(\mathsf{sk}_{i-1}+\bar{\mathsf{sk}}_i, .)}(\mathsf{pk}_i, \xi_{\mathsf{Sub}}) : \mathsf{Vpk}(\mathsf{pk}_i, \mathsf{pk}_{i-1}, \Pi_i) = 1\\ \wedge\ \mathsf{pk}_i = \mathsf{pk}_{i-1} \cdot \mu(\bar{\mathsf{sk}}_i) \wedge \mathsf{SigVerify}(\mathsf{pk}, m^*, \sigma^*) = 1 \wedge m^* \notin \mathcal{Q}^{\mathsf{Sign}}\end{array}\right] = \mathsf{negl}(\lambda),$$

where μ is an efficiently computable map from the secret key to the public key space, and $\mathcal{Q}^{\mathsf{Sign}}$ is the list of queries and responses to the signing oracle.

We also require one-time signature schemes in our construction.

Definition 14 (Strong One-Time Signature Scheme). *A strong one-time signature scheme Σ_{OT} is a signature scheme Σ which satisfies the following unforgeability notion: for all PPT adversaries $\mathcal{A}$*

$$\Pr\left[\begin{array}{l}(\mathsf{sk}, \mathsf{pk}) \leftarrow \mathsf{KG}(1^\lambda), (m^*, \sigma^*) \leftarrow \mathcal{A}^{\mathsf{Sign}(\mathsf{sk}, .)}(\mathsf{pk})\\ \mathsf{SigVerify}(\mathsf{pk}, m^*, \sigma^*) = 1 \wedge (m^*, \sigma^*) \notin \mathcal{Q}^{\mathsf{Sign}}\end{array}\right] = \mathsf{negl}(\lambda),$$

where the oracle $\mathsf{Sign}(\mathsf{sk}; m) := \Sigma.\mathsf{Sign}(\mathsf{sk}, m)$ *can only be called once.*

We now recall the notion of key-homomorphic signatures [17]. We assume that the secret key space $\mathbb{H}$ and the public key space $\mathbb{E}$ are groups with two operations that we will denote by $+$ and $\cdot$ respectively, by convention.

Definition 15 (Secret Key to Public Key Homomorphism). *A signature scheme* $\Sigma = (\mathsf{KG}, \mathsf{Sign}, \mathsf{SigVerify})$ *provides a secret key to public key homomorphism if there is an efficiently computable homomorphism $\mu : \mathbb{H} \rightarrow \mathbb{E}$ such that for all key pairs* $(\mathsf{sk}, \mathsf{pk}) \leftarrow \mathsf{KG}(1^\lambda)$ *one has* $\mathsf{pk} = \mu(\mathsf{sk})$.

Definition 16 (Key-Homomorphic Signatures). *A signature scheme is called key-homomorphic, if it provides a secret key to public key homomorphism and an additional PPT algorithm* Adapt, *defined as:*
$\mathsf{Adapt}(\mathsf{pk}, m, \sigma, \Delta)$: *Given a public key* pk, *a message m, a signature σ, and a shift amount Δ outputs a public key* pk' *and a signature σ', such that for all $\Delta \in \mathbb{H}$ and all* $(\mathsf{sk}, \mathsf{pk}) \leftarrow \mathsf{KG}(1^\lambda)$, *all messages $m \in \mathcal{M}$ and all* $\sigma \leftarrow \mathsf{Sign}(\mathsf{sk}, m)$ *and* $(\mathsf{pk}', \sigma') \leftarrow \mathsf{Adapt}(\mathsf{pk}, m, \mathsf{Sign}(\mathsf{sk}, m))$ *it holds that*

$$Pr[\mathsf{SigVerify}(\mathsf{pk}', m, \sigma') = 1] = 1 \wedge \mathsf{pk}' = \mu(\Delta) \cdot \mathsf{pk}.$$

Definition 17 (Adaptability of Signatures). *A key-homomorphic signature scheme provides adaptability of signatures, if for every $\lambda \in \mathbb{N}$ and every message $m \in \mathcal{M}$, it holds that* $[(\mathsf{sk}, \mathsf{pk}), \mathsf{Adapt}(\mathsf{pk}, m, \mathsf{Sign}(\mathsf{sk}, m), \Delta)]$, *where* $(\mathsf{sk}, \mathsf{pk}) \leftarrow \mathsf{KG}(1^\lambda), \Delta \leftarrow \mathbb{H}$, *and* $[(\mathsf{sk}, \mu(sk)), (\mu(sk) \cdot \mu(\Delta), \mathsf{Sign}(\mathsf{sk} + \Delta, m))]$, *where* $\mathsf{sk} \leftarrow \mathbb{H}, \Delta \leftarrow \mathbb{H}$, *are identically distributed.*

3 Bellare et al.'s Sub-ZK NIZK Can Achieve U-SND

In this section, we show that the technique proposed by Bellare, Fuchsbauer and Scafuro [8] to build Sub-ZK NIZK arguments can be expanded to build NIZK arguments with updatable and universal SRS. In order to build a Sub-ZK and sound NIZK argument from NI zaps, they defined an SRS as a tuple of knowledge assumption, namely $([x]_1, [y]_1, [xy]_1)$, and let a proof for a statement x prove that either there is a witness for x or one knows x or y. They proved knowledge by adding a ciphertext C (of linear encryption) and using a perfectly sound NI zap to prove that either $\mathsf{x} \in \mathbf{L}$ or C encrypts x or y. Their construction uses NI zap of Groth, Ostrovsky and Sahai [29].

In the resulting NIZK argument, ZK is achieved since by encrypting the trapdoor x (or y) proofs can be simulated, and by IND-CPA of C and WI of the NI zap, they are indistinguishable from the real ones. Soundness is achieved since by soundness of the NI zap, a proof for a wrong statement must contain encryption of x or y, which is hard to obtain from an honestly generated SRS. They defined the SRS, as a tuple of a knowledge assumption in bilinear groups, which is *publicly verifiable* by paring, such that they can extract either x or y from an SRS subverter, and simulate the proofs without the need for a trusted third party, consequently achieving Sub-ZK. Nowadays, the mentioned technique is used in all Sub-ZK NIZK arguments, e.g. [1,2,4,20,28]. In nutshell, to achieve Sub-ZK, one first check the well-formedness of SRS elements by pairing equations, and then relying on a knowledge assumption extracts the simulation trapdoors from the SRS subverter and provides to the simulation algorithm constructed in the proof of (standard) ZK. In Bellare, Fuchsbauer and Scafuro's construction [8], another important point to achieve Sub-ZK was that the keys of the encryption scheme were generated with the prover, rather than the subverter. Therefore a subverter or verifier does not have access to the secret key to decrypt C and learn the witness, but the reduction allows non-black-box extraction under a knowledge assumption. We refer to the original work for further details [8].

Expanding Bellare, Fuchsbauer and Scafuro's OR Technique to Achieve U-SND. The folklore OR technique, introduced by [9], is shown to be a prominent technique for designing various cryptographic primitives. As reviewed above, Bellare, Fuchsbauer and Scafuro [8] showed that using such techniques with a NI zap and a *trapdoor-extractable* SRS, e.g. tuple of a knowledge assumption, one can build NIZK argument that can achieve Sub-ZK and SND. As a part of our contribution, we noticed that using NI zaps (resp. NI-ZoKs) with a similar OR language but with an *updatable* and trapdoor-extractable SRS, we can build Sub-ZK NIZK arguments (of knowledge) with *universal* and *updatable* SRS.

The universality of the resulting NIZK argument is inherited from the input NI zap. Particular about their construction [8], one can see that given the SRS, which includes the tuple of DH-KE assumption, namely $([x]_1, [y]_1, [xy]_1)$, a prover needs to prove that either there is a witness for x or he knows x or y, by sending a ciphertext C that encrypts x or y. In other words, the SRS is generated independently of the statement to be proved, and the same SRS can

SRS Generator, $\mathsf{K_{srs}}(\mathbf{R_L})$: $(p, \mathbb{G}_1, \mathbb{G}_T, \hat{e}, [1]_1) \leftarrow \mathsf{BGgen}(1^\lambda)$; Sample $x_0, y_0, t_0 \leftarrow\$ \mathbb{Z}_p$, where x_0, y_0 are the simulation trapdoors; Set the string $\mathsf{srs}_0 := ([t_0]_1, [x_0]_1, [y_0]_1, [x_0 y_0]_1)$ and the well-formedness proof $\pi_0 := (([x_0]_1, [y_0]_1, [x_0 y_0]_1), ([x_0]_1, [y_0]_1, [x_0 y_0]_1))$; Return (srs_0, π_0).

SRS Update, $\mathsf{SU}(\mathbf{R_L}, \mathsf{srs}_{i-1}, \{\pi_j\}_{j=0}^{i-1})$: Given (a potentially updated) srs_{i-1}, parse $\mathsf{srs}_{i-1} := ([t_{i-1}]_1, [x_{i-1}]_1, [y_{i-1}]_1, [x_{i-1} y_{i-1}]_1)$; Sample $t'_i, x'_i, y'_i \leftarrow\$ \mathbb{Z}_p$; Set $[t_i]_1 := t'_i [t_{i-1}]_1$, $[x_i]_1 := x'_i [x_{i-1}]_1$, $[y_i]_1 := y'_i [y_{i-1}]_1$, $[x_i y_i]_1 := x'_i y'_i [x_{i-1} y_{i-1}]_1$; Set the string $\mathsf{srs}_i := ([t_i]_1, [x_i]_1, [y_i]_1, [x_i y_i]_1)$ and the proof $\pi_i := (([x_i]_1, [y_i]_1, [x_i y_i]_1), ([x'_i]_1, [y'_i]_1, [x'_i y'_i]_1))$; Return (srs_i, π_i).

SRS Verification, $\mathsf{SV}(\mathsf{srs}_i, \{\pi_j\}_{j=0}^{i})$: Given $(\mathsf{srs}_i, \{\pi_j\}_{j=0}^{i})$, in order to verify the well-formedness of srs_i, act as follows:

- If $i = 0$: parse $\mathsf{srs}_0 := ([t_0]_1, [x_0]_1, [y_0]_1, [x_0 y_0]_1)$ and $\pi_0 := (([x_0]_1, [y_0]_1, [x_0 y_0]_1), ([x_0]_1, [y_0]_1, [x_0 y_0]_1))$ and do the following:
  1. Check if $[x_0]_1 \bullet [y_0]_1 = [1]_1 \bullet [x_0 y_0]_1$;
  2. Check if $([t_0]_1 \neq 1) \cap ([t_0]_1 \in \mathbb{G}_1)$;
- If $i \geq 1$: parse $\mathsf{srs}_i := ([t_i]_1, [x_i]_1, [y_i]_1, [x_i y_i]_1)$ and $\{\pi_j := (([x_j]_1, [y_j]_1, [x_j y_j]_1), ([x'_j]_1, [y'_j]_1, [x'_j y'_j]_1))\}_{j=0}^{i}$ and do the following:
  1. Check if $[x_0]_1 = [x'_0]_1$, $[y_0]_1 = [y'_0]_1$, and $[x_0 y_0]_1 = [x'_0 y'_0]_1$;
  2. Check if $[x'_j]_1 \bullet [y'_j]_1 = [x'_j y'_j]_1 \bullet [1]_1$ for $j = 0, 1, \cdots, i$;
  3. Check if $[x_j]_1 \bullet [1]_1 = [x_{j-1}]_1 \bullet [x'_j]_1$ for $j = 1, 2, \cdots, i$;
  4. Check if $[y_j]_1 \bullet [1]_1 = [y_{j-1}]_1 \bullet [y'_j]_1$ for $j = 1, 2, \cdots, i$;
  5. Check if $[x_j y_j]_1 \bullet [1]_1 = [x_{j-1} y_{j-1}]_1 \bullet [x'_j y'_j]_1$ for $j = 1, 2, \cdots, i$;
  6. Check if $[x_i]_1 \bullet [y_i]_1 = [1]_1 \bullet [x_i y_i]_1$;
  7. Check if $([t_i]_1 \neq 1) \cap ([t_i]_1 \in \mathbb{G}_1)$;

return 1 if all the checks pass (srs_i is well-formed), otherwise $\perp$.

Fig. 1. The SRS generation $\mathsf{K_{srs}}$, SRS updating SU, and SRS verification SV algorithms for the Sub-ZK NIZK argument of Bellare, Fuchsbauer and Scafuro [8].

be used to prove different statements defined in the first clause. Note that in the resulting NIZK argument $[t_i]_1$ is used to prove the soundness of scheme under CDH assumption, and to achieve Sub-ZK, we only need to extract one of the simulation trapdoors x_i or y_i from the Sub (a malicious SRS generator).

For updatability, next we describe an updating algorithm for the Sub-ZK NIZK argument of Bellare, Fuchsbauer and Scafuro [8] that allows one (e.g. a verifier) to update the SRS and bypass the need for a trusted setup by injecting his share to the generation of SRS. After updating the SRS, the updater needs to return a proof to show that the SRS updating was done honestly and the updated SRS is well-formed. As we discuss later, verifying this proof is necessary to achieve Sub-ZK and U-SND. Figure 1 describes the SRS generation $\mathsf{K_{srs}}$, SRS verification SV, and our proposed SRS updating SU algorithms for the Sub-ZK NIZK argument of [8]. For the description of the proof generation and proof verification algorithms we refer to the original paper [8].

Efficiency. From the description of algorithms (in Fig. 1) one can see that the SRS generation algorithm requires 4 exponentiations in $\mathbb{G}_1$. Similarly, to update an SRS the SU algorithm requires 4 exponentiations in $\mathbb{G}_1$. The SU algorithm also requires 3 additional exponentiations in $\mathbb{G}_1$ to generate a well-formedness proof π_i. Finally, to verify an i-time updated SRS srs_i, $i \geq 1$, the SRS verification algorithm SV needs to compute $8i + 4$ pairings, which mostly are batchable.

Security Proof. Bellare, Fuchsbauer and Scafuro [8], showed that their NIZK argument satisfies SND under DH-KE and Computational Diffie-Hellman (CDH) assumptions; and Sub-ZK under DH-KEA and DLin assumption. Next, we show that their construction can also achieve U-SND. To this end, first, we recall a corollary from [24, Lemma 6], and then give a lemma which is used in the security proof. The lemma proves that in their construction even when given an honestly generated SRS as input, updaters need to know their injected share to the (simulation) trapdoor. In this way security against the updater is linked to an honest SRS.

Corollary 1. *In the updatable SRS model, single adversarial updates imply full updatable security [24, Lemma 6].*

Lemma 1 (Trapdoor Extraction from Updated SRS). *Considering the algorithms in Fig. 1, suppose that there exists a PPT adversary $\mathcal{A}$ such that given $(\mathsf{srs}_0, \pi_0) \leftarrow \mathsf{K}_{\mathsf{srs}}(\mathbf{R_L})$, $\mathcal{A}$ returns the updated SRS (srs_i, π_i), where $\mathsf{SV}(\mathsf{srs}_i, \{\pi_j\}_{j=0}^{1}) = 1$ with non-negligible probability. Then, the DH-KE assumption implies that there exists a PPT extractor $\mathsf{Ext}_{\mathcal{A}}$ that, given the randomness of $\mathcal{A}$ as input, outputs x'_1 or y'_1 such that $[x_1]_1 = x'_1[x_0]$, $[y_1]_1 = y'_1[y_0]$, and $[x_1 y_1]_1 = x'_1 y'_1 [x_0 y_0]$.*

Proof. Considering Corollary 1, we consider the case that $\mathcal{A}$ makes only one update to the SRS, but similar to [24, Lemma 6], it can be generalized. Parse π_0 as containing $([x_0]_1, [y_0]_1, [x_0 y_0]_1)$ and parse srs_0 as containing $\mathsf{srs}_0 := ([t_0]_1, [x_0]_1, [y_0]_1, [x_0 y_0]_1)$. We consider an $\mathcal{A}$, that given srs_0, returns an updated SRS, srs_1, where it contains $([t_1]_1, [x_1]_1, [y_1]_1, [x_1 y_1]_1)$ and its proof π_1 contains $(([t_1]_1, [x_1]_1, [y_1]_1, [x_1 y_1]_1), ([x'_1]_1, [y'_1]_1, [x'_1 y'_1]_1))$. If the SRS verification accepts the updated SRS, namely if $\mathsf{SV}(\mathsf{srs}_i, \{\pi_j\}_{j=0}^{1}) = 1$, then the following equations hold,

$$[x'_0]_1 \bullet [y'_0]_1 = [1]_1 \bullet [x'_0 y'_0]_1, \quad [x'_1]_1 \bullet [y'_1]_1 = [1]_1 \bullet [x'_1 y'_1]_1, \quad [x_1]_1 \bullet [1]_1 = [x_0]_1 \bullet [x'_1]_1,$$

$$[y_1]_1 \bullet [1]_1 = [y_0]_1 \bullet [y'_1]_1, \quad [x_1 y_1]_1 \bullet [1]_1 = [x_0 y_0]_1 \bullet [x'_1 y'_1]_1, \quad [x_1]_1 \bullet [y_1]_1 = [1]_1 \bullet [x_1 y_1]_1,$$

By the equations, $[x'_0]_1 \bullet [y'_0]_1 = [1]_1 \bullet [x'_0 y'_0]_1$, under the DH-KE assumption, there exists an extraction algorithm that can extract either x'_0 or y'_0. Similarly, by the equations $[x'_1]_1 \bullet [y'_1]_1 = [1]_1 \bullet [x'_1 y'_1]_1$, and $[x_1]_1 \bullet [y_1]_1 = [x_1 y_1]_1 \bullet [1]_1$ under the DH-KE assumption, there exists an extraction algorithm $\mathsf{Ext}_{\mathcal{A}}$ that given the randomness of $\mathcal{A}$, can extract x_0 or y_0, x'_1 or y'_1, and x_1 or y_1. The other equations check the consistency and the well-formedness of SRS and imply that $x_1 = x_0 x'_1 = x'_0 x'_1$ and $y_1 = y_0 y'_1 = y'_0 y'_1$. □

Given the constructed SU and SV algorithms (in Fig. 1), the following theorem shows that their construction can also achieve U-SND under the same assumption used in the security proof of the protocol.

Theorem 1. *Given the* SU *and* SV *algorithms described in Fig. 1, the Sub-ZK and SND NIZK argument proposed by Bellare, Fuchsbauer and Scafuro [8] additionally satisfies U-SND assuming the DH-KE and CDH assumptions hold.*

Proof. Considering Corollary 1, to prove this it suffices to prove security in the case that $\mathcal{A}$ makes only one update to the SRS. Imagine we have a PPT adversary $\mathcal{A}$ that given honestly sampled $(\mathsf{srs}_0, \pi_0) \leftarrow \mathsf{K}_{\mathsf{srs}}(\mathbf{R_L}, 1^\lambda)$, returns an updated SRS (srs_i, π_i) (along with a well-formedness proof) and a pair of (x, π) that get accepted; i.e., such that $\mathsf{SV}(\mathsf{srs}_i, \{\pi_j\}_{j=0}^{i}) = 1$, and also the verifier of NIZK argument accepts π as a valid proof for the statement x, $\mathsf{V}(\mathbf{R_L}, \mathsf{srs}_i, \mathsf{x}, \pi) = 1$. By Lemma 1, because the updated SRS verifies, there exists an extractor $\mathsf{Ext}_{\mathcal{A}}$ that outputs the SRS trapdoors τ, such that running the SU algorithm with trapdoors τ returns (srs_i, π_i). The rest of proof is the same as the proof of soundness, which is given in [8]. □

Remark 1. The above theorem showed that the Sub-ZK NIZK argument of Bellare, Fuchsbauer and Scafuro [8] can also achieve U-SND. It is worth mentioning that their original construction was instantiated with the NI zap of Groth, Ostrovsky and Sahai [29] that is proven to achieve (Sub-)WI and (Sub-)SND. By instantiating their construction with the NI-ZoK of Fuchsbauer and Orru [21], which is a variant of [29], one can obtain a Sub-ZK NIZK argument of *knowledge* that can satisfy KS. Then, using our proposed SU and SV algorithms, one will obtain a NIZK argument that will satisfy Sub-ZK and U-KS.

4 Sub-ZK and U-{SS, SE} NIZKs from NI Zaps

In Sect. 3, we showed that the Sub-ZK NIZK argument of Bellare, Fuchsbauer and Scafuro [8], built with a NI zap argument and a trapdoor-extractable SRS, can also achieve U-SND. Moreover, it can be instantiated with a NI-ZoK [21] to build a Sub-ZK and U-KS NIZK argument. The resulting NIZK arguments are universal and have a succinct updatable SRS, which allows both the prover and verifier to efficiently update and bypass the need for a TTP. However, in practice one may require updatable NIZK arguments with even stronger security guarantees than U-SND and U-KS, so-called Updatable Simulation Soundness (U-SS) [7] and U-SE [2]. SS and SE imply SND and KS, respectively, even if the adversary sees a polynomial number of simulated proofs. Both notions guarantee the non-malleability of proofs [16] which is necessary for various applications. As in U-SND and U-KS, in the U-SS and U-SE, the adversary is also allowed to update the SRS, while the notions ensure that SS and SE are achieved as long as the initial SRS generation or one of SRS updates is done by an honest party.

As mentioned in the introduction, one of our key insights is that once we use NI zaps and define an OR language, then the NI zap does not have an SRS, and if the SRS of the second clause be the public key of a key-updatable signature scheme, then we can achieve even stronger security notions in the resulting Sub-ZK NIZK argument. In this section, we show that Bellare, Fuchsbauer and Scafuro's approach can be expanded to build an OR-based compiler that uses NI zaps and allows one to build Sub-ZK NIZK arguments with *succinct*, *universal* and *updatable* SRS that can satisfy U-SS or U-SE. To this end, we revise the OR-based compiler of Derler and Slamanig [17], which is presented to build SE NIZK arguments with *black-box* extractability, and present a new variant that can be used to build Sub-ZK NIZK arguments with succinct, universal and updatable SRS that can achieve U-SS or U-SE with *non-black-box* extraction. In [2], Abdolmaleki, Ramacher and Slamanig also presented a new variant of Derler and Slamanig's compiler [17], so-called LAMASSU , that allows one to lift any Sub-ZK and U-KS zk-SNARK to a Sub-ZK and U-SE one. LAMASSU is particularly designed for updatable zk-SNARKs, and as discussed in ([2], Theorem 4), it requires the input zk-SNARK to satisfy U-ZK which is a stronger requirement than (sub-)WI that NI zaps achieve, and we require it in the new compiler. Considering the negative result that Sub-ZK and black-box extractability cannot be achieved at the same time [7,8], Sub-ZK and U-SE with non-black-box extraction is the best achievable if we aim to retain Sub-ZK [7].

In Derler and Slamanig's OR-based construction [17], they use a EUF-CMA secure adaptable key-homomorphic signature scheme Σ and a strongly unforgeable one-time signature (sOTS) scheme Σ_{OT} to achieve non-malleability in the input KS NIZK argument Π, which results in a SE NIZK argument, but under a trusted setup. A key point about their construction is that the prover does not need to prove that a signature verifies under the verification key given in the SRS, as done in Groth's constructions [26]. Instead, the prover needs to prove that he knows the secret key of the public key given in the SRS, which he has used to adapt signatures produced with Σ_{OT}, to the ones valid under the public key given in the SRS. Next, we present a variant of their construction that given a NI zap, an sOTS scheme, and a *key-updatable* signature scheme allows one to build NIZK arguments with universal and updatable SRS. Key-updatable signature schemes are an extension of key-homomorphic signatures, where their keys are updatable, and they can guarantee unforgeability as long as at least one of the key updates or the key generation will be done honestly [2].

For the compiler, let $\mathbf{L}$ be an arbitrary NP-language $\mathbf{L} = \{x \mid \exists \mathsf{w} : \mathbf{R_L}(\mathsf{x}, \mathsf{w}) = 1\}$, for which we aim to construct a Sub-ZK and U-SS (or U-SE) NIZK, and let $\mathbf{L}'$ be the language for lifted construction, such that, $((\mathsf{x}, \mathsf{cpk}, \mathsf{pk}), (\mathsf{w}, \mathsf{csk} - \mathsf{sk})) \in \mathbf{R_{L'}}$, iff:

$$(\mathsf{x}, \mathsf{w}) \in \mathbf{R_L} \vee \mathsf{cpk} = \mathsf{pk} \cdot \mu(\mathsf{csk} - \mathsf{sk}),$$

where μ is an efficiently computable map, $(\mathsf{cpk}, \mathsf{csk})$ is a key pair for a key-updatable signature scheme, $(\mathsf{sk}, \mathsf{pk})$ is a key pair for an sOTS scheme. Let $\Sigma_{OT} = (\mathsf{KG}, \mathsf{Sign}, \mathsf{SigVerify})$ be an sOTS scheme, $\Sigma = (\mathsf{KG}, \mathsf{Upk}, \mathsf{Vpk}, \mathsf{Sign}, \mathsf{SigVerify})$ be a key-updatable signature scheme, and $\Psi := (\mathsf{P}, \mathsf{V})$ be a NI zap (or NI-ZoK) arguments. Then, Fig. 2 presents the resulting NIZK argument for $\mathbf{L}$ with PPT algorithms $(\mathsf{K}'_{\mathsf{srs}}, \mathsf{SU}', \mathsf{SV}', \mathsf{P}', \mathsf{V}', \mathsf{Sim}')$, where we later show that it can achieve Sub-ZK and U-SS or U-SE, depending on the input NI zap.

SRS Generation, $(\mathsf{srs}'_0, \Pi'_{\mathsf{srs}_0}) \leftarrow \mathsf{K}'_{\mathsf{srs}}(\mathbf{R_L})$**:** Run the key generator of the key-updatable signature scheme $(\mathsf{csk}_0, \mathsf{cpk}_0, \Pi_{\mathsf{cpk}_0}) \leftarrow \Sigma.\mathsf{KG}(1^\lambda)$; Set $\mathsf{srs}'_0 := \mathsf{cpk}_0$, $\Pi'_{\mathsf{srs}_0} := \Pi_{\mathsf{cpk}_0}$, and $\mathsf{ts}_0 = \mathsf{csk}_0$; Return $(\mathsf{srs}'_0, \Pi'_{\mathsf{srs}_0})$.

SRS Updating, $(\mathsf{srs}'_i, \Pi'_{\mathsf{srs}_i}) \leftarrow \mathsf{SU}'(\mathbf{R_L}, \mathsf{srs}'_{i-1}, \{\Pi'_{\mathsf{srs}_j}\}_{j=0}^{i-1})$**:** Parse $\mathsf{srs}'_{i-1} := \mathsf{cpk}_{i-1}$; Run $(\mathsf{csk}_i, \mathsf{cpk}_i, \Pi_{\mathsf{cpk}_i}) \leftarrow \Sigma.\mathsf{KU}(\mathsf{cpk}_{i-1})$; Set $(\mathsf{srs}'_i \parallel \Pi'_{\mathsf{srs}_i}) := (\mathsf{cpk}_i \parallel \Pi_{\mathsf{cpk}_i})$, where Π'_{srs_i} is the well-formedness proof; Return $(\mathsf{srs}'_i, \Pi'_{\mathsf{srs}_i})$.

SRS Verify, $(\perp/1) \leftarrow \mathsf{SV}'(\mathbf{R_L}, \mathsf{srs}'_i, \{\Pi'_{\mathsf{srs}_j}\}_{j=0}^{i})$**:** Given $\mathsf{srs}'_i := (\perp, \mathsf{cpk}_i)$, and $\{\Pi'_{\mathsf{srs}_j} := \Pi_{\mathsf{cpk}_j}\}_{j=0}^{i}$ act as follows: if $\{\Sigma.\mathsf{KV}(\mathsf{cpk}_{j-1}, \mathsf{cpk}_j, \Pi_{\mathsf{cpk}_j}) = 1\}_{j=1}^{i}$ return 1 (i.e., the srs'_i is well-formed), otherwise $\perp$.

Prover, $(\pi'/\perp) \leftarrow \mathsf{P}'(\mathbf{R_L}, \mathsf{srs}'_i, \mathsf{x}, \mathsf{w})$**:** Parse $\mathsf{srs}'_i := \mathsf{cpk}_i$; Return $\perp$ if $(\mathsf{x}, \mathsf{w}) \notin \mathbf{R_L}$; generate $(\mathsf{sk}, \mathsf{pk}) \leftarrow \Sigma.\mathsf{KG}(1^\lambda)$ and $(\mathsf{sk}_{OT}, \mathsf{pk}_{OT}) \leftarrow \Sigma_{OT}.\mathsf{KG}(1^\lambda)$; generate $\pi \leftarrow \mathsf{P}(\mathcal{R}_\mathbf{L}, \perp, (\mathsf{x}, \mathsf{cpk}_i, \mathsf{pk}), (\mathsf{w}, \perp))$; sign $\sigma \leftarrow \Sigma.\mathsf{Sign}(\mathsf{sk}, \mathsf{pk}_{OT})$ and $\sigma_{OT} \leftarrow \Sigma_{OT}.\mathsf{Sign}(\mathsf{sk}_{OT}, (\mathsf{x}, \mathsf{pk}, \pi, \sigma))$; and return $\pi' := (\pi, \mathsf{pk}, \sigma, \mathsf{pk}_{OT}, \sigma_{OT})$.

Verifier, $(0/1) \leftarrow \mathsf{V}'(\mathbf{R_L}, \mathsf{srs}'_i, \mathsf{x}, \pi')$**:** Parse $\mathsf{srs}'_i := \mathsf{cpk}_i$ and $\pi' := (\pi, \mathsf{pk}, \sigma, \mathsf{pk}_{OT}, \sigma_{OT})$; return 1 if the following holds and 0 otherwise: $\mathsf{V}(\mathbf{R_L}, \perp, (\mathsf{x}, \mathsf{cpk}_i, \mathsf{pk}), \pi) = 1 \wedge \Sigma.\mathsf{SigVerify}(\mathsf{pk}, \mathsf{pk}_{OT}, \sigma_{OT}) = 1 \wedge \Sigma_{OT}.\mathsf{SigVerify}(\mathsf{pk}_{OT}, (\mathsf{x}, \mathsf{pk}, \pi, \sigma), \sigma_{OT}) = 1$.

Simulator, $(\pi') \leftarrow \mathsf{Sim}'(\mathbf{R_L}, \mathsf{srs}'_i, \mathsf{x}, \mathsf{ts}'_i)$**:** Parse $\mathsf{srs}'_i := \mathsf{cpk}_i$ and $\mathsf{ts}'_i := \mathsf{ts}_i$; generate $(\mathsf{sk}, \mathsf{pk}) \leftarrow \Sigma.\mathsf{KG}(1^\lambda)$ and $(\mathsf{sk}_{OT}, \mathsf{pk}_{OT}) \leftarrow \Sigma_{OT}.\mathsf{KG}(1^\lambda)$; generate $\pi \leftarrow \mathsf{P}(\mathcal{R}_\mathbf{L}, \perp, (\mathsf{x}, \mathsf{cpk}_i, \mathsf{pk}), (\perp, \mathsf{csk}_i - \mathsf{sk}))$; sign $\sigma \leftarrow \Sigma.\mathsf{Sign}(\mathsf{sk}, \mathsf{pk}_{OT})$ and $\sigma_{OT} \leftarrow \Sigma_{OT}.\mathsf{Sign}(\mathsf{sk}_{OT}, (\mathsf{x}, \mathsf{pk}, \pi, \sigma))$; and return $\pi' := (\pi, \mathsf{pk}, \sigma, \mathsf{pk}_{OT}, \sigma_{OT})$.

Fig. 2. A construction for building Sub-ZK and U-SE (or U-SS) NIZK arguments from a NI zap (or NI-ZoK) with PPT algorithms (P, V).

As it can be seen in Fig. 2, every time P' uses Σ to certify the public key of a fresh key pair $(\mathsf{sk}, \mathsf{pk})$ of the Σ_{OT} sOTS scheme. It uses sk_{OT} to sign the proof and achieve non-malleability. By adaptability of the key-updatable signature scheme Σ, the prover can use fresh keys of Σ for each proof. Due to OR construction of $\mathbf{R_{L'}}$, one needs to know the secret key csk to shift such signatures to the valid ones under cpk given in the SRS. On the other side, honest P can use his witness w to generate valid proof, without knowledge of the csk. However, given csk, one can simulate the proofs and pass the verification using the second clause of OR relation. Next, we show how one can exploit NI zaps along with the described construction (in Fig. 2) and build universal and updatable NIZK arguments.

Theorem 2. *Let Ψ be a NI-ZoK, which satisfies completeness, (Sub-)KS and (Sub)-WI. Let Σ be a EUF-CMA secure key-updatable and adaptable signature scheme, and Σ_{OT} be a strongly unforgeable one-time signature scheme. Then, the universal and updatable NIZK argument constructed in Fig. 2 satisfies (i) completeness, (ii) Sub-ZK, and (iii) U-SE.*

Proof. The completeness is straight forward from the description of the resulting NIZK argument given in Fig. 2.

Subversion Zero-Knowledge (Sub-ZK). Considering the fact that NI zap arguments do not have an SRS, the SRS of the resulting NIZK argument is just the public key of the key-updatable signature scheme σ. Suppose that there exists a PPT subvertor $\mathcal{A}$ that outputs a srs' and $\Pi_{\mathsf{srs}'}$ such that $\{\mathsf{SV}'(\mathbf{R_L}, \mathsf{srs}'_i, \Pi'_{\mathsf{srs}_j}) = 1\}_{j=0}^{i}$. From the definition of key-updatable signatures, it then implies that there exists a PPT extractor $\mathsf{Ext}_{\mathcal{A}}$ that given the source code of the adversary and under a proper knowledge assumption (e.g. BDH-KE in our case, Definition 11), it can extract the simulation trapdoor $\mathsf{ts}_i := \mathsf{csk}_i$ associated with the updated SRS srs'_i. Then, given the SRS trapdoor ts_i, we can run the simulator algorithm Sim' described in Fig. 2, and simulate the proofs. This concludes the proof of Sub-ZK.

Updatable Simulation Extractability (U-SE). The proof of U-SE is a modified version of the proof of Theorem 4 in [2], where for each game change based on the ZK property of the zk-SNARK, we now exploit the (Sub-)WI property of the NI-ZoK argument. For the steps relying on the knowledge soundness of zk-SNARK, we rely on the knowledge soundness of NI-ZoK. For the sake of completeness, we present the proof below.

Considering Corollary 1, we prove the theorem in the case that Sub makes only a single update to the SRS after an honest setup. One could also consider the case that Sub generate the SRS, and then we do a single honest update on it. From the definition of a secure key updatable signature, Definition 13, it is possible to use $\mathsf{Ext}_{\mathsf{Sub}}$ and extract the subverter's contribution to the trapdoor when it updates the SRS. Note that in order to collapse all the honest updates into an honest setup, we assume that the trapdoor contributions of setup and update commute. Due to this fact, we use a chain of honest updates, and a single honest setup interchangeably. As we mentioned earlier, NI zaps, do not have an SRS, and we use csk_i of Σ to simulate the proofs.

Relying on the updatable EUF-CMA of Σ, if Sub (or $\mathcal{A}$) return an updated SRS $\mathsf{srs}_i := \mathsf{cpk}_i$ and the corresponding proof Π_i, then (relying on a knowledge assumption, e.g. BDH-KE in our case, given in Definition 11) there exists a PPT extractor $\mathsf{Ext}_{\mathsf{Sub}}$, that given the randomness of Sub as input, outputs $\mathsf{ts}_i := \mathsf{csk}_i$. It is important to note that in the U-SE (given in Definition 7), in addition to accessing the simulation oracle $\mathsf{O}(\mathsf{ts}_i, ...)$ that returns simulated proofs, an adversary $\mathcal{A}$ (or subverter Sub) is allowed to update or generate the initial SRS, which is examined below in experiment $\mathsf{Exp.}$ 2. Following the Definition 13, we use the subverter Sub for updating the SRS and the adversary $\mathcal{A}$ against SE. However, Sub and $\mathcal{A}$ can communicate and $\mathsf{RND}(\mathsf{Sub}) = \mathsf{RND}(\mathcal{A})$, or can be the same entity. The definition of U-SE and the simulation oracle are presented in Definition 7 and Fig. 2, respectively. Next, we write some consecutive games, starting from the real experiment, and highlight the changes, and show that they all are indistinguishable from each other.

Exp. 0. This is the original experiment given in Definition 7 and Fig. 2.
Exp. 1. This experiment is the same as Exp. 0., but Sim' uses the simulation trapdoor $\mathsf{ts}_i := \mathsf{csk}_i$, which is extracted by $\mathsf{Ext}_{\mathsf{Sub}}$, and generate the simulated proof π as $\pi \leftarrow \mathsf{P}(\mathcal{R}_{\mathbf{L}}, \perp, (\mathsf{x}, \mathsf{cpk}_i, \mathsf{pk}), (\perp, \mathsf{csk}_i - \mathsf{sk}))$ (shown in Fig. 2).

Winning Condition. Let Q be the set of (x, π) pairs, and let T be the set of verification keys generated by $\mathsf{O}(.)$. The experiment returns 1 iff: $(\mathsf{x}, \pi) \notin Q \wedge \mathsf{V}(\mathbf{R_L}, \mathsf{srs}_i, \mathsf{x}, \pi) = 1 \wedge \mathsf{pk}_{OT} \notin T \wedge \mathsf{cpk}_i = \mathsf{pk} \cdot \mu(\mathsf{csk} - \mathsf{sk})$.
Exp. 0. $\rightarrow$ Exp. 1.: If the underlying OT signature is strongly unforgeable, and that the underlying NI-ZoK is knowledge sound and WI, then we have $\Pr[\mathsf{Exp.\ 0.}] \leq \Pr[\mathsf{Exp.\ 1.}] + \mathsf{negl}(\lambda)$. The reason is that if $(\mathsf{x}, \pi) \notin Q$ and pk_{OT} has been generated by $\mathsf{O}(.)$, then the $(\mathsf{x}, \pi, \mathsf{pk})$ is a valid message/signature pair. Hence by the unforgeability of the σ_{OT}, we know that the case $(\mathsf{x}, \pi) \notin Q$ and pk_{OT} generated by $\mathsf{O}(.)$, happens with probability $\mathsf{negl}(\lambda)$, which allows us to focus on $\mathsf{pk}_{OT} \notin T$.

The extracted w is unique for all valid witnesses. Further, if some witness is valid for $\mathbf{L}$ and that $(\mathsf{x}, \mathsf{w}) \notin \mathbf{R_L}$, we know it must be the case that due to the WI property of the NI-ZoK and the property of the updating procedure that if SV' outputs 1, then there exists an extractor that extracts the $\mathsf{ts}_i := \mathsf{csk}_i$ (i.e., the trapdoor extraction for the key-updatable signature scheme implies that it is possible to extract the trapdoor when the adversary generates the $\mathsf{srs}_i := \mathsf{cpk}_i$ itself). Given, $\mathsf{ts}_i := \mathsf{csk}_i$, one can use Sim' (given in Fig. 2) and simulate the proofs in a way that no PPT adversary can distinguish them.
Exp. 2. This experiment is the same as Exp. 1., but the only difference is that Sub generates the srs and then we have an honest update.
Exp. 1. $\rightarrow$ Exp. 2.: From the property of the updating procedure in key-updatable signature schemes, we know that if SV' outputs 1, then there exists an $\mathsf{Ext}_{\mathsf{Sub}}$ that can extract the $\mathsf{ts}_i := \mathsf{csk}_i$ (relying on a knowledge assumption). Considering that and also from the WI property of the NI-ZoK argument we have $\Pr[\mathsf{Exp.\ 0.}] \leq \Pr[\mathsf{Exp.\ 1.}] + \mathsf{negl}(\lambda)$.
Exp. 3. This experiment is the same as Exp. 2., but the $\Delta \leftarrow\!\!\$\ \mathbb{H}$ is replaced in $\mathsf{cpk} = \mu(\Delta) \cdot \mathsf{pk}$, where $\Delta \leftarrow\!\!\$\ \mathbb{H}$ and $\mathsf{srs}_i := (\mathsf{cpk} \cdot \mu(\Delta))$ and $\mathsf{ts}_i := \mathsf{csk}_i$.

Winning Condition. Let Q be the set of (x, π) pairs, and let T be the set of verification keys generated by the $\mathsf{O}(.)$. The experiment returns 1 iff: $(\mathsf{x}, \pi) \notin Q \wedge \mathsf{V}(\mathcal{R}_{\mathbf{L}}, \mathsf{srs}_i, \mathsf{x}, \pi) = 1 \wedge \mathsf{pk}_{OT} \notin T \wedge \mathsf{cpk}_i \cdot \mu(\Delta) = \mathsf{pk} \cdot \mu(\Delta) \cdot \mu(\mathsf{csk}_i - \mathsf{sk})$, where relying on the adaptable and updatable EUF-CMA property of the underlying key-updatable signature scheme Σ, it is $\mathsf{negl}(\lambda)$. □

Theorem 3. *Let Ψ be a NI zap, which satisfies (Sub-)SND and (Sub)-WI. Let Σ be a EUF-CMA secure key-updatable and adaptable signature scheme, and Σ_{OT} be a strongly unforgeable one-time signature scheme. Then, the universal and updatable NIZK argument constructed in Fig. 2 satisfies (i) completeness, (ii) Sub-ZK, and (iii) U-SS.*

Proof. The proofs of completeness and Sub-ZK are the same as in the proof of Theorem 2. The proof of U-SS is analogous to the proof of U-SE in the same theorem, which again can be considered as a minimally modified version of the proof of Theorem 4 in [2], where for each game change based on the ZK property of the zk-SNARK, we now use the (Sub-)WI property of the NI zap, and for the steps relying on the knowledge soundness of the zk-SNARK, we rely on the soundness of NI zap, but only achieve U-SS instead of U-SE. □

Instantiations. Next, we instantiate the construction presented in Fig. 2 and obtain Sub-ZK NIZK arguments (resp. of knowledge) with an updatable SRS, that can satisfy U-SS and U-SE.

Considering Theorem 2, to obtain a Sub-ZK and U-SE NIZK argument of knowledge, we instantiate the NI-ZoK Ψ with the one proposed in [21], and the key-updatable signature scheme Σ with the one proposed in [2], and the strongly unforgeable one-time signature scheme Σ_{OT} with Groth's scheme [26].

Similarly, considering Theorem 3, to build a Sub-ZK and U-SS NIZK argument, we instantiate the NI zap Ψ with the one proposed in [29], and again the key-updatable signature scheme Σ from [2], and the one-time signature scheme Σ_{OT} from [26]. In both cases, the resulting NIZK argument will have an *updatable* SRS containing only two group elements, which are the public key of the key-updatable signature scheme, which can be updated and verified efficiently.

5 Conclusion

In this paper, we first showed that the Sub-ZK NIZK argument proposed by Bellare et al. [8], can also satisfy U-SND, which reduces the trust in the third parties even more. By using our proposed SRS updating algorithm, the verifier can update the SRS one time and then bypass the need for a TTP.

Then, we show that one can expand their idea and construct a general construction based on NI zaps that can be used to build universal and updatable NIZK arguments in a modular way. To this end, we presented a compiler based on the construction of Derler and Slamanig [17], which allows one to use NI zaps and build NIZK arguments with succinct, universal, and updatable SRS, that can achieve Sub-ZK, U-SND, U-KS, U-SS, and U-SE. We instantiated our compiler with some NI zaps [21,29] and presented some universal and updatable NIZK arguments that all have succinct SRS.

Due to the currently available options, we instantiated our scheme with the DL-based NI zaps, key-updatable signatures, and one-time secure signatures. Building the mentioned primitives from Post-Quantum (PQ) secure assumptions can be an interesting future research question, as they would allow for the building of universal and updatable NIZK arguments from the PQ assumptions.

Acknowledgement. We thank the anonymous reviewers for their valuable comments and suggestions. The authors also thank Chaya Ganesh for shepherding the final version of the paper. This work has been supported in part by the Defense Advanced Research Projects Agency (DARPA) under contract No. HR001120C0085, and by CyberSecurity Research Flanders with reference number VR20192203, and by the Norwegian Research Council. Navid Ghaedi Bardeh has been supported by Norwegian Research Council project number 288545.

References

1. Abdolmaleki, B., Baghery, K., Lipmaa, H., Zając, M.: A subversion-resistant SNARK. In: Takagi, T., Peyrin, T. (eds.) ASIACRYPT 2017. LNCS, vol. 10626, pp. 3–33. Springer, Cham (2017). https://doi.org/10.1007/978-3-319-70700-6_1
2. Abdolmaleki, B., Ramacher, S., Slamanig, D.: Lift-and-shift: obtaining simulation extractable subversion and updatable SNARKs generically. In: ACM SIGSAC Conference on Computer and Communications Security, CCS 2020 (2020). http://eprint.iacr.org/2020/062
3. Abdolmaleki, B., Slamanig, D.: Subversion-resistant quasi-adaptive NIZK and applications to modular Zk-SNARKs. In: Conti, M., Stevens, M., Krenn, S. (eds.) CANS 2021. LNCS, vol. 13099, pp. 492–512. Springer, Cham (2021). https://doi.org/10.1007/978-3-030-92548-2_26
4. Baghery, K.: Subversion-resistant simulation (Knowledge) sound NIZKs. In: Albrecht, M. (ed.) IMACC 2019. LNCS, vol. 11929, pp. 42–63. Springer, Cham (2019). https://doi.org/10.1007/978-3-030-35199-1_3
5. Baghery, K., Bardeh, N.G.: Updatable NIZKs from non-interactive zaps. Cryptology ePrint Archive, Paper 2022/1214 (2022). http://eprint.iacr.org/2022/1214
6. Baghery, K., Pindado, Z., Ràfols, C.: Simulation extractable versions of Groth's zk-SNARK revisited. In: Krenn, S., Shulman, H., Vaudenay, S. (eds.) CANS 2020. LNCS, vol. 12579, pp. 453–461. Springer, Cham (2020). https://doi.org/10.1007/978-3-030-65411-5_22
7. Baghery, K., Sedaghat, M.: TIRAMISU: black-box simulation extractable NIZKs in the updatable CRS model. In: Conti, M., Stevens, M., Krenn, S. (eds.) CANS 2021. LNCS, vol. 13099, pp. 531–551. Springer, Cham (2021). https://doi.org/10.1007/978-3-030-92548-2_28
8. Bellare, M., Fuchsbauer, G., Scafuro, A.: NIZKs with an untrusted CRS: Security in the face of parameter subversion. In: Cheon, J.H., Takagi, T. (eds.) ASIACRYPT 2016. LNCS, vol. 10032, pp. 777–804. Springer, Heidelberg (2016). https://doi.org/10.1007/978-3-662-53890-6_26
9. Bellare, M., Goldwasser, S.: New paradigms for digital signatures and message authentication based on non-interactive zero knowledge proofs. In: Brassard, G. (ed.) CRYPTO 1989. LNCS, vol. 435, pp. 194–211. Springer, New York (1990). https://doi.org/10.1007/0-387-34805-0_19
10. Ben-Sasson, E., Chiesa, A., Tromer, E., Virza, M.: Succinct non-interactive arguments for a von neumann architecture. Cryptology ePrint Archive, Report 2013/879 (2013). http://eprint.iacr.org/2013/879
11. Blum, M., Feldman, P., Micali, S.: Non-interactive zero-knowledge and its applications. In: Proceedings of the Twentieth Annual ACM Symposium on Theory of Computing, pp. 103–112. ACM (1988)
12. Boneh, D., Boyen, X., Shacham, H.: Short group signatures. In: Franklin, M. (ed.) CRYPTO 2004. LNCS, vol. 3152, pp. 41–55. Springer, Heidelberg (2004). https://doi.org/10.1007/978-3-540-28628-8_3
13. Campanelli, M., Faonio, A., Fiore, D., Querol, A., Rodríguez, H.: Lunar: a toolbox for more efficient universal and updatable zkSNARKs and commit-and-prove extensions. In: Tibouchi, M., Wang, H. (eds.) ASIACRYPT 2021. LNCS, vol. 13092, pp. 3–33. Springer, Cham (2021). https://doi.org/10.1007/978-3-030-92078-4_1

14. Chiesa, A., Hu, Y., Maller, M., Mishra, P., Vesely, N., Ward, N.: Marlin: preprocessing zkSNARKs with universal and updatable SRS. In: Canteaut, A., Ishai, Y. (eds.) EUROCRYPT 2020. LNCS, vol. 12105, pp. 738–768. Springer, Cham (2020). https://doi.org/10.1007/978-3-030-45721-1_26
15. Damgård, I.: Towards practical public key systems secure against chosen ciphertext attacks. In: Feigenbaum, J. (ed.) CRYPTO 1991. LNCS, vol. 576, pp. 445–456. Springer, Heidelberg (1992). https://doi.org/10.1007/3-540-46766-1_36
16. De Santis, A., Di Crescenzo, G., Ostrovsky, R., Persiano, G., Sahai, A.: Robust non-interactive zero knowledge. In: Kilian, J. (ed.) CRYPTO 2001. LNCS, vol. 2139, pp. 566–598. Springer, Heidelberg (2001). https://doi.org/10.1007/3-540-44647-8_33
17. Derler, D., Slamanig, D.: Key-homomorphic signatures and applications to multiparty signatures. Cryptology ePrint Archive, Report 2016/792 (2016). http://eprint.iacr.org/2016/792
18. Dwork, C., Naor, M.: Zaps and their applications. In: 41st FOCS, pp. 283–293. IEEE Computer Society Press, November 2000
19. Feige, U., Shamir, A.: Witness indistinguishable and witness hiding protocols. In: 22nd ACM STOC, pp. 416–426. ACM Press, May 1990
20. Fuchsbauer, G.: Subversion-zero-knowledge SNARKs. In: Abdalla, M., Dahab, R. (eds.) PKC 2018. LNCS, vol. 10769, pp. 315–347. Springer, Cham (2018). https://doi.org/10.1007/978-3-319-76578-5_11
21. Fuchsbauer, G., Orrù, M.: Non-interactive zaps of knowledge. In: Preneel, B., Vercauteren, F. (eds.) ACNS 2018. LNCS, vol. 10892, pp. 44–62. Springer, Cham (2018). https://doi.org/10.1007/978-3-319-93387-0_3
22. Gabizon, A., Williamson, Z.J., Ciobotaru, O.: PLONK: permutations over lagrange-bases for oecumenical noninteractive arguments of knowledge. Cryptology ePrint Archive, Report 2019/953 (2019). http://eprint.iacr.org/2019/953
23. Ganesh, C., Khoshakhlagh, H., Kohlweiss, M., Nitulescu, A., Zajac, M.: What makes Fiat-Shamir zkSNARKs (updatable SRS) simulation extractable? Cryptology ePrint Archive, Report 2021/511 (2021). http://eprint.iacr.org/2021/511
24. Garg, S., Mahmoody, M., Masny, D., Meckler, I.: On the round complexity of OT extension. In: Shacham, H., Boldyreva, A. (eds.) CRYPTO 2018. LNCS, vol. 10993, pp. 545–574. Springer, Cham (2018). https://doi.org/10.1007/978-3-319-96878-0_19
25. Goldwasser, S., Micali, S., Rackoff, C.: The knowledge complexity of interactive proof systems. SIAM J. Comput. **18**(1), 186–208 (1989)
26. Groth, J.: Simulation-sound NIZK proofs for a practical language and constant size group signatures. In: Lai, X., Chen, K. (eds.) ASIACRYPT 2006. LNCS, vol. 4284, pp. 444–459. Springer, Heidelberg (2006). https://doi.org/10.1007/11935230_29
27. Groth, J.: On the size of pairing-based non-interactive arguments. In: Fischlin, M., Coron, J.-S. (eds.) EUROCRYPT 2016. LNCS, vol. 9666, pp. 305–326. Springer, Heidelberg (2016). https://doi.org/10.1007/978-3-662-49896-5_11
28. Groth, J., Kohlweiss, M., Maller, M., Meiklejohn, S., Miers, I.: Updatable and universal common reference strings with applications to zk-SNARKs. In: Shacham, H., Boldyreva, A. (eds.) CRYPTO 2018. LNCS, vol. 10993, pp. 698–728. Springer, Cham (2018). https://doi.org/10.1007/978-3-319-96878-0_24
29. Groth, J., Ostrovsky, R., Sahai, A.: Non-interactive zaps and new techniques for NIZK. In: Dwork, C. (ed.) CRYPTO 2006. LNCS, vol. 4117, pp. 97–111. Springer, Heidelberg (2006). https://doi.org/10.1007/11818175_6

30. Maller, M., Bowe, S., Kohlweiss, M., Meiklejohn, S.: Sonic: Zero-knowledge SNARKs from linear-size universal and updatable structured reference strings. In: Cavallaro, L., Kinder, J., Wang, X., Katz, J. (eds.) ACM CCS 2019, pp. 2111–2128. ACM Press, New York (2019)
31. Parno, B., Howell, J., Gentry, C., Raykova, M.: Pinocchio: nearly practical verifiable computation. In: 2013 IEEE Symposium on Security and Privacy, pp. 238–252. IEEE Computer Society Press, May 2013
32. Ràfols, C.: Stretching Groth-Sahai: NIZK proofs of partial satisfiability. In: Dodis, Y., Nielsen, J.B. (eds.) TCC 2015. LNCS, vol. 9015, pp. 247–276. Springer, Heidelberg (2015). https://doi.org/10.1007/978-3-662-46497-7_10
33. Ràfols, C., Zapico, A.: An algebraic framework for universal and updatable SNARKs. In: Malkin, T., Peikert, C. (eds.) CRYPTO 2021. LNCS, vol. 12825, pp. 774–804. Springer, Cham (2021). https://doi.org/10.1007/978-3-030-84242-0_27

Through the Looking-Glass: Benchmarking Secure Multi-party Computation Comparisons for ReLU's

Abdelrahaman Aly[1,2](✉), Kashif Nawaz[1], Eugenio Salazar[1], and Victor Sucasas[1]

[1] Cryptography Research Centre, Technology Innovation Institute, Abu Dhabi, UAE
{abdelrahaman.aly,kashif.nawaz,eugenio.salazar,victor.sucasas}@tii.ae
[2] imec-COSIC, KU Leuven, Leuven, Belgium

Abstract. Comparisons or Inequality Tests are an essential building block of Rectified Linear Unit functions (ReLU's), ever more present in Machine Learning, specifically in Neural Networks. Motivated by the increasing interest in privacy-preserving Artificial Intelligence, we explore the current state of the art of privacy preserving comparisons over Multi-Party Computation (MPC). We then introduce constant round variations and combinations, which are compatible with customary fixed point arithmetic over MPC. Our main focus is implementation and benchmarking; hence, we showcase our contributions via an open source library, compatible with current MPC software tools. Furthermore, we include a comprehensive comparative analysis on various adversarial settings. Our results improve running times in practical scenarios. Finally, we offer conclusions about the viability of these protocols when adopted for privacy-preserving Machine Learning.

Keywords: Secure multi-party computation · ReLU Functions · Applied cryptography

1 Introduction

Secure Multi-Party Computation has continued to evolve across the years, becoming more practical and useful. This is specially true in the last few years, when fundamental results have considerably reduced computing times. It was just logical for researchers to start asking questions regarding how to build realistic applications. New results followed, introducing novel approaches to achieve basic functionalities for the vast array of applications that could make use of MPC.

Among them, Privacy Preserving Machine Learning (PPML) has gathered attention, due to the strong privacy requirements from machine learning model owners and clients. This has highlighted the need for faster performing protocols for a variety of different tasks, especially for inequality tests(INQ) and fixed point arithmetic. Note how both of them are indispensable building blocks to

A. R. Beresford et al. (Eds.): CANS 2022, LNCS 13641, pp. 44–67, 2022.
https://doi.org/10.1007/978-3-031-20974-1_3

implement activation functions such as ReLU's. We can mention for instance, the contributions from Makri et al. [1] and Catrina and De Hoogh [2] on INQ tests and, Catrina et al. [3] on fixed point arithmetic.

Modern Multiparty frameworks, such as the popular SCALE-MAMBA [4] or MP-SPDZ [5], already incorporate some of these results, (specifically [2,3]). The aim of these tools is to give developers the opportunity to build and deploy applications that incorporate state of the art MPC. In this work, we continue these efforts and provide researchers and implementers with a more complete view of the state of the art of INQ protocols. Among them, the results from Makri et al., commonly referred to as Rabbit, as well as other families of comparisons. We go a step further and, besides the conventional flavors, we offer our own variations and combinations, improving performance. Notice that our main interest is the implementation of fast performing ReLU's (for which we also include a basic formulation in Appendix Sect. 2).

Furthermore, and thanks to recent contributions such as Zaphod [6], we show how comparison protocols can be implemented in constant rounds[1], using mixed circuits in a multiparty setting.

Finally, we aim to provide implementers with useful tools for protocol selection. For this reason, we have included an exhaustive benchmarking (under various adversarial settings) to answer the questions: *i).* What do we need to implement state of the art comparison protocols *ii).* How can we improve them and, *iii).* What protocols perform better in the context of implementing ReLU's mixed with fixed point arithmetic.

1.1 Related Work

Putting aside the large existing body of work related to secure comparisons for MPC for instance, the seminal work from Damgård et al. [7], we focus our attention on both of the most recent contributions that motivated this work, i.e. Makri et al. [1] or Rabbit, and Escudero et al. [8]. Both introduced comparison mechanisms that reduce communication complexity, by mixing Boolean and Arithmetic circuit evaluations via edaBits. In this section we discuss some of the key differences:

On Fixed Point and the Use of Slack: One of the main contributions from Rabbit [1] is that the protocols do not require slack (unused domain space required to achieve statistical security). This implies, for instance, that private comparisons of 64 bits integers require a 64 bits domain. However, inequality tests (INQ) are common tools for applications that extensively use fixed point arithmetic. The current state of the art on the topic [3] still needs extended domains. More precisely, it requires the presence of slack during truncation (the precision adjustment after multiplication). Additionally, albeit slack might not be present in the protocols for comparisons, it is still present in several protocols that are

[1] Following MPC analysis common practices, we evaluate protocols using round complexity as metric.

required by Rabbit, e.g. edaBits [8]. These factors still force application designers to use larger prime sizes. Hence, our work pursues to exploit the advantages of Rabbit whilst still bounded to the realities of state of the art and of practical deployments.

On Round Evaluation: Our novel combinations assimilate a selection of the most efficient elements from Makri et al. and Escudero et al. to reduce round complexity. We also incorporate Zaphod as means to achieve constant round complexity (via the multiparty garbled circuit evaluation of boolean components). For instance, we mix the protocol structure used by Catrina and De Hoogh [2], with the bitwise LTEQZ (Less Than Equal to Zero) test explored by Rabbit and make use the upgraded version of daBits from Zaphod, to sample randomness.

Tool Selection: We aim to produce comparison protocols compatible with commonly used results for fixed point arithmetic [3] and circuit evaluation, i.e. Zaphod. Both of which are only present in SCALE-MAMBA. To the best of our knowledge, MP-SPDZ currently does not implement conversion between their BMR and LSSS processors.

1.2 Our Contributions

- We present a series of constant round variations and adaptations of the privacy preserving comparison protocols, introduced by Makri et al. [1]. Our designs are focused on the implementation of ReLU's in the context of fixed point arithmetic. We introduce, implement and benchmark three different flavors using, in the two first instances, techniques that were succinctly mentioned by the authors, but not fully explored. Let q be a sufficiently large prime e.g. 128 bits, then the variations are the following:
  i) **Conventional Rabbit:** Our closest interpretation to traditional Rabbit. Here, bitwise sampling happens either from above i.e. $\lceil \log_2 q \rceil$ or below i.e. $\lfloor \log_2 q \rfloor$, as suggested by the original authors. It is assumed that q is close to a power of 2. This makes Rabbit probabilistic in nature.
  ii) **Rejection List Rabbit:** For any field $\mathbb{F}_q$, we sample randomness in $\mathbb{Z}_{2^{\lceil \log_2 q \rceil}}$, and reject samples that are above q.
  iii) **Slack Rabbit:** A variation of the protocol where we relax security (becoming statistical instead of information theoretic, from an ideal perspective). We do this so that it can exploit the setup of protocols that require slack to instantiate fixed point representation.
- Much in the style of Escudero et al. [8], we adapt and optimize the commonly used comparison construction of Catrina et al. [2], more precisely:
  i) We transform it into a constant round construction, thanks to Aly et al. Zaphod [6] and Hazay et al. [HSS17] [9];
  ii) we replace the fundamental bitwise-less-than (LT) construction, by the recently introduced bitwise, less than equal (LTEQ) protocol from [1] and;
  iii) we incorporate share conversion when needed.

- A thorough benchmark aimed for implementers. It includes the aforementioned Rabbit constructions and results, together with the optimized comparison protocol for ReLU's from [1]. We also consider different compilation styles[2] (VHDL to Bristol Fashion) of the same bitwise `LTEQ` circuit, including:
  i) `AND_XOR`'*s*: The circuit *as presented* in [1], mixing `xor` with `and` gates to benefit from *free-xor*.
  ii) `AND_NOT`'*s*: The same circuit as it would be typically derived by commonly used synthesizers. The circuit in this case, is entirely made of `and` mixed with `not` gates.
- We give special emphasis to **Usability**. Hence, we provide open source ReLU and comparison libraries on publicly available repositories, written for `SCALE-MAMBA`.

1.3 Outline

This work is structured as follows: In Sect. 1, we present the main motivations for this work as well some basic comparison with the state of the art. Section 2, introduces some generalities needed for understanding our contributions. Sections 3 and 4 explore our novel Rabbit and non-Rabbit protocol combinations. Finally, we include an extensive benchmarking on Sect. 5 and some further discussion and our conclusions in Sect. 6. We have also included comprehensive Appendices, explaining in detail the background and inner workings of Rabbit and of our privacy preserving ReLU protocol.

2 Preliminaries

2.1 Notation

Let q be a sufficiently large prime such that: *i).* It can instantiate the underlying MPC protocol; *ii).* Supports fixed point arithmetic with a public bitwise precision p and; *iii).* Allows for a sufficiently large statistical security parameter sec.

We make use of the same integer representation employed by the existing tooling, e.g. `SCALE-MAMBA` and `MP-SPDZ`. That is, we identify the finite field F_q with the centered (integer) interval $[-\frac{q-1}{2}, \frac{q-1}{2}) \cap \mathbb{Z}$ and similarly, the ring $\mathbb{Z}_{2^k}$ with $[-2^{k-1}, 2^{k-1}) \cap \mathbb{Z}$, often assumed to be $k = 64$.

We encode any negative number x on $\mathbb{F}_q$ as: $q - |x|$, e.g. -1 becomes $q - 1$. In $\mathbb{Z}_{2^{64}}$, we use a similar formulation $2^{64} - |x|$ e.g. $2^{64} - 1$. Because of the requirements of fixed point arithmetic, a typical mantissa of 40 bits would require larger q's, in this case, of at least 121 bits, as we see later on. Note that the sizes of the 2 domains are vastly different. We choose this homogenic representation, albeit it complicates the design of protocols of this kind, as this is more in line with the available tooling.

[2] Note that, as stated in Zaphod, `SCALE-MAMBA` adjusts the number of rounds (based on the circuit depth) when the setup is honest majority, instead of Full Threshold.

Additionally, we differentiate between secret shared fixed point elements ($\langle x \rangle$) and secret integers ($[\![y]\!]$), by the use square brackets. Integers can be secret shared in both $\mathbb{F}_q$ and $\mathbb{Z}_{2^k}$, whereas fixed points only in $\mathbb{F}_q$.

Inputs on $\mathbb{F}_q$ can be expressed either implicitly ($[\![x]\!]$) or explicitly ($[\![x]\!]_q$). Whereas, inputs base 2^k, are explicitly indicated by using the suffix 2^k i.e. $[\![x]\!]_{2^k}$. Values on $\mathbb{F}_2$ follow the same principle and use the explicit suffix 2 i.e. $[\![x]\!]_2$. More precisely, we adopt the fixed point representation introduced by Catrina and Saxena [3] used by `SCALE-MAMBA` and `MP-SPDZ`. Let $[\![v]\!]$ be a mantissa bounded by some 2^l, and p the bitwise fixed point precision. We can have a secret shared fixed point number $\langle x \rangle$ such that:

$$\langle x \rangle = [\![v]\!] \cdot 2^p \texttt{ mod } q. \tag{1}$$

For simplicity and w.l.g. we also assume $l = 40$. This way multiplications can be supported whilst using typical prime size selections, e.g. a 128 bits prime. This is because the bitsize of the multiplication (before truncation) could double i.e. 80 bits. Furthermore, extra `sec` bits (typically $\texttt{sec} = 40$), need to be added as well. This comes from the probabilistic truncation protocol introduced in [3]. Hence, in regards to the field size, q should be much larger than $2^{2 \cdot l + \texttt{sec}}$ for $\mathbb{F}_q$.

Finally, following convention, constants and vectors are uppercased. For completeness, in this work we differentiate our protocols security parameter κ from `sec`. However, in practice they are the same.

2.2 Arithmetic Black Box

To simplify the theoretical analysis of our constructions, we abstract the underlying MPC protocols via an ideal *arithmetic black box* ($\mathcal{F}_{ABB}$). The original concept was introduced by [10] and it is flexible enough to allow extensions. This technique has been adopted by other works in the area e.g. [7,11,12]. Furthermore, it has been employed by works of similar nature, with an emphasis on implementation e.g. [13]. In our case, the extensions correspond to (ideally extendable): fixed point arithmetic functionality and, a set of complex building blocks. We also specify the UC secure [14] realizations we based this functionality from. We define our arithmetic black box or $\mathcal{F}_{ABB}$, as specified in Table 1.

Invoking Rabbit (`rabbit_sint(`$[\![y]\!]$`)`): For simplicity, we provide an encapsulation of the invocation of Rabbit. The method is just an abstraction tool, for the invocation of any of the variations of Rabbit presented in this work. The method simply extracts the system parameters and then invokes any desired Rabbit construction. Let `sint` be a register type for elements in $\mathbb{F}_q$, then the construction can be simply expressed as indicated by Fig. 1.

Table 1. Secure Arithmetic operations provided by the $\mathcal{F}_{ABB}$.

Functionality	Description	Rounds	Prot.
$x \leftarrow [\![x]\!]$	Opening secret field element	1	-
$[\![x]\!] \leftarrow x$	Storing public input in a secret field element	1	-
$[\![z]\!] \leftarrow [\![x]\!] + [\![y]\!]$	Addition: of secret inputs	0	-
$[\![z]\!] \leftarrow [\![x]\!] + y$	Addition: (mixed) secret and public inputs	0	-
$[\![z]\!] \leftarrow [\![x]\!] \cdot [\![y]\!]$	Multiplication: of secret inputs	1	-
$[\![z]\!] \leftarrow [\![x]\!] \cdot y$	Multiplication: (mixed) secret and public inputs	0	-
$\langle z \rangle \leftarrow \langle x \rangle + \langle y \rangle$	Addition: secret fixed point	0	-
$\langle z \rangle \leftarrow \langle x \rangle + y$	Addition: (mixed) secret and public fixed point	0	-
$\langle z \rangle \leftarrow [\![x]\!] + \langle y \rangle$	Addition: secret fixed point with secret input	0	-
$\langle z \rangle \leftarrow \langle x \rangle \cdot \langle y \rangle$	Multiplication: secret fixed point	2	[2,3]
$\langle z \rangle \leftarrow \langle x \rangle \cdot y$	Multiplication: (mixed) secret and public fixed point	1	[2,3]
$\langle z \rangle \leftarrow [\![x]\!] \cdot \langle y \rangle$	Multiplication: secret fixed point with secret input	2	[2,3]
Complex Building Blocks			
$[\![\mathfrak{r}]\!]_q, [\![\hat{\mathfrak{R}}]\!]_q, [\![\mathfrak{r}]\!]_{2^k}, [\![\hat{\mathfrak{R}}]\!]_2 \leftarrow$ `get_r_from_dabits_list(size)`	Returns daBits list of size **size**, and their respective combination	0	Trivial
$[\![\hat{\mathfrak{R}}]\!]_q, [\![\hat{\mathfrak{R}}]\!]_2 \leftarrow$ `get_dabits_list(size)`	Returns vector of daBits of size **size**	0	Trivial
$[\![\mathfrak{r}]\!]_q, [\![\mathfrak{r}]\!]_{2^k} \leftarrow$ `combine_dabits(`$[\![\hat{\mathfrak{R}}]\!]_q, [\![\hat{\mathfrak{R}}]\!]_2$`)`	Returns vector combinations of $[\![\hat{\mathfrak{R}}]\!]_q$, $[\![\hat{\mathfrak{R}}]\!]_2$, daBits	0	Trivial
$[\![r_\kappa]\!] \leftarrow$ `PRandInt(size)`	Returns some randomness in $[0, 2^{\mathtt{size}})$	0	[2,3]
$[\![x]\!]_q \leftarrow$ `conv_sint(`$[\![y]\!]_2$`)`	Conversion from $\mathbb{Z}_2$ to $\mathbb{F}_q$	1	[4,6,15]
$[\![c]\!]_q \leftarrow$ `rabbit_sint(`$[\![y]\!]$`)`	Rabbit encapsulation routine	4	This Work
$[\![c]\!]_q \leftarrow$ `bitwise_lteq(`$[\![y]\!]_q$`)`	bitwise LTEQZ circuit evaluation	2	[1]

Arithmetic Black Box in Practice. The abstraction, albeit useful from a theoretical perspective, meets some limitations in practice. In reality, an implementer has to adjust to what is provided by the tooling, e.g. `SCALE-MAMBA`. MPC frameworks of this kind tend to operate storing secret and public inputs, in the form of registers. Frameworks also include a selection of instructions (**RISC** and **CISC**), to interact with registers. In the most ambitious setting, our constructions require constant round multiparty evaluation of Garbled Circuits (hence, Boolean Circuits), mixing them with arithmetic operations over Full Threshold, using High Gear Overdrive [16] (a member of the `SPDZ`'s family of protocols). Zaphod [6] achieves this, allowing us to combine a variation of [9,17], for modulo 2 arithmetic, and [16] on modulo q via daBits. As mentioned, `SCALE-MAMBA`, is the only framework currently available, implementing Zaphod, hence the one used by this work.

On the Conversion $\mathbb{Z}_2 \leftarrow \mathbb{F}_q$ (`conv_sint(`$[\![y]\!]_2$`)`)*:* Just in the same way as in Rabbit [1], the protocols in this work return results on $\mathbb{F}_2$. However, they can be trivially converted to $\mathbb{F}_q$, by using a single daBit. This process is also explained in `SCALE-MAMBA`'s documentation, and is derived from [15]. Let $[\![y]\!]_2$ be a secret element in $\mathbb{F}_2$. We locally calculate the `xor` , between a fresh daBit (modulo rabbit_sint($[\![x]\!]$)

```
1  //instantiate vector params
2  //with system parameters for default rabbit mode.
3   PARAMS[] := get_system_params(rabbit.mode);
4   c := rabbit.mode(PARAMS, x);
5   return: type(c) != sint ? conv_sint(c): c;
```

Fig. 1. Rabbit encapuslation

2) and $[\![y]\!]_2$. We then, simply open the result and `xor` the result again, just that this time with the daBits modulo q. The process requires a single round. We refer the reader to [4], for a more detailed description.

2.3 ReLU

Rectified Linear Unit functions are simple activation functions, popular in deep learning. They are of special interest for PPML, given that their linearity makes their performance more competitive versus sigmoidal functions. A ReLU can be defined as follows:

$$\mathsf{ReLU}(x) = \begin{cases} 0 & \text{for}(x < 0); \\ x & \text{for}(x \geq 0). \end{cases} \tag{2}$$

From this definition, It is clear that a ReLU can be derived from any LTEQZ protocol. For context, a ReLU activation layer is part of a whole Neural Network architecture, composed by linear transformations, folding layers and more complex activation functions frequently based on exponential operations (e.g. sigmoid or softmax). Thus, the LTEQZ protocol adopted for ReLU's must be compatible with the MPC protocols supporting the operations for the other layers. This implies slack and fixed point arithmetic [3].

3 Ad(a/o)pting Rabbit

We explore our novel protocol combinations and discuss various aspects, necessary for their adoption in practice. For a complete revision on the definitions of Rabbit that are used in this section, we kindly refer the reader to Appendix Sect. 1.

3.1 Inequality Tests

Our main interest is the implementation of Less than Equal Zero (LTEQZ) tests. By using LTEQZ we can trivially instantiate any other form of INQ test. We can define the problem as follows:

$$\mathsf{LTEQ}(x,0) \rightarrow \mathsf{LTEQZ}(x) : \mathbb{Z} \rightarrow \{0,1\} \subseteq: \begin{cases} \mathsf{LTEQZ}(x) = 1 & \text{if}(x \leq 0); \\ \mathsf{LTEQZ}(x) = 0 & \text{otherwise}. \end{cases} \tag{3}$$

3.2 Beyond Rabbit

Let us consider one of the main protocols introduced by [1], an INQ between a secret shared value and some public scalar. In this section, We discuss 3 flavors of such protocol, including one novel slack based version, later in this section. Note that the protocols in this section work directly on the mantissa of any fixed point value $\langle z \rangle$.

Conventional Rabbit. Following the discussion from Marki et al. [1]: Consider the sampling distribution of the random masks the protocol uses. It is clear, that the vanilla Rabbit construction, as presented by the authors cannot achieve perfect security[3], when implemented over $\mathbb{F}_q$. To address this, authors succinctly mentioned possible alternatives, namely: *i).* selecting a prime close to a power of 2 and, *ii).* the use of a rejection list for sampling. We therefore provide our own constant-round understanding of these 2 scenarios.

Probabilistic (Statistical Security): Protocol 1 proposes a version of Rabbit, in line (as is) with the original contributions outlined by [1]. This is the simplest of the constructions shown by this work. It is our interpretation of the author's original intent. We do include some minor adaptations, namely the use of constant round building blocks and the domain shifting, in order to make it compatible with fixed point arithmetic.

Notice that the selection of the prime field $\mathbb{F}_q$ is of importance. For security reasons, it has to be close to a power of 2. This is motivated by the fact that, as indicated by the original work [1], the gap defined as $|q - \lceil \log_2(q) \rceil|$ affects its security. We take this into account in our implementation and benchmarking. Furthermore, depending on the implementation, it could also affect correctness given that oversampling of the bitwise mask could cause incongruousness, i.e. sampled randomness is bigger than q causing discrepancies between its value in $\mathbb{F}_q$ and its bit expansion. Our design addresses this latter concern as well.

Correctness: The protocol is correct, as demonstrated by [1]. We revise these principles on Appendix Sect. 1.

Complexity: Complexity is constant, with 2 parallel invocations of `bitwise_lteq` (2 rounds). We also have to take into account the opening in *line 9*. Note that the result given is modulo 2, hence an extra round for conversion is required for a total of 4 rounds. This last step is critical because we have to operate on fixed point arithmetic.

Discussion: As noted in previous sections, we deal with the domain shift, by adding `R` in places such as *line 13*. Besides this, and for implementation purposes, we have to trivially adapt the protocol so that it can discard/reduce a bit from

[3] Furthermore, current implementations of protocols for share conversion can only achieve statistical security.

Protocol 1: Simple Rabbit (rabbit_fp)

Input: The prime: (q), the prime flag: (above), and secret input: ($[\![x]\!]_q$).
Output: secret shared LTEQZ (x) in $\mathbb{F}_2$
Pre:
1 $k = \texttt{int}(\lfloor \log_2(q) \rfloor) + 1$; // `int converts to integer`
2 $\mathtt{R} = \lceil (q-1)/2 \rceil$
3 **if** above $== 1$ **then**
4 $\quad [\![\mathtt{r}]\!]_q, [\![\hat{\mathtt{R}}]\!]_q, [\![\mathtt{r}]\!]_{2^k}, [\![\hat{\mathtt{R}}]\!]_2 \leftarrow$ `get_r_from_dabits_list(k)`;
5 **else**
6 $\quad [\![\hat{\mathtt{R}}]\!]_q, [\![\hat{\mathtt{R}}]\!]_2 \leftarrow$ `get_dabits_list(k − 1)`;
7 $\quad [\![\mathtt{r}]\!]_q, [\![\mathtt{r}]\!]_{2^k} \leftarrow$ `combine_dabits`$([\![\hat{\mathtt{R}}]\!]_q, [\![\hat{\mathtt{R}}]\!]_2)$;
Pos:
8 $[\![a]\!] \leftarrow ([\![\mathtt{r}]\!]_q + [\![x]\!]_q)$;
9 $a \leftarrow [\![a]\!]$;
10 $b = (a + q - \mathtt{R})$;
11 $[\![w_1]\!]_2 \leftarrow$ `bitwise_lteq` $(a, [\![\hat{\mathtt{R}}]\!]_2, k)$;
12 $[\![w_2]\!]_2 \leftarrow$ `bitwise_lteq` $(b, [\![\hat{\mathtt{R}}]\!]_2, k)$;
13 $w_3 = b + \mathtt{R} < \texttt{cint}(q - \mathtt{R}) + \mathtt{R}$; //`cint converts to register`
14 **return** $[\![w_1]\!]_2 - [\![w_2]\!]_2 + w_3$;
15 in return `conv_sint converts to` $\mathbb{F}_q$

Protocol 1. Rabbit for $\mathbb{F}_q$ with statistical security

the randomness sampling. We also include some specificities from SCALE-MAMBA, e.g. (cint invocation to transform input to a SCALE-MAMBA register). *Security* follows directly from [1], i.e. simulation remains the same given that we do not perform any additional opening and the $\mathcal{F}_{ABB}$ functionality is ideally modeled. Thus trivially secure under composition as in the original proofs (we remind the reader that the hybrid model allows us to replace UC secure realizations for ideal ones [14]). This is also true for all constructions present in this work, hence we do not come back to it later. For specificities regarding the statistical properties of the security proof, we refer the reader to the original work in [1].

Rejection List: We extend the previous construction by modifying the sampling, and incorporating a rejection list. We show how to perform this inclusion in a way that, from an ideal perspective, gives this construction perfect security. We present our interpretation of Rabbit rejection list in Protocol 2.

Correctness: The correctness, once again follows from [1]. In this case, no further adaptations to the sampling are needed, as it always returns some randomness bounded by q. After sampling, Rabbit then proceeds as expected.

Complexity: We still have the 4 original invocations (one opening and 2 rounds from the parallel calls to `bitwise_lteq` and 1 for the conversion). However, because of the rejection list (that involves additional calls to `bitwise_lteq`), performance depends on the prime, where probability (ϕ) of every subsequent 2 rounds can be defined as:

$$\phi = \frac{2^{\lceil \log_2(q) \rceil} - q}{2^{\lceil \log_2(q) \rceil}}. \tag{4}$$

Protocol 2: Rejection List Rabbit (`req_list`)

Input: The prime: (q)
and secret input ($[\![x]\!]_q$).
Output: secret shared LTEQZ (x) in $\mathbb{F}_2$
Pre:
1 $k = \texttt{int}(\lfloor \log_2(q) \rfloor) + 1$; // `int converts to integer`
2 $\texttt{R} = \lceil (q-1)/2 \rceil$;
3 **repeat**
4 $[\![\hat{\texttt{R}}]\!]_q, [\![\hat{\texttt{R}}]\!]_2 \leftarrow \texttt{fill\_dabits\_array(k)}$;
5 $[\![\texttt{above}]\!]_2 \leftarrow \texttt{bitwise\_lteq}\ (q, [\![\hat{\texttt{R}}]\!]_2, k)$;
6 $\texttt{above} \leftarrow [\![\texttt{above}]\!]_2$;
7 **until** ($\texttt{above} == 1$);
8 $[\![\hat{\texttt{r}}]\!]_q, [\![\hat{\texttt{r}}]\!]_{2^k} \leftarrow \texttt{combine\_dabits}([\![\hat{\texttt{R}}]\!]_q, [\![\hat{\texttt{R}}]\!]_2)$;
Pos:
9 $[\![a]\!] \leftarrow ([\![\hat{\texttt{r}}]\!]_q + [\![x]\!]_q)$;
10 $a \leftarrow [\![a]\!]$;
11 $b = (a + q - \texttt{R})$;
12 $[\![w_1]\!]_2 \leftarrow \texttt{bitwise\_lteq}\ (a, [\![\hat{\texttt{R}}]\!]_2, k)$;
13 $[\![w_2]\!]_2 \leftarrow \texttt{bitwise\_lteq}\ (b, [\![\hat{\texttt{R}}]\!]_2, k)$;
14 $w_3 = b + \texttt{R} < \texttt{cint}(q - \texttt{R}) + \texttt{R}$; //`cint converts to register`
15 **return** $[\![w_1]\!]_2 - [\![w_2]\!]_2 + [\![w_3]\!]$;
16 //in return `conv_sint converts to` $\mathbb{F}_q$

Protocol 2. *Perfect Secure* Rabbit for $\mathbb{F}_q$.

Discussion: As before, the prime selection is also important although for different reasons i.e. the prime should not be far below the immediate next power of 2, as the sampling, will have a lower probability of requiring extra rounds per execution. *Security,* as indicated before, trivially follows from [1]. Moreover, as it is shown in the original work, the incorporation of the rejection list, is the only method available by which any Rabbit variation can (ideally) achieve prefect security over $\mathbb{F}_q$.

Slack Rabbit. We also propose novel a variation of Rabbit that reduces the sizes of the bitwise inequality tests `bitwise_lteq`. This significantly reduces the number of daBits the protocol requires whilst still working on larger q's. We achieve this by borrowing and adapting the bitwise sampling of randomness from Catrina and De Hoogh. Further adaptations were required to incorporate, among other things, shifts in the numeric domain that originated by the now shorter circuits, as we later explain. The protocol is described as follows:

Protocol 3: Slack Rabbit (`rabbit_slack`)

Input: The prime: (q), input size: (k), `sec param`: (κ), and secret input: $([\![x]\!]_q)$.
Output: secret shared LTEQZ (x) in $\mathbb{F}_2$
Pre:
1 $\mathtt{M} = 2^k$;
2 $\mathtt{R} = \lceil \frac{\mathtt{M}_2}{2} \rceil - 1$;
3 $[\![r_\kappa]\!] \leftarrow \mathtt{PRandInt}(\kappa)$;
4 $[\![\hat{\mathtt{r}}]\!]_q, [\![\hat{\mathtt{R}}]\!]_q, [\![\hat{\mathtt{r}}]\!]_{2^k}, [\![\hat{\mathtt{R}}]\!]_2 \leftarrow \mathtt{get\_r\_from\_dabits\_list(k)}$;
Pos:
5 $[\![z]\!] \leftarrow [\![x]\!]_q + \mathtt{R}$;
6 $[\![a]\!] \leftarrow ([\![\hat{\mathtt{r}}]\!]_q + [\![z]\!]) + [\![r_\kappa]\!] \cdot 2^k$;
7 $a \leftarrow [\![a]\!]$;
8 $b \leftarrow a + \mathtt{M} - \mathtt{R}$;
9 $\mathrm{a}' = a \bmod 2^k$;
10 $\mathrm{b}' = b \bmod 2^k$;
11 //comparisons
12 $[\![w_1]\!]_2 \leftarrow \mathtt{bitwise\_lteq}\ (a', [\![\hat{\mathtt{R}}]\!]_2, k)$;
13 $[\![w_2]\!]_2 \leftarrow \mathtt{bitwise\_lteq}\ (b', [\![\hat{\mathtt{R}}]\!]_2, k)$;
14 $w_3 = b - \mathtt{cint}(\mathtt{M} + \mathtt{R}) < 0$; //cint converts to register
15 **return** $1 - ([\![w_1]\!]_2 - [\![w_2]\!]_2 + [\![w_3]\!])$;

Protocol 3. Rabbit on statistical security.

Correctness: The protocol uses the same principles from Rabbit, from previous protocols (see Appendix Sect. 1). Note that changes were applied to the generation of the random mask. As indicated in [18] and [2], by using black box random bit generation (via daBits), combined with PRandInt, we can build a statistically hiding mask. At the same time, we also hold the bit decomposition of the relevant sections of the randomness.

Complexity: Complexity remains the same, i.e. constant round $\mathcal{O}(1)$ and 4 rounds in total. The improvement comes from a reduction on the number of daBits invocations. In this case we require k, instead of $\lceil \log_2(q) \rceil$. Furthermore, the size of the circuit used by the `bitwise_lteq`'s invocations is reduced to k, e.g. 64 bits.

Discussion: The protocol begins by reconstructing some bounded randomness. It combines k daBits (that are later used as the bit expansion of $r \leftarrow \mathbb{Z}_{2^k}$, i.e. 64 bits) and `PRandInt` (on the size of our security parameter κ). After some domain switching (see Sect. 2.1), which is further complicated by the types limitations in `SCALE-MAMBA` (negative number encoding), the protocol proceeds to the familiar flow of Rabbit. A relevant observation, is that the bitwise comparisons can be done over a smaller domain e.g. 2^k, rather than in $\log_2(q)$. A fact that we exploit on *lines 12) and 13)*. *Security* analysis is also trivial, as it follows directly from the discussion on [2,18].This is also the case for the statistical properties of the mask.

3.3 Optimized Rabbit for ReLU's

For completeness we also explore the optimized comparison protocol designed specifically for ReLU's from Makri et al. [1]. Authors imagine scenarios where w.l.o.g. the 64 bits domain coincides with the ring size. The protocol itself is quite different to the constructions we present in this paper. In fairly general terms it can be summarized as follows:

1. Conversion of some secret $[\![x]\!]_q$ to modulo 2^k (if needed).
2. Extract the MSB from $[\![x]\!]_{2^k}$.
3. Interpret and return the MSB as the result of the comparison.

The protocol proposes challenges when used in the context of the applications explored by this work. More precisely, to make it compatible with $\mathbb{F}_q$, and with the results from Catrina and Saxena [3] (fixed point arithmetic), we have to rely on the rather expensive $\mathbb{F}_q$ to $\mathbb{Z}_{2^{64}}$ conversion primitive from Zaphod[4]. We have implemented this variation as well for benchmarking purposes. We call this construction `rabbit_conv`.

4 Constant Round Catrina and De Hoogh

In this section, we explore our constant round adaptation of the commonly used LTZ formulation from Catrina and De Hoogh [2], combined with some of the enhancements introduced by Rabbit. More formally, we present 2 protocols to: Solve the modulo 2^m of any secret shared input and then, an oblivious LTZ construction based on the former.

---

[4] The details of the conversion and its development are also explored in detail in `SCALE-MAMBA`.

4.1 Modulo 2^m (mod2m)

We start, by discussing our `mod2m` construction, in Protocol 4. It reflects the same process flow of its namesake protocol from Catrina and De Hoogh [2]. However, we introduced some notable changes:

- **Randomness**: We sample the random mask using daBits in the first k bits, instead of the construction from [7]. A notable difference with other adaptation efforts i.e. [8] is that we can make use of `PRandInt(k')` to generate the slack.
- **Bitwise INQ**: We replace the original bitwise LTZ provided by Catrina and De Hoogh, by the low complexity LTEQZ test provided by Rabbit. This change forces us to further adapt the protocol so that it can still mimic the original result.
- **Conversion to $\mathbb{F}_q$**: The result of the bitwise comparison is obtained via distributed Garbled Circuits [HSS17], with an output on $\mathbb{Z}_2$. Hence, we invoke `conv_sint`($[\![x]\!]$) to transform the output back to $\mathbb{F}_q$.

Protocol 4: constant round mod 2^m (mod2m)

Input: the bit length of inputs:(k), a power of Two: (m), sec param: (κ), and secret input: ($[\![x]\!]_p$).
Output: secret shared LTZ (x) in $\mathbb{F}_q$
Pre:
1 // size of κ + non_dabits bits,
2 // if any e.g. 40 + 1
3 $k' = k + \kappa - m$;
4 $[\![r_\kappa]\!] \leftarrow$ PRandInt(k');
5 $[\![\mathtt{r}]\!]_q, [\![\hat{\mathtt{R}}]\!]_q, [\![\mathtt{r}]\!]_{2^k}, [\![\hat{\mathtt{R}}]\!]_2 \leftarrow$ get_r_from_dabits_list(m);
6 $[\![\hat{\mathtt{r}}]\!]_q = [\![\mathtt{r}]\!]_q + 1$;
Pos:
7 $[\![a]\!] \leftarrow 2^{k-1} + [\![\mathtt{r}]\!]_q + [\![x]\!]_q + [\![r_\kappa]\!] \cdot 2^m$;
8 $a \leftarrow [\![a]\!]$;
9 $a' = a \bmod 2^m$;
10 $[\![w]\!]_2 \leftarrow$ bitwise_lteq $(a', [\![\hat{\mathtt{R}}]\!]_2, k)$;
11 $[\![w]\!]_q \leftarrow$ conv_sint($[\![w]\!]_2$) ;
12 **return** $a' - [\![\mathtt{r}]\!]_q + (2^m) \cdot [\![w]\!]_q$;

Protocol 4. Constant round Catrina and De Hoogh mod 2^m.

Correctness: Correctness follows directly from Catrina and De Hoogh [2]. Note the change of the bitwise INQ test, from an LTZ to LTEQZ (on *line 6*). To obtain the equivalent behaviour, we add a 1 to the value that is secretly contained in

$[\![\mathfrak{r}]\!]_q$. This small change propagates to a. As a result, the composition of a' is altered i.e. $[\![\hat{\mathfrak{r}}]\!]_q + 1$ instead of $[\![\mathfrak{r}]\!]_q$. This suffices for $a' \leq [\![\mathfrak{r}]\!]_q$ to match the expected behaviour. Besides this, all other changes introduced to the protocol are orthogonal to its correctness.

Complexity: The protocol has a constant round complexity, similar to other protocols studied in this paper (4 rounds). An opening, 1 invocation of a Garbled circuit (2 rounds), and 1 extra round for the conversion in *line 11*. Hence, results are delivered in $\mathbb{F}_q$.

Discussion: Protocol keeps the basic and simple flow, that made it so popular to use with fixed point values. *Security* and the statistical properties of the mask trivially follow from [2]. Simulation is the same, given that there are no additional openings, and the generation of the random mask and conversion are modeled as ideal functionalities. As a technical observation, we could envision a circuit that merges *line 10*, and *line 11*, and thus further reducing the round count by 1. Note that, in practice this means that the typical 40 bits of security present in frameworks such as `SCALE-MAMBA` can remain unchanged.

4.2 Catrina and De Hoogh Constant Round LTZ (`cons_ltz`)

We can now make use of our `mod2m` construction to build the INQ protocol introduced by Catrina and De Hoogh. For simplicity, we synthesize their results and produce a single protocol, replacing the modulo 2^m invocation by our own `mod2m`. Traditionally, the Catrina and de Hoogh construction returns LTZ. We note that it can be trivially adapted to return a LTEQZ instead (by reverting the input size and negating the output). The Protocol can be constructed as follows:

Protocol 5: constant round LTZ (`cons_ltz`)

Input: the bitlength of inputs:(k) `sec param`: (κ), and secret input: ($[\![x]\!]_q$).
Output: secret shared LTZ (x) in $\mathbb{F}_q$
1 $[\![x']\!] \leftarrow$ `mod2m` $(k, k-1, \kappa, [\![x]\!])$;
2 $[\![z]\!] = \frac{[\![x]\!]-[\![x']\!]}{2^m}$ `mod` q;
3 **return** $-[\![z]\!]$;

Protocol 5. Constant round Catrina and Hoogh.

Correctness: It follows directly from [2]. We have replaced some elements in the `mod2m` construction, namely the bitwise INQ test. However, as previously stated the behaviour does mimic the original. This protocol can be seen as the integration of the truncation and the LTZ primitives introduced by Catrina and De Hoogh.

Complexity: It is bound to mod2m. As it does not feature any additional operation that requires round based computations i.e. 4 rounds. Its complexity matches all Rabbit constructions introduced by this work. However, we reduce the number of invocations of bitwise_lteq to 1.

Discussion: The protocol is intuitive and simple. It can also be trivially adapted to derive a probabilistic truncation protocol. *Security* follows directly from mod2m, as there are no other openings originated by the protocol. As a reminder, simulation in this case is trivial (hybrid model [14]), given that, there is no opening and we only compose it with ideal functionalities.

5 Benchmarking

In this section, we provide a performance evaluation geared towards implementers of all our protocols. This section also provides details regarding our testing environment and our prototype.

5.1 Prototype

Our implementation was built on top of SCALE-MAMBA version 1.13 and it is compatible with version 1.14. This open source framework is commonly used for experimentation by various applications, including on topics related to machine learning [13,19]. On setups, the framework offers several protocol flavours that can be combined with Boolean circuit evaluation thanks to Zaphod. We are particularly interested in two: *i).* High Gear Overdrive, a member of the SPDZ's family [16], what we call from this point forward Full Threshold configuration (FT) and *ii).* A custom made SCALE-MAMBA adaptation to evaluate the case when Garbling is done offline, as originally intended in HSS17 [9], referred to in this section as FT(OG). For completeness, we have included the Shamir based protocol from Smart and Wood [20], simply referred to as Shamir. Note that we can only use Garbled Circuits via HSS17 in combination with FT setups. It is worth commenting that there are no high level functionalities available in MAMBA related to daBits (except for the instruction itself). Hence, our prototype required to build all the daBits apparatus described by our $\mathcal{F}_{ABB}$. More formally, our prototype comprises of the following:

- Extensions to library.py, for random sampling using the daBits instruction.
- Extensions to comparison.py, where we incorporate bitwise_lteq constructions using $\mathbb{Z}_2$ instructions, i.e. reactive.
- Two precompiled VHDL circuit versions of bitwise_lteq (Bristol Fashion). We add few minor manual edits to conform to circuit design. They were generated via the limited tooling already available in SCALE-MAMBA. Both target rabbit_slack and cons_ltz (our fastest protocols), note that they make use the GC instruction in 64 bits. More precisely:

i). AND_XOR: Circuit from [1] as is. Convenient for [HSS17] [9][5].
ii). AND_NOT: With a simple depth reduction. Convenient for LSSS [20](see footnote 5).

- Library rabbit_lib.py. Implements all INQ tests described in this paper.
- Library relu_lib.py. Implements variations of ReLU's, specifically for Machine Learning, including 2 and 3 dimensional ReLU's.
- Extensive test programs for all the functionality presented/required by this work.

For completeness, we have also incorporated in our benchmarking the original LTZ from Catrina and De Hoogh [2], which is already present in SCALE-MAMBA. This protocol works exclusively over LSSS in $\mathbb{F}_q$. In our tests, we refer to this protocol as lsss_ltz. Finally, we note the prototype is fully available as open source[6].

Performance Evaluation Setup: Our test bed comprises of 5 locally managed, physical servers connected with Gigabit LAN connections. Each one has a static fixed memory allocation of 512 GB of RAM memory. All servers are equipped with 2 Intel(R) Xeon(R) Silver 4208 @ 2.10GH CPUs. All machines are running Ubuntu 18. The approximate default ping time is 0.15 ms. This allows us to control network conditions by tuning latency via /sbin/tc. In terms of the SCALE-MAMBA configuration (default), we use a prime q of 128 bits, with a matching sec and $\kappa = 40$, and a $k = 64$, for all our protocols. The size of the mantissa for fixed point is 40. It is also worth commenting that all times (expressed in ms) in our performance evaluation correspond exclusively to the online phase.

It is important to note that the setup considers the smallest party subsets supported by Smart and Wood [20] and Hazay et al. [9] i.e. 3 and 2 parties, respectively. Any setup with additional parties can then be extrapolated.

5.2 Results

Table 2 shows the performance evaluation in one machine, with no real communications. Time complexity is entirely dominated by computation costs. As expected, Shamir outperforms FT for all protocols. This is due to the extra costs related to operating with information theoretic MACs, circuit garbling and evaluation. On the other hand, the LSSS version of Catrina and De Hoogh (lsss_ltz) remained mostly the same in both configurations. This is because it does not require Garbled Circuits. It is worth noting that Rabbit rejection list req_list, Rabbit with conversion rabbit_conv and simple Rabbit rabbit_fp protocols significantly underperform the rest. This phenomena is due to the large size of their corresponding circuits for the evaluation of $\mathbb{F}_q$ elements.

Regarding the circuit choice, AND_XOR underperfoms AND_NOT on Shamir. This is explained by the higher circuit depth, which translates into more rounds

[5] See SCALE-MAMBA documentation.
[6] https://github.com/Crypto-TII/beyond_rabbit.

Table 2. Performance evaluation (ms) in one machine

Protocol	Circuit	No comms		
		Shamir	FT	FT(OG)
rabbit_slack	AND_NOT	2.3	8.5	1.4
cons_ltz	AND_NOT	1.3	4.2	1.2
rabbit_slack	AND_XOR	3.1	8.1	1.3
cons_ltz	AND_XOR	1.5	4.0	1.0
rabbit_conv	–	8.4	12.7	–
req_list	–	44.0	119.7	–
rabbit_fp	–	30.7	64.0	–
lsss_ltz	–	1.7	1.8	–

Table 3. Performance evaluation (ms) with 2/3 machines (FT/ Shamir)

Protocol	Circuit	D = 10 ms			D = 20 ms		
		Shamir	FT	FT(OG)	Shamir	FT	FT(OG)
rabbit_slack	AND_NOT	623.1	297.6	124.7	1236.2	577.2	245.1
cons_ltz	AND_NOT	317.7	148.6	62.6	627.7	289.1	122.7
rabbit_slack	AND_XOR	1031.5	295.7	124.7	2045.2	575.2	244.6
cons_ltz	AND_XOR	522.0	148.6	62.5	1033.0	288.1	122.5
lsss_ltz	–	74.9	75.2	-	144.9	144.6	–

(see [4]). On the other hand, for FT there is no meaningful difference between both circuits when applied in both rabbit_slack and cons_ltz, given their small size($\approx$ less than 200 gates). From the results it is also clear that our variation of Catrina and De Hoogh (cons_ltz) outperforms the original lsss_ltz on Shamir. However, this is the opposite on FT, mainly due to the time spent for garbling in cons_ltz. This is clear when observing the results for the case when the garbling is done offline, i.e. FT(OG). In such case, the proposed cons_ltz is noticeably more efficient than lsss_ltz (and slightly more efficient than rabbit_slack).

Table 3 shows the results when the protocols run on several machines with real communications. Specifically, with two different latencies 10 ms and 20 ms (one-way latency). We restrict the evaluation to rabbit_slack, cons_ltz and lsss_ltz since the other Rabbit versions are clearly less efficient. Results show that rabbit_slack and cons_ltz are more affected by delay on Shamir than on FT. Indeed, with only 10ms delay, FT configuration becomes faster than Shamir. This is explained by the fact that Shamir incurs in more communication rounds per bitwise circuit evaluation.

When considering the case for garbling offline our proposed cons_ltz outperforms all other protocols, including lsss_ltz. This result is consistent on both latencies 10 ms and 20 ms (Table 3).

In the case of the FT configuration, `lsss_ltz` is faster than its counterparts. Increasing the delay does not favour `cons_ltz` over `lsss_ltz`. This may be counter-intuitive, since `lsss_ltz` has 7 rounds and `cons_ltz` has only 4, hence increasing the latency should render `cons_ltz` more efficient. However, this is not the case because the TCP throughput is affected by latency and the quantity of transmitted data is higher in `cons_ltz` than in `lsss_ltz`. The intuition when implementing MPC protocols dictates that higher latency favours protocols with lesser rounds. This is not necessarily the case when the communication channel implements TCP e.g. TLS, because TCP throughput is heavily affected by latency and packet loss rate. This is due to TCP's congestion control mechanisms and its slow start procedure. To solve this, framework designers could apply secure communications protocols based on UDP, such as QUIC, since UDP throughput is unaffected by latency. Although such profound change falls out of the scope of this work, we believe it is an interesting unexplored research avenue. Hence, we strongly encourage framework developers, namely for SCALE-MAMBA and MP-SPDZ, to incorporate it in future releases.

5.3 Practical Scenarios

Realistically, frameworks such as SCALE-MAMBA rely on circuit optimizers to reduce the number of communication rounds during compilation time. Without them, round complexity for the Catrina and de Hoogh (`lsss_ltz`) protocol increases drastically. Namely, the construction requires as many rounds as multiplications which, for a 128 bit prime implies 121 rounds instead of 7. It has to be stressed that because of their nature, optimizers require to load the dependency graph to memory, becoming impractical for large circuits e.g. neural networks (see [4]). In such scenarios, `cons_ltz` (with AND_NOT) becomes the far better alternative in all configurations. We tested this case by compiling the comparisons without such optimizations[7]. We show these results in Table 4. While `cons_ltz` performance remains unaffected by this new configuration, `lsss_ltz`'s performance is significantly impaired.

Table 4. Performance evaluation (ms) with 2/3 machines (FT/ Shamir)

Protocol	Circuit	No comms		D = 10 ms		D = 20 ms	
		Shamir	FT	Shamir	FT	Shamir	FT
`cons_ltz`-O1	AND_NOT	1.3	4.6	317.8	148.6	627.7	289.2
`cons_ltz`-O1	AND_XOR	1.6	3.9	522.1	148.6	1033.0	288.2
`lsss_ltz`-O1	-	4.1	4.0	1243.8	1238.8	2453.8	2449.2

[7] We achieve this via the `-O1` compilation flag, as recommended by the SCALE-MAMBA documentation [4].

6 Conclusion, Discussion and Future Work

We presented a series of variations and novel combinations of Rabbit and other comparison protocols for MPC, with ReLU's in mind. Our results are compatible with the current state of the art for fixed point arithmetic [3] and constant round evaluation of Boolean circuits i.e. Zaphod [6]. We accompany our findings with thorough benchmarking and provide an open source implementation. Our results show that:

i) The conventional Rabbit variations studied in this work underperform our novel slack based formulation for large primes.
ii) As latency increases, all constructions perform worse than the original Catrina and De Hoogh `lsss_ltz` when Garbling is done Online.
iii) Our `cons_ltz` performs better than classical LSSS Catrina and De Hoogh and any other protocol when Garbling is performed Offline. This is true for all latency configurations.
iv) When compiling without optimizations, `cons_ltz` and `rabbit_slack` are a far better choice (by orders of magnitude) than classic Catrina and De Hoogh `lsss_ltz` under any setup i.e. Shamir, FT and FT(OG). This is specially relevant for Machine Learning, due to the severe compiler limitations of `SCALE-MAMBA` for large circuits.

Regarding future work, we believe that the use of QUIC can be an interesting avenue of research for framework developers. Notice that this work also raises novel questions regarding the process of compiling Boolean circuits i.e. Circuit optimization via hardware oriented synthesizers.

Acknowledgements. Authors would like to thank Dragos Rotaru, Titouan Tanguy, Chiara Marcolla, Eduardo Soria-Vazquez and Santos Merino for their fruitful discussion, that undoubtedly raised the quality of this work.

Appendix

1 Rabbit Definitions

1.1 The Problem

The majority of previous works have proposed mechanisms for comparisons based on bit decomposition. Such constructions tend to be expensive in terms of multiplicative depth. In general terms, they are compatible with both MPC and Homomorphic Encryption (HE) schemes. They also tend to have sublinear cost on the inputs size with some associated non-negligible constant. An example of this, is the seminal work from Damgård et al. [7] previously mentioned by this work.

To solve this issue, the literature has proposed to relax the security model, as a trade-off for efficiency e.g. [2,18]. The principle is to reduce the impact of bit decomposition in exchange of security under statistical constraints, i.e. statistical security. This statistical security should not be confused with cryptographic security, and it rather relates to the probability distribution over masked inputs.

1.2 The Rabbit Principle

The method itself is based on the commutative properties of addition. It formulates 2 different but equivalent equations. Generally speaking, the authors derive a simplified algebraic construction comprised of 3 INQ's, one of which relies exclusively on public inputs. The other 2 depend on public inputs and secret shared precomputed randomness. Furthermore, they can be all executed in parallel. This construction is equivalent to an LTEQZ on secret inputs.

To generate randomness, Rabbit authors rely on edaBits [8] (which is exclusively present on MP-SPDZ). For the purpose of this section, we abstract edaBits, as a construction that allows us to generate (together with its bit expansion) some bounded randomness in $\mathbb{Z}_{2^k}$.

Let $\mathbb{Z}_M$ be some commutative ring bounded by $M \in \mathbb{Z}$, $[\![x]\!]$ and $[\![r]\!]$ be some secret shared input and randomness in $\mathbb{Z}_M$ and, R be some public element of $\mathbb{Z}_M$. Then we can establish the following:

$$B = M - R, \tag{5}$$
$$[\![a]\!] = [\![x]\!] + [\![r]\!], \tag{6}$$
$$[\![b]\!] = [\![x]\!] + [\![r]\!] + B, \tag{7}$$
$$[\![c]\!] = [\![x]\!] + B. \tag{8}$$

If we observe carefully the constructions above, we can appreciate that B is simply the complement of R. Prior discussing the algebraic elements of Rabbit, let us now consider the following statement:

$$[x+y] = \begin{cases} [\![x]\!] + [\![y]\!] - M \cdot \mathsf{LT}([\![x]\!] + [\![y]\!], [\![x]\!]); \\ [\![x]\!] + [\![y]\!] - M \cdot \mathsf{LT}([\![x]\!] + [\![y]\!], [\![y]\!]). \end{cases} \tag{9}$$

Which is always true for any element of $\mathbb{Z}_M$. Given the equations above, we can establish the following relations, let us start with $([\![a]\!] + B)$:

$$\begin{aligned} [\![b]\!] &= [\![a]\!] + B \\ &= [\![a]\!] + B - M \cdot ([\![a+B]\!] < B) \\ &= [\![x]\!] + [\![r]\!] - M \cdot ([\![x+r]\!] < [\![r]\!]) + B - M \cdot ([\![a+B]\!] < B). \end{aligned}$$

When we expand $[\![c+r]\!]$ in the same fashion we can derive the following:

$$\begin{aligned} [\![b]\!] &= [\![c+r]\!] \\ &= [\![c]\!] + r - M \cdot ([\![c+r]\!] < [\![r]\!]) \\ &= [\![x]\!] + [\![b]\!] - M \cdot ([\![x+B]\!] < [\![r]\!]) + [\![r]\!] - M \cdot ([\![c+r]\!] < [\![r]\!]). \end{aligned}$$

If we equate both expansions of $[\![b]\!]$, using $[\![a+B]\!]$ and $[\![c]\!] + [\![r]\!]$, we can obtain the following (after simplifications):

$$[\![a < r]\!] + [\![b < B]\!] = [\![c < B]\!] + [\![b < r]\!].$$

Let us now replace $[\![a]\!]$, $[\![b]\!]$ and $[\![c]\!]$, and express the equation above, in terms of $[\![x]\!]$ and $[\![r]\!]$:

$$\begin{aligned} [\![x+r]\!] < [\![r]\!] + [\![c+r]\!] < B = [\![x+B]\!] < B + [\![x+r+B]\!] < [\![r]\!], \\ [\![x+B]\!] < B = [\![x+r]\!] < [\![r]\!] + [\![x+B+r]\!] < B - [\![x+r+B]\!] < [\![r]\!]. \end{aligned}$$

The INQ that we have conveniently now placed on the left of the equation, expresses the relation between x and the complement of R. In this case the INQ would be true, only if x is greater than R. Note that we are still working on $\mathbb{Z}_M$, meaning that any excess over R would force an overflow and a subsequent wraparound. Now, let us abuse the notation and consider R to be some public element on $\mathbb{Z}_M$ e.g. 0.

Given that we can freely disclose the masked secret $[\![x]\!] + [\![r]\!]$ without compromising security, the equation above would finally look like:

$$[\![x+B]\!] < B = (x+r) < [\![r]\!] + (x+B+r) < B - (x+r+B) < [\![r]\!].$$

As previously stated both inequalities can be calculated in parallel. The inequality tests themselves are executed bitwise, using for instance, $\mathsf{edaBits}$ or any other mean to obtain the bit decomposition offline.

2 Constant Round ReLU Protocol

Our proposed ReLU construction, follows the same line of thought from the contribution sections of this work. Indeed, Catrina and Saxena's fixed point representation is heavily interlinked with the protocol. In fact, Protocol 6, optimizes the fixed point multiplication needed by the ReLU, extracting the mantissa from $\langle x \rangle$.

In line with the definitions, introduced in Sect. 2.3. Our constant round ReLU can be trivially implemented as follows:

Protocol 6: constant round ReLU (relu(x))

Input: $\langle x \rangle$ (with a mantissa $[\![v]\!]_q$ and precision p).
Output: secret shared relu($\langle$x$\rangle$) in $\mathbb{F}_q$

1 $[\![v]\!]_q \leftarrow [\![x.v]\!]_q$;
2 $[\![c]\!]_q \leftarrow 1 -$ rabbit_sint(v)$_q$;
3 $[\![x.v]\!]_q \leftarrow [\![c]\!]_q \cdot [\![v]\!]_q$; // **zero otherwise**
4 **return** $\langle x \rangle$;

Protocol 6. Constant round protocol for ReLU's.

Complexity: The protocol has constant round complexity ($\mathcal{O}(1)$). It consists of 1 round (from the multiplication on *line 3)*, plus what is added by any selected comparison mechanism introduced by this work i.e. 4 rounds.

Discussion: Our ReLU itself does not require to invoke PRTrunc, ever present in fixed point multiplications. Note that ReLU's are typically surrounded by more complex fixed point operations, that do require conventional fixed point multiplications e.g. [21] (hence the presence of slack and an invocation of PRTrunc per multiplication gate).

References

1. Makri, E., Rotaru, D., Vercauteren, F., Wagh, S.: Rabbit: efficient comparison for secure multi-party computation. In: Borisov, N., Diaz, C. (eds.) FC 2021. LNCS, vol. 12674, pp. 249–270. Springer, Heidelberg (2021). https://doi.org/10.1007/978-3-662-64322-8_12
2. Catrina, O., de Hoogh, S.: Improved primitives for secure multiparty integer computation. In: Garay, J.A., De Prisco, R. (eds.) SCN 2010. LNCS, vol. 6280, pp. 182–199. Springer, Heidelberg (2010). https://doi.org/10.1007/978-3-642-15317-4_13
3. Catrina, O., Saxena, A.: Secure computation with fixed-point numbers. In: Sion, R. (ed.) FC 2010. LNCS, vol. 6052, pp. 35–50. Springer, Heidelberg (2010). https://doi.org/10.1007/978-3-642-14577-3_6
4. Aly, A., et al.: SCALE and MAMBA v1.14: Documentation (2021). https://homes.esat.kuleuven.be/~nsmart/SCALE/
5. Keller, M.: MP-SPDZ: a versatile framework for multi-party computation. In: Ligatti, J., Ou, X., Katz, J., Vigna, G. (eds.) ACM CCS 2020, pp. 1575–1590. ACM Press, November 2020

6. Aly, A., Orsini, E., Rotaru, D., Smart, N.P., Wood, T.: Zaphod: efficiently combining lsss and garbled circuits in scale. In: Proceedings of the 7th ACM Workshop on Encrypted Computing & Applied Homomorphic Cryptography. WAHC 2019, pp. 33–44. Association for Computing Machinery, New York (2019)
7. Damgård, I., Fitzi, M., Kiltz, E., Nielsen, J.B., Toft, T.: Unconditionally secure constant-rounds multi-party computation for equality, comparison, bits and exponentiation. In: Halevi, S., Rabin, T. (eds.) TCC 2006. LNCS, vol. 3876, pp. 285–304. Springer, Heidelberg (2006). https://doi.org/10.1007/11681878_15
8. Escudero, D., Ghosh, S., Keller, M., Rachuri, R., Scholl, P.: Improved primitives for MPC over mixed arithmetic-binary circuits. In: Micciancio, D., Ristenpart, T. (eds.) CRYPTO 2020. LNCS, vol. 12171, pp. 823–852. Springer, Cham (2020). https://doi.org/10.1007/978-3-030-56880-1_29
9. Hazay, C., Scholl, P., Soria-Vazquez, E.: Low cost constant round MPC combining BMR and oblivious transfer. In: Takagi, T., Peyrin, T. (eds.) ASIACRYPT 2017. LNCS, vol. 10624, pp. 598–628. Springer, Cham (2017). https://doi.org/10.1007/978-3-319-70694-8_21
10. Damgård, I., Nielsen, J.B.: Universally composable efficient multiparty computation from threshold homomorphic encryption. In: Boneh, D. (ed.) CRYPTO 2003. LNCS, vol. 2729, pp. 247–264. Springer, Heidelberg (2003). https://doi.org/10.1007/978-3-540-45146-4_15
11. Aly, A., Abidin, A., Nikova, S.: Practically efficient secure distributed exponentiation without bit-decomposition. In: Meiklejohn, S., Sako, K. (eds.) FC 2018. LNCS, vol. 10957, pp. 291–309. Springer, Heidelberg (2018). https://doi.org/10.1007/978-3-662-58387-6_16
12. Atapoor, S., Smart, N.P., Alaoui, Y.T.: Private liquidity matching using MPC. In: Galbraith, S.D. (ed.) CT-RSA 2022. LNCS, vol. 13161, pp. 96–119. Springer, Cham (2022). https://doi.org/10.1007/978-3-030-95312-6_5
13. Aly, A., Smart, N.P.: Benchmarking privacy preserving scientific operations. In: Deng, R.H., Gauthier-Umaña, V., Ochoa, M., Yung, M. (eds.) ACNS 2019. LNCS, vol. 11464, pp. 509–529. Springer, Cham (2019). https://doi.org/10.1007/978-3-030-21568-2_25
14. Canetti, R.: Security and composition of multiparty cryptographic protocols. J. Cryptol. **13**(1), 143–202 (2000)
15. Rotaru, D., Wood, T.: MArBled Circuits: mixing arithmetic and boolean circuits with active security. In: Hao, F., Ruj, S., Sen Gupta, S. (eds.) INDOCRYPT 2019. LNCS, vol. 11898, pp. 227–249. Springer, Cham (2019). https://doi.org/10.1007/978-3-030-35423-7_12
16. Keller, M., Pastro, V., Rotaru, D.: Overdrive: making SPDZ great again. In: Nielsen, J.B., Rijmen, V. (eds.) EUROCRYPT 2018. LNCS, vol. 10822, pp. 158–189. Springer, Cham (2018). https://doi.org/10.1007/978-3-319-78372-7_6
17. Wang, X., Ranellucci, S., Katz, J.: Authenticated garbling and efficient maliciously secure two-party computation. In: Thuraisingham, B.M., Evans, D., Malkin, T., Xu, D. (eds.) ACM CCS 2017, pp. 21–37. ACM Press, October/November 2017
18. Lipmaa, H., Toft, T.: Secure equality and greater-than tests with sublinear online complexity. In: Fomin, F.V., Freivalds, R., Kwiatkowska, M., Peleg, D. (eds.) ICALP 2013. LNCS, vol. 7966, pp. 645–656. Springer, Heidelberg (2013). https://doi.org/10.1007/978-3-642-39212-2_56
19. Makri, E., Rotaru, D., Smart, N.P., Vercauteren, F.: EPIC: efficient private image classification (or: learning from the masters). In: Matsui, M. (ed.) CT-RSA 2019. LNCS, vol. 11405, pp. 473–492. Springer, Cham (2019). https://doi.org/10.1007/978-3-030-12612-4_24

20. Smart, N.P., Wood, T.: Error detection in monotone span programs with application to communication-efficient multi-party computation. In: Matsui, M. (ed.) CT-RSA 2019. LNCS, vol. 11405, pp. 210–229. Springer, Cham (2019). https://doi.org/10.1007/978-3-030-12612-4_11
21. LeCun, Y., et al.: Backpropagation applied to handwritten zip code recognition. Neural Comput. **1**(4), 541–551 (1989)

Public-Key Infrastructure

Oh SSH-it, What's My Fingerprint? A Large-Scale Analysis of SSH Host Key Fingerprint Verification Records in the DNS

Sebastian Neef(✉) and Nils Wisiol

Security in Telecommunications, Technische Universität Berlin, Berlin, Germany
{neef,nils.wisiol}@tu-berlin.de

Abstract. The SSH protocol is commonly used to access remote systems on the Internet, as it provides an encrypted and authenticated channel for communication. If upon establishing a new connection, the presented server key is unknown to the client, the user is asked to verify the key fingerprint manually, which is prone to errors and often blindly trusted. The SSH standard describes an alternative to such manual key verification: using the Domain Name System (DNS) to publish the server key information in SSHFP records.

In this paper, we conduct a large-scale Internet study to measure the prevalence of SSHFP records among DNS domain names. We scan the Tranco 1M list and over 500 million names from the certificate transparency log over the course of 26 d. The results show that in two studied populations, about 1 in 10,000 domains has SSHFP records, with more than half of them deployed without using DNSSEC, drastically reducing security benefits.

Keywords: DNS · DNSSEC · SSH · PKI · Internet security

1 Introduction

The Secure Shell (SSH) protocol allows to securely establish connections to remote servers over insecure transport channels [24]. It was standardized in Request for Comments (RFCs) 4250ff more than 15 years ago and is widely adopted on the Internet. In May 2022, the Internet scanning service Shodan reports close to 21 million active SSH-based services found in the IPv4 space [3] (most of them using TCP port 22). Common use-cases include remotely administering computer systems, copying files between systems, tunneling TCP connections or graphical sessions, and many others [4].

The SSH protocol defines a server and a client component. The former offers a service, usually on a remote system, and the latter is used to connect to such services. Upon establishing a connection, the client ought to verify the server's identity, which is done using public-key cryptography. To verify the server's identity, the client requires the (fingerprint of the) server's public key. If the client

A. R. Beresford et al. (Eds.): CANS 2022, LNCS 13641, pp. 71–88, 2022.
https://doi.org/10.1007/978-3-031-20974-1_4

has no public key on record for the given host name, the key is retrieved from the server without authentication and presented to the user for manual verification, as can be seen in Fig. 1. Only if the user chooses to trust the key, a connection is established. The client then stores the server's host name and fingerprint information and uses it to verify host keys presented in future connection attempts. This Trust On First Use (TOFU) principle makes this initial interaction pivotal to the security of all SSH connections from this client to this host name. An adequate validation requires the user to obtain the host key fingerprint through an out-of-band channel, i.e., asking the server's administrator. However, using these channels is not always feasible or comfortable. Thus users might accept fraudulent host keys or unknowingly perform human errors while comparing the fingerprints, as anecdotal evidence shows according to [16].

The risks associated with blindly trusting SSH host keys are many-fold. For example, if password-based authentication is used, a malicious SSH server can collect and store the user's password in plain text using publicly available tools [30]. Further, the OpenSSH client sends all of the client's public keys to the server, which can be used to personally identify the user through correlation with other sources [33]. Although alternative, password-less authentication methods mitigate the credentials-stealing attacks, in an online scenario, attackers in an unauthenticated connection can still use the user's credentials to obtain access to the SSH service under attack and deposit the attacker's key as trusted into the client's key database.

One approach to avoid manual verification of SSH server keys is to store the server's host key fingerprints in the Domain Name System (DNS) and let the SSH client use this out-of-band channel to retrieve them. RFCs 4251 and 4255 described the use of such SSHFP records in detail [15,24]. With DNSSEC seeing more widespread adoption [8,12], information retrieved via the DNS can be verified to be authentic as provided by the entity that owns the host name of SSH server. Consequently, the SSHFP specification mandates that the information obtained from the DNS can only be trusted if DNSSEC is used [15]. Hence, to enable host key verification based on SSHFP, DNS name owners are responsible for setting up the correct SSHFP records and securing their zone using DNSSEC.

1.1 Related Work

Different aspects of SSH were covered by academic work in the past. The widely used OpenSSH server and client implementation were studied with respect to their security. [10] presents a variety of plaintext-recovering attacks against SSH, while [25] reports on the security measures to make OpenSSH more resilient against vulnerabilities. The vulnerability database *CVE details* lists less than 100 discovered security issues in over 20 years to this date [2]. Since OpenSSH bases its cryptographic guarantees on underlying libraries, such as OpenSSL, it is affected by issues in those. An extensively studied incident is a bug in OpenSSL which lead to predictable random numbers endangering SSL/TLS and SSH servers [9,19,36]. A recent study analyzed OpenSSH's update patterns and

```
$ ssh server
The authenticity of host 'server (192.168.10.24)' can't be established.
ED25519 key fingerprint is SHA256:t0n0+3Gn9cwdke/WV66eC2zJUH197eWaxhnDnHS9JZQ.
+--[ED25519 256]--+
|              .. |
|             oE +|
|          . . + X|
|         . o + B*|
|        S + . *+o|
|         o * + *+|
|          o B BoB|
|           . + XX|
|             .B+B|
+----[SHA256]-----+
This key is not known by any other names
Are you sure you want to continue connecting (yes/no/[fingerprint])?
```

Fig. 1. An example of an SSH client prompting the user to verify the SSH server's host public key fingerprint the first time a connection is established.

discovered that many servers lag behind current patches, rendering them vulnerable [35]. Further, privacy implications of SSH authentication mechanisms were studied by [20] and [33].

While the previously mentioned work shows that SSH is being studied intensively, there is little research on the crucial first step of using SSH: The first connection to a server and its host key verification. As outlined in the introduction, improper handling of the initial verification puts users at risk. To the best of our knowledge, only [14] performed a large-scale analysis of SSH servers and SSHFP records. They report that only 660 of 2,070 domains with SSHFP records can be authenticated using DNSSEC and thus highlight the importance of correctly securing these records. Although [17,21] and [11] have contributed work to facilitate DNS-based host key verification, this method appears to be lacking adoption or proper security configuration.

1.2 Contributions

In this paper, we set out to analyze the current situation of DNS-based host key verification information on a large scale. In essence, we answer the following research questions:

1. How common are DNS-based host key verification records (SSHFP)?
2. Do the SSHFP records match their service counterpart?
3. Are these records properly secured using DNSSEC?

We answer these questions with large-scale, in-the-wild measurements with respect to the prevalence, correctness, and authenticity of SSHFP resource records according to the respective RFCs based on the Tranco Top 1M domains as well as more than 500 million domains obtained from the certificate transparency log over the course of 26 d, complementing and updating prior work.

2 Background

2.1 Host Key Verification

Server-Side Keys. A set of key pairs is required to run an SSH server. The keys are used for authentication of the server against the connecting user. If no keys are given, OpenSSH generates several key pairs using different algorithms (ECDSA, ED25519, and RSA) on the first start-up [6]. Previous versions of OpenSSH also featured DSA key pairs [7].

Fingerprints. The host key verification process requires validating if the server's public key matches the expected one. This check is performed each time a connection to the server is being established. To ease the process for the user, in OpenSSH, the verification of the host key fingerprint is facilitated using a hashed and encoded format using SHA256 and base64.

Client-Side Verification. When connecting to an SSH server, the server's public host key is sent to the client, which then tries to verify it [6]. There are three possible outcomes:

1. The host key is known and trusted.
2. The host key is unknown, and no entry for the host name exists in the local database.
3. The host key is unknown, but there is an entry for the host name in the local database.

In case 1, the user connects to a server whose host key is already trusted and stored in its local database. Both, the host names and key information match, and the connection succeeds.

If the server key cannot be found in the local database (case 2), the user is asked to verify the server's host key. This step is prone to human error, i.e., misreading the fingerprint, ignoring it due to inconvenience or other factors [16]. However, it is crucial for the TOFU principle to confirm that the fingerprint corresponds to the server's identity. Listing 1.1 displays the OpenSSH's prompt to verify the host key. If the user accepts the host key, it will be permanently stored in its local database.

```
1  The authenticity of host 'server (192.168.10.24)' can't
       be established.
2  ECDSA key fingerprint is SHA256:
       jq3V6ES34fNDKdn5L1sbmhoyJ5MN9afd9wIS1Upaldc.
3  This key is not known by any other names
4  Are you sure you want to continue connecting (yes/no/[
       fingerprint])?
```

Listing 1.1. On the first connection, the user is informed that the authenticity cannot be established and asked to verify the host key fingerprint.

When a connection to a known host name is established, but the presented server host keys do not match the record on file, either due to administrative changes on the server or an attacker performing a man-in-the-middle attack, the host key fingerprint comparison will fail due to a mismatch. In this case (3), the OpenSSH client implementation displays an eye-catching warning as seen in Listing 1.2. The user is made aware of that issue, and the connection is aborted. To resolve the issue, the user can either remove the known fingerprint and re-accept the key or add the correct fingerprint to their database (leading to prior scenarios).

In the previously discussed cases 2 and 3, the user needs to obtain the host key fingerprints for the server using an authenticated out-of-band channel. The RFC 4251 ([24]) suggests obtaining the key via telephone or the DNS. To avoid human error and in order to enable cryptographic authentication of the obtained fingerprint, RFC 4255 [15] standardizes the key exchange using DNS with security extensions. This functionality is included in the OpenSSH client, but not enabled by default [5]. If enabled, OpenSSH attempts to retrieve fingerprints for unknown host names via DNS, and if a successful match is produced, the user is asked to continue connecting without a manual fingerprint verification.

```
1 @@@@@@@@@@@@@@@@@@@@@@@@@@@@@@@@@@@@@@@@@@@@@@@@@@@@@@@@@@@
2 @    WARNING: REMOTE HOST IDENTIFICATION HAS CHANGED!     @
3 @@@@@@@@@@@@@@@@@@@@@@@@@@@@@@@@@@@@@@@@@@@@@@@@@@@@@@@@@@@
4 IT IS POSSIBLE THAT SOMEONE IS DOING SOMETHING NASTY!
5 Someone could be eavesdropping on you right now (man-in-the
      -middle attack)!
6 It is also possible that a host key has just been changed.
7 The fingerprint for the ECDSA key sent by the remote host
      is
8 SHA256:jq3V6ES34fNDKdn5L1sbmhoyJ5MN9afd9wIS1Upaldc.
9 Please contact your system administrator.
10 Add correct host key in ~/.ssh/known_hosts to get rid of
      this message.
11 Offending ED25519 key in ~/.ssh/known_hosts:121
12 Password authentication is disabled to avoid man-in-the-
      middle attacks.
13 Keyboard-interactive authentication is disabled to avoid
      man-in-the-middle attacks.
14 UpdateHostkeys is disabled because the host key is not
      trusted.
15 server: Permission denied (publickey,password).
```

Listing 1.2. A large warning is displayed and the connection aborted when the host key fingerprints do not match.

2.2 SSHFP Records

Format. Publication of SSH server key fingerprint in the DNS is done using the *SSHFP* resource records type and is documented in RFC 4255 [15]. SSHFP records include three fields; Listing 1.3 shows the structure.

```
1   SSHFP <KEY-ALGO> <HASH-TYPE> <FINGERPRINT>
```

Listing 1.3. SSHFP record presentation format [15].

The first field, `KEY-ALGO`, is an identifier for the host key's cryptographic algorithm. The second field, `HASH-TYPE`, encodes the hashing algorithm used to generate the fingerprint as an integer. Finally, the third field, `FINGERPRINT`, contains the actual fingerprint. Table 1 and 2 provide an exhaustive mapping of valid `KEY-ALGO` and `HASH-TYPE` values, according to the Internet standards [15,18,26,32].

Table 1. Values for the SSHFP `KEY-ALGO` field.

Value	Algorithm	RFC
0	Reserved	4255
1	RSA	4255
2	DSA	4255
3	ECDSA	6594
4	ED25519	7479
5	unassigned [1]	–
6	ED448	8709

Table 2. Values for the SSHFP `HASH-TYPE` field.

Value	Algorithm	RFC
0	Reserved	4255
1	SHA1	4255
2	SHA256	6594

Matching. Several conditions must be met when matching SSHFP records with server-side host keys. Unless all the following conditions are fulfilled, the connection is vulnerable to man-in-the-middle attacks [15]: (1) The key algorithms must match. (2) The key's fingerprints, calculated using the designated hashing algorithm, must match. (3) The SSHFP records must be trustworthy, i.e., received and validated using DNS with DNSSEC or another secure transport channel.

DNSSEC. In light of additional administrative efforts, the adoption of DNSSEC is only progressing very slowly [13,34]. If records have been authenticated, this is indicated by the AD bit in the DNS response, which assumes that the network between client and DNS resolver is trusted. One goal of this paper is to establish whether SSHFP records are correctly configured and secured.

3 Methodology

3.1 Data Collection

To collect bulk data from the DNS and SSH servers, we implemented a scanner using Python and multiprocessing that can be easily extended for other collection tasks and is available on GitHub under a free license [27]. Figure 2 shows the stages of our methodology.

Domain Input. For our study, we relied on two sources for domain names: First, the Tranco list [23], which includes 1 million popular domain names (as of 6 Dec 2021, ID: G8KK). Second, names published in the certificate transparency log [22], which includes all names for which certificates have been issued over the course of 26 d (22 Dec 2021 to 18 Jan 2022). Together, we scanned about 515 million domain names for the presence of SSHFP records.

This methodology based on domain names complements prior work ([14]), which studied the prevalence of SSHFP records in the entire IPv4 Internet, but relied on reverse lookups, i.e., names associated with an IPv4 address. The limitation of this methodology is that not for all addresses of SSH servers, the reverse lookup pointing to a domain name is correctly configured. The limitation of the methodology used in this work, in contrast, is that not all SSH server addresses appear in our sample of domain names.

Query Pipeline. The Query Pipeline workers query a domain for SSHFP records using a shared PowerDNS[1] recursive DNS resolver. For any given domain

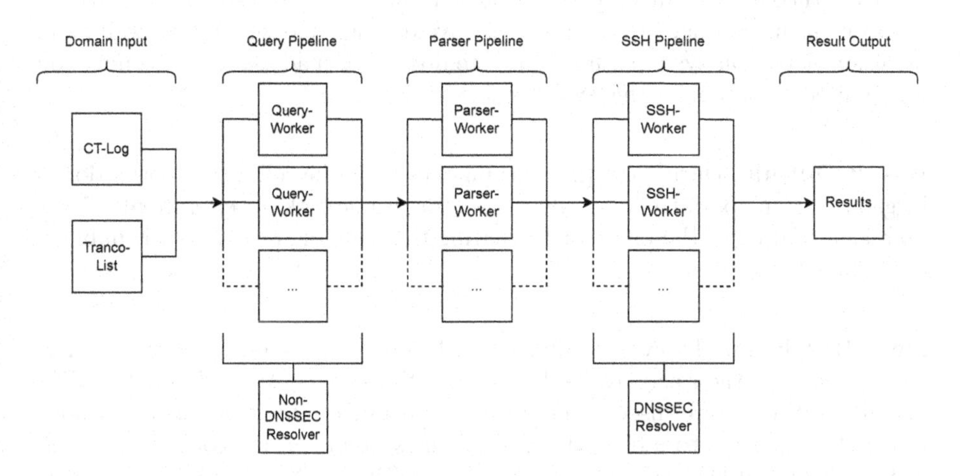

Fig. 2. The data collection tool consists of multiple pipelines used for scanning and analyzing the domains for SSHFP records.

[1] https://www.powerdns.com/.

name, this step returns zero or more SSHFP records. If records are present, the data is passed on to the next stage. Otherwise, the domain is omitted from further processing. Our scanning configuration consisted of 50 Query workers.

Parser Pipeline. The third stage parses a domain's SSHFP records and checks them for syntactical correctness, i.e., if a record adheres to the format described in Sect. 2.2 and if the fingerprint length matches the output length of the hash function specified in the given `HASH-TYPE`. Erroneous and syntactical correct records are logged; domains with syntactically correct records are passed to the SSH Pipeline.

SSH Pipeline. For each given domain name, all associated Internet addresses are determined by retrieving the A record sets for the given name. For each IPv4 address, the SSH fingerprints are collected using `ssh-keyscan`[2]. (To avoid expensive port scans, we only consider SSH services on TCP port 22.) Unless the set of these fingerprints is empty, i.e., no SSH Server was reachable, they are saved for later comparison. Additionally, the SSHFP query is repeated, but this time through the DNSSEC-validating resolver (cf. Fig. 2) to determine whether these records can be authenticated. Again, the results, including the failure-cases, are logged to a file for later analysis. We did not contact IP v6 SSH services due to a lack of support in our measurement network. Of 17,759 domain names with SSHFP records studied in this work, 8,200 had IPv4 and IPv6 addresses assigned and are thus only partially included (but note that it is common for dual-stack setups that v4 and v6 address point to the same service); 182 domain names (1%) are fully excluded as they only had v6 addresses.

All SSH connection attempts were made from a single host in our institution's network, using a single IP address. To avoid being blocked by firewalls and intrusion detection systems, no login attempts were made, and the connection was limited to obtaining the SSH key fingerprints.

Result Output. During the previous pipeline step, the collected information is logged as JSON-formatted lines by the logging framework in separate files. This data is later used as the basis for evaluating the scanning results and is publicly available [29].

DNS Resolvers. To avoid problems with direct upstream resolvers, we ran two instances of the freely available PowerDNS resolvers. Apart from DNSSEC, default settings were used. The primary instance was configured without DNSSEC validation to reduce the load on the system and network. The second instance featured DNSSEC validation to establish the SSHFP records' security, but the workload was assumed to be much lower due to the previous filtering steps.

[2] `ssh-keyscan -D -4 -t dsa,rsa,ecdsa,ed25519 -T 5 <IP>`.

Ethical Considerations. We minimized the risk and harm to the Internet caused by our research by taking the following steps.

First, we scanned from our university's network using a single IP address to make the network traffic easily recognizable as research activity. Further, we set up a website stating our intentions and research activities on that particular IP address. It included a point of contact to have all scanning activities ceased and have the domain removed from our lists.

Second, we used locally hosted recursive DNS resolvers to distribute the query-load on the respective upstream name servers. Our query-per-second rate averaged in the low hundreds, which we assume not to cause any harm to any network.

Third, SSH connection attempts were only performed if several prerequisites were met, i.e., an SSHFP and A record were found, thereby significantly reducing the number of connections. In particular, our SSH connections only query the server's host keys and do not attempt a login that might trigger various intrusion detection systems.

3.2 Data Analysis

Empirical Data and Quantitative Analysis. As stated previously, we empirically collected data to analyze the prevalence of SSHFP records on the Internet. Since the analysis of the Tranco 1M domains only showed an extremely small prevalence, we proceeded to evaluate a larger data set of domain names used in the wild, obtained from the global certificate transparency log ([22]).

We approach the resulting data sets with quantitative analysis and aim to answer our research questions with basic statistical methods. All data and analyses are available to the public ([29]).

SSHFP library All code related to handling SSHFP records was implemented as a stand-alone Python library, which will be published to facilitate current and future research [28]. It covers all basic functionality to work with SSHFP records and their structure. For example, records can be checked for validity, manipulated, or created. The library complements the functionality of other python DNS libraries, such as dnspython[3].

3.3 Replicability

All code used in data collection and analysis for this work is available on GitHub [27,28] and is suitable to replicate our work. As data collection results may change over time, we also provide the data we collected [29].

[3] https://dnspython.readthedocs.io/.

4 Evaluation

4.1 Tranco 1M

DNS Scanning. The scanning process finished within roughly 1.5 h. For 953,147 out of the 1,000,000 domains, we received a DNS response without error (response status `NOERROR`), of which only 105 (0.011%) had one or more SSHFP records. In total, 465 records were collected.

DNS Data Analysis. Out of the 465 records, 2 were invalid due to specifying an incorrect value for `KEY-ALGO`, and thus removed from further processing.

As each domain can have multiple SSHFP records (i.e., for each `KEY-ALGO` or `HASH-TYPE`), the comparison of the individual record sets revealed 11 identical and 94 unique, with the most common set counted 3 times.

For single SSHFP records, we discover 422 to be unique, with 3 repetitions at most. Considering only these unique records, Table 3 displays the distribution of the key algorithms and hash types.

SSH Scanning and Matching. For 72 of the 105 domain names, we successfully obtained fingerprints from the corresponding SSH services from at least one of the given IPv4 addresses. In total, we counted 380 fingerprints received via SSH connections from 75 different IPv4 addresses.

For 66 out of 75 hosts reached under these addresses (providing a total of 256 fingerprints), we found at least one fingerprint match in the DNS data corresponding to the domain name that led us to this address. In contrast, for 9 hosts (totaling 124 fingerprints), there was no match with the fingerprint records given in the DNS.

Table 3 shows the key algorithms and hash types for the matching and mismatching server-side fingerprints and Fig. 3a displays the distribution of Tranco domain names with full, partial, and no matching SSHFP records.

Finally, of a total of 953,147 existing domain names taken from the Tranco list, 28 (0.0029%) had matching SSHFP records deployed securely.

Table 3. Distribution of `KEY-ALGO` and `HASH-TYPE` values for the Tranco 1M list

Data from	Key Algorithm						Hash Type	
	RESERVED	RSA	DSA	ECDSA	ED25519	ED448	SHA1	SHA256
DNS	0	131	79	109	103	0	245	177
SSH	0	138	22	106	114	0	190	190
– Matching	0	93	10	74	79	0	151	105
– Mismatching	0	45	12	32	35	0	39	85

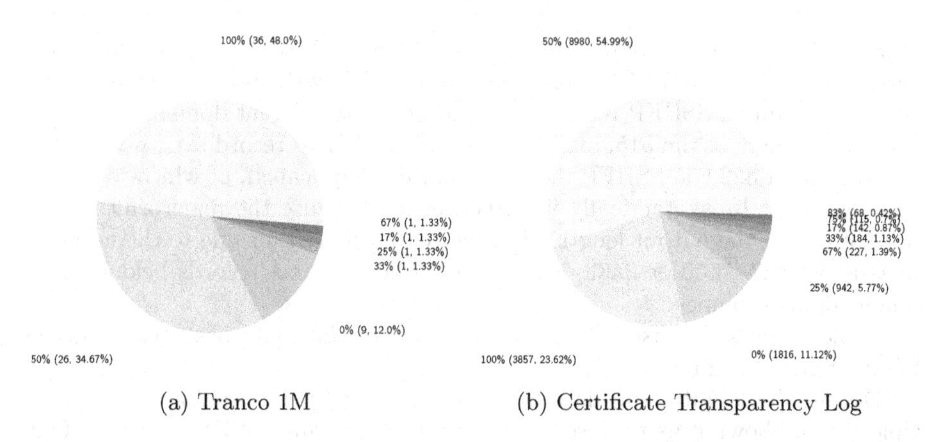

(a) Tranco 1M

(b) Certificate Transparency Log

Fig. 3. Proportion of domain names that have full, partial, and no match with the fingerprint we retrieved using the SSH protocol. 100% indicates that all fingerprints matched (implying that the same number of fingerprints was retrieved via DNS and SSH), whereas 0% denotes no matches.

4.2 Certificate Transparency Logs

The evaluation for the certificate transparency (CT) log is more nuanced since the log features domains using wildcards as well as domains using many labels (i.e., `*.label2.label1.tld`). To avoid counting duplicates, we skipped all domains using wildcards. For all other domains, to shorten domains with many labels, we identified the public suffix of each domain name. Together with the label immediately below the public suffix, the *registrable domain name*, sometimes also known as eTLD+1, is derived (in above example, `label1.tld`). If a domain occurred multiple times in the CT log, it was also scanned multiple times. On average, domain names showed up 3.8 times over the course of 26 d (median: 3). Some domains showed up frequently, and the most frequent name was seen 6 million times.

DNS Scanning. This scanning process is open-ended in its nature since the CT log continuously provides new data. Therefore, we stopped the data collection process after roughly 600 million domain names and a collection time frame of 26 d between 2021-12-22 and 2022-01-18.

After removing approximately 84.6 million wildcard domains, we issued DNS requests for the SSHFP record set for each domain name, resulting in over 515.5 million queries. This number includes queries for the same domain name if it appears multiple times in the CT log. In total, we queried only slightly over 136.5 million *unique* domain names, which belong to about 45 million unique registrable domains.

DNS Data Analysis. Within the 136.5 million unique non-wildcard domains, we found a total of 17,672 (0.013%) SSHFP record sets belonging to 7,007 unique registrable domains or subdomains. Many SSHFP record sets are deployed for several names: out of 17,672 record sets, we only observed 5,961 unique sets, with the most common SSHFP record set found at 1,670 different domain names.

In the course of the 515.5 million queries for SSHFP record sets, we found a grand total of 323,655 SSHFP records (counting duplicates), of which we found 365 records to be syntactically incorrect, either because the fingerprint length did not match the output length of the stated hash type, or due to the usage of unassigned `KEY-ALGO` or `HASH-TYPE` values. The incorrect records belong to 18 unique domain names.

Table 4 shows the distribution of the key algorithms and hash types for the unique SSHFP records.

Due to the longitudinal data collection, some domains were analyzed multiple times, allowing us to observe changes to a domain's SSHFP records. Out measurements show 543 changes in the record sets of registrable domains. In particular, the whole record set was replaced in 539 cases. In the other 4 cases, we observed two partial removals and two partial replacements.

Table 4. Distribution of `KEY-ALGO` and `HASH-TYPE` values for the Certificate Transparency Logs

Data From	Algorithm						Hash Type	
	RESERVED	RSA	DSA	ECDSA	ED25519	ED448	SHA1	SHA256
DNS	1	7,536	2,367	6,726	7,191	2	9,054	14,769
SSH	0	26,974	5,680	19,562	20,296	0	36,256	36,256
– Matching	0	15,190	1,528	11,972	12,211	0	21,871	19,030
– Mismatching	0	11,784	4,152	7,590	8,085	0	14,385	17,226

SSH Scanning and Matching. We obtained 16,331 IPv4 addresses by querying the A records for all 17,672 domain names for which we found SSHFP records. Contacting all addresses via SSH yielded a total of 72,512 fingerprints belonging to 11,524 unique domain names (with the remainder of domains having no reachable SSH service on port 22).

Under 14,515 addresses, an SSH service presented at least one fingerprint matching an SSHFP record published under the associated domain name (89%). This accounts for 10,378 of 11,524 unique domain names (90%) with SSHFP records.

Again, Table 4 presents the key algorithms and hash types for the matching and mismatching server-side fingerprints, and Fig. 3b shows the distribution of domain names with full, partial, and no matching SSHFP records.

Finally, for the certificate transparency data set, only 3,896 (0.0029%) out of the 136.5 million domains had matching SSHFP records deployed securely.

5 Discussion

5.1 Prevalence of SSHFP Records

Our data provides an estimate for the prevalence of SSHFP records on the Internet based on the Tranco 1M list and our study of over 500 million domain names. In both cases, the rate of domain names having SSHFP records is on the order of 1 in 10,000. For the Tranco 1M list, which portrays itself "a research oriented top sites ranking hardened against manipulation" [23], where reasonable security best practices could be expected, only 0.0105% registrable domains have SSHFP records. For the certificate transparency data set, only 0.0014% unique registrable domains feature SSHFP records.

While SSHFP records are not strictly required for each domain, our expectation of a more widespread adoption was not met. The records are a sensible security best practice when the domain's delegated server systems operate an SSH service. This is not the case in, for example shared web hosting environments, where direct access to the SSH servers is nonexistent or even permitted.

In prior work, Gasser et al. [14] found 2,070 domain names with SSHFP records by considering the reverse lookup information for all IPv4 addresses with active SSH hosts. From the 10,483 domain names with SSHFP records that we identified, we found that 1,931 have reverse lookup information setup for their address. We conclude that limiting the attention to addresses with reverse lookup information excludes a large proportion of deployed SSHFP from the analysis. Furthermore, due to the different limitations of methodology, our results do not allow a direct comparison w.r.t. the prevalence of SSHFP records to the numbers obtained by Gasser et al. beyond the fact that both ours and their numbers constitute lower bounds for the total number of domain names having SSHFP record sets.

The low prevalence of SSHFP records is in spite of support for SSHFP being implemented in the commonly used OpenSSH client for nearly 20 years (although not enabled by default). With `ssh -o VerifyHostKeyDNS=ask example.com`, the client will retrieve the SSHFP records and use them for verification. Also, the openssh-package comes with a tool which outputs a server's SSHFP records to facilitate importing them into a DNS zone (`ssh-keyscan -D example.com`).

5.2 Security and Privacy

By specification, SSH clients can only validate fingerprints obtained via SSHFP records if they can be authenticated. The only automatic approach for authentication standardized is DNSSEC.

Among the Tranco 1 million domain names, out of the 72 domain names that have SSHFP records provisioned, 63 presented at least one matching fingerprint in SSH connection attempts. Of these, 28 domain names published their SSHFP records securely (i.e., with DNSSEC enabled), and 35 did so insecurely (i.e., without authenticity guaranteed through DNSSEC). Among the 137M domain names that appeared in the CT log during our study, out of the

17,654 unique domain names that have SSHFP records provisioned, 10,378 presented at least one matching fingerprint in SSH connection attempts. Of these, 3,896 domain names published their SSHFP records securely, and 6482 did so insecurely. Figure 4 compares the number of domains with matching fingerprints with the numbers for the Tranco domain names by DNSSEC security status.

For both populations, we find that about 88% of SSH servers that we reached under domain names with SSHFP records actually presented matching key fingerprints. But only around half of these SSHFP records, the client can check authenticity using DNSSEC. Further, Fig. 3a and 3b show that at most around half of SSHFP records represent a full match with the fingerprints collected from the respective SSH servers. While this could be attributed to ongoing key rollovers or the precautionary deployment of emergency keys, the large prevalence of such configurations indicates that misconfigurations may be in place. The latter is supported by the observation that some mismatching records have a correct fingerprint but incorrect key algorithm or hash values.

Nonetheless, compared to [14], we find fewer matching records (94% vs. 88%), which may be caused by the different methodology. We also observe a higher adoption rate of DNSSEC (31.8% vs. $\geq 44\%$), which can be expected due to the overall increase in DNSSEC adoption in the 8 years since their study.

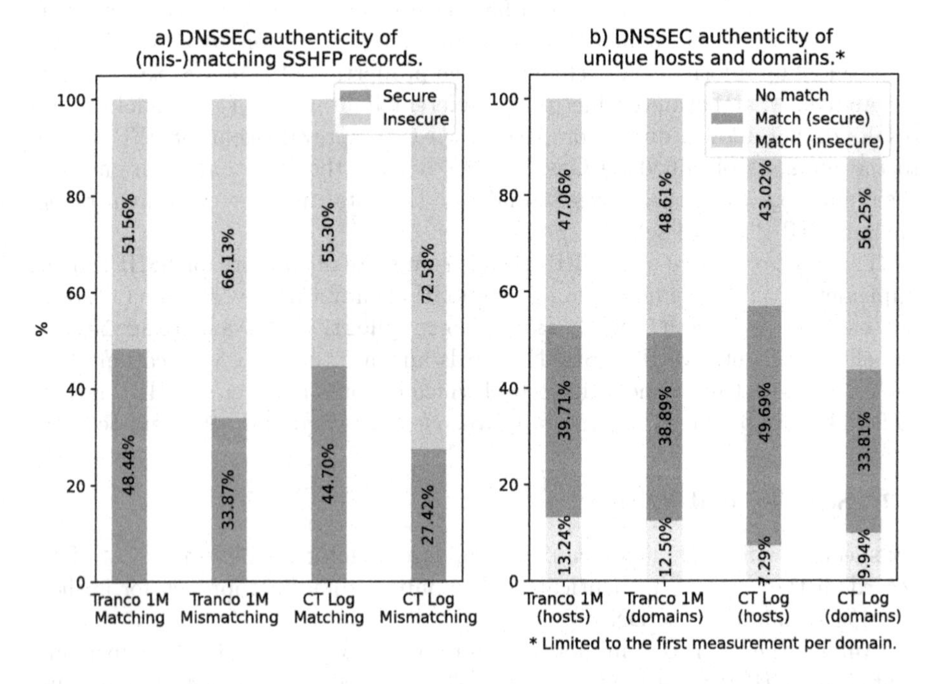

Fig. 4. Overview of the DNSSEC security status of (a) SSHFP records and (b) SSHFP record sets for associated domain names and hosts (identified by IPv4 address). If multiple measurements of the same domain name are available, only the first one is considered.

An additional insight into the used key and hash algorithms is offered by Tables 3 and 4. Modern key algorithms and hash types, such as ones based on elliptic curves and SHA-256, respectively, are still behind RSA, DSA, and SHA-1. However, the former provides higher security as, for example, the security of SHA-1 is seriously threatened [31]. An interesting fact is the low number of discovered ED448 keys, despite the RFC being published more than 2 years ago, which we attribute to the default key algorithm settings of OpenSSH.

Finally, we found duplicates of several SSHFP records under various domain names, with the most popular fingerprint appearing 1,776 times. This allows identifying related domains by observing names that share one or more host key fingerprints, which may impact privacy. If fingerprints are identical for SSH services running on different machines, bad security practice by reusing keys is indicated.

5.3 Limitations

While running this study, we noticed that a significant proportion of our initial DNS queries for SSHFP record sets of new domain names resulted in errors. Out of 516M queries, an error condition was met in 26M cases (5%). For 16M cases (including 14k from Tranco), our resolver determined that the domain name does not exist (`NXDOMAIN`). In 10M cases, we did not receive a reply within 5 s (albeit retries of the resolver) or all received replies were broken.

We attribute these error conditions to faulty configuration of authoritative name servers, but caution that unreliable network links to distant servers may also play a role. In the latter case, errors during the initial query for the SSHFP record set would incorrectly eliminate a candidate domain name from further processing; and a failed re-query at the end of the SSH-stage using the validating resolver would hinder the security assessment. For completeness, a detailed list of such errors is available along with all data captured for this study.

Additionally, we noticed interruptions in the data provided by the certificate transparency log, due to which data in short periods of time in the study period is missing from the analysis. The total duration of missing data is less than 3% of the total time the study ran.

5.4 Future Work

A longitudinal study should be performed to better understand the evolution of SSHFP record deployment on the Internet. In addition, alternative data sources to obtain a widespread insight in the DNS or server-side host keys are an interesting area for future work, as well as ways to a more resilient analysis process, e.g., using redundant DNS resolvers or different network locations for measurements.

Additionally, the causes of the low prevalence of SSHFP records should be studied. For example, is it an unawareness of these possibilities, the unwillingness to properly establish a server's authenticity, or technical issues (i.e., DNSSEC) which hinder the usage of SSHFP records? Similarly, improvements for easier deployment of SSHFP records should be discussed in future work.

6 Summary and Conclusion

We provided an overview of the SSHFP specification and conducted a large-scale analysis of such records on the Internet. To that end, we collected key fingerprint information for domains from the Tranco 1M list as well as more than 500 million domains over the course of a month from certificate transparency logs. Furthermore, we obtained the corresponding key fingerprints via SSH from the addresses associated with the domain names for comparison and checked if the SSHFP records are secured by using DNSSEC.

Our data shows that SSHFP records are still a niche occurrence lacking widespread adoption, although it was mentioned early in the SSH standardization process. While a few thousand domains successfully use these records, almost 50% do not securely transmit them, violating the standard and drastically reducing security benefits. Nevertheless, if used correctly, SSHFP records have the potential to mitigate many risks associated with SSH's TOFU approach.

The OpenSSH software package already supports the generation and verification of SSHFP records. We complement this by publishing all code used in this work to facilitate future work in this area.

References

1. DNS Sshfp Resource Record Parameters. https://www.iana.org/assignments/dns-sshfp-rr-parameters/dns-sshfp-rr-parameters.xhtml
2. Openbsd Openssh : CVE security vulnerabilities, versions and detailed reports. https://www.cvedetails.com/product/585/Openbsd-Openssh.html?vendor_id=97
3. Shodan Search. https://www.shodan.io/search?query=ssh
4. ssh(1) - OpenBSD manual pages. https://man.openbsd.org/ssh
5. ssh_config(5) - OpenBSD manual pages. https://man.openbsd.org/ssh_config.5
6. sshd(8) - OpenBSD manual pages. https://man.openbsd.org/sshd
7. sshd(8) - OpenBSD manual pages. https://man.openbsd.org/OpenBSD-6.0/sshd
8. Why has DNSSEC increased in some economies and not others? (Jul 2020). https://blog.apnic.net/2020/07/10/why-has-dnssec-increased-in-some-economies-and-not-others/
9. Ahmad, D.: Two years of broken crypto: Debian's Dress rehearsal for a global PKI compromise. IEEE Security Priv. **6**(5), 70–73 (2008). https://doi.org/10.1109/MSP.2008.131
10. Albrecht, M.R., Paterson, K.G., Watson, G.J.: Plaintext Recovery Attacks against SSH. In: 2009 30th IEEE Symposium on Security and Privacy, pp. 16–26 (May 2009). https://doi.org/10.1109/SP.2009.5, ISSN: 2375-1207
11. Buijsman, M., Cuylaerts, P.: Automatic SSH public key fingerprint retrieval and publication in DNSSEC, p. 43
12. Chung, T., et al.: A Longitudinal, End-to-End View of the DNSSEC Ecosystem, pp. 1307–1322 (2017). https://www.usenix.org/conference/usenixsecurity17/technical-sessions/presentation/chung

13. Decker, S., Liedtka, D.: "A Reproduction of A Longitudinal End-to-End View of the DNSSEC Ecosystem", p. 6 (2020)
14. Gasser, O., Holz, R., Carle, G.: A deeper understanding of SSH: results from Internet-wide scans. In: 2014 IEEE Network Operations and Management Symposium (NOMS), pp. 1–9 (May 2014). https://doi.org/10.1109/NOMS.2014.6838249, ISSN: 2374-9709
15. Griffin, W., Schlyter, J.: Using DNS to Securely Publish Secure Shell (SSH) Key Fingerprints. Request for Comments RFC 4255, Internet Engineering Task Force (Jan 2006). https://doi.org/10.17487/RFC4255,https://datatracker.ietf.org/doc/rfc4255, num Pages: 9
16. Gutmann, P.: Do Users Verify SSH Keys? p. 2
17. Hardaker, W., Krishnaswamy, S.: Enabling DNSSEC in Open Source Applications, p. 8
18. Harris, B., Velvindron, L.: Ed25519 and Ed448 Public Key Algorithms for the Secure Shell (SSH) Protocol. Request for Comments RFC 8709, Internet Engineering Task Force (Feb 2020). https://doi.org/10.17487/RFC8709,https://datatracker.ietf.org/doc/rfc8709, num Pages: 7
19. Heninger, N., Durumeric, Z., Wustrow, E., Halderman, J.A.: Mining Your Ps and Qs: Detection of Widespread Weak Keys in Network Devices, p. 16
20. Kannisto, J., Harju, J.: The time will tell on you: exploring information leaks in SSH Public Key authentication. In: Yan, Z., Molva, R., Mazurczyk, W., Kantola, R. (eds.) NSS 2017. LNCS, vol. 10394, pp. 301–314. Springer, Cham (2017). https://doi.org/10.1007/978-3-319-64701-2_22
21. Krishnaswamy, S., Hardaker, W., Mundy, R.: DNSSEC in practice: using DNSSEC-Tools to deploy DNSSEC. In: 2009 Cybersecurity Applications Technology Conference for Homeland Security. pp. 3–15 (Mar 2009). https://doi.org/10.1109/CATCH.2009.21
22. Laurie, B., Langley, A., Kasper, E.: Certificate Transparency. Request for Comments RFC 6962, Internet Engineering Task Force (Jun 2013). https://doi.org/10.17487/RFC6962,https://datatracker.ietf.org/doc/rfc6962, num Pages: 27
23. Le Pochat, V., Van Goethem, T., Tajalizadehkhoob, S., Korczyński, M., Joosen, W.: Tranco: A Research-Oriented Top Sites Ranking Hardened Against Manipulation. In: Proceedings of the 26th Annual Network and Distributed System Security Symposium, NDSS 2019 (Feb 2019). https://doi.org/10.14722/ndss.2019.23386
24. Lonvick, C.M., Ylonen, T.: The Secure Shell (SSH) Protocol Architecture. Request for Comments RFC 4251, Internet Engineering Task Force (Jan 2006). https://doi.org/10.17487/RFC4251,https://datatracker.ietf.org/doc/rfc4251, num Pages: 30
25. Miller, D.: Security measures in OpenSSH, p. 6
26. Moonesamy, S.: Using Ed25519 in SSHFP Resource Records. Request for Comments RFC 7479, Internet Engineering Task Force (Mar 2015). https://doi.org/10.17487/RFC7479,https://datatracker.ietf.org/doc/rfc7479, num Pages: 4
27. Neef, S.: gehaxelt/sshfp-dns-measurement: Code used for the "oh ssh-it, what's my fingerprint? a large-scale analysis of ssh host key fingerprint verification records in the dns" paper. https://github.com/gehaxelt/sshfp-dns-measurement
28. Neef, S.: libsshfp · pypi. https://pypi.org/project/libsshfp/, version 0.0.2
29. Neef, S.: Source and result datasets for ""Oh SSH-it, what's my fingerprint? A Large-Scale Analysis of SSH Host Key Fingerprint Verification Records in the DNS" (Aug 2022). https://doi.org/10.5281/zenodo.6993096
30. Oosterhof, M.: Cowrie (Apr 2022). https://github.com/micheloosterhof/cowrie-dev, original-date: 2021-10-17T15:56:32Z

31. Stevens, M., Bursztein, E., Karpman, P., Albertini, A., Markov, Y.: The First collision for Full SHA-1. In: Katz, J., Shacham, H. (eds.) CRYPTO 2017. LNCS, vol. 10401, pp. 570–596. Springer, Cham (2017). https://doi.org/10.1007/978-3-319-63688-7_19
32. Surý, O.: Use of the SHA-256 Algorithm with RSA, Digital Signature Algorithm (DSA), and Elliptic Curve DSA (ECDSA) in SSHFP Resource Records. Request for Comments RFC 6594, Internet Engineering Task Force (Apr 2012). https://doi.org/10.17487/RFC6594,https://datatracker.ietf.org/doc/rfc6594, num Pages: 9
33. Valsorda, F.: whoami.filippo.io (Apr 2022). https://github.com/FiloSottile/whoami.filippo.io, original-date: 2015-08-04T01:44:29Z
34. Wander, M.: Measurement survey of server-side DNSSEC adoption. In: 2017 Network Traffic Measurement and Analysis Conference (TMA), pp. 1–9 (Jun 2017). https://doi.org/10.23919/TMA.2017.8002913
35. West, J.C., Moore, T.: Longitudinal Study of Internet-Facing OpenSSH Update Patterns. In: Hohlfeld, O., Moura, G., Pelsser, C. (eds.) PAM 2022. LNCS, vol. 13210, pp. 675–689. Springer, Cham (2022). https://doi.org/10.1007/978-3-030-98785-5_30
36. Yilek, S., Rescorla, E., Shacham, H., Enright, B., Savage, S.: When private keys are public: results from the 2008 Debian OpenSSL vulnerability. In: Proceedings of the 9th ACM SIGCOMM conference on Internet measurement, IMC 2009, pp. 15–27. Association for Computing Machinery, New York (Nov 2009). https://doi.org/10.1145/1644893.1644896

Attribute-Based Anonymous Credential: Optimization for Single-Use and Multi-Use

Kwan Yin Chan(✉) and Tsz Hon Yuen

The University of Hong Kong, Hong Kong, Hong Kong
{kychan,thyuen}@cs.hku.hk

Abstract. User attributes can be authenticated by an attribute-based anonymous credential while keeping the anonymity of the user. Most attribute-based anonymous credential schemes are designed specifically for either multi-use or single-use. In this paper, we propose a unified attribute-based anonymous credential system, in which users always obtain the same format of credential from the issuer. The user can choose to use it for an efficient multi-use or single-use show proof. It is a more user-centric approach than the existing schemes.

Technically, we propose an interactive approach to the credential issuance protocol using a two-party computation with an additive homomorphic encryption. At the same time, it keeps the security property of impersonation resilience, anonymity, and unlinkability. Apart from the interactive protocol, we further design the show proofs for efficient single-use credentials which maintain the user anonymity.

Keywords: Anonymous credential · Zero-knowledge proof · Single-use · Multi-use

1 Introduction

Anonymous credentials provide a secure approach for transmitting trust signals while protecting the anonymity of the users simultaneously in a cryptographic way. Starting from the idea from Chaum [11], the development of anonymous credentials has been last for decades. Attribute-based access control is already implemented by the industry[1] Hence, attribute-based anonymous credential (ABC) with efficient show proofs for complex statements are important [40].

[1] AWS: https://docs.aws.amazon.com/IAM/latest/UserGuide/introduction_attribute-based-access-control.html. Azure: https://docs.microsoft.com/en-us/azure/role-based-access-control/conditions-overview.

A. R. Beresford et al. (Eds.): CANS 2022, LNCS 13641, pp. 89–121, 2022.
https://doi.org/10.1007/978-3-031-20974-1_5

Looking at the typical design of an attribute-based credential, it contains several attributes from the user who is being authenticated (e.g., age = 20, gender = male, ZIP code = 123456). A full disclosure of attributes may compromise the identity of the user. For example, 87% of the population in U.S. can be uniquely identified based on ZIP code, date of birth, and gender [36]. With the help of zero-knowledge show proofs, ABC allows the minimal number of user attributes to be disclosed during authentication and maintains strong privacy. Verifiers could verify the zero-knowledge proof from a user without knowing the content of the credential. Therefore, the credentials can be used multiple times with anonymity.

q-SDH-Based Anonymous Credential System. Tan *et al.* [40] introduced an attribute-based anonymous credential (ABC) system, which supports the needs of showing proofs for complex statements. The system generates credentials with the self-introduced *MoniPoly* commitment scheme and the SDH-based Camenisch-Lysyanskaya (CL) signature [7]. The proposed scheme includes a series of zero-knowledge proofs, which proves the relationship between the attribute set in the credential A and the attribute set of the verifier A'. The authors proposed AND, ANY/OR, NAND/NOT and NANY proofs concretely. The ABC system also achieves impersonation resilience, anonymity, and unlinkability.

Single-use and Multi-use Credentials. Considering the (un)linkability of the anonymous credentials, they could be classified into *single-use* credentials and *multi-use* credentials. A *multi-use* credential can be used more than once without revealing any linkage between different authenticated sessions. We could find many protocols are in the type of *multi-use* credentials in recent research [12,23,40] which aim to reduce the number of credentials issued from the issuer.

If an *single-use* credential is used to authenticate two different sessions, the two sessions are linked (while the anonymity of the attributes is still preserved). The traditional application of *single-use* credentials can be shown in U-Prove [32], also it could be very useful under the situation of e-voting (double voting can be detected). Existing research work of *single-use* credentials could be found in [14,18,26], and they are usually more efficient than *multi-use* credentials during the authentication protocol. On the other hand, if the linkage of sessions is undesirable in the application, the issuer has to generate a new credential for each communication. The cost of the authentication protocol is switched to the credential generation protocol in this case.

1.1 Motivation

In this paper, we design a unified attribute-based anonymous credential system supporting efficient single-use and multi-use credential. In the existing ABC systems, the choice of single-use or multi-use credential is selected by the one who design and implement the system (which may be the issuer). In this paper, we design a unified ABC system, in which this choice is chosen by the *user* or depending on the real world application. The issuer, which is usually an authority managing identities, does not need to care about the underlying use case of the credential system.

Consider the example of anonymous discussion forum. Users can be authenticated by anonymous credential before posting messages. The user can choose to use a multi-use credential if he wants all his posts remain unlinked to each other. The user can also choose to use a single-use credential to keep all his posts linked in the same thread/topic. In this case, the choice of single-use of multi-use is chosen by the user.

Building an efficient attribute-based anonymous credential system supporting both single-use and multi-use credential is a non-trivial task. Many existing single-use credentials are constructed from symmetric key primitives [14,26] and hence it is not efficient to use a zero-knowledge proof to convert it into a multi-use credential. On the other hand, most existing multi-use credentials are fully or partially known by the issuer [7,12,17,23,27,40]. Simply presenting this credential as a show proof of a single-use credential compromise the anonymity with respect to the issuer.

1.2 Our Contributions

In this paper, we propose an attribute-based anonymous credential system which support efficient single-use and multi-use show proof. In particular, the choice of single-use or multi-use is chosen by the user, instead of the issuer. As compared to the state-of-the-art scheme from Tan *et al.* [40], our system has the contributions below:

User-Centric Anonymous Credentials. Based on the system proposed by Tan *et al.* [40], we propose a interactive credential issuance protocol using two-party computation and additive homomorphic encryption. Following this interactive approach, the full content of the credential is only known by the user, not by the issuer. It enables the user to use the credential as a single-use or multi-use later. The interactive approach does not affect any of the multi-use show proof presentation protocol in [40]. Our multi-use show proof credential system achieves impersonation resilience, anonymity, and unlinkability.

If the user choose to use a single-use show proof, he can also choose to use a subset of his attributes when generating that single-use credential. For example, if Alice has 100 attributes and she is going to use 3 attributes in a single-use anonymous authentication, she just needs to request a credential with these 3 attributes only. It can significantly reduce the computation and communication complexity, especially when the user has a large number of attributes.

Clear Role for the Issuer. In [40], the attributes from users are committed using the *MoniPoly* commitment scheme. The commitment is sent to the issuer and the issuer generates credential upon the commitment. Tan *et al.* claimed that their scheme achieved perfectly hiding of attributes with respect to the issuer. However, we find it unrealistic for the issuer (e.g., the identity authority) for not knowing the attributes (e.g., gender, date of birth, etc.) when it issues credential. Generally, the issuer knows the content of the attribute set from a user, and what attribute(s) that the user would like to authenticate in each credential. This prevents some malicious users issue the credentials with some unexpected attributes.

In our proposed protocol, we set that the issuer knows the attributes of a particular user. Although this approach breaks the perfectly hiding of attributes among the issuing protocol between the issuer and the user, it maintains the power that the issuer understands what it is authenticating and that is its only role. The issuer does not need to care about the choice of single-use or multi-use in the system.

Show Proofs for Single-use Credentials. We further design the show proofs with logic statements for single-use credentials. Since the single-use credentials are aimed to use once only, a prover could hide less information in order to decrease computation costs while maintaining anonymity. With the single-use setting, we further proposed batch credentials issuance in order to minimize the communication rounds.

1.3 Overview of Our Scheme

To fill the aforementioned research gap, we propose a modified attribute-based credential system from Tan *et al.* [40], with a new two-party computation approach to generating the credential.

The protocol proposed by Tan *et al.* [40] is a state-of-the-art attribute-based anonymous credential system, with *multi-use* credentials. Furthermore, it provides different show proofs to prove the credential with a statement, comparing the requirement from the verifiers and the authenticated attributes from the users. The credential in [40] is essentially a Camenisch-Lysyanskaya (CL) signature [7]. Suppose that C is the commitment of the user attributes, x is the issuer's secret key, b, c are system parameters. The credential is

$$(t, \quad s, \quad v = (C \cdot b^s \cdot c)^{\frac{1}{x+t}}),$$

in which t is chosen by the issuer, and s is jointly chosen by the issuer and the user. Simply presenting (t, s, v) as a single-use credential violates anonymity since t is known to the issuer.

In this paper, we design a new two-party computation protocol to generate the CL signature, such that the issuer has no information about the entire credential (t, s, v). If we can obtain such credential, we can design an efficient show proof for the single-use credentials. The major technical difficulty is the computation of $1/(x+t)$ in the exponent without the full knowledge of t by the issuer. We take advantage of the multiplicative to additive (MtA) protocol [20] to achieve such computations between the two parties.

Share Conversion Protocol. Gennaro *et al.* [20] generalized the multiplicative to additive (MtA) share conversion protocol using additive homomorphic encryption. This protocol shares secrets between two parties in the form of $\alpha + \beta = ab$, where a (and α) and b (and β) are the secrets (and additive shares) kept by Alice and Bob, respectively.

In our scheme, we adopt the MtA protocol during the interactive generation of credentials between the issuer and the user. Now the issuer knows the secret key x and the user chooses a random t. They engage in the MtA protocol and obtain a, b such that $x + t = ab$. The issuer computes $v' = (C \cdot b^s \cdot c)^{\frac{1}{a}}$ and the user can recover $v = v'^{\frac{1}{b}}$. By the security of the MtA protocol, the issuer has no information of t and v.

1.4 Related Works

We remark that Tan *et al.* [40] provides a detailed comparisons between recent works. Apart from the q-SDH-based anonymous credential system, various systems are using different cryptographic approaches. Recently, some research [12,17,23] focus on the anonymous credential system using the structure-preserving signatures on equivalence classes. Moreover, some are designed using different kind of signatures such as Camenisch and Lysyanskaya (CL) Signature [7,27,40], Abe-Haralambiev-Ohkubo signature [1,31] and BLS signature [21,35]. Moreover, there are various systems are designed with special functionalities, such as multi-authority credentials [2,24], anonymous credentials with redactable signature [37], blacklistable anonymous credentials [1,30,41,42], anonymous credentials with accumulator-based revocation [3], updatable anonymous credentials [22], and delegatable anonymous credentials [3,4,13]. Taking advantages from the anonymous credential protocols, many applications were being proposed and applied on different aspects such as direct anonymous attestation (DAA) [6], application on Smart City [5,28,29,34], smart cards [16], IoT devices [8,33,39], and blockchain [15]. And, the real-time message application *Signal* adopts anonymous credential [9].

Organization. The organization of this paper is as follows. In Sect. 2, we briefly introduce the mathematical background and the secure models. We define the security requirement of our ABC scheme in Sect. 3, the construction in Sect. 4, and the security proofs in Sect. 5. We further propose the zero-knowledge proofs for single-use credentials and the security proofs in Sect. 6. We give a conclusion in Sect. 7.

2 Preliminaries

2.1 Bilinear Pairing

Consider $\mathbb{G}_1$, $\mathbb{G}_2$, $\mathbb{G}_T$ be cyclic groups of prime order p such that $\mathsf{e} : \mathbb{G}_1 \times \mathbb{G}_2 \rightarrow \mathbb{G}_T$. Assuming $g_1 \in \mathbb{G}_1$, $g_2 \in \mathbb{G}_2$ and $x, y \in \mathbb{Z}_p$, the bilinear pairing function follows the properties below:

1. Bilinearity: $\mathsf{e}(g_1^x, g_2^y) = \mathsf{e}(g_1^y, g_2^x) = \mathsf{e}(g_1, g_2)^{xy}$
2. Non-degeneracy: $\mathsf{e}(g_1, g_2) \neq 1$

3. Efficiency: e is efficiently computable.

Galbraith *et al.* [19] classified the types of pairing: (1) Type 1: $\mathbb{G}_1 = \mathbb{G}_2$; (2) Type 2: $\mathbb{G}_1 \neq \mathbb{G}_2$ where there exists an efficient isomorphism ψ; and (3) Type 3: $\mathbb{G}_1 \neq \mathbb{G}_2$ with no isomorphism exists. In this work, we take Type 3 pairings.

2.2 Security Assumptions

Definition 1. *Discrete logarithm Assumption (DLOG): An algorithm $\mathcal{C}$ $(t_{\mathsf{dlog}}, \epsilon_{\mathsf{dlog}})$-breaks the DLOG assumption if $\mathcal{C}$ runs with a negligible probability ϵ_{dlog} such that:*

$$\Pr[x \in \mathbb{Z}_p : \mathcal{C}(g, g^x) = x)] \geq \epsilon_{\mathsf{dlog}}$$

and runs in time at most t_{dlog}. It is said that the DLOG assumption is $(t_{\mathsf{dlog}}, \epsilon_{\mathsf{dlog}})$-secure is there are no algorithm $(t_{\mathsf{dlog}}, \epsilon_{\mathsf{dlog}})$-solves the DLOG problem.

Definition 2. *q-Strong Diffie-Hellman Assumption (SDH) [38]: An algorithm $\mathcal{C}$ $(t_{\mathsf{sdh}}, \epsilon_{\mathsf{sdh}})$-breaks the SDH assumption if $\mathcal{C}$ runs with a negligible probability ϵ_{sdh} such that:*

$$\Pr[x \in \mathbb{Z}_p, c \in \mathbb{Z}_p \setminus \{-x\} : \mathcal{C}(g_1, g_1^x, ..., g_1^{x^q}, g_2, g_2^x) = (g_1^{\frac{1}{x+c}}, c)] \geq \epsilon_{\mathsf{sdh}}$$

and runs in time at most t_{sdh}. It is said that the SDH assumption is $(t_{\mathsf{sdh}}, \epsilon_{\mathsf{sdh}})$-secure is there are no algorithm $(t_{\mathsf{sdh}}, \epsilon_{\mathsf{sdh}})$-solves the SDH problem.

Definition 3. *q-co-Strong Diffie-Hellman Assumption (co-SDH) [10]: An algorithm $\mathcal{C}$ $(t_{\mathsf{cosdh}}, \epsilon_{\mathsf{cosdh}})$-breaks the co-SDH assumption if $\mathcal{C}$ runs with a negligible probability $\epsilon_{\mathsf{cosdh}}$ such that:*

$$\Pr[x \in \mathbb{Z}_p, c \in \mathbb{Z}_p \setminus \{-x\} : \mathcal{C}(g_1, g_1^x, ..., g_1^{x^q}, g_2, g_2^x, ..., g_2^{x^q}) = (g_1^{\frac{1}{x+c}}, c)] \geq \epsilon_{\mathsf{cosdh}}$$

and runs in time at most t_{cosdh}. It is said that the co-SDH assumption is $(t_{\mathsf{cosdh}}, \epsilon_{\mathsf{cosdh}})$-secure is there are no algorithm $(t_{\mathsf{cosdh}}, \epsilon_{\mathsf{cosdh}})$-solves the co-SDH problem.

2.3 The SDH-Based Camenisch and Lysyanskaya (CL) Signature

We recall a pairing-based signature schemes introduced by Camenisch and Lysyanskaya [7] as follows:

$\mathsf{KeyGen}(1^k)$: Construct three cyclic groups $\mathbb{G}_1$, $\mathbb{G}_2$, $\mathbb{G}_T$ of order p based on an bilinear-based elliptic curve with the bilinear pairing $\mathsf{e} : \mathbb{G}_1 \times \mathbb{G}_2 \to \mathbb{G}_T$. Sample randon generators $a, b, c \in \mathbb{G}_1$, $g_2 \in \mathbb{G}_2$ and a secret value $x \in \mathbb{Z}_p^*$. This alrogithm outputs the public key $pk = (\mathsf{e}, \mathbb{G}_1, \mathbb{G}_2, \mathbb{G}_T, p, a, b, c, g_2, X = g_2^x)$ and the secret key $sk = x$.

$\mathsf{Sign}(m, pk, sk)$: The algorithm intakes message m, chooses random values $s, t \in \mathbb{Z}_p$ for computing $v = (a^m b^s c)^{\frac{1}{x+t}}$. If the rare case with $x + t = 0 \mod p$ occurs, reselect random t. It outputs the signature $sig = (t, s, v)$.

$\mathsf{Verify}(m, sig, pk)$: The algorithm verify the signature sig with

$$\mathsf{e}(v, X g_2^t) = \mathsf{e}((a^m b^s c)^{\frac{1}{x+t}}, g_2^{x+t}) = \mathsf{e}(a^m b^s c, g_2).$$

It outputs 1 for a successful verification, 0 otherwise.

2.4 Share Conversion Protocol

Gennaro *et al.* [20] generalized the multiplicative to additive (MtA) share conversion protocol. Assume that Alice and Bob holding a, b respectively, attempt to share the secret in the form of $\alpha + \beta = ab$ using the homomorphic encryption with the mechanism below. We omit the details of the range proof and the zero-knowledge proof without loss of generality. However, we emphasize that all the proofs are required for a particular homomorphic cryptosystem.

1. Alice computes $c_A = \mathsf{Enc}_A(a)$, and sends c_A to Bob.
2. Bob picks β' uniformly randomly and computes $c_B = b \times c_A + \mathsf{Enc}_A(\beta') = \mathsf{Enc}_A(ab + \beta')$, where $\beta = -\beta'$. Bob replies Alice with c_B.
3. Alice decrypts c_B and gets α', such that $\alpha = \alpha'$.

Alice and Bob eventually reveal α and β to each other and compute $\alpha + \beta$ on their own.

3 Security Requirements for Attribute-Based Anonymous Credential

In this section, we generally introduce the security models of impersonation resilience, anonymity, and unlinkability. The attribute-based anonymous credential system is divided into the algorithms as follows:

1. $\mathsf{KeyGen}(1^k, 1^n) \rightarrow (pk, sk)$: Executed by the issuer with the security parameter k and the attributes upper bound n, it generates a key pair (pk, sk).
2. $(\mathsf{Obtain}(pk, A), \mathsf{Issue}(pk, sk, T)) \rightarrow (cred \text{ or } \perp)$: Interactively executed by the issuer and the user, these two algorithms form the credential issuing protocol. Obtain is invoked by the user with the public key of issuer pk and an attribute set A. With the request from user, the issuer executed the Issue algorithm with the public key pk, the secret key sk, and the attributes table T. The protocol outputs a valid credential $cred$ or a null value $\perp$ otherwise.
3. $(\mathsf{Prove}(pk, cred, \phi_{\mathsf{stmt}}), \mathsf{Verify}(pk, \phi_{\mathsf{stmt}}) \rightarrow b)$: These two algorithms form the credential presentation protocol. An access policy ϕ is formed by an attribute set A from prover, with a statement stmt that specifies the relation between A and A' from the verifier. The details of this protocol remains unchanged in this work, please refer to [40] for details.

3.1 Impersonation Resilience

The property of impersonation resilience requires that it is infeasible to get accepted by the verifier for an adversary in the show proof. We recap the definition the security model as the security against impersonation under active and concurrent attacks (imp-aca) between an adversary $\mathcal{A}$ and a challenger $\mathcal{C}$ in **Game** 1 from Tan *et al.* [40] as follows:

Game 1 (imp-aca($\mathcal{A}$, $\mathcal{C}$))

1. ***Setup:*** *$\mathcal{C}$ runs* KeyGen(1^k, n) *and sends pk to $\mathcal{A}$.*
2. ***Phase 1:*** *$\mathcal{A}$ is able to play the role of user, prover and verifier, respectively. He can issue concurrent queries to the* Obtain, Prove *and* Verify *oracles on any attribute set A_i of his choice in the i-th query. And, $\mathcal{A}$ can issue queries to the* IssueTranscript *oracle which takes in A_i and returns the corresponding transcripts of the issuing protocol.*
3. ***Challenge:*** *$\mathcal{A}$ output the challenge attribute set A^* and its corresponding access policy ϕ^*_{stmt} such that $\phi^*_{\mathsf{stmt}}(A_i) = 0$ and $\phi^*_{\mathsf{stmt}}(A^*) = 1$ for every A_i queried to the* Obtain *oracle during Phase 1.*
4. ***Phase 2:*** *With the restriction that $\mathcal{A}$ cannot query an attribute set A_i to* Obtain *such that $\phi^*_{\mathsf{stmt}}(A_i) = 1$, it can continue to query the oracles as in Phase 1.*
5. ***Impersonate:*** *$\mathcal{A}$ completes a show proof as the prover with $\mathcal{C}$ as the verifier for the access policy $\phi^*_{\mathsf{stmt}}(A^*) = 1$. $\phi^*_{\mathsf{stmt}}(A^*) = 1$ wins the game if $\mathcal{C}$ outputs 1, otherwise 0.*

Definition 4. *An adversary $\mathcal{A}$ is said to $(t_{\mathsf{imp}}, \epsilon_{\mathsf{imp}})$-break the* imp-aca *security of an ABC system if $\mathcal{A}$ runs in time at most t_{imp} and wins **Game** 1 for a negligible probability ϵ_{imp} such that:*

$$\Pr[(\mathcal{A}, \mathsf{Verify}(pk, \phi^*_{\mathsf{stmt}})) = 1] \geq \epsilon_{\mathsf{imp}}.$$

A particular ABC system is imp-aca*-secure if there are no adversary $(t_{\mathsf{imp}}, \epsilon_{\mathsf{imp}})$-wins **Game** 1.*

3.2 Anonymity

The property of anonymity requires an adversary cannot recover the identity of a user from the show proofs. We introduce the security model for anonymity under active and concurrent attacks (anon-aca) in **Game** 2 between an adversary $\mathcal{A}$ and a challenger $\mathcal{C}$:

Game 2 (anon-aca($\mathcal{A}$, $\mathcal{C}$))

1. ***Setup:*** *$\mathcal{C}$ runs* KeyGen(1^k, n) *and sends pk, sk to $\mathcal{A}$.*

2. ***Phase 1:*** *$\mathcal{A}$ is able to play the role of user, issuer, prover and verifier, respectively. He can issue concurrent queries to the* Obtain, Issue, Prove *and* Verify *oracles on any attribute set A_i of his choice in the i-th query. And, $\mathcal{A}$ can issue queries to the* Corrupt *oracle which takes in transcript of presentation protocol from prover which is $\mathcal{C}$ and returns the entire internal state, including the random seed used by $\mathcal{C}$ in the transcript.*
3. ***Challenge:*** *$\mathcal{C}$ selects two credentials from* IssueTranscript *oracle which contains the credentials created with $\mathcal{A}$ as a Issuer.*

$$(\mathsf{Otain}(pk, A_0), \mathsf{Issue}(pk, sk)) \rightarrow cred_0, \quad (\mathsf{Otain}(pk, A_1), \mathsf{Issue}(pk, sk)) \rightarrow cred_1.$$

The two selected credentials hold with equal length, and the access policy ϕ^*_{stmt} which aim to challenge such that $\phi^*_{\mathsf{stmt}}(A_0) = \phi^*_{\mathsf{stmt}}(A_1) = 1$. $\mathcal{C}$ responds a random bit $b \in \{0,1\}$ and interacts as the prover with $\mathcal{A}$ as verifier to complete the protocol:

$$(\mathsf{Prove}(pk, cred_b, \phi^*_{\mathsf{stmt}}), \mathsf{Verify}(pk, \phi^*_{\mathsf{stmt}})) \rightarrow 1.$$

4. ***Phase 2:*** *With the restriction that $\mathcal{A}$ cannot query transcript of the challenged show proofs to* Corrupt, *it can continue to query the oracles as in Phase 1.*
5. ***Guess:*** *$\mathcal{A}$ wins the game with guess b' if $b' = b$.*

Definition 5. *An adversary $\mathcal{A}$ is said to $(t_{\mathsf{ano}}, \epsilon_{\mathsf{ano}})$-break the* anon-aca *security of an ABC system if $\mathcal{A}$ runs in time at most t_{ano} and wins **Game** 2 for a negligible probability ϵ_{ano} such that:*

$$\Pr[b = b'] - \frac{1}{2} \geq \epsilon_{\mathsf{ano}}$$

A particular ABC system is anon-aca*-secure if there are no adversary $(t_{\mathsf{ano}}, \epsilon_{\mathsf{ano}})$-wins **Game** 2.*

3.3 Unlinkability

The property of unlinkability requires an adversary cannot link the attributes or instances among the presentation protocols. We introduce the security model for unlinkability under active and concurrent attacks (unl-aca) in **Game** 3 between an adversary $\mathcal{A}$ and a challenger $\mathcal{C}$, which requires an adversary cannot distinguish the sequence of two attribute sets after being involved in the generation of a list of credentials:

Game 3 (unl-aca($\mathcal{A}$, $\mathcal{C}$))

1. ***Setup:*** *$\mathcal{C}$ runs* KeyGen(1^k, n) *and sends pk, sk to $\mathcal{A}$.*
2. ***Phase 1:*** *$\mathcal{A}$ is able to play the role of user, issuer, prover and verifier, respectively. He can issue concurrent queries to the* Obtain, Issue, Prove *and* Verify *oracles on any attribute set A_i of his choice in the i-th query. And, $\mathcal{A}$ can issue queries to the* Corrupt *oracle which takes in transcript of presentation protocol from prover which is $\mathcal{C}$ and returns the entire internal state, including the random seed used by $\mathcal{C}$ in the transcript.*

3. ***Challenge:*** *$\mathcal{C}$ responds a random bit $b \in \{0,1\}$ and selects two credentials from* IssueTranscript *oracle which contains the credentials created with $\mathcal{A}$ as a Issuer.*

$$(\mathsf{Otain}(pk, A_b), \mathsf{Issue}(pk, sk)) \rightarrow cred_b, \quad (\mathsf{Otain}(pk, A_{1-b}), \mathsf{Issue}(pk, sk)) \rightarrow cred_{1-b}.$$

The two selected credentials hold with equal length, and the access policy ϕ^*_{stmt} which aim to challenge such that $\phi^*_{\mathsf{stmt}}(A_0) = \phi^*_{\mathsf{stmt}}(A_1) = 1$. $\mathcal{C}$ interacts as the prover with $\mathcal{A}$ as verifier to complete the protocol:

$$(\mathsf{Prove}(pk, cred_b, \phi^*_{\mathsf{stmt}}), \mathsf{Verify}(pk, \phi^*_{\mathsf{stmt}})) \rightarrow 1,$$

$$(\mathsf{Prove}(pk, cred_{1-b}, \phi^*_{\mathsf{stmt}}), \mathsf{Verify}(pk, \phi^*_{\mathsf{stmt}})) \rightarrow 1.$$

4. ***Phase 2:*** *With the restriction that $\mathcal{A}$ cannot query transcript of the challenged show proofs to* Corrupt*, it can continue to query the oracles as in Phase 1.*
5. ***Guess:*** *$\mathcal{A}$ wins the game with guess b' if $b' = b$.*

Definition 6. *An adversary $\mathcal{A}$ is said to $(t_{\mathsf{unl}}, \epsilon_{\mathsf{unl}})$-break the* unl-aca *security of an ABC system if $\mathcal{A}$ runs in time at most t_{imp} and wins **Game** 3 for a negligible probability ϵ_{unl} such that:*

$$\Pr[b = b'] - \frac{1}{2} \geq \epsilon_{\mathsf{unl}}$$

A particular ABC system is unl-aca*-secure if there are no adversary $(t_{\mathsf{unl}}, \epsilon_{\mathsf{unl}})$-wins **Game** 3.*

4 Our Construction on Credential Issuance

In this section, we illustrate our modification towards Tan *et al.* [40]. In our construction, we utilize the share conversion protocol (MtA), trying to share secrets between the issuer and the user during the credential issuance protocol.

Generally, the issuer knows the content of the attribute set from a user, and what attribute(s) that the user would like to authenticate in each credential. This prevents some malicious users issue the credentials with some unexpected attributes. Therefore, we further allow the issuer holds table T which maintains the attributes of a particular user.

The user credential is an q-SDH-based CL signature, with the use of *MoniPoly* commitment C with its attribute set A. Precisely, an attribute m_i is an attribute-value pair (attribute=value) and $A = \{m_0, ..., m_{n-1}\}$ is an attribute set. And, we assume A'' be a set of attributes without value (attribute), where the attributes in A and A'' are the same. An access policy ϕ is formed by an attribute set A with a statement that specifies the relation between A and A'.

4.1 Key Generation

$\mathsf{KeyGen}(1^k,\ n)$: Construct three cyclic groups $\mathbb{G}_1$, $\mathbb{G}_2$, $\mathbb{G}_T$ of order p based on an bilinear-based elliptic curve with the bilinear pairing $\mathsf{e} : \mathbb{G}_1 \times \mathbb{G}_2 \to \mathbb{G}_T$. Sample random generators $a, b, c \in \mathbb{G}_1$, $g_2 \in \mathbb{G}_2$ and two secret values $x, x' \in \mathbb{Z}_p$. Compute parameters $a_0 = a, a_1 = a^{x'}, ..., a_n = a^{x'^n}$, $X = g_2^x, X_0 = g_2, X_1 = g_2^{x'}, ..., X_n = g_2^{x'^n}$. The Issuer also generates the key pair for homomorphic encryption E by running $(\mathsf{sk}, \mathsf{pk}) \leftarrow \mathsf{E.KeyGen}()$. The homomorphic key pair is generated with corresponding range proofs and zero-knowledge proofs, depending on the adopted homomorphic cryptosystem. This algorithm outputs the public key $pk = (\mathsf{e}, \mathbb{G}_1, \mathbb{G}_2, \mathbb{G}_T, p, b, c, \{a_i, X_i\}_{0 \le i \le n}, X, \mathsf{pk})$ and the secret key $sk = (x, x', \mathsf{sk})$. The Issuer also maintains a table T of its users and their corresponding attributes.

4.2 Issue of Credentials

$(\mathsf{Obtain}(pk,\ A),\ \mathsf{Issue}(pk, sk, T))$: The algorithm instantiates an interaction between the user and the issuer, generating a user credential *cred* on an attribute set $A = \{m_0, ..., m_{n-1}\}$. The algorithm operates in the following steps:

1. User samples a random opening value $o \in \mathbb{Z}_p$ to compute $C = \prod_{j=0}^{n} a_j^{\mathsf{m}_j} = \mathsf{Commit}(pk, A, o)$. Subsequently, user selects random $s_1 \in \mathbb{Z}_p$ to initialize the issuing protocol by completing the ZK protocol π_s with Issuer:

$$PK\{s_1 : M = C \cdot b^{s_1}\}.$$

   User sends (A'', M, C, o, π_s) to Issuer.
2. Issuer receives (A'', M, C, o, π_s) and generates the corresponding attribute set A from A'' using its own table T. Issuer proceeds to next step if π_s is verified and $\mathsf{Open}(pk, C, A, o) = 1$. Else, issuer outputs $\perp$ and halts.
3. Issuer chooses a random value $u_1, \Delta \in \mathbb{Z}_p$, and sets

$$z_{u_1} = \mathsf{Enc}_{\mathsf{pk}}(u_1), \quad z_{\hat{x}} = \mathsf{Enc}_{\mathsf{pk}}(x + \Delta).$$

   Issuer sends z_{u_1} and $z_{\hat{x}}$ to User.
4. User selects $t', u_2, \gamma_2 \xleftarrow{\$} \mathbb{Z}_p$. User computes

$$z_1 = \mathsf{Enc}_{\mathsf{pk}}(t' \cdot u_1 + (x + \Delta) \cdot u_2 - \gamma_2) = t' \cdot z_{u_1} + u_2 \cdot z_{\hat{x}} + \mathsf{Enc}_{\mathsf{pk}}(-\gamma_2),$$
$$\omega_2 = \gamma_2 + t' \cdot u_2.$$

   User sends z_1, ω_2 and a ZK proof π_U of (t', u_2, γ_2) to Issuer.
5. After validating π_U, Issuer calculates

$$\gamma_1 = \mathsf{Dec}_{\mathsf{sk}}(z_1), \quad \omega_1 = \gamma_1 + (x + \Delta) \cdot u_1, \quad \beta = \omega_1 + \omega_2, \quad \delta_I = u_1 \cdot \beta^{-1}.$$

   Issuer selects $s_2 \xleftarrow{\$} \mathbb{Z}_p$ and generates a partial SDH-CL signature for M as

$$sig' = (\Delta, s_2, v_1 = (Mb^{s_2}c)^{\delta_I}).$$

   Issuer sends sig' and β to User.

6. User calculates $v_2 = (Mb^{s_2}c)^{\delta_U}$, where $\delta_U = u_2 \cdot \beta^{-1}$. User sets

$$t = t' + \Delta, \quad v = v_1 \cdot v_2 = (Mb^{s_2}c)^{\delta_I + \delta_U} = (Mb^{s_2}c)^{\frac{1}{(x+\Delta)+t'}} = (Mb^{s_2}c)^{\frac{1}{x+t}}$$

and generates a full SDH-CL signature for M as $sig = (t, s_2, v)$.
If sig is not a valid signature on $A \cup \{o\}$, User outputs $\perp$ and stops. Else, user outputs the credential as $cred = (t, s, v, A = A \cup \{o\})$ where:

$$s = s_1 + s_2, \quad v = \left(a_0^{\prod_{j=1}^{n}(x'+m_j)} b^s c\right)^{1/(x+t)}.$$

4.3 Zero-Knowledge Proofs for Multi-use Show Proof

Tan *et al.* [40] proposed the proof of possession, AND, ANY/OR, NAND/NOT and NANY show proofs concretely. The details of these proofs are remain unchanged with the aforementioned modifications, i.e. the presentation protocol $((\mathsf{Prove}(pk, cred, \phi_{\mathsf{stmt}}), \mathsf{Verify}(pk, \phi_{\mathsf{stmt}})) \rightarrow b$ unchanged, where $b \in \{0, 1\}$. Under the perspective of the verifier, there are no differences between the original t in Tan *et al.* [40] and the t in this work, the MtA protocol is independent to the verifier.

5 Security

5.1 Impersonation Resilience

In the security proof, we first classify 3 different types of adversary and use different simulation strategies for each of them to solve the SDH problem. In all proofs, we will extract the credential (s^*, t^*, v^*, A^*) that the adversary used to win the security game. Denote (s_i, t_i, v_i, A_i) as the credential used in the i-th Obtain or Verify oracle query. We have:

- Adversary $\mathcal{A}_1$: $t^* \neq t_i$ for all i.
- Adversary $\mathcal{A}_2$: $t^* = t_i$ for some i and $s^* \neq s_i$.
- Adversary $\mathcal{A}_3$: $t^* = t_i$ for some i and $s^* = s_i$.

We will use any of these adversaries to solve the SDH problem.

In the simulation, there is a special case that is common for all types of adversaries: $v^* = v_i$ for some i. We first describe it here and we do not repeat it throughout the simulation with $\mathcal{A}_1$, $\mathcal{A}_2$ and $\mathcal{A}_3$. This case is handled by solving the DLOG problem first. Assuming $M^* = \prod_{j=i}^{n}(x' + m_j^*)$ and $M_i = \prod_{j=i}^{n}(x' + m_{i,j})$ for attribute sets $A^* = \{m_j^*\}$ and $A_i = \{m_j\}$ respectively. Assume that $b = a_0^{\tau}$ and $c = a_0^{\gamma}$ for some $\tau, \gamma \in \mathbb{Z}_p$. Whenever v^* produced by $\mathcal{A}$ is the same as v_i produced by $\mathcal{C}$, the DLOG problem can be solved such that:

$$\begin{aligned}
\because v^* &= v_i \\
(a_0^{M^*} b^{s^*} c)^{\frac{1}{x+t^*}} &\equiv (a_0^{M_i} b^{s_i} c)^{\frac{1}{x+t_i}} \\
(a_0^{M^* + s^*\tau + \gamma})^{\frac{1}{x+t^*}} &\equiv (a_0^{M_i + s_i\tau + \gamma})^{\frac{1}{x+t_i}} \\
\therefore \frac{M^* + s^*\tau + \gamma}{x + t^*} &\equiv \frac{M_i + s_i\tau + \gamma}{x + t_i} \mod p,
\end{aligned}$$

which leads to:

$$x \equiv \frac{t^* M_i - t_i M^* + \tau(t^* s_i - t_i s^*) + \gamma(t^* - t_i)}{M^* - M_i + \tau(s^* - s_i)} \mod p.$$

$\mathcal{C}$ can solve the SDH problem using x if $M^* - M_i + \tau(s^* - s_i) \neq 0$. Next consider two cases for $M^* - M_i + \tau(s^* - s_i) = 0$.

1. $M^* \neq M_i$ or $s^* \neq s_i$: It happens with negligible probability of $1/p$ with the random choice of τ.
2. $M^* = M_i$ and $s^* = s_i$. This case only applies to $\mathcal{A}_1$ and $\mathcal{A}_3$ defined above. It implies $A^* = A_i$. In the security model, it is restricted that A^* cannot be the same as A_i used in the Obtain oracle. On the other hand, if $A^* = A_i$ used in the IssueTranscript queries or Verify queries. If the view of $\mathcal{A}$ is independent of the choice s_i of $\mathcal{C}$, there exists a probability of $1 - 1/p$ such that $s^* \neq s_i$, which means that it happens with negligible probability $1/p$ such that the simulation fails.

We present Lemma 1, 2 and 3 representing the adversaries $\mathcal{A}_1$, $\mathcal{A}_2$, and $\mathcal{A}_3$ as follows. Please refer to Appendix A for the proofs.

Theorem 1. *If an adversary $\mathcal{A}$ $(t_{\mathsf{imp}}, \epsilon_{\mathsf{imp}})$-breaks the* imp-aca-*security of the proposed anonymous credential system, then there exists an algorithm $\mathcal{C}$ which $(t_{\mathsf{cosdh}}, \epsilon_{\mathsf{cosdh}})$-breaks the co-SDH problem such that:*

$$\frac{\epsilon_{\mathsf{cosdh}}}{t_{\mathsf{cosdh}}} = \frac{\epsilon_{\mathsf{imp}}}{t_{\mathsf{imp}}},$$

or an algorithm $\mathcal{C}$ which $(t_{\mathsf{sdh}}, \epsilon_{\mathsf{sdh}})$-breaks the SDH problem such that:

$$\epsilon_{\mathsf{imp}} \leq \sqrt[N]{\sqrt{\epsilon_{\mathsf{sdh}}} - 1} + \frac{1 + (q-1)!/p^{q-2}}{p} + 1, \quad t_{\mathsf{imp}} \leq t_{\mathsf{sdh}}/2N - T(q^2),$$

where N is the total adversary instance, $q = Q_{(O,I)} + Q_{(P,V)}$ is the total query made to the Obtain *and* Verify *oracles, while $T(q^2)$ is the time parameterized by q to setup the simulation environment and to extract the SDH solution. Consider the dominant time elements t_{imp} and t_{sdh} only, we have:*

$$\left(1 - \left(1 - \epsilon_{\mathsf{imp}} + \frac{1 + (q-1)!/p^{q-2}}{p}\right)^N\right)^2 \leq \epsilon_{\mathsf{sdh}}, \quad 2N t_{\mathsf{imp}} \approx t_{\mathsf{sdh}}.$$

Let $N = (\epsilon_{\mathsf{imp}} - \frac{1+(q-1)!/p^{q-2}}{p})^{-1}$, we get $\epsilon_{\mathsf{sdh}} \geq (1 - e^{-1})^2 \geq 1/3$ and the success ratio is:

$$\frac{\epsilon_{\mathsf{sdh}}}{t_{\mathsf{sdh}}} \geq \frac{1}{3 \cdot 2N t_{\mathsf{imp}}}$$

$$\frac{6\epsilon_{\mathsf{sdh}}}{t_{\mathsf{sdh}}} \geq \frac{\epsilon_{\mathsf{imp}}}{t_{\mathsf{imp}}} - \frac{1 + (q-1)!/p^{q-2}}{t_{\mathsf{imp}} p}$$

which gives a tight reduction.

We follow the setting from Tan *et al.* [40] to use Multi-Instance Reset Lemma [25] as the knowledge extractor which requires an adversary $\mathcal{A}_1$ to run N parallel instances under active and concurrent attacks. The challenger can fulfil this requirement by simulating the $N-1$ instances from the SDH instance. It suffices to describe the simulation for a single instance of impersonation. Our security reduction proof is as follows.

Lemma 1. *If an adversary $\mathcal{A}_1$ $(t_{\mathsf{imp}}, \epsilon_{\mathsf{imp}})$-breaks the* imp-aca-*security of the proposed anonymous credential system, then there exists an algorithm $\mathcal{C}$ which $(t_{\mathsf{cosdh}}, \epsilon_{\mathsf{cosdh}})$-breaks the co-SDH problem such that:*

$$\epsilon_{\mathsf{imp}} \leq \sqrt[N]{\sqrt{\epsilon_{\mathsf{sdh}}} - 1 + \frac{1 + (q-1)!/p^{q-2}}{p}} + 1, \quad t_{\mathsf{imp}} \leq t_{\mathsf{sdh}}/2N - T(q^2),$$

where N is the total adversary instance, $q = Q_{(O,I)} + Q_{(P,V)}$ is the total number of query made to the Obtain *and* Verify *oracles, while $T(q^2)$ is the time parameterized by q to setup the simulation environment and to extract the SDH solution.*

Lemma 2. *If an adversary $\mathcal{A}_2$ $(t_{\mathsf{imp}}, \epsilon_{\mathsf{imp}})$-breaks the* imp-aca-*security of the proposed anonymous credential system, then there exists an algorithm $\mathcal{C}$ which $(t_{\mathsf{cosdh}}, \epsilon_{\mathsf{cosdh}})$-breaks the co-SDH problem such that:*

$$\epsilon_{\mathsf{imp}} \leq \sqrt[N]{\sqrt{\epsilon_{\mathsf{sdh}}} - 1 + \frac{1 + (q-1)!/p^{q-2}}{p}} + 1, \quad t_{\mathsf{imp}} \leq t_{\mathsf{sdh}}/2N - T(q^2),$$

where N is the total adversary instance, $q = Q_{(O,I)} + Q_{(P,V)}$ is the total number of query made to the Obtain *and* Verify *oracles, while $T(q^2)$ is the time parameterized by q to setup the simulation environment and to extract the SDH solution.*

Lemma 3. *If an adversary $\mathcal{A}_3$ $(t_{\mathsf{imp}}, \epsilon_{\mathsf{imp}})$-breaks the* imp-aca-*security of the proposed anonymous credential system, then there exists an algorithm $\mathcal{C}$ which $(t_{\mathsf{cosdh}}, \epsilon_{\mathsf{cosdh}})$-breaks the co-SDH problem such that:*

$$\epsilon_{\mathsf{imp}} \leq \sqrt[N]{\sqrt{\epsilon_{\mathsf{sdh}}} - 1 + \frac{1 + (q-1)!/p^{q-2}}{p}} + 1, \quad t_{\mathsf{imp}} \leq t_{\mathsf{sdh}}/2N - T(q^2),$$

where N is the total adversary instance, $q = Q_{(O,I)} + Q_{(P,V)}$ is the total number of query made to the Obtain *and* Verify *oracles, while $T(q^2)$ is the time parameterized by q to setup the simulation environment and to extract the SDH solution.*

Combining Theorem 3 from [40], Lemma 1, 2, and 3 in this work gives Theorem 1 as required.

5.2 Anonymity

In this security proof, we prove that the proposed interactive anonymous credential system achieves anonymity under active and concurrent attack (anon-aca). In our modification, the Issuer contains the attribute sets of Users, therefore, the anonymity among the issuing protocol is exploited, while we keep the anonymity among the presentation protocol.

Before proving the anonymity and unlinkability of the new proposed interactive ABC system, we note that committed attributes and the randomized credentials maintain the properties of perfectly hiding. Similarly, the issuing protocol and the presentation protocol achieve self-reducibility [40]. Please refer to Appendix B for the proof.

Theorem 2. *The proposed interactive anonymous credential system is* anon-aca-*secure under the presentation protocol.*

5.3 Unlinkability

With a similar approach, we prove that the proposed interactive anonymous credential system achieves unlinkability under active and concurrent attack (unl-aca). As aforementioned, the unlinkability among the issuing protocol is exploited, while we keep the unlinkability among the presentation protocol. Please refer to Appendix C for the proof.

Theorem 3. *The proposed interactive anonymous credential system is* unl-aca-*secure under the presentation protocol.*

6 Single-Use Credential and Anonymity Proof

Recall that a user credential *cred* is an SDH-CL signature on the MoniPoly Commitment C of his attribute set A and opening o (i.e., $C \leftarrow \mathsf{MoniPoly.Commit}(pk, A, o)$). The show proofs of a multi-use ABC system is a proof of knowledge for some predicate $Pred = \{\mathsf{Intersection}, \mathsf{Difference}\}$ with respect to an attribute set A' and length l:

$$\begin{aligned} PK\{(cred, C, P, W) : 1 = \mathsf{SDH{-}CL.Verify}(pk, C, cred) \wedge \\ 1 = \mathsf{MoniPoly.Verify}Pred(pk, C, P, W, (A', l))\}, \end{aligned}$$

where $(P, W) \leftarrow \mathsf{MoniPoly.Open}Pred(pk, C, A, o, (A', l))$.

For the credential system in [40], the credential is $cred = (t, s, v)$, in which t, s, v are all known to the issuer. Hence, a zero-knowledge proof on (t, s, v) should be used in order to provide anonymity against the issuer, even if the credential is used once only. Hence, the zero-knowledge proof in [40] is complicated if we apply it to a single-use credential system.

6.1 Proof of Possession of Single-Use Credential

In our Issue and Obtain protocol, the issuer and the user runs a two-party computation protocol, such that the issuer cannot obtain any information about C and $cred = (t, s, v)$ for the attribute set A. As a result, we can formulate an efficient show proof for a single-use credential *cred*.

In order to give a show proof to an attribute set A' and length l, the prover first runs $(P, W) \leftarrow \mathsf{MoniPoly.Open}Pred(pk, C, A, o, (A', l))$ for some predicate $Pred = \{\mathsf{Intersection}, \mathsf{Difference}\}$. The prover can simply output $(cred, C, P, W)$ as the show proof. The verifier can validate the show by checking if $1 = \mathsf{SDH\text{-}CL.Verify}(pk, C, cred)$ and $1 = \mathsf{MoniPoly.Verify}Pred(pk, C, P, W, (A', l))$.

6.1.1 and Proof. We give a simple demonstration on a single AND clause. The prover can prove its ownership without disclosing any attribute as follows.

1. Verifer requests a proof of possession with an AND proof for the attribute set $A' = \{m_1, \ldots, m_l\}$ with length l. Denote $\{\mathsf{m}_j\}_{0 \leq j \leq l} = \mathsf{MPEncode}(A')$.
2. If A' is not a subset of the prover's attribute set A (where $|A| = n$), the prover aborts and the verifier outputs 0.
3. The prover computes $\{\mathsf{w}'_j\}_{0 \leq j \leq n-l} = \mathsf{MPEncode}(A - A')$ and sets $W = \prod_{j=0}^{n-l} a_j^{\mathsf{w}'_j}$. The prover outputs the intersection set $P = A'$, the witness W, the commitment C and the credential (t, s, v).
4. The verifier outputs 1 if:

$$\hat{e}(W, \prod_{j=0}^{l} X_j^{\mathsf{m}_j}) = \hat{e}(C, X_0).$$

Otherwise, it outputs 0. The correctness for the equation is shown in Appendix E.1.

6.1.2 ANY and OR Proof. We give a simple implementation on a single ANY/OR clause, proving that the prover has l attributes $\{m_j\}_{1 \leq j \leq l} \in (A' \cap A)$, where $|A| = n$ and $|A'| = k$. The prover can prove its ownership without disclosing any attribute as follows.

1. Verifier requests a proof of possession with an ANY/OR proof for the attribute set $A' = \{m_1, \ldots, m_k\}$ with length k.
2. The prover tries to generate a l-attribute intersection set $I \in (A' \cap A)$, the prover aborts and the verifier outputs 0 if no such I can be formed.
3. The prover computes $\{\mathsf{w}'_j\}_{0 \leq j \leq n-l} = \mathsf{MPEncode}(A - I)$ and sets $W = \prod_{j=0}^{n-l} a_j^{\mathsf{w}'_j}$. Also, the prover computes $\{\mathsf{m}'_{2,j}\}_{0 \leq j \leq k-l} = \mathsf{MPEncode}(A' - I)$ and sets $W' = \prod_{j=0}^{k-l} a_j^{\mathsf{m}'_{2,j}}$. The prover outputs the witness W, the commitment C and the credential (t, s, v).
4. The verifier outputs 1 if:

$$\hat{e}(W'W, \prod_{j=0}^{l} X_j^{\iota_j}) = \hat{e}(C \cdot \prod_{j=0}^{k} a_j^{\mathsf{m}_{1,j}}, X_0)$$

where $\{\mathsf{m}'_{1,j}\}_{0 \leq j \leq k} = \mathsf{MPEncode}(A')$, $\{\iota'_j\}_{0 \leq j \leq l} = \mathsf{MPEncode}(I)$. Otherwise, it outputs 0. The correctness for the equation is shown in Appendix E.2.

6.1.3 NAND and NOT Proof. We give a simple demonstration on a single NAND clause, proving that an attribute set A' is disjoint with the set A in his credential, where $|A| = n$ and $|A'| = k$. If $|A'| = 1$, the NAND proof becomes a NOT proof. The prover can prove its ownership without disclosing any attribute as follows.

1. Verifier requests a proof of possession with an NAND proof for the attribute set $A' = \{m_1, \ldots, m_k\}$ with length k. Denote $\{\mathsf{m}_j\}_{0 \le j \le k} = \mathsf{MPEncode}(A')$.
2. If $|A' - A| < k$, the prover aborts and the verifier outputs 0.
3. The prover computes $(\{\mathsf{w}'_j\}_{0 \le j \le n-k}, \{\mathsf{r}'_j\}_{0 \le j \le k-1}) = \mathsf{MPEncode}(A)/\mathsf{MPEncode}(A')$, and set $W = \prod_{j=0}^{n-k} a_j^{\mathsf{w}'_j}$. The prover outputs the witness W, the commitment C and the credential (t, s, v).
4. The verifier outputs 1 if:

$$\prod_{j=0}^{k-1} a_j^{\mathsf{r}'_j} \neq 1_{\mathbb{G}_1}, \quad \hat{e}(W, \prod_{j=0}^{k} X_j^{\mathsf{m}_j}) = \hat{e}(C \cdot \prod_{j=0}^{k-1} a_j^{-\mathsf{r}'_j}, X_0)$$

   Otherwise, it outputs 0. The correctness for the equation is shown in Appendix E.3.

6.1.4 NANY Proof. We give a simple implementation on a single NANY clause, proving that the prover has an l-attribute set $D \subseteq (A' - A)$ are not in the credential, where $|A| = n$ and $|A'| = k$. The prover can prove its ownership without disclosing any attribute as follows.

1. Verifier requests a proof of possession with an NANY proof for the attribute set $A' = \{m_1, \ldots, m_k\}$ with length k.
2. Prover generates a l-attribute difference set $D \in (A' - A)$. The prover aborts and the verifier outputs 0 if no such D can be formed.
3. The prover computes $(\{\mathsf{w}'_j\}_{0 \le j \le n-l}, \{\mathsf{r}'_j\}_{0 \le j \le l-1}) = \mathsf{MPEncode}(A)/\mathsf{MPEncode}(D)$, and set $W = \prod_{j=0}^{n-l} a_j^{\mathsf{w}'_j}$. Also, the prover computes $\{\mathsf{m}'_{2,j}\}_{0 \le j \le k-l} = \mathsf{MPEncode}(A' - D)$ and sets $W' = \prod_{j=0}^{k-l} a_j^{\mathsf{m}'_{2,j}}$. The prover outputs the witness $(W, \{\mathsf{r}'_j\}_{0 \le j \le l-1})$, the commitment C and the credential (t, s, v).
4. With $\{\mathsf{m}'_{1,j}\}_{0 \le j \le k} = \mathsf{MPEncode}(A')$, $\{\delta_j\}_{0 \le j \le l} = \mathsf{MPEncode}(D)$, the verifier outputs 1 if:

$$\prod_{j=0}^{l-1} a_j^{\mathsf{r}'_j} \neq 1_{\mathbb{G}_1}, \quad \hat{e}(W'W, \prod_{j=0}^{l} X_j^{\delta_j}) = \hat{e}(C \cdot \prod_{j=0}^{k} a_j^{\mathsf{m}_{1,j}} \cdot \prod_{j=0}^{l-1} a_j^{-\mathsf{r}'_j}, X_0)$$

   Otherwise, it outputs 0. The correctness for the equation is shown in Appendix E.4.

6.2 Proof of Anonymity

In this subsection, we give the full prove of anonymity towards the aforementioned single use credentials. Please refer to Appendix D for the proof.

Theorem 4. *The proposed single use interactive anonymous credential is* anon-aca*-secure under the presentation protocol.*

6.3 Batch the Single-use Credentials

The single-use credential can only be used once in order to maintain the unlinkability. Therefore, under the scenario that the single-use credentials are being adopted, the batched version of our proposed credential system may alleviate the tedious operations of creating credentials one by one. Suppose the User would like to invoke l creations of the proposed single-use credentials, using the same attribute set. This action could be done by batch MtA, with only one instance of the key generation algorithm. Instead of sending a single value of a variable in each communication, a list (vector) with length l of each variable could be used in the batched single-use credential issuance. This approach could decrease the number of communication rounds from $4l$ to 4.

7 Conclusion and Further Extensions

In this work, we optimize the existing q-SDH-based attribute-based anonymous credential system with an interactive credential issuance. Moreover, we further design the show proofs between credentials in a single-use manner. We further point out that our interactive approach could be extended to other q-SDH-based credential systems.

Interactive Setup. In this work, we proposed an interactive approach between the Issuer and User under the q-SDH-based anonymous credential system [40]. This setup decentralizes the original centralized approach in the existing literature. The interactive approach could be applicable to other q-SDH-based anonymous credential systems and maybe some related protocols. Here, we give an example of the possible protocol which is the q-SDH-based direct anonymous attestation [6]. However, due to the limitation of the computation power of the TPM, the interactive setup could not be adopted at this moment.

From the perspective of security requirements, we exploit the full anonymity, full attribute unlinkability, and full protocol unlinkability in [40], since our interactive approach requires both the issuer and the user to know the content inside a particular credential. With this setting, we further prove that our protocol achieves anonymity and unlinkability among the presentation protocol.

A Proof of Theorem 1

A.1 Proof of Lemma 1

Proof. In this proof, we show that if $\mathcal{A}_1$ exists, there exists an algorithm $\mathcal{C}$ which output $(g_1^{\frac{1}{x+t}}, t)$ by acting the simulator for the ABC system. Given a q-SDH instance $(g_1, g_1^x, g_1^{x^2}, ..., g_1^{x^q}, g_2, g_2^x)$ where $q = Q_{(O,I)} + Q_{(P,V)}$ is the number of queries made to the Obtain and Verify oracles. The reduction games are as follows:

Game$_0$. Let S be the event of a successful impersonation. Attacking by $\mathcal{A}$ on N real instances of anonymous credential system, by assumption, we have:

$$\Pr[S_0] = \epsilon_{\mathsf{imp}}. \tag{1}$$

Game$_1$. This game simulates the environment of the modified ABC system. $\mathcal{C}$ uniformly selects unique $t_0, t_0', t_0'', x', t_1, ..., t_q \in \mathbb{Z}_p^*$. Next, let $f(x)$ be the polynomial $f(x) = \prod_{k=1}^{q}(x + t_k) := \sum_{k=0}^{q} \rho_k x^k$ for some coefficient ρ_k, $f_i(x)$ be the polynomial $f_i(x) = \prod_{k=1,k\neq i}^{q}(x + t_k) := \sum_{k=0}^{q-1} \lambda_k x_k$ for some coefficient λ_k, and thus $g_1^{f(x)} = \prod_{k=0}^{q}(g_1^{x^k})^{\rho_k}$. $\mathcal{C}$ additionally generates the key pair $(\mathsf{sk}, \mathsf{pk}) \leftarrow \mathsf{E.KeyGen}()$ under the key generation protocol of homomorphic cryptosystem E and sends $(\mathsf{e}, \mathbb{G}_1, \mathbb{G}_2, \mathbb{G}_T, p, a_0 = g_1^{f(x)t_0}, a_1 = a_0^{x'}, ..., a_n = a_0^{x'^n}, b = g_1^{f(x)t_0'}, c = g_1^{f(x)t_0''}, X = g_2^x, X_0 = g_2, X_1 = X_0^{x'}, ..., X_n = X_0^{x'^n}, \mathsf{pk})$ as the public key to $\mathcal{A}_1$. $\mathcal{C}$ also creates two empty lists $L_{(O,I)}$ and $L_{(P,V)}$ which stores the corrupted credentials simulated during the issuing protocol and the non-corrupted credentials simulated during the presentation protocol, respectively. Note that t_0, t_0', t_0'', x' are uniformly random (including the corresponding random self-reducible $N-1$ instances and the variables in the homomorphic encryption schemes), the distribution of the simulated public key is the same as that of the original scheme, thus:

$$\Pr[S_1] = \Pr[S_0]. \tag{2}$$

Game$_2$. $\mathcal{A}_1$ plays the role of multiple users in this game, and concurrently interact with the issuer simulated by $\mathcal{C}$. We assume every user i uses different attribute set A_i without loss of generality. $\mathcal{C}$ produces a credential $cred_i$ for $\mathcal{A}_1$'s chosen $A_i = \{m_{1,i}, ...m_{n-1,i}, o_i\}$, if the i-th session of an issuing protocol ends successfully. Their interaction is as follows:

1. $\mathcal{A}_1$ concurrently initializes the issuing protocol with $\mathcal{C}$ by running the zero-knowledge protocol $\pi_{s,i}$:

$$PK\{s_{1,i} : M_i = C_i \cdot b^{s_{1,i}}\}$$

   $\mathcal{A}_1$ sends $(A_i'', M_i, C_i, o_i, \pi_{s,i})$ to $\mathcal{C}$. If the ZK proof $\pi_{s,i}$ is valid, $\mathcal{C}$ can successfully extract the secret exponents $s_{1,i}$ used by $\mathcal{A}_1$ in the protocol.
2. $\mathcal{C}$ validates (A_i'', C_i, o_i) with its own data set T. The protocol proceed if $\mathsf{Open}(pk, C_i, A_i, o_i) = 1$ where A_i is generated locally by $\mathcal{C}$ using A_i'' and T.

3. $\mathcal{C}$ chooses a random value $u_{1,i} \in \mathbb{Z}_p$, and sets

$$z_{u_{1,i}} = \mathsf{Enc}_{\mathsf{pk}}(u_{1,i}).$$

   $\mathcal{C}$ chooses a random ciphertext $z_{\hat{x},i}$. $\mathcal{C}$ sends $(z_{u_{1.i}}, z_{\hat{x},i})$ to $\mathcal{A}_1$.
4. $\mathcal{A}_1$ sends $z_{1,i}, \omega_{2,i}$ and a ZK proof $\pi_{U,i}$ to $\mathcal{C}$. By the knowledge extractor of the ZK proof, $\mathcal{C}$ can obtain $(t'_i, u_{2,i}, \gamma_{2,i})$.
5. $\mathcal{C}$ picks a random $\beta_i, s_{2,i} \xleftarrow{\$} \mathbb{Z}_p$, calculates $\Delta_i = t_i - t'_i$ and generates a partial SDH-CL signature for M_i as $sig'_i = (\Delta_i, s_{2,i}, v_{1,i})$, where

$$\begin{aligned} v_{1,i} &= (M_i b^{s_{2,i}} c)^{\delta_{I,i}} \\ &= (\prod_{j=0}^{n} a_j^{\alpha_{j,i}} b^{\sigma_i} b^{s_{2,i}} c)^{\frac{1}{x+t_i} - \delta_{U,i}} \\ &= (\prod_{j=0}^{n} g_1^{f(x) t_0 x'^j \alpha_{j,i} + f(x) t'_0 (\sigma_i + s_{2,i}) + f(x) t''_0})^{\frac{1}{x+t_i} - \frac{u_{2,i}}{\beta_i}} \\ &= (\prod_{j=0}^{n} g_1^{f(x)[t_0 x'^j \alpha_{j,i} + t'_0(\sigma_i + s_{2,i}) + t''_0]})^{\frac{1}{x+t_i} - \frac{u_{2,i}}{\beta_i}}. \end{aligned}$$

   Observe that the above $v_{1,i}$ can be calculated by using $g_1^{f_i(x)}$. $\mathcal{C}$ sends sig'_i and β_i to $\mathcal{A}_1$.
   Since $\mathcal{C}$ has extracted t'_i and $u_{2,i}$ from the ZK proof $\pi_{U,i}$, $\mathcal{C}$ can also calculate the full SDH-CL signature (t_i, s_i, v_i). $\mathcal{C}$ will check if $(\mathsf{m}_{0,i}, ..., \mathsf{m}_{n,i}, t_i, s_i, v_i) \in L_{(P,V)}$, $\mathcal{C}$ removes it from $L_{(P,V)}$ and adds to $L_{(O,I)}$.

Since $\mathcal{C}$'s choices of $s_{2,i}$ are independent of $\mathcal{A}_1$'s view, we have $s_i \neq s_j$ for some $i, j \leq q$ with overwhelming probability. Since $t_i \neq t_j$, a collision $v_i = v_j$ for some $i, j \leq q$ in $\mathcal{A}$'s concurrent queries happens with a negligible probability of $\Pr[Col] = 1/p$ in which $\mathcal{A}_1$ can compute the discrete logarithm x. Else, $\mathcal{C}$ simulates the issuing protocol perfectly for every concurrent query and $\mathcal{A}_1$ can formulate its credential $cred_i$ as in the original issuing protocol. This gives:

$$\begin{aligned} \Pr[S_2] &= \Pr[S_1] + \Pr[Col] \\ &\leq \Pr[S_1] + \prod_{i=1}^{q-1} 1/p \\ &\leq \Pr[S_1] + (q-1)!/p^{q-1}. \end{aligned} \tag{3}$$

Game$_3$. This game $\mathcal{C}$ plays as a verifier and $\mathcal{A}_1$ plays as multiple provers which concurrently interact with $\mathcal{C}$. Without loss of generality, assume that every prover i uses a valid $cred_i$ to execute the corresponding show proof on ϕ_{stmt_i} such that $\phi_{\mathsf{stmt}_i}(A_i) = 1$. $\mathcal{C}$ simulates Verify orcale accordingly and thus:

$$\Pr[S_3] = \Pr[S_2]. \tag{4}$$

Game$_4$. This game $\mathcal{A}_1$ plays as a verifier and $\mathcal{C}$ plays as multiple provers which concurrently interact with $\mathcal{A}_1$. $\mathcal{C}$ interacts with $\mathcal{A}_1$ using a $cred_i$ where $\phi_{\mathsf{stmt}_i}(A_i) = 1$ when $\mathcal{A}_1$ requests for a show proof. With the assumption that $\mathcal{C}$

has appropriate credentials for these queries already. Also, $\mathcal{C}$ simulates $(\mathsf{m}_{0,i}, ..., \mathsf{m}_{n,i}, \Delta_i, s_{2,i}, v_{1,i})$ as in **Game**$_2$ and adds it to $L_{(P,V)}$ before the interaction with $\mathcal{A}_1$. This results:

$$\Pr[S_4] = \Pr[S_3]. \tag{5}$$

Game$_5$. $\mathcal{A}_1$ tries to impersonate the prover in this game. The attribute set of the prover is $A^* = \{m_1^*, ..., m_n^*\} \neq A_i \in L_{(O,I)}$ using the access policy $\phi^*_{\mathsf{stmt}_i}$ where $\phi^*_{\mathsf{stmt}_i}(A^*) = 1$ and $\phi^*_{\mathsf{stmt}_i}(A_i) = 0$. $\mathcal{A}_1$ is still allowed to query the oracles as in **Game**$_2$, **Game**$_3$ and **Game**$_4$ with restriction that $\phi^*_{\mathsf{stmt}_i}(A_i) \neq 1$ for the Obtain oracle. The aim of $\mathcal{A}_1$ is to complete the proof with $(\mathcal{A}_1^{\mathsf{Prove}}(pk, \cdot, \phi^*_{\mathsf{stmt}_i}(A^*)), \mathcal{C}^{\mathsf{Verify}}(pk, \phi^*_{\mathsf{stmt}_i}(A^*))) = 1$. $\mathcal{C}$ may further obtain two valid transcripts and regenerate the secret values to extract the credentials components (t^*, s^*, v^*) if the show proof could be verified again after resetting $\mathcal{A}_1$ by $\mathcal{C}$ to the time after sending witnesses.

$\mathcal{A}_1$ is required to output $t^* \notin \{t_1, ..., t_q\}$. If $v^* \notin L_{(O,I)} \cup L_{(P,V)}$, $\mathcal{C}$ can construct a polynomial $c(x)$ of degree $n-1$ where $f(x) = c(x)(x+t^*) + d$ to compute:

$$\begin{aligned} v^{*\frac{1}{(t_0 \sum_{j=0}^{n} x'^j \mathsf{m}_j^* + t'_0 s^* + t''_0)\cdot d}} g_1^{\frac{-c(x)}{d}} &= g_1^{\frac{f(x)\cdot(t_0 \sum_{j=0}^{n} x'^j \mathsf{m}_j^* + t'_0 s^* + t''_0)}{(x+t^*)\cdot(t_0 \sum_{j=0}^{n} x'^j \mathsf{m}_j^* + t'_0 s^* + t''_0)\cdot d} - \frac{c(x)}{d}} \\ &= g_1^{\frac{c(x)(x+t^*)+d}{d\cdot(x+t^*)} - \frac{c(x)}{d}} \\ &= g_1^{\frac{1}{x+t^*}} \end{aligned}$$

and outputs $(g^{\frac{1}{x+t^*}}, t^*)$ as the solution for the SDH instance. On the other hand, if we have $v^* \in L_{(O,I)} \cup L_{(P,V)}$, $\mathcal{C}$ can extract the discrete logarithm x to break the SDH assumption.

Let $\Pr[Res]$ be the probability of $\mathcal{C}$ resets successfully, and $\Pr[Acc]$ be the probability of $\mathcal{C}$ outputs 1 in the presentation protocol with $\mathcal{A}_1$, by Multi-Instance Reset Lemma [25], we have:

$$\begin{aligned} \Pr[S_5] &\leq \Pr[S_4] + \Pr[Acc] \\ &\leq \Pr[S_4] + \sqrt[N]{\Pr[Res] - 1} + \frac{1}{p} + 1 \\ &\leq \Pr[S_4] + \sqrt[N]{\sqrt{\epsilon_{\mathsf{sdh}}} - 1} + \frac{1}{p} + 1, \end{aligned} \tag{6}$$

and summing up the probability from (1) to (6), we have $\epsilon_{\mathsf{imp}} \leq \sqrt[N]{\sqrt{\epsilon_{\mathsf{sdh}}} - 1} + \frac{1+(q-1)!/p^{q-2}}{p} + 1$ as required. The time taken by $\mathcal{C}$ is at least $2Nt_{\mathsf{imp}}$ due to reset and interacting with N parallel impersonation instances, in additional to the environment setup and the final SDH soltion extraction that cost $T(q^2)$. □

A.2 Proof of Lemma 2

Proof. In this proof, we show that if $\mathcal{A}_2$ exists, there exists an algorithm $\mathcal{C}$ which output $(g_1^{\frac{1}{x+t}}, t)$ by acting the simulator for the ABC system. Given a q-SDH instance $(g_1, g_1^x, g_1^{x^2}, ..., g_1^{x^q}, g_2, g_2^x)$ where $q = Q_{(O,I)} + Q_{(P,V)}$ is the number of queries made to the Obtain and Verify oracles. The reduction games are as follows:

Game$_0$. There are no differences between this game and **Game$_0$** in Lemma 1 such that:

$$\Pr[S_0] = \epsilon_{\mathsf{imp}}. \tag{7}$$

Game$_1$. This game follows **Game$_1$** in Lemma 1 with exceptions that $\mathcal{C}$ additionally checks $X = g_2^{-t_i}$ for $i \in \{1, ..., q\}$. If t_i is found, $\mathcal{C}$ outputs the solution towards the SDH instance using the discrete logarithm $x = -t_i$. $\mathcal{C}$ also computes $f_{i,j}(x) = \prod_{k=1,k\neq i,j}^{q}(x+t_k) = \sum_{k=0}^{q-2}\gamma_k x^k$ and uniformly selects random distinct $s_1, ..., s_q \in \mathbb{Z}_p$. $\mathcal{C}$ sends $(\mathsf{e}, \mathbb{G}_1, \mathbb{G}_2, \mathbb{G}_T, p, a_0 = g_1^{f(x)t_0}, a_1 = a_0^{x'}, ..., a_n = a_0^{x'^n}, b = g_1^{f(x)t'_0 - \sum_{j=1}^{q} f_j(x)}, c = g_1^{f(x)t''_0 + \sum_{j=1}^{q} s_j f_j(x)}, X = g_2^x, X_0 = g_2, X_1 = X_0^{x'}, ..., X_n = X_0^{x'^n}, \mathsf{pk})$ as the public key to $\mathcal{A}_2$. Thus,

$$\Pr[S_1] \leq \Pr[S_0]. \tag{8}$$

Game$_2$. This game is the same as **Game$_2$** in Lemma 1 except in step 5, $\mathcal{C}$ picks a random $\beta_i \xleftarrow{\$} \mathbb{Z}_p$ and calculates $\Delta_i = t_i - t'_i$, $s_{2,i} = s_i - s_{1,i}$. $\mathcal{C}$ simulates the partial SDH-CL signature $sig'_i = (\Delta_i, s_{2,i}, v_{1,i})$ on $M_i = a_0^{(x'+o_i)\prod_{j=1}^{n-1}(x'+m_{j,i})} b^{s_{1,i}}$ for $A_i = \{m_{1,i}, ..., m_{n-1,i}, o_i\}$ after reset of $\mathcal{A}_2$ such that:

$$\begin{aligned}
v_{1,i} &= (M_i b^{s_{2,i}} c)^{\delta_{I,i}} \\
&= (a_0^{\prod_{j=1}^{n}(x'+m_{j,i})} b^{s_{1,i}+(s_i - s_{1,i})} c)^{\frac{1}{x+t_i} - \delta_{U,i}} \\
&= \left(g_1^{f(x)t_0\prod_{j=1}^{n}(x'+m_{j,i})} g_1^{s_i(f(x)t'_0 - \sum_{j=1}^{q} f_j(x))} g_1^{f(x)t''_0 + \sum_{j=1}^{q} s_j f_j(x)}\right)^{\frac{1}{x+t_i} - \frac{u_{2,i}}{\beta_i}} \\
&= \left(g_1^{f(x)[t_0\prod_{j=1}^{n}(x'+m_{j,i}) + s_i t'_0 + t''_0]} g_1^{\sum_{j=1,j\neq i}^{q}(s_j - s_i) f_j(x)}\right)^{\frac{1}{x+t_i} - \frac{u_{2,i}}{\beta_i}}.
\end{aligned}$$

Observe that the above $v_{1,i}$ can be calculated by using $g_1^{f_i(x)}$ and $g_1^{f_{i,j}(x)}$. $\mathcal{C}$ sends sig'_i and β_i to $\mathcal{A}_2$. Since $\mathcal{C}$ simulates the issuing protocol perfectly, this gives:

$$\Pr[S_2] \leq \Pr[S_1] + (q-1)!/p^{q-1}. \tag{9}$$

Game$_3$. There are no differences between this game and **Game$_3$** in Lemma 1 such that:

$$\Pr[S_3] = \Pr[S_2]. \tag{10}$$

Game$_4$. There are no differences between this game and **Game$_4$** in Lemma 1 such that:

$$\Pr[S_4] = \Pr[S_3]. \tag{11}$$

Game$_5$. Similar to the **Game$_5$** in Lemma 1, $\mathcal{C}$ can reset $\mathcal{A}_2$ to extract the elements (t^*, s^*, v^*) of $cred^*$ where v^* has the form:

$$v^* = \left(g_1^{f(x)[t_0\prod_{j=1}^{n}(x'+m_{j,i}) + s^* t'_0 + t''_0] + \sum_{j=1,j\neq i}^{q}(s_j - s^*) f_j(x) + (s_i - s^*) f_i(x)}\right)^{\frac{1}{x+t_i}}.$$

Since $\mathcal{A}_2$ must output $t^* = t_i \in \{t_1, ..., t_q\}$ but $s^* \neq s_i \in \{s_1, ..., s_q\}$ for $i \in \{1, ..., q\}$, $\mathcal{C}$ proceeds to compute $c(x)$ of degree $q-2$ and $d \in \mathbb{Z}_p$ from the knowledge of $\{t_1, ..., t_q\}$ such that $f_i(x) = c(x)(x + t_i) + d$ (since $x \neq -t_i$ in **Game**$_1$). Moreover, it will be the case that $v \notin L_{(O,I)} \cup L_{(P,V)}$ as discussed in the special case. $\mathcal{C}$ then calculates:

$$\left(v^{*\frac{1}{f_i(x)[t_0 \sum_{j=0}^{n} \mathsf{m}_j^* x'^j + s^* t'_0 + t''_0] + \sum_{j=1, j\neq i}^{q} (s_j - s^*) f_{j,i}(x) + (s_i - s^*) c(x)}} \right)^{\frac{1}{d(s_i - s^*)}}$$
$$= g_1^{\frac{(f_i(x) - c(x)(x+t_i))(s_i - s^*)}{d(s_i - s^*)(x+t_i)}}$$
$$= g_1^{\frac{1}{x+t_i}},$$

and outputs $(g_1^{\frac{1}{x+t_i}}, t_i)$ as the solution for the SDH instance. Therefore, we have:

$$\Pr[S_5] \leq \Pr[S_4] + \sqrt[N]{\sqrt{\epsilon_{\mathsf{sdh}}} - 1} + \frac{1}{p} + 1, \tag{12}$$

and summing up the probability from (7) to (12), we have $\epsilon_{\mathsf{imp}} \leq \sqrt[N]{\sqrt{\epsilon_{\mathsf{sdh}}} - 1} + \frac{1+(q-1)!/p^{q-2}}{p} + 1$ as required. The time taken by $\mathcal{C}$ is at least $2Nt_{\mathsf{imp}}$ due to reset and interacting with N parallel impersonation instances, in additional to the environment setup and the final SDH solution extraction that cost $T(q^2)$. □

A.3 Proof of Lemma 3

Proof. In this game, we show that if $\mathcal{A}_3$ exists, there exists an algorithm $\mathcal{C}$ which output $(g_1^{\frac{1}{x+t}}, t)$ by acting the simulator for the ABC system. Given a q-SDH instance $(g_1, g_1^x, g_1^{x^2}, ..., g_1^{x^q}, g_2, g_2^x)$ where $q = Q_{(O,I)} + Q_{(P,V)}$ is the number of queries made to the Obtain and Verify oracles, The reduction games are as follows:

Game$_0$. There are no differences between this game and **Game**$_0$ in Lemma 1 such that:

$$\Pr[S_0] = \epsilon_{\mathsf{imp}}. \tag{13}$$

Game$_1$. This game follows **Game**$_1$ in Lemma 2 with exceptions that $\mathcal{C}$ sends $(\mathsf{e}, \mathbb{G}_1, \mathbb{G}_2, \mathbb{G}_T, p, a_0 = g_1^{f(x)t_0 - \sum_{j=1}^{q} f_j(x)}, a_1 = a_0^{x'}, ..., a_n = a_0^{x'^n}, b = g_1^{f(x)t'_0 - \sum_{j=1}^{q} f_j(x)}, c = g_1^{f(x)t''_0 + \sum_{j=1}^{q} z_j f_j(x)}, X = g_2^x, X_0 = g_2, X_1 = X_0^{x'}, ..., X_n = X_0^{x'^n}, \mathsf{pk})$ as the public key to $\mathcal{A}_3$, where $z_1, ..., z_q \in \mathbb{Z}_p$ is randomly chosen with uniform distribution. Thus,

$$\Pr[S_1] \leq \Pr[S_0]. \tag{14}$$

Game$_2$. This game is the same as **Game**$_2$ in Lemma 1 except in step 5, $\mathcal{C}$ picks a random $\beta_i \xleftarrow{\$} \mathbb{Z}_p$ and calculates $\Delta_i = t_i - t'_i$, $s_{2,i} = s_i - s_{1,i}$. $\mathcal{C}$ simulates the partial SDH-CL signature $sig'_i = (\Delta_i, s_{2,i}, v_{1,i})$ on $M_i = a_0^{(x'+o_i)\prod_{j=1}^{n-1}(x'+m_{j,i})} b^{s_{1,i}}$ for

$A_i = \{m_{1,i}, ..., m_{n-1,i}, o_i\}$ after reset of $\mathcal{A}_3$ such that:

$$\begin{aligned}
v_{1,i} &= (a_0^{\prod_{j=1}^{n}(x'+m_{j,i})} b^{s_{1,i}+(s_i-s_{1,i})} c)^{\frac{1}{x+t_i}-\delta_{U,i}} \\
&= \left(g_1^{(f(x)t_0-\sum_{j=1}^{q} f_j(x))(\prod_{j=1}^{n}(x'+m_{j,i}))} g_1^{s_i(f(x)t_0'-\sum_{j=1}^{q} f_j(x))} g_1^{f(x)t_0''+\sum_{j=1}^{q} z_j f_j(x)}\right)^{\frac{1}{x+t_i}-\frac{u_{2,i}}{\beta_i}} \\
&= \left(g_1^{f(x)[t_0 \prod_{j=1}^{n}(x'+m_{j,i})+s_i t_0'+t_0'']} g_1^{\sum_{j=1, j\neq i}^{q}(z_j-z_i)f_j(x)}\right)^{\frac{1}{x+t_i}-\frac{u_{2,i}}{\beta_i}}.
\end{aligned}$$

Observe that the above $v_{1,i}$ can be calculated by using $g_1^{f_i(x)}$. $\mathcal{C}$ sends sig_i' and β_i to $\mathcal{A}_2$. Since $\mathcal{C}$ simulates the Issue oracle perfectly, this gives:

$$\Pr[S_2] \leq \Pr[S_1] + (q-1)!/p^{q-1}. \tag{15}$$

Game$_3$. There are no differences between this game and **Game$_3$** in Lemma 1 such that:

$$\Pr[S_3] = \Pr[S_2]. \tag{16}$$

Game$_4$. There are no differences between this game and **Game$_4$** in Lemma 1 such that:

$$\Pr[S_4] = \Pr[S_3]. \tag{17}$$

Game$_5$. This game requires $\mathcal{A}_3$ to output $t^* = t_i \in \{t_1, ..., t_q\}$ and $s^* = s_i \in \{s_1, ..., s_q\}$ for $i \in \{1, ..., q\}$. Note that the output must be the case that $v \notin L_{(O,I)} \cup L_{(P,V)}$ or $\mathcal{C}$ already found $x = -t_i$ during **Game$_1$**. $\mathcal{C}$ aborts with the unlikely case of forgery $(A^*, s^*, t^*, v^*) \in L_{(P,V)}$ which happens with probability $1/p$. Similar to the **Game$_5$** in Lemma 1, $\mathcal{C}$ can reset $\mathcal{A}_3$ to extract the elements (t^*, s^*, v^*) of *cred** where v^* is in form of

$$v^* = \left(g_1^{f(x)(t_0 \sum_{j=0}^{n} \mathsf{m}_{j,i} x'^j + s_i t_0' + t_0'')} g_1^{\sum_{j=1, j\neq i}^{q}(z_j-z^*)f_j(x)+(z_i-z^*)f_i(x)}\right)^{\frac{1}{x+t_i}}.$$

$\mathcal{C}$ proceeds to compute $c(x)$ of degree $q-2$ and $d \in \mathbb{Z}_p$ from the knowledge of $\{t_1, ..., t_q\}$ such that $f_i(x) = c(x)(x+t_i) + d$. $\mathcal{C}$ subsequently computes:

$$\begin{aligned}
&\left(v^{*\frac{1}{f_i(x)(t_0 \sum_{j=0}^{n} \mathsf{m}_j^* x'^j + s^* t_0' + t_0'') + \sum_{j=1, j\neq i}^{q}(z_j-z^*)f_{j,i}(x)+(z_i-z^*)c(x)}}\right)^{d(z_i-z^*)} \\
&= g_1^{\frac{(f_i(x)-c(x)(x+t_i))(z_i-z^*)}{d(z_i-z^*)(x+t_i)}} \\
&= g_1^{\frac{1}{x+t_i}},
\end{aligned}$$

and outputs $(g_1^{\frac{1}{x+t_i}}, t_i)$ as the solution for the SDH instance. Therefore, we have:

$$Pr[S_5] \leq Pr[S_4] + \sqrt[N]{\sqrt{\epsilon_{\mathsf{sdh}}} - 1} + 1, \tag{18}$$

and summing up the probability from (13) to (18), we have $\epsilon_{\mathsf{imp}} \leq \sqrt[N]{\sqrt{\epsilon_{\mathsf{sdh}}} - 1} + \frac{(q-1)!}{p^{q-1}} + 1$ as required. The time taken by $\mathcal{C}$ is at least $2Nt_{\mathsf{imp}}$ due to reset and interacting with N parallel impersonation instances, in additional to the environment setup and the final SDH soltion extraction that cost $T(q^2)$. $\square$

B Proof of Theorem 2

Proof. We prove that with respect to the ABC system simulator $\mathcal{C}$, an adversary $\mathcal{A}$ wins the game with anon-aca-security only with a negligible advantage ϵ_{aunl}.

Game$_0$. Attacking on the original ABC system, we have

$$\Pr[S_0] \leq \epsilon_{\mathsf{anon}} + \frac{1}{2} \tag{19}$$

by definition, where S_0 is denoted as a successful distinguishing attempt.

Game$_1$. As in the original algorithm, $\mathcal{C}$ generates (pk, sk). The key pair is forwarded to $\mathcal{A}$ so that it can play the role as user and issuer. Moreover, $\mathcal{C}$ holds two lists $L_{(O,I)}$ and $L_{(P,V)}$ for corrupted issuing protocol and presentation protocol, respectively. Since the actions do not alter the key generation algorithm, thus:

$$\Pr[S_1] = \Pr[S_0]. \tag{20}$$

Game$_2$. Acting as an issuer, $\mathcal{A}$ interact with $\mathcal{C}$ concurrently, who simulates the Obtain oracle to produce a credential $cred_i$ for the user in the i-th session. Assume every user uses different attributes set $A_i = \{m_{1,i}, ..., m_{n-1,i}, o_i\}$ without loss of generality. The interaction is as follows:

1. $\mathcal{C}$ initials the issuing protocol for use in the i-th session of the concurrent interactions by running the zero-knowledge protocol:

$$PK\{s_{1,i} : M_i = C_i \cdot b^{s_{1,i}}\}.$$

   $\mathcal{C}$ sends $(A_i'', M_i, C_i, o_i, \pi_{s,i})$ to $\mathcal{A}$. If the ZK proof $\pi_{s,i}$ is valid, $\mathcal{A}$ can successfully extract the secret exponents $s_{1,i}$ used by $\mathcal{C}$ in the protocol.
2. $\mathcal{A}$ validates (A_i'', C_i, o_i) with its own data set T. The protocol proceed if $\mathsf{Open}(pk, C_i, A_i, o_i) = 1$ where A_i is generated locally by $\mathcal{A}$ using A_i'' and T.
3. $\mathcal{A}$ chooses a random value $u_{1,i} \in \mathbb{Z}_p$, and sets

$$z_{u_{1,i}} = \mathsf{Enc}_{\mathsf{pk}}(u_{1,i}).$$

   $\mathcal{A}$ chooses a random ciphertext $z_{\hat{x},i}$. $\mathcal{A}$ sends $(z_{u_{1.i}}, z_{\hat{x},i})$ to $\mathcal{C}$.
4. $\mathcal{C}$ sends $z_{1,i}, \omega_{2,i}$ and a ZK proof $\pi_{U,i}$ to $\mathcal{A}$. By the knowledge extractor of the ZK proof, $\mathcal{A}$ can obtain $(t_i', u_{2,i}, \gamma_{2,i})$.
5. $\mathcal{A}$ picks a random $\beta_i, s_{2,i} \xleftarrow{\$} \mathbb{Z}_p$, calculates $\Delta_i = t_i - t_i'$ and generates a partial SDH-CL signature for M_i as $sig_i' = (\Delta_i, s_{2,i}, v_{1,i})$, where $v_{1,i} = (M_i b^{s_{2,i}} c)^{\delta_{I,i}}$. $\mathcal{A}$ sends sig_i' and β_i to $\mathcal{C}$. Since $\mathcal{A}$ has extracted t_i' and $u_{2,i}$ from the ZK proof $\pi_{U,i}$, $\mathcal{A}$ can also calculate the full SDH-CL signature (t_i, s_i, v_i). $\mathcal{C}$ adds $cred_i = (t_i, s_i, v_i, A_i)$ to $L_{(O,I)}$.

From the view of $\mathcal{A}$, the issuing protocol is the same as the original one. For every M_i and its witness, they achieve the property of perfectly hiding. Also, each protocol session is uniformly distributed. The arguments are valid for the case where $\mathcal{A}$ concurrently runs the issuing protocol on the same attribute set. Since $\mathcal{A}$ do not gain more information than acting as an issuer, we ignore the case where $\mathcal{A}$ acts as a user in the issuing protocol. This gives

$$\Pr[S_2] = \Pr[S_1]. \tag{21}$$

Game$_3$. $\mathcal{A}$ queries the issuing protocol transcript of the i-th sesion to the Corrupt oracle additionally. $\mathcal{C}$ searches in $L_{(O,I)}$ and returns the internal state and the random exponents used. Since the issuing protocol achieves self-reducibility [40], for any two witness sets:

$$(\tilde{s}_{1,i,1}, \tilde{m}_{0,i,1}, ..., \tilde{m}_{n,i,1}), (\tilde{s}_{1,i,2}, \tilde{m}_{0,i,2}, ..., \tilde{m}_{n,i,2})$$

in the issuing protocol returned by Corrupt, the distribution of their transcripts are identical to each other from the view of $\mathcal{A}$. Following the perfectly hiding property among the committed attributes and the corresponding witness, o_i and $s_{1,i}$ are hidden, thus the non-uniformed distributes attributes are also identical to each other from the view of $\mathcal{A}$. Since $\mathcal{A}$ does not gain any advantage, we have:

$$\Pr[S_3] = \Pr[S_2]. \tag{22}$$

Game$_4$. $\mathcal{A}$ acts as the verifier and concurrently interact with $\mathcal{C}$ as the prover for multiple credentials. $\mathcal{C}$ runs the i-th session of a show proof for $cred_i = (t_i, s_i, v_i, A_i = \{m_{1,i}, ...m_{n-1,i}, o_i\})$. We assume the $\mathcal{A}$ always request for successful show proofs where $\phi_{\mathsf{stmt}}(A_i) = 1$. From the view of $\mathcal{A}$, the interaction is the same as the original show proofs. With the property that the randomized credential in the presentation protocol is perfectly hiding, and the presentation protocol of the credential system offers random self-reducibility [40], this gives:

$$\Pr[S_4] = \Pr[S_3]. \tag{23}$$

Game$_5$. $\mathcal{A}$ also queries to the presentation transcript of the i-th session to the Corrupt oracle. $\mathcal{C}$ searches in $L_{(P,V)}$ to return the internal state and the random exponents used in completing the protocol. The presentation protocol is an extension to the initialization in the issuing protocol where $\mathcal{C}$ additionally prove the knowledge of the blinding factors used to randomize the credential. Specifically, $\mathcal{C}$ proves the validity of the randomized credential element v_i' in a witness-hiding protocol, such that it consists of the corresponding randomized attributes $(\mathsf{m}'_{0,i}, ..., \mathsf{m}'_{n,i})$, the blinded credential elements t_i', s_i' and the blinding factors (r_i, y_i). Therefore, following the property that the presentation protocol of the credential system offers random self-reducibility [40], for any two witness sets in a presentation protocol returned by Corrupt, the distribution of their transcripts are identical form the view of $\mathcal{A}$. Following the property that the randomized credential in the presentation protocol is perfectly hiding [40], this is true even if $\mathcal{A}$ knows $(t_i, s_{2,i}, v_i)$ that have been exposed during the issuing protocol, which now have been perfectly hidden by (r_i, y_i). $\mathcal{A}$ also act as a prover in which it does not gain useful information, and any advantage from the query.

The same argument applies on show proofs with access policy of composite clauses and thus:

$$\Pr[S_5] = \Pr[S_4], \tag{24}$$

Game$_6$. $\mathcal{C}$ plays the role of user to run the challenge issuing protocol with A_0 and A_1, respectively. When the issuing protocol is completed, $\mathcal{C}$ obtains two credentials $cred_0$ and $cred_1$. $\mathcal{C}$ randomly selects a bit $b \in \{0, 1\}$ and completes the challenge show proof with $\mathcal{A}$ as the verifier using $cred_b$. $\mathcal{A}$ can request polynomially many times of show proofs. With the restriction that $\mathcal{A}$ cannot query to the challenge transcripts to Corrupt, $\mathcal{A}$ can query to oracles as before. Finally, $\mathcal{A}$ is requested to make a guess on b. It breaks the anonymity of the ABC system with correctly guessing $b' = b$ with the probability that:

$$\begin{aligned} \Pr[S_6] &= \Pr[S_5] \\ &= \Pr[b' = b] \\ &= \frac{1}{2} + \epsilon_{\mathsf{anon}}. \end{aligned} \tag{25}$$

Combining the Eqs. 19 to 25, we have a negligible ϵ_{anon} as required and $\mathcal{A}$ runs in time t_{anon}. □

C Proof of Theorem 3

Proof. The proof is the same as that of Theorem 2 except **Game**$_6$.

Game$_6$. $\mathcal{C}$ randomly selects a bit $b \in \{0, 1\}$ and plays the role of user to run the challenge issuing protocol with A_b and A_{1-b}, respectively. When the issuing protocol is completed, $\mathcal{C}$ obtains two credentials $cred_b$ and $cred_{1-b}$. $\mathcal{C}$ completes the challenge show proof with $\mathcal{A}$ as the verifier using the same order of $cred_b$ and $cred_{1-b}$. $\mathcal{A}$ can request polynomially many times of show proofs. With the restriction that $\mathcal{A}$ cannot query to the challenge transcripts to Corrupt, $\mathcal{A}$ can query to oracles as before. Finally, $\mathcal{A}$ is requested to make a guess on b. It breaks the anonymity of the ABC system with correctly guessing $b' = b$ with the probability that:

$$\begin{aligned} \Pr[S_6] &= \Pr[S_5] \\ &= \Pr[b' = b] \\ &= \frac{1}{2} + \epsilon_{\mathsf{unl}}. \end{aligned} \tag{26}$$

Therefore, we have a negligible ϵ_{unl} as required and $\mathcal{A}$ runs in time t_{unl}. □

D Proof of Theorem 4

Proof. The proof is the same as that of Theorem 2 except **Game**$_4$ to **Game**$_6$.

Game$_4$. $\mathcal{A}$ acts as the verifier and concurrently interact with $\mathcal{C}$ as the provers for multiple credentials. $\mathcal{C}$ runs the i-th session of a show proof for $cred_i =$

$(t_i, s_i, v_i, A_i = \{m_{1,i}, ...m_{n-1,i}, o_i\})$. We assume the $\mathcal{A}$ always request for successful show proofs where $\phi_{\mathsf{stmt}}(A_i) = 1$. From the view of $\mathcal{A}$, the interaction is the same as the original show proofs. We note that the credential in the presentation protocol is being revealed to the verifier, thus the perfectly hiding property is exploited. With the property that the presentation protocol of the credential system offers random self-reducibility [40], this gives: This gives:

$$\Pr[S_4] = \Pr[S_3]. \tag{27}$$

Game$_5$. $\mathcal{A}$ also queries to the presentation transcript of the i-th session to the $\mathsf{Corrupt}$ oracle. $\mathcal{C}$ searches in $L_{(P,V)}$ to return the internal state and the random exponents used in completing the protocol. $\mathcal{A}$ also act as a prover in which it does not gain useful information, and any advantage from the query. The same argument applies on show proofs with access policy of composite clauses and thus:

$$\Pr[S_5] = \Pr[S_4], \tag{28}$$

Game$_6$. It is the same as **Game**$_6$ in Theorem 2.

Therefore, we have a negligible ϵ_{anon} as required and $\mathcal{A}$ runs in time t_{anon}.

E Correctness for the Equations from Section 6.1

E.1 And proof (Sect. 6.1.1)

$$\begin{aligned}
\hat{e}(W, \prod_{j=0}^{l} X_j^{\mathsf{m}_j}) &= \hat{e}(\prod_{j=0}^{n-l} a_j^{\mathsf{w}'_j}, \prod_{j=0}^{l} (g_2^{x'^j})^{\mathsf{m}_j}) \\
&= \hat{e}(a^{\prod_{j=l+1}^{n}(x'+m_j)}, g_2^{\prod_{j=1}^{l}(x'+m_j)}) \\
&= \hat{e}(a^{\prod_{j=1}^{n}(x'+m_j)}, g_2) \\
&= \hat{e}(\prod_{j=0}^{n} a_j^{\mathsf{m}_j}, g_2) \\
&= \hat{e}(C, X_0)
\end{aligned}$$

E.2 ANY proof (Sect. 6.1.2)

$$\begin{aligned}
\hat{e}(W'W, \prod_{j=0}^{l} X_j^{\iota_j}) &= \hat{e}(\prod_{j=0}^{k-l} a_j^{\mathsf{m}'_{2,j}} \cdot \prod_{j=0}^{n-l} a_j^{\mathsf{w}'_j}, \prod_{j=0}^{l} X_j^{\iota_j}) \\
&= \hat{e}(\prod_{j=0}^{k-l} a_j^{\mathsf{m}'_{2,j}}, \prod_{j=0}^{l} X_j^{\iota_j}) \cdot \hat{e}(\prod_{j=0}^{n-l} a_j^{\mathsf{w}'_j}, \prod_{j=0}^{l} X_j^{\iota_j}) \\
&= \hat{e}(a^{\sum_{j=l+1}^{n} x'^j \mathsf{m}'_{2,j}}, g_2^{\sum_{j=0}^{l} x'^j \iota_j}) \cdot \hat{e}(a^{\sum_{j=l+1}^{n} x'^j \mathsf{w}'_j}, g_2^{\sum_{j=0}^{l} x'^j \iota_j}) \\
&= \hat{e}(a^{\prod_{j=1}^{n}(x'+m_j)}, g_2) \cdot \hat{e}(a^{\prod_{j=1}^{n}(x'+\hat{m}_j)}, g_2) \\
&= \hat{e}(\prod_{j=0}^{k} a_j^{\mathsf{m}_{1,j}}, g_2) \cdot \hat{e}(C, g_2) \\
&= \hat{e}(C \cdot \prod_{j=0}^{k} a_j^{\mathsf{m}_{1,j}}, X_0)
\end{aligned}$$

E.3 NAND proof (Sect. 6.1.3)

Note that C could be rewritten as $C = a_0^{f(x')}$ where $f(x') = d(x')q(x') + r(x')$. Let $d(x') = \sum_{j=0}^{n-k} x'^j \mathsf{w}'_j$, $q(x') = \sum_{j=0}^{k} x'^j \mathsf{m}_j$, and $r(x') = \sum_{j=0}^{k-1} x'^j \mathsf{r}'_j$.

$$\begin{aligned}
\hat{e}(W, \prod_{j=0}^{k} X_j^{\mathsf{m}_j}) &= \hat{e}(\prod_{j=0}^{n-k} a_j^{\mathsf{w}'_j}, \prod_{j=0}^{k} X_j^{\mathsf{m}_j}) \\
&= \hat{e}(a^{\sum_{j=0}^{n} x'^j \mathsf{w}'_j}, g_2^{\sum_{j=0}^{k} x'^j \mathsf{m}_j}) \\
&= \hat{e}(a^{d(x')q(x')+r(x')} \cdot a^{-r(x')}, X_0) \\
&= \hat{e}(C \cdot \prod_{j=0}^{k-1} a_j^{-\mathsf{r}'_j}, X_0)
\end{aligned}$$

E.4 NANY proof (Sect. 6.1.4)

$$\begin{aligned}
\hat{e}(W'W, \prod_{j=0}^{l} X_j^{\delta_j}) &= \hat{e}(\prod_{j=0}^{k-l} a_j^{\mathsf{m}'_{2,j}} \cdot \prod_{j=0}^{n-l} a_j^{\mathsf{w}'_j}, \prod_{j=0}^{l} X_j^{\delta_j}) \\
&= \hat{e}(\prod_{j=0}^{k-l} a_j^{\mathsf{m}'_{2,j}}, \prod_{j=0}^{l} X_j^{\delta_j}) \cdot \hat{e}(\prod_{j=0}^{n-l} a_j^{\mathsf{w}'_j}, \prod_{j=0}^{l} X_j^{\delta_j}) \\
&= \hat{e}(a_0^{\prod_{m_j \in (A'-D)}(x'+m_j)}, X_0^{\prod_{m_j \in (D)}(x'+m_j)}) \cdot \hat{e}(a_0^{d(x')q(x')}, X_0) \\
&= \hat{e}(a_0^{\prod_{m_j \in A'}(x'+m_j)}, X_0) \cdot \hat{e}(a_0^{d(x')q(x')+r(x')} \cdot a_0^{-r(x')}, X_0) \\
&= \hat{e}(\prod_{j=0}^{k} a_j^{\mathsf{m}_{1,j}}, X_0) \cdot \hat{e}(C \cdot \prod_{j=0}^{l-1} a_j^{-\mathsf{r}'_j}, X_0) \\
&= \hat{e}(C \cdot \prod_{j=0}^{k} a_j^{\mathsf{m}_{1,j}} \cdot \prod_{j=0}^{l-1} a_j^{-\mathsf{r}'_j}, X_0)
\end{aligned}$$

References

1. Aikou, Y., Sadiah, S., Nakanishi, T.: An efficient blacklistable anonymous credentials without ttps using pairing-based accumulator. In: 2017 IEEE 31st International Conference on AINA, pp. 780–786 (2017)
2. Anada, H.: Decentralized multi-authority anonymous credential system with bundled languages on identifiers. In: Maimut, D., Oprina, A.-G., Sauveron, D. (eds.) SecITC 2020. LNCS, vol. 12596, pp. 71–90. Springer, Cham (2021). https://doi.org/10.1007/978-3-030-69255-1_6
3. Begum, N., Nakanishi, T.: An accumulator-based revocation in delegatable anonymous credentials. In: CANDARW 2020, pp. 314–320 (2020)
4. Blömer, J., Bobolz, J.: Delegatable attribute-based anonymous credentials from dynamically malleable signatures. In: Preneel, B., Vercauteren, F. (eds.) ACNS 2018. LNCS, vol. 10892, pp. 221–239. Springer, Cham (2018). https://doi.org/10.1007/978-3-319-93387-0_12
5. Camenisch, J., Drijvers, M., Dzurenda, P., Hajny, J.: Fast keyed-verification anonymous credentials on standard smart cards. In: Dhillon, G., Karlsson, F., Hedström, K., Zúquete, A. (eds.) SEC 2019. IAICT, vol. 562, pp. 286–298. Springer, Cham (2019). https://doi.org/10.1007/978-3-030-22312-0_20
6. Camenisch, J., Drijvers, M., Lehmann, A.: Anonymous attestation using the strong diffie hellman assumption revisited. In: Franz, M., Papadimitratos, P. (eds.) TRUST, pp. 1–20. Springer, Cham (2016)
7. Camenisch, J., Lysyanskaya, A.: Signature schemes and anonymous credentials from bilinear maps. In: Franklin, M. (ed.) CRYPTO 2004. LNCS, vol. 3152, pp. 56–72. Springer, Heidelberg (2004). https://doi.org/10.1007/978-3-540-28628-8_4
8. Casanova-Marqués., R., Pascacio., P., Hajny., J., Torres-Sospedra., J.: Anonymous attribute-based credentials in collaborative indoor positioning systems. In: SECRYPT, pp. 791–797. INSTICC, SciTePress (2021)

9. Chase, M., Perrin, T., Zaverucha, G.: The signal private group system and anonymous credentials supporting efficient verifiable encryption. In: CCS 2020, p. 1445–1459. ACM, New York (2020)
10. Chatterjee, S., Menezes, A.: On cryptographic protocols employing asymmetric pairings - the role of ψ revisited. Discret. Appl. Math. **159**(13), 1311–1322 (2011)
11. Chaum, D.: Security without identification: Transaction systems to make big brother obsolete. Commun. ACM **28**(10), 1030–1044 (1985)
12. Connolly, A., Lafourcade, P., Perez Kempner, O.: Improved constructions of anonymous credentials from structure-preserving signatures on equivalence classes. In: Hanaoka, G., Shikata, J., Watanabe, Y. (eds.) Public-Key Cryptography - PKC 2022, pp. 409–438. Springer, Cham (2022). https://doi.org/10.1007/978-3-030-97121-2_15
13. Crites, E.C., Lysyanskaya, A.: Delegatable anonymous credentials from mercurial signatures. In: Matsui, M. (ed.) CT-RSA 2019. LNCS, vol. 11405, pp. 535–555. Springer, Cham (2019). https://doi.org/10.1007/978-3-030-12612-4_27
14. Davidson, A., Goldberg, I., Sullivan, N., Tankersley, G., Valsorda, F.: Privacy pass: Bypassing internet challenges anonymously. Proc. Privacy Enhan. Technol. **2018**, 164–180 (2018)
15. Deng, X., Tian, C., Chen, F., Xian, H.: Designated-verifier anonymous credential for identity management in decentralized systems. Mobile Information Systems 2021, article ID 2807395
16. Dzurenda, P., Hajny, J., Malina, L., Ricci, S.: Anonymous credentials with practical revocation using elliptic curves. In: SECRYPT 2017, pp. 534–539 (2017)
17. Fuchsbauer, G., Hanser, C., Slamanig, D.: Structure-preserving signatures on equivalence classes and constant-size anonymous credentials. JOC **32**, 498–546 (2019)
18. Fuchsbauer, G., Hanser, C., Slamanig, D.: Practical round-optimal blind signatures in the standard model. In: Gennaro, R., Robshaw, M. (eds.) CRYPTO 2015. LNCS, vol. 9216, pp. 233–253. Springer, Heidelberg (2015). https://doi.org/10.1007/978-3-662-48000-7_12
19. Galbraith, S.D., Paterson, K.G., Smart, N.P.: Pairings for cryptographers. Discret. Appl. Math. **156**, 3113–3121 (2006)
20. Gennaro, R., Goldfeder, S.: Fast multiparty threshold ecdsa with fast trustless setup. In: CCS 2018, p. 1179–1194. ACM (2018)
21. Guo, N., Gao, T., Park, H.: Random oracle-based anonymous credential system for efficient attributes proof on smart devices. Soft. Comput. **20**, 1781–1791 (2016)
22. Haböck, U., Krenn, S.: Breaking and fixing anonymous credentials for the cloud. In: Mu, Y., Deng, R.H., Huang, X. (eds.) CANS 2019. LNCS, vol. 11829, pp. 249–269. Springer, Cham (2019). https://doi.org/10.1007/978-3-030-31578-8_14
23. Hanzlik, L., Slamanig, D.: With a little help from my friends: Constructing practical anonymous credentials. In: CCS 2021, p. 2004–2023. ACM (2021)
24. Hébant, C., Pointcheval, D.: Traceable constant-size multi-authority credentials. Cryptology ePrint Archive, Paper 2020/657 (2020). https://eprint.iacr.org/2020/657
25. Kiltz, E., Masny, D., Pan, J.: Optimal Security Proofs for Signatures from Identification Schemes. In: Robshaw, M., Katz, J. (eds.) CRYPTO 2016. LNCS, vol. 9815, pp. 33–61. Springer, Heidelberg (2016). https://doi.org/10.1007/978-3-662-53008-5_2
26. Kreuter, B., Lepoint, T., Orrù, M., Raykova, M.: Anonymous tokens with private metadata bit. In: Micciancio, D., Ristenpart, T. (eds.) CRYPTO 2020. LNCS, vol.

12170, pp. 308–336. Springer, Cham (2020). https://doi.org/10.1007/978-3-030-56784-2_11
27. Krzywiecki, Ł, Wszoła, M., Kutyłowski, M.: Brief announcement: Anonymous credentials secure to ephemeral leakage. In: Dolev, S., Lodha, S. (eds.) CSCML 2017. LNCS, vol. 10332, pp. 96–98. Springer, Cham (2017). https://doi.org/10.1007/978-3-319-60080-2_7
28. Lin, C., He, D., Zhang, H., Shao, L., Huang, X.: Privacy-enhancing decentralized anonymous credential in smart grids. Computer Standards & Interfaces 75 (2021), article ID: 103505
29. Liu, D., Wu, H., Ni, J., Shen, X.: Efficient and anonymous authentication with succinct multi-subscription credential in sagvn. IEEE Trans. Intell. Transp. Syst. **23**(3), 2863–2873 (2022)
30. Nakanishi, T., Kanatani, T.: Efficient blacklistable anonymous credential system with reputation using a pairing-based accumulator. IET Inf. Secur. **14**(6), 613–624 (2020)
31. Okishima, R., Nakanishi, T.: An anonymous credential system with constant-size attribute proofs for cnf formulas with negations. In: Attrapadung, N., Yagi, T. (eds.) IWSEC 2019. LNCS, vol. 11689, pp. 89–106. Springer, Cham (2019). https://doi.org/10.1007/978-3-030-26834-3_6
32. Paquin, C., Zaverucha, G.: U-prove cryptographic specification v1.1 (revision 3) (December 2013). https://www.microsoft.com/en-us/research/publication/u-prove-cryptographic-specification-v1-1-revision-3/
33. Pinjala, S.K., Vivek, S.S., Sivalingam, K.M.: Delegated anonymous credentials with revocation capability for iot service chains (dancis). IEEE Internet Things J. **9**(5), 3729–3742 (2022)
34. Pussewalage, H.S.G., Oleshchuk, V.A.: An anonymous delegatable attribute-based credential scheme for a collaborative e-health environment. ACM Trans. Internet Technol. **19**(3), 1–22 (2019)
35. Rondelet, A.: A note on anonymous credentials using BLS signatures. CoRR abs/arXiv: 2006.05201 (2020)
36. Samarati, P., Sweeney, L.: Protecting privacy when disclosing information: k-anonymity and its enforcement through generalization and suppression. Tech. rep. (1998)
37. Sanders, O.: Efficient redactable signature and application to anonymous credentials. In: Kiayias, A., Kohlweiss, M., Wallden, P., Zikas, V. (eds.) PKC 2020, pp. 628–656 (2020)
38. Schäge, S.: Tight proofs for signature schemes without random oracles. In: Paterson, K.G. (ed.) EUROCRYPT 2011. LNCS, vol. 6632, pp. 189–206. Springer, Heidelberg (2011). https://doi.org/10.1007/978-3-642-20465-4_12
39. Srinivas, J., Das, A.K., Kumar, N., Rodrigues, J.J.P.C.: Tcalas: Temporal credential-based anonymous lightweight authentication scheme for internet of drones environment. IEEE Trans. Veh. Technol. **68**(7), 6903–6916 (2019)
40. Tan, S.-Y., Groß, T.: MoniPoly—an expressive q-SDH-based anonymous attribute-based credential system. In: Moriai, S., Wang, H. (eds.) ASIACRYPT 2020. LNCS, vol. 12493, pp. 498–526. Springer, Cham (2020). https://doi.org/10.1007/978-3-030-64840-4_17
41. Wang, W., Liu, J., Qin, Y., Feng, D.: Formal analysis of a ttp-free blacklistable anonymous credentials system. In: Qing, S., Mitchell, C., Chen, L., Liu, D. (eds.) Information and Communications Security, pp. 3–16. Springer, Cham (2018). https://doi.org/10.1007/978-3-319-89500-0_1

42. Yang, R., Au, M.H., Xu, Q., Yu, Z.: Decentralized blacklistable anonymous credentials with reputation. Comput. Sec. **85**, 353–371 (2019)

Auditable Asymmetric Password Authenticated Public Key Establishment

Antonio Faonio[1], Maria Isabel Gonzalez Vasco[2], Claudio Soriente[3](✉), and Hien Thi Thu Truong[3]

[1] EURECOM, Sophia Antipolis, France
antonio.faonio@eurecom.fr
[2] Universidad Rey Juan Carlos, MACIMTE, Móstoles, Spain
mariaisabel.vasco@urjc.es
[3] NEC Laboratories Europe GmbH, Heidelberg, Germany
claudio.sorient@neclab.eu

Abstract. Non-repudiation of user messages is a desirable feature in a number of online applications, but it requires digital signatures and certified cryptographic keys. Unfortunately, the adoption of cryptographic keys often results in poor usability, as users must either carry around their private keys (e.g., in a smart-card) or store them in all of their devices. A user-friendly alternative, adopted by several companies and national administrations, is based on so-called "cloud-based PKI certificates". In a nutshell, each user has a certified key-pair stored at a server in the cloud; users authenticate to the server—via passwords or one-time codes—and ask it to sign messages on their behalf. However, moving the key-pair from user-private storage to the cloud impairs non-repudiation. In fact, users can always deny having signed a message, by claiming that the signature was produced by the allegedly malicious server without their consent. In this paper we present Auditable Asymmetric Password Authenticated Public Key Establishment ($\mathsf{A^2PAKE}$), a cloud-based solution to allow users to manage their signing key-pairs that (i) has the same usability of cloud-based PKI certificates, and (ii) guarantees non-repudiation of signatures. We do so by introducing a new ideal functionality in the Universal Composability framework named $\mathcal{F}_{\mathsf{A^2PAKE}}$. The functionality is password-based and allows to generate asymmetric key-pairs, where the public key is output to all the parties, but the secret key is the private output of a single one (e.g., the user). Further, the functionality is *auditable*: given a public key output by the functionality, a server can prove to a third party (i.e., a judge) that the corresponding secret key is held by a specific user. Thus, if a user signs messages with the secret key obtained via $\mathsf{A^2PAKE}$, then signatures are non-repudiable. We provide an efficient instantiation based on distributed oblivious pseudo-random functions for signature schemes based on DLOG. We also develop a prototype implementation of our instantiation and use it to evaluate its performance in realistic settings.

Keywords: Public key cryptography · Password authentication · Server-aided key generation · Oblivious pseudorandom functions

A. R. Beresford et al. (Eds.): CANS 2022, LNCS 13641, pp. 122–142, 2022.
https://doi.org/10.1007/978-3-031-20974-1_6

1 Introduction

Imagine an online application where users sign their messages so that, later on, they can be held accountable. For example, in an online banking application, the banking server may ask a user to sign her requests to transfer funds to other accounts. Later on, in case of dispute, the server may wish to prove to a third party (i.e., in court) that the user had indeed requested a specific transfer operation.

Most applications, however, do not ask users to sign their messages, mainly because of the usability issues of (certified) cryptographic keys—since users must carry around their private keys (e.g., in a smart-card) or store them in all of their devices.

The most popular solution to allow users to sign their messages is based on so-called "cloud-based PKI certificates". In a nutshell, each user has a certified key-pair stored at a server in the cloud; users authenticate to the server—via passwords or one-time codes—and ask it to sign messages on their behalf. Owing to their usability, cloud-based PKI certificates are used by a number of companies [2,3,35] and national administration authorities [20]. Some of those companies are included as certification authorities—or so called "qualified e-signature service providers"—in the single framework for digital signatures promoted by the European Union eIDAS Regulation [14].

Cloud-based PKI certificates, however, impair non-repudiation of messages signed by a user. In particular, a third party may not be able to tell if signatures issued by the server on behalf of a user, had been actually authorized by that user. Since the server holds a user key-pair and could sign any message on her behalf, that user could deny having signed a message (i.e., by claiming that the signature was produced by the server without her consent).

An ideal solution to enable users to sign their messages and to guarantee non-repudiation would (i) retain the usability of password-only techniques like cloud-based PKI certificates, and (ii) ensure that no server can impersonate or frame a user by issuing a signature on her behalf.

We note that available password-based protocols to derive cryptographic keys are ill-suited for the problem at hand. For example, techniques that derive cryptographic keys from low-entropy passwords (e.g., the PBKDF2 key derivation function) are vulnerable to off-line brute-force attacks. In particular, an adversary with access to the user public key could easily enumerate the passwords until it finds the corresponding secret key. Further, online protocols like Password-Authenticated Key Establishment (PAKE) cannot guarantee non-repudiation. In particular, PAKE allows two parties — e.g., a user and a server — to derive a symmetric key from a common password. As such, if a PAKE-derived key is used for signing messages, one may not ascribe the signature to the user as the signature may have been produced by the server. Further, by holding the user password, the server can compute the signing key offline and frame the user at will. The same shortcoming holds in case of "asymmetric" PAKE protocols (e.g., [25])—where the server holds a one-way function of the user password: a malicious server could brute-force the password (off-line) and use it to compute the signing key.

1.1 Our Contributions

In this paper we define, instantiate and evaluate a cryptographic protocol named Auditable Asymmetric Password Authenticated Public Key Establishment ($\mathsf{A^2PAKE}$), that enable users to obtain certified key-pairs. The protocol is "password-only", as users are only required to remember a (low-entropy) password. At the same time, the protocol ensures non-frameability of honest users. Hence, if keys obtained via $\mathsf{A^2PAKE}$ are used to sign messages, signatures are non repudiable and users can be held accountable for the messages they sign. Further, the protocol is *auditable*. Namely, a third party with input a public key produced by an execution of $\mathsf{A^2PAKE}$ and the corresponding protocol transcript, can tell whether the protocol execution went through correctly and produced the alleged public key.

As in threshold PAKE protocols [26–28, 31], we use multiple servers to ensure that no single server can run an off-line brute-force attack on the user password and obtain her signing key. More in detail, we consider a setting where there are two servers. The "main" server helps users obtain their keys-pairs, whereas the "secondary" server supports its peer in authenticating users and cooperates to produce auditing evidence. As long as one of the servers is honest, (i) the other malicious server cannot run off-line brute-force attacks on user passwords, and (ii) a third party can pinpoint a public key output by the protocol to the user that engaged in that protocol execution. In more detail, we make the following contributions:

New Ideal Functionality. We introduce the $\mathsf{A^2PAKE}$ ideal functionality. The functionality captures the security requirements of non-repudiation of keys generated by a (possibly malicious) user and non-frameability from a malicious server. $\mathsf{A^2PAKE}$ allows for the generation of fresh and auditable key-pairs for registered users and provides forward-security, namely, secret keys generated in the past are secure even if the user password is leaked. We defer further discussion to Sect. 4.

Efficient Universal-Composable Secure Protocol. We provide a protocol that realizes the $\mathsf{A^2PAKE}$ functionality and prove it secure against static adversaries in the universal composability framework of Canetti [11]. The main ingredient of our protocol is a distributed oblivious pseudo-random function (TOPRF) introduced by Jarecki *et al.* [23]. Roughly speaking, the user inputs their password to the TOPRF protocol to derives a long-term secret key for a signature scheme, which public key was previously certified by the two servers. Once the long-term key is available to the user, we achieve forward-security by running a distributed key-generation protocol so the user obtains a fresh key-pair that she certifies using their long-term key. We defer more details on how we can provide auditability to Sect. 5.

Implementation. As our last contribution, we provide a prototype implementation written in Python and present the results of an evaluation carried out to assess throughput, latency, and communication overhead. We defer more details to Sect. 6.

A Note on Identities. We note that auditing a protocol transcript—i.e., ascribing a public key to an identity—requires establishing and verifying user "identities". In other words, each user registering to the system must prove her identity, so that key-pairs created using $\mathsf{A^2PAKE}$ can be later attributed to such identity. In our solution, this requirements translate to a registration phase that runs over an authenticated channel; nevertheless, all communication after the registration phase uses unauthenticated channels. We note that many password-based protocols require authenticated channels during user registration [24, 31]. Our protocol is, however, agnostic to how the identity of the registering user is established. For example, identities could be bound to an ID by asking the user to submit a copy of her ID during registration [3, 35]. If the registering user holds an eIDs, it can be used to sign the registration transcript with a smart-card reader attached to a PC [20]. Later on, during auditing, a public key can be ascribed to the holder of the ID (or eID) used during registration. Another option would be for users to register with an email address: during registration, the user must prove ownership of an email address (e.g., by receiving a one-time code in her inbox). During auditing, a public key can be attributed to the holder of the email address used during registration. In a similar fashion, identities can be verified by means of mobile phone numbers and one-time codes sent via SMS messages.

2 Related Work

There is a vast literature on password-based cryptography. The basic idea is to design protocols with strong cryptographic guarantees by relying solely on low-entropy passwords.

The popular PKCS#5 [32] standard shows how to use passwords to derive symmetric keys to be used for (symmetric) encryption or message authentication. Password-Authenticated Key Exchange (PAKE) [6, 7] enables two parties, holding the same password, to authenticate mutually and to establish a symmetric key. In the client-server settings, compromise of the password database at the server may be mitigated by splitting passwords among multiple servers, typically in a threshold manner [26–28].

Password-Authenticated Public-Key Encryption (PAPKE) [8] enhances public-key encryption with passwords. In particular, generation of a key-pair is bound to a password and so is encryption. Hence, decryption of a ciphertext reveals the original message only if the password used at encryption time matches the one used when the public key was generated. Thus, PAPKE preserves confidentiality despite a man-in-the-middle that replaces the public key of the receiver (as long as the adversary does not guess the receiver's password when generating its public key). Password-based signatures were proposed in [17] where the signature key is split between the user and a server and the user's share is essentially their password—so that the user can create signatures with the help of the server. We note that in [17] the server does not authenticate users and that it could recover the full signing key of any user by brute-forcing the password. User authentication and resistance to brute-force attacks for password-based signatures were introduced in [9], that requires users to carry a personal device such as a smart card. Password-hardening services [15, 29, 30, 34] enable password-based authentication while mitigating the consequences of password database leak. The idea behind these is to pair the authentication server with a "cryptographic service" that blindly computes (keyed) hashes of the passwords. The password database at the authentication service stores such hashes so that a leak of the database does not reveal passwords, unless the key of the cryptographic service is also compromised. PASTA by Agrawal *et al.* [1] and PESTO by Baum *et al.* [5] propose password-based threshold token-based authentication where the role of an identity provider in a protocol such as OAuth[1] is

[1] https://oauth.net/.

distributed across several parties and the user obtains an authentication token only by authenticating to a threshold number of servers; both protocols are based on threshold oblivious pseudo-random functions [23].

To the best of our knowledge, the closest cryptographic primitive to $\mathsf{A^2PAKE}$ is Password-Protected Secret Sharing [4,10,21–23]. PPSS allows users to securely store shares of a secret—e.g., a cryptographic key— on a set of servers while reconstruction is only feasible by using the right password or by corrupting more than a given threshold of servers. In principle, PPSS may be used to design a password-based signature scheme (without auditability or forward-security) as follows. During the PPSS registration phase, a user generates a key-pair and secret-shares the signing key across the participating servers. During the PPSS reconstruction phase, that user inputs their password to recover the signing key; the latter could be used to produce signatures that can be verified by whoever holds the corresponding verification key. This design has, however, a number of shortcomings. First, the PPSS functionality [21] does not authenticate users: as shown in [13], lack of user authentication provides a bigger surface for online guessing attacks as the server cannot distinguish adversarial attempts to guess a password from a request to reconstruct the secret by a legitimate user. Similarly, PPSS does not account for auditability. Finally, using PPSS to recover a signing-key does not provide forward-secrecy. That is, if a password is leaked the adversary could forge signatures also for past sessions. Our definition of $\mathsf{A^2PAKE}$ explicitly allows the main server to authenticate the user, caters for auditability, and ensures forward secrecy.

Looking ahead, we notice that our protocol realizing $\mathsf{A^2PAKE}$ makes use of an authenticated channel for the registration phase and of a TOPRF, also used in the protocol realizing the PPSS proposed in [22]. Indeed, with some adjustments we could have based our protocol on the PPSS functionality directly, instead of the combination of TOPRF and authenticated channels. However, this might hide an important design choice of our scheme (i.e., the need of an authenticated channel at registration time) without significantly simplifying the proof of security. In our opinion, the protocol presented using OPRF and authenticated channels as primitives is more clear and easy to understand.

3 Preliminaries

Digital Signatures. A signature scheme is a triple of probabilistic polynomial time algorithms $(\mathsf{KGen}, \mathsf{Sign}, \mathsf{Vf})$. We consider the standard notion of correctness and existential unforgeability under chosen-messages attacks [18].

NIZK Proof of Knowledge. A non-interactive zero-knowledge (NIZK) proof system for a relation $\mathcal{R}$ is a tuple $\mathcal{NIZK} = (\mathsf{Init}, \mathsf{P}, \mathsf{V})$ of PPT algorithms such that: Init on input the security parameter outputs a (uniformly random) common reference string $\mathsf{crs} \in \{0,1\}^\lambda$; $\mathsf{P}(\mathsf{crs}, x, w)$, given $(x, w) \in \mathcal{R}$, outputs a proof π; $\mathsf{V}(\mathsf{crs}, x, \pi)$, given instance x and proof π outputs 0 (reject) or 1 (accept). In this paper we consider the notion of *NIZK with labels*[2], that are NIZKs where P and V additionally take as input a

[2] In our protocol the client sends a NIZK proof-of-knowledge of discrete log, to avoid that the adversary re-uses such proofs in different protocol executions we label the NIZKs using the session identifiers of the protocol executions.

label $L \in \mathcal{L}$ (e.g., a binary string). A NIZK (with labels) is *correct* if for every $\mathsf{crs} \in_\$ \mathsf{Init}(1^\lambda)$, any label $L \in \mathcal{L}$, and any $(x, w) \in \mathcal{R}$, we have $\mathsf{V}(\mathsf{crs}, L, x, \mathsf{P}(\mathsf{crs}, L, x, w)) = 1$. We consider a property called *simulation-extractable soundness*. Roughly speaking, the definition of simulation extractable soundness assumes the existence of a Init algorithm that, additionally to the common reference string, outputs a *simulation trapdoor* tp_s that allows to simulate proofs, and a *extraction trapdoor* tp_e that allows to extract the witness from valid (no-simulated) proofs. The security guarantee is that, even in presence of an oracle that simulates proofs, an adversary cannot produce a valid proof that cannot be extracted. Further we require the NIZK to be adaptive composable zero-knowledge—by now the standard zero-knowledge notion for NIZK, first considered by Groth [19].

Universal Composability. We use the Universal Composability model (Canetti [11]) to define security. As opposed to other game-based definitions, the simulation-based security offered by the UC model allows to formulate security statements that do not need to make any assumptions on the distribution of the passwords (see Canetti *et al.* [12] for further discussion). We review some basic notions of the UC model. In a nutshell, a protocol Π UC-realizes an ideal functionality $\mathcal{F}$ with setup assumption $\mathcal{G}$ if there exists a PPT simulated adversary $\mathcal{B}^*$ (also called the simulator) such that no PPT environment $\mathcal{Z}$ can distinguish an execution of the protocol Π which can interact with the setup assumption $\mathcal{G}$ from a joint execution of the simulator $\mathcal{B}^*$ with the ideal functionality $\mathcal{F}$. The environment $\mathcal{Z}$ provides the inputs to all the parties of the protocols, decides which parties to corrupt (we consider static corruption, where the environment decides the corrupted parties before the protocol starts), and schedules the order of the messages in the networks. When specifying an ideal functionality, we use the "delayed outputs" terminology of Canetti [11]. Namely, when a functionality $\mathcal{F}$ *sends a public (resp. private) delayed output* M *to party* $\mathcal{P}_i$ we mean that M is first sent to the simulator (resp. the simulator is notified) and then forwarded to $\mathcal{P}_i$ only after acknowledgement by the simulator. We sometimes say *the ideal functionality* $\mathcal{F}$ *registers the tuple* X *(resp. retrieves* X*)*, in this case we assume that the ideal functionality is stateful and keeps an internal database where stores all the registered tuples.

4 A²PAKE

We start by recalling the settings and high-level goals of our primitive. We assume a number of clients $\{\mathcal{C}_1, \ldots, \mathcal{C}_n\}$, and two servers $\mathcal{S}_1, \mathcal{S}_2$.[3]

The goal is to design a password-only protocol that allows clients to obtain a key-pair that can be used, e.g., to sign messages. Server $\mathcal{S}_1$ is designated as the "main" server. It is the one that learns the client's public key as output by the protocol—so it can verify messages signed by the client. The other server is designated as "support" server and helps the main one to authenticate clients and, most importantly, to produce auditing evidence.

Obtained key-pairs should be forward secure, i.e., leakage of a password should not compromise key-pairs computed before leakage took place. Further, the protocol should

[3] For simplicity, we consider only the two-server scenario, and leave the extension of the ideal functionality to more than two servers as future work.

Functionality $\mathcal{F}_{\mathsf{A^2PAKE}}$:

The functionality interacts with clients $\mathcal{C}_1, \ldots, \mathcal{C}_n$, two servers $\mathcal{S}_1$ and $\mathcal{S}_2$, an auditor $\mathcal{A}$, and an adversary $\mathcal{B}$.

Registration: On $(\mathtt{register}, \mathsf{sid}, \mathsf{pw})$ from $\mathcal{C}_j$.
If there is no record of the form $(\mathsf{sid}, C_j, *) \in \mathcal{D}_{\mathsf{pw}}$ then create a fresh record $(\mathsf{sid}, C_j, \mathsf{pw})$ in $\mathcal{D}_{\mathsf{pw}}$.
Send delayed output $(\mathtt{registered}, \mathsf{sid}, C_j)$ to $\mathcal{S}_1, \mathcal{S}_2$.

Init: On $(\mathtt{init}, \mathsf{sid}, j, \mathsf{qid}, \mathsf{pw})$ from a party $\mathcal{P} \in \{\mathcal{C}_j, \mathcal{S}_1, \mathcal{S}_2\}$: //pw is empty if $\mathcal{P} \in \{\mathcal{S}_1, \mathcal{S}_2\}$
Send $(\mathtt{init}, \mathsf{sid}, j, \mathsf{qid}, \mathcal{P})$ to $\mathcal{B}$.
Record that $\mathcal{P}$ initialized the session.
If $\mathcal{C}_j, \mathcal{S}_1$ and $\mathcal{S}_2$ initialized the session, then record the session $(\mathsf{sid}, j, \mathsf{qid})$ is active for $\mathcal{S}_1$ and $\mathcal{C}_j$.
If $\mathcal{P} = \mathcal{C}_j$ and $(\mathsf{sid}, C_j, \mathsf{pw}) \notin \mathcal{D}_{\mathsf{pw}}$ then record the session $(\mathsf{sid}, j, \mathsf{qid})$ is invalid and notify the adversary.
Sample $(\mathsf{pk}, \mathsf{sk}) \in_{\$} \mathsf{KGen}(1^\lambda)$ and register $(\mathsf{sid}, j, \mathsf{qid}, \mathsf{sk}, \mathsf{pk})$.
If $(\mathtt{corrupt}(\mathsf{sid}, j) \vee \mathcal{C}_j \in \mathbb{C})$ then send $(\mathsf{sid}, j, \mathsf{qid}, \mathsf{pk}, \mathsf{sk})$ to the adversary, else send $(\mathsf{sid}, j, \mathsf{qid}, \mathsf{pk})$.

Test Password: On $(\mathtt{test}, \mathsf{sid}, j, \mathsf{qid}, \mathsf{pw}')$ from $\mathcal{B}$.
Assert $\mathcal{S}_1$ and $\mathcal{S}_2$ have initialized the session $(\mathsf{sid}, j, \mathsf{qid})$ or $\mathcal{S}_1, \mathcal{S}_2 \in \mathbb{C}$.
If $(\mathsf{sid}, C_j, \mathsf{pw}') \in \mathcal{D}_{\mathsf{pw}}$ then reply $\mathcal{B}$ with $\mathtt{correct}$ and set $\mathtt{corrupt}(\mathsf{sid}, j) \leftarrow 1$,
else set the session $(\mathsf{sid}, j, \mathsf{qid})$ as invalid and reply $\mathcal{B}$ with $\mathtt{wrong}$.

New Key: On message $(\mathtt{newkey}, \mathsf{sid}, j, \mathsf{qid}, \mathcal{P}, \tilde{\mathsf{pk}}, \tilde{\mathsf{sk}})$ from $\mathcal{B}$.
Assert $\mathcal{P} \in \{\mathcal{C}_j, \mathcal{S}_1\}$ and that session $(\mathsf{sid}, j, \mathsf{qid})$ is active for $\mathcal{P}$;
Mark session $(\mathsf{sid}, j, \mathsf{qid})$ for $\mathcal{P}$ as finalized;
If $\mathcal{P} \in \mathbb{C} \vee \mathtt{corrupt}(\mathsf{sid}, j)$ then set $(\mathsf{pk}, \mathsf{sk}) := (\tilde{\mathsf{pk}}, \tilde{\mathsf{sk}})$ else retrieve $(\mathsf{sid}, j, \mathsf{qid}, \mathsf{pk}, \mathsf{sk})$.
If the session $(\mathsf{sid}, j, \mathsf{qid})$ is invalid set $\mathsf{pk} = \perp$,
if $\mathcal{P} = \mathcal{S}_1$ and session valid then register $(\mathsf{sid}, \mathsf{qid}, C_j, \mathsf{pk})$ in $\mathcal{D}_{\mathsf{pk}}$;
If $\mathcal{P} = \mathcal{S}_1$ then send $(\mathtt{output}, \mathsf{sid}, j, \mathsf{qid}, \mathsf{pk})$ to $\mathcal{S}_1$;
If $\mathcal{P} = \mathcal{C}_j$ then send $(\mathtt{output}, \mathsf{sid}, j, \mathsf{qid}, \mathsf{sk})$ to $\mathcal{C}_j$;

Invalid: On message $(\mathtt{invalid}, \mathsf{sid}, j, \mathsf{qid}, \mathcal{P})$ from $\mathcal{B}$ and $\mathcal{P} \in \{\mathcal{C}_j, \mathcal{S}_1\}$.
Send $(\mathtt{output}, \mathsf{sid}, j, \mathsf{qid}, \perp)$ to $\mathcal{P}$ and mark the session finalized for $\mathcal{P}$.

Audit: On message $(\mathtt{audit}, \mathsf{sid}, \mathsf{qid}, j, \mathsf{pk})$ from party $\mathcal{S}_1$.
NON-FRAMEABILITY. If $\mathcal{C}_j, \mathcal{S}_2 \in \mathbb{H} \wedge \neg \mathtt{corrupt}(\mathsf{sid}, j) \wedge (\mathsf{sid}, \mathsf{qid}, C_j, \mathsf{pk}) \notin \mathcal{D}_{\mathsf{pk}}$ then set $b \leftarrow 0$.
NON-REPUDIABILITY. If $\mathcal{S}_1 \in \mathbb{H} \wedge \mathcal{C}_j \in \mathbb{C} \wedge (\mathsf{sid}, \mathsf{qid}, C_j, \mathsf{pk}) \in \mathcal{D}_{\mathsf{pk}}$ then set $b \leftarrow 1$.
All other cases wait for a bit b' from the adversary $\mathcal{B}$ and set $b \leftarrow b'$.
Send to the auditor $\mathcal{A}$ the message $(\mathtt{audit}, \mathsf{sid}, \mathsf{qid}, j, \mathsf{pk}, b)$.

Fig. 1. Ideal functionality $\mathcal{F}_{\mathsf{A^2PAKE}}$

be audible. That is, any third party should be able to tell, given a protocol transcript π and the corresponding public key pk, if the protocol execution went through correctly and should be able to ascribe the public key to the user, say u, involved in π. Thus, if signatures verify with respect to the public key pk, then u cannot repudiate signed messages.

The ideal functionality that realizes $\mathsf{A^2PAKE}$, namely $\mathcal{F}_{\mathsf{A^2PAKE}}$, is depicted in Fig. 1. The functionality is parameterised by a security parameter λ and an asymmetric public key generation algorithm KGen. It receives from the environment the set $\mathbb{C}$ of corrupted parties. Let $\mathbb{H}$ be the set of honest parties (that is, the complement of $\mathbb{C}$). Let $\mathcal{D}_{\mathsf{pk}}$ (resp. $\mathcal{D}_{\mathsf{pw}}$) be the database of the completed sessions (resp. of registered passwords). Both $\mathcal{D}_{\mathsf{pk}}$ and $\mathcal{D}_{\mathsf{pw}}$ are initialized to empty.

The **Registration** interface allows a client to register her passwords pw. Notice that, even if both servers are corrupted, the password is not leaked. Similarly to the notion of strong asymmetric PAKE [25], the only way for an attacker to leak the password is by using the "test password" interface. Note that each password is registered together with a sid and an identifier for the client, which will thereafter thus be used as an identifier for the password that is linked to the client after registration.

Any party can initialize a session via the **Init** interface. In case **Init** is called by a client, it must also submit her password; in case the password has not been registered, the session is marked as invalid. Once a client and the two servers have initialized the same session (identified by qid), the session is marked as active and a fresh key pair is sampled, if either the password or the client are corrupted then the secret key is revealed to the adversary. Note that qid is actually an identifier linked to a concrete signing key generation session; the complete tuple $\mathsf{sid}\|\mathsf{qid}\|\jmath$ will be used later as a global session identifier (for instance, as input to the **Audit** phase.)

The ideal functionality needs inputs from both servers whenever the adversary uses the **Test Password** interface, which captures password guessing attacks. That is, the adversary must wait that the honest server initializes a new session to be able to test a password during such session), therefore: (i) if at least one of the server is honest then only "online" brute-force attacks on the password are possible; (ii) if both servers are corrupted then the attacker can carry out "off-line" brute-force attack on the password. The latter property requires the simulator of our protocol, playing the role of the ideal-model adversary, to be able to detect off-line password tests made by the real-world adversary. However, when both the servers are corrupted, the adversary can carry out the tests locally, namely without sending any message. Thus, this seems to require a non-black-box assumption which would allow the simulator to extract a password test from the adversary. PAKEs based on OPRFs, such as [25], face similar extractability issues. To the best of our knowledge, the random oracle model offers the most natural solution to these issues.

The **New Key** interface accepts inputs from the adversary of the form

$$(\mathtt{newkey}, \mathsf{sid}, \jmath, \mathsf{qid}, \mathcal{P}, \tilde{\mathsf{sk}}, \tilde{\mathsf{pk}}).$$

As a result, a signing key pair will be registered for client $\jmath$ linked to the corresponding identifier $\mathsf{sid}, \jmath, \mathsf{qid}$. This new key generation can be influenced by the adversary in different ways: (1) it can decide when the parties receive the outputs, as we assume that the adversary has complete control over the network, (2) when the client is corrupted or its password is corrupted (resp. the server is corrupted) then the adversary can decide the outputs of the functionality for the client (resp. the server). In this case the output of the client $\mathcal{C}_\jmath$ (resp. the corrupted server) at session $(\mathsf{sid}, \mathsf{qid}, \jmath)$ is $\tilde{\mathsf{sk}}$ (resp. $\tilde{\mathsf{pk}}$). We stress that this is unavoidable when the parties are corrupted, as the adversary has full control of them, and thus of their outputs. When the password is corrupted but the client is honest, for simplicity, we let the adversary decide the output of the client anyway because the security properties of our functionality cannot be guaranteed, since the adversary could impersonate the client.

Notice that by design, the functionality guarantees a form of forward-secrecy for the generated secret keys: even if a client password is leaked by the adversary, the key-pairs output before password leakage took place are still unknown to the adversary. We elaborate further on this at the end of this section. Also notice that the ideal functionality registers the key-pair in the database of key-pairs only when the server $\mathcal{S}_1$ is honest. Indeed, when the server $\mathcal{S}_1$ is corrupted, it can always deny to have executed the protocol.

Finally, the ideal functionality assures non-frameability and non-repudiablity. For the former, an auditor cannot be convinced that a public key belongs to an honest client if that client did not actually produced the key-pair jointly with the servers. This holds as long as the password of the client is not corrupted. We stress that both servers could be malicious but still cannot frame the client, if, for example, the password of the client has high-entropy. For non-repudiability, an honest server with a transcript of an execution with a (possibly malicious) client, can always convince the auditor that the secret key matching the public key in the transcript belongs to that client. Technically, both non-frameability and non-repudiability are enforced by the ideal functionality by maintaining the database $\mathcal{D}_{\mathsf{pk}}$ of the registered public keys. For non-frameability, the ideal functionality makes the auditor $\mathcal{A}$ output 0 whenever the client is honest (and the its password is not leaked) and the alleged public key is not present in the database of the registered public keys. For non-repudiability the ideal functionality makes the auditor output 1 whenever the server is honest and the tuple client/associated public key is present in database (with the corresponding $\mathsf{sid}\|\mathsf{qid}$ tags). In all the other cases, the adversary can set the output as it prefers. The reason is that non-frameability is a property aiming to protect an honest client, while non-repudiability cannot hold when a malicious server refutes to engage in the audit protocol.

A Note on Forward-Secrecy. As we mentioned, the functionality $\mathcal{F}_{\mathsf{A^2PAKE}}$ guarantees a form of forward-secrecy, as key-pairs output before password leakage took place are still private. Yet, as our envisioned use of the functionality is to generate keys for a digital signature scheme, forward-secrecy alone would not be enough to prevent an adversary from "back-dating" a signature. In particular, an adversary that has learned the password of a honest client at time t, may still obtain a fresh key-pair, and sign messages with an arbitrary date (e.g., earlier than t). As in any forward-secure signature scheme, we need a mechanism to bound a key-pair to an "epoch", so that only signatures that verify under the public key of the current epoch are considered valid. Such mechanism may be realized using the field qid of the command `init` of the functionality. In particular, some well-defined bits of qid could be used to encode the current epoch—notice that the three parties $\mathcal{C}_j$, $\mathcal{S}_1$ and $\mathcal{S}_2$ must agree on the qid (thus the epoch) to successfully conclude a key generation and that the generated public key is binded to qid. Finally, the verification procedure of the signature scheme would have to check the association between the public key and the epoch, which we can achieve using the audit interface offered by the functionality.

Our functionality can guarantees forward-secrecy even when both the servers are corrupts. The main reason is that our functionality assumes that only the clients can register themselves. However, looking ahead in our protocol, we need to assume an authenticated channel to enforce such a strong condition. We notice that if we

Functionality $\mathcal{F}_{\mathtt{TOPRF}}$:

The functionality is parametrized by a positive integer t and runs with a client C servers $\mathcal{S}_1, \mathcal{S}_2$, and an adversary $\mathcal{A}$. It maintains a table $T(\cdot,\cdot)$ initialized with null entries and a vector $tx(\cdot)$ initialized to 0.

Initialization:

- On $(\mathtt{Init}, \mathsf{sid})$ from S_i, $i \in \{1,2\}$
  - send $(\mathtt{Init}, \mathsf{sid}, S_i)$ to the adversary $\mathcal{A}$,
  - mark S_i active.
- On $(\mathtt{Init}, \mathsf{sid}, \mathcal{A}, k)$ from $\mathcal{A}$
  - check that k is unused and $k \neq 0$
  - record $(\mathsf{sid}, \mathcal{A}, k)$
  - return $(\mathtt{Init}, \mathsf{sid}, \mathcal{A}, k)$ to the adversary $\mathcal{A}$.
- On $(\mathtt{InitComplete}, \mathsf{sid}, S_i)$ for $i \in \{1,2\}$ from the adversary $\mathcal{A}$, if $\mathcal{S}_i$ is active
  - send $(\mathtt{InitComplete}, \mathsf{sid})$ to S_i
  - mark S_i as *initialized.*

Evaluation:

- On $(\mathtt{eval}, \mathsf{sid}, \mathsf{ssid}, x)$ from $\mathcal{P} \in \{C, \mathcal{A}\}$,
  - if tuple $(\mathsf{ssid}, \mathcal{P}, *)$ already exists, ignore.
  - Else, record $(\mathsf{ssid}, \mathcal{P}, x)$ and send $(\mathtt{eval}, \mathsf{sid}, \mathsf{ssid}, \mathcal{P})$ to $\mathcal{A}$.
- On $(\mathtt{SndrComplete}, \mathsf{sid}, \mathsf{ssid}, i)$ for $i \in \{1,2\}$ from $\mathcal{A}$
  - ignore if S_i is not initialized.
  - Else set $tx(i) := tx(i) + 1$ and send $(\mathtt{SndrComplete}, \mathsf{sid}, \mathsf{ssid})$ to S_i.
- On $(\mathtt{RcvComplete}, \mathsf{sid}, \mathsf{ssid}, \mathcal{P}, p^*)$ for $\mathcal{P} \in \{C, \mathcal{A}\}$ from $\mathcal{A}$,
  - retrieve $(\mathsf{ssid}, \mathcal{P}, x)$ if it exists, and ignore this message if there is no such tuple or if any of the following conditions fails:
    (i) if $p^* = 0$ then $tx(1) > 0$ and $tx(2) > 0$,
    (ii) if both servers are honest then $p^* = 0$.
  - If $p^* = 0$ then set $tx(1) := tx(1) - 1$ and $tx(2) := tx(2) - 1$.
  - If $T(p^*, x)$ is null, pick ρ uniformly at random from $\{0,1\}^t$ and set $T(p^*, x) := \rho$.
  - Send $(\mathtt{eval}, \mathsf{sid}, \mathsf{ssid}, T(p^*, x))$ to $\mathcal{P}$.

Fig. 2. Ideal functionality $\mathcal{F}_{\mathrm{TOPRF}}$ (adapted from [23]). Label 0 is reserved for the honest execution.

additionally let the adversary register the clients, we would loose forward-secrecy when the servers are both corrupts, since the adversary could re-register a client and could produce a valid key for the attacked client for a given epoch. The only way to avoid this generic attack seems to carefully define forward-secrecy in our context, which we defer for future works.

5 UC-secure Protocol

5.1 Setup Assumptions

We leverage functionalities $\mathcal{F}_{\mathsf{AUTH}}, \mathcal{F}_{\mathsf{KRK}}, \mathcal{F}_{\mathsf{RO}}$ and $\mathcal{F}_{\mathsf{CRS}}$, which model authenticated channels, key-registration, random oracle, and common reference string (see the full version of the paper for their formal definitions). The authenticated channel is used only once by each client at registration time. The key-registration functionality allows to create a PKI between the servers and the auditor. Note that we do not need a *global* functionality for the PKI functionality. Indeed, in our protocol we just need that the messages signed by the second server could be verified by the first server during registration time and by the auditor to achieve non-repudiation. We need a common reference string for the NIZK that we make use of, while we use $\mathcal{F}_{\mathtt{RO}}$ for the coin-tossing part of our protocol.

Additionally and more crucially, we use a threshold oblivious pseudo-random function, formalized by the ideal functionality $\mathcal{F}_{\mathrm{TOPRF}}$. In Fig. 2, we present a simplified version of the functionality of Jarecki et al. in [23] which fits our purpose. The ideal functionality $\mathcal{F}_{\mathrm{TOPRF}}$ produces uniformly random outputs, even in case of adversarial choice of the involved private key and also maintains a table $T(\cdot,\cdot)$ storing the PRF evaluations and a counter vector $tx(\cdot)$ for each server, used to ensure the involvement of the 2 servers on each completed evaluation. In particular, note that in Fig. 2 the adversary may initialize servers with a fixed key of his choice through `Init` or without choosing the key himself (using `InitComplete`). The counter is thus controled by him through `SndrComplete`, while the PRF evaluation is completed (and possibly sent to the client) in `RcvComplete`.

Our protocol makes use of the multi-session extension of the ideal functionality $\mathcal{F}_{\mathrm{TOPRF}}$ (that we identify with the *hatted* functionality $\hat{\mathcal{F}}_{\mathrm{TOPRF}}$). When the functionality $\hat{\mathcal{F}}_{\mathrm{TOPRF}}$ is called we thus include a sub-session identifier ssid. Specifically, on input $(\mathsf{sid}, \mathsf{ssid}, m)$ to $\hat{\mathcal{F}}_{\mathrm{TOPRF}}$, the functionality first checks there is a running copy of $\mathcal{F}_{\mathrm{TOPRF}}$ with session identifier ssid and, if so, activates that copy with message m. Otherwise, it invokes a new copy of $\mathcal{F}_{\mathrm{TOPRF}}$ with input (ssid, m), and links to this copy the sub-session identifier ssid. For further details, see [11]. In our concrete usage (see Figs. 3 and 4) there are two layers of executions: the client's index (j) is used as the sub-session identifier when calling $\hat{\mathcal{F}}_{\mathrm{TOPRF}}$ (thus in the protocol each client uses a different instance of $\mathcal{F}_{\mathrm{TOPRF}}$); the query identifier qid (used in the command `init` of $\mathcal{F}_{\mathsf{A^2PAKE}}$), is used as the sub-sub-session identifier when calling $\hat{\mathcal{F}}_{\mathrm{TOPRF}}$.

5.2 Generic Description of Our Protocol

An high-level description of our protocol realizing $\mathcal{F}_{\mathsf{A^2PAKE}}$ from the setup assumptions $\mathcal{F}_{\mathtt{RO}}, \mathcal{F}_{\mathrm{AUTH}}, \mathcal{F}_{\mathrm{KRK}}, \mathcal{F}_{\mathrm{TOPRF}}$ and $\mathcal{F}_{\mathsf{CRS}}$ is given in Figs. 3 to 5. The protocol consists of three phases: *registration*, in which the client registers with the two servers, *authentication*, in which the client and the server $\mathcal{S}_1$ produce a fresh and authenticated key pair, and *audit*, in which the server can prove to the auditor the relation between clients and public keys.

At registration of a new client, the servers initialize a new fresh instance of $\mathcal{F}_{\mathrm{TOPRF}}$ by calling $\hat{\mathcal{F}}_{\mathrm{TOPRF}}$ with sub-session identifier the index relative to the client. Then, the client and the two servers run the $\hat{\mathcal{F}}_{\mathrm{TOPRF}}$ (on sub-sub-session identifier a special string `signup` used for registration), where the client's private input is the password whereas each server uses its secret key share as private input. The client receives the evaluation of the OPRF that is parsed as a secret key $\mathsf{sk}^* \in \mathbb{Z}_q$ for a DLOG-based signature scheme[4]. The client, using the interfaces provided by $\mathcal{F}_{\mathrm{AUTH}}$, can send an authenticated

[4] The choice of the signature scheme is arbitrary and taken for the sake of simplicity. Indeed, with minor modifications to the protocol we could use any EUF-CMA secure signature scheme.

Registration Phase

Protocol for Client $\mathcal{C}_j$:

- On $(\mathtt{register}, \mathsf{sid}, \mathsf{pw})$
  - send $(\mathtt{eval}, \mathsf{sid}, j, \mathtt{signup}, \mathsf{pw})$ to $\hat{\mathcal{F}}_{\text{TOPRF}}$
  - send $(\mathtt{CRS}, \mathsf{sid}, \mathcal{C}_j)$ to $\mathcal{F}_{\text{CRS}}$
  - Wait to receive:
    - $(\mathtt{CRS}, \mathsf{sid}, \mathsf{crs})$ from $\mathcal{F}_{\text{CRS}}$
    - $(\mathtt{eval}, \mathsf{sid}, j, \mathtt{signup}, \rho)$ from $\hat{\mathcal{F}}_{\text{TOPRF}}$
  - set $\mathsf{pk}^* = g^\rho$ and $\mathsf{sk}^* = \rho$
  - send $(\mathtt{round1} - \mathtt{reg}, \mathsf{sid}, j, \mathsf{pk}^*)$ using $\mathcal{F}_{\text{AUTH}}$ to $\mathcal{S}_1$ and $\mathcal{S}_2$

Protocol for Server $\mathcal{S}_1$:

- On $(\mathtt{register}, \mathsf{sid}, j)$
  - send $(\mathtt{Init}, \mathsf{sid}, j)$ to $\hat{\mathcal{F}}_{\text{TOPRF}}$,
  - send $(\mathtt{CRS}, \mathsf{sid}, C_j, S_1)$ to $\mathcal{F}_{\text{CRS}}$
  - wait to receive:
    - $(\mathtt{CRS}, \mathsf{sid}, \mathsf{crs})$ from $\mathcal{F}_{\text{CRS}}$
    - $(\mathtt{InitComplete}, \mathsf{sid}, j)$ from $\hat{\mathcal{F}}_{\text{TOPRF}}$
    - $(\mathtt{SndrComplete}, \mathsf{sid}, j, \mathtt{signup})$ from $\hat{\mathcal{F}}_{\text{TOPRF}}$
    - $(\mathtt{round1} - \mathtt{reg}, \mathsf{sid}, j, \mathsf{pk}^*)$ from $\mathcal{F}_{\text{AUTH}}$
    - $(\mathtt{round2} - \mathtt{reg}, \sigma_2)$ from $\mathcal{S}_2$
  - assert $\mathsf{Vf}(pk_2, \mathsf{sid}\|j\|\mathsf{pk}^*, \sigma_2) = 1$ and store $(\mathsf{sid}, j, \mathsf{pk}^*, \sigma_2)$

Protocol for Server $\mathcal{S}_2$:

- At first activation
  - sample $s_2 \in_\$ \mathbb{Z}_q$
  - send $(\mathtt{register}, \mathsf{sid}, s_2)$ to $\mathcal{F}_{\text{KRK}}$
- On $(\mathtt{register}, \mathsf{sid}, j)$
  - send $(\mathtt{init}, \mathsf{sid}, j)$ to $\hat{\mathcal{F}}_{\text{TOPRF}}$
  - wait to receive:
    - $(\mathtt{InitComplete}, \mathsf{sid}, j)$ from $\hat{\mathcal{F}}_{\text{TOPRF}}$
    - $(\mathtt{SndrComplete}, \mathsf{sid}, j, \mathtt{signup})$ from $\hat{\mathcal{F}}_{\text{TOPRF}}$
    - $(\mathtt{round1} - \mathtt{reg}, \mathsf{sid}, j, \mathsf{pk}^*)$ from $\mathcal{F}_{\text{AUTH}}$
  - compute $\sigma_2 \leftarrow \mathsf{Sign}(\mathsf{sk}_2, \mathsf{sid}\|j\|\mathsf{pk}^*)$
  - send $(\mathtt{round2} - \mathtt{reg}, \sigma_2)$ to $\mathcal{S}_1$.

Fig. 3. Part of the protocol realizing the registration phase of the functionality $\mathcal{F}_{\mathsf{A^2PAKE}}$

message to both servers with the public key $\mathsf{pk}^* = g^{\mathsf{sk}^*}$. We notice that using the $\mathcal{F}_{\text{AUTH}}$ setup assumption for the last step is necessary, to bind a client identity with public key pk^*, moreover, this is the only step where we use an authenticated channel. Finally, the server $\mathcal{S}_2$ signs the public key pk^* produced and sends such signature to $\mathcal{S}_1$, thus witnessing the successful registration of the client.

During authentication, a registered client and the two servers run again the instance of the $\mathcal{F}_{\text{TOPRF}}$ associated to the client. Once again, the secret input of the client is a password whereas each server inputs the secret key share picked during registration. Thus, the client recovers the secret key sk^*. Concurrently, client and server run a simple coin-tossing protocol to produce a DLOG key pair. Such protocol ensures randomly

Authentication Phase

Protocol for Client C_j:

- On $(\texttt{init}, \mathsf{sid}, j, \mathsf{qid})$
  - set $\mathsf{sid}' := (\mathsf{sid}\|\mathsf{qid}\|j)$
  - sample $x_C \leftarrow \mathbb{Z}_q$ and set $y_C \leftarrow g^{x_C}$
  - compute $\pi \leftarrow \mathsf{P}(\mathsf{crs}, \mathsf{sid}', y_C, x_C)$
  - send $(\texttt{RO}, \mathsf{sid}'\|y_C\|\pi)$, receive $(\texttt{RO}, h)$ from $\mathcal{F}_{\texttt{RO}}$
  - send $(\texttt{round1}, \mathsf{sid}', h)$
- On $(\texttt{round2}, \mathsf{sid}', x_S)$ from $\mathcal{S}_1$
  - set $\mathsf{pk} = g^{x_C \cdot x_S}$
  - compute $\sigma_C \leftarrow \mathsf{Sign}(\mathsf{sk}^*, \mathsf{sid}'\|\mathsf{pk})$
  - send $(\texttt{round3}, \mathsf{sid}', y_C, \pi, h, \mathsf{pk}, \sigma_C)$ to $\mathcal{S}_1$
  - output $\mathsf{sk} = x_C \cdot x_S$

Protocol for Server $\mathcal{S}_1$:

- On $(\texttt{init}, \mathsf{sid}, j, \mathsf{qid})$,
  - set $\mathsf{sid}' := (\mathsf{sid}\|\mathsf{qid}\|j)$
  - wait to receive $(\texttt{SndrComplete}, \mathsf{sid}, j, \mathsf{qid})$ from $\hat{\mathcal{F}}_{\texttt{TOPRF}}$
  - sample $x_S \in_\$ \mathbb{Z}_q$
  - send $(\texttt{round2}, \mathsf{sid}', x_S)$ to C_j.
- On $(\texttt{round3}, \mathsf{sid}', y_C, \pi, h, \mathsf{pk}, \sigma_C)$ from C_j
  - assert the output $(\texttt{RO}, h')$ of $\mathcal{F}_{\texttt{RO}}$ on input $(\mathsf{sid}'\|y_C\|\pi)$ fulfills $h' = h$
  - assert $\mathsf{V}(\mathsf{crs}, \mathsf{sid}', y_C, \pi) = 1$
  - assert $\mathsf{Vf}(\mathsf{pk}^*, \mathsf{sid}'\|\mathsf{pk}, \sigma_C) = 1$
  - assert $\mathsf{pk} = y_C^{x_S}$
  - register the tuple $(\mathsf{sid}, \mathsf{qid}, j, \mathsf{pk})$

Protocol for Server $\mathcal{S}_2$:

- On $(\texttt{Init}, \mathsf{sid}, \mathsf{qid}, j)$,set $\mathsf{sid}' := (\mathsf{sid}\|\mathsf{qid}\|j)$, wait to receive $(\texttt{SndrComplete}, \mathsf{sid}, j, \mathsf{qid})$ from $\hat{\mathcal{F}}_{\texttt{TOPRF}}$

Fig. 4. Part of the protocol realizing the authentication of $\mathcal{F}_{\mathsf{A^2PAKE}}$.

generated keys. Additionally, the last message of the client, which defines uniquely the key-pair, is authenticated with a signature under the key pk^*. Server $\mathcal{S}_1$ accepts the public key only if it were correctly generated by the client and the signature on that public key verifies under key pk^*.

At auditing time, if server $\mathcal{S}_1$ wants to prove that a public key pk belongs to a client C_j, the server can simply show to the auditor (1) the signature received by $\mathcal{S}_2$ at registration time on pk^* and the client's identity j, and (2) the signature received by the client at authentication time on pk. In this way the auditor checks that $\mathcal{S}_2$ witnessed the registration of pk^* by client C, and that pk was certified by pk^*. More in detail, the auditor checks that σ_C is a valid signature of $\mathsf{sid}\|\mathsf{qid}\|j\|\mathsf{pk}$ under key pk^*, and that σ_2 is a valid signature of the message $\mathsf{sid}\|j\|\mathsf{pk}^*$ under key pk_2—the public key of $\mathcal{S}_2$. If both checks succeed, the auditor concludes that pk belongs to client C.

Theorem 1. *Let* KGen *be the algorithm that upon input the description of a group outputs* $\mathsf{pk} = g^{\mathsf{sk}}$ *and* $\mathsf{sk} \in_\$ \mathbb{Z}_q$. *The protocol described in Figs. 3 to 5* UC-realizes

Audit Phase

Protocol for Server $\mathcal{S}_1$:

- On $(\texttt{audit}, \mathsf{sid}, \mathsf{qid}, j)$
  - retrieve $(\mathsf{sid}, j, \mathsf{pk}^*, \sigma_2)$ and $(\mathsf{sid}, \mathsf{qid}, j, \mathsf{pk}, \sigma_C)$
  - send $(\texttt{audit}, \mathsf{sid}, \mathsf{qid}, j, \mathsf{pk}^*, \sigma_2, \mathsf{pk}, \sigma_C)$ to $\mathcal{A}$

Protocol for Audit $\mathcal{A}$:

- On $(\texttt{audit}, \mathsf{sid}, \mathsf{qid}, j, \mathsf{pk}^*, \sigma_2, \mathsf{pk}, \sigma_C)$ from $\mathcal{S}_1$
  - send $(\texttt{retrieve}, \mathsf{sid}, \mathcal{S}_2)$ to $\mathcal{F}_{\text{KRK}}$ and receive $(\mathsf{sid}, \mathcal{S}_2, \mathsf{pk}_2)$
  - compute $b_0 \leftarrow \mathsf{Vf}(\mathsf{pk}_2, \mathsf{sid}\|j\|\mathsf{pk}^*, \sigma_2)$ $b_1 \leftarrow \mathsf{Vf}(\mathsf{pk}^*, \mathsf{sid}\|\mathsf{qid}\|j\|\mathsf{pk}, \sigma_C)$
  - output $b_0 \wedge b_1$

Fig. 5. Part of the protocol realizing the audit of $\mathcal{F}_{\mathsf{A^2PAKE}}$.

the ideal functionality $\mathcal{F}_{\mathsf{A^2PAKE}}$ *parametrized by* KGen *against static adversaries with setup assumptions* $\mathcal{F}_{\mathtt{RO}}$, $\mathcal{F}_{AUTH}$, $\mathcal{F}_{KRK}$, $\mathcal{F}_{CRS}$ *and* $\hat{\mathcal{F}}_{TOPRF}$.

We give some intuitions behind the proof; the formal proof is in the full version [16]. To prove security we need to show a simulated adversary $\mathcal{B}^*$ that interacts with the ideal functionality $\mathcal{F}_{\mathsf{A^2PAKE}}$ and an environment $\mathcal{Z}$, such that the environment cannot distinguish such interaction with an interaction with the real protocol. First we show how non-frameability and no-repudiability are guaranteed in the real world as they are in the ideal world.

Non-frameability. Suppose that $\mathcal{Z}$ instructs the corrupted server $\mathcal{S}_1$ to engage the audit phase, $\mathcal{Z}$ feeds the server with an input $(\mathsf{sid}, \mathsf{qid}, C_j, \tilde{\mathsf{pk}})$ and the client C_j is honest. Moreover, the public key $\tilde{\mathsf{pk}}$ was never produced as the output of an interaction between the client C_j and the servers. Thus, unless the password of the client C_j was corrupted, in the ideal world, the auditor will surely output 0. We claim that, unless the password of the client was corrupted, also in the real world, the auditor will output 0 with overwhelming probability. The reason is that, by the security of the $\mathcal{F}_{\mathtt{TOPRF}}$ the secret key $\mathsf{sk}^* = \mathtt{TOPRF}(\mathsf{pw})$ associated to the client C_j is known only by the honest client C_j. Notice that, not even the environment knows the secret key since it does not have direct access to the outputs of $\mathcal{F}_{\mathtt{TOPRF}}$ during a protocol execution. However, the environment could send an `eval` commands to the OPRF (for example through a man-in-the-middle attack) with the password of the client and obtain the secret key. In this case our simulator sends the same password to the test interface of $\mathcal{F}_{\mathsf{A^2PAKE}}$, and in case of a correct guess reveal the secret key of the signature scheme to the environment. Thus the environment gets to know the secret key only when the password is corrupted. In the case where the password was not corrupted the environment does not know the secret key, the only way to make the auditor accept is to forge a signature, which we can reduce to the existential unforgeability of the signature scheme.

Non-repudiability. The honest server can make the auditor output 1 in the real world by sending a valid signature on the tuple client/public key. In the ideal world, the auditor outputs 1 if the tuple was registered by the ideal functionality. Thus, the simulator needs to enforce that a new public key is recorded in the database of the public key of the ideal functionality only when the malicious client sends the message `round3` which contains a valid signature on the client-public-key tuple.

Equivocate, Extract Inputs and Simulate Key Generation. Equivocate and extract the inputs during registration phase is rather straightforward. Indeed, the inputs of the clients are directly sent to the ideal functionality $\mathcal{F}_{\mathrm{TOPRF}}$. The most interesting part is to make sure the key pair output by the ideal functionality $\mathcal{F}_{\mathsf{A2PAKE}}$ does agree with the transcript generated by the simulator. Recall that in this part of the protocol first the client sends $h = \mathtt{RO}(\mathsf{sid}'\|y_c\|\pi)$, then the server sends x_S and finally the client sends (y_c, π). When the client is honest and the server $\mathcal{S}_1$ is malicious, the simulator chooses the value y_C adaptively once received both the message x_S from the server and the public key from the ideal functionality. Notice it can do so by programming the random oracle and by simulating the NIZK of knowledge of x_C. When the client is malicious and the server $\mathcal{S}_1$ is honest, we can extract the value x_C from the client thanks to the extractability of the NIZK and the observability of the random oracle, and then simulate x_S setting it to be $\mathsf{sk} - x_C$.

5.3 Concrete Instantiation

We now describe a concrete instantiation of $\mathcal{F}_{\mathsf{A2PAKE}}$ that generated DLOG-based key-pairs and that is based on the 2HashDH instantiation of $\mathcal{F}_{\mathrm{TOPRF}}$, presented in [23]. For concreteness, we use the same cyclic group to generate key-pairs as output by $\mathcal{F}_{\mathsf{A2PAKE}}$ and to instantiate the underlying distributed OPRF.

Let G be a cyclic group of prime order p with generator g. Also let H, H_1, and H_2 be three hash functions ranging over $\{0,1\}^\ell$, G, and $\mathbb{Z}_q$, respectively. Given an input x and a key k from $\mathbb{Z}_q$, function $f_k(x)$ is defined as $H_2(x, H_1(x)^k)$ (where key k is shared among the servers). Figure 6 describes the full protocol. Note that, for clarity, Fig. 6 assumes a direct communication channel between $\mathcal{S}_1$ and $\mathcal{S}_2$. In a real deployment scenario those two parties may not have a long-lasting connection and the client may proxy messages from one server to another; the latter settings is the one we have used in the evaluation of Sect. 6. We substitute the index j of the client from the generic description of the protocol with a unique username. During registration, client $\mathcal{C}$ and servers $\mathcal{S}_1$, and $\mathcal{S}_2$, run the OPRF protocol. The private input for the client is password pw, while the private input for server $\mathcal{S}_i$ is a freshly sampled key share k_i (for $i \in \{1,2\}$). The private client's output is set as its secret key sk^* with corresponding public key pk^*. The public key is sent by the client to both servers via an authenticated channel so that pk^* can be bound to a client identity. We do not specify how this channel should be implemented and gave a few examples in Sect. 1. One option is for the client to sign pk^* with its digital ID so to bound the public key to an ID number. Server $\mathcal{S}_2$ signs the public key received by the client and provides $\mathcal{S}_1$ with the signature—thereby providing a witness of a correct client registration. At the end of the registration, the user must only remember username $\mathcal{C}$ and password pw; $\mathcal{S}_2$ remembers the client's username and the key-share k_2, whereas $\mathcal{S}_1$ stores the tuple $(\mathcal{C}, k_1, \mathsf{pk}^*, \sigma_2)$. During authentication, the distributed OPRF protocol is run (as during registration) so that the client can recover

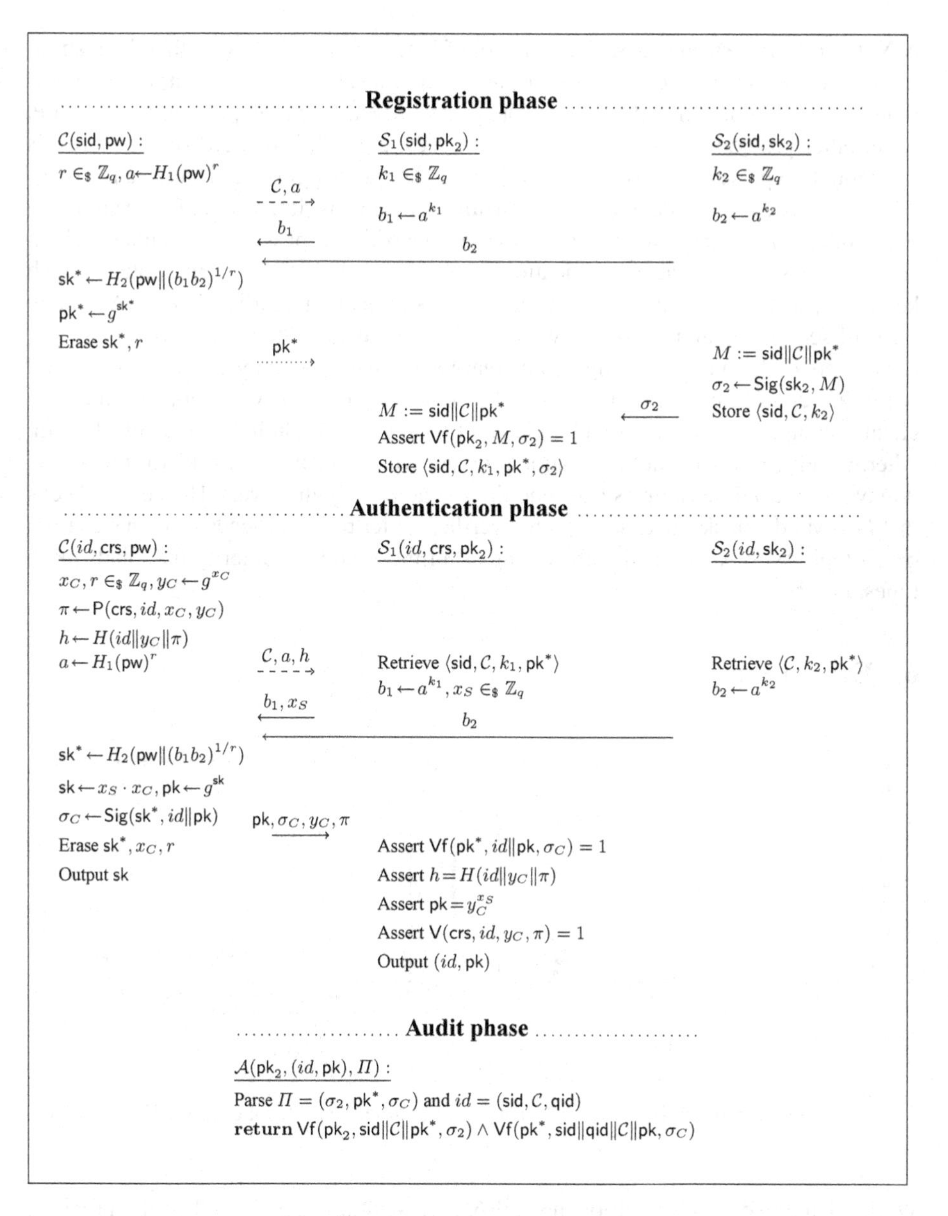

Fig. 6. Concrete instantiation of $\mathsf{A^2PAKE}$. Dashed arrows depict broadcast messages. The dotted arrow in the registration phase denotes an authenticated channel. In the authentication phase the three parties receive in input an identifier $id = (\mathsf{sid}, \mathcal{C}, \mathsf{qid})$.

sk^*. We consider the audit phase as a non-interactive procedure where the auditor takes in input the public key of the server $\mathcal{S}_2$, the tuple (id, pk) describing the client and its public key and a proof Π that pk is indeed its public key.

A Note on Forward-Secrecy. The protocol of Fig. 6 realizes $\mathcal{F}_{\mathsf{A^2PAKE}}$, thereby guaranteeing forward-secrecy: even if a user password is leaked, key-pairs output by executions of the authentication protocol before password leakage took place are still secure. As in other protocols that ensure forward-secrecy, e.g., [33], forward-secrecy alone is not enough to prevent an adversary from "back-dating" a signature. That is, a notion of "time" is needed to decide whether a signature can be considered valid. For example, in our application scenario, an adversary that has learned the password of a honest client at time t, may still run the authentication protocol on behalf of the client, obtain a fresh key-pair, and sign messages with arbitrary timestamps (e.g., earlier than t). As in any forward-secure signature scheme, we need a mechanism to bound a key-pair $\mathsf{sk}_t, \mathsf{pk}_t$ to an "epoch" t, so that only signatures that verify under the public key of the current epoch are considered valid. This could be achieved in many ways. For example, the client may upload key-pairs to a public and timestamped bulletin board or blockchain. Alternatively, during the authentication protocol when the client uses sk^* to sign $id\|\mathsf{pk}$, it may include a timestamp ts and send the signature to both servers. Hence, $\mathcal{S}_2$ checks that ts is valid, checks that the signature verifies under pk^*, and sends its own signature over $id\|\mathsf{pk}\|ts$ to party $\mathcal{S}_1$, thereby acting as a timestamping authority that binds pk to timestamp ts.

6 Evaluation

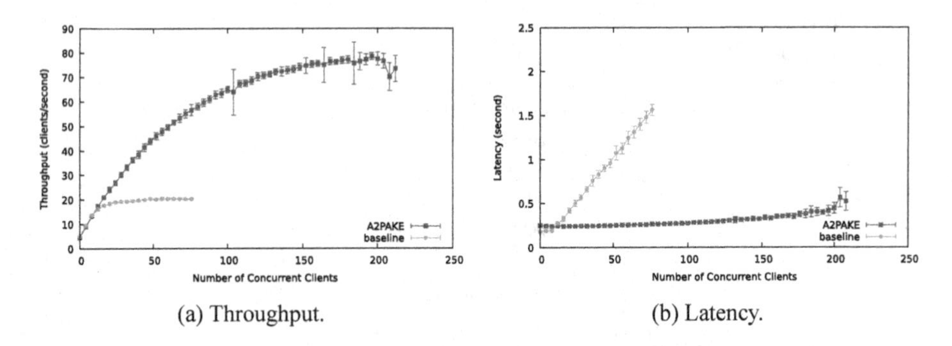

(a) Throughput. (b) Latency.

Fig. 7. Comparison of $\mathsf{A^2PAKE}$ versus the baseline protocol over WAN.

We implemented a prototype of the $\mathsf{A^2PAKE}$ instantiation presented in the previous section. The prototype was written in Python with the Charm-crypto[5] library for cryptographic operations. We instantiated ECDSA over elliptic curve `prime192v1` as the digital signature scheme; thus signature generation and verification take one and two point multiplications, respectively. Further each signature amounts to two elements in $\mathbb{Z}_q$. We used the same curve to instantiate the $\mathsf{2HashDH}$ [23] distributed OPRF. Random oracles were instantiated with SHA256.

[5] http://charm-crypto.io/.

Theoretical Overhead. We now provide a theoretical evaluation of the computation and communication overhead of the protocols in Fig. 6. For elliptic curve operations, we only report the number of point multiplications (mults), including there the computation of multiples of a given point. During registration, the client computes 4 mults and 2 hashes. Apart from a username, the client sends two group elements and a signature. This signature is the one that $\mathcal{S}_2$ sends to $\mathcal{S}_1$ at the end of the registration protocol in Fig. 6; we decide to use the client as a proxy between the two servers because in a real deployment the two servers will not likely have a long-lasting connection (and may not even know their end-points). During authentication, the client computes 6 mults, one signature and 3 hashes. Apart from a username, the client sends 3 group elements, a signature, a proof of knowledge of discrete log (one group element and one element in $\mathbb{Z}_q$), and one hash. At registration time, server $\mathcal{S}_1$ computes a single exponentiation and verifies the validity of a signature; it sends one group element. During authentication, $\mathcal{S}_1$ computes one exponentiation and one hash. It also verifies a signature and a proof-of-knowledge of discrete log (two mults). $\mathcal{S}_1$ sends one group element and one element in $\mathbb{Z}_q$. During registration, server $\mathcal{S}_2$ computes one exponentiation and one signature; it sends one group element and a signature (to the client that will forward it to $\mathcal{S}_1$). During authentication, $\mathcal{S}_2$ computes one exponentiation and sends one group element.

Baseline Comparison. As a baseline comparison for $\mathsf{A^2PAKE}$, we implement a simple client-server protocol that allows the server to authenticate the client and both of them to generate an asymmetric key pair—where the secret key is only learned by the client. In particular, client and server run a distributed coin-tossing protocol similar to the one of Fig. 6 (e.g., the client sends g^{x_C} for random x_C, the server sends random x_S, the client sets $\mathsf{sk} = x_C \cdot x_S$ and $\mathsf{pk} = g^{\mathsf{sk}}$). Further, the client derives a MAC key from the password (by using PBKDF2) and authenticates the public key pk. The server uses the password to derive the same MAC key and accepts pk only if the MAC sent by the client is valid. Note that such protocol does not ensure non-repudiation (since either party could have created and MACed a key-pair), but it is a straightforward example of how to authenticate clients and create fresh key-pairs by using passwords.

Experiments. We setup the two servers on two Amazon EC2 machines (t3a.2xlarge instances) and use four laptops (Intel i7-6500U, 16GB RAM) to instantiate clients. With this setup at hand, we measure latency and throughput for $\mathsf{A^2PAKE}$ and for the baseline protocol. In particular, we send a number of concurrent client requests from the laptops and measure the end-to-end time for a client to complete; we keep increasing the number of requests until the aggregated throughput saturates. Figures 7a and 7b provide average and standard deviations for throughput and latency, respectively. In all of the figures, one data-point is the average resulting from measuring 30 runs.

Results. Latency of $\mathsf{A^2PAKE}$ (from 0.25s with few clients up to 0.56s right before the main server saturates) is slightly higher than the one of the baseline protocol (from 0.18s with few clients up to 0.50s right before the server saturates). However, the baseline protocol saturates the server with a smaller number of clients compared to $\mathsf{A^2PAKE}$. A closer look at the timings showed that most of the overhead in the baseline protocol is due to the PBKDF2 key derivation function. Indeed, this function is designed to slow-down the computation, in order to discourage brute-force attacks. Replacing this function with, say SHA256, would definitely improve the performance, but would pose passwords at greater risk in case of compromise of the password database, and is discouraged according to PKCS series. Using a two-server settings—as in $\mathsf{A^2PAKE}$—allows us to use faster hashes like SHA256 because compromise of a single server does make brute-force attacks any easier. We also measured the time it takes to run the registration protocol of Fig. 6. Since this procedure is executed once per client, we are not interested in throughput but just in latency. We use one client laptop and two servers and measure 100 executions. Registration takes 0.14s on average (standard deviation 0.004s); most of the time is taken by network latency, especially because the client must proxy a signature from the secondary server to the main one.

Acknowledgements. M.I.G. Vasco is supported by research grant PID2019- 109379RB-100 from Spanish MINECO. Antonio Faonio is partially supported by the MESRI-BMBF French-German joint project named PROPOLIS (ANR-20-CYAL-0004–01).

References

1. Agrawal, S., Miao, P., Mohassel, P., Mukherjee, P.: PASTA: PASsword-based threshold authentication. In: ACM CCS 2018. ACM Press (2018)
2. Aruba S.p.A.: Firma Digitale Remota (2019) www.aruba.it
3. Ascertia Limited: SignHub (2019). https://www.signinghub.com/
4. Bagherzandi, A., Jarecki, S., Saxena, N., Lu, Y.: Password-protected secret sharing. In: ACM CCS 2011. ACM Press (2011)
5. Baum, C., Frederiksen, T.K., Hesse, J., Lehmann, A., Yanai, A.: PESTO: proactively secure distributed single sign-on, or how to trust a hacked server. In: IEEE EuroS&P, pp. 587–606. IEEE (2020). https://doi.org/10.1109/EuroSP48549.2020.00044,https://doi.org/10.1109/EuroSP48549.2020.00044
6. Bellare, M., Pointcheval, D., Rogaway, P.: Authenticated key exchange secure against dictionary attacks. In: Preneel, B. (ed.) EUROCRYPT 2000. LNCS, vol. 1807, pp. 139–155. Springer, Heidelberg (2000). https://doi.org/10.1007/3-540-45539-6_11
7. Boyko, V., MacKenzie, P., Patel, S.: Provably secure password-authenticated key exchange using Diffie-Hellman. In: Preneel, B. (ed.) EUROCRYPT 2000. LNCS, vol. 1807, pp. 156–171. Springer, Heidelberg (2000). https://doi.org/10.1007/3-540-45539-6_12
8. Bradley, T., Camenisch, J., Jarecki, S., Lehmann, A., Neven, G., Xu, J.: Password-authenticated public-key encryption. In: Deng, R.H., Gauthier-Umaña, V., Ochoa, M., Yung, M. (eds.) ACNS 2019. LNCS, vol. 11464, pp. 442–462. Springer, Cham (2019). https://doi.org/10.1007/978-3-030-21568-2_22
9. Camenisch, J., Lehmann, A., Neven, G., Samelin, K.: Virtual smart cards: how to sign with a password and a server. In: Zikas, V., De Prisco, R. (eds.) SCN 2016. LNCS, vol. 9841, pp. 353–371. Springer, Cham (2016). https://doi.org/10.1007/978-3-319-44618-9_19
10. Camenisch, J., Lysyanskaya, A., Neven, G.: Practical yet universally composable two-server password-authenticated secret sharing. In: ACM CCS 2012. ACM Press (2012)
11. Canetti, R.: Universally composable security: A new paradigm for cryptographic protocols. In: 42nd FOCS. IEEE Computer Society Press (2001)
12. Canetti, R., Halevi, S., Katz, J., Lindell, Y., MacKenzie, P.: Universally composable password-based key exchange. In: Cramer, R. (ed.) EUROCRYPT 2005. LNCS, vol. 3494, pp. 404–421. Springer, Heidelberg (2005). https://doi.org/10.1007/11426639_24

13. Das, P., Hesse, J., Lehmann, A.: DPaSE: Distributed password-authenticated symmetric encryption. Cryptology ePrint Archive, Report 2020/1443 (2020). https://eprint.iacr.org/2020/1443
14. EU Parliament: eIDAS Regulation (Regulation (EU) N 910/2014) (2014). https://cutt.ly/TCn4MhM
15. Everspaugh, A., Chatterjee, R., Scott, S., Juels, A., Ristenpart, T.: The pythia PRF service. In: USENIX Security 2015. USENIX Association (2015)
16. Faonio, A., González Vasco, M.I., Soriente, C., Truong, H.T.T.: Auditable asymmetric password authenticated public key establishment. Cryptology ePrint Archive, Report 2020/060 (2020). https://eprint.iacr.org/2020/060
17. Petkova-Nikova, S., Pashalidis, A., Pernul, G. (eds.): EuroPKI 2011. LNCS, vol. 7163. Springer, Heidelberg (2012). https://doi.org/10.1007/978-3-642-29804-2
18. Goldwasser, S., Micali, S., Rivest, R.L.: A digital signature scheme secure against adaptive chosen-message attacks. SIAM J. Comput. /textbf17(2), 281–308 (1988)
19. Groth, J.: Simulation-sound nizk proofs for a practical language and constant size group signatures. In: Lai, X., Chen, K. (eds.) ASIACRYPT 2006. LNCS, vol. 4284, pp. 444–459. Springer, Heidelberg (2006). https://doi.org/10.1007/11935230_29
20. Identidad Electrónica para las Administraciones - Gobierno de España: Clave Firma (2019). https://clave.gob.es/clave_Home/dnin.html
21. Jarecki, S., Kiayias, A., Krawczyk, H.: Round-optimal password-protected secret sharing and t-pake in the password-only model. In: Sarkar, P., Iwata, T. (eds.) ASIACRYPT 2014. LNCS, vol. 8874, pp. 233–253. Springer, Heidelberg (2014). https://doi.org/10.1007/978-3-662-45608-8_13
22. Jarecki, S., Kiayias, A., Krawczyk, H., Xu, J.: Highly-efficient and composable password-protected secret sharing (or: How to protect your bitcoin wallet online). In: IEEE EuroS&P, pp. 276–291. IEEE (2016)
23. Jarecki, S., Kiayias, A., Krawczyk, H., Xu, J.: TOPPSS: cost-minimal password-protected secret sharing based on threshold oprf. In: Gollmann, D., Miyaji, A., Kikuchi, H. (eds.) ACNS 2017. LNCS, vol. 10355, pp. 39–58. Springer, Cham (2017). https://doi.org/10.1007/978-3-319-61204-1_3
24. Jarecki, S., Krawczyk, H., Shirvanian, M., Saxena, N.: Device-enhanced password protocols with optimal online-offline protection. In: ASIACCS 16. ACM Press (2016)
25. Jarecki, S., Krawczyk, H., Xu, J.: OPAQUE: an asymmetric pake protocol secure against pre-computation attacks. In: Nielsen, J.B., Rijmen, V. (eds.) EUROCRYPT 2018. LNCS, vol. 10822, pp. 456–486. Springer, Cham (2018). https://doi.org/10.1007/978-3-319-78372-7_15
26. Katz, J., MacKenzie, P., Taban, G., Gligor, V.: Two-server password-only authenticated key exchange. In: Ioannidis, J., Keromytis, A., Yung, M. (eds.) ACNS 2005. LNCS, vol. 3531, pp. 1–16. Springer, Heidelberg (2005). https://doi.org/10.1007/11496137_1
27. Katz, J., Ostrovsky, R., Yung, M.: Efficient password-authenticated key exchange using human-memorable passwords. In: Pfitzmann, B. (ed.) EUROCRYPT 2001. LNCS, vol. 2045, pp. 475–494. Springer, Heidelberg (2001). https://doi.org/10.1007/3-540-44987-6_29
28. Kiefer, F., Manulis, M.: Distributed smooth projective hashing and its application to two-server password authenticated key exchange. In: Boureanu, I., Owesarski, P., Vaudenay, S. (eds.) ACNS 2014. LNCS, vol. 8479, pp. 199–216. Springer, Cham (2014). https://doi.org/10.1007/978-3-319-07536-5_13
29. Lai, R.W.F., Egger, C., Reinert, M., Chow, S.S.M., Maffei, M., Schröder, D.: Simple password-hardened encryption services. In: USENIX Security 2018. USENIX Association (2018)
30. Lai, R.W.F., Egger, C., Schröder, D., Chow, S.S.M.: Phoenix: Rebirth of a cryptographic password-hardening service. In: USENIX Security 2017. USENIX Association (2017)

31. MacKenzie, P., Shrimpton, T., Jakobsson, M.: Threshold password-authenticated key exchange. J. Cryptology **19**(1), 27–66 (2005). https://doi.org/10.1007/s00145-005-0232-5
32. Moriarty, K., Kaliski, B., Rusch, A.: Pkcs#5: Password-based cryptography specification version 2.1. Tech. Rep. RFC8010, Internet Engineering Task Force (IETF) (2017). https://tools.ietf.org/html/rfc8018
33. Park, D.G., Boyd, C., Moon, S.-J.: Forward secrecy and its application to future mobile communications security. In: Imai, H., Zheng, Y. (eds.) PKC 2000. LNCS, vol. 1751, pp. 433–445. Springer, Heidelberg (2000). https://doi.org/10.1007/978-3-540-46588-1_29
34. Schneider, J., Fleischhacker, N., Schröder, D., Backes, M.: Efficient cryptographic password hardening services from partially oblivious commitments. In: ACM CCS 2016. ACM Press (2016)
35. Step Over International: WebSignatureOffice (2019). https://www.websignatureoffice.com/us/

(Augmented) Broadcast Encryption from Identity Based Encryption with Wildcard

Anaïs Barthoulot[1,2(✉)], Olivier Blazy[3], and Sébastien Canard[1]

[1] Orange Innovation, Caen, France
{anais.barthoulot,sebastien.canard}@orange.com
[2] Université de Limoges, XLim, Limoges, France
[3] École Polytechnique, Palaiseau, France
olivier.blazy@polytechnique.edu

Abstract. Several broadcast encryption (BE) constructions have been proposed since Fiat and Naor introduced the concept, some achieving short parameters size while others achieve better security. Since 1994, a lot of alternatives to BE have moreover been additionally proposed, such as the broadcast and trace (BT) primitive which is a combination of broadcast encryption and traitor tracing. Among the other variants of BE, the notion of augmented BE (AugBE), introduced by Boneh and Waters in 2006, corresponds to a BE scheme with the particularity that the encryption algorithm takes an index as an additional parameter. If an AugBE scheme is both message and index hiding, it has been proved that it can generically be used to construct a secure BT scheme. Hence, any new result related to the former gives an improvement to the latter. In this paper, we first show that both BE and AugBE can be obtained by using an identity-based encryption scheme with wildcard (WIBE). We also introduce the new notion of anonymous AugBE, where the used users set is hidden, and prove that it implies index hiding. We then provide two different WIBE constructions. The first one has constant size ciphertext and used to construct a new constant size ciphertext BE scheme with adaptive CPA security, in the standard model (under the SXDH assumption). The second WIBE provides pattern-hiding, a new definition we introduced, and serves as a basis for the first anonymous AugBE scheme (and subsequently a BT scheme since our scheme is also index hiding by nature) in the literature, with adaptive security in the standard model (under the XDLin assumption).

Keywords: Broadcast encryption · Augmented broadcast encryption · Broadcast and trace · Identity based encryption with wildcard

1 Introduction

Broadcast Encryption. Broadcast Encryption (BE), defined by Fiat and Naor [14], is a public key encryption scheme in which the encryption algorithm takes

A. R. Beresford et al. (Eds.): CANS 2022, LNCS 13641, pp. 143–164, 2022.
https://doi.org/10.1007/978-3-031-20974-1_7

as input the public key pk, a message m, a subset $S \subseteq [N]$ of users (N being the number of users in the system), and such that the output ciphertext can be decrypted by any user in the subset S. Regarding related work, Boneh *et al.* ([7]) were the first to achieve constant size ciphertext (i.e., independent of the number of users in the set), but the security was only selective and proven in the generic group model. Recently, Agrawal *et al.* ([3]) achieves constant size parameters with selective security proven in the standard model, combining both pairings and lattices. Lastly, Gay *et al.* ([16]) proposes a scheme based on pairings with constant size ciphertext. As far as we know, this is the only BE scheme with a constant-size ciphertext and providing adaptive security in the standard model.

Augmented Broadcast Encryption. In 2006, Boneh and Waters [9] introduced *Augmented* Broadcast Encryption (AugBE), in which the encryption algorithm takes as additional input an index $\mathsf{ind} \in [N+1]$. As for any BE scheme, the output ciphertext can be decrypted by any user in the subset S, but it is additionally required that the user's index is greater or equal to ind. In particular, if $\mathsf{ind} = N+1$, no one can decrypt. Regarding security, an AugBE scheme should verify both some indistinguishability security (usually called message-hiding in this context), and some index-hiding security to protect the index. Both properties can be defined in a selective or in an adaptive way. The first AugBE constructions [9,15] give a ciphertext's size in $O(\sqrt{N})$. In [17], using both pairings and lattices, Goyal *et al.* propose a selectively secure construction with ciphertext size in $O(N^\epsilon)$ $(0 < \epsilon \leq 1/2)$. Goyal *et al.* also propose in [18] a generic construction of an AugBE based on Positional Witness Encryption (PWE). Their scheme is the first one providing constant parameters. However, currently only few instantiations of PWE exist and all rely on multilinear maps.

Broadcast and Trace. Another variant of BE is the Broadcast and Trace (BT) primitive, i.e., the combination of BE and Traitor Tracing (a message is encrypted for the whole subset $[N]$ but if some subset of traitors uses their secret keys to produce a pirate decoder, then the tracing procedure can identify at least one of the traitors). In [9,18], it was demonstrated that a BT scheme can be constructed from any message and index-hiding AugBE. As for traitor tracing, BT schemes can achieve either public (anyone can find the traitors) or private (traitors can only be retrieved by the owner of a specific master key) traceability, and both cases are useful for different kinds of use cases. Theoretically speaking, public traceability is however known to be harder to achieve [8]. By construction, the Boneh-Waters AugBE definition [9] gives a publicly traceable BT scheme. Goyal *et al.* [17] have recently given another definition of AugBE that is suitable for the private case, where two encryption algorithms called $\mathsf{Encrypt}$ and $\mathsf{Index\text{-}Encrypt}$ need to be defined. Their resulting BT is based on pairings and lattices, has ciphertext in $O(N^\epsilon)$, for $0 < \epsilon \leq 1/2$, and is secretly traceable. In 2020, Zhandry [27] proposed a secretly traceable BT scheme based only on pairings, that has constant size ciphertext, but is only secure in the generic group model. In this paper, we only focus on the Boneh-Waters' AugBE definition.

Our Contributions. In this paper, our idea is to use identity based encryption with wildcard (WIBE) [2] to construct BE schemes. In a WIBE scheme, private keys and ciphertexts are created for vectors of size L (called patterns) over a set $\mathcal{U}$, which contains a wildcard symbol "$\star$". A message encrypted for a pattern $\boldsymbol{P}$ can be decrypted by a secret key made for a pattern $\boldsymbol{P}'$ such that $\boldsymbol{P}'$ belongs to $\boldsymbol{P}$, i.e. if for all $i \in [L]$, $P_i = \star$ or $P_i = P_i'$. More precisely, we provide two main contributions to broadcast encryption:

- we prove (Sect. 3.1) that WIBE can be used to construct BE schemes. Then, any new result on WIBE gives an improvement in the BE setting;
- we also prove (Sect. 3.2) that if WIBE satisfies some additional specific security property it can be used to construct AugBE schemes.

As a complement to those two results, we additionally provide the following minor contributions:

- we propose (Sect. 4) two new WIBE schemes, in the pairing setting and adaptively secure in the standard model. One has constant size ciphertext while the other achieves pattern hiding, a new property we introduced;
- our first WIBE construction gives a constant-size ciphertext BE scheme with adaptive security, proven in the standard model and using only pairings. Compared to the only existing equivalent construction [16], ours does not have constant size secret keys but has shorter public key (Table 1);
- our second WIBE construction gives us the first AugBE scheme, based on pairings, which is adaptively secure in the standard model. Using the generic transformation [9,18], this gives us a BT scheme with similar characteristics. Compare to the state-of-the-art (Table 2), and especially Zhandry's BT scheme [27], we do not reach constant-size ciphertext, but we provide the harder publicly traceable property (while Zhandry's scheme is secretly traceable), and we prove the security of our construction in the standard model while Zhandry's is only proven secure in the generic group model.

Details on our Generic Constructions. We first remark that any subset $S^* \subseteq [N]$ can be represented as a pattern in $\boldsymbol{P} \in \{0, \star\}^N$, where for $j \in [\![1, N]\!]$, $P_j = \star$ if $j \in S^*$ and $P_j = 0$ otherwise. This fact can then be used to associate such pattern to the BE encryption set S. Additionally, any user identity $i \in [N]$ can be represented as a pattern $\boldsymbol{P}^i \in \{0, 1\}^N$ such that for $j \in [\![1, N]\!]$, $P^i_j = 1$ if $i = j$ and $P^i_j = 0$ otherwise. This finally gives us that $i \in S$ iff $\boldsymbol{P}^i$ belongs to $\boldsymbol{P}$. Regarding AugBE, we have noticed that the decrypting condition $i \geq \mathsf{ind}$ for any $i \in [N]$, $\mathsf{ind} \in [N+1]$ can be rewritten as $i \in \{\mathsf{ind}, \mathsf{ind}+1, \cdots, N+1\}$. It follows that the AugBE decrypting condition becomes $i \in S \cap \{\mathsf{ind}, \mathsf{ind}+1, \cdots, N+1\}$. Then, we can associate encryption and key patterns as for the BE scheme to build our AugBE. From that, our generic constructions are then quite straightforward, and the security also comes directly, assuming that the used WIBE is indistinguishable. But in order to obtain AugBE security, we need a WIBE scheme that does not give information about the pattern used in encryption. For this purpose, we introduce such definition that we call *pattern-hiding*, and which may be of independent interest. We finally remark that using a pattern-hiding WIBE, we additionally freely obtain for the AugBE that the used user set is hidden into the ciphertext: this is the anonymity property, which has never been considered until now for AugBE. Saying that, it remains us to build such (pattern-hiding) WIBE.

Details on our WIBE Constructions. We started from the paper of Kim *et al.* [20], who proposes a selectively secure WIBE scheme with constant size ciphertext. We have first adapted it to our keys and ciphertexts patterns, and using [19]'s idea to use composite order bilinear groups we obtained adaptive security. Afterwards, we have moved it from a symmetric bilinear group setting to an asymmetric prime order one, thanks to the combination of the work on Dual Pairing Vector Spaces by Lewko [21] with the one of Chen *et al.* [13].[1] Our first scheme is then adaptively secure under the Symmetric External Diffie-Hellman assumption. We have then modified this first scheme to achieve the pattern-hiding property. Inspired by the work of [25] on attribute-hiding inner product encryption scheme, we used the orthogonality of dual pairing vector spaces to obtain a new WIBE scheme that is adaptively pattern-hiding in the standard model, based on the External Decisional Linear Assumption in $\mathbb{G}_1$ and $\mathbb{G}_2$. We used elements of a base $\mathbb{B}^*$ to build user secret key and elements of base $\mathbb{B}$ for the ciphertext. By choosing wisely the elements of $\mathbb{B}, \mathbb{B}^*$ to use according to the patterns, we obtained that if the secret key pattern belongs to the ciphertext pattern, thanks to the orthogonality property, the elements in the key and in the ciphertext will cancel with each other. However, as we are using dual orthonormal bases of size L, each element of the bases has size L which results in a scheme with linear (in the number of user in the scheme) ciphertext and secret keys, and with quadratic public key.

Broadcast Encryption Efficiency Comparison. In Table 1, we give a comparison between our BE scheme (obtained from the WIBE scheme of Sect. 4.1) and existing BE schemes;

Table 1. BE comparison; "GGM", "Sym" and "Asym" stand for "Generic Group Model", "Symmetric" and "Asymmetric" respectively. Here $t \in \mathbb{N}$, such that t divides N.

Scheme	$\|\mathsf{pk}\|$	$\|\mathsf{sk}_i\|$	$\|\mathsf{ct}\|$	Security	Assumption	Model	Settings
Sect. 4.1	$O(N)$	$O(N)$	$O(1)$	Adaptive	SXDH	Standard	Asym pairings
[3]	$O(\lambda)$	$O(\lambda)$	$O(\lambda)$	Selective	LWE, KOALA	Standard	Lattices
[16]	$O(N^2)$	$O(1)$	$O(1)$	Adaptive	k-Lin	Standard	Asym pairings
[12]	$O(t+N/t)$	$O(N/t)$	$O(t)$	Adaptive	k-Lin	Standard	Asym pairings
[7]	$O(N)$	$O(1)$	$O(1)$	Selective	N-BDHE	GGM	Sym pairings

[1] [4] proposed generic methods to transfer a composite order group scheme into a prime order group scheme via computational pair encodings. We do not used this method as the less general method of [21] and [13] is enough as we are considering simple predicates and encodings.

Our scheme is not as efficient as [3]'s scheme, the most efficient BE scheme in the literature currently. However, our scheme satisfies the stronger adaptive security notion, and is proven secure under standard assumption. Compare to the adaptively secure scheme of [16], we have a bigger user secret key (sk_i) size, but a shorter public key (pk) size. To be exhaustive, [10] proposed a scheme with all parameters in $\mathsf{poly}(\log(N))$, with adaptive security. However, this scheme is using multilinear maps and its security is proven in the GGM. [11] proposed a scheme with all parameters in $\mathsf{poly}(n, \log(N))$ using lattices, but no security proof is given.

Augmented BE and Broadcast and Trace Efficiency Comparison. Using our generic construction and our WIBE instantiation from Sect. 4.2 with $L = N$ we obtain an instantiation of AugBE. The resulting scheme is the first proven adaptively secure in the standard model. Our scheme can itself be turned into a BT scheme, using the generic construction given in [9,18]. Table 2 gives a comparison between our resulting BT and existing ones.

Table 2. BT comparison; tk, "p.o", "c.o", "PWE", "std" "Multi", "P" and "S" mean tracing key, "prime order" "composite order", "Positional Witness Encryption", "standard", "multilinear", "public" and "secret" respectively, $0 < \epsilon \leq 1/2$.

Scheme	$\|\mathsf{pk}\|$	$\|\mathsf{sk}_i\|$	$\|\mathsf{ct}\|$	Users set	Security	Model	tk	Object
Sect. 4.2	$O(N^2)$	$O(N)$	$O(N)$	$\times$	Adaptive	Std	P	Pairings p.o
[27]	$O(N)$	$O(N)$	$O(1)$	Given	Adaptive	GGM	S	Pairings p.o
[17]	$\Omega(N)$	$\Omega(N^2)$	$O(N^\epsilon)$	Given	Selective	GGM	S	Pairing, lattices
[18]	$\mathsf{poly}(1^\lambda)$	$\mathsf{poly}(1^\lambda)$	$\mathsf{poly}(1^\lambda)$	Given	Adaptive	Multi	P	PWE
[9]	$O(\sqrt{N})$	$O(\sqrt{N})$	$O(\sqrt{N})$	Given	Adaptive	GGM	P	Pairing c.o

As we can see our scheme is the first BT scheme (as far as we know) that does not need the description of the user sets to be able to decrypt, and that has security proven in the standard model. Moreover, our scheme is publicly traceable, and uses pairings in prime order group while other existing publicly traceable schemes are using either pairings in composite order group (less secure), or positional witness encryption. Regarding efficiency, our resulting BT scheme has a complexity similar to a "trivial" scheme [26] (with all parameters sizes linear in the number of users). However, the claimed of our work is not to provide a new efficient Broadcast and Trace scheme, but a new generic way to build AugBE schemes, and our generic construction could be more efficient than a "trivial" BT scheme, even if our current instantiation is not. Moreover, we also consider that our proposal has the additional feature of anonymity, that the trivial construction could not have without being less efficient than ours. With such property, the users set is included in the ciphertext and no longer given in the clear which leads to a linear additional computational cost during decryption. Anonymity in the context of BT seems to be an overkill, but we think that for some applications, it might be a real interest to use an anonymous scheme. Please refer to Appendix D of the full version of the paper [5] for more details about anonymity in the context of Broadcast (and Trace) Encryption.

2 Preliminaries

Notations. Let "PPT" denotes "probabilistic polynomial-time" and unless specified, we consider that any PPT adversary $\mathcal{A}$ has output in $\{0,1\}$. For $a, b \in \mathbb{N}$ we denote $\{1, 2, \cdots, a\}$ as $[a]$, and $\{a, a+1, \cdots, b\}$ as $[\![a, b]\!]$. For every finite set S, $x \leftarrow S$ denotes a uniformly random element x from the set S. The security parameter of our schemes is denoted by 1^λ, where $\lambda \in \mathbb{N}$. Vectors are written with **bold face** lower case letters, patterns and matrices with **bold face** upper case letters. Regarding security definitions, we always present them in the adaptive way; the selective version can easily be derived. We also consider in this work only security against Chosen Plaintext Attacks (CPA), and do not consider the *multi-challenge* setting ([16]) for BE. In each security definition, adversary is allowed to query at most $Q \in \mathbb{N}$ secret keys. For BE and its variants, we have chosen to put the description of the target S as an input of the decryption algorithm. A consequence is that for any scheme, the size of S is not taken into account for the computation of the ciphertext's size, unless specified.

2.1 Broadcast Encryption

Definition 1. ***Broadcast Encryption*** *[14,16]. A broadcast encryption scheme consists of algorithms (*$\mathsf{Setup}, \mathsf{KeyGen}, \mathsf{Encrypt}, \mathsf{Decrypt}$*):*

- $\mathsf{Setup}(1^\lambda, 1^N) \rightarrow (\mathsf{pk}, \mathsf{msk})$. *This algorithm takes as input* 1^λ*, the number of users* 1^N *and outputs the public key* pk *and the master secret key* msk.
- $\mathsf{KeyGen}(\mathsf{msk}, i) \rightarrow \mathsf{sk}_i$. *This algorithm gets as input the master secret key* msk *and an index* $i \in [N]$. *It outputs the secret key* sk_i *for user* i.
- $\mathsf{Encrypt}(\mathsf{pk}, S, \mathsf{m}) \rightarrow \mathsf{ct}_S$. *This algorithm gets as input* pk*, a message* m *and a subset* $S \subseteq [N]$. *It outputs a ciphertext* ct_S.
- $\mathsf{Decrypt}(\mathsf{pk}, S, i, \mathsf{sk}_i, \mathsf{ct}_S) \rightarrow \mathsf{m}$ *or* $\perp$. *This algorithm gets as input* $\mathsf{pk}, S, i, \mathsf{sk}_i$ *and* ct_S. *It outputs message* m *or reject symbol* $\perp$.

BE correctness definition is straightforward and given in [5].

Definition 2. ***Adaptive security*** *(IND-CPA-BE) [16]. A BE scheme is said* adaptively secure *(or satisfying* $\mathsf{IND\text{-}CPA\text{-}BE}$ *security) if all PPT adversaries* $\mathcal{A}$ *have at most negligible advantage in the game presented in Fig. 1, where* $\mathcal{A}$*'s advantage is defined as* $\mathsf{Adv}_{\mathcal{A}}^{\mathsf{IND\text{-}CPA\text{-}BE}}(\lambda) := \left|\Pr\left[b' = b\right] - 1/2\right|$.

SETUP: challenger $\mathcal{C}$ runs $\mathsf{Setup}(1^\lambda, 1^N)$ to generate pk and msk, and gives pk to $\mathcal{A}$.
KEY QUERY: $\mathcal{A}$ issues queries to $\mathcal{C}$ for index $i \in [N]$. $\mathcal{C}$ returns $\mathsf{sk}_i \leftarrow \mathsf{KeyGen}(\mathsf{msk}, i)$.
CHALLENGE: $\mathcal{A}$ selects messages $\mathsf{m}_0, \mathsf{m}_1$ and set $S^* \subseteq [N]$ of users. We require that $\mathcal{A}$ has not issued key queries for any $i \in S^*$. $\mathcal{A}$ passes $\mathsf{m}_0, \mathsf{m}_1$ and S^* to $\mathcal{C}$. The latter picks $b \in \{0,1\}$ random and computes $\mathsf{ct}^* \leftarrow \mathsf{Encrypt}(\mathsf{pk}, S^*, \mathsf{m}_b)$ which is returned to $\mathcal{A}$.
KEY QUERY: $\mathcal{A}$ makes queries for index $i \in [N]$ with the restriction that $i \notin S^*$.
GUESS: $\mathcal{A}$ outputs its guess $b' \in \{0,1\}$ for b, and wins the game if $b' = b$.

Fig. 1. IND-CPA-BE security game.

2.2 Augmented Broadcast Encryption

Definition 3. ***Augmented Broadcast Encryption Scheme*** *(AugBE) [9, 18]. An AugBE scheme is a tuple of algorithms (*Setup, Encrypt, Decrypt*):*
- Setup $(1^\lambda, 1^N) \rightarrow (msk, pk, \{sk_1, \cdots, sk_N\})$. *This algorithm takes as input* 1^λ *and the number of users* N. *It outputs a master secret key* msk, *a public key* pk *and secret keys* $\{sk_1, \cdots, sk_N\}$, *where* sk_i *is the secret key for user* i.
- Encrypt $(pk, S, m, \mathsf{ind}) \rightarrow \mathsf{ct}$. *It takes as input the public key* pk, *a set of users* $S \subseteq [N]$, *a message* m, *an index* $\mathsf{ind} \in [N+1]$, *and outputs a ciphertext* ct.
- Decrypt $(pk, sk_i, S, ct) \rightarrow m$ *or* $\bot$. *This algorithm takes as input the public key* pk, *the secret key for* i^{th} *user* sk_i, *a set of users* $S \subseteq [N]$, *a ciphertext* ct *and outputs a message* m *or reject symbol* $\bot$.

AugBE correctness definition is straightforward and given in [5].

Definition 4. ***Message Hiding Security*** *[18]. An AugBE scheme satisfies* adaptive message hiding security *if for every stateful PPT adversary* $\mathcal{A}$, *there exists a negligible function* $\mathsf{negl}(.)$ *such that for every* $\lambda \in \mathbb{N}$, *the advantage of* $\mathcal{A}$ *to win the game presented in Fig. 2 is lower or equal to* $1/2 + \mathsf{negl}(\lambda)$.

SETUP: challenger $\mathcal{C}$ runs $\mathsf{Setup}(1^\lambda, 1^N)$ to get $\mathsf{msk}, \mathsf{pk}, \{\mathsf{sk}_i\}_{i\in[N]}$ and gives pk to $\mathcal{A}$.
KEY QUERY: $\mathcal{A}$ chooses an index $i \in [N]$ and sends it to $\mathcal{C}$, who responds with sk_i.
CHALLENGE: $\mathcal{A}$ chooses messages $\mathsf{m}_0, \mathsf{m}_1$ and a challenge set S^* and sends it to $\mathcal{C}$. $\mathcal{C}$ chooses $b \in \{0,1\}$, runs $\mathsf{ct}^* \leftarrow \mathsf{Encrypt}(\mathsf{pk}, S^*, \mathsf{m}_b, N+1)$ and gives ct^* to $\mathcal{A}$.
KEY QUERY: $\mathcal{A}$ chooses an index $i \in [N]$ and sends it to $\mathcal{C}$, who responds with sk_i.
GUESS: $\mathcal{A}$ outputs its guess $b' \in \{0,1\}$ for b, and wins the game if $b' = b$.

Fig. 2. Adaptive message hiding security game.

Definition 5. ***Index Hiding Security*** *[18]. An AugBE scheme satisfies* adaptive index hiding security *if for every stateful PPT adversary* $\mathcal{A}$, *there exists a negligible function* $\mathsf{negl}(.)$ *such that for every* $\lambda \in \mathbb{N}$, *the advantage of* $\mathcal{A}$ *to win the game presented in Fig. 3 is lower or equal to* $1/2 + \mathsf{negl}(\lambda)$.

SETUP: challenger $\mathcal{C}$ runs $\mathsf{Setup}(1^\lambda, 1^N)$ to get $\mathsf{pk}, \mathsf{msk}, \{\mathsf{sk}_i\}_{i\in[N]}$ and gives pk to $\mathcal{A}$.
KEY QUERY: at each query, $\mathcal{A}$ chooses an index $i \in [N]$ and sends it to $\mathcal{C}$. $\mathcal{C}$ responds with sk_i. Let S be the set of indices for which a key is queried by $\mathcal{A}$.
CHALLENGE: $\mathcal{A}$ chooses a message m, a challenge set S^* and an index $\mathsf{ind} \in [N]$ and sends them to $\mathcal{C}$. If $\mathsf{ind} \in S \cap S^*$, $\mathcal{C}$ aborts. Otherwise, $\mathcal{C}$ chooses $b \in \{0,1\}$, runs $\mathsf{ct}^* \leftarrow \mathsf{Encrypt}(\mathsf{pk}, S^*, \mathsf{m}, \mathsf{ind} + b)$ and gives ct^* to $\mathcal{A}$.
KEY QUERY: at each query, $\mathcal{A}$ chooses an index $i \in [N]$ and sends it to $\mathcal{C}$ who adds i to S. If $\mathsf{ind} \in S \cap S^*$, $\mathcal{C}$ aborts. Otherwise $\mathcal{C}$ responds with sk_i.
GUESS: $\mathcal{A}$ outputs its guess $b' \in \{0,1\}$ for b, and wins the game if $b' = b$.

Fig. 3. Adaptive index hiding security game.

Finally, we introduce a new security property for AugBE: **anonymity**. The definition, close to the one for BE schemes ([24]), provides the adaptive version.

Definition 6. ***Anonymous*** *AugBE (*ANO-AUGE-BE*). We say that an AugBE scheme is adaptively* anonymous *if all adaptive PPT adversaries $\mathcal{A}$ have at most negligible advantage in the game presented in Fig. 4, where $\mathcal{A}$'s advantage is defined as* $\mathsf{Adv}_{\mathcal{A}}^{\text{ano-augbe}}(\lambda) = \left|\Pr\left[b' = b\right] - 1/2\right|$.

SETUP: challenger $\mathcal{C}$ runs $\mathsf{Setup}(1^\lambda, 1^N)$ to get pk, msk, $\{\mathsf{sk}_i\}_{i\in[N]}$, and gives pk to $\mathcal{A}$.
KEY QUERY: $\mathcal{A}$ can issue queries to $\mathcal{C}$ for index $i \in [N]$. $\mathcal{C}$ responds with sk_i.
CHALLENGE: $\mathcal{A}$ selects a message m, two distinct sets $S^0, S^1 \subseteq [N]$ of users and an index $\mathsf{ind} \in [N+1]$. We impose that $\mathcal{A}$ has not issued key queries for any $i \geq \mathsf{ind}$ such that $i \notin S^0 \cap S^1$. The adversary $\mathcal{A}$ passes $\mathsf{m}, S^0, S^1, \mathsf{ind}$ to $\mathcal{C}$. The latter picks a random bit $b \in \{0,1\}$ and computes $\mathsf{ct}^* \leftarrow \mathsf{Encrypt}(\mathsf{pk}, S^b, \mathsf{m}, \mathsf{ind})$ which is returned to $\mathcal{A}$.
KEY QUERY: $\mathcal{A}$ makes queries for index $i \in [N]$ such that if $i \geq \mathsf{ind}$ then $i \in S^0 \cap S^1$.
GUESS: $\mathcal{A}$ outputs its guess $b' \in \{0,1\}$ for b, and wins the game if $b' = b$.

Fig. 4. ANO-AUGE-BE security game.

In the following theorem, we then prove that this new anonymity property is enough to obtain an index-hiding AugBE.

Theorem 1. *If an AugBE scheme is anonymous, then it is also index hiding.*

Proof. Let $\mathcal{C}$ be a challenger and $\mathcal{B}$ be an adversary that wins the index hiding security game with non negligible advantage. Informally, index hiding means that an adversary cannot distinguish between an encryption to index ind and one to index $\mathsf{ind}+1$ without the key $\mathsf{sk}_{\mathsf{ind}}$ and that an adversary cannot distinguish an encryption to index ind and one to index $\mathsf{ind}+1$ when ind is not in the target set S^* ([9]). Thus $\mathcal{B}$ can either distinguish which index was used in encryption when

$\mathsf{ind} \in S^*$ and without knowing $\mathsf{sk}_{\mathsf{ind}}$, or he can distinguish the encryption index when $\mathsf{ind} \notin S^*$, knowing $\mathsf{sk}_{\mathsf{ind}}$. Therefore he either chooses $\mathsf{ind} \in S^*$ or $\mathsf{ind} \notin S^*$ but in this case he asks $\mathsf{sk}_{\mathsf{ind}}$ otherwise he would have advantage equal to $1/2$. We construct, in Fig. 5, an adversary $\mathcal{A}$ that wins the anonymous security game with non negligible advantage.

SETUP: $\mathcal{C}$ runs $\mathsf{Setup}(1^\lambda, 1^N) \to (\mathsf{msk}, \mathsf{pk}, \mathsf{sk}_1, \cdots, \mathsf{sk}_N)$, and sends pk to $\mathcal{A}$, and $\mathcal{B}$.
KEY QUERY: $\mathcal{B}$ chooses $i \in [N]$, sends it to $\mathcal{A}$ who sends it to $\mathcal{C}$. The later sends sk_i to $\mathcal{A}$ who sends it to $\mathcal{B}$.
CHALLENGE: $\mathcal{B}$ chooses a message m, a set S^* of users and an index $\mathsf{ind} \in [N]$ and sends $\mathsf{m}, S^*, \mathsf{ind}$ to $\mathcal{A}$. The latter creates the sets $S^0 = S^* \cap \{\mathsf{ind}, \cdots, N\}$ and $S^1 = S^* \cap \{\mathsf{ind}+1, \cdots, N\}$. $\mathcal{A}$ sends m, S^0, S^1 to $\mathcal{C}$. If for any queried i, $i \in S^0 \wedge i \notin S^1$ then $\mathcal{C}$ aborts. Otherwise, it chooses $b \leftarrow \{0,1\}$ and sets $\mathsf{ct}^* \leftarrow \mathsf{Encrypt}(\mathsf{pk}, S^b, \mathsf{m}, 1)$. It sends ct^* to $\mathcal{A}$ who sends it to $\mathcal{B}$.
KEY QUERY: $\mathcal{A}$ and $\mathcal{B}$ act like in the previous KEY QUERY step. If $i \in S^0 \wedge i \notin S^1$, $\mathcal{C}$ aborts. Otherwise, it sends sk_i to $\mathcal{A}$ who sends it to $\mathcal{B}$.
GUESS: $\mathcal{B}$ outputs its guess b' to $\mathcal{A}$, who outputs it as its guess.

Fig. 5. Construction of ANO-AUGE-BE adversary from index hiding adversary.

We have that if all $\mathcal{B}$'s queries satisfy the game constraints, then all $\mathcal{A}$'s queries have the same property. Thus $\mathcal{A}$'s simulation is perfect and the advantage of $\mathcal{A}$ is the same as $\mathcal{B}$'s. This concludes the proof.

Note 1. If $\mathsf{ind} \in S^*$, then $\mathsf{ind} \in S^0 \wedge \mathsf{ind} \notin S^1$ thus adversary cannot query $\mathsf{sk}_{\mathsf{ind}}$. If $\mathsf{ind} \notin S^*$, then $\mathsf{ind} \notin S^0 \wedge \mathsf{ind} \notin S^1$ thus adversary can query $\mathsf{sk}_{\mathsf{ind}}$ Also index hiding does not imply anonymous. Indeed, in the index hiding security game, in the case where ind is not in the challenge, knowing the challenge set does not help determining if ind or ind + 1 was used for encryption.

2.3 Identity-Based Encryption with Wildcard

Definition 7. *A pattern $\boldsymbol{P}$ is a vector $(P_1, \cdots, P_L) \in \mathcal{U}^L$, where $\mathcal{U}$ is a set with a special wildcard symbol "$\star$", and $L \in \mathbb{N}$. A pattern $\boldsymbol{P}' = (P'_1, \cdots, P'_L)$* belongs *to $\boldsymbol{P}$, denoted $\boldsymbol{P}' \in_\star \boldsymbol{P}$, iff $\forall i \in \{1, \cdots, L\}$, $(P'_i = P_i) \vee (P_i = \star)$. For a pattern $\boldsymbol{P} \in \mathcal{U}^L$, $W(\boldsymbol{P}) = \{i \in [L] | P_i = \star\}$, and $\overline{W}(\boldsymbol{P})$ is the complementary set.*

Definition 8. ***Identity-based Encryption with Wildcard** (WIBE) [2,20]. A WIBE scheme consists of four algorithms:*

- $\mathsf{Setup}(1^\lambda, 1^L)$*: the setup algorithm takes as input 1^λ and the pattern length $L \in \mathbb{N}$. It outputs a public key pk and a master secret key msk.*
- $\mathsf{KeyDer}(\mathsf{msk}, \boldsymbol{P})$*: the key derivation algorithm takes as input msk and a pattern $\boldsymbol{P}$ and create a secret key $\mathsf{sk}_{\boldsymbol{P}}$ for $\boldsymbol{P}$. It can also take as input a secret key $\mathsf{sk}_{\boldsymbol{P}'}$ for a pattern $\boldsymbol{P}'$ instead of msk and derive a secret key for any pattern $\boldsymbol{P} \in_\star \boldsymbol{P}'$.*

- $\mathsf{Encrypt}(\mathsf{pk}, \boldsymbol{P}, \mathsf{m})$: *this algorithm takes as input the public key* pk, *a pattern* $\boldsymbol{P}$ *and a message* m. *It outputs ciphertext* ct *for pattern* $\boldsymbol{P}$.
- $\mathsf{Decrypt}(\mathsf{sk}_{\boldsymbol{P}}, \mathsf{ct}, \boldsymbol{P}')$: *the decryption algorithm takes as input a user secret key* $\mathsf{sk}_{\boldsymbol{P}}$ *for a pattern* $\boldsymbol{P}$ *and a ciphertext* ct *for a pattern* $\boldsymbol{P}'$. *Any user in possession of the secret key for a pattern* $\boldsymbol{P}$ *that belongs to* $\boldsymbol{P}'$ *can decrypt the ciphertext using* $\mathsf{sk}_{\boldsymbol{P}}$, *and the algorithm outputs message* m.

WIBE correctness definition is straightforward and given in [5]. We introduce a new security definition for WIBE: adaptive pattern-hiding security. For lack of space we present both IND-WID-CPA (adaptive indistinguishability CPA security of WIBE) and pattern-hiding security games in one.

Definition 9. ***Adaptive security.*** *The advantage of an adversary* $\mathcal{A}$ *in the game presented in Fig. 6 is defined as* $\mathsf{Adv}_{\mathcal{A}}^{WIBE}(\lambda) = \Pr[\mathcal{A} \text{ wins }] - 1/2$ *for any* $\lambda \in \mathbb{N}$. *A WIBE scheme is* adaptively secure *if for all PPT adversaries* $\mathcal{A}$, *all* $\lambda \in \mathbb{N}$, $\mathsf{Adv}_{\mathcal{A}}^{WIBE}(\lambda)$ *is negligible. For each run of the game, we define a variable* s *as* $s = 0$ *if* $\mathsf{m}^0 \neq \mathsf{m}^1$ *and* $\boldsymbol{P}^0 = \boldsymbol{P}^1 = \boldsymbol{P}^*$, *and* $s = 1$ *if* $\mathsf{m}^0 = \mathsf{m}^1 = \mathsf{m}$ *and* $P^0 \neq P^1$. *The case* $s = 0$ *corresponds to* IND-WID-CPA *security, and the case* $s = 1$ *corresponds to pattern-hiding security. Let* $\mathcal{C}$ *be a challenger.*

Note 2. [1] introduced **anonymous** WIBE, which differs from our definition as in anonymous security game the adversary can only query keys that do not decrypt the challenge ciphertext. In our definition, adversary can query keys that decrypt the challenge ciphertext for both challenge patterns. Also notice that if a WIBE is pattern-hiding, then the decryption algorithm does no longer take as input the pattern associated to the ciphertext.

SETUP: $\mathcal{C}$ runs $\mathsf{Setup}(1^\lambda, 1^L)$ to get pk and msk, and pk is given to $\mathcal{A}$.
KEY QUERY: $\mathcal{A}$ may adaptively query a key for pattern $\boldsymbol{P}$. In response, $\mathcal{A}$ is given the corresponding secret key $\mathsf{sk}_{\boldsymbol{P}} \leftarrow \mathsf{KeyGen}(\mathsf{msk}, \boldsymbol{P})$.
CHALLENGE: $\mathcal{A}$ outputs challenge patterns $\boldsymbol{P}^0, \boldsymbol{P}^1$ and challenge messages $\mathsf{m}_0, \mathsf{m}_1$, subject to the following restrictions:
- if $s = 0$, $\boldsymbol{P} \notin_\star \boldsymbol{P}^*$ for all the key queried pattern $\boldsymbol{P}$.
- if $s = 1$, any key query $\boldsymbol{P}$ verifies one of the following conditions:
  - $\boldsymbol{P} \in_\star \boldsymbol{P}^0 \wedge \boldsymbol{P} \in_\star \boldsymbol{P}^1$
  - $\boldsymbol{P} \notin_\star \boldsymbol{P}^0 \wedge \boldsymbol{P} \notin_\star \boldsymbol{P}^1$

A random bit b is chosen. $\mathcal{A}$ is given $\mathsf{ct}^* \leftarrow \mathsf{Encrypt}(\mathsf{pk}, \boldsymbol{P}^b, \mathsf{m}^b)$.
KEY QUERY: The adversary may continue to issue key queries for additional pattern $\boldsymbol{P}$, subject to the restrictions given above. $\mathcal{A}$ is given the corresponding key $\mathsf{sk}_{\boldsymbol{P}} \leftarrow \mathsf{KeyGen}(\mathsf{msk}, \boldsymbol{P})$.
GUESS: $\mathcal{A}$ outputs a bit b', and wins if $b' = b$.

Fig. 6. Adaptive security game.

2.4 Other Definitions

Definition 10. ***Asymmetric bilinear pairing groups*** *[13].* Asymmetric bilinear groups $\Gamma = (p, \mathbb{G}_1, \mathbb{G}_2, \mathbb{G}_T, g_1, g_2, e)$ *are tuple of prime* p*, cyclic (multiplicative) groups* $\mathbb{G}_1, \mathbb{G}_2$*,* $\mathbb{G}_T$ *of order* p*,* $g_1 \neq 1 \in \mathbb{G}_1$*,* $g_2 \neq 1 \in \mathbb{G}_2$*, and a polynomial-time computable non-degenerate bilinear pairing* $e : \mathbb{G}_1 \times \mathbb{G}_2 \rightarrow \mathbb{G}_T$*, i.e.* $e(g_1^s, g_2^t) = e(g_1, g_2)^{st}$ *and* $e(g_1, g_2) \neq 1$*.*

Note 3. For any group element $g \in \mathbb{G}$, and any vector $\boldsymbol{v}$ of size $l \in \mathbb{N}$, we denote by $g^{\boldsymbol{v}}$ the vector $(g^{v_1}, \cdots, g^{v_l})$. Let $\boldsymbol{u}, \boldsymbol{v}$ be two vectors of length L. Then by $g^{\boldsymbol{u}\cdot\boldsymbol{v}}$, we denote the element g^{α}, where $\alpha = \boldsymbol{u} \cdot \boldsymbol{v} = u_1 \cdot v_1 + u_2 \cdot v_2 + \cdots + u_L \cdot v_L$.

Definition 11. ***Dual pairing vector spaces*** *(DPVS) [13]. For a prime* p *and a fixed (constant) dimension* n*, we choose two random bases* $\mathbb{B} = (\boldsymbol{b}_1, \cdots, \boldsymbol{b}_n)$ *and* $\mathbb{B}^* = (\boldsymbol{b}_1^*, \cdots, \boldsymbol{b}_n^*)$ *of* $\mathbb{Z}_p^n$*, subject to the constraint that they are* ***dual orthonormal****, meaning that* $\boldsymbol{b}_i \cdot \boldsymbol{b}_j^* = 0 \pmod{p}$ *whenever* $i \neq j$*, and* $\boldsymbol{b}_i \cdot \boldsymbol{b}_i^* = \psi \pmod{p}$ *for all* i*, where* ψ *is a uniformly random element of* $\mathbb{Z}_p$*. Here the elements of* $\mathbb{B}, \mathbb{B}^*$ *are vectors and* $\cdot$ *corresponds to the scalar product. We denote such algorithm as* $\mathsf{Dual}(\mathbb{Z}_p^n)$*. For generators* $g_1 \in \mathbb{G}_1$ *and* $g_2 \in \mathbb{G}_2$*, we note that* $e(g_1^{\boldsymbol{b}_i}, g_2^{\boldsymbol{b}_j^*}) = 1$ *whenever* $i \neq j$*.*

Definition 12. ***Symmetric External Diffie-Hellman*** *(SXDH) [13]. The SXDH assumption holds if DDH problems are intractable in both* $\mathbb{G}_1$ *and* $\mathbb{G}_2$*.*

Definition 13. ***eXternal Decision Linear 1 Assumption*** *(XDLin1) [6]. Let* $\mathbb{G}_1, \mathbb{G}_2$ *be cyclic groups of prime order, with generators* (g_1, g_2)*, and* $e : \mathbb{G}_1 \times \mathbb{G}_2 \rightarrow \mathbb{G}_T$ *be a bilinear map. The XDLin1 assumption states that given a tuple* $(g_1, g_1^x, g_1^y, g_1^{ax}, g_1^{by}, g_2, g_2^x, g_2^y, g_2^{ax}, g_2^{by}, g_1^c)$ *it is hard to decide if* $c = a + b$ *or not, for random* $a, b, x, y \in \mathbb{Z}_p$*.*

The **eXternal Decision Linear 2 Assumption** (XDLin2) is defined similarly, except that the last element of the tuple is equal to g_2^c.

3 Generic Construction of AugBE from WIBE

This section presents two generic broadcast encryption constructions from identity based encryption with wildcard: one for a basic BE scheme and the other for an AugBE scheme. For sake of simplicity, we present all proofs in adaptive way (selective way can be adapted) and admit that the number of keys queried is always lower or equal to the maximal number Q of keys that an adversary is allowed to query. The length of patterns is $L \in \mathbb{N}$.

3.1 Broadcast Encryption from WIBE

Let $\mathcal{WIBE} = (w.\mathsf{Setup}, w.\mathsf{KeyDer}, w.\mathsf{Encrypt}, w.\mathsf{Decrypt})$ be an identity based encryption with wildcard scheme for key pattern space $\{0,1\}^L \setminus \{\mathbf{0}^L\}$ and ciphertext pattern space $\{0,\star\}^L \setminus \{\mathbf{0}^L\}$. Let $N \in \mathbb{N}$ be the number of users in the scheme. We construct a BE scheme BE = (Setup, Encrypt, Decrypt) in Fig. 7.

- $\mathsf{Setup}(1^\lambda, 1^N)$: set $L = N$, run $w.\mathsf{Setup}(1^\lambda, 1^N)$ and set $\mathsf{pk} = w.\mathsf{pk}$ and $\mathsf{msk} = w.\mathsf{msk}$.
- $\mathsf{KeyGen}(\mathsf{msk}, i \in [N])$: define $\boldsymbol{P}' \in \{0,1\}^N$ such that for $j \in [\![1, N]\!]$, $P'_j = 0$ if $j \neq i$ and $P'_j = 1$ if $i = j$. Then set $\mathsf{sk}_i = w.\mathsf{KeyDer}(w.\mathsf{msk}, \boldsymbol{P}')$. It outputs sk_i.
- $\mathsf{Encrypt}(\mathsf{pk}, S, \mathsf{m})$: first, associate S with a pattern $\boldsymbol{P}$ in $\{0,\star\}^N$ such that for $j \in [\![1, N]\!]$, $P_j = \star$ if $j \in S$ and $P_j = 0$ otherwise. Finally compute $\mathsf{ct} = w.\mathsf{Encrypt}(\mathsf{pk}, \boldsymbol{P}, \mathsf{m})$ and outputs ct.
- $\mathsf{Decrypt}(\mathsf{pk}, \mathsf{sk}_i, \mathsf{ct}, S)$: gets $\mathsf{m} \leftarrow w.\mathsf{Decrypt}(\mathsf{sk}_i, \boldsymbol{P}, \mathsf{ct})$ if $i \in S$, $\perp$ otherwise.

Fig. 7. Generic construction of BE from WIBE.

Note 4. Encryption for pattern $\mathbf{0}^L$ is not relevant as it means that no one can decrypt, that is why we excluded this pattern of encryption pattern space. Secret key for pattern $\mathbf{0}^L$ is not relevant either as it corresponds to none of the users.

The proof that correctness of the obtained BE follows the one of the underlying WIBE is straightforward. Refer to full version [5] for more details.

Theorem 2. *If $\mathcal{WIBE}$ satisfies adaptive (resp selective)* IND-WID-CPA *security, the obtained BE satisfies adaptive (resp selective)* IND-CPA-BE *security.*

Proof. Let $\mathcal{B}$ be an adversary against IND-CPA-BE security, that wins with non negligible advantage. In Fig. 8 we construct $\mathcal{A}$ from $\mathcal{B}$, and wins against IND-WID-CPA with non negligible advantage. Let $\mathcal{C}$ be a challenger.
If all $\mathcal{B}$'s queries satisfy the game constraints, then all $\mathcal{A}$'s queries have the same property. Thus, $\mathcal{A}$'s simulation is perfect and the advantage of $\mathcal{A}$ is the same as $\mathcal{B}$'s.

3.2 Augmented Broadcast Encryption from WIBE

Let $\mathcal{WIBE} = (w.\mathsf{Setup}, w.\mathsf{KeyDer}, w.\mathsf{Encrypt}, w.\mathsf{Decrypt})$ be an identity based encryption with wildcard scheme for key pattern space $\{0,1\}^L \setminus \{\mathbf{0}^L\}$ and ciphertext pattern space $\{0,\star\}^L$. Let $N \in \mathbb{N}$ be the number of users in the scheme. We construct an AugBE scheme AugBE = (Setup, Encrypt, Decrypt) in Fig. 9.

SETUP: $\mathcal{C}$ runs $\mathsf{Setup}(1^\lambda, 1^N) \to (\mathsf{msk}, \mathsf{pk})$ and gives pk to $\mathcal{A}$, who gives it to $\mathcal{B}$.
KEY QUERY: $\mathcal{B}$ chooses an index $i \in [N]$ and sends it to $\mathcal{A}$, who creates $\boldsymbol{P}^i$, for $j \in [\![1, N]\!]$, such that $P^i_j = 1$ if $i = j$ and $P^i_j = 0$ otherwise. $\mathcal{A}$ sends $\boldsymbol{P}^i$ to $\mathcal{C}$. The latter runs $\mathsf{KeyDer}(\mathsf{msk}, \boldsymbol{P}^i) \to \mathsf{sk}_{\boldsymbol{P}^i}$ and sends $sk_{\boldsymbol{P}^i}$ to $\mathcal{A}$, who sends it as sk_i to $\mathcal{B}$.
CHALLENGE: $\mathcal{B}$ chooses $\mathsf{m}_0, \mathsf{m}_1$ and a set S^*; it sends it to $\mathcal{A}$ who creates the pattern $\boldsymbol{P}^*$, for $j \in [\![1, N]\!]$ s.t. $\boldsymbol{P}^*_j = 0$ if $j \notin S^*$, $P^*_j = \star$ otherwise, and sends $\boldsymbol{P}^*, \mathsf{m}_0, \mathsf{m}_1$ to $\mathcal{C}$. If for any queried $\boldsymbol{P}^i$, $\boldsymbol{P}^i \in_\star \boldsymbol{P}^*$ then $\mathcal{C}$ aborts. Otherwise it chooses $b \in \{0, 1\}$ and runs $\mathsf{ct}^* \leftarrow \mathsf{Encrypt}(\mathsf{pk}, \boldsymbol{P}^*, \mathsf{m}_b)$. It sends ct^* to $\mathcal{A}$ who sends it to $\mathcal{B}$.
KEY QUERY: $\mathcal{B}$ chooses index $i \in [N]$, sends it to $\mathcal{A}$, who creates $\boldsymbol{P}^i$, for $j \in [\![1, N]\!]$, s.t. $P^i_j = 1$ if $i = j$ and $P^i_j = 0$ otherwise. $\mathcal{A}$ sends $\boldsymbol{P}^i$ to $\mathcal{C}$. If $\boldsymbol{P}^i \in_\star \boldsymbol{P}^*$, aborts. Otherwise $\mathcal{C}$ runs $\mathsf{KeyDer}(\mathsf{msk}, \boldsymbol{P}^i) \to \mathsf{sk}_{\boldsymbol{P}^i}$ and sends $sk_{\boldsymbol{P}^i}$ to $\mathcal{A}$, who sends it as sk_i to $\mathcal{B}$.
GUESS: $\mathcal{B}$ outputs a bit b' to $\mathcal{A}$ who outputs it as its guess.

Fig. 8. Construction of IND-WID-CPA adversary from IND-CPA-BE adversary.

- $\mathsf{Setup}(1^\lambda, 1^N)$: set $L = N$, and run $w.\mathsf{Setup}(1^\lambda, 1^N)$ to obtain $w.\mathsf{pk}, w.\mathsf{msk}$. Then for each $i \in [N]$, define $\boldsymbol{P}' \in \{0, 1\}^N$ such that for $j \in [\![1, N]\!]$, $P'_j = 0$ if $j \neq i$ and $P'_j = 1$ if $i = j$. Then set $\mathsf{sk}_i = w.\mathsf{KeyDer}(w.\mathsf{msk}, \boldsymbol{P}')$, $(\mathsf{pk}, \mathsf{msk}) = (w.\mathsf{pk}, w.\mathsf{msk})$. It outputs msk, pk and $\{\mathsf{sk}_i\}_{i \in [N]}$.
- $\mathsf{Encrypt}(\mathsf{pk}, S, \mathsf{ind}, \mathsf{m})$: here $\mathsf{ind} \in [N+1]$. Associate S with a pattern $\boldsymbol{P}^*$ in $\{0, \star\}^N$ such that for $j \in [\![1, N]\!]$, $P^*_j = \star$ if $j \in S$ and $P^*_j = 0$ otherwise. Then define the pattern $\boldsymbol{P}^{\mathsf{ind}} \in \{0, \star\}^N$ such that for $j \in [\![1, N]\!]$, $P^{\mathsf{ind}}_j = 0$ if $j < \mathsf{ind}$ and $P^{\mathsf{ind}}_j = \star$ otherwise. Finally, define $\boldsymbol{P} \in \{0, \star\}^N$ such that for $j \in [\![1, N]\!]$, $P_j = P^*_j \wedge P^{\mathsf{ind}}_j$ with the following rule : $\star \wedge 0 = 0$. Finally compute $\mathsf{ct} = w.\mathsf{Encrypt}(\mathsf{pk}, \boldsymbol{P}, \mathsf{m})$ and outputs ct.
- $\mathsf{Decrypt}(\mathsf{pk}, \mathsf{sk}_i, \mathsf{ct})$: compute $\mathsf{m} \leftarrow w.\mathsf{Decrypt}(\mathsf{sk}_i, \mathsf{ct})$ if $i \in S \wedge i \geq ind$, $\perp$ otherwise.

Fig. 9. Generic construction of AugBE from WIBE.

Note 5. Encryption for pattern $\mathbf{0}^L$ corresponds to encryption for index $N+1$. Also as the underlying WIBE is pattern-hiding, the AugBE decryption algorithm does not take as input the set for which the message was encrypted.

The proof that correctness of the obtained AugBE follows the one of the underlying WIBE is straightforward. Refer to full version [5] for more details.

Theorem 3. *If WIBE satisfies adaptive (resp. selective)* IND-WID-CPA *security, then the obtained AugBE scheme satisfies adaptive (resp. selective) message hiding security.*

Proof. Let $\mathcal{B}$ be an adversary against message hiding security, that wins with non negligible advantage. In Fig. 10 we construct $\mathcal{A}$ from $\mathcal{B}$, that wins against IND-WID-CPA with non negligible advantage. Let $\mathcal{C}$ be a challenger.

If all $\mathcal{B}$'s queries satisfy the game constraints, then all $\mathcal{A}$'s queries have the same property. Thus $\mathcal{A}$'s simulation is perfect and the advantage of $\mathcal{A}$ is the same as $\mathcal{B}$'s. This concludes the proof.

SETUP: $\mathcal{C}$ runs $\mathsf{Setup}(1^\lambda, 1^N) \to (\mathsf{msk}, \mathsf{pk})$ and sends pk to $\mathcal{A}$, who sends it to $\mathcal{B}$.
KEY QUERY: $\mathcal{B}$ chooses $i \in [N]$, sends it to $\mathcal{A}$ who creates the pattern $\boldsymbol{P}^i$ such that for $j \in [\![1, N]\!]$, $P^i_j = 1$ if $i = j$, $P^i_j = 0$ otherwise. $\mathcal{A}$ sends $\boldsymbol{P}^i$ to $\mathcal{C}$, who responds with $\mathsf{sk}_{\boldsymbol{P}^i} \leftarrow \mathsf{KeyDer}(\mathsf{msk}, \boldsymbol{P}^i)$. $\mathcal{A}$ sends $\mathsf{sk}_{\boldsymbol{P}^i}$ to $\mathcal{B}$ as sk_i.
CHALLENGE: $\mathcal{B}$ chooses messages $\mathsf{m}_0, \mathsf{m}_1$ and a set S^*. It sends $\mathsf{m}_0, \mathsf{m}_1, S^*$ to $\mathcal{A}$, who creates pattern $\boldsymbol{P}^*$, such that for $j \in [\![1, N]\!]$, $P^*_j = 0$. $\mathcal{A}$ sends $\mathsf{m}_0, \mathsf{m}_1, P^*$ to $\mathcal{C}$, who chooses $b \leftarrow \{0,1\}$ and runs $\mathsf{ct}^* \leftarrow \mathsf{Encrypt}(\mathsf{pk}, \boldsymbol{P}^*, \mathsf{m}_b)$. $\mathcal{C}$ gives ct^* to $\mathcal{A}$, who sends it to $\mathcal{B}$.
KEY QUERY: $\mathcal{A}, \mathcal{B}, \mathcal{C}$ act like in the previous KEY QUERY step.
GUESS: $\mathcal{B}$ outputs its guess b' to $\mathcal{A}$, who outputs it as its guess.

Fig. 10. Construction of IND-WID-CPA adversary from message hiding adversary.

Note 6. Pattern $\boldsymbol{P}^*$ is equal to $\mathbf{0}^N$. Then, for all $i \in [N]$, $\boldsymbol{P}^i \notin_\star \boldsymbol{P}^*$: the WIBE adversary's constraint is always verified and we do not specify it in the proof.

Theorem 4. *If WIBE satisfies adaptive (resp. selective) pattern-hiding security, the obtained AugBE satisfies adaptive (resp. selective) anonymous security.*

Proof. Let $\mathcal{C}$ be a challenger and $\mathcal{B}$ an adversary that wins the anonymous security game with non negligible advantage. We build, in Fig. 11, an adversary $\mathcal{A}$ that uses $\mathcal{B}$ and wins the pattern-hiding security game with non negligible advantage.

SETUP: $\mathcal{C}$ runs $\mathsf{Setup}(1^\lambda, 1^N) \to (\mathsf{msk}, \mathsf{pk})$ and sends pk to $\mathcal{A}$, who sends it to $\mathcal{B}$.
KEY QUERY: $\mathcal{B}$ chooses $i \in [N]$, sends it to $\mathcal{A}$ who creates the pattern $\boldsymbol{P}^i$ such that for $j \in [\![1, N]\!]$, $P^i_j = 1$ if $i = j$, $P^i_j = 0$ otherwise. $\mathcal{A}$ sends $\boldsymbol{P}^i$ to $\mathcal{C}$, who responds with $\mathsf{sk}_{\boldsymbol{P}^i} \leftarrow \mathsf{KeyDer}(\mathsf{msk}, \boldsymbol{P}^i)$. $\mathcal{A}$ sends $\mathsf{sk}_{\boldsymbol{P}^i}$ to $\mathcal{B}$ as sk_i.
CHALLENGE: $\mathcal{B}$ chooses a message m, two sets S^0, S^1 and sends m, S^0, S^1 to $\mathcal{A}$. The latter creates the patterns $\boldsymbol{P}^0$, $\boldsymbol{P}^1$ such that for $j \in [\![1, N]\!]$, $P^0_j = \star$ if $j \in S^0$, $P^0_j = 0$ otherwise, and $P^1_j = \star$ if $j \in S^1$, $P^1_j = 0$ otherwise. $\mathcal{A}$ sends $\mathsf{m}, \boldsymbol{P}^0, \boldsymbol{P}^1$ to $\mathcal{C}$. If for any queried $\boldsymbol{P}^i$, $\boldsymbol{P}^i \in_\star \boldsymbol{P}^0 \wedge \boldsymbol{P}^i \notin_\star \boldsymbol{P}^1$ or $\boldsymbol{P}^i \notin_\star \boldsymbol{P}^0 \wedge \boldsymbol{P}^i \in_\star \boldsymbol{P}^1$, $\mathcal{C}$ aborts. Otherwise, it chooses $b \leftarrow \{0,1\}$ and sets $\mathsf{ct}^* \leftarrow \mathsf{Encrypt}(\mathsf{pk}, \boldsymbol{P}^b, \mathsf{m})$. It sends ct^* to $\mathcal{A}$ who sends it to $\mathcal{B}$.
KEY QUERY: $\mathcal{A}$ and $\mathcal{B}$ act like in the previous KEY QUERY step. If $\boldsymbol{P}^i \in_\star \boldsymbol{P}^0 \wedge \boldsymbol{P}^i \notin \boldsymbol{P}^1$ or $\boldsymbol{P}^i \notin_\star \boldsymbol{P}^0 \wedge \boldsymbol{P}^i \in \boldsymbol{P}^1$, $\mathcal{C}$ aborts. Otherwise, it runs $\mathsf{KeyDer}(\mathsf{msk}, \boldsymbol{P}^i) \to \mathsf{sk}_{\boldsymbol{P}^i}$ and sends $\mathsf{sk}_{\boldsymbol{P}^i}$ to $\mathcal{A}$ who sends it as sk_i to $\mathcal{B}$.
GUESS: $\mathcal{B}$ outputs its guess b' to $\mathcal{A}$, who outputs it as its guess.

Fig. 11. Construction of pattern-hiding adversary from AugBE anonymous adversary.

If all $\mathcal{B}$'s queries satisfy the game constraint, then all $\mathcal{A}$'s queries have the same property. Thus $\mathcal{A}$'s simulation is perfect, and the advantage of $\mathcal{A}$ is the same as $\mathcal{B}$'s. This concludes the proof.

Combining Theorems 1 and 4 we obtain that if WIBE satisfies adaptive (resp. selective) pattern-hiding security then the AugBE scheme obtained from the WIBE satisfies adaptive (resp. selective) index hiding security.

4 Instantiations of WIBE

In this section, we first present a WIBE that has constant-size ciphertext, then a second scheme which does not have constant-size ciphertext but is proved to be pattern-hiding. Both do not allow key derivation for a pattern from another pattern's key (thus KeyDer algorithm will be written KeyGen). As in the previous section, both schemes have key pattern space equal to $\{0,1\}^L \setminus \{\mathbf{0}^L\}$, and ciphertext pattern space is equal to $\{0,\star\}^L \setminus \{\mathbf{0}^L\}$ for the first scheme and to $\{0,\star\}^L \setminus \{\star^L\}$ for our second scheme. Let $\boldsymbol{P}' \in \{0,1\}^L \setminus \{\mathbf{0}^L\}$ and $\boldsymbol{P} \in \{0,\star\}^L$ be patterns. We define $\mathcal{I} = \left\{i \in [L] | P_i' = 1\right\}$ and $\mathcal{O} = \left\{i \in [L] | P_i' = 0\right\}$; notice that $[L] = \mathcal{I} \cup \mathcal{O}$. Also notice that $\boldsymbol{P}' \in_\star \boldsymbol{P} \Longrightarrow \forall i \in [L]$, if $P' = 1$ then $P_i = \star$ and thus $\mathcal{I} \subseteq W(\boldsymbol{P})$.

4.1 WIBE with Constant Size Ciphertext

We start by our first WIBE scheme (Fig. 12), which has a constant-size ciphertext, and can be used to instantiate a BE scheme as in the previous section.

- $\mathsf{Setup}(1^\lambda, 1^L)$: generate an asymmetric bilinear pairing group $\Gamma = (p, \mathbb{G}_1, \mathbb{G}_2, \mathbb{G}_T, g_1, g_2, e)$ for sufficiently large prime order p. Sample random dual orthonormal bases $(\mathbb{D}, \mathbb{D}^*) \leftarrow \mathsf{Dual}(\mathbb{Z}_p^4)$. Let $\boldsymbol{d}_1, \cdots, \boldsymbol{d}_4$ denote the elements of $\mathbb{D}$ and $\boldsymbol{d}_1^*, \cdots, \boldsymbol{d}_4^*$ denote the elements of $\mathbb{D}^*$. Pick $\alpha, a_1, \cdots, a_L \leftarrow \mathbb{Z}_p$. The public key is computed as: $\mathsf{pk} = (\Gamma, p, e(g_1, g_2)^{\alpha \boldsymbol{d}_1 \cdot \boldsymbol{d}_1^*}, g_1^{\boldsymbol{d}_1}, \boldsymbol{h}_1 = g_1^{a_1 \cdot \boldsymbol{d}_2}, \cdots, \boldsymbol{h}_L = g_1^{a_L \cdot \boldsymbol{d}_2})$ and the master secret key is $\mathsf{msk} = (\alpha, g_2^{\boldsymbol{d}_1^*}, g_2^{\boldsymbol{d}_2^*}, a_1, \cdots, a_L)$.
- $\mathsf{KeyGen}(\mathsf{msk}, \boldsymbol{P}')$: pick $r \leftarrow \mathbb{Z}_p$. Compute $\boldsymbol{a} = g_2^{\alpha \boldsymbol{d}_1^* + r \cdot \sum_{i \in \mathcal{I}} a_i \cdot \boldsymbol{d}_1^* - r \cdot \boldsymbol{d}_2^*}$ and $\boldsymbol{b}_i = g_2^{r \cdot a_i \cdot \boldsymbol{d}_1^*}$ for $i \in \mathcal{O}$. The secret key is $\mathsf{sk}_{\boldsymbol{P}'} = (\boldsymbol{a}, \{\boldsymbol{b}_i\}_{i \in \mathcal{O}})$.
- $\mathsf{Encrypt}(\mathsf{pk}, \boldsymbol{P}, \mathsf{m} \in \mathbb{G}_T)$: choose $s \leftarrow \mathbb{Z}_p$ and compute $\mathsf{ct} = (c_1, \boldsymbol{c}_2)$ where $c_1 = \mathsf{m} \cdot (e(g_1, g_2)^{\alpha \boldsymbol{d}_1^* \cdot \boldsymbol{d}_1})^s$, $\boldsymbol{c}_2 = g_1^{s \boldsymbol{d}_1} \cdot \prod_{i \in W(\boldsymbol{P})} \boldsymbol{h}_i^s$.
- $\mathsf{Decrypt}(\mathsf{sk}_{\boldsymbol{P}'}, \boldsymbol{P}, \mathsf{ct})$: compute $\boldsymbol{a}' = \boldsymbol{a} \prod_{i \in W(\boldsymbol{P}) \cap \mathcal{O}} \boldsymbol{b}_i$ and finally $\boldsymbol{C}_1 \cdot \frac{1}{e(\boldsymbol{c}_2, \boldsymbol{a}')}$.

Fig. 12. An adaptive WIBE in prime order group, with constant size ciphertext.

The scheme correctness is straightforward. See [5] for more details.

Theorem 5. *If SXDH holds then our scheme satisfies adaptive* IND-WID-CPA.

Our proof is based on the ones of [21] (Sect. 4.6) and [13] (Sect. 4) and is using **dual system encryption** ([23]). We introduce a second form of keys and ciphertexts: semi functional keys and semi functional ciphertexts. Let $\mathsf{sk} = (\boldsymbol{a}, \{\boldsymbol{b}_i\}_{i\in\mathcal{O}})$ be a normal key, and $t_3, t_4, \{t_{b,i}\}_{i\in\mathcal{O}}$ be random elements of $\mathbb{Z}_p$. We define a semi functional key as $\mathsf{sk}' = (\boldsymbol{a}', \left\{\boldsymbol{b}_i'\right\}_{i\in\mathcal{O}})$ where $\boldsymbol{a}' = \boldsymbol{a} \cdot g_2^{t_3\cdot \boldsymbol{d}_3^*+t_4\cdot \boldsymbol{d}_4^*}$ and $\boldsymbol{b}_i' = \boldsymbol{b}_i \cdot g_2^{t_{b,i}\cdot \boldsymbol{d}_3^*}$ for $i \in \mathcal{O}$. Let $\mathsf{ct} = (c_1, \boldsymbol{c}_2)$ be a normal ciphertext, and $z_3, z_4 \leftarrow \mathbb{Z}_p$. A semi functional ciphertext is $\mathsf{ct}' = (c_1', \boldsymbol{c}_2')$ where $c_1' = c_1$ and $\boldsymbol{c}_2' = \boldsymbol{c}_2 \cdot g_1^{z_3\cdot \boldsymbol{d}_3+z_4\cdot \boldsymbol{d}_4}$. We prove Theorem 5 with a sequence of $Q+3$ games.

- Game_0: is the real IND-WID-CPA security game (Definition 9 for $s=0$).
- Game_1: is as Game_0 except that the challenge ciphertext is semi-functional.
- Game_{2-j}: for j from 1 to Q, Game_{2-j} is the same as Game_1 except that the first j keys are semi-functional and the remaining keys are normal.
- Game_3: is the same as Game_{2-Q}, except that the challenge ciphertext is a semi-function encryption of a random message in $\mathbb{G}_T$.

For lack of space, we only give an overview of the proofs of indistinguishability between these games (refer to Appendix B of [5] for full proofs). Moving from symmetric pairings to asymmetric pairings is not an issue if elements are taken in the correct group ($\mathbb{G}_1$ for ciphertext and public key elements, and $\mathbb{G}_2$ for secret keys elements). The proofs are using assumptions called DS1 and DS2, presented in Appendix A of [5]. Here is the idea of the proofs, for $\mathcal{A}$ an adversary.

- If $\mathcal{A}$ can distinguish Game_0 from Game_1 then we can build an adversary with non-negligible advantage against DS1 with $k=2$ and $n=4$.
- If $\mathcal{A}$ can distinguish $\mathsf{Game}_{2-(j-1)}$ from Game_{2-j} then we can build an adversary with non-negligible advantage against DS2 with $k=2$ and $n=4$.
- If $\mathcal{A}$ can distinguish Game_{2-Q} from Game_3 then we can build an adversary with non-negligible advantage against DS1 with $k=1$ and $n=4$. We prove this in two steps, by randomizing each appearance of s in the $\boldsymbol{c}_2$ term. The end result is a semi-functional encryption of a random message. We consider an intermediary game, called $\mathsf{Game}_{2-Q'}$, that is exactly like Game_{2-Q}, except that in the $\boldsymbol{c}_2$ term of the challenge ciphertext the coefficient of $\boldsymbol{d}_2$ is changed from being $s\sum_{i\in W(P)} a_i$ to a fresh random value in $\mathbb{Z}_p$. Then we prove that
  - If $\mathcal{A}$ can distinguish Game_{2-Q} from $\mathsf{Game}_{2-Q'}$, we can build an adversary with non-negligible advantage against DS1 with $k=1$ and $n=4$.
  - If $\mathcal{A}$ can distinguish $\mathsf{Game}_{2-Q'}$ from Game_3 then we can build an adversary with non-negligible advantage against DS2 with $k=1$ and $n=4$

4.2 Pattern Hiding WIBE

We describe our scheme (Fig. 13), which can be used to obtain an instantiation of our AugBE scheme given in Sect. 3.

- $\mathsf{Setup}(1^\lambda, 1^L)$: generate an asymmetric bilinear pairing group $\Gamma = (p, \mathbb{G}_1, \mathbb{G}_2, \mathbb{G}_T, g_1, g_2, e)$ for sufficiently large prime order p. Sample random dual orthonormal bases $(\mathbb{B}, \mathbb{B}^*) \leftarrow \mathsf{Dual}(\mathbb{Z}_p^{4L+2})$. Let $\boldsymbol{b}_0, \cdots, \boldsymbol{b}_{4L+1}$ denote the elements of $\mathbb{B}$. Pick $\alpha \leftarrow \mathbb{Z}_p$. The public key is computed as: $\mathsf{pk} = (\Gamma, p, e(g_1, g_2)^{\alpha \boldsymbol{b}_0 \cdot \boldsymbol{b}_0^*}, g_1^{\boldsymbol{b}_0}, g_1^{\boldsymbol{b}_{4L+1}}, \boldsymbol{h}_1 = g_1^{\boldsymbol{b}_1}, \cdots, \boldsymbol{h}_L = g_1^{\boldsymbol{b}_L})$ and the master secret key is $\mathsf{msk} = (\alpha, g_2^{\boldsymbol{b}_0^*}, g_2^{\boldsymbol{b}_1^*}, \cdots g_2^{\boldsymbol{b}_L^*}, g_2^{\boldsymbol{b}_{3L+1}^*} \cdots, g_2^{\boldsymbol{b}_{4L}^*})$.
- $\mathsf{KeyGen}(\mathsf{msk}, \boldsymbol{P}')$: pick $\boldsymbol{r}, \boldsymbol{\eta} \in \mathbb{Z}_p^L$. The secret key is $\mathsf{sk}_{\boldsymbol{P}'} = g_2^{\alpha \boldsymbol{b}_0^* + \sum_{j \in \mathcal{I}} r_j \boldsymbol{b}_j^* + \sum_{l=1}^{L} \eta_l \cdot \boldsymbol{b}_{3L+l}^*}$.
- $\mathsf{Encrypt}(\mathsf{pk}, \boldsymbol{P}, \mathsf{m} \in \mathbb{G}_T)$: choose $s_1, s_2, s_3 \leftarrow \mathbb{Z}_p$ and compute $\mathsf{ct} = (c_1, \boldsymbol{c}_2)$ where
$c_1 = \mathsf{m} \cdot (e(g_1, g_2)^{\alpha \boldsymbol{b}_0^* \cdot \boldsymbol{b}_0})^{s_1}$, $\boldsymbol{c}_2 = g_1^{s_1 \boldsymbol{b}_0 + s_2 \boldsymbol{b}_{4L+1}} \cdot \prod_{i \in \bar{W}(\boldsymbol{P})} \boldsymbol{h}_i^{s_3}$.
- $\mathsf{Decrypt}(\mathsf{sk}_{\boldsymbol{P}'}, \mathsf{ct})$: compute $c_1 \cdot \frac{1}{e(\boldsymbol{c}_2, \mathsf{sk}_{\boldsymbol{P}'})}$.

Fig. 13. An adaptive WIBE in prime order group, satisfying pattern-hiding.

The scheme correctness is straightforward. See [5] for more details.

Theorem 6. *If* $\mathsf{XDLin1}, \mathsf{XDLin2}$ *hold, then our scheme is adaptively pattern-hiding secure, in the standard model.*

Our proof is inspired by the one of [25] (Sect. 4.3) for their IPE scheme: the security is proven throughout a series of games. We start those two:

- Game_0 is the original game of the WIBE security definition (Definition 9).
- $\mathsf{Game}_{0'}$ is the same as Game_0 except that a coin $t \in \{0,1\}$ is chosen before setup, and the game is aborted in challenge step if $t \neq s$.

First, we execute a preliminary game transformation from Game_0 to $\mathsf{Game}_{0'}$. We define that adversary $\mathcal{A}$ wins with probability $1/2$ when the game is aborted (and the advantage in $\mathsf{Game}_{0'}$ is $\Pr[\mathcal{A} \text{ wins}] - 1/2$ as well). Since t is independent from s, the game is aborted with probability $1/2$. Hence, the advantage in $\mathsf{Game}_{0'}$ is a half of that in Game_0, i.e., $\mathsf{Adv}_{\mathcal{A}}^{0'}(\lambda) = 1/2 \cdot \mathsf{Adv}_{\mathcal{A}}^{0}(\lambda)$. Moreover, $\Pr[\mathcal{A} \text{ wins}] = 1/2 \cdot (\Pr[\mathcal{A} \text{ wins}|t = 0] + \Pr[\mathcal{A} \text{ wins}|t = 1])$ in $\mathsf{Game}_{0'}$ since t is uniformly and independently generated. For lack of space, we only present the idea of the proofs when $t = 0$ and $t = 1$. For the full proofs, refer to Appendix B of [5].

$\mathsf{IND\text{-}WID\text{-}CPA}$ **security ($t = 0$).** This proof is similar to the one of [22] (Sect. 3.5.2); it uses a series of $Q + 2$ games, for challenge plaintexts $(\mathsf{m}_0, \mathsf{m}_1)$ and pattern $\boldsymbol{P}^*$:

- Game_1: is the same as $\mathsf{Game}_{0'}$ except that the challenge ciphertext $(c_1, \boldsymbol{c}_2)$ is changed into **temporal 1** form: $s_1, s_2, s_3, t_1, \cdots, t_L \leftarrow \mathbb{Z}_p, b \leftarrow \{0,1\}$, and requires that $P_1^* \neq \star$,

$$c_1 = \mathsf{m}_b \cdot e(g_1, g_2)^{\alpha \boldsymbol{b}_0 \cdot \boldsymbol{b}_0^* s_1}, \ \boldsymbol{c}_2 = g_1^{s_1 \boldsymbol{b}_0 + s_2 \boldsymbol{b}_{4L+1} + s_3 \sum_{i \in \bar{W}(\boldsymbol{P}^*)} \boldsymbol{b}_i + \sum_{l=1}^{L} t_l \boldsymbol{b}_{L+l}} \quad (1)$$

- Game_{2-k} ($k \in [\![1, Q]\!]$): is the same as $\mathsf{Game}_{2-(k-1)}$ (for $k = 1$, $\mathsf{Game}_{2-(k-1)}$ is Game_1) except that the reply to the k-th key queried for $\boldsymbol{P}$ is changed into **temporal 1** form: $\alpha, \{r_j\}_{j\in\mathcal{I}}, \{\eta_i, x_i\}_{i\in[\![1,L]\!]} \leftarrow \mathbb{Z}_p$,

$$\boldsymbol{sk_P} = g_2^{\alpha\boldsymbol{b}_0^* + \sum_{j\in\mathcal{I}} r_j\boldsymbol{b}_j^* + \sum_{l=1}^{L} x_l\boldsymbol{b}_{L+l}^* + \sum_{l=1}^{L} \eta_l\boldsymbol{b}_{3L+l}^*} \tag{2}$$

- Game_3: is the same as Game_{2-Q} except that the challenge ciphertext $(c_1, \boldsymbol{c}_2)$ is changed into **unbiased** form: $s_1', \{\tilde{s}_i\}_{i\in[\![1,L]\!]} \leftarrow \mathbb{Z}_p$

$$c_1 = \mathsf{m}_b \cdot e(g_1, g_2)^{\alpha\boldsymbol{b}_0\cdot\boldsymbol{b}_0^* s_1}, \;\; \boldsymbol{c}_2 = g_1^{s_1'\boldsymbol{b}_0 + s_2\boldsymbol{b}_{4L+1} + \sum_{i=1}^{L} \tilde{s}_i\boldsymbol{b}_i + \sum_{l=1}^{L} t_l\boldsymbol{b}_{L+l}} \tag{3}$$

and all the other variables are generated as in Game_{2-Q}.

Indistinguishability is proven using intermediate problems (defined in Appendix A of [5]) that hold if $\mathsf{XDLin1}, \mathsf{XDLin2}$ hold. If an adversary can distinguish $\mathsf{Game}_{0'}$ from Game_1, $\mathsf{Game}_{2-(k-1)}$ from Game_{2-k} then Problems 1 and 2 can be broken. Finally the advantage of an adversary in winning Game_{2-Q} is the same than the one of an adversary winning Game_3; and the latter is equal to 0. The original proofs are min the symmetric pairing settings but they can be turned into the asymmetric setting by taking elements in the correct group.

Pattern Hiding Security ($t = 1$). The proof is done as in [25] (Sect. 4.3.3), except that it is turned into the asymmetric setting (easily when considering elements in the correct group). It uses a sequence of $4Q + 2$ games using different forms of ciphertexts $\boldsymbol{c}_2$ and keys that we introduce. The different forms of ciphertext are defined according to challenge patterns $\boldsymbol{P}^0, \boldsymbol{P}^1$.

- Game_1: is as $\mathsf{Game}_{0'}$ except that the ciphertext is changed to **temporal 0** form: let $b \in \{0, 1\}, t \in \mathbb{Z}_p$ and suppose that $P_1^b = 0$. Define $\boldsymbol{c}_2$ as

$$g_1^{s_1\boldsymbol{b}_0 + s_2\boldsymbol{b}_{4L+1} + s_3 \sum_{i\in\overline{W}(\boldsymbol{P}^b)} \boldsymbol{b}_i + t\boldsymbol{b}_{L+1}} \tag{4}$$

- For $1 \leq h \leq Q$ (the number of keys queried), we define the following 4 games:
  - Game_{2-h-1}: in this game, the challenge ciphertext is changed to **temporal 1** form: let $b \in \{0, 1\}, t, u, \tilde{u} \in \mathbb{Z}_p$. Define $\boldsymbol{c}_2$ as g_1 with exponent

$$s_1\boldsymbol{b}_0 + s_2\boldsymbol{b}_{4L+1} + s_3 \sum_{i\in\overline{W}(\boldsymbol{P}^b)} \boldsymbol{b}_i + t \sum_{i\in\overline{W}(\boldsymbol{P}^b)} \boldsymbol{b}_{L+i} + u \sum_{i\in\overline{W}(\boldsymbol{P}^0)} \boldsymbol{b}_{2L+i} + \tilde{u} \sum_{i\in\overline{W}(\boldsymbol{P}^1)} \boldsymbol{b}_{2L+i} \tag{5}$$

  and the first $h - 1$ keys are **temporal 1** forms, while remaining keys are normal. Let $\boldsymbol{x} \in \mathbb{Z}_p^L$ be a random vector; temporal 1 key is defined as

$$g_2^{\alpha\boldsymbol{b}_0^* + \sum_{j\in\mathcal{I}} r_j\boldsymbol{b}_j^* + \sum_{j\in\mathcal{I}} x_j\boldsymbol{b}_{2L+j}^* + \sum_{l=1}^{L} \eta_l\cdot\boldsymbol{b}_{3L+l}^*} \tag{6}$$

- Game_{2-h-2}: in this game the h-th key is changed to **temporal 2** form, while remaining keys and challenge ciphertext are as in Game_{2-h-1}. Let $\boldsymbol{z} \in \mathbb{Z}_p^L$ be a random vector; temporal 2 key is defined as

$$g_2^{\alpha \boldsymbol{b}_0^* + \sum_{j \in \mathcal{I}} r_j \boldsymbol{b}_j^* + \sum_{j \in \mathcal{I}} z_j \boldsymbol{b}_{L+j}^* + \sum_{l=1}^{L} \eta_l \cdot \boldsymbol{b}_{3L+l}^*} \tag{7}$$

- Game_{2-h-3}: in this game, challenge ciphertext is changed to **temporal 2** form: let $b \in \{0,1\}, t, \tilde{t}, u, \tilde{u} \in \mathbb{Z}_p$. Define $\boldsymbol{c}_2$ as g_1 with exponent

$$\begin{aligned} & s_1 \boldsymbol{b}_0 + s_2 \boldsymbol{b}_{4L+1} + s_3 \sum_{i \in \bar{W}(\boldsymbol{P}^b)} \boldsymbol{b}_i + t \sum_{i \in \bar{W}(\boldsymbol{P}^0)} \boldsymbol{b}_{L+i} \\ & + \tilde{t} \sum_{i \in \bar{W}(\boldsymbol{P}^1)} \boldsymbol{b}_{L+i} + u \sum_{i \in \bar{W}(\boldsymbol{P}^0)} \boldsymbol{b}_{2L+i} + \tilde{u} \sum_{i \in \bar{W}(\boldsymbol{P}^1)} \boldsymbol{b}_{2L+i} \end{aligned} \tag{8}$$

  while all the queried keys are the same as in Game_{2-h-2}.
- Game_{2-h-4}: in this game, the h-th key is changed to **temporal 2** form (Eq. 6), remaining keys and the challenge ciphertext are as in Game_{2-h-3}.

- Game_3: the challenge ciphertext is changed to **unbiased form**: let $b \in \{0,1\}, w, \tilde{w}, t, \tilde{t}, u, \tilde{u} \in \mathbb{Z}_p$. Define $\boldsymbol{c}_2$ as g_1 with the following exponent while all the queried keys are **temporal 2** form (Eq. 6). In this game, the advantage of adversary is 0.

$$\begin{aligned} & s_1 \boldsymbol{b}_0 + s_2 \boldsymbol{b}_{4L+1} + w \sum_{i \in \bar{W}(\boldsymbol{P}^0)} \boldsymbol{b}_i + \tilde{w} \sum_{i \in \bar{W}(\boldsymbol{P}^1)} \boldsymbol{b}_i + t \sum_{i \in \bar{W}(\boldsymbol{P}^0)} \boldsymbol{b}_{L+i} \\ & + \tilde{t} \sum_{i \in \bar{W}(\boldsymbol{P}^1)} \boldsymbol{b}_{L+i} + u \sum_{i \in \bar{W}(\boldsymbol{P}^0)} \boldsymbol{b}_{2L+i} + \tilde{u} \sum_{i \in \bar{W}(\boldsymbol{P}^1)} \boldsymbol{b}_{2L+i} \end{aligned} \tag{9}$$

Indistinguishability between games is proven using intermediate problems (defined in Appendix A of [5]) that hold if $\mathsf{XDLin1}, \mathsf{XDLin2}$ hold:

- If there exists an adversary that can distinguish $\mathsf{Game}_{0'}$ from Game_1 then there exists an adversary that breaks Problem 1.
- $\mathsf{Game}_{2-(h-1)-4}$ can conceptually be changed into Game_{2-h-1}. The advantage of an adversary in distinguishing theses games is equal to $4/p$ when $h = 1$, otherwise it is equal to $3/p$.
- If there exists an adversary that can distinguish Game_{2-h-1} from Game_{2-h-2} then there exists an adversary that breaks Problem 2.
- If there exists an adversary that can distinguish Game_{2-h-3} from Game_{2-h-4} then there exists an adversary that breaks Problem 3.
- Game_{2-Q-4} can conceptually be changed into Game_3. The advantage of an adversary in distinguishing theses games is equal to $3/p$.

The original proof of indistinguishability between Game_{2-h-2} and Game_{2-h-3} cannot be applied here. Indeed, [25] proved that Game_{2-h-2} can be conceptually changed to Game_{2-h-3} with a change of bases and an intermediate game. However, with their change of bases $\mathbb{B}, \mathbb{B}^*$ to $\mathbb{D}, \mathbb{D}^*$, the h-th key of our scheme can no longer decrypt the ciphertext. Thus, the adversary can distinguish the different games as in one case the h-th key decrypts the challenge ciphertext but not in the other case. That is because, with the definition of $\mathbb{D}, \mathbb{D}^*$, some elements of $\mathbb{B}$ (resp. $\mathbb{B}^*$) are now linear combination of elements of $\mathbb{D}$ (resp. $\mathbb{D}^*$). Thus, the set $\bar{W}(\boldsymbol{P}^b) \cap \mathcal{I}$ is no longer equal to $\varnothing$ (the decryption condition) but is equal to $\bar{W}(\boldsymbol{P}^b)$. So we change the way the new dual orthonormal bases are computed, following the idea of the last lemma in the original proof. Let $\theta_i, \tau_i \leftarrow \mathbb{Z}_p$ and for $i \in [\![1, L]\!]$ set $\boldsymbol{d}_i = \tau_i^{-1}\boldsymbol{b}_i + \theta_i \boldsymbol{b}_{L+i}$, $\boldsymbol{d}_{L+i} = \tau_i \boldsymbol{b}_{L+i}$, $\boldsymbol{d}_i^* = \tau_i \boldsymbol{b}_i^*$, $\boldsymbol{d}_{L+i}^* = -\theta_i \boldsymbol{b}_i^* + \tau_i^{-1}\boldsymbol{b}_{L+i}^*$ and $\mathbb{D} = (\boldsymbol{b}_0, \boldsymbol{d}_1 \cdots, \boldsymbol{d}_L, \boldsymbol{d}_{L+1}, \cdots, \boldsymbol{d}_{2L}, \boldsymbol{b}_{2L+1} \cdots \boldsymbol{b}_{4L+1})$, and $\mathbb{D}^* = (\boldsymbol{b}_0^*, \boldsymbol{d}_1^*, \cdots, \boldsymbol{d}_L^*, \boldsymbol{b}_L^*, \boldsymbol{d}_{L+1}^*, \cdots, \boldsymbol{d}_{2L}^*, \boldsymbol{b}_{2L+1}^*, \cdots, \boldsymbol{b}_{4L+1}^*)$. This solves the issue raised by our scheme's construction and allows us to prove the indistinguishability between the two games.

Acknowledgements. We would like to thank Sherman S. M. Chow and anonymous reviewers for their helpful discussions and valuable comments. Part of this work has received funding from the French National Research Agency (ANR), PRESTO project number ANR-19-CE39-0011-01.

References

1. Abdalla, M., Caro, A.D., Phan, D.H.: Generalized key delegation for wildcarded identity-based and inner-product encryption. IEEE Trans. Inf. Forensics Secur. **7**(6), 1695–1706 (2012). https://doi.org/10.1109/TIFS.2012.2213594
2. Abdalla, M., Catalano, D., Dent, A.W., Malone-Lee, J., Neven, G., Smart, N.P.: Identity-based encryption gone wild. In: Bugliesi, M., Preneel, B., Sassone, V., Wegener, I. (eds.) ICALP 2006, Part II. LNCS, vol. 4052, pp. 300–311. Springer, Heidelberg (2006). https://doi.org/10.1007/11787006_26
3. Agrawal, S., Wichs, D., Yamada, S.: Optimal broadcast encryption from LWE and pairings in the standard model. In: Pass, R., Pietrzak, K. (eds.) TCC 2020, Part I. LNCS, vol. 12550, pp. 149–178. Springer, Cham (2020). https://doi.org/10.1007/978-3-030-64375-1_6
4. Attrapadung, N.: Dual system encryption framework in prime-order groups via computational pair encodings. In: Cheon, J.H., Takagi, T. (eds.) ASIACRYPT 2016, Part II. LNCS, vol. 10032, pp. 591–623. Springer, Heidelberg (2016). https://doi.org/10.1007/978-3-662-53890-6_20
5. Barthoulot, A., Blazy, O., Canard, S.: Augmented broadcast encryption from identity based encryption with wildcard. Cryptology ePrint Archive, Paper 2022/1192 (2022). https://eprint.iacr.org/2022/1192
6. Blazy, O., Kakvi, S.A.: Skipping the q in group signatures. In: Bhargavan, K., Oswald, E., Prabhakaran, M. (eds.) INDOCRYPT 2020. LNCS, vol. 12578, pp. 553–575. Springer, Cham (2020). https://doi.org/10.1007/978-3-030-65277-7_25
7. Boneh, D., Gentry, C., Waters, B.: Collusion resistant broadcast encryption with short ciphertexts and private keys. In: Shoup, V. (ed.) CRYPTO 2005. LNCS, vol. 3621, pp. 258–275. Springer, Heidelberg (2005). https://doi.org/10.1007/11535218_16
8. Boneh, D., Sahai, A., Waters, B.: Fully collusion resistant traitor tracing with short ciphertexts and private keys. In: Vaudenay, S. (ed.) EUROCRYPT 2006. LNCS, vol. 4004, pp. 573–592. Springer, Heidelberg (2006). https://doi.org/10.1007/11761679_34

9. Boneh, D., Waters, B.: A fully collusion resistant broadcast, trace, and revoke system. In: Juels, A., Wright, R.N., De Capitani di Vimercati, S. (eds.) ACM CCS 2006, pp. 211–220. ACM Press, October/November 2006. https://doi.org/10.1145/1180405.1180432
10. Boneh, D., Waters, B., Zhandry, M.: Low overhead broadcast encryption from multilinear maps. In: Garay, J.A., Gennaro, R. (eds.) CRYPTO 2014, Part I. LNCS, vol. 8616, pp. 206–223. Springer, Heidelberg (2014). https://doi.org/10.1007/978-3-662-44371-2_12
11. Brakerski, Z., Vaikuntanathan, V.: Lattice-inspired broadcast encryption and succinct ciphertext-policy ABE. Cryptology ePrint Archive, Report 2020/191 (2020). https://ia.cr/2020/191
12. Chen, J., Gay, R., Wee, H.: Improved dual system ABE in prime-order groups via predicate encodings. In: Oswald, E., Fischlin, M. (eds.) EUROCRYPT 2015, Part II. LNCS, vol. 9057, pp. 595–624. Springer, Heidelberg (2015). https://doi.org/10.1007/978-3-662-46803-6_20
13. Chen, J., Lim, H.W., Ling, S., Wang, H., Wee, H.: Shorter IBE and signatures via asymmetric pairings. In: Abdalla, M., Lange, T. (eds.) Pairing 2012. LNCS, vol. 7708, pp. 122–140. Springer, Heidelberg (2013). https://doi.org/10.1007/978-3-642-36334-4_8
14. Fiat, A., Naor, M.: Broadcast encryption. In: Stinson, D.R. (ed.) CRYPTO 1993. LNCS, vol. 773, pp. 480–491. Springer, Heidelberg (1994). https://doi.org/10.1007/3-540-48329-2_40
15. Garg, S., Kumarasubramanian, A., Sahai, A., Waters, B.: Building efficient fully collusion-resilient traitor tracing and revocation schemes. In: Al-Shaer, E., Keromytis, A.D., Shmatikov, V. (eds.) ACM CCS 2010, pp. 121–130. ACM Press, October 2010. https://doi.org/10.1145/1866307.1866322
16. Gay, R., Kowalczyk, L., Wee, H.: Tight adaptively secure broadcast encryption with short ciphertexts and keys. In: Catalano, D., De Prisco, R. (eds.) SCN 2018. LNCS, vol. 11035, pp. 123–139. Springer, Cham (2018). https://doi.org/10.1007/978-3-319-98113-0_7
17. Goyal, R., Quach, W., Waters, B., Wichs, D.: Broadcast and trace with N^{ε} ciphertext size from standard assumptions. In: Boldyreva, A., Micciancio, D. (eds.) CRYPTO 2019, Part III. LNCS, vol. 11694, pp. 826–855. Springer, Cham (2019). https://doi.org/10.1007/978-3-030-26954-8_27
18. Goyal, R., Vusirikala, S., Waters, B.: Collusion resistant broadcast and trace from positional witness encryption. In: Lin, D., Sako, K. (eds.) PKC 2019, Part II. LNCS, vol. 11443, pp. 3–33. Springer, Cham (2019). https://doi.org/10.1007/978-3-030-17259-6_1
19. Kim, J., Lee, J., Lee, S., Oh, H.: Scalable wildcarded identity-based encryption with full security. Electronics **9**, 1453 (2020)
20. Kim, J., Lee, S., Lee, J., Oh, H.: Scalable Wildcarded identity-based encryption. In: Lopez, J., Zhou, J., Soriano, M. (eds.) ESORICS 2018, Part II. LNCS, vol. 11099, pp. 269–287. Springer, Cham (2018). https://doi.org/10.1007/978-3-319-98989-1_14
21. Lewko, A.: Tools for simulating features of composite order bilinear groups in the prime order setting. In: Pointcheval, D., Johansson, T. (eds.) EUROCRYPT 2012. LNCS, vol. 7237, pp. 318–335. Springer, Heidelberg (2012). https://doi.org/10.1007/978-3-642-29011-4_20

22. Lewko, A., Okamoto, T., Sahai, A., Takashima, K., Waters, B.: Fully secure functional encryption: attribute-based encryption and (hierarchical) inner product encryption. In: Gilbert, H. (ed.) EUROCRYPT 2010. LNCS, vol. 6110, pp. 62–91. Springer, Heidelberg (2010). https://doi.org/10.1007/978-3-642-13190-5_4
23. Lewko, A., Waters, B.: New techniques for dual system encryption and fully secure HIBE with short ciphertexts. In: Micciancio, D. (ed.) TCC 2010. LNCS, vol. 5978, pp. 455–479. Springer, Heidelberg (2010). https://doi.org/10.1007/978-3-642-11799-2_27
24. Libert, B., Paterson, K.G., Quaglia, E.A.: Anonymous broadcast encryption: adaptive security and efficient constructions in the standard model. In: Fischlin, M., Buchmann, J., Manulis, M. (eds.) PKC 2012. LNCS, vol. 7293, pp. 206–224. Springer, Heidelberg (2012). https://doi.org/10.1007/978-3-642-30057-8_13
25. Okamoto, T., Takashima, K.: Adaptively attribute-hiding (hierarchical) inner product encryption. In: Pointcheval, D., Johansson, T. (eds.) EUROCRYPT 2012. LNCS, vol. 7237, pp. 591–608. Springer, Heidelberg (2012). https://doi.org/10.1007/978-3-642-29011-4_35
26. Phan, D.H.: Some Advances in Broadcast Encryption and Traitor Tracing. Habilitation à diriger des recherches, Ecole normale supérieure - ENS PARIS, November 2014. https://tel.archives-ouvertes.fr/tel-02384086
27. Zhandry, M.: New techniques for traitor tracing: size $N^{1/3}$ and more from pairings. In: Micciancio, D., Ristenpart, T. (eds.) CRYPTO 2020, Part I. LNCS, vol. 12170, pp. 652–682. Springer, Cham (2020). https://doi.org/10.1007/978-3-030-56784-2_22

Attacks and Countermeasures

Passive Triangulation Attack on ORide

Shyam Murthy(✉) and Srinivas Vivek

International Institute of Information Technology Bangalore, Bengaluru, India
{shyam.sm,srinivas.vivek}@iiitb.ac.in

Abstract. Privacy preservation in Ride Hailing Services is intended to protect privacy of drivers and riders. ORide is one of the early RHS proposals published at USENIX Security Symposium 2017. In the ORide protocol, riders and drivers, operating in a zone, encrypt their locations using a Somewhat Homomorphic Encryption scheme (SHE) and forward them to the Service Provider (SP). SP homomorphically computes the squared Euclidean distance between riders and available drivers. Rider receives the encrypted distances and selects the optimal rider after decryption. In order to prevent a triangulation attack, SP randomly permutes the distances before sending them to the rider.

In this work, we use propose a passive attack that uses triangulation to determine coordinates of all participating drivers whose permuted distances are available from the points of view of multiple honest-but-curious adversary riders. An attack on ORide was published at SAC 2021. The same paper proposes a countermeasure using noisy Euclidean distances to thwart their attack. We extend our attack to determine locations of drivers when given their permuted and noisy Euclidean distances from multiple points of reference, where the noise perturbation comes from a uniform distribution.

We conduct experiments with different number of drivers and for different perturbation values. Our experiments show that we can determine locations of all drivers participating in the ORide protocol. For the perturbed distance version of the ORide protocol, our algorithm reveals locations of about 25% to 50% of participating drivers. Our algorithm runs in time polynomial in the number of drivers.

Keywords: Ride Hailing Services · Privacy and censorship · Attack · ORide · Triangulation

1 Introduction

Ride-Hailing Services (RHS) and Ride-Sharing Services (RSS) have become popular world over. RHS are typically managed by big organizations like Uber, Ola, etc. RSS tend to be carpool or vanpool services offered by individuals in a peer-to-peer car sharing model like Sidecar, Relay Rides, etc. There are many advantages of both these services like being environment friendly as well as being cost-effective. In order to provision their services, RHS Service Providers (SP)

A. R. Beresford et al. (Eds.): CANS 2022, LNCS 13641, pp. 167–187, 2022.
https://doi.org/10.1007/978-3-031-20974-1_8

gather personal information from users, where users are both riders and drivers. Such information is needed for billing and statistics as well as to comply with regulatory requirements. This might lead to a breach of privacy either due to negligence on part of the SP [15,22] or by the SP itself trying to snoop user information for advertising or other purposes. Therefore, privacy concerns of users need to be addressed in order make RHS/RSS secure.

A number of works are available in the literature that deal with privacy preservation in RHS (PP-RHS). While rider privacy concerns have received a lot of attention in PP-RHS literature, there are not many works that deal with driver privacy. There have been many instances in the media where driver safety is compromised. The article [16] reports of how a gang makes use of ride-hailing apps to harvest driver locations for robbery. Another article [6], claims that some regular (non-SP) taxi drivers, pretending to be customers, located Uber vehicles to attack them. These incidents provide a motivation to consider driver-threat models that leak locations of drivers to riders.

ORide [12] is one of the early RHS proposals which primarily aims to provide secure and efficient ride matching between riders and participating drivers. ORide and many subsequent PP-RHS solutions make use of homomorphic encryption schemes as their primary cryptographic construct. Homomorphic encryption schemes allow computation on ciphertexts such that the result of computation is available only after decryption. A Fully Homomorphic Encryption (FHE) scheme allows homomorphic addition and multiplication any number of times at the cost of large ciphertexts and huge computation latency. A Somewhat Homomorphic Encryption (SHE) scheme also allows addition and multiplication but only for a pre-defined number of times with the advantage of much smaller ciphertext size and lesser computational latency. Hence, SHE schemes are more popular in practical solutions, e.g., ORide in which the FV SHE scheme [4] is used to provide 112-bit security. Most of the PP-RHS solutions use semantically secure encryption schemes in their protocol. However, possible side-effects of adapting these encryption schemes to RHS applications need to be considered carefully which otherwise might give scope for adversarial attacks.

In the ORide protocol, described in more detail in Sect. 2.1, rider and drivers rely on SHE to send their encrypted locations to the SP. SP then homomorphically computes the encrypted squared Euclidean distances between rider and drivers. These encrypted distances are received by the rider who decrypts the distances, selects the smallest among them and informs the index of the selected driver. SP notifies the driver and helps establish a secure channel between rider and the selected driver after which both the parties proceed with ride completion. The paper considers drivers' location-harvesting attacks where a malicious rider might try to triangulate drivers by making three simultaneous fake ride requests and obtain distances. They propose a countermeasure where SP permutes the list of drivers' indices before forwarding to rider. This is aimed to thwart the ability of the adversary to correlate driver distances and hence perform triangulation. However, we show that four colluding adversary riders, by using only the uncorrelated driver distances available to each of them as per the

ORide protocol, and using triangulation, can reveal the coordinates of all the participating drivers.

Alongside the RHS proposals, a number of attacks on some of the works are also available in the literature, a few of them are mentioned in Sect. 5. We note here that the attacks are important to help make the protocols more robust and thus aid in development of truly privacy-preserving versions of RHS protocols. The work by Kumaraswamy *et al.* [8] proposes a location-harvesting attack on the ORide protocol, where they show that a rider can determine the exact locations of 45% of the responding drivers. They make use of the fact that the planar coordinates in the ORide protocol are integers and obtain all lattice points inside a circle of radius n_d centered at rider's actual location, where n_d is the distance computed by rider between herself and driver d. They then reduce the number of potential locations, to about 2 on average, using topology information of the region and by making use of the fact that a driver must be at a motorable location in rider's zone. They propose a countermeasure to thwart this attack where the driver, instead of encrypting her actual location, encrypts a uniform random location within a perturbation distance ρ from her original location to respond to rider's request. In effect, using anonymised driver location will result in the rider decrypting a *noisy distance* between herself and the driver but all the other steps in the original ORide protocol remain unchanged, and we term this as the *noisy* variant of ORide. They show that by using such anonymised locations, drivers are successful in preserving their anonymity against their attack.

In this paper, we show that a sufficient number of adversary riders colluding with one another and using only the *uncorrelated noisy distances* available to them, can reveal locations of about 25% to 50% of participating drivers. Each of our successfully recovered locations will be a distance at most 2ρ from a driver's original location. Our solution neither makes use of topology information of the region nor relies on encoding mechanism of driver coordinates. While the attack of [8] on the ORide protocol reveals coordinates of about 45% of participating drivers, our attack on the same reveals the coordinates of all participating drivers.

1.1 Triangulation

Triangulation is a well-known method in navigation and surveying where the position of an object can be determined based on angles measured from multiple points of reference. The term triangulation has been used in different contexts. In the field of image processing and computer vision, the term triangulation refers to the process of finding the position of a point in space by using its position in two images taken with different cameras [5]. In computational geometry, polygon triangulation is a basic algorithm where a polygon is decomposed into a set of non-intersecting triangles [13]. In this paper, we use the term triangulation to mean determining the planar coordinates of an object based on distances measured from multiple reference points.

1.2 Threat Model

As mentioned earlier, users in RHS can either be drivers who sign up with the SP to offer rides for profit or riders who wish to avail ride services for a fee. Either of the three entities, namely the SP, driver or rider can be an adversary trying to learn more about other parties. The SP, holding personal user information, has a reputation to maintain and hence would typically refrain from taking an active adversarial role, except that it is curious. Riders can be subjected to profiling or even physical attacks, where drivers are the adversary entities. Riders or other outsiders masquerading as legitimate riders can be the adversary entities trying to obtain driver information like location, identity etc. In the ORide protocol, riders and drivers are modeled as active adversaries and SP is an honest-but-curious adversary. Riders and drivers do not collude with SP and that the SP does not provide the users with malicious apps.

In this work, we consider the adversarial model as that of ORide. We look at driver location-harvesting attacks by adversary rider entities. In other words, the rider is the adversary trying to glean location information about participating drivers and the SP is unaware of presence of such an adversary. The adversary, in this case, will follow the protocol correctly but uses the information gathered during the protocol to infer more than what is ordinarily available in the protocol. Multiple adversary riders participate in the attack, share information with one another and thus collude among themselves to perform driver location-harvesting attack. In a practical scenario, a competitor SP can masquerade as a set of riders with the intention of gleaning location information about drivers working for other SP(s).

1.3 Our Contribution

We present two driver location-harvesting attacks, one on the ORide protocol and another on the variant of the ORide protocol suggested as countermeasure in the attack paper of [8].

Our first attack algorithm, given in Sect. 3.3, makes use of triangulation to harvest drivers' locations. The ORide protocol claims to preserve driver anonymity in addition to providing an efficient and privacy-preserving ride hailing protocol. In particular, they claim to provide a countermeasure for driver triangulation attack by malicious riders. This is done by randomly permuting driver responses before forwarding them to requesting riders, thus preventing the rider adversaries from correlating distances between the adversary and responding drivers. Our attack uses four honest-but-curious passive adversary riders in collusion, where each adversary gets uncorrelated drivers' distances in random permuted order. We experimentally show that our algorithm is successful in obtaining exact coordinates of all drivers who respond to ride requests, thus negating one of the security claims of the ORide paper. Our attack recovers coordinates of all responding drivers, by picking points that are at exact distances received by atleast three adversaries, and is independent of the underlying road topology, whereas the attack in [8] uses road information and recovers about half the number of responding drivers.

We next consider an attack on the *noisy* variant of the ORide protocol which was proposed in [8] as a countermeasure mechanism for a topology-based driver location-harvesting attack proposed in the same paper. In the countermeasure solution, each rider obtains uncorrelated and noisy (squared) distances to anonymised locations within a circle of radius ρ, the perturbation distance, around each of the responding drivers, which is the noisy variant of the ORide protocol. In Sect. 3.4, we provide an algorithm to recover locations of responding drivers in the noisy variant of the ORide protocol. We use 12 colluding adversaries in this attack where each adversary is honest-but-curious and passive, all of whom receive permuted n noisy distances from n participating drivers. Using n such distances each from two adversaries, our attack looks at all intersecting $2n^2$ points and then does a brute force over distances available with all other adversaries and eliminates unsuitable points. We run our experiments for different values of ρ and for different zone sizes as described in Sect. 4. Our results are tabulated in Tables 2 and 3 which show that we obtain coordinates of about 25% to 50% of participating drivers. Each of our successfully recovered coordinates will be at a distance at most 2ρ from a driver's original location.

Our algorithms are heuristic in nature and each runs in time $\mathcal{O}(dn^3)$, for d adversaries and n drivers participating in the protocol. Our attack can result in large-scale inference of drivers' locations which might lead to unwanted consequences. We note here that our attack does not reveal anything about the driver private information other than their location. Our attacks are independent of the underlying encryption scheme and the coordinate encoding mechanism.

The rest of the paper is organized as follows. Section 2.1 describes the ORide protocol and its noisy variant. Section 3 explains the attacks followed by our experiments and results in Sect. 4. Related works in Sect. 5 gives some details of literature that identify vulnerabilities in PP-RHS solutions. The algorithm for the two attacks are given in Appendix A.

2 Overview of ORide [12] and Its Noisy Variant [8]

In this section, we begin with a brief overview of ORide and present only those details that are needed to demonstrate our attacks. Next, we describe the *noisy* variant of the ORide protocol which mitigates a location-harvesting attack from [8].

2.1 ORide [12]

ORide is a privacy-preserving ride-hailing service protocol. The protocol is summarized in the following steps:

1. There are three parties involved in the protocol: rider, service provider (SP) and drivers.

2. SP does not collude with rider or drivers. Drivers and riders are honest-but-curious adversaries trying to learn more about the other party than what is expected from the protocol. The protocol aims to preserve the identity and location information of drivers and riders from SP and from each other.
3. During initialization, SP creates and publishes zones in its area of operation. Zones are demarcated based on historical driver and ride densities (*aka* anonymity set) in the region and such information is available to all drivers and riders alike.
4. Rider, wanting to hail a ride, picks a (public key, private key) pair for a semantically secure SHE scheme, encrypts her locations using the public key and sends the ciphertext and public key to SP requesting a ride. The authors use the FV SHE scheme [4] to demonstrate the working of the protocol. Since the basic SHE scheme (without HEEAN/CKKS extensions [3]) works on integers, locations are encoded as integers in UTM[1] format.
5. SP forwards the request to all drivers in rider's zone.
6. Available drivers encrypt their locations using the public key and send the ciphertext to SP.
7. SP does not have the secret keys to decrypt the received ciphertexts. The semantic security of the underlying SHE scheme ensures the privacy of the encrypted data with respect to SP.
8. SP uses the homomorphic properties of the SHE scheme to securely compute the squares of the Euclidean distances between each of the received drivers' encrypted locations and the encrypted rider location.
9. SP randomly permutes the results before forwarding them to rider. This is done to prevent correlation of driver responses by rider and thus helps to prevent triangulation attack by multiple colluding riders trying to derive driver locations.
10. Rider uses the SHE private key to decrypt the distances, sorts the resulting plaintext, chooses the index associated with the smallest value and informs the SP.
11. SP enables the rider and selected driver to establish a secure communication channel between each other. Following this, the rider and driver complete their ride establishment privately.
12. In addition to the aforementioned features, the protocol also provides convenience features like ride payment, reputation rating, accountability etc., which are not relevant for the attack in our paper. The interested reader is referred to the original paper for more details.

In Section 8 of the ORide paper, the authors consider location-harvesting attacks by outsiders. They consider triangulation attack on drivers where the adversary can obtain driver coordinates by making three simultaneous ride requests from different locations. They consider two methods to mitigate the attack. The first one is to make it financially expensive, wherein they impose

[1] Universal Transverse Mercator: a map-projection system for geographical locations [20].

a charge on riders who issue ride requests followed by cancellations. The second method is to permute the list of drivers' indices for each ride request so as to thwart the ability of the adversary to correlate rider request with driver responses. In this paper, we provide an attack on the second mitigation method mentioned above.

2.2 Noisy Variant of ORide [8]

The paper [8] proposes a location-harvesting attack on the ORide protocol. Their attack describes a method where a rider in ORide, by issuing a single ride request, is able to determine the exact locations of about 40% of the responding drivers. Their method uses the topology, terrain and road network information of the area to mount the attack. Their method is a variant of the classical Gauss' circle problem of finding lattice points on a circle of known radius. They find integer coordinates on a circle of radius equal to the distance between rider and responding driver, with center of circle being the rider location. They then reduce the number of possible locations by using road network information by picking points that lie only on motorable areas. In the same paper, in order to thwart the attack mentioned therein, the authors propose a simple countermeasure where each driver anonymises her location by choosing a random location within a distance ρ from her original location. In other words, in response to a ride request, a driver instead of encrypting her actual location, would pick a random anonymised location inside a circle of radius ρ around her actual location and sends the encryption of that anonymised location. The value of ρ is determined by the ride-hailing application provided by SP based on observed driver density in the specific zone, available to both drivers and riders. SP then homomorphically computes the squared Euclidean distance between the rider location and the anonymised location and forwards the same to rider. After decryption, rider would thus obtain a noisy distance between herself and the responding driver.

The maximum distance between the actual location and the random anonymised location is the perturbation distance ρ. Due to this perturbation, the authors of [8] show a marked increase in driver anonymity with respect to rider. Note that increasing the perturbation distance would decrease accuracy of selected closest driver, thereby requiring the SP to select the perturbation distance carefully to prevent customer dis-satisfaction. Finally, the authors give recommendation for perturbation distance based on grid size. We term this variation of ORide as *noisy* ORide.

We also give an attack on noisy ORide to try and recover coordinates of participating drivers.

3 Location Harvesting Attacks

In this section, we describe our location-harvesting attacks on the ORide protocol. We start with a basic triangulation attack wherein the received responses can be correlated to the respective drivers. As mentioned in Sect. 2.1, the ORide protocol has a mechanism to thwart such an attack; so we propose an attack which is an adaptation of the basic triangulation attack to recover driver coordinates of all participating drivers in the ORide protocol. We then look at the attack on the noisy version of ORide. Our attack, in this case, will try to recover a point within the perturbation circle around the driver's actual location. The algorithms of our attack are given in Appendix A as Algorithms 1 and 2.

3.1 Preliminaries

We consider the honest-but-curious adversary model in our attack. The adversary rider follows the protocol and tries to obtain more information based on driver response than is ordinarily available as per the protocol. SP does not collude with any of the parties. Multiple adversaries participate in the attack and all of them collude among themselves. RHS providers operate in specific geographic areas and for ease of management, the SP demarcates the area into suitably sized zones. Based on their location, the SP associates riders and drivers to a specific zone for purposes of ride hailing and ride availability advertisements, respectively.

Definition: Adversary Circle: Adversary circle w.r.t adversary A_α, at location α, and i^{th} driver D_i, denoted by $\mathcal{K}_{\alpha,R_{\alpha,i}}$, is a circle centered at α with radius $R_{\alpha,i}$, the squared Euclidean distance between A_α and D_i (at her original or anonymised location).

Definition: Perturbation Circle: Perturbation circle w.r.t a driver's (actual or potential) location χ, denoted by $\mathcal{P}_{\chi,n\rho}$, is a circle centered at χ and radius equal to $n\rho$ ($n \in \mathbb{R}$), and ρ is the perturbation distance. In the ORide protocol, driver would set n to 0 since there is no perturbation being added to her original location. In the noisy variant of ORide, driver would set $n = 1$ when responding to ride request. Adversary rider would set $n = 2$ while executing the procedures from Algorithm 2.
Remarks:

1. None of the attacks described in this paper make use of any geographical information or road network topology in the area of operation.
2. The location and identity of the entity requesting a ride are encrypted, hence the SP will not be able to distinguish between an adversary ride request from a legitimate one.
3. Each adversary entity is indistinguishable from one another. In a practical attack, there might be just one single physical device masquerading as multiple adversaries.
4. UTM coordinates are used by the ORide protocol since they use integer based BFV-SHE scheme [4] in their protocol. ORide could possibly be adapted to use CKKS FHE scheme [3] to encrypt real number coordinates in (latitude, longitude) format. Our attack is agnostic of the underlying encryption scheme or coordinate scheme since it only uses Euclidean distances computed between drivers and adversaries.

3.2 Basic Triangulation Attack

In the basic triangulation attack, three colluding riders located sufficiently close to one another issue ride requests simultaneously. Each rider computes the distance values using responses obtained from the SP, for each responding driver. The drivers' locations can be computed easily as long as the distances corresponding to a specific driver can be correlated with respect to each of the riders. If A_α, A_β and A_γ be three adversary riders, $R_{\alpha,i}$, $R_{\beta,i}$ and $R_{\gamma,i}$ be distances computed for driver D_i by each of the adversaries, respectively, then the point of intersection of $\mathcal{K}_{\alpha,R_{\alpha,i}}$, $\mathcal{K}_{\beta,R_{\beta,i}}$ and $\mathcal{K}_{\gamma,R_{\gamma,i}}$ would give the location of driver D_i. The ORide paper specifically mentions a possible triangulation attack and provides a mechanism to thwart the same as described in Sect. 2.1. In the following section, we describe our attack to overcome the same.

3.3 Attack on ORide Protocol

As described in Sect. 2.1, ORide provides a mechanism to thwart the basic rider triangulation attack. They prevent the ability of adversary rider to correlate the computed distances without which the basic triangulation attack described in Sect. 3.2 would not be possible. Our attack uses triangulation and involves multiple adversaries placed far away from one another. Our algorithm runs in time $\mathcal{O}(dn^3)$, for d adversaries and n drivers. In our experiments, four adversary entities were enough to reveal all responding drivers' locations. Each adversary entity issues a ride request (almost) simultaneously following the ORide protocol. SP then computes distances homomorphically from the received responses, permutes the order of received responses and forwards the set of encrypted distances to each requester, respectively. Hence, each adversary obtains n distances in random permuted order. Each adversary colludes with one another to execute Algorithm 1. A brief description of the algorithm is given below.

Description of Algorithm 1

- Let A_α denote the adversary rider, where $\alpha \in [1, 4]$. For n responding drivers, each A_α would receive n distances.
- Two adversary entities, say, A_1 and A_2 w.l.o.g, each use their respective n distance values to form $\mathcal{K}_{1,R_{1,i}}$ and $\mathcal{K}_{2,R_{2,i}}$, for $i \in [1, n]$, respectively.
- A_1 and A_2 collude and intersect $\mathcal{K}_{1,R_{1,i}}$, for $i \in [1, n]$, and $\mathcal{K}_{2,R_{2,j}}$, for $j \in [1, n]$, to obtain a set L of $2n^2$ intersection points. This is done in the procedure `ObtainCircleIntersectionPoints`.
- Each of the other two adversary entities A_3 and A_4 use their respective n distance values to form $\mathcal{K}_{3,R_{3,i}}$ and $\mathcal{K}_{4,R_{4,i}}$, for $i \in [1, n]$, respectively.
- A_3 and A_4 each check if points in the L set lie on their respective circles.
- Points that do not lie on either of the circles are filtered out from L. This is done in procedure `FilterInCorrectCoordinates`.
- At the end of this procedure only valid drivers' coordinates are present in the set L.

3.4 Attack on Noisy Version of ORide

As described in Sect. 2.2, [8] gives a location-harvesting attack on ORide paper and a countermeasure solution for their attack. In this section, we give an attack on the solution proposed in that paper. Our attack uses a variation of triangulation and involves multiple adversaries placed far away from one another. Our algorithm runs in time $\mathcal{O}(dn^3)$, for d adversaries and n drivers. In our experiments, we use 12 adversary entities for the attack.

Formally, let A_i be the ith adversary rider, $i \in [1, 12]$ at location (x_{A_i}, y_{A_i}). Each A_i issues a ride request (almost) simultaneously following the ORide protocol. As part of the attack mitigation given in [8], a driver at location (x_D, y_D), upon receiving the request, picks a uniformly random location $(\hat{x}_{D_i}, \hat{y}_{D_i})$ inside a perturbation circle of radius ρ centered at (x_D, y_D), encrypts that random location and responds to the ride request. SP receives the response, uses it to homomorphically compute the squared Euclidean distance between (x_{A_i}, y_{A_i}) and $(\hat{x}_D, \hat{y}_D)$ and forwards the same to A_i. A_i then uses the secret key to decrypt the computed distances to obtain the noisy distances between itself and each of the responding drivers. The adversaries collude with one another and execute Algorithm 2. The steps of the algorithm are described below.

Remark: The distances received by each adversary are in random order of drivers. Hence, the subscript j in $R_{\alpha,j}$ is just an enumeration and not a driver identifier.

Description of Algorithm 2

- Each adversary A_α, for $\alpha \in [1, m]$, is placed at a location far away from one another inside the zone, and each one receives noisy Euclidean distances from each of the participating drivers D_i, for $i \in [1, n]$.
- Let $R_\alpha = \{R_{\alpha,1}, \ldots, R_{\alpha,n}\}$ be the list of distances received by adversary A_α from n drivers in some random order.
- Two adversary entities, say, A_1 and A_2 w.l.o.g, each use their respective n distance values to form $\mathcal{K}_{1,R_{1,i}}$ and $\mathcal{K}_{2,R_{2,i}}$, for $i \in [1, n]$, respectively.
- A_1 and A_2 collude and intersect $\mathcal{K}_{1,R_{1,i}}$, for $i \in [1, n]$, and $\mathcal{K}_{2,R_{2,j}}$, for $j \in [1, n]$, to obtain the set L_1 of $2n^2$ intersection points, n (to be determined) of which are potential points inside each driver's perturbation circle. This is done in the procedure `ObtainCircleIntersectionPoints`.
- For driver locations that are close to being collinear with locations of A_1 and A_2, there is a high probability that the adversary circles do not intersect. In order to retrieve such points, we pick two other adversaries A_3 and A_4 located at points that are non-collinear to locations of both A_1 and A_2.
- A_3 and A_4 collude and intersect $\mathcal{K}_{3,R_{3,i}}$, for $i \in [1, n]$, and $\mathcal{K}_{4,R_{4,j}}$, for $j \in [1, n]$, to obtain the set L_2 of $2n^2$ intersection points as mentioned above.
- We pick the first point p from L_1. We draw perturbation circle $\mathcal{P}_{p,2\rho}$. (The radius of the perturbation circle is set this way since two points in the driver's perturbation circle of radius ρ will be at a distance at most 2ρ from one another.)
- Using each of the n distances available at next adversary A_α, we look for intersection of $\mathcal{P}_{p,2\rho}$ and $\mathcal{K}_{\alpha,R_{\alpha,i}}$, for $i \in [1, n]$. If none of the $\mathcal{K}$ circles intersect

$\mathcal{P}_{p,2\rho}$ at real points, we discard p. Otherwise, it is retained. This is done in procedure `FilterOutSuperfluousPoints`.
- The above step is repeated for each point in L_1 as well as in L_2 and over each adversary circle of every adversary.
- At the end of the previous step, we are left with two sets of filtered points in L_1 and L_2.
- The procedures `FilterOutNearbyInvalidPoints` and `SelectLikelyPoints` take τ as an input parameter. It is the threshold distance between two points to filter out nearby points. In case of small zone size and/or large number of drivers, we end up with a large number of points in L_1 and L_2 close to each other. In such cases we set τ to $< 2\rho$ so as to enable filtering out more number of points.
- Within each L_i, $i \in [1, 2]$, we discard points that are at a distance $\leq \tau$ from one another. In procedure `FilterOutNearbyInvalidPoints`, we find such points and pick only one of such nearby points.
- Finally, in the procedure `SelectLikelyPoints`, we compute the distance between each point in L_1 with each point in L_2 and pick only those points in L_1 that are at a distance $\leq \tau$ from at least one point in L_2. These picked points are output by the algorithm.

3.5 Correctness and Time Complexity

The correctness of Algorithm 1 is based on the fact that given exact distances between driver and adversary locations, all the adversary circles intersect at the driver location.

Our attack in Algorithm 2 relies on the fact that when given adversaries located sufficiently far from one another and driver locations that are picked uniformly random within the perturbation circle of radius ρ centered around the respective driver original location, then with a high probability the intersection of two such sets of adversary circles would have an intersection point inside the perturbation circle of *some* driver, as shown in Fig. 1. Since the maximum distance between two points inside a circle of radius ρ is 2ρ, we use one such intersection point as center of a circle of radius 2ρ and then look for the remaining adversary circles that will intersect this circle (of radius 2ρ).

However, when two adversary locations and a driver's actual location are close to being collinear then there is a high probability that the circles w.r.t that particular driver do not intersect. Hence, we pick two other adversaries that are located in such a way so as to obtain successful intersection of the adversary circles corresponding to the *missed* drivers.

Algorithms 1 and 2, given in Appendix A and described in Sect. 3, each run in time $\mathcal{O}(dn^3)$, for d adversaries and n drivers.

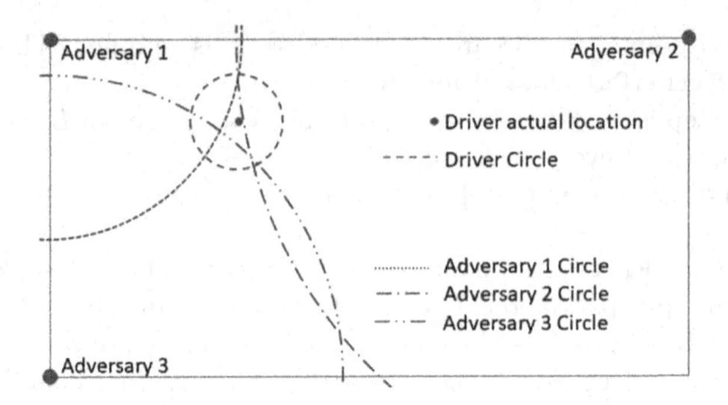

Fig. 1. Grid showing three adversary circles intersecting within a driver circle.

3.6 Mobile Drivers in the ORide Protocol

In Sects. 3.2 and 3.3, we consider the case of a driver at a location (x_D, y_D). It is possible that a driver in the ORide protocol looking to offer a ride might be mobile on the road. In this section, we consider such non-static drivers who respond to ride requests.

We feel it is reasonable to consider the driving speed of a driver looking for a ride to be about 25 kmph. This would translate to about 7 m per second. Assuming that the average turnaround time between ride request and response is less than 10 s, the driver would have travelled about 70 m. This would imply that the actual location of the driver would be off by at most ±70 m from the derived location obtained as described in Sect. 3.3 which is a reasonable approximation of driver's actual location. This problem of harvesting locations of mobile ORide drivers can also be seen as a problem in the noisy ORide variant where the perturbation ρ is about 75 m. Hence, we can apply Algorithm 2 to obtain locations of mobile drivers in the ORide protocol.

4 Experiments and Results

Sagemath 8.6 [14] was used to implement the procedures mentioned in Algorithms 1 and 2. Our experiments were run on a commodity HP Pavilion laptop with 512 GB SSD and AMD Ryzen 5 processor. Our experiments take about 2 s to complete for 25 drivers and about 300 s to complete for 100 drivers. The Sagemath code for our attacks in Algorithms 1 and 2 are available at https://github.com/shyamsmurthy/cans2022.

4.1 Experiment Details

Our experiments were run for two zone sizes, 100 km^2 and 25 km^2, which we term as large and small zone sizes, respectively. For the large zone size, we ran experiments for perturbation values, ρ, of 0, 50, 75, 100, 125 and 150 m. Perturbation value of 0 corresponds to our attack described in Sect. 3.3 and others

Table 1. Percentage of driver locations recovered for the ORide protocol (zero perturbation)

Zone size	Number of drivers = 25, 50, 75, 100
25 km^2	100
100 km^2	100

Table 2. Percentage of driver locations recovered for zone size of 100 km^2

Number of drivers	Perturbation radius (in meters)				
	$\rho = 50$	$\rho = 75$	$\rho = 100$	$\rho = 125$	$\rho = 150$
25	60.8	59.7	51.6	49.3	42.8
50	50.1	43.8	42.5	35.4	33.3
75	46.9	35.7	30.9	27.9	28.2
100	38.7	29.1	25.1	25.2	24.8

Table 3. Percentage of driver locations recovered for zone size of 25 km^2

Number of drivers	Perturbation radius (in meters)		
	$\rho = 50$	$\rho = 75$	$\rho = 100$
25	49.4	43.2	40.5
50	38.5	35.4	30.0
75	31.3	27.8	27.5
100	24.9	24.5	24.4

Table 4. Percentage of driver locations recovered for different adversary count for perturbation distance = 50 m and number of drivers = 75

Adversary count	Zone size = 100 km^2	Zone size = 25 km^2
4	6.1	6.6
8	22.8	18.7
12	**46.9**	**31.3**
16	50.5	26.0

correspond to our attack in Sect. 3.4. For the small zone, we have considered perturbation values, ρ, of 0, 50, 75 and 100 m. These values are inline to what is mentioned in Sect. 3.2 of [8], where the perturbation values are so chosen as to maintain sufficient anonymity and also to provide good accuracy of driver selection in a given zone size. For each combination of (zone, ρ) we set n, the number of drivers, to 25, 50, 75 and 100.

At the start of each run of the experiment, the algorithm takes the zone coordinates and generates n uniformly distributed random points, namely the driver original locations, inside the zone. For a driver original location χ, and per adversary, a new uniform random point p is picked at a distance $\leq \rho$ from χ. The squared Euclidean distance between p and adversary location is given to the adversary in random order. For n drivers, each adversary will have n distance values. As is evident, this exactly mimics the rider scenario in the ORide protocol where, after decryption, the rider receives the squared Euclidean distances to each driver from herself. As described in Sect. 3.3, each adversary will collude with one another and execute the steps described in Algorithm 2 to obtain a set of η coordinates.

4.2 Discussion of Results

In our experiments for the attack on ORide protocol described in Sect. 3.3, we exactly recover n locations corresponding to each of the n drivers participating in the ORide RHS protocol and are given in Table 1.

The results from our experiments to recover driver locations for the attack described in Sect. 3.4, namely *noisy* ORide, are given in Tables 2 and 3. Each table gives the percentage of driver coordinates that are *valid*, averaged over 20 runs. By valid, we mean that the recovered driver coordinates are at a distance $\leq 2\rho$ from an original driver location. Determining the set of valid locations is done during post-processing of the results as explained in Sect. 4.3. We see that as the number of drivers increases, the number of valid locations revealed decreases. This is due to the fact that the number of circle intersections increases as square of number of drivers, hence, resulting in a large number of false positives, thus decreasing the accuracy of the results. In our experiments, we use τ as a parameter, to filter out values in procedures `FilterOutNearbyAlliedPoints` and `SelectLikelyPoints` in Algorithm 2.

Table 4 gives the percentage of successfully recovered driver locations, out of 75 participating drivers and perturbation distance of 50 m, for varying number of adversary entities of 4, 8, 12 and 16. We see that with 12 adversaries we get an optimum recovery percentage. With lesser number of adversaries, fewer points get eliminated resulting in lower success rate. With higher number of adversary circles and with a smaller grid size, far too many points get eliminated also resulting in a lower success rate. Although, with zone size of 100 km^2 the recovery percentage is better for 16 adversaries, the gain is not proportional to the extra overhead, hence we choose to keep the number of adversaries as 12.

In Tables 5 and 6, we give a summary comparison of our attacks with that of [8] and the triangulation attack considered in the ORide paper [12], respectively.

Table 5. Comparison of our attack with the attack of [8]

	Success percentage of attack on ORide protocol	Topology information	Integer encoding
Attack of [8]	40	Required	Required
Our attack	100	Not required	Not required

Table 6. Summary comparison of our attacks with triangulation attack considered in ORide paper [12]

	Attack conditions
ORide paper [12] (Sect. 8)	Rider can correlate driver with respective exact distance
Our attack (Algorithm 1)	Drivers' exact distances are randomly permuted by SP
Our attack (Algorithm 2)	Drivers' perturbed distances are randomly permuted by SP

4.3 Post-processing of Our Experiment Results

At the end of each run, the experiment will return η number of coordinates, where η may or may not be equal to n. As mentioned earlier, at the start of every run, n original driver locations are generated. During post-processing, we compare each of the η values with n and pick only those that is at a distance $\leq 2\rho$ from one of the n values. These picked values are deemed *valid* driver locations.
Remark: To obtain the percentage of valid locations we divide the number of valid driver locations by $max(n, \eta)$.

5 Related Works

5.1 Ride-Hailing Services

Zhao *et al.* [22] perform a systematic study of leakage of drivers' sensitive data and show that large scale data harvesting of such information is possible. They analyze apps provided to drivers by Uber, Lyft and other popularly deployed SPs and show that a malicious outsider SP can harvest driver data using the apps. ORide is one of the early PP-RHS solutions that not only uses a semantically secure SHE scheme to encrypt user and driver locations to enable an SP to anonymously match drivers with riders, but also supports RHS features like easy payment, reputation rating, accountability etc. Kumaraswamy *et al.* [8] give a location-harvesting attack on ORide. Using a single ride request they demonstrate that a rider can reveal locations of up to 40% of participating drivers. Their attack makes use of the geography and road network of the area to identify motorable areas to determine likely driver locations. They provide a countermeasure to thwart the attack while preserving sufficient anonymity.

Wang *et al.* propose *TRACE* [19], a privacy-preserving dynamic spatial query solution using bilinear pairing to encrypt locations of drivers and riders. Kumaraswamy and Vivek [9] disprove the privacy claims of the TRACE protocol. Their attack exploits shared randomness used across different messages and recovers masked plaintext used in the initial part of the RHS protocol. *lpRide* by Yu *et al.* [21] uses modified Paillier cryptosystem [11] for encrypting RNE transformed locations of riders and drivers. All homomorphic distance computations and optimum driver selection operations are performed on a single SP server. [17] propose an attack on the modified Paillier scheme used in lpRide, allowing the service provider to recover locations of all riders and drivers in the region. Vivek [18] gives an attack on the lpRide protocol. Their attack does cryptanalysis of the modified version Paillier cryptosystem and show that any rider/driver will be able to learn the location of any other rider participating in the RHS.

5.2 Triangulation

Triangulation is a popular technique used in recovering 2 and 3-dimensional structure of an object using images from multiple points of reference. This problem is non-trivial in the presence of noise [5]. There are a number of works in the field of computer vision that work on recovering points in space when given image coordinates perturbed by noise, and using camera matrices [5,10]. In the field of computational geometry, the term polygon triangulation means decomposition of a polygon into a set of triangles [1,2,7].

6 Conclusion and Future Work

In this paper, we presented driver location-harvesting attacks on the ORide paper based on passive triangulation. We recover coordinates of all participating drivers in the ORide protocol. We also look at an attack on a *noisy* version of the ORide protocol where we recover about 25% to 50% of participating drivers' locations.

One possible method to decrease the effectiveness of our attack might be for a driver to vary, within some known bounds, the radius of her perturbation circle for each response. This would force us to use the largest possible perturbation radius in our attack algorithm, possibly reducing its effectiveness. However, this might also have an effect on the driver selection algorithm. Therefore, both the countermeasure solution and our attack on the same need to be experimentally evaluated, which we leave for future work.

As part of a future work, our method of adapting triangulation attack can be explored for other protocols that make use of uncorrelated distances for privacy preservation. Our method and analysis are based on heuristics, a theoretical analysis would be very useful to correlate successful driver location recovery with perturbation radius.

Acknowledgements. We thank the anonymous reviewers for their invaluable comments and suggestions, which helped us improve the manuscript. This work was partly funded by the INSPIRE Faculty Award (DST, Govt. of India) and the Infosys Foundation Career Development Chair Professorship grant for Srinivas Vivek.

A Algorithms for Triangulation Attack

Algorithm 1. Retrieve coordinates using Triangulation

```
1: procedure MAIN(R_1, ..., R_m)
2:     Input : R_1, ..., R_m: the list of distances received by adversaries A_1, ..., A_m in that
   order
3:     Output : Set of likely driver coordinates

4:     L ← ObtainCircleIntersectionPoints( R_1, R_2 )
5:     for i ← 3, m do
6:                    ▷ Use other adversary distances to filter in correct intersection points
7:         L ← FilterInCorrectCoordinates( R_i, L )
8:     end for
9:     return L
10: end procedure

11: procedure OBTAINCIRCLEINTERSECTIONPOINTS(R_α, R_β)
12:     Input : R_α, R_β: the list of distances received by adversaries A_α and A_β, respectively
13:     Output : Set of circle intersection points

14:     L ← null
15:     for i ← 1, len(R_α) do                ▷ len(X) gives number of elements in list X
16:         for j ← 1, len(R_β) do
17:             p_1, p_2 = Circle_Intersection_Points(K_{α,R_{α,i}}, K_{β,R_{β,j}})
18:             if p_1 ≠ null then
19:                 Add p_1 and p_2 to L
20:             end if
21:         end for
22:     end for
23:     return L
24: end procedure

25: procedure FILTERINCORRECTCOORDINATES(R_γ, L)
26:     Input : R_γ: the list of distances received by adversary A_γ, L: current set of intersection
   points
27:     Output : Filtered set of coordinate points

28:     L_out = null
29:     for i ← 1, len(L) do
30:         for j ← 1, len(R_γ) do
31:             if L[i] lies on K_{γ,R_{γ,i}} then     ▷ Adversary circle, center : γ, radius : R_{γ,i}
32:                 Add L[i] to L_out
33:             end if
34:         end for
35:     end for
36:     return L_out
37: end procedure
```

Algorithm 2. Retrieve coordinates from noisy distances

1: **procedure** MAIN($R_1, \ldots, R_m$)
2: **Input** : $R_1, \ldots, R_m$: the list of distances received by adversaries $A_1, \ldots, A_m$, respectively
3: **Output** : Set of likely driver coordinates

4: ▷ Intersect adversary circles $\mathcal{K}_{1,R_{1,i}}$ and $\mathcal{K}_{2,R_{2,i}}$, for $i \in [1, n]$
5: $L_1 \leftarrow$ `ObtainCircleIntersectionPoints(` R_1, R_2 `)`
6: **for** $i \leftarrow 3, m$ **do** ▷ Use all the other adversary distance lists
7: $L_1 \leftarrow$ `FilterOutSuperfluousPoints(` R_i, L_1 `)`
8: **end for**
9: ▷ Intersect adversary circles $\mathcal{K}_{3,R_{3,i}}$ and $\mathcal{K}_{4,R_{4,i}}$, for $i \in [1, n]$
10: $L_2 \leftarrow$ `ObtainCircleIntersectionPoints(` R_3, R_4 `)`
11: **for** $i \leftarrow 1, 2, 5, m$ **do** ▷ Use all the other adversary distance lists
12: $L_2 \leftarrow$ `FilterOutSuperfluousPoints(` R_i, L_2 `)`
13: **end for**
14: $L_1 \leftarrow$ `FilterOutNearbyInvalidPoints(` L_1, 2ρ `)`
15: $L_2 \leftarrow$ `FilterOutNearbyInvalidPoints(` L_2, 2ρ `)`
16: $L \leftarrow$ `SelectLikelyPoints(` L_1, L_2, 2ρ `)`
17: **return** L
18: **end procedure**

19: **procedure** OBTAINCIRCLEINTERSECTIONPOINTS(R_α, R_β)
20: **Input** : R_α, R_β: the list of distances received by adversaries A_α and A_β respectively.
21: **Output** : Set of circle intersection points

22: $L \leftarrow null$
23: **for** $i \leftarrow 1, len(R_\alpha)$ **do**
24: **for** $j \leftarrow 1, len(R_\beta)$ **do**
25: $p_1, p_2 \leftarrow Circle\_Intersection\_Points(\mathcal{K}_{\alpha,R_{\alpha,i}}, \mathcal{K}_{\beta,R_{\beta,j}})$
26: **if** $p_1 \neq null$ **then**
27: Add p_1 and p_2 to L
28: **end if**
29: **end for**
30: **end for**
31: **return** L
32: **end procedure**

33: **procedure** FILTEROUTSUPERFLUOUSPOINTS(R_γ, L)
34: **Input** : R_γ: the list of distances received by adversary A_γ, L: Current set of filtered circle intersection points
35: **Output** : Filtered set of circle intersection points

36: $resultList \leftarrow null$
37: **for** $i \leftarrow 1, len(L)$ **do**
38: **for** $j \leftarrow 1, len(R_\gamma)$ **do**
39: $q_1, q_2 \leftarrow Circle\_Intersection\_Points(\mathcal{P}_{L[i],(2\rho)}, \mathcal{K}_{\gamma,R_{\gamma,j}})$
40: ▷ Perturbation circle $\mathcal{P}_{L[i],(2\rho)}$: Center : $L[i]$, Radius : 2ρ
41: **if** $q_1 \neq null$ **then**
42: Add $L[i]$ to $returnList$;
43: **break**
44: **end if**
45: **end for**
46: **end for**
47: **return** $resultList$
48: **end procedure**

```
49: procedure FilterOutNearbyInvalidPoints(L, τ)
50:     Input : L: the list of coordinate points, τ: threshold distance to filter out points
51:     Output : Filtered set of coordinate points such that neighbouring points that
        are ≤ threshold distance from points in the filtered set are removed

52:     resultList ← null
53:     for i ← 1, len(L) − 1 do
54:         for j ← i + 1, len(L) do
55:             if Euclidean_distance(L[i], L[j]) ≤ τ then
56:                 Add L[i] to resultList, if not already present
57:             end if
58:         end for
59:     end for
60:     return resultList
61: end procedure

62: procedure SelectLikelyPoints(L1, L2, τ)
63:     Input : L1, L2: the list of filtered coordinate points, τ: distance threshold for
        selection
64:     Output : Set of likely driver coordinate points

65:     L ← null
66:     for i ← 1, len(L1) do
67:         for j ← 1, len(L2) do
68:             if L1[i] == L2[j] then
69:                 continue
70:             end if
71:             if Euclidean_distance(L1[i], L2[j]) ≤ τ then
72:                 Add L1[i] to L, if not already present
73:             end if
74:         end for
75:     end for
76:     return L
77: end procedure
```

References

1. Baker, B.S., Grosse, E., Rafferty, C.S.: Nonobtuse triangulation of polygons. Discrete Comput. Geom. **3**(2), 147–168 (1988). https://doi.org/10.1007/BF02187904
2. Bucher-Karlsson, M.: On minimal triangulations of products of convex polygons. Discrete Comput. Geom. **41**(2), 328–347 (2008). https://doi.org/10.1007/s00454-008-9087-5
3. Cheon, J.H., Kim, A., Kim, M., Song, Y.: Homomorphic encryption for arithmetic of approximate numbers. In: Takagi, T., Peyrin, T. (eds.) ASIACRYPT 2017, Part I. LNCS, vol. 10624, pp. 409–437. Springer, Cham (2017). https://doi.org/10.1007/978-3-319-70694-8_15
4. Fan, J., Vercauteren, F.: Somewhat practical fully homomorphic encryption. Cryptology ePrint Archive (2012). http://eprint.iacr.org/2012/144

5. Hartley, R.I., Sturm, P.: Triangulation. Comput. Vis. Image Underst. **68**(2), 146–157 (1997). https://doi.org/10.1006/cviu.1997.0547. https://www.sciencedirect.com/science/article/pii/S1077314297905476
6. Hurriyet Daily News: Istanbul taxi drivers hunt down, beat up Uber drivers as tensions rise (2018). https://www.hurriyetdailynews.com/istanbul-taxi-drivers-hunt-down-beat-up-uber-drivers-as-tensions-rise-128443. Accessed 11 June 2020
7. Kirkpatrick, D.G., Klawe, M.M., Tarjan, R.E.: Polygon triangulation in$O(n$ log log$n)$ time with simple data structures. Discrete Comput. Geom. **7**(4), 329–346 (1992). https://doi.org/10.1007/BF02187846
8. Kumaraswamy, D., Murthy, S., Vivek, S.: Revisiting driver anonymity in ORide. In: AlTawy, R., Hülsing, A. (eds.) SAC 2021. LNCS, vol. 13203, pp. 25–46. Springer, Cham (2022). https://doi.org/10.1007/978-3-030-99277-4_2
9. Kumaraswamy, D., Vivek, S.: Cryptanalysis of the privacy-preserving ride-hailing service TRACE. In: Adhikari, A., Küsters, R., Preneel, B. (eds.) INDOCRYPT 2021. LNCS, vol. 13143, pp. 462–484. Springer, Cham (2021). https://doi.org/10.1007/978-3-030-92518-5_21
10. Mohr, R., Quan, L., Veillon, F.: Relative 3d reconstruction using multiple uncalibrated images. I. J. Robotic Res. **14**, 619–632 (12 1995). https://doi.org/10.1177/027836499501400607
11. Nabeel, M., Appel, S., Bertino, E., Buchmann, A.: Privacy preserving context aware publish subscribe systems. In: Lopez, J., Huang, X., Sandhu, R. (eds.) NSS 2013. LNCS, vol. 7873, pp. 465–478. Springer, Heidelberg (2013). https://doi.org/10.1007/978-3-642-38631-2_34
12. Pham, A., Dacosta, I., Endignoux, G., Troncoso-Pastoriza, J.R., Huguenin, K., Hubaux, J.: ORide: a privacy-preserving yet accountable ride-hailing service. In: Kirda, E., Ristenpart, T. (eds.) 26th USENIX Security Symposium, USENIX Security 2017, Vancouver, BC, Canada, 16–18 August 2017, pp. 1235–1252. USENIX Association (2017)
13. Siedel, R.: A simple and fast incremental randomized algorithm for computing trapezoidal decompositions and for triangulating polygons. Comput. Geom. Theory Appl. **1**, 51–64 (1991)
14. Stein, W., et al.: Sage Mathematics Software (Version 8.6). The Sage Development Team (2019). http://www.sagemath.org
15. TechCrunch+: Ride-hailing app Careem reveals data breach affecting 14 million people (2018). https://techcrunch.com/2018/04/23/careem-data-breach/. Accessed 01 May 2022
16. thejournal.ie: West Dublin gang using hailing apps to target older taxi drivers (2019). https://www.thejournal.ie/west-dublin-taxi-robbery-4420178-Jan2019/. Accessed 11 June 2020
17. Vivek, S.: Attacks on a privacy-preserving publish-subscribe system and a ride-hailing service. CoRR (2021). https://arxiv.org/abs/2105.04351
18. Vivek, S.: Attacks on a privacy-preserving publish-subscribe system and a ride-hailing service **13129**, 59–71 (2021). https://doi.org/10.1007/978-3-030-92641-0_4
19. Wang, F., et al.: Efficient and privacy-preserving dynamic spatial query scheme for ride-hailing services. IEEE Trans. Veh. Technol. **67**(11), 11084–11097 (2018)
20. Wikipedia contributors: Universal Transverse Mercator coordinate system (2020). https://en.wikipedia.org/wiki/Universal_Transverse_Mercator_coordinate_system. Accessed 27 April 2020
21. Yu, H., Shu, J., Jia, X., Zhang, H., Yu, X.: lpRide: lightweight and privacy-preserving ride matching over road networks in online ride hailing systems. IEEE Trans. Veh. Technol. **68**(11), 10418–10428 (2019)

22. Zhao, Q., Zuo, C., Pellegrino, G., Lin, Z.: Geo-locating drivers: a study of sensitive data leakage in ride-hailing services. In: 26th Annual Network and Distributed System Security Symposium, NDSS 2019, San Diego, California, USA, 24–27 February 2019. The Internet Society (2019). https://www.ndss-symposium.org/ndss-paper/geo-locating-drivers-a-study-of-sensitive-data-leakage-in-ride-hailing-services/

HyperDetector: Detecting, Isolating, and Mitigating Timing Attacks in Virtualized Environments

Musa Sadik Unal, Arsalan Javeed, Cemal Yilmaz(✉), and Erkay Savas

Sabanci University, Istanbul, Turkey
{musa,ajaveed,cyilmaz,erkays}@sabanciuniv.edu

Abstract. We present a generic approach, called HyperDetector, to detect, isolate, and prevent ongoing timing based side-channel attacks that operate by measuring the execution times of short-running operations in virtualized environments. HyperDetector, being implemented at the level of hypervisor, uses a hardware extension for virtualization to intercept the `rdtsc` instructions, such that the consecutive pairs of time readings that are close to each other in time can be detected. Once potentially malicious time measurements are detected, noise is introduced into the measurements to prevent the ongoing attacks and the sequence of such measurements is analyzed at runtime by using a sliding window-based approach to determine the processes involved in the attacks. In the experiments, HyperDetector detected all the malicious processes with a perfect accuracy after these processes made few time measurements, reduced the success rates of the attacks from between 98%–99% to between 0%–0.5%, and did so with a runtime overhead of 1.14%.

Keywords: Cloud security · Virtualization · Microarchitecture · Side-channel attacks · Timing attacks

1 Introduction

Side channel attacks aim to exfiltrate secret information by measuring and analyzing the information unintentionally leaked by a computing system, such as power consumption, execution time, and cache access behavior [1–4]. These attacks can lead to a serious loss of sensitive and private data, including the cryptographic keys, passwords, digital identities, and company/government secrets.

A distinctive branch of side-channel attacks, which is also the focus of this paper, is *timing attacks* [5–7], such as Meltdown [8], Flush+Flush [9], Flush+Reload [10], and Prime+Probe [11]. In a timing attack, the attacker simply measures the execution time of a typically short-running operation and uses the differences between the time measurements to reduce the space of potential values for the secret data. For example, in the well-known Meltdown attack [8], the time it takes to access a memory chunk (typically, a byte) is measured to figure out whether the requested data resides in the cache or not; fetching the

A. R. Beresford et al. (Eds.): CANS 2022, LNCS 13641, pp. 188–199, 2022.
https://doi.org/10.1007/978-3-031-20974-1_9

data from the cache is faster than fetching it from the RAM. The differences in the access times are then used to exfiltrate private data belonging to other processes, for which the attacker does not have any access rights, otherwise.

In our previous work [12], we have developed a general approach, called Detector$^+$, to detect, isolate, and prevent the side-channel attacks that operate by timing the execution times of short-running operations. The aforementioned approach was based on a simple observation: For each measurement in such attacks, the malicious process needs to carry out a pair of successive time readings in a short period of time, such that the difference between the time readings obtained before and after an operation of interest can be associated with the operation. Consequently, Detector$^+$ monitors the time readings at runtime on a per process basis. When two consecutive readings are suspiciously close to each other in time, the respective measurement is marked as suspicious, i.e., potentially malicious. The results of our experiments empirically demonstrated that the time measurement characteristics of the malicious processes are quite different from those of the benign processes, thus the malicious processes, which leverage information unintentionally leaked by the benign processes, ironically leak information by themselves, allowing the timing attacks to be detected, isolated, and prevented at runtime.

An integral part of Detector$^+$ is to monitor the different means of reading the time information, such that the processes issuing the requests can be determined and the Detector$^+$ logic can be implemented. In our previous work [12], we demonstrated that, when the time readings are obtained by using system calls, such as `clock_gettime`, the monitoring task can efficiently and effectively be performed by instrumenting the respective system calls. Therefore, Detector$^+$ was originally implemented in the operating system (OS) kernel.

An important concern that was left as future work, though, was how to monitor the accesses to the time-stamp counter – a hardware register that keeps track of CPU clock cycles since its reset. For example, in `x86` systems, the `rdtsc` instruction can be used to read the current value of the time-stamp counter from all privilege levels, allowing accurate time measurements, of the order of clock cycles. In the remainder of the paper, this instruction and the similar instructions on different platforms will collectively be referred to as the `rdtsc` instruction. Due to its accuracy and fine-grained resolution, the `rdtsc` instruction is, indeed, the preferred way of measuring time in many side-channel attacks [13].

One issue from the perspective of Detector$^+$, however, is that `rdtsc` can be invoked via inline assembly at any point during an execution by any process without even letting the underlying operating system know. And, this makes the monitoring of the `rdtsc` instruction quite challenging. In previous work, we performed the monitoring task by instrumenting the application binaries, such that Detector$^+$ was notified every time the `rdtsc` instruction was executed. This, however, reduces the practicality of the approach as it requires the source code and/or binaries of the applications apriori.

In this work, we present *HyperDetector*, extending our previous work in three ways. First, we develop an efficient and effective mechanism to intercept the `rdtsc` instructions by using a hardware extension for virtualization without requiring the source code and/or binaries of the applications. Second, we demonstrate that the proposed approach can also work in the virtualized environments, such as the Cloud environments. To this end, we implement the approach at the level of hypervisors (i.e., at a lower level than the operating systems). This is important because the virtualized environments, which are rapidly gaining popularity, are also susceptible to the timing attacks [14–17]. Last but not least, we carry out a series of experiments, the results of which confirm our previously reported results [12].

More specifically, we rely on the Intel VT-x technology [18], such that every time an `rdtsc` instruction is executed in a virtual machine (VM), a trap (i.e., a `VM_EXIT` event) is created. The trap is then handled by HyperDetector residing in the underlying hypervisor. In the presence of a suspicious time measurement (characterized by two consecutive time readings that are close to each other in time), random noise is introduced into the measurement to prevent the issuer from infiltrating secret information by analyzing the measurement result. And, if a process frequently carries out suspicious measurements, then an alarm is raised for the offending process.

To evaluate the proposed approach, we carried out a series of experiments by using a number of well-known timing attacks together with a suite of benign applications [19]. In these experiments, HyperDetector detected all the malicious processes without any false positives after a few time measurements were made by these processes and reduced the success rates of the attacks from between 98%–99% to between 0%–0.5%. Furthermore, all of these were achieved with a runtime overhead of 1.14%.

The remainder of the paper is organized as follows: Sect. 2 provides background information on Intel VT-x and KVM; Sect. 3 introduces HyperDetector; Sect. 4 discusses the results of the experiments we carried out to evaluate the proposed approach; Sect. 5 discusses the related work; and Sect. 6 presents the concluding remarks.

2 Background

We use Intel VT-x and KVM to implement HyperDetector.

2.1 Intel VT-x

Intel VT-x, which has been frequently used by many open source and commercial hypervisors, including KVM [20], Oracle VM VirtualBox [21], and VMware Workstation [22], provides architectural support for CPU and memory virtualization. To virtualize CPU, Intel VT-x offers two different CPU modes: i) root-mode and ii) non-root mode. The virtual machines run in the non-root mode, while the hypervisor and the host OS run in the root mode. Switching from the non-root mode to the root mode is referred to as `VM_EXIT`, which can be triggered by various events, including the executions of interrupts, exceptions, and specific instructions [23]. One instruction, which can cause a `VM_EXIT` once VT-x is configured accordingly, is `rdtsc`. This trap is typically used to virtualize the `rdtsc` instruction. In this work, we, on the other hand, use it to capture the executions of the `rdtsc` instruction, so that potentially malicious time measurements can be detected, isolated, and prevented at runtime.

2.2 KVM

KVM is a kernel module that turns the Linux operating system into a hypervisor with the help of the hardware extensions for virtualization, such as Intel VT-x or AMD-V [20]. In this work, we implement HyperDetector in KVM. We chose KVM because it is an open source project with a large user-base supporting multiple architectures. KVM has also been frequently used by commercial cloud providers. Note, however, that HyperDetector can readily be adapted to other hypervisors as the proposed approach is a hypervisor-agnostic approach.

3 HyperDetector

HyperDetector is based on Detector$^+$ [12] as outlined in Algorithm 1. The difference is that HyperDetector is implemented in a hypervisor, rather than in an operating system. Furthermore, HyperDetector utilizes a hardware extension for virtualization to intercept the `rdtsc` instructions at runtime, rather than relying on the availability of the source codes and/or binaries of the applications; such that the `rdtsc` instructions can be instrumented accordingly [12].

To this end, we have modified Linux 5.11.0-38 kernel's KVM source code (i.e., by creating a patch) to implement HyperDetector. KVM's code tree for x86 systems is located under `/arch/x86/kvm`. In particular, we have implemented an `rdtsc` handler in KVM, such that every time an `rdtsc` instruction is executed, the control is passed to the hypervisor, which implements the HyperDetector logic outlined in Algorithm 1. The handler is implemented in the `vmx.c` file.

Once an `rdtsc` instruction is about the execute, we first acquire the ID of the thread issuing the instruction by using the `fs_base` register (line 1). Note that for the Windows-based guest operating systems, one needs to interpret the content of this register in a slightly different manner [24].

Then, the time passed since the last `rdtsc` instruction is computed (line 6). If the two readings are suspiciously close to each other, i.e., if the time lag since the last reading is below a threshold, which we call *delta threshold* (line 6), the measurement is marked as suspicious (line 7). In the presence of a suspicious measurement, we introduce random noise to prevent a potentially malicious measurement (line 22). In the remainder of the paper, the time lag between two consecutive pair of time readings is referred to as *time delta*.

The delta threshold is empirically determined by analyzing the distribution of the time deltas observed in the benign processes. For this work, we opted to use a threshold value (300 clock cycles after subtracting the noise), which was

Algorithm 1: HyperDetector Algorithm

```
Data: This function is implemented in the rdtsc handler in KVM
Input: vcpu of the currently exited virtual machine
1  vm_tid ← vcpu.fs_base_register
2  curr_time ← rdtsc()
3  if vcpu.cpl == user_space then
4      thread ← get_thread_info(vcpu, vm_tid)
5      thread.read_cnt ++
6      if curr_time − thread.last_reading ≤ delta_threshold then
7          thread.suspicious_reads++
8          if thread.read_cnt ≥ window_size then
9              score ← thread.suspicious_reads/thread.read_cnt
10             thread.suspicious_reads ← 0
11             thread.read_cnt ← 0
12             if score ≥ warning_threshold then
13                 thread.warning_cnt ++
14                 if thread.warning_cnt ≥ alarm_threshold then
15                     raise alarm for thread
16                     thread.warning_cnt ← 0
17                 end
18             else
19                 thread.warning_cnt ← 0
20             end
21         end
22         random noise
23     end
24     curr_time ← rdtsc()
25 end
26 return curr_time
```

smaller than all the time deltas in the benign applications. That is, any time delta less than 300 clock cycles was marked as suspicious in the experiments.

Next, to determine the potentially malicious processes, we analyze the sequence of time deltas observed in a process by using a non-overlapping sliding window-based approach. Given a consecutive sequence of s time deltas, where s represents the window size, if ratio of suspicious time deltas in the sequence is above a threshold value, called *warning threshold*, a warning is issued (line 12).

In the experiments, we used 0.5 as the warning threshold. We opted to use this warning threshold because, in a typical scenario where a single malicious measurement is made in every iteration of a loop, only half of the time deltas observed in the loop represent actual malicious measurements. The other half is simply an artifact of the monitoring process caused by measuring the time lag between the last time reading of an iteration and the first time reading of the subsequent iteration. Further discussion can be found in [12].

If the warnings are kept on emitting for a number of consecutive windows indicated by *alarm threshold*, then an alarm is raised for the offending process, which is then marked as potentially malicious (lines 13–16). We set the alarm threshold to 1 in the experiments. Note that the value of this threshold can be increased to reduce the number of false positives. Reducing it, on the other hand, helps mark the malicious processes faster as fewer number of time deltas need to be observed before an alarm can be raised. Consequently, we opted to set the alarm threshold to 1.

Note that, in this work, we run the HyperDetector logic only for the `rdtsc` instructions issued from the user space. Although the ones issued from the kernel space are also intercepted by our `rdtsc` handler in the hypervisor, we chose not to analyze them as they are originating from the ring with the highest privilege. To this end, we use the `vmx_get_cpl` function in KVM and process the user-level instructions where $cpl = 3$ (line 3).

4 Experiments

We carried out experiments to evaluate HyperDetector. In these experiments, we used 4 well-known timing attacks, Prime+Probe [11], Flush+Flush [9], Flush+Reload [10], and Meltdown [8], the implementations of which were obtained from publicly available repositories [25]. And, we utilized the Parsec benchmarking suite [19] as the suite of benign applications. We chose this benchmarking suite because it provides a number of real applications from different domains, including computer animations, data mining, and financial analysis.

All the experiments were carried out on an Intel(R) Core(TM) i5-8250U CPU (Kaby Lake) with 16 GB of RAM, 256 KB of L1, 1 MB of L2, and 6 MB of L3 cache memory. We implemented HyperDetector in KVM with the kernel 5.11.0-38 and used Debian with the kernel 3.2.0-4-amd64 as the guest operating system. Furthermore, we disabled the default mitigation strategies, such that the attacks used in the experiments can successfully be carried out.

Figure 1 presents the distributions of the malicious time deltas (i.e., the time measurements made with malicious intents) obtained from the attacks, where the dashed line represents the delta threshold of 300. When the time deltas observed in benign and malicious applications were considered, the accuracy of correctly determining the malicious deltas with this threshold value, was 0.973.

To determine the malicious processes, we configured the HyperDetector to use non-overlapping sliding windows of size 4 with a warning threshold of 0.5 and an alarm threshold of 1, which was indeed the default configuration used in our previous work [12]. HyperDetector correctly pinpointed all the malicious processes without having any false positives after the 3.75th window, on average. That is, while no warning or alarm was raised for any of the benign processes, the first alarms for the malicious processes were raised after these processes performed about 15 time readings, on average.

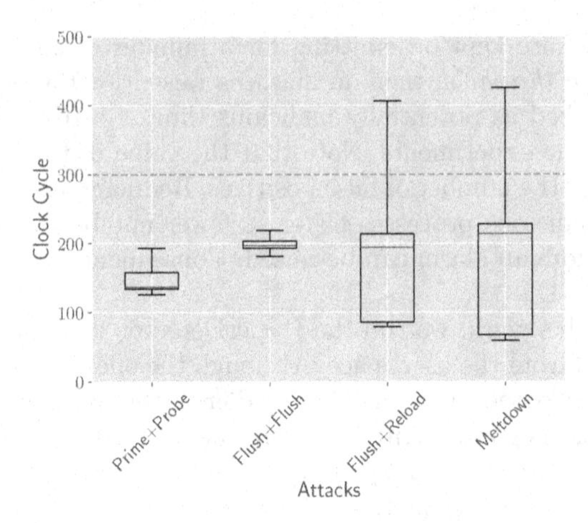

Fig. 1. Distributions of the malicious time deltas obtained in different attacks where the dashed line represents the delta threshold used in the experiments.

We then measured the runtime overhead of the proposed approach by running our subject applications on the original and the instrumented hypervisors. The experiments were repeated at least 5 times. The runtime overhead introduced by HyperDetector was 1.14%, on average. The average overheads on a per subject application basis can be found in Table 1.

Last but not least, we have evaluated the effectiveness of our mitigation strategy. To this end, we used the reliability tool (`reliability.c`), which is distributed with the publicly available source code of Meltdown [26] to measure the success rate of the attack. In the absence of HyperDetector, the success rate of the Meltdown attack was between 98% and 99%. In the presence of HyperDetector, however, the success rate was significantly reduced to between 0% and 0.5%, demonstrating the effectiveness of our mitigation strategy.

One countermeasure against HyperDetector is to increase the gap between the consecutive time readings by inserting dummy instructions, such as NOPs, to stay above the delta threshold. The cost of these instructions can then be factored out from the time measurements to figure out the actual execution times of the operations of interest. In previous work [12], however, we empirically demonstrated that such strategies typically reduce the effectiveness of the attacks due to the noise introduced in the measurements.

5 Related Work

Many approaches have been proposed in the literature to mitigate the timing attacks [27–31], including the coarsification of high resolution clock resources [13,32–34], programming language-based approaches for limiting the amount of information leaked [35–38], formal/static program analysis-based

Table 1. Runtime overheads on the Parsec benchmarking suite.

Application	Domain	Overhead (%)
facesim	Animation programs	0.87
x264	H.264 video encoding	1.54
bodytrack	Computer Vision	0.37
fluidanimate	Animation programs	0.43
ferret	Similarity Search	≈0
canneal	Engineering	2.57
dedup	Enterprise Storage	0.64
streamcluster	Online Clustering	4.36
freqmine	Data Mining	≈0
blackscholes	Financial Analysis	0.69

approaches [39–41], constant-time implementations of cryptographic operations [5,35,42], online monitoring-based mitigation approaches [43–45], and hardware modifications [13,46–50]. Our work generally differs from these works in that we not only mitigate the attacks, but also detect the presence of ongoing attacks and pinpoint the malicious processes involved in them.

Approaches for detecting and isolating the timing attacks have also be studied [48,51–53]. These approaches, however, generally focus on specific types of attacks, such as cache-based timing attacks [51,54–56] and Meltdown attacks [53], by monitoring pre-determined types of resources, such as cache memory [31,48,52,55,56], or events, such as segmentation faults [53,57,58]. HyperDetector, on the other hand, focuses on the common characteristics of the timing attacks with the goal of detecting all the attacks, including the zero-day attacks, which operate by measuring the execution times of short-running operations.

6 Concluding Remarks

In this work, we have developed a generic approach, called HyperDetector, which operates at the level of hypervisors to detect, isolate, and prevent ongoing timing attacks. To this end, we used some of the virtualization features supported by modern CPUs to monitor the executions of the `rdtsc` instructions in an efficient manner at runtime. The results of our experiments confirm our previously reported results [12] in that HyperDetector detected all the malicious processes with a perfect accuracy after these processes made few time measurements and reduced the success rates of the attacks from between 98%–99% to between 0%–0.5%. Furthermore, all of these were achieved with a runtime overhead of 1.14%.

One avenue for future research is to evaluate HyperDetector on other timing attacks. Another avenue is to develop approaches to prevent the malicious parties from determining the presence of HyperDetector by, for example, adjusting the time measurements to factor out the runtime overheads. Furthermore, we continue working on analyzing the essence of the attacks, such that generic approaches can be developed for detecting, isolating, and preventing not just specific attacks, but also classes of attacks, including the zero-day attacks.

References

1. Zander, S., Armitage, G., Branch, P.: A survey of covert channels and countermeasures in computer network protocols. IEEE Commun. Surv. Tutor. **9**(3), 44–57 (2007)
2. Szefer, J.: Survey of microarchitectural side and covert channels, attacks, and defenses. J. Hardw. Syst. Secur. **3**(3), 219–234 (2019)
3. Betz, J., Westhoff, D., Müller, G.: Survey on covert channels in virtual machines and cloud computing. Trans. Emerg. Telecommun. Technol. **28**(6), e3134 (2017)
4. Atici, A.C., Yilmaz, C., Savas, E.: An approach for isolating the sources of information leakage exploited in cache-based side-channel attacks. In: 2013 IEEE Seventh International Conference on Software Security and Reliability Companion, pp. 74–83 (2013)
5. Bernstein, D.J.: Cache-timing attacks on AES (2005)
6. Osvik, D.A., Shamir, A., Tromer, E.: Cache attacks and countermeasures: the case of AES. In: Pointcheval, D. (ed.) CT-RSA 2006. LNCS, vol. 3860, pp. 1–20. Springer, Heidelberg (2006). https://doi.org/10.1007/11605805_1
7. Percival, C.: Cache missing for fun and profit (2005)
8. Lipp, M., et al.: MeltDown: reading kernel memory from user space. In: 27th USENIX Security Symposium (USENIX Security 2018) (2018)
9. Gruss, D., Maurice, C., Wagner, K., Mangard, S.: Flush+Flush: a fast and stealthy cache attack. In: Caballero, J., Zurutuza, U., Rodríguez, R.J. (eds.) DIMVA 2016. LNCS, vol. 9721, pp. 279–299. Springer, Cham (2016). https://doi.org/10.1007/978-3-319-40667-1_14
10. Yarom, Y., Falkner, K.: Flush+reload: a high resolution, low noise, L3 cache side-channel attack. In: Proceedings of the 23rd USENIX Conference on Security Symposium, ser. SEC 2014, pp. 719–732. USENIX Association, USA (2014)
11. Liu, F., Yarom, Y., Ge, Q., Heiser, G., Lee, R.B.: Last-level cache side-channel attacks are practical. In: 2015 IEEE Symposium on Security and Privacy, pp. 605–622. IEEE (2015)
12. Javeed, A., Yilmaz, C., Savas, E.: Detector+: an approach for detecting, isolating, and preventing timing attacks. Comput. Secur. **110**, 102454 (2021)
13. Martin, R., Demme, J., Sethumadhavan, S.: TimeWarp: rethinking timekeeping and performance monitoring mechanisms to mitigate side-channel attacks. In: 2012 39th Annual International Symposium on Computer Architecture (ISCA), pp. 118–129. IEEE (2012)
14. Li, P., Gao, D., Reiter, M.K.: Stopwatch: a cloud architecture for timing channel mitigation. ACM Trans. Inf. Syst. Secur. (TISSEC) **17**(2), 1–28 (2014)
15. Wu, J., Ding, L., Lin, Y., Min-Allah, N., Wang, Y.: XenPump: a new method to mitigate timing channel in cloud computing. In: 2012 IEEE Fifth International Conference on Cloud Computing, pp. 678–685. IEEE (2012)
16. Moon, S.-J., Sekar, V., Reiter, M.K.: Nomad: mitigating arbitrary cloud side channels via provider-assisted migration. In: Proceedings of the 22nd ACM SIGSAC Conference on Computer and Communications Security, pp. 1595–1606 (2015)

17. Varadarajan, V., Ristenpart, T., Swift, M.: Scheduler-based defenses against {Cross-VM} side-channels. In: 23rd USENIX Security Symposium (USENIX Security 2014), pp. 687–702 (2014)
18. Neiger, G., Santoni, A., Leung, F., Rodgers, D., Uhlig, R.: Intel virtualization technology: hardware support for efficient processor virtualization. Intel Technol. J. **10**(3) (2006)
19. The parsec benchmark suite. https://parsec.cs.princeton.edu/
20. Kivity, A., Kamay, Y., Laor, D., Lublin, U., Liguori, A.: KVM: the linux virtual machine monitor. In: Proceedings of the Linux Symposium, Dttawa, Ontorio, Canada, vol. 1, no. 8, pp. 225–230 (2007)
21. https://www.virtualbox.org/
22. VMware workstation pro, June 2022. https://www.vmware.com/products/workstation-pro/workstation-pro-evaluation.html
23. Bugnion, E., Nieh, J., Tsafrir, D.: Hardware and Software Support for Virtualization. Synthesis Lectures on Computer Architecture, vol. 12, pp. 1–206. Springer, Cham (2017)
24. https://docs.microsoft.com/en-us/windows/win32/api/winternl/ns-winternl-teb
25. IAIK: Flush + flush (2016). https://github.com/IAIK/flush_flush
26. IAIK: Meltdown (2018). https://github.com/IAIK/meltdown
27. Spreitzer, R., Moonsamy, V., Korak, T., Mangard, S.: Systematic classification of side-channel attacks: a case study for mobile devices. IEEE Commun. Surv. Tutor. **20**(1), 465–488 (2017)
28. Ge, Q., Yarom, Y., Cock, D., Heiser, G.: A survey of microarchitectural timing attacks and countermeasures on contemporary hardware. J. Cryptogr. Eng. **8**(1), 1–27 (2018)
29. Biswas, A.K., Ghosal, D., Nagaraja, S.: A survey of timing channels and countermeasures. ACM Comput. Surv. (CSUR) **50**(1), 1–39 (2017)
30. Zhang, Q., Gong, H., Zhang, X., Liang, C., Tan, Y.-A.: A sensitive network jitter measurement for covert timing channels over interactive traffic. Multimedia Tools Appl. **78**(3), 3493–3509 (2019)
31. Qureshi, M.K.: New attacks and defense for encrypted-address cache. In: 2019 ACM/IEEE 46th Annual International Symposium on Computer Architecture (ISCA), pp. 360–371. IEEE (2019)
32. Canella, C., et al.: Fallout: leaking data on meltdown-resistant CPUs. In: Proceedings of the 2019 ACM SIGSAC Conference on Computer and Communications Security, pp. 769–784 (2019)
33. Oren, Y., Kemerlis, V.P., Sethumadhavan, S., Keromytis, A.D.: The spy in the sandbox: practical cache attacks in javascript and their implications. In: Proceedings of the 22nd ACM SIGSAC Conference on Computer and Communications Security, pp. 1406–1418 (2015)
34. Hu, W.-M.: Reducing timing channels with fuzzy time. J. Comput. Secur. **1**(3–4), 233–254 (1992)
35. Almeida, J.B., Barbosa, M., Barthe, G., Dupressoir, F., Emmi, M.: Verifying constant-time implementations. In: 25th USENIX Security Symposium (USENIX Security 2016), pp. 53–70 (2016)
36. Zhang, D., Wang, Y., Suh, G.E., Myers, A.C.: A hardware design language for timing-sensitive information-flow security. ACM SIGPLAN Not. **50**(4), 503–516 (2015)
37. Li, X., et al.: Sapper: a language for hardware-level security policy enforcement. In: Proceedings of the 19th International Conference on Architectural Support for Programming Languages and Operating Systems, pp. 97–112 (2014)

38. Porter, D.E., Bond, M.D., Roy, I., McKinley, K.S., Witchel, E.: Practical fine-grained information flow control using laminar. ACM Trans. Program. Lang. Syst. (TOPLAS) **37**(1), 1–51 (2014)
39. Doychev, G., Köpf, B., Mauborgne, L., Reineke, J.: CacheAudit: a tool for the static analysis of cache side channels. ACM Trans. Inf. Syst. Secur. (TISSEC) **18**(1), 1–32 (2015)
40. Cock, D., Ge, Q., Murray, T., Heiser, G.: The last mile: an empirical study of timing channels on seL4. In: Proceedings of the 2014 ACM SIGSAC Conference on Computer and Communications Security, pp. 570–581 (2014)
41. Rodrigues, B., Quintão Pereira, F.M., Aranha, D.F.: Sparse representation of implicit flows with applications to side-channel detection. In: Proceedings of the 25th International Conference on Compiler Construction, pp. 110–120 (2016)
42. Barthe, G., Betarte, G., Campo, J., Luna, C., Pichardie, D.: System-level non-interference for constant-time cryptography. In: Proceedings of the 2014 ACM SIGSAC Conference on Computer and Communications Security, pp. 1267–1279 (2014)
43. Gruss, D., Maurice, C., Mangard, S.: Rowhammer.js: a remote software-induced fault attack in JavaScript. In: Caballero, J., Zurutuza, U., Rodríguez, R.J. (eds.) DIMVA 2016. LNCS, vol. 9721, pp. 300–321. Springer, Cham (2016). https://doi.org/10.1007/978-3-319-40667-1_15
44. Nomani, J., Szefer, J.: Predicting program phases and defending against side-channel attacks using hardware performance counters. In: Proceedings of the Fourth Workshop on Hardware and Architectural Support for Security and Privacy, pp. 1–4 (2015)
45. Zhang, X., Xiao, Y., Zhang, Y.: Return-oriented flush-reload side channels on arm and their implications for android devices. In: Proceedings of the 2016 ACM SIGSAC Conference on Computer and Communications Security, pp. 858–870 (2016)
46. Andrysco, M., Kohlbrenner, D., Mowery, K., Jhala, R., Lerner, S., Shacham, H.: On subnormal floating point and abnormal timing. In: 2015 IEEE Symposium on Security and Privacy, pp. 623–639. IEEE (2015)
47. Domnitser, L., Jaleel, A., Loew, J., Abu-Ghazaleh, N., Ponomarev, D.: Non-monopolizable caches: low-complexity mitigation of cache side channel attacks. ACM Trans. Archit. Code Optim. (TACO) **8**(4), 1–21 (2012)
48. Kiriansky, V., Lebedev, I., Amarasinghe, S., Devadas, S., Emer, J.: DAWG: a defense against cache timing attacks in speculative execution processors. In: 2018 51st Annual IEEE/ACM International Symposium on Microarchitecture (MICRO), pp. 974–987. IEEE (2018)
49. Wang, Z., Lee, R.B.: New cache designs for thwarting software cache-based side channel attacks. In: Proceedings of the 34th Annual International Symposium on Computer Architecture, pp. 494–505 (2007)
50. Page, D.: Partitioned cache architecture as a side-channel defence mechanism. Cryptology ePrint Archive (2005)
51. Fletchery, C.W., Ren, L., Yu, X., Van Dijk, M., Khan, O., Devadas, S.: Suppressing the oblivious ram timing channel while making information leakage and program efficiency trade-offs. In: 2014 IEEE 20th International Symposium on High Performance Computer Architecture (HPCA), pp. 13–224. IEEE (2014)
52. Wang, S., Wang, P., Liu, X., Zhang, D., Wu, D.: CacheD: identifying Cache-Based timing channels in production software. In: 26th USENIX Security Symposium (USENIX Security 2017), pp. 235–252 (2017)

53. Akyildiz, T.A., Guzgeren, C.B., Yilmaz, C., Savas, E.: MeltdownDetector: a runtime approach for detecting meltdown attacks. Futur. Gener. Comput. Syst. **112**, 136–147 (2020)
54. Kim, T., Peinado, M., Mainar-Ruiz, G.: STEALTHMEM: system-Level protection against Cache-Based side channel attacks in the cloud. In: 21st USENIX Security Symposium (USENIX Security 2012), pp. 189–204 (2012)
55. Kulah, Y., Dincer, B., Yilmaz, C., Savas, E.: SpyDetector: an approach for detecting side-channel attacks at runtime. Int. J. Inf. Secur. **18**(4), 393–422 (2018). https://doi.org/10.1007/s10207-018-0411-7
56. Chiappetta, M., Savas, E., Yilmaz, C.: Real time detection of cache-based side-channel attacks using hardware performance counters. Appl. Soft Comput. **49**, 1162–1174 (2016)
57. Zhang, Y., Reiter, M.K.: Düppel: retrofitting commodity operating systems to mitigate cache side channels in the cloud. In: Proceedings of the 2013 ACM SIGSAC Conference on Computer & Communications Security, pp. 827–838 (2013)
58. Payer, M.: HexPADS: a platform to detect "Stealth" attacks. In: Caballero, J., Bodden, E., Athanasopoulos, E. (eds.) ESSoS 2016. LNCS, vol. 9639, pp. 138–154. Springer, Cham (2016). https://doi.org/10.1007/978-3-319-30806-7_9

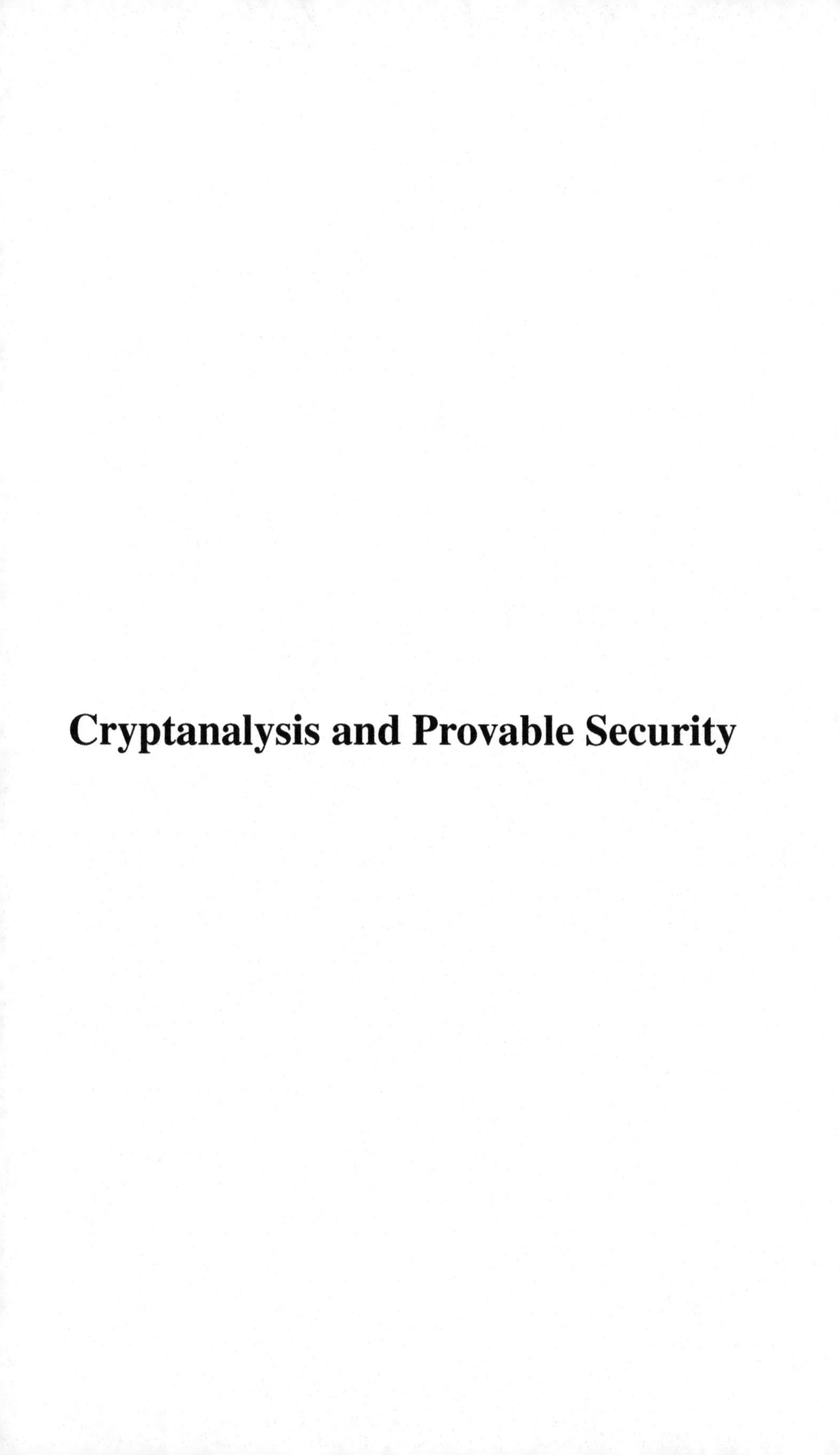

Cryptanalysis and Provable Security

The Construction and Application of (Related-Key) Conditional Differential Neural Distinguishers on KATAN

Dongdong Lin[1(✉)], Shaozhen Chen[1,2], Manman Li[1,2], and Zezhou Hou[1,2]

[1] Information Engineering University, Zhengzhou, China
Alin_lin_20@163.com
[2] State Key Laboratory of Cryptology, Beijing, China

Abstract. At CRYPTO 2019, Ghor applied deep learning to the cryptanalysis of block ciphers and presented neural distinguishers instead of purely differential distinguishers, which improved key recovery attacks of Speck32/64 using Bayesian optimization. In this paper, the authors attempt to improve the performance of neural distinguishers (NDs) and apply new NDs to present practical key recovery attacks on KATAN ciphers. First, with the help of MILP model, we present a (related-key) conditional differential neural distinguishers ((RK)CDNDs) of KATAN ciphers. The (RK)CDNDs use a new data format, combining with conditions and multiple differences. Compared to previous work, we greatly improve the number of rounds and the accuracy of NDs in both single-key and related-key scenarios. Moreover, a related-key conditional differential cryptanalysis framework based on deep learning is proposed with the RKCDNDs, resulting in a significant improvement from the previous. We present a practical key recovery attack on the 125-round KATAN32. The data complexity is $2^{15.7}$ and the time complexity is $2^{19.9}$. We also present 106-round KATAN48 and 95-round KATAN64 practical key recovery attacks. The extension of key recovery attack improves the results for two more rounds by calculating the wrong key response profile in parallel. Our work not only increases the number of attack rounds and the recoverable key bits, but also reduces the computational complexity.

Keywords: Deep learning · Block cipher · KATAN ciphers · Related-Key conditional differential cryptanalysis · Neural distinguishers

1 Introduction

Deep learning has been widely applied in image recognition, natural language processing, machine translation and other areas to solve a series of challenging problems [18], which was proposed by Hinton in 2006 [12]. Neural networks automatically extract features from the data and make feature engineering efficient and concise. The convolutional neural networks [17] and recurrent neural networks [21] had greatly enhanced the learning ability of neural networks.

A. R. Beresford et al. (Eds.): CANS 2022, LNCS 13641, pp. 203–224, 2022.
https://doi.org/10.1007/978-3-031-20974-1_10

At ICLR 2018, Aidan *et al.* [10] proposed a method of using generative adversarial networks (GANs) to decrypt the Vigenère cipher. At CRYPTO 2019, Ghor [9] applied deep learning to the cryptanalysis of block ciphers for the first time. He presented a powerful neural distinguisher which improved the 11-round key recovery attack of Speck32/64. In 2021, Bao *et al.* [1] introduced the generalized neutral bits into Ghor's key recovery framework and first proposed a practical key recovery attack of 13-round Speck32/64 and 16-round Simon32/64. At EUROCRYPT 2021, Benamira *et al.* [2] presented a convincing explanation of neural network distinguishers, showing that neural distinguishers rely on the differential distribution of ciphertext pairs and the differential distribution in the penultimate and antepenultimate rounds. Chen *et al.* [7] proposed a new neural distinguisher by using multiple ciphertext pairs which are constructed from different keys. Hou *et al.* [13] presented a new neural distinguisher using multiple output differences. However, they can't improve the results of key recovery attack with their neural distinguishers. In [9,10], the researchers improved neural distinguishers by changing data format. Inspired by these, we propose a (related-key) conditional differential neural distinguisher((RK)CDND) of KATAN ciphers, combining with the conditions and multiple differences.

Table 1. Summary of related-key attacks on KATAN ciphers

Cipher	Technique	Rounds	Time	Data	Reference
KATAN32	RKCD	120	2^{31}	2^{31} CP	[16]
	RKCD(*)	158	$2^{77.97}$	2^{20} CP	[19]
	Boomerang Attacks(*)	174	$2^{78.8}$	$2^{27.6}$ CP	[14]
	Boomerang Attacks(*)	187	$2^{78.4}$	$2^{31.8}$ CP	[6]
	RKCDDL	**125**	$\mathbf{2^{19.9}}$	$\mathbf{2^{15.7}}$ **CP**	**Section** 4.2
KATAN48	RKCD	103	2^{25}	2^{25} CP	[16]
	RKCD(*)	140	$2^{77.4}$	2^{27} CP	[19]
	Boomerang Attacks(*)	145	$2^{78.5}$	$2^{38.4}$ CP	[14]
	Boomerang Attacks(*)	150	$2^{77.6}$	$2^{47.2}$	[6]
	RKCDDL	**106**	$\mathbf{2^{17.0}}$	$\mathbf{2^{12.8}}$ **CP**	**Section** 5.1
KATAN64	RKCD	90	2^{27}	2^{27} CP	[16]
	RKCD(*)	126	$2^{79.19}$	2^{25} CP	[19]
	Boomerang Attacks(*)	130	$2^{78.1}$	$2^{53.1}$ CP	[14]
	Boomerang Attacks(*)	133	$2^{78.5}$	$2^{58.4}$CP	[6]
	RKCDDL	**95**	$\mathbf{2^{14.2}}$	$\mathbf{2^{15.2}}$**CP**	**Section** 5.2

CP: chosen plaintext KP: known plaintext *: theoretical attacks.
RKCD: related-key conditional differential cryptanalysis.
RKCDDL: related-key conditional differential cryptanalysis based on deep learning.

KATAN family is a lightweight block cipher based on nonlinear feedback shift registers (NLFSRs), designed by Cannière *et al.* [8] and published at CHES 2009. It is a hardware-oriented lightweight block cipher which is highly compact and offers adequate security. In 2011, Knellwolf *et al.* [16] proposed a related-key conditional differential (RKCD) cryptanalysis method of KATAN ciphers. In the related-key scenario, there are some theoretical attack results of KATAN family [6,14,19]. We improve the related-key conditional differential cryptanalysis by using RKCDNDs. We call it 'related-key conditional differential cryptanalysis based on deep learning (RKCDDL)'. In the related-key scenario, our work is the best result in the practical key recovery attack on KATAN family as known so far. All the results are summarized in Table 1.

Our Contributions. In the study, we present a (related-key) conditional differential neural distinguishers((RK)CDNDs) of KATAN ciphers. Using RKCDNDs, we propose a related-key conditional differential cryptanalysis method on KATAN ciphers.

First, we introduce a new data format combined with conditions and multiple differences. Based on the new data format, the input shape and hyperparameters of the deep residual neural network are adjusted. We propose a (related-key) conditional differential neural distinguisher, which improves the accuracy and rounds of the neural distinguishers. Based on MILP model, we search appropriate plaintext differences, key differences (in the related-key scenario) and conditions to find differential characteristics with probability 1 for KATAN ciphers. Compared to previous NDs, the CDNDs improve at least 22 rounds in the single-key scenario and the RKCDNDs improve at least 46 rounds in the related-key scenario. Although conditions will reduce the plaintext space, we control the number of conditions to ensure that the remaining plaintext space is large enough to present practical key recovery attacks.

Second, a related-key conditional differential cryptanalysis framework based on RKCDNDs is proposed. In [16], related-key conditional differential cryptanalysis only can recover a few discontinuous key bits and the computational complexity of cryptanalysis is high. With the help of RKCDNDs, we improve the results of related-key conditional differential cryptanalysis. We present practical key recovery attacks against 125/106/95 rounds KATAN32/48/64, which can recover 30/30/22 continuous subkey bits. Message modification technology reduces the computational complexity at the plaintext filtering stage. By optimizing the calculation of the wrong key response profile, we extend our practical key recovery attacks for two more rounds. The attacks of KATAN ciphers are presented as the best known practical results so far.

Outline. The remainder of the structure is as follows: Section 2 provides some preliminaries, a brief description of KATAN ciphers, related-key cryptanalysis and differential cryptanalysis based on deep learning. Section 3 introduces the construction of (related-key) conditional differential neural distinguishers in detail. Section 4 proposes a practical key recovery attack of related-key conditional differential cryptanalysis based on deep learning on KATAN32. In Sect. 5, we present practical key recovery attacks against KATAN48/64 ciphers and extend the attacks of KATAN family. The summary is in Sect. 6.

2 Preliminaries

2.1 Notation

Table 2. The notations of the paper

Symbol	Definition
P, C, K	Plaintext, ciphertext and master key
L_t, R_t	The states of two NLFSRs at round t
p_i, c_i, k_i, l_{t+i}, r_{t+i}	the i-th bits of P, C, K, L_t and R_t
ΔP, ΔC, ΔK, ΔL_t, ΔR_t	differences of P, C, K, L_t and R_t
P^{block}, C^{block}	a P^{block} (C^{block}) consists of 32 plaintext (ciphertext) pairs
$P_{structure}$, $C_{structure}$	a $P_{structure}$ ($C_{structure}$) consists of 2^s P^{block} (C^{block})

2.2 Description of KATAN

KATAN ciphers have three versions: KATAN32, KATAN48 and KATAN64. The three versions have block sizes of 32, 48 and 64 bits. The family of ciphers shares the same key schedule, master key length, encryption rounds and NLFSRs.

The master key $K = (k_0, \cdots, k_{79})$ of KATAN family is 80 bits. The key schedule uses an 80-bit linear feedback shift register (LFSR) and the feedback polynomial is an 80-bit primitive polynomial. The ciphers use two key bits per round. The maximal number of consecutive rounds that key difference does not introduce differences is 39 rounds.

$$k_{i+80} = k_i \oplus k_{i+19} \oplus k_{i+30} \oplus k_{i+67}, \quad 0 \leq i \leq 427 \tag{1}$$

The structure of KATAN is shown in Fig. 1.

Taking KATAN32 as an example, the block size of KATAN32 is 32 bits. The lengths of registers L and R are 13 bits and 19 bits. The plaintext is loaded into L and R:

$$(p_{31}, p_{30}, \cdots, p_{19}) \rightarrow (l_0, l_1, \cdots, l_{12})$$

$$(p_{18}, p_{17}, \cdots, p_0) \rightarrow (r_0, r_1, \cdots, r_{18})$$

The round functions in each round are two nonlinear functions which are defined as follows:

$$r_{t+19} = l_t \oplus l_{t+5} \oplus (l_{t+4} l_{t+7}) \oplus l_{t+9} a_t \oplus k_{2t} \tag{2}$$

$$l_{t+13} = r_t \oplus r_{t+11} \oplus (r_{t+6} r_{t+8}) \oplus (r_{t+10} r_{t+15}) \oplus k_{2t+1} \tag{3}$$

where a_t is a round constant which has the initial value $(1, 1, 1, 1, 1, 1, 1, 0)$ and is updated by feedback polynomial $a_{t+8} = a_t + a_{t+1} + a_{t+3} + a_{t+5}, t \geq 8$. k_{2t+1}

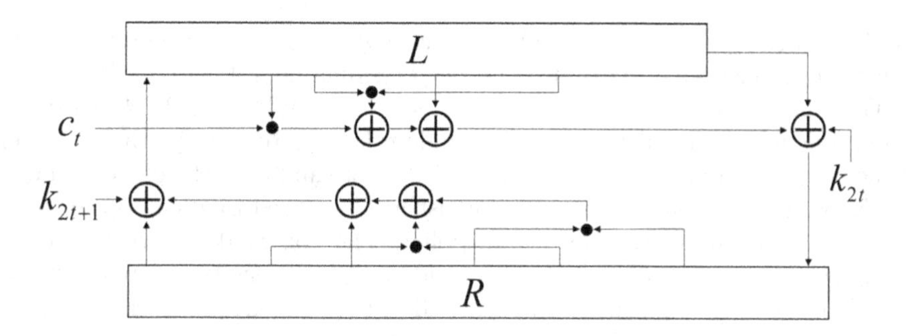

Fig. 1. The structure of KATAN

and k_{2t} are two subkeys. Nonlinear functions are different in various versions. KATAN48 applies the functions twice by using the same subkeys in one round. For KATAN64, the functions are applied three times each round. After 254 rounds of encryption, the states in the registers L and R are output as the ciphertext.

2.3 Related-Key Cryptanalysis

In 1994, Biham [3] introduced related-key cryptanalysis, which is effective for block ciphers with relatively simple key expansion algorithms. This method is usually used in combination with other attack methods, such as differential cryptanalysis and impossible differential cryptanalysis. In the related-key differential cryptanalysis, researchers can choose differences in plaintext and master key to find the connection of the corresponding encryption algorithm. Related-key differential cryptanalysis successfully attacked many block ciphers, such as [5,15].

2.4 Description of Differential Cryptanalysis Based on Deep Learning

At CRYPTO 2019, Ghor proposed a differential cryptanalysis framework based on deep learning. The neural distinguishers of the round-reduced Speck32/64 are constructed based on the neural network and trained with the input difference and ciphertext pairs. At the key recovery stage, combined with the Bayesian optimization algorithm [20], Ghor proposed an 11-round Speck32/64 key recovery attack by using neural distinguishers.

First, we introduce Ghor's construction method of neural distinguishers. The plaintext difference is $\Delta P = 0x00400000$. The plaintext pair and the ciphertext pair are (P, P') and (C, C'). The input of the neural network is ciphertext pairs. Generate $0-1$ data as label Y for ciphertext pairs randomly. The value of P' is decided by label Y. If $Y = 1$, $P' = P \oplus \Delta$. If $Y = 0$, P' is generated randomly. Put the ciphertext pairs and their labels into the neural distinguisher. If the distinguisher can correctly distinguish the labels with the accuracy $\geq 50\%$, a useable neural distinguisher is trained. Ghor trained neural distinguishers of the round-reduced Speck32/64 by using a deep residual neural network [11].

Ghor performed a key recovery attack on $r+1$-round Speck32/64 by using an r-round neural distinguisher. Use the random key K_r to decrypt the ciphertext of the $r+1$-round Speck32/64 for one round. Score and rank the current random key K_r with the r-round neural distinguisher. Ghor used Bayesian optimization algorithm to optimize the key search policy. The non-random structure of the wrong key response value distribution generated the wrong key response profile. To enhance the distinguishers' response, Ghor used s neutral bits [4] to generate a plaintext structure consisting of 2^s plaintext pairs, which passed the first two rounds differential together. Ghor partially decrypted each ciphertext pair by using all final-round subkeys and used the response value of ciphertext structure to rank all subkeys. The Algorithm 1 sums up the algorithm.

Algorithm 1. $R+1$-round Bayesian key search strategy

Require: Ciphertext structure $C = \{C_0, C_1, \cdots, C_{2^s-1}\}$, R-round multi-differential neural distinguisher ND_R, number of iterations l, number of the set of subkey candidates n.

$S := \{k_0, k_1, \cdots, k_{n-1}\} \leftarrow$ choose at random without replacement from the set of all subkey candidates.

$L \leftarrow \{\}$

for $j \in \{0, 1, \cdots, l-1\}$ **do**

  $P_{i,k} \leftarrow Decrypt(C_i, k)$, for all $C_i \in C, k \in S$

  $v_{i,k} \leftarrow ND_R(P_{i,k}, k)$, for all i, k

  $w_{i,k} \leftarrow log_2(v_{i,k}/(1-v_{i,k}))$, for all i, k

  $w_k \leftarrow \sum_{i=0}^{n-1} v_{i,k}$, $k \in S$

  $L \leftarrow L||[(k, w_k)]$, $k \in S$

  $m_k \leftarrow \sum_{i=0}^{n-1} v_{i,k}/n$, $k \in S$

  $\lambda_k \leftarrow \sum_{i=0}^{n-1} (m_i - \mu_{k \oplus k_i})^2 / \sigma_{k \oplus k_i}^2$, $k \in \{0, 1, \cdots, 2^{16}-1\}$

  $S \leftarrow argsort_k(\lambda)[0 : n-1]$

end for

return L

3 (Related-Key) Conditional Differential Neural Distinguishers Based on MILP

The core idea of cryptanalysis based on deep learning is to train neural distinguishers. A well-behaved neural distinguisher can effectively increase the rounds of the key recovery attack. At the same round, the higher the accuracy of the neural distinguisher is, the lower the computational complexity of the key recovery attack is. In [13], Hou *et al.* constructed MOD neural distinguishers. Using multiple differences, they improved the accuracy of the neural distinguishers and increase its number of rounds. However, the multiple differences lead to an exponential decrease in the probability of prepended differential, which do not improve the key recovery attack. We apply conditions to the training of the neural distinguishers to further increase the rounds of the neural distinguishers. Based on the multiple differences and conditions, we introduce a new data format.

3.1 Data Format of (Related-Key) Conditional Differential Neural Distinguishers

Since deep learning is a data-driven technology, the quality of data plays a key role in the quality of the neural model. For neural distinguishers, Data format directly affects the accuracy. The conditions filter the plaintext to prevent the propagation of differences, which can increase the rounds of neural distinguishers. The construction of (related-key) conditional differential data is shown in Fig. 2.

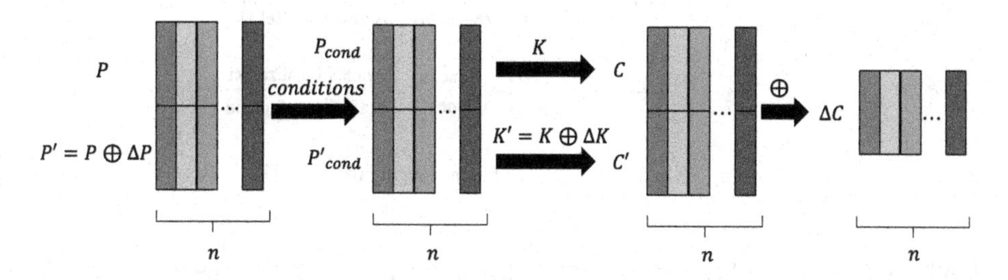

Fig. 2. Data format of (related-key) conditional differential neural distinguishers

As shown in Fig. 2, we generate n plaintext P randomly and $P' = P \oplus \Delta P$, where ΔP is input difference. After filtering plaintext pairs by conditions, we get new plaintext pairs (P_{cond}, P'_{cond}), where $P'_{cond} = P_{cond} \oplus \Delta P$. In the single-key scenario, (P_{cond}, P'_{cond}) is encrypted by K. In the related-key scenario, P'_{cond} is encrypted by K', where $K' = K \oplus \Delta K$. The resulting ciphertext pairs and ciphertext differences are (C, C') and ΔC. The ciphertext differences ΔC are the input of the neural network. Generate $0 - 1$ data as label Y for ciphertext pair sets randomly, If $Y = 1$, $P' = P \oplus \Delta P$. If $Y = 0$, P' is generated randomly. Based on the new data format, we design a neural network on KATAN ciphers.

3.2 Neural Network Structure

In this section, we design a deep residual neural network based on the data format of KATAN ciphers. The specific structure is shown in Fig. 3.

Our neural network is similar to Ghor's [9] work. The neural network mainly consists of three parts: the input layer, the iterative layer, and the output layer. The input layer receives KATAN's ciphertext differences data and reshape the data into a matrix form. The symbol bs and n stand for the block size of different

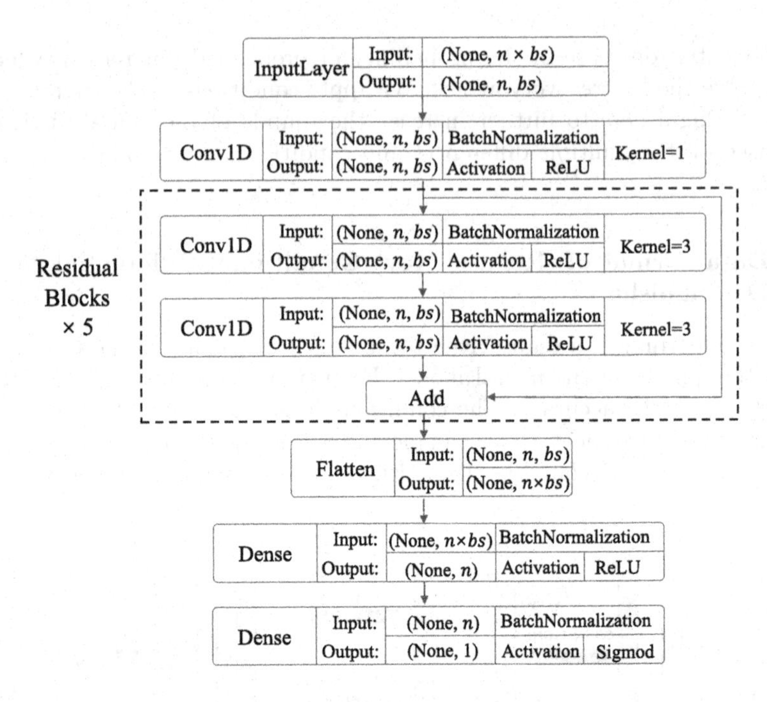

Fig. 3. Neural network structure

KATAN versions and the number of multiple differences. Then, the data passes a conv1d layer. The main part of neural network is iterative layer. In the iterative layer, the neural network uses 5 residual blocks. Each residual block contains two conv1d layers and each conv1d layer is followed by a batchnormalization layer and an activation layer. The output of the residual block and the input are added. The result is passed as the input for the next block. The output layer consists of a flatten layer, a fully connected layer and an output unit. The hyperparameters of the neural network are given below. The convolutional kernel is 1 in the input layers and 3 in the iterative layers. The number of filters in the convolutional layers is n (block size). We use MSE(Mean-Squared-Error) loss function and Adam optimization. The training set size and validation set size are 10^7 and 10^6. We set that batch size and epochs are 1000 and 200.

The deep residual network is originally used in the image recognition field, which has advantages in recognizing matrix data. To take advantage of the characteristics of the deep residual network, we concatenate the differences into a matrix. The neural network extracts not only the features in each difference, but also the connection between different differences. In Sect. 3.3, we take KATAN32 as an example to show how to choose conditions in the related-key scenario and compare the effects of various neural distinguishers on KATAN ciphers in detail.

3.3 MILP Model of KATAN Family

Conditions. For KATAN ciphers, the difference of updated bits in each round is determined by the partial bits and the differences of the previous round. Applying the conditions, the partial differential bits can be controlled to prevent the propagation of differences. Conditions are generally used to prevent the differential propagation in the initial rounds. In [16], the conditions are classified into three types:

I. Conditions only involve plaintext bits p_i.
II. Conditions involve plaintext bits p_i and key bits k_i.
III. Conditions only involve key bits k_i.

Construction of MILP Model. The MILP model can search an appropriate input difference and conditions for neural distinguishers. In [22], Xing *et al.* proposed a MILP model of KATAN32 in the single-key scenario. KATAN family shares the same round functions, while KATAN32 applies the functions once, KATAN48 applies the functions twice and KATAN64 applies the functions three times.

In the single-key scenario, we use the sets of linear inequalities described in [22]. KATAN48 and KATAN64 apply the round function multiple times with the same key. Since neural distinguishers are sensitive to the input differences and require the input data to satisfy the same input differences, we add some equalities to constrain the output differences of prepended differential.

In the related-key scenario, we should rebuild the linear inequalities. Taking KATAN32 as an example, for Eq. (2) and (3), Δr_{t+19} is generated by 6 bits in the 13-bit NLFSR of round t and Δl_{t+13} is generated by 7 bits in the 19-bit NLFSR of round t. Let c denote whether a condition is applied or not. In Eq. (2), there is a constant a_t at each round. We model two cases to simplify constraints of the MILP model. When $a_t = 0$, we show all values of the vector $(\Delta l_t, \Delta l_{t+5}, \Delta l_{t+4}, \Delta l_{t+7}, \Delta k_{2t}, \Delta r_{t+19}, c)$ in Appendix Table 9. When $a_t = 1$, we show all values of the vector $(\Delta l_t, \Delta l_{t+5}, \Delta l_{t+4}, \Delta l_{t+7}, \Delta l_{t+9}, \Delta k_{2t}, \Delta r_{t+19}, c)$ in Appendix Table 10. In Eq. (3), Δl_{t+13} depends on the values and the differences of the 7 bits. We show all values of the vector $(\Delta r_t, \Delta r_{t+11}, \Delta r_{t+6}, \Delta r_{t+8}, \Delta l_{t+10}, \Delta r_{t+15}, \Delta k_{2t+1}, \Delta l_{t+13}, c)$ in Appendix Table 11. We use SageMath to model three vectors and obtain three sets of linear inequalities in Appendix (10), (11) and (12). Then, we expand the linear inequalities to the selected rounds to obtain the constraints of MILP model. Other settings are similar to [22]. With these methods, we build a MILP model for KATAN32 in the related-key scenario. In the same way, KATAN48 and KATAN64's MILP models are built.

3.4 (Related-Key) Conditional Differential Neural Distinguishers

In the following experiments, we verify the advantages of (related-key) conditional differential neural distinguishers ((RK)CDNDs). We compare our

(RK)CD-NDs with neural distinguishers (NDs) in [9] and Multiple Output Differences neural distinguishers (MODNDs) in [13]. The NDs and MODNDs only applied on Speck and Simon family in [9,13]. Based on experimental experience, we search the input differences of neural distinguishers with low hamming distance and choose appropriate input differences for NDs and MODNDs on KATAN ciphers. The input size of the neural network is $(None, n \times bs)$ and the hyperparameter settings are shown in Sect. 3.2. We only show the highest round and accuracy of each neural distinguisher.

Table 3. Comparison of neural distinguishers on KATAN ciphers

Cipher	Distinguishers	ΔP	ΔK	Conditions	n	Rounds	Accuracy
KATAN32	ND	$0x00002000$	–	–	–	51	53.3%
	MODND	$0x00002000$	–	–	64	59	57.5%
	CDND	$0x61082200$	–	18	64	**85**	56.0%
	RKCDND	$0x00049248$	ΔK_1	19	64	**112**	64.7%
KATAN48	ND	$0x040000000000$	–	–	–	40	58.0%
	MODND	$0x040000000000$	–	–	48	50	54%
	CDND	$0x610010080402$	–	25	48	**72**	58.2%
	RKCDND	$0x0C0000845000$	ΔK_2	19	48	**96**	62.5%
KATAN64	ND	$0x000000200000$	–	–	–	31	71.8%
	MODND	$0x000000200000$	–	–	64	36	54.8%
	CDND	$0x2480482010080400$	–	26	64	**61**	61.3%
	RKCDND	$0x9201208F40380000$	ΔK_3	30	64	**86**	72.8%

ND:neural distinguishers.
MODND:Multiple Output Differences neural distinguishers.
CDND:conditional differential neural distinguishers.
RKCDND:related-key conditional differential neural distinguishers.
$\Delta K_1 = 0x00080801000020000000$ $\Delta K_2 = 0x08010000200000000000$.
$\Delta K_3 = 0x00400008000000000000$ n:the number of multiple differences.

For KATAN32, based on the 18 conditions and plaintext difference $\Delta P = 0x61082200$, we get a 85-round CDND against KATAN32 with 56.0% accuracy. We also get a 112-round RKCDND againist KATAN32 with 64.7%, based on 19 conditions, $\Delta P = 0x00049248$ and ΔK_1. For KATAN48, we get a 72-round CDND and a 96-round RKCDND with 58.2% and 62.5% accuracy, respectively. For KATAN64, we obtain a 61-round CDND and an 86-round RKCDND with 61.3% and 72.8% accuracy, respectively. The results are shown in Table 3. Compared with previous work, we greatly improve the number of rounds and the accuracy of neural distinguishers in both single-key and related-key scenarios. Although conditions will reduce the plaintext space, the remaining plaintext space is large enough to present practical key recovery attacks. Taking RKCDNDs as an example, the remaining plaintext space of KATAN32/48/64 is $2^{13}/2^{29}/2^{34}$, respectively.

4 Key Recovery Attack of KATAN32

Related-Key conditional differential cryptanalysis prevents the propagation of differences by controlling the state of NLFSRs with conditions. The basic idea is as follows: Firstly, search the key difference ΔK which is not introduce differences for 39 rounds after round r. Secondly, find the conditions and a plaintext difference ΔP to cancel the differences introduced by ΔK. Thirdly, impose the conditions to filter plaintexts which can lead to bias on some update bit differences. Key recovery attacks are proposed using the bias.

Although related-key conditional differential cryptanalysis increases the rounds of differential attack, only a few discontinuous key bits can be recovered. Based on the related-key conditional neural distinguishers proposed in Sect. 3, we present related-key conditional differential cryptanalysis based on deep learning.

4.1 Training of Related-Key Conditional Differential Neural Distinguishers

We use MILP model to search for a 66-round related-key differential characteristic with 14 conditions for KATAN32. The differential characteristic and conditions are presented in Table 4. The plaintext difference is $\Delta P = 0x00049248$ and the key difference is $\Delta K_1 = 0x00080801000020000000$. After imposing 14 conditions, a 66-round differential characteristic with $\Delta P = 0x00049248 \xrightarrow[\Delta K]{prob.=1} \Delta = 0x00000001$ is found. To get the plaintexts that satisfy all 14 conditions, we need to spend plenty of time to filter the plaintexts. For training neural distinguishers, the train set size and validation set size are 10^7 and 10^6, which is impossible to filter one by one. To solve this problem, we reshape the conditions to reduce the computational complexity of filtering the plaintexts and modify each randomly generated plaintext with the reshaped conditions. For example, condition $r_{20} = 0$ is reshaped.

$$p_{30} = p_{25} \oplus p_{26}p_{23} \oplus p_{21} \oplus k_2 \tag{4}$$

The final plaintexts satisfy all the conditions. The plaintext bits in the reshaped conditions can't be modified in the following conditions. To make all the conditions modifiable, we add 5 conditions.

$$p_{26} = 0, p_{24} = 0, p_{21} = 0, r_{19} = 1, r_{25} = 0 \tag{5}$$

After imposing 19 conditions, we have a 66-round differential characteristic with $\Delta P = 0x00049248 \xrightarrow[\Delta K]{prob.=1} \Delta = 0x00000001$.

The accuracy of the related-key conditional neural distinguishers of KATAN32 is shown in Table 5.

The RKCDNDs with accuracy almost 50% respond weakly to wrong keys. In the related-key conditional differential cryptanalysis based on deep learning, we have to use RKCDNDs with low accuracy to attack more rounds. To boost

Table 4. Related-key differential characteristic and conditions of KATAN32

Round	ΔK	Difference state	Condition
0		0000000000000 1001001001001001000	
1		0000000000000 0010010010010010000	$p_{10} = 0$
2		0000000000000 0100100100100100000	$p_{11} = 0$
3		0000000000001 1001001001001000000	$p_1 = 1$
4		0000000000010 0010010010010000000	$p_7 = 1$
5		0000000000100 0100100100100000000	$p_8 = 1$
6		0000000001000 1001001001000000000	$r_{20} = 0$
7	k_{12}	0000000010000 0010010010000000000	$p_4 = 1$
8		0000000100001 0100100100000000000	$p_5 = 1$
9		0000001000010 1001001000000000000	$p_{19} = 0$
10		0000010000100 0010010000000000000	
11	k_{20}	0000100001000 0100100000000000000	
12		0001000010000 1001000000000000000	$l_{18} = 1$
13		0010000100001 0010000000000000000	
14		0100001000010 0100000000000000000	$l_{17} = 0$
15		1000010000100 1000000000000000000	
16	k_{31}	0000100001000 0000000000000000000	
17		0001000010000 0000000000000000000	$l_{23} = 0$
18		0010000100000 0000000000000000000	
19		0100001000000 0000000000000000000	$l_{22} = 0$
20		1000010000000 0000000000000000000	
21		0000100000000 0000000000000000000	
22		0001000000000 0000000000000000000	$l_{28} = 0$
23		0010000000000 0000000000000000000	
24		0100000000000 0000000000000000000	
25	k_{50}	1000000000000 0000000000000000000	
26		0000000000000 0000000000000000000	
..		....	
65		0000000000000 0000000000000000000	
66		0000000000000 0000000000000000001	

ΔK : master key difference.

Table 5. The accuracy of RKCDNDs of KATAN32

Round	105	106	107	108	109	110	111	112
Accuracy	95.1%	94.2%	92.1%	75.5%	72.8%	68.3%	65.4%	64.9%

the response of RKCDNDs, we attempt to use s neutral bits to create a plaintext structure expected to pass the initial 66-round differential characteristic together. However, the 66-round differential characteristic is too long to apply neutral bits. We use the concept of simultaneous-neutral bit-sets in [1].

Plaintext structures are generated by simultaneous-neutral bit-sets, which pass the initial 66-round differential characteristic together with probability 1. For KATAN32, 6 bits $[28, 27, 23, 18, 9, 0]$ are only shown in the last condition. Hence, $\{28, 15\}$, $\{27, 15\}$, $\{23, 15\}$, $\{18, 15\}$, $\{9, 15\}$, $\{0, 15\}$ (p_{15} is modified in the last condition) are 6 simultaneous-neutral bit-sets of KATAN32. Randomly generating a plaintext block P^{block}, we can use 6 simultaneous-neutral bit-sets to generate a plaintext structure $P_{structure}$ consisting of 2^6 plaintext blocks.

4.2 125-Round Practical Key Recovery Attack of KATAN32

The process of 125-round practical key recovery attack is as follows:

The plaintext is $P = (p_{31}, p_{30}, \cdots, p_0)$ and the input difference of plaintext is $\Delta P = 0x61082200$. The key difference is ΔK_1. The plaintext pair is (P, P'). After filtering plaintext pairs by conditions, we get new plaintext pairs (P_{cond}, P'_{cond}), where $P'_{cond} = P_{cond} \oplus \Delta P$. Randomly generate a plaintext block P^{block} consisting of 64 different (P_{cond}, P'_{cond}) with the same ΔP. We use 6 *weak neutral bit sets* to generate a plaintext structure $P_{structure}$ consisting of 64 P^{block}. After 125-round encryption, we get the resulting ciphertext structure $C_{structure}$.

The output difference of the 112 rounds is expressed by the 125-round ciphertext and subkeys. The output difference of the 112-round KATAN32 is:

$$\Delta L_{112} = (\Delta l_{112}, \Delta l_{113}, \cdots, \Delta l_{124}) \tag{6}$$

$$\Delta R_{112} = (\Delta r_{112}, \Delta r_{113}, \cdots, \Delta r_{130}) \tag{7}$$

After all output differences are expressed by 112-round ciphertext and subkeys, no subkeys are contained in the expressions of Δr_{125} - Δr_{130}. Therefore, 32 expressions only involve 16 bit subkeys $k_{232}, k_{234}, k_{236}$ - k_{249}. The wrong key response profiles are shown in Fig. 4, which contain the empirical mean and standard deviation. We only show the empirical mean in Fig. 4. The wrong key response profile of 125-round KATAN32 with the 112-round related-key conditional neural distinguisher is shown in Fig. 4(a).

Using Algorithm 1, we partially decrypt the ciphertext structure $C_{structure}$ with each candidate key and score each candidate key we tried. If the score is higher than a cutoff threshold c_1, we use the corresponding key bits k_{236} - k_{249} to decrypt 7 rounds and get a 118-round ciphertext structure $C'_{structure}$. The process is repeated for another 13 rounds with the 105-round related key conditional neural distinguisher. The output difference of the 105-round KATAN32 is:

$$\Delta L_{105} = (\Delta l_{105}, \Delta l_{106}, \cdots, \Delta l_{117}) \tag{8}$$

$$\Delta R_{105} = (\Delta r_{105}, \Delta r_{106}, \cdots, \Delta r_{124}) \tag{9}$$

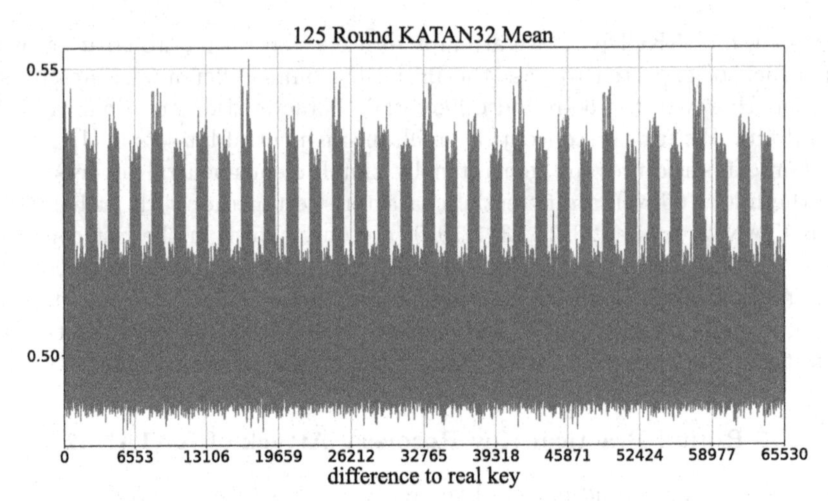

(a) Wrong key response profile of 125-round KATAN32 with 112-round related key conditional neural distinguisher

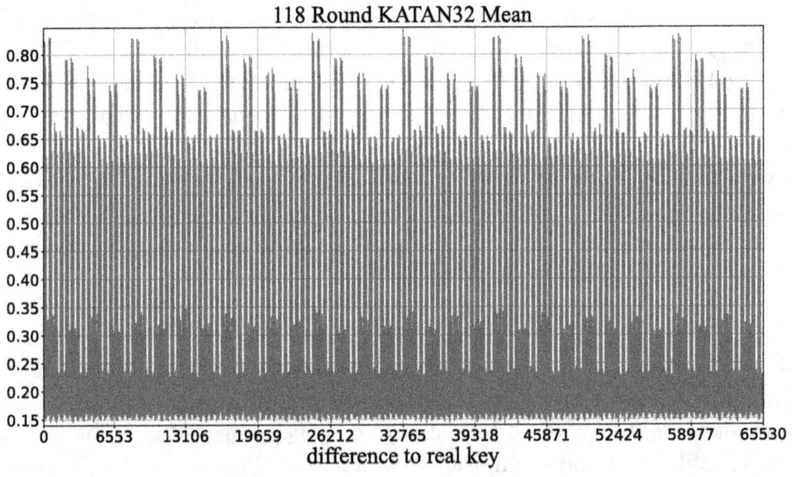

(b) Wrong key response profile of 118-round KATAN32 with 105-round related key conditional neural distinguisher

Fig. 4. Wrong key response profiles of KATAN32

No subkeys are contained in the expressions of Δr_{118} - Δr_{124}. The 32 expressions only involve 16 bit subkeys $k_{218}, k_{220}, k_{222}$ - k_{235}. k_{232} and k_{234} have been recovered. We only need to recover 14 key bits. The wrong key response profile 118-round KATAN32 is shown in Fig. 4(b). Using Algorithm 1, we partially decrypt the $C'_{structure}$ with each candidate key and score each candidate key we tried. If the score is higher than a cutoff threshold c_2, we terminate the search and return the key guess. All subkeys of the last 14 rounds k_{222} - k_{249} and part of subkeys of the last 15 and 16 rounds k_{218} and k_{220} can be recovered.

We count a success if the last 16 key bits are guessed wrong for at most 1 bit and the second 16 key bits are wrong for no more than 3 bits. The cutoff threshold parameters of key recovery attack are $c_1 = 10, c_2 = 400$. The key recovery attack is successful in 67 out of 100 trials. The success rate is 67%.

We analysis the data and time complexity of the attacks. The data complexity is on average $2^{15.7}$ in each attack. For the time complexity, the average time of 100 trials is 1811.7 s. It costs 1.95 s to encrypt 2^{10} 125-round KATAN32 for our hardware (Intel Xeon 6226R@2.90 Ghz, Nvidia GeForce RTX3090). The time complexity is $1811.7s/(\frac{1.95s}{2^{10}}) \approx 2^{19.9}$.

5 Key Recovery Attack of KATAN48 and KATAN64

The key recovery procedures of KATAN48 and KATAN64 are similar to KATAN32. We present the practical key recovery attacks of 106-round KATAN48 and 95-round KATAN64 in this section. By optimizing the calculation of the wrong key response profile, we extend our practical key recovery attacks for two more rounds.

5.1 106-Round Practical Key Recovery Attack of KATAN48

We use MILP model to search for the smallest number of conditions with the input difference $\Delta P = 0x0C0000845000$ and key difference ΔK_2. A 57-round differential characteristic with 14 conditions has been searched. After message modification, we should apply another 5 conditions to reduce the computational complexity for filtering the plaintext. After imposing 19 conditions, we have a 57-round differential characteristic with $\Delta P = 0x0C0000845000 \xrightarrow[\Delta K]{prob.=1} \Delta = 0x000000000003$. We use $\{46,30\}, \{43,30\}, \{42,30\}, \{24,30\}$, $\{22,30\}$ to boost the response of the related-key conditional neural distinguishers. The accuracy of the related-key conditional neural distinguishers of KATAN48 is shown in Table 6.

We use 89-round and 96-round related-key conditional neural distinguishers to present a 106-round practical key recovery attack of KATAN48. Using Algorithm 1, we can recover all subkeys of the last 14 rounds k_{184} - k_{211} and part of subkeys of the last 15 and 16 rounds k_{180} and k_{182}. The cutoff threshold parameters of key recovery attack are $c_1 = 0, c_2 = 50$. The key recovery attacks are successful in 79 out of 100 trials. The success rate is 79%. We analyze the data and time complexity of the attacks. The data complexity is $2^{12.8}$ in each trial. The time complexity is $338.7s/(\frac{2.65s}{2^{10}}) \approx 2^{17.0}$.

Table 6. The accuracy of RKCDNDs of KATAN48

Round	89	90	91	92	93	94	95	96
Accuracy	98.3%	96.7%	96.5%	73.5%	72.2%	70.4%	67.8%	62.5%

5.2 95-Round Practical Key Recovery Attack of KATAN64

We use MILP model to search for the smallest number of conditions with the input difference $\Delta P = 0x9201208F40380000$ and key difference ΔK_3. We get a 54-round differential characteristic with 22 conditions and apply 8 conditions additionally to reduce the computational complexity. After imposing 30 conditions, we have a 54-round differential characteristic with $\Delta P = 0x9201208F40380000 \xrightarrow[\Delta K]{prob.=1} \Delta = 0x0000000000000007$. We use $\{60,44\}, \{45,44\}, \{40,44\}, \{35,44\}, \{26,44\}$ to boost the response of the related-key conditional neural distinguishers. The accuracy of the related-key conditional neural distinguishers of KATAN64 is shown in Table 7.

Table 7. The accuracy of RKCDNDs of KATAN64

Round	83	84	85	86	87
Accuracy	88.3%	81.7%	78.3%	72.8%	51.4%

We use 83-round and 86-round related-key conditional neural distinguishers to present a 95-round practical key recovery attack of KATAN64. Using Algorithm 1, we can recover all subkeys of the last 11 rounds k_{168} - k_{189}. The cutoff threshold parameters of key recovery attack are $c_1 = 0, c_2 = 100$. The key recovery attacks are successful in 99 out of 100 trials. The success rate is 99%. The data complexity is $2^{15.2}$ in each attack. The time complexity is $59.4s/(\frac{3.16s}{2^{10}}) \approx 2^{14.2}$.

5.3 Extension of Key Recovery Attack

By optimizing the calculation of the wrong key response profile, we can extend the above 125/106/95-round practical key recovery attack for two more rounds, respectively.

In the offline phase of key recovery attack, the most time-consuming step is to calculate the wrong key response profile, which is the necessary step for key recovery attack. For 16 bit of subkeys, we need to exhaustively enumerate 2^{16} wrong keys, calculate empirical mean and standard deviation of 2000 trials for each wrong key. This process usually spends almost 1 day. To improve the key recovery attack for two rounds, we need to calculate the wrong key response profile for 20 bit of subkeys, which takes at least 16 days. It is one of the difficulties of improving our practical key recovery attack results. To optimize this process,

Table 8. Summary of practical related-key attacks on KATAN ciphers

Cipher	Technique	Rounds	Recoverable key bits	Time	Data	Reference
KATAN32	RKCD	120	10	2^{31}	2^{31}CP	[16]
	RKCDDL	**125**	**30**	$\mathbf{2^{19.9}}$	$\mathbf{2^{15.7}}$**CP**	**Section** 4.2
KATAN48	RKCD	103	3	2^{25}	2^{25}CP	[16]
	RKCDDL	**106**	**30**	$\mathbf{2^{17.0}}$	$\mathbf{2^{12.8}}$**CP**	**Section** 5.1
KATAN64	RKCD	90	1	2^{27}	2^{27}CP	[16]
	RKCDDL	**95**	**22**	$\mathbf{2^{14.2}}$	$\mathbf{2^{15.2}}$**CP**	**Section** 5.2

we calculate the wrong key response profile in parallel. Since the response values for 2^{20} wrong keys are not correlated with each other, we take 2^{16} wrong keys as a group and divide 2^{20} wrong keys into 16 groups. Each 4 consecutive groups are allocated to 1 GPU. Using 4 GPUs for computation in parallel, we can complete all computations in about 4 days. We combine the results to form the complete result of the wrong key response profile for 20 bit of subkeys.

We improved the results of KATAN ciphers by calculating the wrong key response profile in parallel. For KATAN32/48/64, we present a 127/108/97-round practical key recovery attack with recovering 34/34/26 key bits. In fact, based on the computing resources, our key recovery framework can be further extended. We only need to spend more time for pre-computation and ensure the computational complexity is not too large.

6 Conclusion

In the study, We propose a (related-key) conditional differential neural distinguisher by modifying the neural network structure and the data format and apply the new neural distinguishers on KATAN ciphers. The process of choosing conditions and differences is optimized by the MILP model. Compared to the previous work, the study improves the accuracy and rounds of neural distinguishers. Moreover, we present a related-key conditional differential cryptanalysis on KATAN ciphers based on deep learning. Message modification technology and key search strategy are applied to reduce the computational complexity of the key recovery attack. The extension of key recovery attack extend the results for two more rounds. In Table 8, we summarize the results of practical key recovery attacks on KATAN ciphers in the related-key scenario.

Compared with the results in [16], our attacks improve the number of recoverable key bits and have advantages in time complexity and data complexity. As shown in Table 8, our work is the best result in the practical key recovery attack on KATAN ciphers so far.

Deep learning methods will not supplant traditional cryptanalysis. However, we believe it's meaningful to combine deep learning methods with traditional cryptanalysis. In the future, We attempt to combine our neural distinguishers with other cryptanalysis methods, such as higher order differential, impossible differential and linear cryptanalysis. We also want to apply (related-key) conditional differential neural distinguishers to other block ciphers.

Acknowledgements. State Key Laboratory of Mathematical Engineering and Advanced Computation Open Foundation (2019A08).

A Appendix

In, Sect. 3.3, we construct MILP Models for KATAN cipers. In Appendix, we present the vectors and sets of linear inequalities mentioned in page 9. When $a_t = 0$, the difference state $(\Delta l_t, \Delta l_{t+5}, \Delta l_{t+4}, \Delta l_{t+7}, \Delta k_{2t})$ can take on one of 2^5 values. According to the equation (2), we get all 32 values of the 7-demensional vector $(\Delta l_t, \Delta l_{t+5}, \Delta l_{t+4}, \Delta l_{t+7}, \Delta k_{2t}, \Delta r_{t+19}, c)$, which is shown in Table 9. We use SageMath to model vectors and obtain a set of linear inequalities. After a simple reduction, we get a set of linear inequalities (10).

Table 9. 32 vectors $(\Delta l_t, \Delta l_{t+5}, \Delta l_{t+4}, \Delta l_{t+7}, \Delta k_{2t}, \Delta r_{t+19}, c)$

(0,0,0,0,0,0,0)	(0,1,0,1,1,0,1)	(1,0,1,1,0,0,1)	(0,0,0,0,1,1,0)	(0,1,1,0,0,0,1)
(1,0,1,1,1,0,1)	(0,0,0,1,0,0,1)	(0,1,1,0,1,0,1)	(1,1,0,0,0,0,0)	(0,0,0,1,1,0,1)
(0,1,1,1,0,0,1)	(1,1,0,0,1,1,0)	(0,0,1,0,0,0,1)	(0,1,1,1,1,0,1)	(1,1,0,1,0,0,1)
(0,0,1,0,1,0,1)	(1,0,0,0,0,1,0)	(1,1,0,1,1,0,1)	(0,0,1,1,0,0,1)	(1,0,0,0,1,0,0)
(1,1,1,0,0,0,1)	(0,0,1,1,1,0,1)	(1,0,0,1,0,0,1)	(1,1,1,0,1,0,1)	(0,1,0,0,0,1,0)
(1,0,0,1,1,0,1)	(1,1,1,1,0,0,1)	(0,1,0,0,1,0,0)	(1,0,1,0,0,0,1)	(1,1,1,1,1,0,1)
(0,1,0,1,0,0,1)	(1,0,1,0,1,0,1)			

$$
\begin{cases}
-\Delta l_{i+7} + c \geq 0, \\
-\Delta l_{i+4} + c \geq 0, \\
\Delta l_{i+4} + \Delta l_{i+7} - c \geq 0, \\
\Delta l_i + \Delta l_{i+5} - \Delta l_{i+4} - \Delta l_{i+7} - \Delta k_{2i} - \Delta r_{i+19} + c + 2 \geq 0, \\
\Delta l_i + \Delta l_{i+5} + \Delta k_{2i} - \Delta r_{i+19} + c \geq 0, \\
\Delta l_i + \Delta l_{i+5} + \Delta l_{i+7} - \Delta k_{2i} + \Delta r_{i+19} \geq 0, \\
-\Delta l_i + \Delta l_{i+5} + \Delta k_{2i} + \Delta r_{i+19} + c \geq 0, \\
\Delta l_{i+5} + \Delta l_{i+7} - \Delta k_{2i} + \Delta r_{i+19} - c + 1 \geq 0, \\
\Delta l_i - \Delta l_{i+5} + \Delta k_{2i} + \Delta r_{i+19} + c \geq 0, \\
-\Delta l_i - \Delta l_{i+5} + \Delta k_{2i} - \Delta r_{i+19} + c + 2 \geq 0, \\
-\Delta l_i + \Delta l_{i+5} + \Delta l_{i+7} - \Delta k_{2i} - \Delta r_{i+19} + 2 \geq 0, \\
\Delta l_i - \Delta l_{i+5} - \Delta k_{2i} - \Delta r_{i+19} + c + 2 \geq 0, \\
-\Delta l_i - \Delta l_{i+5} - \Delta k_{2i} + \Delta r_{i+19} + c + 2 \geq 0,
\end{cases}
\tag{10}
$$

When $a_t = 1$, the difference state $(\Delta l_t, \Delta l_{t+5}, \Delta l_{t+4}, \Delta l_{t+7}, \Delta l_{t+9}, \Delta k_{2t})$ can take on one of 2^6 values. According to the Eq. (2), we get all 64 values of the 8-demensional vector $(\Delta l_t, \Delta l_{t+5}, \Delta l_{t+4}, \Delta l_{t+7}, \Delta l_{t+9}, \Delta k_{2t}, \Delta r_{t+19}, c)$, which is shown in Table 10. We use SageMath to model vectors and obtain a set of linear inequalities. After a simple reduction, we get a set of linear inequalities (11).

Table 10. 64 vectors $(\Delta l_t, \Delta l_{t+5}, \Delta l_{t+4}, \Delta l_{t+7}, \Delta l_{t+9}, \Delta k_{2t}, \Delta r_{t+19}, c)$

(0,0,0,0,0,0,0,0)	(0,1,0,1,1,0,0,1)	(1,0,1,1,0,0,0,1)	(0,0,0,0,0,1,1,0)	(0,1,0,1,1,1,0,1)
(1,0,1,1,0,1,0,1)	(0,0,0,0,1,0,1,0)	(0,1,1,0,0,0,0,1)	(1,0,1,1,1,0,0,1)	(0,0,0,0,1,1,0,0)
(0,1,1,0,0,1,0,1)	(1,0,1,1,1,1,0,1)	(0,0,0,1,0,0,0,1)	(0,1,1,0,1,0,0,1)	(1,1,0,0,0,0,0,0)
(0,0,0,1,0,1,0,1)	(0,1,1,0,1,1,0,1)	(1,1,0,0,0,1,1,0)	(0,0,0,1,1,0,0,1)	(0,1,1,1,0,0,0,1)
(1,1,0,0,1,0,1,0)	(0,0,0,1,1,1,0,1)	(0,1,1,1,0,1,0,1)	(1,1,0,0,1,1,0,0)	(0,0,1,0,0,0,0,1)
(0,1,1,1,1,0,0,1)	(1,1,0,1,0,0,0,1)	(0,0,1,0,0,1,0,1)	(0,1,1,1,1,1,0,1)	(1,1,0,1,0,1,0,1)
(0,0,1,0,1,0,0,1)	(1,0,0,0,0,0,1,0)	(1,1,0,1,1,0,0,1)	(0,0,1,0,1,1,0,1)	(1,0,0,0,0,1,0,0)
(1,1,0,1,1,1,0,1)	(0,0,1,1,0,0,0,1)	(1,0,0,0,1,0,0,0)	(1,1,1,0,0,0,0,1)	(0,0,1,1,0,1,0,1)
(1,0,0,0,1,1,1,0)	(1,1,1,0,0,1,0,1)	(0,0,1,1,1,0,0,1)	(1,0,0,1,0,0,0,1)	(1,1,1,0,1,0,0,1)
(0,0,1,1,1,1,0,1)	(1,0,0,1,0,1,0,1)	(1,1,1,0,1,1,0,1)	(0,1,0,0,0,0,1,0)	(1,0,0,1,1,0,0,1)
(1,1,1,1,0,0,0,1)	(0,1,0,0,0,1,0,0)	(1,0,0,1,1,1,0,1)	(1,1,1,1,0,1,0,1)	(0,1,0,0,1,0,0,0)
(1,0,1,0,0,0,0,1)	(1,1,1,1,1,0,0,1)	(0,1,0,0,1,1,1,0)	(1,0,1,0,0,1,0,1)	(1,1,1,1,1,1,0,1)
(0,1,0,1,0,0,0,1)	(1,0,1,0,1,0,0,1)	(0,1,0,1,0,1,0,1)	(1,0,1,0,1,1,0,1)	

$$
\begin{cases}
-\Delta l_{i+7} + c \geq 0, \\
-\Delta l_{i+4} + c \geq 0, \\
-\Delta l_i - \Delta l_{i+5} - \Delta l_{i+9} + \Delta k_{2i} + \Delta r_{i+19} + c + 2 \geq 0, \\
\Delta l_i + \Delta l_{i+5} - \Delta l_{i+9} - \Delta k_{2i} - \Delta r_{i+19} + c + 2 \geq 0, \\
-2\Delta l_i + \Delta l_{i+5} + 2\Delta l_{i+7} - 2\Delta l_{i+9} - 2\Delta k_{2i} + \Delta r_{i+19} - c + 5 \geq 0, \\
-\Delta l_i + \Delta l_{i+5} + \Delta l_{i+4} + \Delta l_{i+9} + \Delta k_{2i} - \Delta r_{i+19} + c \geq 0, \\
-\Delta l_i - \Delta l_{i+5} + \Delta l_{i+9} - \Delta k_{2i} + \Delta r_{i+19} + c + 2 \geq 0, \\
\Delta l_i + \Delta l_{i+5} + \Delta l_{i+4} + \Delta l_{i+9} - \Delta k_{2i} + \Delta r_{i+19} \geq 0, \\
\Delta l_i - \Delta l_{i+5} - \Delta l_{i+4} - \Delta l_{i+7} + \Delta l_{i+9} - \Delta k_{2i} - \Delta r_{i+19} + 2c + 2 \geq 0, \\
\Delta l_i + \Delta l_{i+5} - \Delta l_{i+9} + \Delta k_{2i} + \Delta r_{i+19} + c \geq 0, \\
\Delta l_i - \Delta l_{i+5} + \Delta l_{i+9} + \Delta k_{2i} + \Delta r_{i+19} + c \geq 0, \\
\Delta l_i - \Delta l_{i+5} - \Delta l_{i+9} - \Delta k_{2i} + \Delta r_{i+19} + c + 2 \geq 0, \\
\Delta l_{i+4} + \Delta l_{i+7} - c \geq 0, \\
\Delta l_i - \Delta l_{i+5} - \Delta l_{i+9} + \Delta k_{2i} - \Delta r_{i+19} + c + 2 \geq 0, \\
-\Delta l_i - \Delta l_{i+5} - \Delta l_{i+9} - \Delta k_{2i} - \Delta r_{i+19} + c + 4 \geq 0,
\end{cases}
\tag{11}
$$

According to the Eq. (3), the difference state $(\Delta r_t, \Delta r_{t+11}, \Delta r_{t+6}, \Delta r_{t+8}, \Delta l_{t+10}, \Delta r_{t+15}, \Delta k_{2t+1})$ can take on one of 2^7 values. We get all 128 values of the 9-demensional vector $(\Delta r_t, \Delta r_{t+11}, \Delta r_{t+6}, \Delta r_{t+8}, \Delta l_{t+10}, \Delta r_{t+15}, \Delta k_{2t+1}, \Delta l_{t+13}, c)$, which is shown in Table 11. We use SageMath to model vectors and obtain a set of linear inequalities. After a simple reduction, we get a set of linear inequalities (12).

Table 11. 128 vectors $(\Delta r_t, \Delta r_{t+11}, \Delta r_{t+6}, \Delta r_{t+8}, \Delta l_{t+10}, \Delta r_{t+15}, \Delta k_{2t+1}, \Delta l_{t+13}, c)$

(0,0,0,0,0,0,0,0,0)	(0,0,0,0,0,0,1,1,0)	(0,0,0,0,0,1,0,0,1)	(0,0,0,0,0,1,1,0,1)	(0,0,0,0,1,0,0,0,1)
(0,0,0,0,1,0,1,0,1)	(0,0,0,0,1,1,0,0,1)	(0,0,0,0,1,1,1,0,1)	(0,0,0,1,0,0,0,0,1)	(0,0,0,1,0,0,1,0,1)
(0,0,0,1,0,1,0,0,1)	(0,0,0,1,0,1,1,0,1)	(0,0,0,1,1,0,0,0,1)	(0,0,0,1,1,0,1,0,1)	(0,0,0,1,1,1,0,0,1)
(0,0,0,1,1,1,1,0,1)	(0,0,1,0,0,0,0,0,1)	(0,0,1,0,0,0,1,0,1)	(0,0,1,0,0,1,0,0,1)	(0,0,1,0,0,1,1,0,1)
(0,0,1,0,1,0,0,0,1)	(0,0,1,0,1,0,1,0,1)	(0,0,1,0,1,1,0,0,1)	(0,0,1,0,1,1,1,0,1)	(0,0,1,1,0,0,0,0,1)
(0,0,1,1,0,0,1,0,1)	(0,0,1,1,0,1,0,0,1)	(0,0,1,1,0,1,1,0,1)	(0,0,1,1,1,0,0,0,1)	(0,0,1,1,1,0,1,0,1)
(0,0,1,1,1,1,0,0,1)	(0,0,1,1,1,1,1,0,1)	(0,1,0,0,0,0,0,1,0)	(0,1,0,0,0,0,1,0,0)	(0,1,0,0,0,1,0,0,1)
(0,1,0,0,0,1,1,0,1)	(0,1,0,0,1,0,0,0,1)	(0,1,0,0,1,0,1,0,1)	(0,1,0,0,1,1,0,0,1)	(0,1,0,0,1,1,1,0,1)
(0,1,0,1,0,0,0,0,1)	(0,1,0,1,0,0,1,0,1)	(0,1,0,1,0,1,0,0,1)	(0,1,0,1,0,1,1,0,1)	(0,1,0,1,1,0,0,0,1)
(0,1,0,1,1,0,1,0,1)	(0,1,0,1,1,1,0,0,1)	(0,1,0,1,1,1,1,0,1)	(0,1,1,0,0,0,0,0,1)	(0,1,1,0,0,0,1,0,1)
(0,1,1,0,0,1,0,0,1)	(0,1,1,0,0,1,1,0,1)	(0,1,1,0,1,0,0,0,1)	(0,1,1,0,1,0,1,0,1)	(0,1,1,0,1,1,0,0,1)
(0,1,1,0,1,1,1,0,1)	(0,1,1,1,0,0,0,0,1)	(0,1,1,1,0,0,1,0,1)	(0,1,1,1,0,1,0,0,1)	(0,1,1,1,0,1,1,0,1)
(0,1,1,1,1,0,0,0,1)	(0,1,1,1,1,0,1,0,1)	(0,1,1,1,1,1,0,0,1)	(0,1,1,1,1,1,1,0,1)	(1,0,0,0,0,0,0,1,0)
(1,0,0,0,0,0,1,0,0)	(1,0,0,0,0,1,0,0,1)	(1,0,0,0,0,1,1,0,1)	(1,0,0,0,1,0,0,0,1)	(1,0,0,0,1,0,1,0,1)
(1,0,0,0,1,1,0,0,1)	(1,0,0,0,1,1,1,0,1)	(1,0,0,1,0,0,0,0,1)	(1,0,0,1,0,0,1,0,1)	(1,0,0,1,0,1,0,0,1)
(1,0,0,1,0,1,1,0,1)	(1,0,0,1,1,0,0,0,1)	(1,0,0,1,1,0,1,0,1)	(1,0,0,1,1,1,0,0,1)	(1,0,0,1,1,1,1,0,1)
(1,0,1,0,0,0,0,0,1)	(1,0,1,0,0,0,1,0,1)	(1,0,1,0,0,1,0,0,1)	(1,0,1,0,0,1,1,0,1)	(1,0,1,0,1,0,0,0,1)
(1,0,1,0,1,0,1,0,1)	(1,0,1,0,1,1,0,0,1)	(1,0,1,0,1,1,1,0,1)	(1,0,1,1,0,0,0,0,1)	(1,0,1,1,0,0,1,0,1)
(1,0,1,1,0,1,0,0,1)	(1,0,1,1,0,1,1,0,1)	(1,0,1,1,1,0,0,0,1)	(1,0,1,1,1,0,1,0,1)	(1,0,1,1,1,1,0,0,1)
(1,0,1,1,1,1,1,0,1)	(1,1,0,0,0,0,0,0,0)	(1,1,0,0,0,0,1,1,0)	(1,1,0,0,0,1,0,0,1)	(1,1,0,0,0,1,1,0,1)
(1,1,0,0,1,0,0,0,1)	(1,1,0,0,1,0,1,0,1)	(1,1,0,0,1,1,0,0,1)	(1,1,0,0,1,1,1,0,1)	(1,1,0,1,0,0,0,0,1)
(1,1,0,1,0,0,1,0,1)	(1,1,0,1,0,1,0,0,1)	(1,1,0,1,0,1,1,0,1)	(1,1,0,1,1,0,0,0,1)	(1,1,0,1,1,0,1,0,1)
(1,1,0,1,1,1,0,0,1)	(1,1,0,1,1,1,1,0,1)	(1,1,1,0,0,0,0,0,1)	(1,1,1,0,0,0,1,0,1)	(1,1,1,0,0,1,0,0,1)
(1,1,1,0,0,1,1,0,1)	(1,1,1,0,1,0,0,0,1)	(1,1,1,0,1,0,1,0,1)	(1,1,1,0,1,1,0,0,1)	(1,1,1,0,1,1,1,0,1)
(1,1,1,1,0,0,0,0,1)	(1,1,1,1,0,0,1,0,1)	(1,1,1,1,0,1,0,0,1)	(1,1,1,1,0,1,1,0,1)	(1,1,1,1,1,0,0,0,1)
(1,1,1,1,1,0,1,0,1)	(1,1,1,1,1,1,0,0,1)	(1,1,1,1,1,1,1,0,1)		

$$\begin{cases} -\Delta r_{i+6}+c\geq 0, \\ -\Delta r_{i+8}+c\geq 0, \\ -\Delta r_{i+10}+c\geq 0, \\ -\Delta r_{i+15}+c\geq 0, \\ -\Delta r_i-\Delta r_{i+11}-\Delta r_{i+6}-\Delta r_{i+8}-\Delta r_{i+10}+\Delta r_{i+15}+\Delta k_{2i+1}-\Delta l_{i+13}+3c+2\geq 0, \\ -\Delta r_i-\Delta r_{i+11}-\Delta r_{i+6}+\Delta r_{i+8}-\Delta r_{i+10}-\Delta r_{i+15}+\Delta k_{2i+1}+\Delta l_{i+13}+2c+2\geq 0, \\ \Delta r_{i+6}+\Delta r_{i+8}+\Delta r_{i+10}+\Delta r_{i+15}-c\geq 0, \\ -\Delta r_i-\Delta r_{i+11}+\Delta r_{i+6}+\Delta r_{i+8}+\Delta r_{i+15}-\Delta k_{2i+1}+\Delta l_{i+13}+2\geq 0, \\ -\Delta r_i-\Delta r_{i+11}+\Delta r_{i+6}-\Delta r_{i+8}+\Delta r_{i+10}-\Delta r_{i+15}+\Delta k_{2i+1}-\Delta l_{i+13}+2c+2\geq 0, \\ \Delta r_i-\Delta r_{i+11}-\Delta k_{2i+1}+\Delta l_{i+13}+2c\geq 0, \\ -\Delta r_i+\Delta r_{i+11}-\Delta r_{i+6}+\Delta r_{i+8}-\Delta r_{i+10}-\Delta r_{i+15}+\Delta k_{2i+1}-\Delta l_{i+13}+2c+2\geq 0, \\ -\Delta r_i+\Delta r_{i+11}+\Delta k_{2i+1}+\Delta l_{i+13}+c\geq 0, \\ \Delta r_i-\Delta r_{i+11}+\Delta r_{i+8}+\Delta r_{i+10}+\Delta r_{i+15}+\Delta k_{2i+1}-\Delta l_{i+13}-c+2\geq 0, \\ \Delta r_i+\Delta r_{i+11}-\Delta r_{i+6}-\Delta r_{i+8}-\Delta r_{i+10}+\Delta r_{i+15}+\Delta k_{2i+1}-\Delta l_{i+13}+3c\geq 0, \\ \Delta r_i+\Delta r_{i+11}+\Delta r_{i+6}-\Delta r_{i+8}+\Delta r_{i+10}-\Delta r_{i+15}+\Delta k_{2i+1}-\Delta l_{i+13}+2c\geq 0, \\ \Delta r_i+\Delta r_{i+11}+\Delta r_{i+8}+\Delta r_{i+10}+\Delta r_{i+15}+\Delta k_{2i+1}+\Delta l_{i+13}-c\geq 0, \\ -\Delta r_i+\Delta r_{i+11}-\Delta k_{2i+1}-\Delta l_{i+13}+c\geq 0, \\ \Delta r_i-\Delta r_{i+11}-\Delta r_{i+6}+\Delta r_{i+8}+\Delta r_{i+10}-\Delta r_{i+15}+\Delta k_{2i+1}+\Delta l_{i+13}+2c\geq 0, \\ -\Delta r_i+\Delta r_{i+11}+\Delta r_{i+6}+\Delta r_{i+8}+\Delta r_{i+10}-\Delta k_{2i+1}+\Delta l_{i+13}-c+2\geq 0, \\ -\Delta r_i+\Delta r_{i+11}+\Delta r_{i+6}+\Delta r_{i+8}+\Delta r_{i+15}+\Delta k_{2i+1}-\Delta l_{i+13}-c+2\geq 0, \\ -\Delta r_i-\Delta r_{i+11}-\Delta r_{i+6}-\Delta r_{i+8}-\Delta r_{i+10}-\Delta r_{i+15}-\Delta k_{2i+1}-\Delta l_{i+13}+3c+4\geq 0, \end{cases} \tag{12}$$

References

1. Bao, Z., Guo, J., Liu, M., Ma, L., Tu, Y.: Conditional differential-neural cryptanalysis. Cryptology ePrint Archive, Paper 2021/719 (2021). https://eprint.iacr.org/2021/719
2. Benamira, A., Gerault, D., Peyrin, T., Tan, Q.Q.: A deeper look at machine learning-based cryptanalysis. In: Canteaut, A., Standaert, F.-X. (eds.) EUROCRYPT 2021. LNCS, vol. 12696, pp. 805–835. Springer, Cham (2021). https://doi.org/10.1007/978-3-030-77870-5_28
3. Biham, E.: New types of cryptanalytic attacks using related keys. J. Cryptol. **7**(4), 229–246 (1994). https://doi.org/10.1007/BF00203965
4. Biryukov, A., De Cannière, C., Quisquater, M.: On multiple linear approximations. In: Franklin, M. (ed.) CRYPTO 2004. LNCS, vol. 3152, pp. 1–22. Springer, Heidelberg (2004). https://doi.org/10.1007/978-3-540-28628-8_1
5. Biryukov, A., Nikolić, I.: Automatic search for related-key differential characteristics in byte-oriented block ciphers: application to AES, Camellia, Khazad and Others. In: Gilbert, H. (ed.) EUROCRYPT 2010. LNCS, vol. 6110, pp. 322–344. Springer, Heidelberg (2010). https://doi.org/10.1007/978-3-642-13190-5_17
6. Chen, J., Teh, J.S., Su, C., Samsudin, A., Fang, J.: Improved (related-key) attacks on round-reduced KATAN-32/48/64 based on the extended boomerang framework. In: Liu, J.K., Steinfeld, R. (eds.) ACISP 2016. LNCS, vol. 9723, pp. 333–346. Springer, Cham (2016). https://doi.org/10.1007/978-3-319-40367-0_21

7. Chen, Y., Shen, Y., Yu, H., Yuan, S.: A new neural distinguisher considering features derived from multiple ciphertext pairs. Comput. J. (2022). https://doi.org/10.1093/comjnl/bxac019
8. De Cannière, C., Dunkelman, O., Knežević, M.: KATAN and KTANTAN—a family of small and efficient hardware-oriented block ciphers. In: Clavier, C., Gaj, K. (eds.) CHES 2009. LNCS, vol. 5747, pp. 272–288. Springer, Heidelberg (2009). https://doi.org/10.1007/978-3-642-04138-9_20
9. Gohr, A.: Improving attacks on round-reduced Speck32/64 using deep learning. In: Boldyreva, A., Micciancio, D. (eds.) CRYPTO 2019. LNCS, vol. 11693, pp. 150–179. Springer, Cham (2019). https://doi.org/10.1007/978-3-030-26951-7_6
10. Gomez, A.N., Huang, S., Zhang, I., Li, B.M., Osama, M., Kaiser, L.: Unsupervised cipher cracking using discrete GANs. CoRR abs/1801.04883 (2018). http://arxiv.org/abs/1801.04883
11. He, K., Zhang, X., Ren, S., Sun, J.: Deep residual learning for image recognition. In: Proceedings of the IEEE Conference on Computer Vision and Pattern Recognition, pp. 770–778 (2016). https://doi.org/10.48550/arXiv.1512.03385
12. Hinton, G.E., Osindero, S., Teh, Y.W.: A fast learning algorithm for deep belief nets. Neural Comput. **18**(7), 1527–1554 (2006). https://doi.org/10.1162/neco.2006.18.7.1527
13. Hou, Z., Ren, J., Chen, S.: Improve neural distinguisher for cryptanalysis. Cryptology ePrint Archive, Paper 2021/1017 (2021). https://eprint.iacr.org/2021/1017
14. Isobe, T., Sasaki, Yu., Chen, J.: Related-key boomerang attacks on KATAN32/48/64. In: Boyd, C., Simpson, L. (eds.) ACISP 2013. LNCS, vol. 7959, pp. 268–285. Springer, Heidelberg (2013). https://doi.org/10.1007/978-3-642-39059-3_19
15. Jakimoski, G., Desmedt, Y.: Related-key differential cryptanalysis of 192-bit key AES variants. In: Matsui, M., Zuccherato, R.J. (eds.) SAC 2003. LNCS, vol. 3006, pp. 208–221. Springer, Heidelberg (2004). https://doi.org/10.1007/978-3-540-24654-1_15
16. Knellwolf, S., Meier, W., Naya-Plasencia, M.: Conditional differential cryptanalysis of Trivium and KATAN. In: Miri, A., Vaudenay, S. (eds.) SAC 2011. LNCS, vol. 7118, pp. 200–212. Springer, Heidelberg (2012). https://doi.org/10.1007/978-3-642-28496-0_12
17. Lawrence, S., Giles, C., Tsoi, A.C., Back, A.: Face recognition: a convolutional neural-network approach. IEEE Trans. Neural Networks **8**(1), 98–113 (1997). https://doi.org/10.1109/72.554195
18. LeCun, Y., Bengio, Y., Hinton, G.: Deep learning. Nature **521**(7553), 436–444 (2015). https://doi.org/10.1038/nature14539
19. Liu, A., Wang, M., Li, Y.: Related-key conditional differential cryptanalysis of katan. J. Cryptol. Res. **2**(1), 77–91 (2015). https://doi.org/10.13868/j.cnki.jcr.000062. (in Chinese)
20. Pelikan, M., Goldberg, D.E., Cantú-Paz, E.: BOA: the Bayesian optimization algorithm. In: Proceedings of the 1st Annual Conference on Genetic and Evolutionary Computation-Volume 1, pp. 525–532 (1999)
21. Williams, R.J., Zipser, D.: A learning algorithm for continually running fully recurrent neural networks. Neural Comput. **1**(2), 270–280 (1989). https://doi.org/10.1162/neco.1989.1.2.270
22. Xing, Z., Zhang, W., Han, G.: Improved conditional differential analysis on NLFSR based block cipher KATAN32 with MILP. In: Wang, D., Meng, W., Han, J. (eds.) SPNCE 2020. LNICST, vol. 344, pp. 370–393. Springer, Cham (2021). https://doi.org/10.1007/978-3-030-66922-5_26

How to Design Authenticated Key Exchange for Wearable Devices: Cryptanalysis of AKE for Health Monitoring and Countermeasures via Distinct SMs with Key Split and Refresh

Łukasz Krzywiecki[1] and Hannes Salin[2](✉)

[1] Department of Fundamentals of Computer Science, Wrocław University of Science and Technology, Wrocław, Poland
lukasz.krzywiecki@pwr.edu.pl

[2] Department of Information and Communication Technology, Swedish Transport Administration, Borlänge, Sweden
hannes.salin@trafikverket.se

Abstract. We provide a cryptanalysis of a certain type of an authenticated key exchange protocol (AKE) for wearable devices. Subsequently, we propose a secure construction based on a modified SIGMA protocol with strengthened signature blocks and an additional out-of-bound channel. Specifically, we propose a signature scheme with an additive split of the signing key with a refresh mechanism. We analyze the security of the scheme, assuming that partial keys are stored in distinct hardware signature modules of the signing devices. We use these constructions for strengthening the SIGMA key exchange protocol. Refreshing the partial key shares in each protocol execution protects against potential key leakage from a single SM. Such leakages can occur due to unintended errors in implementations, or malicious hardware manufacturers. We give a formal security analysis in our strengthen Canetti-Krawczyk (CK) model with long-term secret key splitting and refresh over two separated signature modules.

Keywords: Authenticated key exchange · Signatures · Cryptanalysis

1 Introduction

Wearables, Internet of Medical Things (IoMT) and Wireless Body Area Networks (WBAN) [25], provide new opportunities in the healthcare sector, e.g. remote monitoring [23] and advanced, aggregated real-time healthcare monitoring using many types of sensory data sources [29]. Moreover, healthy lifestyle and wellness measures through fitness trackers and smartwatches [21] are now a reality with

A. R. Beresford et al. (Eds.): CANS 2022, LNCS 13641, pp. 225–244, 2022.
https://doi.org/10.1007/978-3-031-20974-1_11

consumer-friendly prices. For many of these types of devices, especially those that use short-range wireless communication protocols such as Bluetooth, NFC, RFID etc., require a certain *pairing* to connect two devices. For example a wearable and a smartphone, or a sensory device and a smart monitor. A typical scenario for pairing two devices, if they have display capabilities, is to generate a numeric that is displayed on one device. Then a human manually verifies/enters that code in the second device to complete the pairing. This out-of-band communication, which requires human interaction, gives rise to a set of problems: how to ensure that the correct device is participating in a key agreement protocol, how to authenticate the devices correctly in the case of a third malicious device trying to impersonate a party (as shown in Fig. 1 (a)), and how to mitigate long-term key leakage in cases where side-channel attacks are possible. There is no guarantee that a smart home or a hospital will provide a reliable and secure network. On the contrary, we may suspect such networks are compromised, thus pairing a device connected to these networks suffers from a risk of exposure. Moreover, an attacker could even physcially get close or install malicious hardware near devices in order to exploit information leakage or vulnerable protocols.

Security Implications and Problem Statement. Connected e-health devices, both wearables and smart monitors, plays an important role for patient safety. The usage of a compromised device, which transfer incorrect monitoring data, can result in faulty diagnosis and put a patient's life in danger. Authenticated Key Exchange (AKE) protocols allow devices to coin a *session secret* used for subsequent encryption of data to be transferred. AKE augmented with an out-of-band (OOB) communication channel allows for confirmation that the session secret is the same on both channel-endpoints. Usage of secure hardware modules for storing long-term secret keys, and enforcing users to verify OOB information, should increase, at least in theory, the difficulty of potential attacks. However, we find that some AKE protocols proposed for wearables are still vulnerable to certain impersonation attacks.

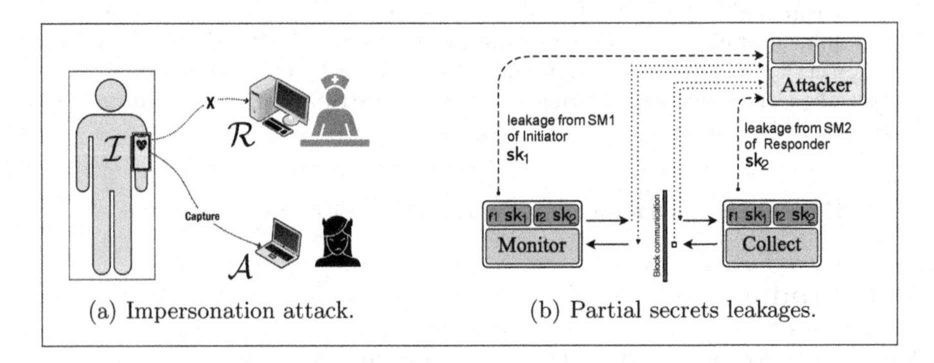

(a) Impersonation attack. (b) Partial secrets leakages.

Fig. 1. Impersonation attack and threat model.

Signing Modules and Secret Keys. Traditionally, computer systems with high security requirements, e.g. within the finance and military sector, use hardware security modules for storing keys and computing specific functions. Specifically, signing modules (SM) could be used for signing procedures. The aim of using SMs is to provide secure storage and signing operations within otherwise potentially untrusted systems. With the rapid development of smaller devices, IoT and smartphones, the demand for using such secure storage and computational units seems to increase. Today we find secure units in both Apple (Secure Enclave) [2] and Android (StrongBox) [9] devices. These are supported by current research for IoT devices [4,30,31]. In the rest of the paper, by SM we denote a tamper resistant module storing a secret key sk used for *signing functionality* f.

Security Enhancing Techniques. A *secret key split* technique splits one initial secret key into several partial secrets stored independently in separate SMs, coming from different vendors. Having at least one trusted/fair vendor mitigates potential secret key compromising, even if a subset of SMs allow for partial secret leakages. A *partial secret refresh* technique changes the partial secrets synchronously, in a way that the final signing functionality performed collectively by SMs using partial secrets, can be verified with a single public key. The public key corresponds to the initial secret key (as it was before split). The goal of the continuous refreshing is to mitigate leakages that could occur from different SMs in different signing sessions, and to protect against side channel and timing attacks targeting operations involving secrets, that would potentially leave energy, voltage or radio frequency traces. This strategy is sometimes referred to as key blinding, or rather *key splitting* [8,14,28], where a subprotocol refreshes the key shares. We consider scenarios (after [34]) with a dual SM setup, with $\mathsf{f1}$ and $\mathsf{f2}$ signing functionalities respectively. We denote the relation between those SMs as a *pipeline*. It defines the order of execution of $\mathsf{f1}$ and $\mathsf{f2}$ in each SM, as well as the combined operation on their respective results. As in [34] an *additive* key splitting scheme is used where the secret key is split into two random shares $\mathsf{sk} = \mathsf{sk}_1^i + \mathsf{sk}_2^i$. The device is now able to erase sk and store $\mathsf{sk}_1^i, \mathsf{sk}_2^i$. These shares are refreshed synchronously, i.e. $\mathsf{sk}_1^{i+1} = \mathsf{sk}_1^i - r$ and $\mathsf{sk}_2^{i+1} = \mathsf{sk}_2^{i+1} + r$ for some random value $r \xleftarrow{\$} \mathbb{Z}_q^*$. An *OOB confirmation* technique is used for two devices with short range connectivity, e.g. IoT or wearables. It is not unusual to pair them using an optical OOB channel for initial authentication and security configurations. Typical scenarios cover pairing an IoT device with a smart monitor or hub, or a wearable device with the user's smartphone. During the pairing phase, the user may verify codes or authentication messages displayed on the devices. Therefore, the OOB confirmation involves human interaction and final accepting or rejecting the devices.

1.1 Contribution

As a starting point of our contribution we provide a cryptanalysis of the AKE construction from [34]. We argue that this vulnerable construction is a result of some high level design *bad choices*, where the authentication of identities is not strictly bound to the usage of secret keys. To mitigate similar design pitfalls we propose to apply a modular approach to AKE constructions where authenticity and session key secrecy are achieved by combining provably secure building blocks, chosen in order to achieve required functionalities. The detailed contribution is the following:

- We discovered and demonstrate an *effective attack* on the AKE scheme for health monitoring wearable devices proposed in [34].
- We propose a *generic solution* to mitigate similar attacks, based on provable secure modular AKE protocols augmented with a long-term secret key split and refresh mechanism, stored in two distinct SMs. We argue that it is valid for a variety of SIG-based protocols like [15,18,32].
- We propose a stronger *modified Canetti-Krawczyk* (mCK) model, in which the adversary can issue additional type of queries per session, called "Partial-Key-Reveal", which returns computation results from both SMs, and additionally one current secret stored in a single SM chosen by the adversary.
- We propose *a modified SIGMA* based on the regular SIGMA from [6], and on the Schnorr signatures with additive secret key split and refreshment from [22]. We provide a *formal security analysis* of our specific construction in our strengthen (mCK) model.

1.2 Related Work

A *Leakage-Resilient Authenticated Key Exchange* (LR-AKE) scheme is secure against leakage of long-term secret keys and/or ephemeral values [1,19]. For example, an attacker running a side-channel attack will not be able to extract any secret information. Several models for leakage resilience has been proposed for AKE schemes. In the *bounded memory-leakage* model the adversary have access to an efficiently computable leakage function f which takes the secret key sk as input. Then $f(\mathsf{sk})$ output bits from the key partially, up to some fixed leakage parameter λ, hence bounded. Several AKE schemes has been proven secure within the bounded model, e.g. [1,19,26]. Another model is the *continuous* (unbounded) leakage model, introduced by Brakerski et al. [3] and Dodis et al. [7]. In the continuous memory-leakage model, no restrictions are set of neither time or memory. When the adversary calls the leakage function, it may only receive at most a specified fraction of the total bits from the internal state of the attacked memory, which consists of the secret key and the entropy source [3].

Key splitting and refresh mechanisms are found in different type of cryptographical schemes, not only additive key splitting is used as in [8,14,28,34] but also more complicated variants; in puncturable encryption where the key is associated with a tag, the secret key sk is refreshed using exponentiations with a set of random values, proven secure with bilinear pairings [10]. We note that the practical implementation in [10] shows that the key refresh function is on average slower than the encryption function. Another type of key splitting is when using trusted third parties, e.g. in [5] where a key generation center issues keys and generates partial randomness used for key splitting and refreshing; again the scheme is secure under pairings. However, the security relies on trusted third parties which are not included in our scenario nor applicable for wearables and e-health devices.

In Fig. 2 we compare different kind of AKE protocols. The complexity is measured by the number of exponentiations on each party's side as well as the number of signatures (S), verifications (V), ring signatures (RS) and ring verifications (RV). We use same notation from [6,13,32]. Note that authentication in [6,13,32] is provided by undeniable signature based schemes that is used for the mutual identification of parties. In [13,32] the BLS signature has been used. It can be denoted as protocols "without NAXOS" and "BLS-HMQV" protocols, respectively.

Paper	Protocol	Complexity	Rounds
[19]	NAXOS	4	2
[24]	E-NAXOS	5	2
[33]	CMQV	3	2
[27]	SMQV	3	2
[13]	without-NAXOS	3	2
[20]	KEA+C	3	3
[16]	HMQV	3	3
[32]	BLS-HMQV	4	3
[6]	SIGMA ver. Σ_0	2 + S + V	3
[17]	mod Σ_0	2 + RS + RV	3
[11]	AMA	4	4
[12]	MRI	3	4

Fig. 2. Protocol comparison.

1.3 Structure of Paper

In Sect. 2 we describe the system setting and threat model. In Sect. 3 we give the details of the attack on the scheme [34]. In Sect. 4 we describe the methodology for securing LR-AKE schemes and recall SIGMA [6] and split Schnorr [22] schemes. In Sect. 5 we propose the modified SIGMA using the key splitting technique. In Sect. 6 we provide the formal security model and analysis. The conclusion is given in Sect. 7.

2 Preliminaries

2.1 System Settings

We analyze scenarios for (wearable) devices, which could be used for continuous health monitoring. A sensor-equipped device is attached to the human body for measuring medical characteristics for further transmission of data to an analysis- and managing central device. A typical setup is shown in Fig. 1 (a). The data is to be encrypted via a fresh symmetric session key each time the devices are paired together. Therefore, prior data transmission, the chosen AKE protocol π is executed on both devices. Architectures of both wearable and central devices include SMs for storing long-term secret keys used for authentication in π. We consider devices equipped with two SMs, where the long-term key is split additively. The functionalities of these SMs, denoted as **f1** and **f2** perform an operation pipeline, realizing the authentication, e.g. a signature, verified with the help of the public key. We illustrate this security architecture in Fig. 1 (b) for which the impersonation threat model is described.

AKE Protocols: Let $\mathcal{I}$ denote an initiator device, and $\mathcal{R}$ a responder device. These two are the only peers in protocol π. The initiator is the party who initiates π and sends the first message. Each party have key-pairs of long-term secret/public keys, $(\mathsf{sk}_{\mathcal{I}}, \mathsf{pk}_{\mathcal{I}})$ and $(\mathsf{sk}_{\mathcal{R}}, \mathsf{pk}_{\mathcal{R}})$ respectively.

Let $\pi(\mathcal{I}(\mathsf{sk}_{\mathcal{I}}, \mathsf{pk}_{\mathcal{R}}), \mathcal{R}(\mathsf{sk}_{\mathcal{R}}, \mathsf{pk}_{\mathcal{I}}))$ denote the protocol execution between $\mathcal{I}$ and $\mathcal{R}$, where each party have access to the other's public key. For the protocol $\pi(\mathcal{I}(\mathsf{sk}_{\mathcal{I}}, \mathsf{pk}_{\mathcal{R}}), \mathcal{R}(\mathsf{sk}_{\mathcal{R}}, \mathsf{pk}_{\mathcal{I}}))$ we set the following *post execution protocol requirements*:

1. Let $\pi(\mathcal{I}(\mathsf{sk}_{\mathcal{I}}, \mathsf{pk}_{\mathcal{R}}), \mathcal{R}(\mathsf{sk}_{\mathcal{R}}, \mathsf{pk}_{\mathcal{I}})) \rightarrow (\mathcal{I}\ \mathtt{accept}\ \mathcal{R})$ denote when $\mathcal{I}$ authenticates $\mathcal{R}$, i.e. the holder of the secret $\mathsf{sk}_{\mathcal{R}}$ corresponds to the public key $\mathsf{pk}_{\mathcal{R}}$. Similarly we denote $\pi(\mathcal{I}(\mathsf{sk}_{\mathcal{I}}, \mathsf{pk}_{\mathcal{R}}), \mathcal{R}(\mathsf{sk}_{\mathcal{R}}, \mathsf{pk}_{\mathcal{I}})) \rightarrow (\mathcal{R}\ \mathtt{accept}\ \mathcal{I})$ for the fact that $\mathcal{R}$ knows the identity of $\mathcal{I}$, i.e. the holder of the secret $\mathsf{sk}_{\mathcal{I}}$ corresponding to the public key $\mathsf{pk}_{\mathcal{I}}$. If both events occur, we say that $\mathcal{I}$ and $\mathcal{R}$ mutually authenticate each other.
2. $\mathcal{I}$ and $\mathcal{R}$ compute same session key K_s.
3. K_s is secret, i.e. it is only known to $\mathcal{I}$ and $\mathcal{R}$.

2.2 Threat Model

The threat model covers attacks against authenticated key establishment (as of AKE protocols) between $\mathcal{I}$ and $\mathcal{R}$ parties. These involves impersonation attacks, and attacks against the session key secrecy, covering a typical *active attacker* $\mathcal{A}$ of the Canetti-Krawczyk (CK) model from [6] with the ability to interfere and block communication between $\mathcal{I}$ and $\mathcal{R}$. $\mathcal{A}$ can modify messages, replace, inject and redirect them towards parties $\mathcal{I}$ and $\mathcal{R}$.

Partial key leakage: Additionally in this paper we consider the *stronger attacker model* which allows $\mathcal{A}$ to access partial secret keys. We assume $\mathcal{A}$ can learn secrets from one SM of a chosen device per signing session, but is able to compromise different SMs of the target device in different sessions (see Fig. 1 (b) - in one session $\mathcal{A}$ accesses sk_1 of $\mathcal{I}$ and sk_2 of $\mathcal{R}$). This reflects additional scenarios of using a SM from untrusted vendors, or with implementation errors, where a malicious device manufacturer allows leakages from one SM per session.

Impersonation: The impersonation attack against the scheme [34], shown in our paper, affects the first post requirement for AKE protocol execution: improper acceptance. Intuitively we demand that each party should use its secret key to perform the protocol and be accepted by its peer party. In the impersonation attack we demonstrate how an active adversary can impersonate another party only with the knowledge of public parameters.

Definition 1. *We say that AKE protocol π is* impersonation vulnerable *if there exists a polynomial-time adversary algorithm $\mathcal{A}$ such that at least one of the probabilities:*

$$\Pr[\pi(\mathcal{I}(\mathsf{sk}_{\mathcal{I}}, \mathsf{pk}_{\mathcal{R}}), \mathcal{A}(\mathsf{pk}_{\mathcal{I}}, \mathsf{pk}_{\mathcal{R}})) \rightarrow (\mathcal{I} \texttt{ accept } \mathcal{A} \text{ as } \mathcal{R})],$$
$$\Pr[\pi(\mathcal{A}(\mathsf{pk}_{\mathcal{I}}, \mathsf{pk}_{\mathcal{R}}), \mathcal{R}(\mathsf{sk}_{\mathcal{R}}, \mathsf{pk}_{\mathcal{I}})) \rightarrow (\mathcal{R} \texttt{ accept } \mathcal{A} \text{ as } \mathcal{I})]$$

is non-negligible. The first event $\mathcal{A}(\mathsf{pk}_{\mathcal{I}}, \mathsf{pk}_{\mathcal{R}})$ denotes adversary $\mathcal{A}$ impersonating $\mathcal{R}$. Similarly, the second event $\mathcal{A}(\mathsf{pk}_{\mathcal{I}}, \mathsf{pk}_{\mathcal{R}})$ is the impersonation of $\mathcal{I}$.

Session Key Secrecy Compromising: In this type of attack the adversary tries to get hold of the session key used between two parties. It could be feasible due to numerous reasons, e.g. by key leakage or bad protocol design allowing for cryptanalysis of the key(s).

2.3 Notation

From the formal perspective we consider AKE protocols based on the Diffie-Hellman (DH) key exchange. We assume that corresponding computations on devices are done within a group $\mathbb{G} = \langle g \rangle$ of prime order q, where the chosen computational assumptions hold. Here we rely on the Discrete Logarithm Problem (DLP), Computational Diffie-Hellman (CDH), and Decisional Diffie-Hellman (DDH). Let X be a finite set. We use notation $x_1 \ldots, x_n \leftarrow_{\$} X$, or $\{x_i\}_1^n \leftarrow_{\$} X$, to specify that each x_i is selected uniformly at random from X. Let λ be a security parameter. We denote negligible values as ϵ. A function $\mathcal{H} : \{0,1\}^* \rightarrow \mathbb{A}$ is a secure hash function that transforms any binary string into an element of a set $\mathbb{A}$.

Definition 2 Discrete Logarithm Problem (DLP)). *Let $k \in \mathbb{N}$ be a security parameter and $\mathbb{G}$ a cyclic group of order $q > 2^k$. Let g be a generator of $\mathbb{G}$. The* DLP *is, given a randomly chosen $y, g \in \mathbb{G}$, to find the unique $x \in \mathbb{Z}_q^*$ such that $y = g^x$.*

Definition 3 (Decisional Diffie-Hellman (DDH)). *Let $\mathbb{G}$ be a cyclic group with generator g and prime order q. Given (g, g^a, g^b, g^c) for some $a, b, c \leftarrow_{\$} \mathbb{Z}_q^*$, it is hard to computationally decide correctly if $c = ab$.*

Definition 4 Computational Diffie-Hellman (CDH)). *Let $\mathbb{G}$ be a cyclic group with generator g and prime order q. Given (g, g^a, g^b) for some $a, b \leftarrow_{\$} \mathbb{Z}_q^*$, it is hard to compute g^{ab}.*

3 An Impersonation Attack on the LR-AKE Scheme

3.1 Original Scheme

The original scheme [34] use public parameters $\mathsf{par} = \{\mathbb{G}, g, q\}$, where $\langle g \rangle = \mathbb{G}$, and $|\mathbb{G}| = q$ is prime. The scheme is constructed over an elliptic curve,

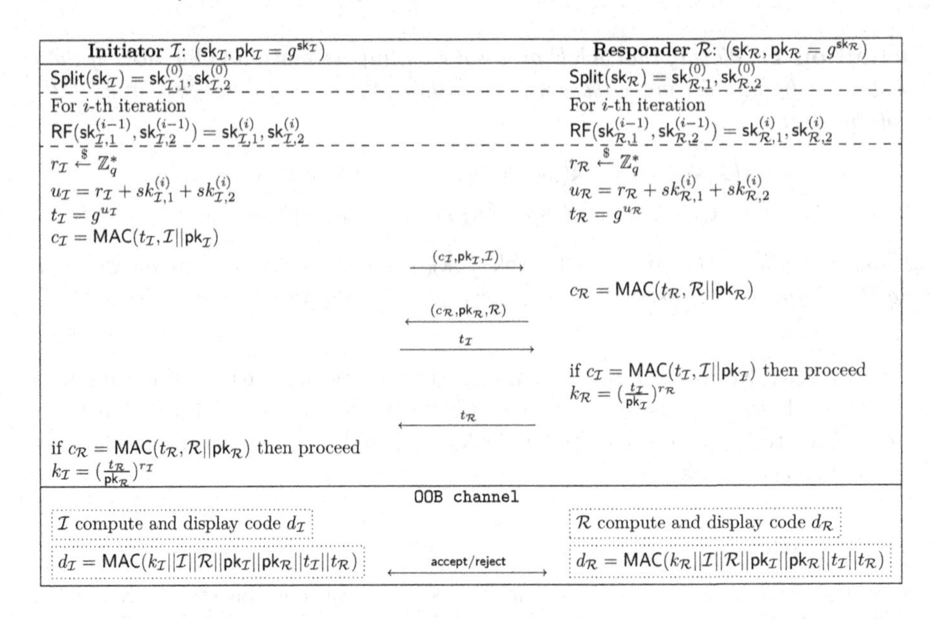

Fig. 3. Original LR-AKE scheme with additive key splitting. OOB communication is used for verifying the display code on both devices, to finalize the pairing; here by the user checking that code $d_{\mathcal{I}}$ shows up and equals $d_{\mathcal{R}}$ on both displays.

using the typical curve "additive" notation. However, in our paper we will use multiplicative group notation for readability and better space compression. Key-pairs for each party is generated as $\mathsf{sk}_{\mathcal{I}} \xleftarrow{\$} \mathbb{Z}_q^*, \mathsf{pk}_{\mathcal{I}} = g^{\mathsf{sk}_{\mathcal{I}}}$ and $\mathsf{sk}_{\mathcal{R}} \xleftarrow{\$} \mathbb{Z}_q^*, \mathsf{pk}_{\mathcal{R}} = g^{\mathsf{sk}_{\mathcal{R}}}$ respectively. Key splitting consists of two sub-protocols:

$\mathsf{Split}(\mathsf{sk}) \rightarrow (\mathsf{sk}_1^{(0)}, \mathsf{sk}_2^{(0)})$: takes a user's secret key sk as input, generates $\mathsf{sk}_1^{(0)} \xleftarrow{\$} \mathbb{Z}_q^*$ and computes $\mathsf{sk}_2^{(0)} = \mathsf{sk} - \mathsf{sk}_1^{(0)}$. Values $\mathsf{sk}_1^{(0)}$ and $\mathsf{sk}_2^{(0)}$ are stored securely and sk is removed from memory since $\mathsf{sk} = \mathsf{sk}_1^{(0)} + \mathsf{sk}_2^{(0)}$.

$\mathsf{RF}(\mathsf{sk}_1^{(i)}, \mathsf{sk}_2^{(i)}) \rightarrow (\mathsf{sk}_1^{(i+1)}, \mathsf{sk}_2^{(i+1)})$: every i-th time (for $i \geq 1$) the splitting values update as follows: $\mathsf{sk}_1^{(i+1)} = \mathsf{sk}_1^{(i)} + s_i$ and $\mathsf{sk}_2^{(i+1)} = \mathsf{sk}_2^{(i)} - s_i$, where $s_i \xleftarrow{\$} \mathbb{Z}_q^*$.

We recall the complete original scheme [34] in Fig. 3.

3.2 Attack Description

Here we consider the attack in which $\mathcal{A}$ impersonate $\mathcal{R}$ in front of $\mathcal{I}$. Note that similar attack in which $\mathcal{A}$ impersonate $\mathcal{I}$ in front of $\mathcal{R}$ can be mounted in a *mutatis mutandis* manner. Let $\mathcal{I}$ and $\mathcal{R}$ setup the devices for the scheme in Fig. 3. When $\mathcal{I}$ starts the protocol towards $\mathcal{R}$, the adversary $\mathcal{A}$ captures $(c_{\mathcal{I}}, pk_{\mathcal{I}}, \mathcal{I})$ and subsequently impersonates $\mathcal{R}$ in front of $\mathcal{I}$, using its own fake device with its own choice of random values. We also note that the shared secret $k_{\mathcal{I}} = k_{\mathcal{R}}$ does not bind the private long-term key in any step (i.e. provide authentication); it rather cancels out via the public key.

$$k_{\mathcal{I}} = \left(\frac{t_{\mathcal{R}}}{\mathsf{pk}_{\mathcal{R}}}\right)^{r_{\mathcal{I}}} = \left(\frac{g^{u_{\mathcal{R}}}}{\mathsf{pk}_{\mathcal{R}}}\right)^{r_{\mathcal{I}}} = \left(\frac{g^{r_{\mathcal{R}}+\mathsf{sk}^{(i)}_{\mathcal{R},1}+sk^{(i)}_{\mathcal{R},2}}}{\mathsf{pk}_{\mathcal{R}}}\right)^{r_{\mathcal{I}}}$$
$$= \left(\frac{g^{r_{\mathcal{R}}}g^{\mathsf{sk}_{\mathcal{R}}}}{\mathsf{pk}_{\mathcal{R}}}\right)^{r_{\mathcal{I}}} = \left(\frac{g^{r_{\mathcal{R}}}\mathsf{pk}_{\mathcal{R}}}{\mathsf{pk}_{\mathcal{R}}}\right)^{r_{\mathcal{I}}} = g^{r_{\mathcal{I}}r_{\mathcal{R}}} = k_{\mathcal{R}}.$$

and similarly

$$k_{\mathcal{R}} = g^{r_{\mathcal{I}}r_{\mathcal{R}}}.$$

Now, the attack is mounted explicitly as follows:

1. $\mathcal{A}$ prepares a fake computing device using only the public parameters.
2. $\mathcal{I}$ sends to $\mathcal{R}$ a tuple $(c_{\mathcal{I}}, \mathsf{pk}_{\mathcal{I}}, \mathcal{I})$.
3. $\mathcal{A}$ intercepts that message. It generates $r_{\mathcal{A}} \xleftarrow{\$} \mathbb{Z}_q^*$, computes $t_{\mathcal{A}} = \mathsf{pk}_{\mathcal{R}} \cdot g^{r_{\mathcal{A}}}$, and $c_{\mathcal{A}} = \mathsf{MAC}(t_{\mathcal{A}}, \mathcal{R}||\mathsf{pk}_{\mathcal{R}})$. and sends to $\mathcal{I}$ the response message $(c_{\mathcal{A}}, \mathsf{pk}_{\mathcal{R}}, \mathcal{R})$, i.e. $\mathcal{A}$ tries to be $\mathcal{R}$ in front of $\mathcal{I}$.
4. $\mathcal{A}$ computes its session key $k_{\mathcal{A}} = \left(\frac{t_{\mathcal{I}}}{\mathsf{pk}_{\mathcal{I}}}\right)^{r_{\mathcal{A}}}$ which will be used instead of the session key of $\mathcal{R}$.
5. $\mathcal{A}$ displays $d_{\mathcal{A}} = \mathsf{MAC}(k_{\mathcal{A}}||\mathcal{I}||\mathcal{R}||\mathsf{pk}_{\mathcal{I}}||\mathsf{pk}_{\mathcal{R}}||t_{\mathcal{I}}||t_{\mathcal{A}})$ code on the fake device.
6. $\mathcal{I}$ computes its session key $k_{\mathcal{I}} = \left(\frac{t_{\mathcal{A}}}{\mathsf{pk}_{\mathcal{R}}}\right)^{r_{\mathcal{I}}}$.
7. $\mathcal{I}$ displays $d_{\mathcal{I}} = \mathsf{MAC}(k_{\mathcal{I}}||\mathcal{I}||\mathcal{R}||\mathsf{pk}_{\mathcal{I}}||\mathsf{pk}_{\mathcal{R}}||t_{\mathcal{I}}||t_{\mathcal{A}})$ code on the device.

The impersonation attack is possible despite the fact that the secret key is split, and the refresh procedure is triggered for each protocol execution. We note that $\mathcal{A}$ impersonates $\mathcal{R}$ in front of $\mathcal{I}$ since:

- in both devices, $\mathcal{I}$ and $\mathcal{A}$ compute the same session key $k_{\mathcal{I}} = k_{\mathcal{A}} = g^{r_{\mathcal{I}}r_{\mathcal{A}}}$, namely

$$k_{\mathcal{I}} = \left(\frac{t_{\mathcal{A}}}{\mathsf{pk}_{\mathcal{R}}}\right)^{r_{\mathcal{I}}} = \left(\frac{\mathsf{pk}_{\mathcal{R}} \cdot g^{r_{\mathcal{A}}}}{\mathsf{pk}_{\mathcal{R}}}\right)^{r_{\mathcal{I}}} = g^{r_{\mathcal{I}}r_{\mathcal{A}}},$$
$$k_{\mathcal{A}} = \left(\frac{t_{\mathcal{I}}}{\mathsf{pk}_{\mathcal{I}}}\right)^{r_{\mathcal{A}}} = \left(\frac{g^{u_{\mathcal{I}}}}{\mathsf{pk}_{\mathcal{I}}}\right)^{r_{\mathcal{A}}} = \left(\frac{g^{r_{\mathcal{I}}+sk^{(i)}_{\mathcal{I},1}+sk^{(i)}_{\mathcal{I},2}}}{\mathsf{pk}_{\mathcal{I}}}\right)^{r_{\mathcal{A}}} = \left(\frac{g^{r_{\mathcal{I}}+\mathsf{sk}_{\mathcal{I}}}}{\mathsf{pk}_{\mathcal{I}}}\right)^{r_{\mathcal{A}}}$$
$$= \left(\frac{g^{r_{\mathcal{I}}} \cdot \mathsf{pk}_{\mathcal{I}}}{\mathsf{pk}_{\mathcal{I}}}\right)^{r_{\mathcal{A}}} = g^{r_{\mathcal{I}}r_{\mathcal{A}}}.$$

- the secret key $\mathsf{sk}_{\mathcal{R}}$ is not necessary when computing the session key $k_{\mathcal{A}}$, since $k_{\mathcal{I}} = k_{\mathcal{A}}$ and both devices will display the same message authentication code $d_{\mathcal{I}} = d_{\mathcal{A}}$,
- the device of $\mathcal{I}$ proceeds as in regular communication with $\mathcal{R}$, making all computations using the public key $\mathsf{pk}_{\mathcal{R}}$ and values received, it "thinks" the computed session key is shared with the device of $\mathcal{R}$, hence "certified" with the public key $\mathsf{pk}_{\mathcal{R}}$,

- a user who inspects the device visually, falsely concludes that they mutually authenticated themselves as the displayed values $d_{\mathcal{I}}$ and $d_{\mathcal{A}}$ are equal.

4 Methodology for Improving LR-AKE

Instead of designing a new protocol from scratch, we integrate new functionalities in existing solutions. Our methodology of improvement relies on provably secure cryptographic building blocks. The fundamental feature is the modular construction of SIGMA, based on signature scheme SIG, message authentication code MAC, and pseudorandom function PRF. The layered architecture enables implementation flexibility based on reuse of existing libraries, already tested in commercial and industrial environments. Alternatively, it is possible to replace the building blocks, with specialized counterparts to achieve additional functionality. This approach was used in several constructions; e.g. in [32] a BLS layer was added on the HMQV protocol to mitigate extended key compromise attacks (eKCI), or in [18], where the regular signature SIG in SIGMA was replaced by anonymous ring signature RSIG to achieve the deniability property. The methodology could be summarised in the following stages:

- **Base AKE choice**: select an existing AKE scheme, preferably one that it is based on SIG and MAC components, which are provable secure in a commonly accepted formal security model.
- **Long-term secret key split**: apply a split-modification on the SIG scheme, i.e. split the long-term signing secret key into two secret sub-key shares.
- **Distinct SMs**: store the shares of the split secret key in two separate SMs, each performing the signing functionality.
- **Key refreshment in SMs**: apply a key refreshment technique in both SMs, each using preferably the same hardware-based source of randomness.
- **OOB channel**: define a protocol step which utilizes an OOB channel.
- **Initial security model adjustment**: adjust the initial security model of the chosen base AKE, to reflect the long-term secret key splitting and refresh mechanism. Adjust the adversary power to the ability of learning partial secrets in different protocol sessions. This would address the risk of secret key-leakage e.g. produced by an untrusted manufacturer of the SMs.
- **Formal proof**: prove the security of the construction in the adjusted model.

4.1 Secure AKE Construction with Signature Components

Let us briefly recall the 3-round version of the SIGMA protocol, denoted as Σ_0 in [6]. Two parties, the initiator $\mathcal{I}$ and responder $\mathcal{R}$, exchange messages using predefined secure building blocks such as a signature function SIG, a message authentication code function MAC, and a pseudorandom function PRF, to identify themselves and to establish a secret session key.

The SIGMA protocol is described in Fig. 4 by rows indicated as `a) original SIGMA`. We briefly recall the steps:

1. Initiator $\mathcal{I}$ generate a session identifier sid, pick at random $x \xleftarrow{\$} \mathbb{Z}_q^*$ and compute an ephemeral DH public key g^x. $\mathcal{I}$ then sends (sid, g^x) to $\mathcal{R}$.
2. $\mathcal{R}$ picks at random $y \xleftarrow{\$} \mathbb{Z}_q^*$ and computes an ephemeral DH public key g^y. Next, a key $(g^x)^y = g^{xy}$ is computed. $\mathcal{R}$ then derive keys $k_0 = \mathsf{PRF}_{g^{xy}}(0)$, and $k_1 = \mathsf{PRF}_{g^{xy}}(1)$. Subsequently, $\mathcal{R}$ erases y and g^{xy} from the device memory and computes MAC_{k_1} ("1", $\mathsf{sid}, ID_{\mathcal{R}}$), and $\mathsf{SIG}_{\mathsf{sk}_{\mathcal{R}}}$("1", sid, g^x, g^y). Finally, $\mathcal{R}$ sends sid, its own identifier $ID_{\mathcal{R}}$, the public key g^y, the signature, and the computed MAC in the response message to $\mathcal{I}$.
3. $\mathcal{I}$ computes the key $(g^y)^x = g^{xy}$ and derives $k_0 = \mathsf{PRF}_{g^{xy}}(0)$, and $k_1 = \mathsf{PRF}_{g^{xy}}(1)$. Subsequently, $\mathcal{I}$ erases x and g^{xy} from the device memory. Next, $\mathcal{I}$ verifies MAC_{k_1} ("1", sid, $ID_{\mathcal{R}}$), retrieves the public key of the party identified by $ID_{\mathcal{R}}$ and verifies $\mathsf{SIG}_{\mathsf{sk}_{\mathcal{R}}}$ ("1", sid, g^x, g^y). If any of the verification procedures fail, $\mathcal{I}$ aborts the session and outputs "reject". If verification is successful, $\mathcal{I}$ computes MAC_{k_1} ("0", $s, ID_{\mathcal{I}}$), and $\mathsf{SIG}_{\mathsf{sk}_{\mathcal{I}}}$ ("0", sid, g^x, g^y). Finally, $\mathcal{I}$ sends sid, $ID_{\mathcal{I}}$, the signature, and the computed MAC to $\mathcal{R}$. $\mathcal{I}$ completes the session with public output $(ID_{\mathcal{I}}, \mathsf{sid}, ID_{\mathcal{R}})$ and the secret session key k_0.
4. $\mathcal{R}$ verifies MAC_{k_1} ("0", $\mathsf{sid}, ID_{\mathcal{I}}$), retrieves the public key $\mathsf{pk}_{\mathcal{I}}$ and verifies signature $\mathsf{SIG}_{\mathsf{sk}_{\mathcal{I}}}$("0", sid, g^x, g^y). If any of the verifications fail, $\mathcal{R}$ aborts the session and outputs "reject", otherwise $\mathcal{R}$ completes the session with public output $(ID_{\mathcal{R}}, \mathsf{sid}, ID_{\mathcal{I}})$ and the session key k_0.

5 Improved LR-AKE Using Split Schnorr Signatures with Key Refresh and OOB Optical Inspection

5.1 Separated SM for Key Splitting

We propose a modified SIGMA with split Schnorr signatures [22], utilizing signature secret/public key pairs $(\mathsf{sk}_{\mathcal{I}}, \mathsf{pk}_{\mathcal{I}} = g^{\mathsf{sk}_{\mathcal{I}}})$ and $(\mathsf{sk}_{\mathcal{R}}, \mathsf{pk}_{\mathcal{R}} = g^{\mathsf{sk}_{\mathcal{R}}})$ for $\mathcal{I}$ and $\mathcal{R}$ respectively, set in an appropriate group $\mathbb{G}$ of computation. Each party's device is augmented with two separate SMs for Schnorr signature functionality, containing signing secret key split shares. These shares are refreshed in each session i in a synchronized way; namely the SM of initiator $\mathcal{I}$ in session i contain keys: $\mathsf{sk}_{\mathcal{I},1}^{(i)}, \mathsf{sk}_{\mathcal{I},2}^{(i)}$. Similarly the SM of responder $\mathcal{R}$ contains $\mathsf{sk}_{\mathcal{R},1}^{(i)}, \mathsf{sk}_{\mathcal{R},2}^{(i)}$. For the key refreshment procedure, each SM is equipped with the pseudo-random number generator PRNG, accessing the hardware based source of randomness $\xi_{\mathcal{I}}$, $\xi_{\mathcal{R}}$ for $\mathcal{I}$ and $\mathcal{R}$ devices respectively. We assume for the security and synchronization purposes, that both SMs access the same source of randomness.

Definition 5 (Signatures with key split and refresh (SIGSRF)). *Signatures with key split and refresh is defined as a tuple of procedures* SIGSRF = (ParGen, KeyGen, $\mathsf{InitSRF}$, SRF, $\mathsf{SignSRF}$, Ver)*:*

$\mathsf{ParGen}(\lambda) \rightarrow \mathsf{par}$*: takes security parameter* λ *and outputs parameters* par*. These are default parameters of the subsequent procedures in the scheme, therefore we omit them for simplicity of notation.*

$\mathsf{KeyGen}(\mathsf{par}) \rightarrow (\mathsf{sk}, \mathsf{pk})$: *takes parameters* par *and output a pair of secret and public keys* sk, pk *respectively.*

$\mathsf{InitSRF}(\mathsf{sk}) \rightarrow (\mathbf{f1}, \mathbf{f2})$: *takes secret key* sk *splits it to parts* $\mathsf{sk}_1, \mathsf{sk}_2$ *and stores it securely in SM1, SM2 with functionalities* $\mathbf{f1}, \mathbf{f2}$ *respectively.*

$\mathsf{SRF}(\mathbf{f1}, \mathbf{f2}) \rightarrow (\mathbf{f1}, \mathbf{f2})$: *takes modules SM1, SM2 with respective functionalities* $\mathbf{f1}, \mathbf{f2}$, *and refreshes the partial keys* $\mathsf{sk}_1, \mathsf{sk}_2$ *stored in these modules.*

$\mathsf{SignSRF}(m, \mathbf{f1}, \mathbf{f2}) \rightarrow \sigma$: *Takes a message* m *and processes it with SM1 and SM2 via* $\mathbf{f1}, \mathbf{f2}$ *respectively, outputting a signature* σ.

$\mathsf{Ver}_{\mathsf{pk}}(m, \sigma) \rightarrow 1/0$: *Returns* 1 *for "accept", or* 0 *for "reject"*

Definition 6 (SIGSRF correctness). *Let* SIGSRF = (ParGen, KeyGen, InitSRF, SRF, SignSRF, Ver) *is a signature scheme with key split and refresh.* SIGSRF *is correct if for any message* m *and any integer* ℓ:

$$\Pr\begin{bmatrix} \mathsf{ParGen}(\lambda) \rightarrow \mathsf{par}, \\ \mathsf{KeyGen}(\mathsf{par}) \rightarrow (\mathsf{sk}, \mathsf{pk}) \\ \mathsf{InitSRF}(\mathsf{sk}) \rightarrow (\mathbf{f1}, \mathbf{f2}) \\ \text{for } i = 1 \textit{ to } \ell \text{ run } \mathsf{SRF}(\mathbf{f1}, \mathbf{f2}) \\ \mathsf{SignSRF}(m, \mathbf{f1}, \mathbf{f2}) \rightarrow \sigma \\ \mathsf{Ver}(m, \sigma, \mathsf{pk}) \rightarrow 1 \end{bmatrix} = 1.$$

To address the scenario with partial secret key leakage, a new, stronger security model for key splitting and refresh is used. In this model a malicious forger $\mathcal{F}$ has the ability to query an additional SignReveal oracle $\mathcal{O}_{\mathsf{SignRev}}(m, j)$ which return the signature over m, all messages T exchanged between modules SM1, SM2, and actual partial secret key stored in module indicating by index j.

Definition 7 (Sign Reveal Unforgeability (SR)). *Let* (ParGen, KeyGen, InitSRF, SRF, SignSRF, Ver) *be a split signature scheme. We define security experiment* $\mathbf{Exp}_{\mathsf{SR}}^{\lambda,\ell}$:

`Init` : $\mathsf{par} \leftarrow \mathsf{ParGen}(\lambda)$ $(\mathsf{sk}, \mathsf{pk}) \leftarrow \mathsf{KeyGen}(\mathsf{par})$.

`SignRev Oracle` : *There are two potential calls:*

- $\mathcal{O}_{\mathsf{SignRev}}(m, 1) \rightarrow (T, \mathsf{sk}_1, \sigma)$ *takes a message* m, *the SM indicator* $j = 1$ *and outputs a transcript* T *of messages exchanged between modules SM1, SM2, the fresh partial secret key stored in SM1, and the final signature* σ *generated with both SM1 and SM2, such that* $\mathsf{Ver}(\sigma, \mathsf{pk}, m) = 1$.
- $\mathcal{O}_{\mathsf{SignRev}}(m, 2) \rightarrow (T, \mathsf{sk}_2, \sigma)$ *similarly as above, where* sk_2 *is the partial secret key stored in SM2.*

The oracle models the device in which partial secret key leakage can happen multiple times in different sessions, but only once and from one SM per signing session (i.e. never from both devices in single signing session).

`Hash Oracle` : *The hash oracle* $\mathcal{O}_{\mathcal{H}}$ *is modeled in ROM.*

`Adversary` : *Let the adversary* $\mathcal{F}_{\mathsf{SR}}^{\mathcal{O}_{\mathsf{SignRev}}, \mathcal{O}_{\mathcal{H}}}(\mathsf{pk})$, *be a malicious algorithm initialized with the public key* pk, *having access to the oracles* $\mathcal{O}_{\mathsf{SignRev}}$ *and* $\mathcal{O}_{\mathcal{H}}$. *It issues* ℓ *number of queries to the oracles. Let* $\mathcal{M} = \{m_i\}_1^{\ell}$, *and* $\Omega = \{\sigma_i\}_1^{\ell}$ *denote the set of the messages, and the corresponding signatures the oracles process.*

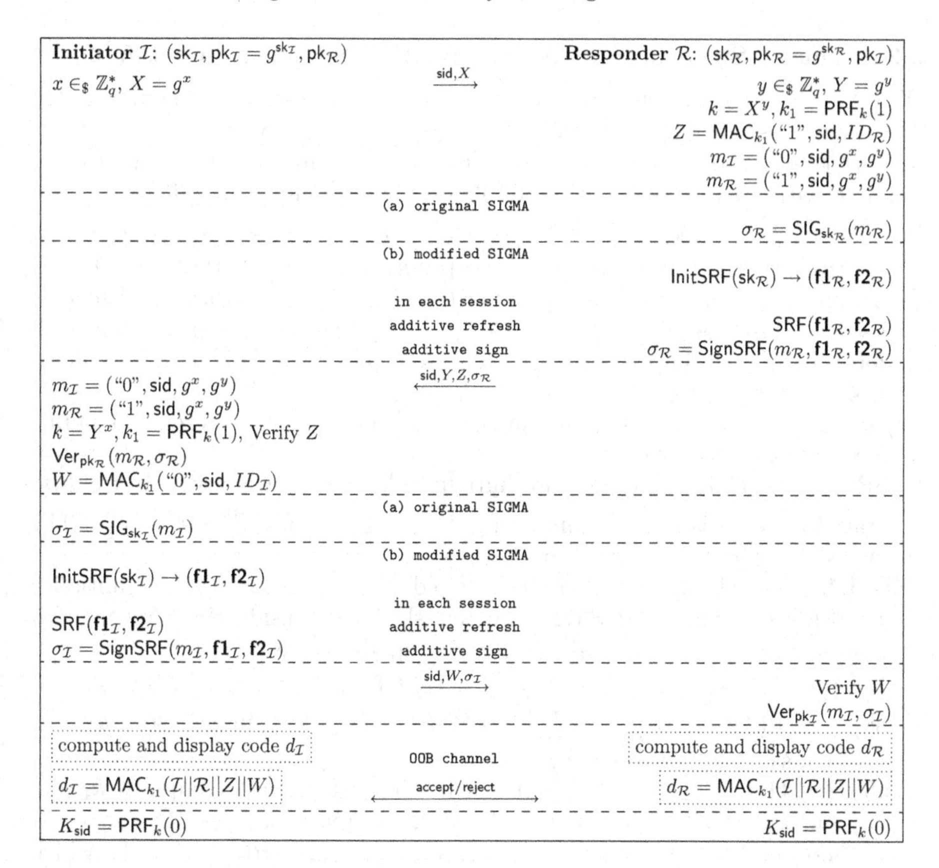

Fig. 4. SIGMA with Schnorr signatures: a) original signature, b) additive split. Keys are stored in two distinct SMs.

`Forgery` : *The adversary generates a tuple:*
$(m^*, \sigma^*) \leftarrow \mathcal{F}_{\mathsf{SR}}^{\mathcal{O}_{\mathsf{SignRev}}, \mathcal{O}_{\mathcal{H}}}(\mathsf{pk})$ *for a new* $m^* \notin \mathcal{M}$*, which was not queried to* $\mathcal{O}_{\mathsf{SignRev}}$ *oracle.*

We say that the signature scheme is secure if for each forgery type, the probability that the adversary produces a valid signature is negligible in parameters λ, ℓ*:*

$$\Pr\left[\begin{array}{l} \mathsf{ParGen}(\lambda) \rightarrow \mathsf{par}, \\ \mathsf{KeyGen}(\mathsf{par}) \rightarrow (\mathsf{sk}, \mathsf{pk}) \\ \mathsf{InitSRF}(\mathsf{sk}) \rightarrow (\mathbf{f1}, \mathbf{f2}) \\ (m^*, \sigma^*) \leftarrow \mathcal{F}_{\mathsf{SR}}^{\mathcal{O}_{\mathsf{SignRev}}, \mathcal{O}_{\mathcal{H}}}(\mathsf{pk}) \\ \mathsf{Ver}(m^*, \sigma^*, \mathsf{pk}) \rightarrow 1 \\ m^* \notin \mathcal{M} \end{array}\right] \leq \epsilon(\lambda, \ell).$$

5.2 Schnorr Signatures with Additive Key Splitting and Refresh

We recall the modification of the Schnorr signature with secret key splitting [22]. The scheme assumes the parties involved in signing (i.e. SM1 and SM2 in our naming convention) share the same source of randomness, e.g. secure PRNG initiated with a hardware based seed. The scheme is defined as follows:

$\mathsf{ParGen}(\lambda) \rightarrow \mathsf{par}$: takes security parameter λ and outputs parameters $\mathsf{par} = (p, q, \langle g \rangle = \mathbb{G})$, where p, q are large primes chosen such that the DLP is assumed hard in a subgroup $\langle g \rangle$, of order q in $\mathbb{Z}_p$. The Schnorr based scheme uses a secure hash function $\mathcal{H} : \{0,1\}^* \rightarrow \mathbb{Z}_q^*$. The signing procedure itself forms a protocol between signing entities, where commitment to a randomness exchange is realized w.l.o.g via $\mathcal{H}$.

$\mathsf{KeyGen}(\mathsf{par}) \rightarrow (\mathsf{sk}, \mathsf{pk})$: takes parameters par and output a secret and public keys sk, pk respectively.

$\mathsf{InitSRF}(\mathsf{sk}) \rightarrow (\mathbf{f1}, \mathbf{f2})$: two SMs are initialized in the following way. In the first stage ($i = 0$) sk is split by computing $\mathsf{sk}_1^{(0)} \xleftarrow{\$} \mathbb{Z}_q$, then $\mathsf{sk}_2^{(0)} = \mathsf{sk} - \mathsf{sk}_1^{(0)}$. The sk_1 is stored in SM1 and sk_2 in SM2.

$\mathsf{SRF}(\mathbf{f1}, \mathbf{f2}) \rightarrow (\mathbf{f1}, \mathbf{f2})$: The hardware based randomness is used to initialize the PRNG of SM1 and SM2. The refreshed keys inside the SMs in each session $i = 1, 2, \ldots$ are based on updating the corresponding values from the previous session by the current output from $\mathsf{PRNG}(i)$, namely: $\mathsf{sk}_1^{(i)} = \mathsf{sk}_1^{(i-1)} + \mathsf{PRNG}(i)$, $\mathsf{sk}_2^{(i)} = \mathsf{sk}_2^{(i-1)} - \mathsf{PRNG}(i)$. Therefore, in each session i the relation $\mathsf{sk} = \mathsf{sk}_1^{(i)} + \mathsf{sk}_2^{(i)}$ holds.

$\mathsf{SignSRF}(m, \mathbf{f1}, \mathbf{f2}) \rightarrow \sigma = (s, r)$: in each i-th session, SM1 computes $k_1 \leftarrow_\$ \mathbb{Z}_q$ and $r_1 = g^{k_1} \bmod p$. Similarily, SM2 computes $k_2 \leftarrow_\$ \mathbb{Z}_q$ and $r_2 = g^{k_2} \bmod p$. Next, SM2 sends the commitment hash $\mathcal{H}(r_2)$ to SM1 which responds with $\mathcal{H}(r_2), r_1$. SM2 verifies the correctness of r_1 by checking if $r_1^q \bmod p$ equals to 1. If successful, SM2 computes $r = r_1 r_2 \bmod p$, $s_2 = k_2 + \mathsf{sk}_2^{(i)} \mathcal{H}(m, r) \bmod q$. SM2 then sends r_1, r_2 and s_2 to SM1. SM1 verifies $\mathcal{H}(r_2)$ and analogously compute $s_1 = k_1 + \mathsf{sk}_1^{(i)} \mathcal{H}(m, r) \bmod q$. In the final step one of the entities outputs the signature $\sigma = (s, r)$, where $s = s_1 + s_2 \bmod q$.

$\mathsf{Ver}_{\mathsf{pk}}(m, \sigma) \rightarrow 1/0$: Returns 1 for "accept", or 0 for "reject" respectively, where the verification procedure by checking that $g^s \stackrel{?}{=} r\mathsf{pk}^{\mathcal{H}(m,r)}$. Note that $r\mathsf{pk}^{\mathcal{H}(m,r)} = g^{(k_1+k_2)} g^{(\mathsf{sk}_1^{(i)} + \mathsf{sk}_2^{(i)})\mathcal{H}(m,r)} \bmod p$.

In [22] the scheme is proved unforgeable against an adversary being able to get partial secrets from different modules in different signing sessions, provided that leakage of partial secret occurs after the key refresh, i.e. the scheme is unforgeable in the sense of Definition 7. We utilize this stronger unforgeability in the modified SIGMA with split Schnorr signatures proposed in Fig. 4.

6 Security Analysis

We provide the formal security analysis with corresponding proofs for our proposed improved scheme, using dual SMs and a key splitting pipeline methodology. As described in [22], an attacker may compromise both SM1 and SM2 given

	$\mathcal{A}$ against mutual identification	$\mathcal{A}$ against session key secrecy
$\mathcal{A}$ goal	Impersonating one party in front of the other party, without the full secret keys (only partial secrets can be leaked). This means impersonating: $\mathcal{I}$ in front of $\mathcal{R}$, and $\mathcal{R}$ in front of $\mathcal{I}$.	Learning the secret session key established in the protocol execution from either the device or communication part of protocol π.
$\mathcal{A}$ power	Active blocking adversary that can: block parties and intercept messages in a Man-in-the-Middle type of attack and extract partial secrets from an SM of parties except both partial secrets of one party in a single seession sid.	For not fully corrupted parties the adversary can exploit partial long term secret key leakage as in: active adversary in the protocol, and passive (observing) adversary
$\mathcal{A}$ oracles	Apart from the regular CK model oracles for an unexposed session s with uncorrupted parties, the active adversary can issue the following combination of queries: **Partial-Key-Reveal**$(\mathcal{I}, \mathsf{sid}, 1)$, **Partial-Key-Reveal**$(\mathcal{R}, \mathsf{sid}, 2)$, or **Partial-Key-Reveal**$(\mathcal{I}, \mathsf{sid}, 2)$, **Partial-Key-Reveal**$(\mathcal{R}, \mathsf{sid}, 1)$.	Adversary can execute oracles as above. The session key is protected by the secrecy of ephemeral values coined by the parties. Executing the *Real-or-Random*-game, issuing the **Test** oracle.
Forbidden combination of queries	Apart from the forbidden CK model oracles for an unexposed test session sid with uncorrupted parties, the active adversary cannot issue the following combination of queries: **Partial-Key-Reveal**$(\mathcal{I}, \mathsf{sid}, 1)$, **Partial-Key-Reveal**$(\mathcal{I}, \mathsf{sid}, 2)$, or **Partial-Key-Reveal**$(\mathcal{R}, \mathsf{sid}, 2)$, **Partial-Key-Reveal**$(\mathcal{R}, \mathsf{sid}, 1)$. These combination would simply reveal the whole secret of parties (as in the case of **Corrupt**$(\mathcal{I}, \mathsf{sid})$, **Corrupt**$(\mathcal{R}, \mathsf{sid})$ queries from CK model which reveal long term secrets) and make the attack trivial.	Adversary cannot execute any oracles that would reveal the ephemeral values, which are used to compute the session key. As in the regular CK model the adversary cannot reveal the *state* of the party - as this would reveal the ephemeral randomness od the parties device.

Fig. 5. Adversary's goal, power, and equivalent oracles in mCK model.

that honest key refreshes are made in-between sessions, however only one SM at the time can be compromised per signature session. We formulate an extention to the Canetti-Krawczyk key exchange model in which we prove impersonation and session key secrecy for our proposed schemes. Note that the regular SIGMA security is based on the unforgeabilty of the underlying signature used. Therefore by replacing the regular signature scheme, with the enhanced scheme secure in the stronger model, we obtain the stronger AKE protocol (Fig. 5).

6.1 Modification of the Canetti-Krawczyk Security Model

To reflect the possibility of the leakage from one SM we introduce the additional oracle "Partial-Key-Reveal" to the regular CK model.

Partial-Key-Reveal$(\mathcal{P}, session, signing\_module)$. This can be used only once in the session sid. If party $\mathcal{P}$ processed computation through SMs pipeline then partial results computations of SMs are returned, and the partial secret key stored in SM indicated by index *signing_module* is revealed. If $\mathcal{P}$ did not process computation through SMs pipeline it returns $\perp$.

Obviously this query is a wrapper for `SignRev Oracle` $\mathcal{O}_{\mathsf{SignRev}}(m,i)$, from our Sign Reveal Unforgeability (SR) model, which could be used for modular AKE protocols which use signature components. With this new query we define that a session sid is **exposed**, not only if the adversary $\mathcal{A}$ issues a *Session-Key-Reveal, State-Reveal* or *Corrupt* query for one of the session's parties, but also if $\mathcal{A}$ makes two partial reveal queries for one party in the same session sid, namely: **Partial-Key-Reveal**($party, \mathsf{sid}, 1$), **Partial-Key-Reveal**($\mathcal{P}, \mathsf{sid}, 2$) which would leak a complete secret key from that party.

Definition 8. *A protocol π provides the session key security if for all adversaries $\mathcal{A}$ the following properties P1 and P2 holds:*

P1: if two uncorrupted parties $\mathcal{I}$ and $\mathcal{R}$, for which ***Partial-Key-Reveal***$(\mathcal{I}, \mathsf{sid}, 1)$, ***Partial-Key-Reveal***$(\mathcal{I}, \mathsf{sid}, 2)$ *and* ***Partial-Key-Reveal***$(\mathcal{R}, \mathsf{sid}, 1)$, ***Partial-Key-Reveal***$(\mathcal{R}, \mathsf{sid}, 2)$ *queries were not issued, complete a matching session* sid, *and correctly identifis peer party in that session, i.e. as* $(\mathcal{I}, \mathsf{sid}, \mathcal{R})$ *and* $(\mathcal{R}, \mathsf{sid}, \mathcal{I})$ *respectively, then the session key K output in these sessions is the same for $\mathcal{I}$ and $\mathcal{R}$ except for a negligible probability.*

P2: an adversary $\mathcal{A}$ succeeds in distinguishing the output from its test query with probability no more than $\frac{1}{2}$ plus a negligible fraction.

6.2 Security Against Impersonation and Session Key Secrecy

The security of the proposed protocols could be proved analogous to the proof of the original SIGMA protocol.

Theorem 1. *Under the the* DDH *assumption in* $\mathbb{G}$, *assuming the security of chosen cryptographic components* $\mathsf{PRF}_k(x)$, MAC_k, *and unforgeability of the underlying Schnorr split signature* $\mathsf{SignSRF}(\mathsf{sk}, m)$, *with refresh function* SRF *in each session realized via distinct* **f1** *and* **f2** *modules, the proposed modified 3-round SIGMA protocol from Sect. 5 is secure in the sense of Def 8.*

Proof. The proof is analogous to the original proof from [6]. It consist of distinct proofs for property P1 and P2 respectively. As we modified the SIGMA scheme by substituting regular signatures with the split signatures with refresh mechanisms, only the proof for P1 requires appropriate adjustment and comments.
Proof of property P1 . We strictly follow the security proof from [6]. Let SignSRF denote the split signing with key refreshing. Let $\mathcal{A}$ denote the attacker having access to the allowed combination of oracles (including **Partial-Key-Reveal**). Let $\mathcal{I}$ and $\mathcal{R}$ denote two uncorrupted entities that complete matching sessions ($\mathcal{I}$, $\mathcal{R}$, sid, *initiator*) and ($\mathcal{I}, \mathcal{R}, \mathsf{sid}, responder$). In order to prove that $\mathcal{I}$ and $\mathcal{R}$ compute the same session key k_0 it suffices to show that both compute the

same DH key g^{xy}, from which k_0 is derived. Let $u_{\mathcal{I}} = g^x$ denote the ephemeral key which $\mathcal{I}$ sends in the first message, and $v_P = g^y$ the ephemeral key which $\mathcal{I}$ receives in the second message. Similarly, we denote $u_{\mathcal{R}} = g^x$ and $v_{\mathcal{R}} = g^y$ as the keys which party $\mathcal{R}$ receives and sends, respectively. Now the signature produced by $\mathcal{R}$ is $\mathsf{SignSRF}_{\mathsf{sk}_{\mathcal{R}}}(\mathsf{sid}, u_{\mathcal{R}}, v_{\mathcal{R}})$ and the signature verified by $\mathcal{I}$ is $\mathsf{SignSRF}_{\mathsf{sk}_{\mathcal{I}}}(\mathsf{sid}, u_{\mathcal{I}}, v_{\mathcal{I}})$. As $\mathsf{SignSRF}_{\mathsf{sk}_{\mathcal{R}}}(\mathsf{sid}, u_{\mathcal{R}}, v_{\mathcal{R}})$ is the only signature made by $\mathcal{R}$ over sid, so arguments to $\mathsf{SignSRF}_{\mathsf{sk}_{\mathcal{R}}}(\mathsf{sid}, u_{\mathcal{R}}, v_{\mathcal{R}})$ and $\mathsf{SignSRF}_{\mathsf{sk}_{\mathcal{I}}}(\mathsf{sid}, u_{\mathcal{I}}, v_{\mathcal{I}})$ have to be the same, or a valid signature over a different pair $u_{\mathcal{I}}, v_{\mathcal{I}}$ was forged by the adversary. In the latter case the adversary can be used to construct an effective forger $\mathcal{F}_{\mathsf{SR}}$ for $\mathsf{SignSRF}$ in the SR model with partial key leakage (as of Def. 7). Thus, if the probability that $\mathcal{A}$ forges a valid a signature for the $\mathsf{SignSRF}$ is negligible, then we have that $u_{\mathcal{I}} = u_{\mathcal{R}}$ and $v_{\mathcal{I}} = v_{\mathcal{R}}$ except for a negligible probability. Similarly, the signature produced by $\mathcal{I}$ is $\mathsf{SignSRF}_{\mathsf{sk}_{\mathcal{I}}}(\mathsf{sid}, u_{\mathcal{I}}, v_{\mathcal{I}})$, and the signature verified by $\mathcal{R}$ is $\mathsf{SignSRF}_{\mathsf{sk}_{\mathcal{I}}}(\mathsf{sid}, u_{\mathcal{R}}, v_{\mathcal{R}})$. As $\mathsf{SignSRF}_{\mathsf{sk}_{\mathcal{I}}}(\mathsf{sid}, u_{\mathcal{I}}, v_{\mathcal{I}})$ is the only signature made by $\mathcal{I}$ over sid, so arguments to these signatures have to be the same, or a valid signature over a different pair $u_{\mathcal{R}}, v_{\mathcal{R}}$ was forged by the adversary $\mathcal{F}_{\mathsf{SR}}$. Thus again, if $\mathcal{A}$ cannot forge a valid a signature for the $\mathsf{SignSRF}$ in the SR model, then we have that $u_I = u_{\mathcal{R}}$ and $v_{\mathcal{I}} = v_{\mathcal{R}}$ except for a negligible probability. So, the DH value computed by $\mathcal{I}$ is $v_{\mathcal{I}}^x = v_{\mathcal{R}}^y = (g^y)^x$ and the DH value computed by $\mathcal{R}$ is $u_{\mathcal{R}}^y = u_{\mathcal{I}}^y = (g^x)^y$. Thus, the session keys for session sid computed by $\mathcal{I}$ and $\mathcal{R}$ are the same.
Proof of property P2 Essentially the same as to proof of the property P2 (*Real-or-Random* indistinguishability) from [6]. □

Corollary 1. *Unless an adversary learns the both partial secrets of one party in a single session (which would enable reconstruction of the long term secret of that party), the proposed modified SIGMA protocol is immune against impersonation attacks.*

Corollary 2. *In order to hijack the session, impersonating some party of chosen identity, and make the peer party to complete the protocol in the accepting state, the active attacker should forge the underlying signature of the impersonated party, or extract both partial key from both SM in one session - which is the equivalent to the whole long term key leakage of that party.*

7 Conclusion

From our analysis we conclude that the proposed key splitting improvements will not increase computational complexity significantly. This indicates that minor algorithmic adjustments, given dual SM properties of the devices, is well justified for increased security against impersonation attacks analyzed in this paper. Our modified unforgeability and CK models allows formal security analysis against impersonation attacks. We argue that same approach could be applied to other AKE protocols with modular architectures, like BLS-HMQV [32].

Acknowledgments. The research was partially financed from the Fundamental Research Fund number 8211104160 of the Wrocław University of Science and Technology.

References

1. Alwen, J., Dodis, Y., Wichs, D.: Leakage-resilient public-key cryptography in the bounded-retrieval model. In: Halevi, S. (ed.) CRYPTO 2009. LNCS, vol. 5677, pp. 36–54. Springer, Heidelberg (2009). https://doi.org/10.1007/978-3-642-03356-8_3
2. Apple: Apple Platform Security Spring 2020 (2020). https://manuals.info.apple.com/MANUALS/1000/MA1902/en_US/apple-platform-security-guide.pdf
3. Brakerski, Z., Kalai, Y.T., Katz, J., Vaikuntanathan, V.: Overcoming the hole in the bucket: public-key cryptography resilient to continual memory leakage. In: 2010 IEEE 51st Annual Symposium on Foundations of Computer Science, pp. 501–510 (2010). https://doi.org/10.1109/FOCS.2010.55
4. Butun, I., Sari, A., Österberg, P.: Hardware security of fog end-devices for the internet of things. Sensors **20**, 5729 (2020)
5. Camenisch, J., Kohlweiss, M., Rial, A., Sheedy, C.: Blind and anonymous identity-based encryption and authorised private searches on public key encrypted data. In: Jarecki, S., Tsudik, G. (eds.) PKC 2009. LNCS, vol. 5443, pp. 196–214. Springer, Heidelberg (2009). https://doi.org/10.1007/978-3-642-00468-1_12
6. Canetti, R., Krawczyk, H.: Security analysis of IKE's signature-based key-exchange protocol. Cryptology ePrint Archive, Report 2002/120 (2002)
7. Dodis, Y., Haralambiev, K., Lopez-Alt, A., Wichs, D.: Cryptography against continuous memory attacks. In: 2010 IEEE 51st Annual Symposium on Foundations of Computer Science, pp. 511–520 (2010). https://doi.org/10.1109/FOCS.2010.56
8. Ferreira, L.C., Dahab, R.: Blinded-key signatures: securing private keys embedded in mobile agents. In: Proceedings of the 2002 ACM Symposium on Applied Computing, SAC 2002, pp. 82–86. Association for Computing Machinery, New York (2002). https://doi.org/10.1145/508791.508808
9. Google: Android Enterprise Security White Paper (2020). https://static.googleusercontent.com/media/www.android.com/sv//static/2016/pdfs/enterprise/Android_Enterprise_Security_White_Paper_2019.pdf
10. Green, M.D., Miers, I.: Forward secure asynchronous messaging from puncturable encryption. In: 2015 IEEE Symposium on Security and Privacy, pp. 305–320 (2015). https://doi.org/10.1109/SP.2015.26
11. Hanzlik, L., Kluczniak, K., Krzywiecki, L., Kutylowski, M.: Mutual chip authentication. In: 12th IEEE International Conference on Trust, Security and Privacy in Computing and Communications, TrustCom 2013 / 11th IEEE International Symposium on Parallel and Distributed Processing with Applications, ISPA-13/12th IEEE International Conference on Ubiquitous Computing and Communications, IUCC-2013, Melbourne, Australia, 16–18 July 2013, pp. 1683–1689. IEEE (2013). https://doi.org/10.1109/TrustCom.2013.209
12. Hanzlik, L., Kluczniak, K., Kutyłowski, M., Krzywiecki, Ł: Mutual restricted identification. In: Katsikas, S., Agudo, I. (eds.) EuroPKI 2013. LNCS, vol. 8341, pp. 119–133. Springer, Heidelberg (2014). https://doi.org/10.1007/978-3-642-53997-8_8

13. Huang, H.: Strongly secure one round authenticated key exchange protocol with perfect forward security. In: Boyen, X., Chen, X. (eds.) ProvSec 2011. LNCS, vol. 6980, pp. 389–397. Springer, Heidelberg (2011). https://doi.org/10.1007/978-3-642-24316-5_28
14. Kiltz, E., Pietrzak, K.: Leakage resilient ElGamal encryption. In: Abe, M. (ed.) ASIACRYPT 2010. LNCS, vol. 6477, pp. 595–612. Springer, Heidelberg (2010). https://doi.org/10.1007/978-3-642-17373-8_34
15. Krawczyk, H.: SIGMA: the "SIGn-and-MAc" approach to authenticated Diffie-Hellman and its use in the IKE protocols. In: Boneh, D. (ed.) CRYPTO 2003. LNCS, vol. 2729, pp. 400–425. Springer, Heidelberg (2003). https://doi.org/10.1007/978-3-540-45146-4_24
16. Krawczyk, H.: HMQV: a high-performance secure Diffie-Hellman protocol. In: Shoup, V. (ed.) CRYPTO 2005. LNCS, vol. 3621, pp. 546–566. Springer, Heidelberg (2005). https://doi.org/10.1007/11535218_33
17. Krzywiecki, Ł: Deniable version of SIGMA key exchange protocol resilient to ephemeral key leakage. In: Chow, S.S.M., Liu, J.K., Hui, L.C.K., Yiu, S.M. (eds.) ProvSec 2014. LNCS, vol. 8782, pp. 334–341. Springer, Cham (2014). https://doi.org/10.1007/978-3-319-12475-9_25
18. Krzywiecki, L., Kluczniak, K., Koziel, P., Panwar, N.: Privacy-oriented dependency via deniable SIGMA protocol. Comput. Secur. **79**, 53–67 (2018). https://doi.org/10.1016/j.cose.2018.08.002
19. LaMacchia, B.A., Lauter, K.E., Mityagin, A.: Stronger security of authenticated key exchange, vol. 2006, p. 73 (2006). http://eprint.iacr.org/2006/073
20. Lauter, K.E., Mityagin, A.: Security analysis of KEA authenticated key exchange protocol, vol. 2005, p. 265 (2005). http://eprint.iacr.org/2005/265
21. Metcalf, D., Milliard, S.T.J., Gomez, M., Schwartz, M.: Wearables and the internet of things for health: wearable, interconnected devices promise more efficient and comprehensive health care. IEEE Pulse **7**(5), 35–39 (2016). https://doi.org/10.1109/MPUL.2016.2592260
22. Nicolosi, A., Krohn, M.N., Dodis, Y., Mazières, D.: Proactive two-party signatures for user authentication. In: NDSS. The Internet Society (2003)
23. Papa, A., Mital, M., Pisano, P., Del Giudice, M.: E-health and wellbeing monitoring using smart healthcare devices: an empirical investigation. Technol. Forecast. Soc. Change **153**, 119226 (2020). https://doi.org/10.1016/j.techfore.2018.02.018. http://www.sciencedirect.com/science/article/pii/S0040162517312696
24. Park, J.H., Chen, H.-H., Atiquzzaman, M., Lee, C., Kim, T., Yeo, S.-S. (eds.): ISA 2009. LNCS, vol. 5576. Springer, Heidelberg (2009). https://doi.org/10.1007/978-3-642-02617-1
25. Qu, Y., Zheng, G., Ma, H., Wang, X., Ji, B., Wu, H.: A survey of routing protocols in WBAN for healthcare applications. Sensors (Basel, Switzerland) **19**(7), 1638 (2019). https://doi.org/10.3390/s19071638. https://pubmed.ncbi.nlm.nih.gov/30959817
26. Ruan, O., Zhang, Y., Zhang, M., Zhou, J., Harn, L.: After-the-fact leakage-resilient identity-based authenticated key exchange. IEEE Syst. J. **12**(2), 2017–2026 (2018). https://doi.org/10.1109/JSYST.2017.2685524
27. Sarr, A.P., Elbaz-Vincent, P., Bajard, J.-C.: A new security model for authenticated key agreement. In: Garay, J.A., De Prisco, R. (eds.) SCN 2010. LNCS, vol. 6280, pp. 219–234. Springer, Heidelberg (2010). https://doi.org/10.1007/978-3-642-15317-4_15

28. Selvi, S.S.D., Paul, A., Rangan, C.P., Dirisala, S., Basu, S.: Splitting and aggregating signatures in cryptocurrency protocols. In: 2019 IEEE International Conference on Decentralized Applications and Infrastructures (DAPPCON), pp. 100–108 (2019). https://doi.org/10.1109/DAPPCON.2019.00021
29. Shuai, M., Liu, B., Yu, N., Xiong, L., Wang, C.: Efficient and privacy-preserving authentication scheme for wireless body area networks. J. Inf. Secur. Appl. **52**, 102499 (2020). https://doi.org/10.1016/j.jisa.2020.102499. http://www.sciencedirect.com/science/article/pii/S2214212619305903
30. Sidhu, S., Mohd, B.J., Hayajneh, T.: Hardware security in IoT devices with emphasis on hardware Trojans. J. Sens. Actuator Netw. **8**(3), 42 (2019)
31. Tahir, H., Tahir, R., McDonald-Maier, K.: On the security of consumer wearable devices in the Internet of Things. PLoS ONE **13**(4), e0195487 (2018)
32. Tang, Q., Chen, L.: Extended KCI attack against two-party key establishment protocols. Inf. Process. Lett. **111**(15), 744–747 (2011)
33. Ustaoglu, B.: Obtaining a secure and efficient key agreement protocol from (H)MQV and NAXOS. Des. Codes Cryptography **46**(3), 329–342 (2008)
34. Zeng, W., Zhang, J.: Leakage-resilient and lightweight authenticated key exchange for E-health. In: 2020 6th International Conference on Information Management (ICIM), pp. 162–166 (2020). https://doi.org/10.1109/ICIM49319.2020.244691

Cryptanalysis of the Multi-Power RSA Cryptosystem Variant

Didier Alquié[1], Guy Chassé[1], and Abderrahmane Nitaj[2](✉)

[1] Académie Militaire de Saint-Cyr Coëtquidan, DGER/CREC, 56381 Guer CEDEX, France
didier.alquie@st-cyr.terre-net.defense.gouv.fr
[2] Normandie Univ, UNICAEN, CNRS, LMNO, 14000 Caen, France
abderrahmane.nitaj@unicaen.fr

Abstract. We study the Multi-Power variant of the RSA cryptosystem where the modulus is of the form $N = p^r q^s$ with $\gcd(r, s) = 1$. We present a method to solve the linear equation $a_1 x_1 + a_2 x_2 \equiv 0 \pmod{p^u q^v}$ where $u < r$, $v < s$, and a_1, a_2 are two integers satisfying $\gcd(a_1 a_2, N) = 1$. We apply the new method to the cryptanalysis of two instances of the Multi-Power RSA. We define a generalization of the CRT-RSA variant of the standard RSA to the Multi-Power RSA, and apply the new method to study its security. The new method is based on Coppersmith's method and lattice reduction techniques.

Keywords: RSA · Multi-Power RSA · Factorization · Lattice reduction · Coppersmith's method

1 Introduction

The RSA cryptosystem [18], designed by Rivest, Shamir and Adleman in 1978 is the most popular asymmetric cryptosystem. It is used to guarantee the security of several industrial applications such as privacy and authenticity. In the standard RSA cryptosystem, the modulus is $N = pq$ where p and q are large prime numbers. To speed up the encryption or the decryption processes, some variants of the RSA cryptosystem have been proposed. In 1998, Takagi [19] proposed a variant of RSA with a modulus of the form $N = p^r q$ with $r \geq 2$. The moduli $N = p^2 q$ have been used in some systems such as the Okamoto-Uchiyama cryptosystem [16], the EPOC and ESIGN schemes [4], and the Schmidt-Samoa [13] cryptosystem. In 2000, Lim et al. [9] proposed to use a modulus of the form $N = p^r q^s$ for $r > s \geq 2$, especially in one of the forms $p^{r+1}q^r$, $p^{r+1}q^{r-1}$, $p^{r+2}q^{r-2}$.

In general, the variants of RSA with a modulus $N = p^r q^s$ use a public exponent e, and a private exponent d satisfying $ed \equiv 1 \pmod{(p-1)(q-1)}$ or $ed \equiv 1 \pmod{p^{r-1}q^{s-1}(p-1)(q-1)}$. For efficiency reasons, the private exponent d should be small. Unfortunately, in many cases, the system can be broken by applying small private exponent attacks. For the standard RSA scheme with a

A. R. Beresford et al. (Eds.): CANS 2022, LNCS 13641, pp. 245–257, 2022.
https://doi.org/10.1007/978-3-031-20974-1_12

modulus $N = pq$, Wiener [20] showed in 1990 that using the continued fraction algorithm, N can be factored if $d < \frac{1}{3}N^{\frac{1}{4}}$. In 1999, Boneh and Durfee applied lattice reduction techniques and Coppersmith's method [2] to show that N can be factored if $d < N^{0.292}$.

For the variants of the RSA cryptosystem with $N = p^r q$ and the equation $ed \equiv 1 \pmod{(p-1)(q-1)}$, Takagi [19] showed in 1998 that N can be factored if $d < N^{\frac{1}{2(r+1)}}$. The former bound was improved in 2004 by May [14] to $d < N^{\max\left(\frac{r}{(r+1)^2}, \frac{(r-1)^2}{(r+1)^2}\right)}$. In 2015, Lu et al. [10] improved this bound to $d < N^{\frac{r(r-1)}{(r+1)^2}}$.

For the variants of RSA with a modulus of the form $N = p^r q^s$, and the equation $ed \equiv 1 \pmod{p^{r-1}q^{s-1}(p-1)(q-1)}$, Lu et al. [11] showed in 2017 that N can be factored if $d < N^{1-\frac{3r+s}{(r+s)^2}}$. One can note that when $s = 1$, the bound reduces to $d < N^{\frac{r(r-1)}{(r+1)^2}}$, which is similar to the bound in [10]. Recently, Nitaj et al. [15] presented an attack on the Multi-Power RSA with a modulus $N = p^r q^s$ when the public exponent e is of the form $e \equiv \frac{z_0}{x_0} \pmod{p^{r-1}q^{s-1}(p-1)(q-1)}$. They showed that N can be factored if $x_0 = N^\delta$, $|z_0| = N^\gamma$ are such that $\delta + \gamma < 1 + \frac{2(r-s)}{r(r+s)^2}\sqrt{s(r+s)} - \frac{2(2r-s)}{r(r+s)}$.

Solving linear equations is useful for cryptanalysis, especially for RSA and its variants [5]. One of the most studied equation is the RSA key equation $ed - k(p-1)(q-1) = 1$. It is the starting point of the majority of the small private exponent attacks. More equations have been used for cryptanalysis such as the equation $a_1x_1 + a_2x_2 \equiv 0 \pmod{p^u}$ where p^u is an unknown factor of N, and a_1, a_2 are integers satisfying $\gcd(a_1a_2, N) = 1$. In [10], the former equation has been used to improve some results on CRT-RSA, a variant of the standard RSA based on the Chinese Remainder Theorem.

In this paper, we study the cryptanalysis of the Multi-Power RSA variant with a modulus of the form $N = p^r q^s$ with $\gcd(r, s) = 1$. Without loss of generality, we assume that p and q are ordered such that $r > s$. We present a method to solve the linear equation $a_1x_1 + a_2x_2 \equiv 0 \pmod{p^u q^v}$ where $u < r$, $v < s$, p^u and q^v are unknown factors of N, and a_1, a_2 are integers satisfying $\gcd(a_1a_2, N) = 1$. We show that one can solve this equation if $|x_1| = N^{\delta_1}$, $|x_2| = N^{\delta_2}$ are such that

$$\delta_1 + \delta_2 < \frac{ru + sv + 2\min(su, rv)}{(r+s)^2}.$$

We apply the new method to show that the bounds in [11] and [15] can be both retrieved by setting $u = r - 1$, and $v = s - 1$.

The CRT-RSA is a variant of the standard RSA where the modulus is $N = pq$, and the public exponent e satisfies two equations, namely $ed_p \equiv 1 \pmod{p-1}$, and $ed_q \equiv 1 \pmod{q-1}$. We present an extension of CRT-RSA to the modulus $N = p^r q^s$ where the public key satisfies the equations $ed_p \equiv 1 \pmod{p^{r-1}(p-1)}$, and $ed_q \equiv 1 \pmod{q^{r-1}(q-1)}$. We show that the new method can be applied to the cryptanalysis of this new variant, and that N can be factored if

$$d_p < N^{\frac{r(r-1)}{(r+s)^2}} \text{ or } d_q < N^{\frac{s(s-1)}{(r+s)^2}}.$$

The remainder of this paper is organized as follows. In Sect. 2, we briefly review lattice reduction technique, and Coppermith's method. In Sect. 3, we present the extension of CRT-RSA to the case of Multi-Power moduli. In Sect. 4, we present the method that solves the linear equation $a_1x_1 + a_2x_2 \equiv 0 \pmod{p^u q^v}$. In Sect. 5, we present three applications of the new method in the cryptanalysis of Multi Power RSA. Finally, we conclude the paper in Sect. 6.

2 Preliminaries

A lattice $\mathcal{L}$ is a discrete subgroup of the form

$$\mathcal{L} = \left\{ \sum_{i=1}^{\omega} \lambda_i b_i \mid \lambda_i \in \mathbb{Z} \right\},$$

where $b_1, \cdots, b_\omega \in \mathbb{R}^n$ are ω linearly independent vectors. The dimension of the lattice is ω with $\omega \leq n$. The determinant of $\mathcal{L}$ is $\det(\mathcal{L}) = \sqrt{|\det(BB^t)|}$ where B is the matrix formed by the rows of the vectors $b_1, \cdots, b_\omega$. In 1982, Lenstra, Lenstra and Lovász [8] proposed a polynomial time algorithm, known as the LLL algorithm, to reduce a lattice. The following result is often used in the cryptanalysis of RSA (see [12]).

Theorem 1. *Let $\mathcal{L}$ be a lattice of dimension ω. In polynomial time, the LLL algorithm outputs a reduced basis $\{u_1, \cdots, u_\omega\}$ satisfying*

$$\|u_1\| \leq \|u_2\| \leq \cdots \leq \|u_i\| \leq 2^{\frac{\omega(\omega-1)}{4(\omega+1-i)}} \det(\mathcal{L})^{\frac{1}{\omega+1-i}},$$

for $1 \leq i \leq \omega$.

In 1996, Coppersmith [2] proposed a method to find the small solutions of a modular univariate polynomial equation with integer coefficients, and a method to find the small roots of a bivariate polynomial with integer coefficients. Coppersmith's method has various applications in cryptanalysis [1,5]. Later, Howgrave-Graham [6] reformulated Coppersmith's method in the following way, where, for $f(x_1, \ldots, x_n) = \sum_{i_1 \cdots i_n} a_{i_1 \cdots i_n} x_1^{i_1} \cdots x_n^{i_n} \in \mathbb{Z}[x_1, \ldots, x_n]$, the Euclidean norm is $\|f(x_1, \ldots, x_n)\| = \sqrt{\sum_{i_1 \cdots i_n} a_{i_1 \cdots i_n}^2}$.

Theorem 2. *Let M be a positive integer, $f(x_1, \ldots, x_n) \in \mathbb{Z}[x_1, \ldots, x_n]$ be a polynomial with at most ω monomials, $X_1, \cdots, X_n$ be positive numbers, and $y_1, \cdots, y_n$ be integers. Suppose that*

$$f(y_1, \ldots, y_n) \equiv 0 \pmod{M},$$
$$|y_1| < X_1, \ldots, |y_n| < X_n,$$
$$\|f(x_1X_1, \ldots, x_nX_n)\| < \frac{M}{\sqrt{\omega}}.$$

Then $f(y_1, \ldots, y_n) = 0$ holds over the integers.

Coppersmith's method serves to find the small solutions $(y_1, \ldots, y_n)$ of the equation $f(x_1, \ldots, x_n) \equiv 0 \pmod{M}$ satisfying $|y_i| < X_i$ for $i = 1, \ldots, n$. First, one builds ω polynomials $g_i(x_1, \ldots, x_n)$, $1 \leq i \leq \omega$ satisfying $g_i(y_1, \ldots, y_n) \equiv 0 \pmod{M}$. Then, one collects the coefficients of the former polynomials to construct a matrix B for a lattice $\mathcal{L}$. Applying lattice reduction techniques via the LLL algorithm, one gets new polynomials $H_i(x_1, \ldots, x_n)$ that share the solution $(y_1, \ldots, y_n)$ over the integers. By applying Gröbner basis techniques or resultant calculations, the solution $(y_1, \ldots, y_n)$ can be obtained. This is possible under the following well-known assumption which is true with overwhelming probability.

Assumption 1. *In Coppersmith's method, the polynomials $H_i(x_1, \ldots, x_n)$, $1 \leq i \leq \omega$, produced by the LLL algorithm are algebraically independent.*

3 The CRT-Multi-Power RSA

In this section, we give a generalization of CRT-RSA to the case where the modulus is of the form $N = p^r q^s$.

CRT-RSA [17] is a variant of the standard RSA based on the Chinese Remainder Theorem. It is devoted to speed up the decryption process in RSA. The CRT-RSA algorithm is as follows.

- **Key Generation**
  1. Generate two prime numbers p and q of the same bit-size.
  2. Compute $N = pq$, and $\phi(N) = (p-1)(q-1)$.
  3. Choose an integer e such that $\gcd(e, \phi(N)) = 1$.
  4. Compute d_p such that $ed_p \equiv 1 \pmod{p-1}$.
  5. Compute d_q such that $ed_q \equiv 1 \pmod{q-1}$.
  6. Compute $q_0 \equiv q^{-1} \pmod{p}$.
  7. The public key is (N, e), and the private key is (p, q, d_p, d_q, q_0).
- **Encryption**
  1. To encrypt a message m, compute $c \equiv m^e \pmod{N}$.
- **Decryption**
  1. To decrypt a ciphertext c, compute $m_p \equiv c^{d_p} \pmod{p}$ and $m_q \equiv c^{d_q} \pmod{q}$.
  2. Compute $M_1 = (m_p - m_q)q_0 \pmod{p}$.
  3. Compute $m = m_q + M_1 q$.

The CRT-RSA can be adapted to the Multi-Power RSA in the following way.

- **Key Generation**
  1. Choose two integers r and s with $\gcd(r, s) = 1$ and $r > s$.
  2. Generate two prime numbers p and q of the same bit-size.
  3. Compute $N = p^r q^s$, and $\phi(N) = p^{r-1}q^{s-1}(p-1)(q-1)$.
  4. Choose an integer e such that $\gcd(e, \phi(N)) = 1$.
  5. Compute d_p such that $ed_p \equiv 1 \pmod{p^{r-1}(p-1)}$.
  6. Compute d_q such that $ed_q \equiv 1 \pmod{q^{s-1}(q-1)}$.
  7. Compute $q_0 \equiv q^{-s} \pmod{p^r}$.

8. The public key is (N, e), and the private key is (p, q, d_p, d_q, q_0).

- **Encryption**
  1. To encrypt a message m, compute $c \equiv m^e \pmod N$.
- **Decryption**
  1. To decrypt a ciphertext c, compute $m_p \equiv c^{d_p} \pmod{p^r}$ and $m_q \equiv c^{d_q} \pmod{q^s}$.
  2. Compute $M_1 \equiv (m_p - m_q)q_0 \pmod{p^r}$.
  3. Compute $m = m_q + M_1 q^s$.

The correctness of the decryption of the CRT-Multi-Power RSA can be proved as follows. Since $ed_p \equiv 1 \pmod{p^{r-1}(p-1)}$, then $ed_p = 1 + p^{r-1}(p-1)u$ with an integer u. Hence

$$m_p \equiv c^{d_p} \equiv m^{ed_p} \equiv m^{1+p^{r-1}(p-1)u} \equiv m \pmod{p^r}.$$

Similarly, we have

$$m_q \equiv m \pmod{q^s}.$$

This induces the system

$$m \equiv \begin{cases} m_p \pmod{p^r}, \\ m_q \pmod{q^s}. \end{cases}$$

Using the Chinese Remainder Theorem, the solution is

$$m \equiv m_q + (m_p - m_q)q_0 q^s \pmod{p^r q^s},$$

where $q_0 \equiv q^{-s} \pmod{p^r}$. Using $M_1 \equiv (m_p - m_q)q_0 \pmod{p^r}$, with $M_1 < p^r$, we get $m = m_q + M_1 q^s$.

4 Solving the Linear Equation

In this section, we present a new method to find the small solutions of the modular equation $a_1x_1 + a_2x_2 \equiv 0 \pmod{p^u q^v}$ when the modulus is $N = p^r q^s$.

Theorem 3. *Let $N = p^r q^s$ be an RSA prime power modulus with $r, s \geq 1$ and $\gcd(r, s) = 1$, where p and q are two prime numbers of the same bit-size. Let $F(x_1, x_2) = a_1x_1 + a_2x_2$ be a homogeneous linear polynomial in two variables whose coefficients are coprime to N. Let u and v be two integers such that $u < r$, and $v < s$. Then one can find all solutions (y_1, y_2) of the equation $F(x_1, x_2) \equiv 0 \pmod{p^u q^v}$ with $|y_1| < N^{\delta_1}$, $|y_2| < N^{\delta_2}$ if*

$$\delta_1 + \delta_2 < \frac{ru + sv + 2\min(su, rv)}{(r+s)^2}.$$

Proof. Let $N = p^r q^s$ with $r, s \geq 1$ and $\gcd(r, s) = 1$. Let $F(x_1, x_2) = a_1x_1 + a_2x_2$ with $\gcd(a_1a_2, N) = 1$. Assume that $F(y_1, y_2) \equiv 0 \pmod{p^u q^v}$ with $u < r$, $v < s$. Then, multiplying by $a_1^{-1} \pmod N$, we get

$$y_1 + ay_2 \equiv 0 \pmod{p^u q^v},$$

where $a \equiv \frac{a_2}{a_1} \pmod N$. Consider the polynomial

$$f(x_1, x_2) = x_1 + ax_2.$$

Then $f(y_1, y_2) \equiv 0 \pmod{p^u q^v}$. Let m, t_1, t_2 be positive integers to be optimised later. To apply Coppersmith's method to solve the equation $f(x_1, x_2) \equiv 0 \pmod{p^u q^v}$, we define the polynomials

$$G_k(x_1, x_2) = x_2^{m-k} f(x_1, x_2)^k N^{\max\left(0, \left\lceil \frac{u(t_1-k)}{r} \right\rceil, \left\lceil \frac{v(t_2-k)}{s} \right\rceil\right)},$$

for $k = 0, \ldots, m$.

Observe that $su \neq vr$, otherwise $\frac{u}{v} = \frac{r}{s}$ which contradicts $u < r$, $v < s$, and $\gcd(r, s) = 1$. Now, suppose that $su > vr$, that is $\frac{u}{r} > \frac{v}{s}$. If $t_1 \geq t_2$, then $\frac{u(t_1-k)}{r} > \frac{v(t_2-k)}{s}$, and

$$\max\left(0, \left\lceil \frac{u(t_1-k)}{r} \right\rceil, \left\lceil \frac{v(t_2-k)}{s} \right\rceil\right) = \max\left(0, \left\lceil \frac{u(t_1-k)}{r} \right\rceil\right),$$

which means that the exponent $\left\lceil \frac{v(t_2-k)}{s} \right\rceil$ will not be used. Consequently, in order to use both exponents $\left\lceil \frac{u(t_1-k)}{r} \right\rceil$ and $\left\lceil \frac{v(t_2-k)}{s} \right\rceil$ alternatively, we assume that $t_1 < t_2$. The following computations show that $G_k(y_1, y_2) \equiv 0 \pmod{p^{ut_1} q^{vt_2}}$.

Case 1. Suppose that $k \geq t_2$. Then

$$\max\left(0, \left\lceil \frac{u(t_1-k)}{r} \right\rceil, \left\lceil \frac{v(t_2-k)}{s} \right\rceil\right) = 0,$$

and

$$\begin{aligned} G_k(y_1, y_2) &= y_2^{m-k} f(y_1, y_2)^k \\ &\equiv 0 \pmod{p^{uk} q^{vk}} \\ &\equiv 0 \pmod{p^{ut_1} q^{vt_2}}. \end{aligned}$$

Case 2. Suppose that $t_2 > k \geq t_1$. Then

$$\max\left(0, \left\lceil \frac{u(t_1-k)}{r} \right\rceil, \left\lceil \frac{v(t_2-k)}{s} \right\rceil\right) = \left\lceil \frac{v(t_2-k)}{s} \right\rceil,$$

and, since $s\left\lceil\frac{v(t_2-k)}{s}\right\rceil \geq v(t_2-k)$, we get

$$\begin{aligned}
G_k(y_1,y_2) &= y_2^{m-k} f(y_1,y_2)^k N^{\left\lceil\frac{v(t_2-k)}{s}\right\rceil} \\
&\equiv 0 \pmod{p^{uk}q^{vk}p^{r\left\lceil\frac{v(t_2-k)}{s}\right\rceil}q^{s\left\lceil\frac{v(t_2-k)}{s}\right\rceil}} \\
&\equiv 0 \pmod{p^{ut_1}q^{vk+s\left\lceil\frac{v(t_2-k)}{s}\right\rceil}} \\
&\equiv 0 \pmod{p^{ut_1}q^{vk+v(t_2-k)}} \\
&\equiv 0 \pmod{p^{ut_1}q^{vt_2}}.
\end{aligned}$$

Case 3. Suppose that $k < t_1$ and $\left\lceil\frac{u(t_1-k)}{r}\right\rceil \leq \left\lceil\frac{v(t_2-k)}{s}\right\rceil$. Then

$$\max\left(0, \left\lceil\frac{u(t_1-k)}{r}\right\rceil, \left\lceil\frac{v(t_2-k)}{s}\right\rceil\right) = \left\lceil\frac{v(t_2-k)}{s}\right\rceil,$$

and

$$\begin{aligned}
G_k(y_1,y_2) &= y_2^{m-k} f(y_1,y_2)^k N^{\left\lceil\frac{v(t_2-k)}{s}\right\rceil} \\
&\equiv 0 \pmod{p^{uk}q^{vk}p^{r\left\lceil\frac{v(t_2-k)}{s}\right\rceil}q^{s\left\lceil\frac{v(t_2-k)}{s}\right\rceil}} \\
&\equiv 0 \pmod{p^{uk}q^{vk}p^{r\left\lceil\frac{u(t_1-k)}{r}\right\rceil}q^{s\left\lceil\frac{v(t_2-k)}{s}\right\rceil}} \\
&\equiv 0 \pmod{p^{uk+u(t_1-k)}q^{vk+v(t_2-k)}} \\
&\equiv 0 \pmod{p^{ut_1}q^{vt_2}}.
\end{aligned}$$

Case 4. Suppose that $k < t_1$ and $\left\lceil\frac{u(t_1-k)}{r}\right\rceil > \left\lceil\frac{v(t_2-k)}{s}\right\rceil$. Then

$$\max\left(0, \left\lceil\frac{u(t_1-k)}{r}\right\rceil, \left\lceil\frac{v(t_2-k)}{s}\right\rceil\right) = \left\lceil\frac{u(t_1-k)}{r}\right\rceil,$$

and

$$\begin{aligned}
G_k(y_1,y_2) &= y_2^{m-k} f(y_1,y_2)^k N^{\left\lceil\frac{u(t_1-k)}{r}\right\rceil} \\
&\equiv 0 \pmod{p^{uk}q^{vk}p^{r\left\lceil\frac{u(t_1-k)}{r}\right\rceil}q^{s\left\lceil\frac{u(t_1-k)}{r}\right\rceil}} \\
&\equiv 0 \pmod{p^{uk}q^{vk}p^{r\left\lceil\frac{u(t_1-k)}{r}\right\rceil}q^{s\left\lceil\frac{v(t_2-k)}{s}\right\rceil}} \\
&\equiv 0 \pmod{p^{uk+u(t_1-k)}q^{vk+v(t_2-k)}} \\
&\equiv 0 \pmod{p^{ut_1}q^{vt_2}}.
\end{aligned}$$

As a consequence, we always have $G_k(y_1,y_2) \equiv 0 \pmod{p^{ut_1}q^{vt_2}}$.

Observe that the inequality $\left\lceil\frac{u(t_1-k)}{r}\right\rceil \leq \left\lceil\frac{v(t_2-k)}{s}\right\rceil$ is satisfied if $k \geq k_0$ where

$$k_0 = \frac{sut_1 - rvt_2}{su - rv}.$$

We have

$$k_0 - t_1 = \frac{rv(t_1 - t_2)}{su - rv} < 0,$$

and, consequently, $\lceil k_0 \rceil \leq t_1$.

Let $X_1 = N^{\delta_1}$ be an upper bound for $|y_1|$, and $X_2 = N^{\delta_2}$ an upper bound for $|y_2|$. We construct a matrix whose rows are the coefficients of the polynomials $G_k(X_1 x_1, X_2 x_2)$ for $k = 0, \ldots, m$. Using this matrix, we build a lattice $\mathcal{L}$ of dimension $\omega = m + 1$. By construction, the matrix is lower triangular, and the determinant of the lattice is the product of the diagonal entries, which is in the form

$$\det(\mathcal{L}) = X_1^{e_1} X_2^{e_2} N^{e_N}, \tag{1}$$

with

$$e_1 = \sum_{k=0}^{m} k = \frac{1}{2} m(m+1),$$
$$e_2 = \sum_{k=0}^{m} (m-k) = \frac{1}{2} m(m+1).$$

Using k_0, the exponent e_N can be computed as

$$e_N = \sum_{k=0}^{\lfloor k_0 \rfloor} \left\lceil \frac{u(t_1 - k)}{r} \right\rceil + \sum_{k=\lfloor k_0 \rfloor + 1}^{t_2} \left\lceil \frac{v(t_2 - k)}{s} \right\rceil.$$

Next, we set $t_1 = \tau_1 m$, $t_2 = \tau_2 m$, $\lfloor k_0 \rfloor = \frac{sut_1 - rvt_2}{su - rv} - c_1$, and $\lceil k_0 \rceil = \frac{sut_1 - rvt_2}{su - rv} + c_2$ with $0 \leq c_1, c_2 < 1$. Then the dominant parts of e_1, e_2, and e_N are

$$\begin{aligned} e_1 = e_2 &= \frac{1}{2} m^2 + o\left(m^2\right), \\ e_N &= \frac{u\left(\tau_1^2 su + \tau_2^2 rv - 2\tau_1\tau_2 rv\right)}{2r(su - rv)} m^2 + o\left(m^2\right). \end{aligned} \tag{2}$$

Applying the LLL algorithm to the lattice $\mathcal{L}$ generated by the matrix whose rows are the coefficients of the polynomials $G_k(X_1 x_1, X_2 x_2)$, we obtain a reduced matrix from which we form ω polynomials $H_k(x_1, x_2)$ satisfying $H_k(y_1, y_2) \equiv 0 \pmod{p^{ut_1} q^{vt_2}}$. In order to combine Theorem 1 with $i = 2$, and Theorem 2, we set

$$2^{\frac{\omega}{4}} \det(\mathcal{L})^{\frac{1}{\omega - 1}} < \frac{p^{ut_1} q^{vt_2}}{\sqrt{\omega}}.$$

or equivalently

$$\det(\mathcal{L}) < \frac{1}{\left(2^{\frac{\omega}{4}} \sqrt{\omega}\right)^{\omega - 1}} \left(p^{ut_1} q^{vt_2}\right)^{\omega - 1}.$$

Since p and q are of the same size, then $p \approx q \approx N^{\frac{1}{r+s}}$. Combining this with (1), we get

$$X_1^{e_1} X_2^{e_2} N^{e_N} < \frac{1}{\left(2^{\frac{\omega}{4}} \sqrt{\omega}\right)^{\omega - 1}} N^{\frac{ut_1 + vt_2}{r+s}(\omega - 1)}, \tag{3}$$

where $X_1 = N^{\delta_1}$, and $X_2 = N^{\delta_2}$. With $t_1 = \tau_1 m$, $t_2 = \tau_2 m$, we get

$$\frac{ut_1 + vt_2}{r+s}(\omega - 1) = \frac{u\tau_1 + v\tau_2}{r+s}m^2 + o(m^2).$$

Combining this with the approximations (2), the inequality (3) can be rewritten as

$$\frac{1}{2}\delta_1 + \frac{1}{2}\delta_1 + \frac{u\left(\tau_1^2 su + \tau_2^2 rv - 2\tau_1\tau_2 rv\right)}{2r(su - rv)} - \frac{u\tau_1 + v\tau_2}{r+s} < -\frac{(m+1)\log\left(2^{\frac{\omega}{4}}\sqrt{\omega}\right)}{m^2\log(N)}.$$

This can be transformed to

$$\delta_1 + \delta_1 < \frac{2(u\tau_1 + v\tau_2)}{r+s} - \frac{u\left(\tau_1^2 su + \tau_2^2 rv - 2\tau_1\tau_2 rv\right)}{r(su - rv)}.$$

The right side is optimized for $\tau_1 = \frac{r(u+v)}{u(r+s)}$, and $\tau_2 = 1$, and the inequality becomes

$$\delta_1 + \delta_2 < \frac{ru + sv + 2rv}{(r+s)^2}.$$

Under this condition, and assuming Assumption 1, we get two algebraically independent polynomials $H_{k_1}(x_1, x_2)$, and $H_{k_2}(x_1, x_2)$ satisfying

$$H_{k_1}(y_1, y_2) = H_{k_2}(y_1, y_2) = 0,$$

with the target solution (y_1, y_2) over the integers. The solution can be obtained by Gröbner basis technique or resultant computations.

Next, suppose that $su < vr$. Then, by interchanging the role of s and r, as well as the role of u and v, the former method works under the condition

$$\delta_1 + \delta_2 < \frac{ru + sv + 2su}{(r+s)^2}.$$

This terminates the proof. □

We note that in [10], Lu et al. proposed a method to solve the equation $a_1x_1 + a_2x_2 \equiv 0 \pmod{p^u}$ when $p > N^\beta$, and p^r is a divisor of N with $u \leq r$, $|x_1| < N^{\delta_1}$, and $|x_2| < N^{\delta_2}$. The main condition for their method is that $\delta_1 + \delta_2 < ru\beta^2$. If we apply this method with $N = p^r q^s$ where p and q are of the same bit-size, the former bound becomes $\delta_1 + \delta_2 < \frac{ru}{(r+s)^2}$. In our method, the equation is $a_1x_1 + a_2x_2 \equiv 0 \pmod{p^u q^v}$, and the bound is $\delta_1 + \delta_2 < \frac{ru+sv+2rv}{(r+s)^2}$, which is more significant than the bound in [10].

In 2015, Coron and Zeitoun [3] proposed a method to factor an RSA modulus $N = p^r q^s$ when $r \geq \log p$. To resist classical factorization methods such as the Elliptic Curve Method for factorization (ECM) [7], the modulus $N = p^r q^s$ should be used with small exponents r and s. In a standard situation, the exponents r and s are small enough so that the method of Coron and Zeitoun can not be applied.

5 Applications of the New Method

In this section, we present three possible applications of the method described in Sect. 4 when the modulus is in the form $N = p^r q^s$.

5.1 Application to the Multi-Power RSA

The Multi-Power RSA is a variant of RSA where the modulus is $N = p^r q^s$ with $r > s$, and $\gcd(r, s) = 1$. In this variant, the Euler totient function is $\phi(N) = p^{r-1}q^{s-1}(p-1)(q-1)$, and the public exponent e and the private exponent d are related by the modular key equation $ed \equiv 1 \pmod{p^{r-1}q^{s-1}(p-1)(q-1)}$. In [11], Lu et al. presented an attack on this variant when $d = N^\delta$ and $\delta < 1 - \frac{3r+s}{(r+s)^2}$.

The modular key equation can be rewritten as $x_1 + ex_2 \equiv 0 \pmod{p^{r-1}q^{s-1}}$ where $x_1 = -1$, and $x_2 = d$. Let $u = r-1$, and $v = s-1$. Then $us-vr = r-s > 0$, and according to Theorem 3 with $\delta_1 = 0$, and $\delta_2 = \delta$, our new method can be applied when

$$\delta < \frac{ru + sv + 2rv}{(r+s)^2} = 1 - \frac{3r+s}{(r+s)^2}.$$

This retrieves the bound as in [11]. As a consequence, our method can be considered as a generalization of the method of Lu et al..

5.2 Application to the Generalization of the Multi-Power RSA

In [15], Nitaj et al. presented an attack on the Multi-Power RSA with a modulus $N = p^r q^s$ with $r > s$ in the following scenario. Assume that there exists two integers x_0 and z_0 such that $\gcd(x_0, z_0 N) = 1$, and $e \equiv \frac{z_0}{x_0} \pmod{p^{r-1}q^{s-1}(p-1)(q-1)}$, or equivalently $ex_0 \equiv z_0 \pmod{p^{r-1}q^{s-1}(p-1)(q-1)}$. They showed that one can factor N if $|x_0| = N^\delta$, and $|z_0| = N^\gamma$ satisfy the condition

$$\delta + \gamma < 1 + \frac{2(r-s)}{r(r+s)^2}\sqrt{s(r+s)} - \frac{2(2r-s)}{r(r+s)}.$$

Observe that $ex_0 \equiv z_0 \pmod{p^{r-1}q^{s-1}(p-1)(q-1)}$ can be rewritten in the form $x_1 + ex_2 \equiv 0 \pmod{p^{r-1}q^{s-1}(p-1)(q-1)}$. Then, using Theorem 3 with $u = r-1$, $v = s-1$, we get $uv - rs = r - s > 0$, and using $|x_1| = N^\gamma$, and $|x_2| = N^\delta$, one can apply the new method to factor N under the condition

$$\delta + \gamma < \frac{ru + sv + 2rv}{(r+s)^2} = 1 - \frac{3r+s}{(r+s)^2}.$$

The difference between the former upper bounds is

$$1-\frac{3r+s}{(r+s)^2}-\left(1+\frac{2(r-s)}{r(r+s)^2}\sqrt{s(r+s)}-\frac{2(2r-s)}{r(r+s)}\right)=\frac{(r-s)\left(r+2s-2\sqrt{r+s}\right)}{r(r+s)^2},$$

which is positive for all positive integers $r > s \geq 1$. This implies that our bound in Theorem 3 supersedes the bound in [15].

5.3 Application to the CRT Multi-power RSA

The following result shows how to apply Theorem 3 to the CRT-Multi-Power RSA variant as defined in Sect. 3.

Theorem 4. *Let $N = p^r q^s$ be a Multi-Power RSA modulus with* $\gcd(r, s) = 1$ *and $r > s$ where p and q are of the same bit-size. Let e be a public exponent satisfying $ed_p \equiv 1 \pmod{p^{r-1}(p-1)}$ and $ed_q \equiv 1 \pmod{q^{s-1}(q-1)}$. If*

$$d_p < N^{\frac{r(r-1)}{(r+s)^2}} \text{ or } d_q < N^{\frac{s(s-1)}{(r+s)^2}},$$

then one can factor N in polynomial time.

Proof. The CRT-Multi-Power RSA shows that the public key satisfies the equations $ed_p \equiv 1 \pmod{p^{r-1}(p-1)}$ and $ed_q \equiv 1 \pmod{q^{s-1}(q-1)}$. The first equation implies that $-1 + ed_p \equiv 0 \pmod{p^{r-1}}$. Set $d_p = N^\delta$. Then, applying Theorem 3 with $u = r-1$, $v = 0$, we get $su - rv = (r-1)s > 0$, and one can find d_p if

$$\delta < \frac{ru+sv+2rv}{(r+s)^2} = \frac{r(r-1)}{(r+s)^2},$$

that is if

$$d_p < N^{\frac{r(r-1)}{(r+s)^2}}.$$

On the other hand, the equation $ed_q \equiv 1 \pmod{q^{s-1}(q-1)}$ implies that $-1 + ed_q \equiv 0 \pmod{q^{s-1}}$. Set $d_q = N^\delta$. Using Theorem 3 with $u = 0$, $v = s-1$, we get $su - rv = -r(s-1) < 0$, and one can find d_q if

$$\delta < \frac{ru+sv+2su}{(r+s)^2} = \frac{s(s-1)}{(r+s)^2},$$

that is if

$$d_q < N^{\frac{s(s-1)}{(r+s)^2}}.$$

This terminates the proof. □

6 Conclusion

In this paper, we studied the Multi-Power RSA variant with a modulus of the form $N = p^r q^s$ where $r > s$. We proposed a method to solve the equation $a_1x_1 + a_2x_2 \equiv 0 \pmod{p^u q^v}$ where $u < r$, $v < s$, and a_1, a_2 are two integers satisfying $\gcd(a_1a_2, N) = 1$. We obtained an explicit condition to efficiently find the solutions, and applied the new method to two known variant of RSA, and proposed a new variant, called CRT-Multi-Power RSA, and studied its cryptanalysis. Our new method was able to retrieve the known results in the cryptanalysis of RSA and some its variants.

References

1. Boneh, D.: Twenty years of attacks on the RSA cryptosystem. Notices Amer. Math. Soc. **46**(2), 203–213 (1999)
2. Coppersmith, D.: Small solutions to polynomial equations, and low exponent RSA vulnerabilities. J. Cryptol. **10**(4), 233–260 (1997)
3. Coron, J.S., Zeitoun, R.: Improved factorization of $N = p^r q^s$, Cryptology ePrint Archive, Report 2016/551 (2016). https://ia.cr/2016/551
4. The EPOC and the ESIGN Algorithms. IEEE P1363: Protocols from Other Families of Public-Key Algorithms (1998)
5. Hinek, M.: Cryptanalysis of RSA and Its Variants. Cryptography and Network Security Series, Chapman & Hall/CRC, Boca Raton (2009)
6. Howgrave-Graham, N.: Finding small roots of univariate modular equations revisited. In: Darnell, M. (ed.) Cryptography and Coding 1997. LNCS, vol. 1355, pp. 131–142. Springer, Heidelberg (1997). https://doi.org/10.1007/BFb0024458
7. Lenstra, H.W., Jr.: Factoring integers with elliptic curves. Ann. Math. **126**, 649–673 (1987)
8. Lenstra, A.K., Lenstra, H.W., Lovász, L.: Factoring polynomials with rational coefficients. Math. Ann. **261**, 513–534 (1982)
9. Lim, S., Kim, S., Yie, I., Lee, H.: A generalized Takagi-cryptosystem with a modulus of the form $p^r q^s$. In: Roy, B., Okamoto, E. (eds.) INDOCRYPT 2000. LNCS, vol. 1977, pp. 283–294. Springer, Heidelberg (2000). https://doi.org/10.1007/3-540-44495-5_25
10. Lu, Y., Zhang, R., Peng, L., Lin, D.: Solving linear equations modulo unknown divisors: revisited. In: Iwata, T., Cheon, J.H. (eds.) ASIACRYPT 2015. LNCS, vol. 9452, pp. 189–213. Springer, Heidelberg (2015). https://doi.org/10.1007/978-3-662-48797-6_9
11. Lu, Y., Peng, L., Sarkar, S.: Cryptanalysis of an RSA variant with moduli $N = p^r q^l$. J. Math. Cryptol. **11**(2), 117–130 (2017)
12. May, A.: New RSA vulnerabilities using lattice reduction methods. Ph.D. thesis, University of Paderborn (2003). http://www.cits.rub.de/imperia/md/content/may/paper/bp.ps
13. Schmidt-Samoa, K.: A new Rabin-type trapdoor permutation equivalent to factoring. Electron. Not. Theor. Comput. Sci. **157**(3), 79–94 (2006). https://eprint.iacr.org/2005/278.pdf
14. May, A.: Secret exponent attacks on RSA-type schemes with moduli $N = p^r q$. In: Bao, F., Deng, R., Zhou, J. (eds.) PKC 2004. LNCS, vol. 2947, pp. 218–230. Springer, Heidelberg (2004). https://doi.org/10.1007/978-3-540-24632-9_16

15. Nitaj, A., Susilo, W., Tonien, J.: A generalized attack on the multi-prime power RSA. In: Batina, L., Daemen, J. (eds.) AFRICACRYPT 2022. LNCS, vol. 13503, pp. 537–549. Springer, Cham (2022). https://doi.org/10.1007/978-3-031-17433-9_23
16. Okamoto, T., Uchiyama, S.: A new public-key cryptosystem as secure as factoring. In: Nyberg, K. (ed.) EUROCRYPT 1998. LNCS, vol. 1403, pp. 308–318. Springer, Heidelberg (1998). https://doi.org/10.1007/BFb0054135
17. Quisquater, J.J., Couvreur, C.: Fast decipherment algorithm for RSA public-key cryptosystem. Electron. Lett. **18**(21), 905–907 (1982)
18. Rivest, R., Shamir, A., Adleman, L.: A Method for obtaining digital signatures and public-key cryptosystems. Commun. ACM **21**(2), 120–126 (1978)
19. Takagi, T.: Fast RSA-type cryptosystem modulo $p^k q$. In: Krawczyk, H. (ed.) CRYPTO 1998. LNCS, vol. 1462, pp. 318–326. Springer, Heidelberg (1998). https://doi.org/10.1007/BFb0055738
20. Wiener, M.: Cryptanalysis of short RSA secret exponents. IEEE Trans. Inf. Theory **36**, 553–558 (1990)

Provable Security of HADES Structure

Yuan Gao[1,2] and Chun Guo[1,2,3](✉)

[1] School of Cyber Science and Technology, Shandong University, Qingdao, Shandong, China
gaoyuanwangan@mail.sdu.edu.cn
[2] Key Laboratory of Cryptologic Technology and Information Security of Ministry of Education, Shandong University, Qingdao 266237, Shandong, China
[3] Shandong Research Institute of Industrial Technology, Jinan 250102 , Shandong, China
chun.guo@sdu.edu.cn

Abstract. The HADES design strategy combines the classical SPN construction with the Partial SPN (PSPN) construction, in which at every encryption round, the non-linear layer is applied to only a part of the state. In a HADES design, a middle layer that consists of PSPN rounds is surrounded by outer layers of SPN rounds. The security arguments of HADES with respect to statistical attacks usually use only the SPN rounds, disregarding the PSPN rounds. There are few results about provable security of HADES and the research on HADES focuses on its designs (the MDS matrix) and attacks (differential and linear). So in this paper, we show that the four-round HADES with the middle two rounds that consist of partial S-boxes surrounded by outer two rounds of SPN, on condition that the linear layer has to be MDS matrix, with independent S-boxes and independent round keys, is birthday bound security.

Keywords: Block cipher · HADES · SPN · PSPN · H-coefficient technique

1 Introduction

1.1 Background

Substitution-permutation network (SPN) is a classical design strategy of cryptographic permutations, used in the AES [1] and in numerous other modern cryptosystems. An SPN iterates many times a sequence of operations called 'round', which consists of a layer of local non-linear operations (S-boxes) and a global linear mixing layer. The wide trail strategy [15] is an approach used to design the round transformations of key-alternating block ciphers that combine efficiency and resistance against differential and linear cryptanalysis. The wide trail strategy, employed in the AES, allows designing SPNs with an easily provable lower bound on the number of active S-boxes in any differential or linear characteristic, thus providing a security guarantee with respect to the most common statistical cryptanalytic attacks.

A. R. Beresford et al. (Eds.): CANS 2022, LNCS 13641, pp. 258–276, 2022.
https://doi.org/10.1007/978-3-031-20974-1_13

In 2013, Gerard et al. [2] proposed the Partial SPN (PSPN) construction, in which the S-box layer is applied to only a part of the state in each round (in exchange for somewhat increasing the number of rounds). This approach, that has obvious performance advantages in various scenarios, was used in the block ciphers Zorro [2] and LowMC [3]. A drawback of this approach is that 'clean' security arguments (like the wide trail strategy) are not applicable for PSPNs, and thus, the security of these designs was argued by more ad-hoc approaches. These turned out to be insufficient, as Zorro was practically broken in [4] and the security of the initial versions of LowMC was shown in [5] to be significantly lower than claimed by the designers.

At Eurocrypt 2020, Grassi et al. [6] proposed the HADES design strategy that combines the classical SPN construction with the PSPN construction. In a HADES design, a middle layer of PSPN rounds is surrounded by two layers of SPN rounds. The scheme allows enjoying 'the best of the two worlds' -the efficiency provided by the PSPN construction, along with the clean security arguments applicable for the SPN construction. The linear layer in the HADES design is implemented by an MDS matrix (see [1]), which guarantees that if the number of S-boxes in any full round is t, then any differential or linear characteristic over two full rounds activates at least $t + 1$ S-boxes. Since the PSPN rounds are not used in the security arguments with respect to statistical attacks, the HADES designers do not impose any restriction on the MDS used in the scheme.

The designers of HADES presented applications of their strategy for securing data transfers with distributed databases using secure multiparty computation (MPC). Subsequently, Grassi et al. proposed Starkad [7] and Poseidon [8] - hash functions whose underlying permutations are instantiations of the HADES methodology, aimed at applications for practical proof systems.

At EUROCRYPT 2021, Keller et al. [9] show that when the MDS is chosen properly, the PSPN rounds can be taken into consideration in the security arguments against differential and linear attacks and a weaker choice of the MDS matrix may lead to existence of huge invariant subspaces for the entire middle layer that do not activate any S-box (for any number of PSPN rounds). They focus on the variants of Starkad and Poseidon suggested in [8] and point out a sharp difference between the cases of a prime field (Poseidon) and a binary field (Starkad).

1.2 Our Results

As briefed before, the research on HADES focuses on its designs (the MDS matrix) and attacks (differential and linear). There are almost no results about provable security of HADES that use the approach (proposed by Luby and Rackoff [10]). Observing this gap, we ask whether it is possible to achieve birthday bound security for four round HADES with the middle two rounds that consists of partial S-boxes surrounded by the outer two rounds of SPN. For this, we focus on HADES with independent S-boxes and independent round keys, and we will focus on the case where $w \geq 4$. Compare to the [12], as the ToSC model only captured "pure" partial SPNs, while our model is closer to HADES or the combination of partial and full SPNs rounds. By considering such a model, our result indicates that combining two different rounds does not create structural weakness. It also sheds lights on on the "roles" of the two different types of SPN rounds. E.g., in our proof, the full SPN rounds in the first and last rounds ensure some sort of "full diffusion". This actually matches some intuitions of HADES, and quite deviates from the "pure" partial SPNs. Besides, 5 partial rounds and our 4-round HADES behave quite differently. The crypto properties of two partial rounds and one full round are quite close (large because they have the same number of S-boxes). Thus, if [12] proved security for 6 partial rounds, then it might implies 4-round HADES. Unfortunately, [12] only proved security for 5 partial rounds. This lack of 1 round actually forced [12] to take a quite different approach from ours. In addition, [12] has to introduce certain conditions into the definition of bad transcripts, which prevents the authors to establish point-wise proximity for 5 partial rounds. In comparison, we did establish point-wise proximity for 4-round HADES. Point-wise proximity is a stronger property than mere indistinguishability.

Concretely, we first characterize conditions on the linear layers that are sufficient for birthday bound security. For a linear transformation T to meet this, it has to be MDS matrix. In addition, in both T and its four matrices $\mathrm{T_{UL}}, \mathrm{T_{UR}}, \mathrm{T_{BL}}, \mathrm{T_{BR}}$ are all MDS (and invertible).

With this, we show that a 4-round HADES is birthday-bound secure, if: (i) 4 independent public random S-boxes are used in the four rounds respectively, and (ii) such a linear permutation layer(MDS matrix) is used in every round, and (iii) the round keys are uniform and independent. Our proof employs the H-coefficient technique [11].

1.3 Organization

We establish notations and models in Sect. 2. Then in Sect. 3, we study the SPRP security of four-round HADES; in Sect. 4, we show an attack to three-round HADES. We finally conclude in Sect. 5.

2 Preliminaries

Throughout this work, we fix positive integers w and n, and let $N = 2^n$. Let $\mathbb{F} := \mathbf{GF}(2^n)$, which is identified with $\{0,1\}^n$. An element x in $\{0,1\}^{wn}$ can be viewed as a concatenation of w blocks of length n. The ith block of this representation will be denoted $x[i]$ for $i = 1, \ldots, w$, so we have $x = x[1]\|x[2]\|\ldots\|x[w]$. For integers $1 \le b \le a$, we write $(a)_b = a(a-1)\cdots(a-b+1)$ and $(a)_0 = 1$ by convention. For an integer $m \ge 1$, the set of all permutations on $\{0,1\}^m$ will be denoted $\mathrm{Perm}(m)$.

MDS Transformations. For any (column) vector $x \in \mathbb{F}^w$, the Hamming weight of x is defined as the number of non-zero entries of x, i.e.,

$$\mathrm{wt}(x) := \Big|\{i | x[i] \neq 0, i = 1, \ldots, w\}\Big|.$$

Let $\mathrm{T} \in \mathbb{F}^{w \times w}$, then the branch number of T (from the viewpoint of differential cryptanalysis) is defined as $\min_{x \in \mathbb{F}^w, x \neq 0}\{\mathrm{wt}(x) + \mathrm{wt}(\mathrm{T} \cdot x)\}$. A matrix $\mathrm{T} \in \mathbb{F}^{w \times w}$ reaching $w + 1$, the upper bound on such branch numbers, is called Maximum Distance Separable (MDS). MDS matrices have been widely used in modern blockciphers including the AES, since the ensured lower bounds on weights typically transform into bounds on the number of active S-boxes (i.e., S-boxes with non-zero input differences).

2.1 The HADES Construction

In this section we briefly describe the structure of a HADES permutation [6].

A block cipher/permutation designed according to the HADES structure employs four types of operations:

1. AddRoundKey, denoted by $\mathrm{ARK}(\cdot)$ - a bitwise XOR of a round subkey (or a round constant for unkeyed designs) with the state;
2. Full S-box Layer, denoted by $\mathrm{S}(\cdot)$ - parallel application of t copies of an identical S-box to the entire state;
3. Partial S-box Layer, denoted by $\mathrm{PS}(\cdot)$ - application of a single S-box to a part of the state, while the rest of the state remains unchanged;
4. Mixing Layer, denoted by $\mathrm{T}(\cdot)$ - multiplication of the entire state.

A full round is defined as $\mathrm{T} \circ \mathrm{S} \circ \mathrm{ARK}(\cdot)$, and a partial round is defined as $\mathrm{T} \circ \mathrm{PS} \circ \mathrm{ARK}(\cdot)$.

2.2 The H-Coefficients Technique

Suppose that a distinguisher $\mathcal{D}$ makes p queries to each of the S-boxes and total q queries to the construction oracles. The queries made to construction oracle is recorded in a query history

$$\mathcal{Q}_C = (i, x_i, y_i)_{1 \le i \le q}.$$

So according to the instantiation, it implies either $\mathrm{HD}_{\mathbf{k}}^{\mathrm{T}}[\mathcal{S}](x_i) = y_i$ or $P(x_i) = y_i$. For $j = 1, \ldots, r$, the queries made to S_j are recorded in a query history

$$\mathcal{Q}_{S_j} = (j, u_{j,i}, v_{j,i})_{1 \le i \le p},$$

where $(j, u_{j,i}, v_{j,i})$ represents the evaluation $S_j(u_{j,i}) = v_{j,i}$ obtained by the ith query to S_j. Let

$$\mathcal{Q}_S = \mathcal{Q}_{S_1} \cup \ldots \cup \mathcal{Q}_{S_r}.$$

Then the pair of query histories

$$\tau = (\mathcal{Q}_C, \mathcal{Q}_S)$$

will be called the transcript of the attack: it contains all the information that $\mathcal{D}$ has obtained at the end of the episode. In this work, we will only consider

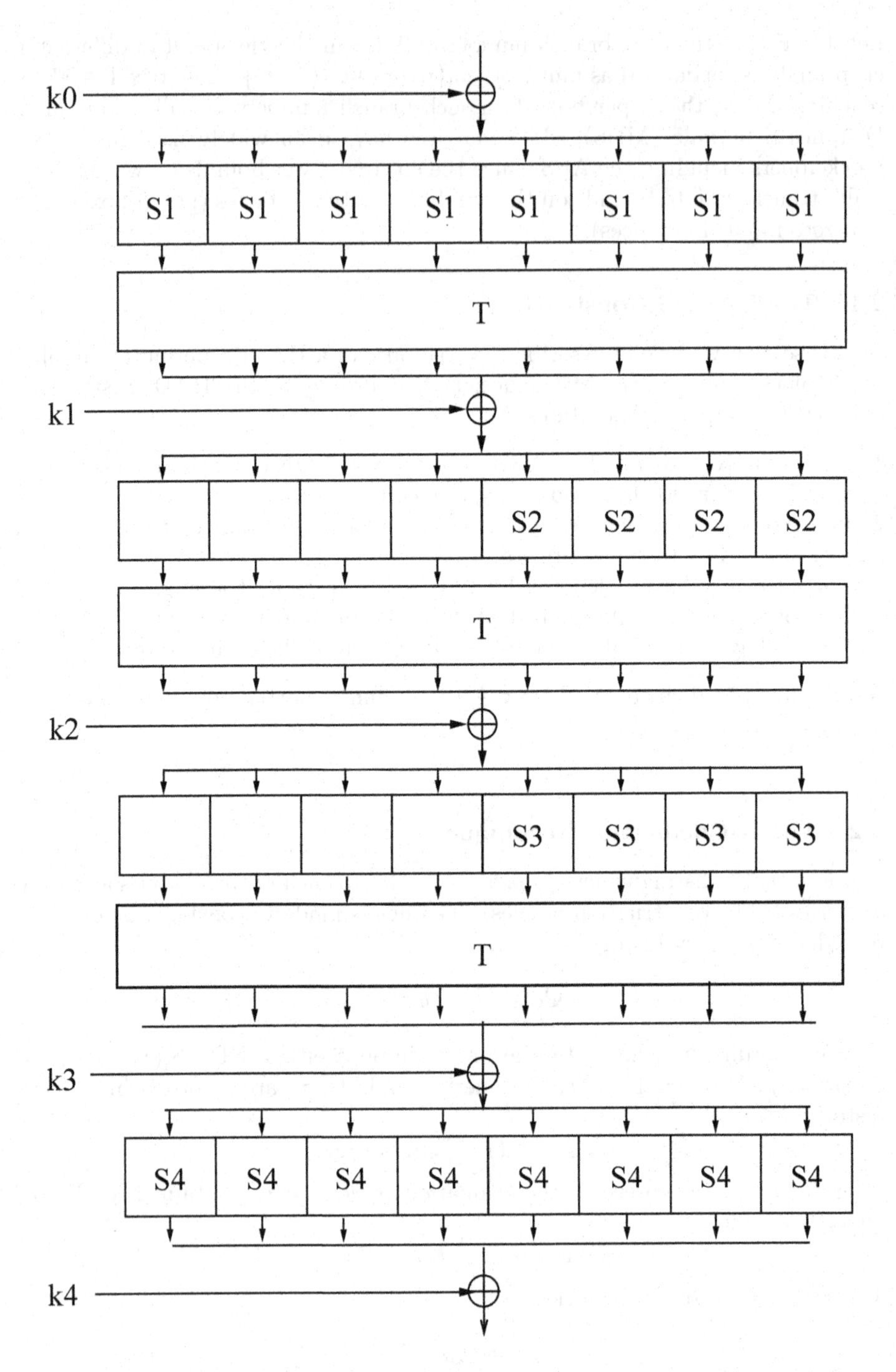

Fig. 1. Four-round HADES with the middle two rounds that consist of partial *S*-boxes surrounded by outer two rounds of SPN.

information-theoretic distinguishers. Therefore we can assume that a distinguisher is deterministic without making any redundant query, and hence the output of $\mathcal{D}$ can be regarded as a function of τ, denoted $\mathcal{D}(\tau)$ or $\mathcal{D}(\mathcal{Q}_C, \mathcal{Q}_S)$.

Fix a transcript $\tau = (\mathcal{Q}_C, \mathcal{Q}_S)$, a key $\mathbf{k} \in \mathcal{K}$, a permutation $P \in \mathsf{Perm}(wn)$, a set of S-boxes $\mathcal{S} = (S_1, \ldots, S_r) \in \mathsf{Perm}(n)^r$ and $j \in \{1, \ldots, r\}$: if $S_j(u_{j,i}) = v_{j,i}$ for every $i = 1, \ldots, p$, then we will write $S_j \vdash \mathcal{Q}_{S_j}$. We will write $\mathcal{S} \vdash \mathcal{Q}_S$ if $S_j \vdash \mathcal{Q}_{S_j}$ for every $j = 1, \ldots, r$. Similarly, if $\mathrm{HD}_{\mathbf{k}}^{\mathrm{T}}[\mathcal{S}](x_i) = y_i$ (resp. $P(x_i) = y_i$) for every $i = 1, \ldots, q$, then we will write $\mathrm{HD}_{\mathbf{k}}^{\mathrm{T}}[\mathcal{S}] \vdash \mathcal{Q}_C$ (resp. $P \vdash \mathcal{Q}_C$).

Let $\mathbf{k} \in \mathcal{K}^{r+1}$, and $P \in \mathsf{Perm}(wn)$, if $\mathrm{HD}_{\mathbf{k}}^{\mathrm{T}}[\mathcal{S}] \vdash \mathcal{Q}_C$ (resp. $P \vdash \mathcal{Q}_C$), then we will write $(\mathrm{HD}_{\mathbf{k}}^{\mathrm{T}}[\mathcal{S}]) \vdash \mathcal{Q}_C$ (resp. $\mathcal{P} \vdash \mathcal{Q}_C$). If there exist $P \in \mathsf{Perm}(wn)$ and $\mathcal{S} \in \mathsf{Perm}(n)^r$ that outputs τ at the end of the interaction with $\mathcal{D}$, then we will call the transcript τ attainable. So for any attainable transcript $\tau = (\mathcal{Q}_C, \mathcal{Q}_S)$, there exist $P \in \mathsf{Perm}(wn)$ and $\mathcal{S} \in \mathsf{Perm}(n)^r$ such that $P \vdash \mathcal{Q}_C$ and $\mathcal{S} \vdash \mathcal{Q}_S$. For an attainable transcript $\tau = (\mathcal{Q}_C, \mathcal{Q}_S)$, let

$$\Pr_{\mathrm{id}}(\tau) = \Pr\left[P \xleftarrow{\$} \mathsf{Perm}(wn), \mathcal{S} \xleftarrow{\$} \mathsf{Perm}(n)^r : P \vdash \mathcal{Q}_C \bigwedge \mathcal{S} \vdash \mathcal{Q}_S\right],$$
$$\Pr_{\mathrm{re}}(\tau) = \Pr\left[\mathbf{k} \xleftarrow{\$} (\{0,1\}^{wn})^{r+1}, \mathcal{S} \xleftarrow{\$} \mathsf{Perm}(n)^r : \mathrm{HD}_{\mathbf{k}}^{\mathrm{T}}[\mathcal{S}] \vdash \mathcal{Q}_C \bigwedge \mathcal{S} \vdash \mathcal{Q}_S\right].$$

With these definitions, the core lemma of the H-coefficients technique (without defining "bad" transcripts) is stated as follows:

Lemma 1. *Let $\varepsilon \geq 0$. Suppose that for any attainable transcript $\tau = (\mathcal{Q}_C, \mathcal{Q}_S)$,*

$$\Pr_{\mathrm{re}}(\tau) \geq (1 - \varepsilon)\Pr_{\mathrm{id}}(\tau). \tag{1}$$

Then one has

$$\mathrm{Adv}_{\mathrm{HD}_{\mathbf{k}}^{\mathrm{T}}}^{\mathrm{sprp}}(\mathcal{D}) \leq \varepsilon.$$

Lemma 2. *Let $\varepsilon : \mathbb{N} \times \mathbb{N} \to \mathbb{R}^{\geq 0}$ be a function such that*

1. *$\varepsilon(x, y) + \varepsilon(x, z) \leq \varepsilon(x, y + z)$ for every $x, y, z \in \mathbb{N}$,*
2. *$\varepsilon(\cdot, z)$ and $\varepsilon(z, \cdot)$ are non-decreasing functions on $\mathbb{N}$ for every $z \in \mathbb{N}$.*

Suppose that for any distinguisher $\mathcal{D}$ in the single-user setting that makes p primitive queries to each of the underlying S-boxes and makes q construction queries, and for any attainable transcript τ obtained by $\mathcal{D}$, one has

$$\Pr_{\mathrm{re}}(\tau) \geq (1 - \varepsilon(p, q))\Pr_{\mathrm{id}}(\tau).$$

3 SPRP Security of 4-Round HADES

In this section, we focus on the SPRP security of four-round HADES. For simplicity, we assume that the width w is even.

Define $\overline{PS^{S_2}}$ and $\overline{PS^{S_3}}$ as the partial S-box of the second and the third round, in order to distinguish the entire S-box of the first and last rounds. And to simplify the expression, below we removed the $\circ$. Concretely, let $\mathrm{HD}_{\mathbf{k}}^{\mathrm{T}}[\mathcal{S}]$ be the four-round HADES using linear transformations T, i.e.

$$\mathrm{HD}_{\mathbf{k}}^{\mathrm{T}}[\mathcal{S}](x) := k_4 \oplus \overline{S_4}\Big(k_3 \oplus \mathrm{T}\Big(\overline{PS^{S_3}}\Big(k_2 \oplus \mathrm{T}\big(\overline{PS^{S_2}}\big(k_1 \oplus \mathrm{T}(\overline{S_1}(k_0 \oplus x))\big)\big)\Big)\Big)\Big), \tag{2}$$

where $\oplus$ is the operation of XORing with the wn-bit round-key k_i and $\circ$ stands for function composition.

We next characterize the properties on T that is sufficient for security. We will frequently write $\mathrm{T} \in \mathbb{F}^{w \times w}$ in the block form of 4 submatrices in $\mathbb{F}^{w/2 \times w/2}$. For this, we follow the convention using U, B, L, R for upper, bottom, left, and right resp., i.e.,

$$\mathrm{T} = \begin{pmatrix} \mathrm{T}_{\mathrm{UL}} & \mathrm{T}_{\mathrm{UR}} \\ \mathrm{T}_{\mathrm{BL}} & \mathrm{T}_{\mathrm{BR}} \end{pmatrix}.$$

Definition 1 (Good Linear Layer for 4 Rounds). *A matrix* $\mathrm{T} \in \mathbb{F}^{w \times w}$ *is* good, *if* T *is MDS,* T *and* T^{-1} *are such that:*

1. *They contain no zero entries, and*
2. *Any column vector of the matrice consists of* w *distinct entries.*

We remark that, as T is MDS, all the four matrices $T_{\mathrm{UL}}, T_{\mathrm{UR}}, T_{\mathrm{BL}}$ and T_{BR} are all MDS (and invertible). Interestingly, the linear layers used in [9] actually satisfy Definition 1.

With such a good T, we have the following theorem on 4-round HADES.

Theorem 1. *Assume* $w \geq 4$, $p + wq \leq N/2$. *Let* $\mathrm{HD}_{\mathbf{k}}^{\mathrm{T}}[\mathcal{S}]$ *be a 4-round* HADES *as defined by Eq. (2). If the round keys* $\mathbf{k} = (k_0, k_1, k_2, k_3, k_4)$ *are uniform and independent, and* T *is good as Definition 1, then*

$$\mathrm{Adv}_{\mathrm{HD}_{\mathbf{k}}^{\mathrm{T}}}^{\mathrm{sprp}}(p, q) \leq \frac{5wpq + 6w^2q^2}{2^n}.$$

The security is birthday bound. All the remaining of this section devotes to prove Theorem 1. The main flow follows the general paradigm of the H-coefficient technique and relies on the following point-wise proximity result and on Lemmas 1 and 2. In detail, we first establish notations in subsect. 3.1. We then complete the two steps defining and analyzing bad transcripts, and peelling off the outer two rounds in subsects. 3.2 and 3.3 resp. Finally we analyze the inner two rounds and bound the ratio $\frac{\Pr_{\mathrm{re}}(\tau)}{\Pr_{\mathrm{id}}(\tau)}$ for good transcripts in subsect. 3.4.

Lemma 3. *Assume* $w \geq 4$ *and* $p + wq \leq N/2$. *Let* $\mathcal{D}$ *be a distinguisher in the single-user setting that makes* p *primitive queries to each of* S_1, S_2, S_3, S_4, *and makes* q *construction queries. Then for any attainable transcript* $\tau = (\mathcal{Q}_C, \mathcal{Q}_S)$, *one has*

$$\frac{\Pr_{\mathrm{re}}(\tau)}{\Pr_{\mathrm{id}}(\tau)} \geq 1 - \frac{5wpq + 6w^2q^2}{2^n}. \tag{3}$$

3.1 Terminology, and Outline of the Proof

Throughout the proof, we fix a distinguisher $\mathcal{D}$ as described in the statement and fix an attainable transcript $\tau = (\mathcal{Q}_C, \mathcal{Q}_S)$ obtained by $\mathcal{D}$. We assume $\mathcal{Q}_C = (x_i, y_i)_{1 \le i \le q}$. Then for $i \in (1, 2, 3, 4, 5)$, let

$$\mathcal{Q}_{S_i}^{(0)} = \{(u, v) \in \{0,1\}^n \times \{0,1\}^n : (i, u, v) \in \mathcal{Q}_S\},$$

and denote the domains and ranges of $\mathcal{Q}_{S_i}^{(0)}$ by

$$U_i^{(0)} = \left\{u_i \in \{0,1\}^n : (i, u_i, v_i) \in \mathcal{Q}_{S_i}^{(0)}\right\},$$
$$V_i^{(0)} = \left\{v_i \in \{0,1\}^n : (i, u_i, v_i) \in \mathcal{Q}_{S_i}^{(0)}\right\}.$$

Extending the Transcripts. Point-wise proximity is usually established by enhancing the transcripts with auxiliary random variables, defining a large enough set of "good" randomness, and then, for each choice of a good random variable, lower bounding the probability of observing this transcript. Such random variables typically include the keys and are usually called good if the adversary cannot use the randomness to follow the path of computation of the encryption/decryption of a query up to a contradiction. To this end, we define an extension of the transcript to gather enough information to allow simple definition of bad randomness. Then, instead of summing over the choice of the randomness, we will define an extension of the transcript, provide the necessary information, and then sum over every possible good extension. In detail, a transcript τ is first extended in the following manner:

- At the end of the interaction between $\mathcal{D}$ and the real world $(\mathcal{S}, \mathrm{HD}_{\mathbf{k}}^{\mathrm{T}}[\mathcal{S}])$, we append τ with the keys $\mathbf{k} = (k_0, k_1, k_2, k_3, k_4)$ and the two random permutations S_1, S_4 in use;
- At the end of the interaction between $\mathcal{D}$ and the ideal world $(\mathcal{S}, P)$, we append τ with randomly sampled keys $\mathbf{k} = (k_0, k_1, k_2, k_3, k_4)$ and the two random permutations S_1, S_4 in use.

Note that, in either case, it is equivalent to sampling two new random permutations S_1, S_4 such that $S_1 \vdash \mathcal{Q}_{S_1}$ and $S_4 \vdash \mathcal{Q}_{S_4}$ and appending them to τ. Because we need to consider the influence of the bad S-box $\overline{S_1}, \overline{S_4}$ and peel off the outer two rounds in the following proof, for any $(x, y) \in \mathcal{Q}_C$, we define

$$a = \mathrm{T}\big(\overline{S_1}(x \oplus k_0)\big), \qquad b = \mathrm{T}^{-1}\big(\overline{S_4^{-1}}(y \oplus k_4)\big).$$

This extends the list $\mathcal{Q}_C$ into a list as follows:

$$\mathcal{Q}'_C = \big((x_1, a_1, b_1, y_1), \ldots, (x_q, a_q, b_q, y_q)\big).$$

With this new list, a colliding query is defined as a construction query $(x, a, b, y) \in \mathcal{Q}'_C$ that fulfills any of the following conditions:

1. there exists an index $i \in \{\frac{w}{2}, \ldots, w\}$ such that $(a \oplus k_1)[i] \in U_2^{(0)}$;
2. there exists an index $i \in \{\frac{w}{2}, \ldots, w\}$ such that $(b \oplus \mathrm{T}^{-1}(k_3))[i] \in V_3^{(0)}$;
3. there exist a construction query $(x', a', b', y') \in \mathcal{Q}'_C$ and two indices $i, j \in \{\frac{w}{2}, \cdots, w\}$ such that $(x, a, i) \neq (x', a', j)$ and $(a \oplus k_1)[i] = (a' \oplus k_1)[j]$;
4. there exist a construction query $(x', a', b', y') \in \mathcal{Q}'_C$ and two indices $i, j \in \{\frac{w}{2}, \cdots, w\}$ such that $(b, y, i) \neq (b', y', j)$ such that $(b \oplus \mathrm{T}^{-1}(k_3))[i] = (b' \oplus \mathrm{T}^{-1}(k_3))[j]$.

Now we further introduce a new set $\mathcal{Q}'_S$ of S-box evaluations to complete the transcript extension. In detail, for each colliding query $(x, a, b, y) \in \mathcal{Q}'_C$, we will add tuples $\big(2, (a \oplus k_1)[i], v'\big)_{\frac{w}{2} \leq i \leq w}$(if (a, b) collides at the input of S_2) or $\big(3, u', (b \oplus \mathrm{T}^{-1}(k_3))[i]\big)_{\frac{w}{2} \leq i \leq w}$ (if (a, b) collides at the output of S_3) to $\mathcal{Q}'_S$ by lazy sampling $v' = \overline{S_2}((a \oplus k_1)[i])$ or $u' = \overline{S_3}^{-1}\big((b \oplus \mathrm{T}^{-1}(k_3))[i]\big)$, as long as it has not been determined by any existing query in $\mathcal{Q}_S$.

An extended transcript of τ includes all the above additional information, i.e.,

$$\tau' = (\mathcal{Q}'_C, \mathcal{Q}_S, \mathcal{Q}'_S, S_1, S_4, \mathbf{k}).$$

For each collision between a construction query and a primitive query, or between two construction queries, the extended transcript will contain enough information to compute a complete round of the evaluation of the HD. This will be useful to lower bound the probability of getting the transcript τ in the real world.

3.2 Bad Transcript Extensions and Probability

The first step is to define the set of bad extended transcripts. Consider an attainable extended transcript $\tau' = (\mathcal{Q}'_C, \mathcal{Q}_S, \mathcal{Q}'_S, S_1, S_4, \mathbf{k})$. For $i = 2, 3$, let

$$\mathcal{Q}_{S_i}^{(1)} = \big\{(u, v) \in \{0,1\}^n \times \{0,1\}^n : (i, u, v) \in \mathcal{Q}_S \cup \mathcal{Q}'_S\big\}.$$

In words, $\mathcal{Q}_{S_i}^{(1)}$ summarizes each constraint that is forced on S_i by $\mathcal{Q}_S$ and $\mathcal{Q}'_S$. For $i = 2, 3$, let

$$U_i^{(1)} = \Big\{u_i \in \{0,1\}^n : (i, u_i, v_i) \in \mathcal{Q}_{S_i}^{(1)}\Big\},$$
$$V_i^{(1)} = \Big\{v_i \in \{0,1\}^n : (i, u_i, v_i) \in \mathcal{Q}_{S_i}^{(1)}\Big\},$$

be the domains and ranges of $\mathcal{Q}_{S_i}^{(1)}$.

We start by upper bounding the probability of getting bad transcripts in the ideal world.

Definition 2. We say an extended transcript τ' is bad if at least one of the following conditions is fulfilled:

(B-1) there exists $(x, y) \in \mathcal{Q}_C, (u_1, v_1) \in U_1^{(0)}, (u_4, v_4) \in U_4^{(0)}$, and index $i, j \in \{1, \ldots, w\}$ such that $(x \oplus k_0)\,[i] = u_1$ or $(y \oplus k_4)\,[j] = v_4$.

(B-2) there exists $(x, y) \in \mathcal{Q}_C$ and distinct indices $i, j \in \{1, \ldots, w\}$ such that $(x \oplus k_0)[i] = (x \oplus k_0)[j]$, or $(y \oplus k_4)[i] = (y \oplus k_4)[j]$.
(B-3) there exists $(x, y), (x', y') \in \mathcal{Q}_C$ and distinct indices $i, j \in \{1, \ldots, w\}$ such that $(x \oplus k_0)[i] = (x' \oplus k_0)[j]$, or $(y \oplus k_4)[i] = (y' \oplus k_4)[j]$.

Any extended transcript that is not bad will be called good. Since these collisions may result in some value of the keys (k_0 or k_4) being parsed or the relationship between the different blocks of the keys (k_0 or k_4) being parsed out. Given an original transcript τ, we denote Θ^1_{good} (resp. Θ^1_{bad}) the set of good (resp. bad) extended transcripts of τ and $\Theta'(\tau)$ the set of all extended transcripts of τ.

We start by upper bounding the probability of getting bad transcripts in the ideal world.

Lemma 4. *One has*

$$\Pr[\tau' \in \Theta^1_{\text{bad}}] \leq \frac{wqp + 2w^2q^2}{N}. \tag{4}$$

Proof. For any fixed construction query $(x, y) \in \mathcal{Q}_C$, now we upper bound the probabilities of the bad extended transcript.
Consider (B-1) first: Since we have at most wqp choices for $(x, y) \in \mathcal{Q}_C$, $(u_1, v_1) \in U_1^{(0)}$ and index $i \in \{1, \ldots, w\}$ and since the random choice of k_0 is independent, one has $\Pr[(x \oplus k_0)[i] = u_1] \leq \frac{wqp}{2^n}$. Similar result follows when $(y \oplus k_4)[j] = v_4$. Then we have $\Pr[(\text{B-1})] \leq \frac{wqp}{2^n}$.
Then consider (B-2). Since the random choice of k_0 and k_4 are independent, then we have $\Pr[(\text{B-2})] \leq \frac{w^2q}{2^n}$. Similarly to (B-3), we have $\Pr[(\text{B-3})] \leq \frac{w^2q^2}{2^n}$. A union bound thus yields

$$\Pr[\tau' \in \Theta^1_{\text{bad}}] \leq \frac{wqp + w^2q + w^2q^2}{2^n} \leq \frac{wqp + 2w^2q^2}{2^n}.$$

3.3 Analysis for Good Transcript

Fix a good transcript and a good round-key vector k, we are to derive a lower bound for the probability $\Pr[\mathcal{S} \xleftarrow{\$} (\mathcal{S}(n))^4 : \text{HD}^{\text{T}}_{\mathbf{k}}[\mathcal{S}] \vdash \mathcal{Q}_C | \mathcal{S} \vdash \mathcal{Q}_S]$. It consists of two steps. In the first step, we will lower bound the probability that a pair of functions (S_1, S_4) satisfies certain "bad" conditions that will be defined. With the values given by a "good" pair of functions (S_1, S_4), a transcript of the distinguisher on 4 rounds can be transformed into a special transcript on 2 rounds; in this sense, we "peel off" the outer two rounds. Then in the second step, assuming (S_1, S_4) is good, we analyze the induced 2-round transcript to yield the final bounds. In the following, each step would take a subsection.

Definition 3. Then we define a predicate Bad(S_1, S_4) on the pair (S_1, S_4), which holds if the corresponding induced set $\mathcal{Q}^*_C(S_1, S_4)$ fulfills at least one of the following three "collision" conditions:

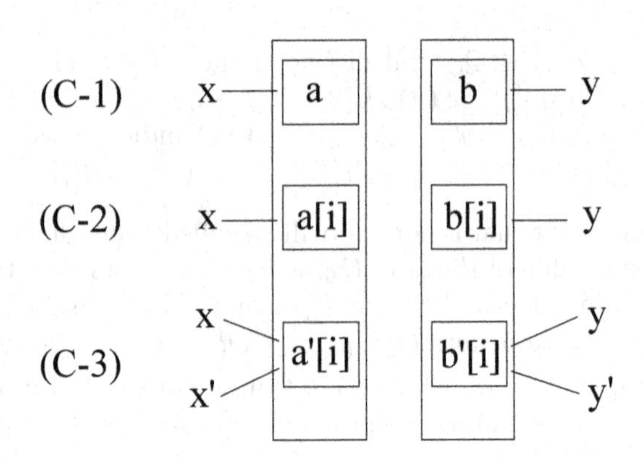

Fig. 2. The three "collision" conditions characterizing a pair of functions $(\overline{S_1}, \overline{S_4})$ such that Bad (S_1, S_4) holds. The values $a, a[i], a'[i], b, b[i], b'[i]$ in squares satisfy $(a \oplus k_1)[i] \in U_2^{(1)}, (a \oplus k_1)[i] = (a \oplus k_1)[i'], (a \oplus k_1)[i] = (a' \oplus k_1)[i'], (b \oplus \mathrm{T}^{-1}(k_3))[j] \in V_3^{(1)}, (b \oplus \mathrm{T}^{-1}(k_3))[i] = (b \oplus \mathrm{T}^{-1}(k_3))[i'], (b \oplus \mathrm{T}^{-1}(k_3))[i] = (b' \oplus \mathrm{T}^{-1}(k_3))[i']$ respectively.

(C-1) there exist $(a, b) \in \mathcal{Q}_C^* (S_1, S_4)$, $i, j \in \{\frac{w}{2}, \ldots, w\}$, $u_2 \in U_2^{(1)}$ and $v_3 \in V_3^{(1)}$ such that $(a \oplus k_1)[i] = u_2$ or $(b \oplus \mathrm{T}^{-1}(k_3))[j] = v_3$.

(C-2) there exist $(a, b) \in \mathcal{Q}_C^* (S_1, S_4)$, distinct $i, i' \in \{\frac{w}{2}, \ldots, w\}$ such that $(a \oplus k_1)$
$[i] = (a \oplus k_1)[i']$ or $(b \oplus \mathrm{T}^{-1}(k_3))[i] = (b \oplus \mathrm{T}^{-1}(k_3))[i']$.

(C-3) There exist distinct pairs $(a, b), (a', b') \in \mathcal{Q}_C^* (S_1, S_4)$ and two indices $i, i' \in \{w/2, \ldots, w\}$ such that
1. $x[\frac{w}{2} + 1..w] \neq x'[\frac{w}{2} + 1..w]$, yet $(a \oplus k_1)[i] = (a' \oplus k_1)[i']$; or
2. $x[\frac{w}{2} + 1..w] = x'[\frac{w}{2} + 1..w], i \neq i'$, yet $(a \oplus k_1)[i] = (a' \oplus k_1)[i']$; or
3. $y[\frac{w}{2} + 1..w] \neq y'[\frac{w}{2} + 1..w]$, yet $(b \oplus \mathrm{T}^{-1}(k_3))[i] = (b' \oplus \mathrm{T}^{-1}(k_3))[i']$; or
4. $y[\frac{w}{2} + 1..w] = y'[\frac{w}{2} + 1..w], i \neq i'$, yet $(b \oplus \mathrm{T}^{-1}(k_3))[i] = (b' \oplus \mathrm{T}^{-1}(k_3))[i']$.

(C-1) captures the case that a 2nd round S-box input or a 3rd round S-box output has been in $\mathcal{Q}'_S$, (C-2) captures collisions among the 2nd round S-box inputs and 3rd round S-box outputs for a single construction query, while (C-3) captures various collisions between the 2nd round S-box inputs, resp. 3rd round S-box outputs, from two distinct queries. Otherwise we say that (S_1, S_4) is good, we denote Θ^2_{good}, (resp. Θ^2_{bad}) the set of good, (resp. bad) pairs of permutations (S_1, S_4) such that $S_1 \vdash \mathcal{Q}_{S_1}, S_4 \vdash \mathcal{Q}_{S_4}$.

In all the following, we denote Θ the set of pairs of permutations (S_1, S_4) such that $S_1 \vdash \mathcal{Q}_{S_1}, S_4 \vdash \mathcal{Q}_{S_4}$. The first step towards studying good transcripts will be to upper bound the probabilities of the five conditions.

Lemma 5. *For any extended* $S_1 \vdash \mathcal{Q}_{S_1}, S_4 \vdash \mathcal{Q}_{S_4}$, *we have*

$$\Pr[\tau_{\text{inner}} \in \Theta^2_{\text{bad}}] \leq \frac{2wpq + 2w^2q^2}{2^n}. \tag{5}$$

Proof. We upper bound the probabilities of the three conditions in turn. We denote Θ_i the set of attainable transcripts satisfying condition (C-i).
Consider the condition (C-1) first. Fix some $(x, a, b, y) \in \mathcal{Q}'_C$ and an index $i \in \{w/2+1..w\}$, $(a \oplus k_1)[w/2+1..w] = \mathrm{T_{BL}} \cdot \overline{S_1}(u_1[1..w/2]) \oplus \mathrm{T_{BR}} \cdot \overline{S_1}(u_1[w/2+1..w]) \oplus k_1[w/2+1..w]$. Since τ is good, $(x \oplus k_0)[i] \notin U_1^{(0)}$ and $(x \oplus k_0)[i] \neq (x \oplus k_0)[i']$ for $i' \neq i$. So the value $S_1((x \oplus k_0)[i])$ for $i \in \{1, \ldots, w\}$ is uniform in a set of size $2^n - p - w + 1$. The MDS property implies that every entry in the wth column of T is nonzero, and thus

$$\Pr[(a \oplus k_1)[i] = u_2] \leq \frac{p}{2^n - p - w + 1} \leq \frac{p}{2^n - p - w}.$$

Similarly by symmetry,

$$\Pr[(b \oplus \mathrm{T}^{-1}(k_3))[j] = v_3] \leq \frac{p}{2^n - p - w}.$$

Summing over $(x, a, b, y) \in \mathcal{Q}'_C, i \in \{w/2+1..w\}$, we reach

$$\Pr[\tau_{\text{inner}} \in \Theta_1] \leq \frac{2 \cdot w/2pq}{2^n - p - w} \leq \frac{wpq}{2^n - p - w}. \tag{6}$$

Next, consider (C-2). Fix $(x, a, b, y) \in \mathcal{Q}'_C$ and $i, i' \in \{w/2+1..w\}$, and let $u_1 = x \oplus k_0, u_2 = a \oplus k_1$. Then the "second half" $u_2[w/2+1..w] = \mathrm{T_{BL}} \cdot \overline{S_1}(u_1[1..w/2]) \oplus \mathrm{T_{BR}} \cdot \overline{S_1}(u_1[w/2+1..w]) \oplus k_1[w/2+1..w]$. Since T is MDS, $\mathrm{T_{BL}}$ and $\mathrm{T_{BR}}$ are also MDS. This means $\mathrm{T_{BR}}$ is invertible, and further that the ith and i'th rows of $\mathrm{T_{BR}}$ are linearly independent and, in particular, there exists an index $j_0 \in \{1, \ldots, w/2\}$ such that the (i, j_0)th and (i', j_0)th entries of $\mathrm{T_{BR}}$ are not equal. Similar to the $\mathrm{T_{BL}}$. Since τ is good, $(x \oplus k_0)[i] \notin U_1^{(0)}$ and $(x \oplus k_0)[i] \neq (x \oplus k_0)[i']$ for $i' \neq i$, then the value of $\overline{S_1}(u_1[1..w/2])$ and $\overline{S_1}(u_1[w/2+1..w])$ are uniform in $2^n - p - w + 1$ values. Therefore,

$$\Pr\left[u_2[\frac{w}{2}+i] = u_2[\frac{w}{2}+i']\right] \leq \frac{1}{2^n - p - w}.$$

Similarly by symmetry, the probability to have $(b \oplus \mathrm{T}^{-1}(k_3))[\frac{w}{2}+i] = (b \oplus \mathrm{T}^{-1}(k_3))[\frac{w}{2}+i']$ is also at most $\frac{1}{2^n-p-w}$. By a union bound over all pairs $(x, a, b, y) \in \mathcal{Q}'_C$ and all $i, i' \in \{1, \ldots, w/2\}$, we reach

$$\Pr[\tau_{\text{inner}} \in \Theta_2] \leq \binom{w/2}{2} \cdot \frac{2q}{2^n - p - w} \leq \frac{w^2 q}{4(2^n - p - w)} \leq \frac{w^2 q^2}{2(2^n - p - w)}. \tag{7}$$

Finally consider (C-3). We first fix $(x, a, b, y), (x', a', b', y') \in \mathcal{Q}'_C$ and $i \neq i' \in \{w/2+1..w\}$ with $x[w/2+1..w] = x'[w/2+1..w]$ for the 2nd condition. While this case concerns with distinct construction queries, the argument is an extension of that of (C-2). In detail, let $u_1 = x \oplus k_0, u_2 = a \oplus k_1, u'_1 = x' \oplus k_0$ and $u'_2 = a' \oplus k_1$. By the analysis for (C-2), we have $\Pr\left[u_2[i] = u_2[i']\right] \leq \frac{1}{N-p-w}$. Since $x[w/2+1..w] = x'[w/2+1..w]$, it can be seen

$$u_2'[i'] = u_2[i'] \oplus \underbrace{(\mathrm{T_{BL}} \cdot (\overline{S_1}(u_1)[1..w/2] \oplus \overline{S_1}(u_1')[1..w/2]))[i' - \frac{w}{2}]}_{\delta}.$$

Since $x[w/2+1..w] = x'[w/2+1..w]$, then there exist $i_0 \in \{1..w/2\}$ such that $x[i_0] \neq x'[i_0]$. Since τ is good, $(x \oplus k_0)[i_0] \neq (x \oplus k_0)[i_1]$ for all $i_1 \neq i_0$ and $(x \oplus k_0)[i_0] \neq (x' \oplus k_0)[i_1]$ for all i_1. So the value of $\overline{S_1}((x \oplus k_0)[i_0])$ is uniform in $\geq 2^n - p - w + 1$ possibilities. Because every entry in the i_0th column of T is nonzero, we have

$$\Pr\big[u_2[i] = u_2'[i']\big] \leq \Pr\big[u_2[i] = u_2[i'] \oplus \delta\big] \leq \frac{1}{2^n - p - w}.$$

We next fix $(x, a, b, y), (x', a', b', y') \in \mathcal{Q}_C'$ and $i, i' \in \{w/2+1, \ldots, w\}$ with $x[w/2+1..w] \neq x'[w/2+1..w]$ for the 1st condition. This means $x[j_0] \neq x'[j_0]$ for some $j_0 \in \{w/2+1, \ldots, w\}$. Since τ is good, $(x \oplus k_0)[j_0] \neq (x \oplus k_0)[j_1]$ for all $j_1 \neq j_0$ and $(x \oplus k_0)[j_0] \neq (x' \oplus k_0)[j_1]$ for all j_1. So the value of $\overline{S_1}((x \oplus k_0)[j_0])$ is uniform in $\geq 2^n - p - w + 1$ possibilities. Then in this situation, if $x[1..w/2] = x'[1..w/2]$, this probability is the same as the previous case. If $x[1..w/2] \neq x'[1..w/2]$, the value of $\overline{S_1}((x \oplus k_0)[j_0'])$ for $j_0' \in \{1..w/2\}$ is also uniform in $\geq 2^n - p - w + 1$. Because every entry in the j_0th and j_0' column of T are nonzero, we have

$$\Pr\big[\,(a \oplus k_1)\,[i] = (a' \oplus k_1)\,[i']\big] \leq \frac{1}{2^n - p - w}.$$

For each choice of $(x, a, b, y), (x', a', b', y')$ the 1st and 2nd conditions are mutual exclusive (i.e., only one may be fulfilled). Hence, summing over all pairs $(x, y, i), (x', y', i') \in \mathcal{Q}_C' \times \{w/2+1, \ldots, w\}$, the probability that either of the two is fulfilled is at most

$$\binom{wq/2}{2} \cdot \frac{2}{2^n - p - w} \leq \frac{w^2 q(q-1)}{8(2^n - p - w)}.$$

Similarly by symmetry, the probability that either the 3rd or the 4th condition is fulfilled is at most $\frac{w^2 q(q-1)}{8(2^n - p - w)}$. Thus

$$\Pr\left[\tau_{\text{inner}} \in \Theta_3\right] \leq \frac{w^2 q(q-1)}{4(2^n - p - w)}. \tag{8}$$

Summing over Eqs. (6),(7),(8), since $p + w \leq 2^n/2$ we reach Eq. (5)

$$\Pr[\tau_{\text{inner}} \in \Theta_{\text{bad}}^2] \leq \frac{2wpq}{2^n - p - w} + \frac{w^2 q^2}{2^n - p - w} \leq \frac{2wpq + 2w^2 q^2}{2^n}.$$

3.4 Analyzing Good Transcript Extensions

We are now ready for the second step of the reasoning. Based on $\mathcal{Q}_C$ and two outer S-boxes $\overline{S_1}, \overline{S_4}$, we derive the 2nd and 3rd rounds intermediate values: these constitute a special transcript $\mathrm{p}_{\mathrm{mid}}(\tau')$ on the middle 2 rounds. We characterize conditions on $\overline{S_1}, \overline{S_4}$ that will ensure certain good properties in the derived $\mathrm{p}_{\mathrm{mid}}(\tau')$, which will ease the analysis. Therefore, we analyze such "good" $\mathrm{p}_{\mathrm{mid}}(\tau')$ to yield the final bounds. Define

$$\mathcal{C}_{\mathbf{k}}^{\mathrm{T}}[\mathcal{PS}](a) := \overline{PS^{S_3}}(\mathrm{T}(\overline{PS^{S_2}}(a \oplus k_1)) \oplus k_2) \oplus \mathrm{T}^{-1}(k_3).$$

For any attainable transcript τ, the ideal world probability is easy to calculate:

$$\begin{aligned}\Pr_{\mathrm{id}}(\tau) &= \Pr\big[(P, \mathcal{S}) \xleftarrow{\$} \mathrm{Perm}(wn) \times \mathrm{Perm}(n)^4 : (P \vdash \mathcal{Q}_C) \wedge (\mathcal{S} \vdash \mathcal{Q}_S)\big] \\ &= \frac{1}{(2^{wn})_q} \cdot \left(\frac{1}{(2^n)_p}\right)^4.\end{aligned}$$

To reach the real world probability $\Pr_{\mathrm{re}}(\tau)$, consider any transcript extension $\tau' = (\mathcal{Q}'_C, \mathcal{Q}_S, \mathcal{Q}'_S, S_1^*, S_4^*, \mathbf{k})$ from τ. Denote

$$\begin{aligned}\mathrm{p}_{\mathrm{re}}(\tau') =& \Pr\Big[(\mathbf{k}', \mathcal{S}) \xleftarrow{\$} (\{0,1\}^{wn})^5 \times \mathrm{Perm}(n)^4 : \Big((S_1 = S_1^*) \wedge (S_4 = S_4^*) \\ & \wedge (S_2 \vdash \mathcal{Q}_{S_2}^{(1)}) \wedge (S_3 \vdash \mathcal{Q}_{S_3}^{(1)}) \wedge (\mathcal{C}_{\mathbf{k}'}^{\mathrm{T}}[\mathcal{PS}] \vdash \mathcal{Q}'_C) \wedge (\mathbf{k}' = \mathbf{k})\Big)\Big],\end{aligned}$$

and

$$\mathrm{p}_{\mathrm{mid}}(\tau') = \Pr\Big[(\mathcal{C}_{\mathbf{k}}^{\mathrm{T}}[\mathcal{PS}] \vdash \mathcal{Q}'_C) \Big| (S_1 = S_1^*) \wedge (S_4 = S_4^*) \wedge (S_2 \vdash \mathcal{Q}_{S_2}^{(1)}) \wedge (S_3 \vdash \mathcal{Q}_{S_3}^{(1)})\Big].$$

and let $\alpha_2 = |\mathcal{Q}_{S_2}^{(1)}| - |\mathcal{Q}_{S_2}^{(0)}| = |\mathcal{Q}_{S_2}^{(1)}| - p$ and $\alpha_3 = |\mathcal{Q}_{S_3}^{(1)}| - p$. With these, we have

$$\begin{aligned}\Pr_{\mathrm{re}}(\tau) &= \Pr\big[(\mathbf{k}, \mathcal{S}) \xleftarrow{\$} (\{0,1\}^{wn})^5 \times \mathrm{Perm}(n)^4 : (\mathrm{HD}_{\mathbf{k}}^{\mathrm{T}}[\mathcal{S}] \vdash \mathcal{Q}_C) \wedge (\mathcal{S} \vdash \mathcal{Q}_S)\big] \\ &\geq \sum_{\tau' \in \Theta_{\mathrm{good}}(\tau)} \mathrm{p}_{\mathrm{re}}(\tau') \\ &\geq \sum_{\tau' \in \Theta_{\mathrm{good}}(\tau)} \frac{1}{2^{5wn}\big((2^n)_{2^n}\big)^2 (2^n)_{p+\alpha_1} (2^n)_{p+\alpha_2}} \cdot \mathrm{p}_{\mathrm{mid}}(\tau').\end{aligned}$$

Therefore

$$\frac{\Pr_{\mathrm{re}}(\tau)}{\Pr_{\mathrm{id}}(\tau)} \geq \sum_{\tau' \in \Theta_{\mathrm{good}}(\tau)} \frac{(2^{wn})_q \cdot \left((2^n)_p\right)^4}{2^{5wn}\left((2^n)_{2^n}\right)^2 (2^n)_{p+\alpha_1}(2^n)_{p+\alpha_2}} \cdot \mathrm{p_{mid}}(\tau')$$
$$\geq \min_{\tau' \in \Theta_{\mathrm{good}}(\tau)} \left((2^{wn})_q \cdot \mathrm{p_{mid}}(\tau')\right)$$
$$\underbrace{\sum_{\tau' \in \Theta_{\mathrm{good}}(\tau)} \frac{1}{2^{5wn}\left((2^n-p)_{2^n-p}\right)^2 (2^n-p)_{\alpha_1}(2^n-p)_{\alpha_2}}}_{B}.$$

Note that, the exact probability of observing the extended transcript τ' is

$$\frac{1}{2^{5wn}\left((2^n-p)_{2^n-p}\right)^2 (2^n-p)_{\alpha_1}(2^n-p)_{\alpha_2}},$$

since:

1. sample keys $k_0, \ldots, k_4 \in \{0,1\}^{wn}$ uniformly and independently at random;
2. sample two random permutations S_1, S_4 from $\mathrm{Perm}(n)$ at uniform, such that $S_1 \vdash \mathcal{Q}^{(0)}_{S_1}, S_4 \vdash \mathcal{Q}^{(0)}_{S_4}$;
3. choose the partial extension of the S-box queries based on the new collisions $\mathcal{Q}'_S$ uniformly at random (meaning that each possible u or v is chosen uniformly at random in the set of its authorized values).

This means the term B captures the probability of good transcript extensions:

$$B = \sum_{\tau' \in \Theta_{\mathrm{good}}(\tau)} \frac{1}{2^{5wn}\left((2^n-p)_{2^n-p}\right)^2 (2^n-p)_{\alpha_1}(2^n-p)_{\alpha_2}}$$
$$= \Pr[\tau' \in \Theta_{\mathrm{good}}(\tau)] \geq 1 - \Pr[\tau' \in \Theta_{\mathrm{bad}}(\tau)],$$

which further implies

$$\frac{\Pr_{\mathrm{re}}(\tau)}{\Pr_{\mathrm{id}}(\tau)} \geq \Pr[\tau' \in \Theta_{\mathrm{good}}(\tau)] \cdot \min_{\tau' \in \Theta_{\mathrm{good}}(\tau)} \left((2^{wn})_q \cdot \mathrm{p_{mid}}(\tau')\right). \tag{9}$$

Definition 4. For $i, i' \in \{w/2+1..w\}$, $\ell \in \{1, \ldots, q\}$, let $\left(\mathrm{T}\left(\overline{PS^{S_2}}(a^{(\ell)} \oplus k_1)\right) \oplus k_2\right)[i] = u_3^{(\ell)}[i]$ and $\left(\mathrm{T}^{-1}\left(\overline{PS^{S_3}}^{-1}(b^{(\ell)} \oplus \mathrm{T}^{-1}(k_3))\right) \oplus k_2\right)[i] = v_2^{(\ell)}$. Then we define $\mathrm{Bad}_2\,(S_1, S_4)$ is fulfilled, if either (E-1) or (E-2) is fulfilled:

(E-1) S_2 or S_3 leads to unfresh intermediate values : there exist $(a,b) \in \mathcal{Q}^*_C\,(S_1, S_4)$, $i, j \in \{\frac{w}{2}, \ldots, w\}$, $u_3 \in U_3^{(1)}$ and $v_2 \in V_2^{(1)}$ such that $u_3^{(\ell)}[i] = u_3$ or $v_2^{(\ell)}[i] = v_2$.

(E-2) S_2 or S_3 leads to colliding intermediate values: there exist distinct pairs $(a,b), (a',b') \in \mathcal{Q}^*_C\,(S_1, S_4)$, distinct $i, i' \in \{\frac{w}{2}+1..w\}$ such that $u_3^{(\ell_1)}[i] = u_3^{(\ell_2)}[i']$ or $v_2^{(\ell_1)}[i] = v_2^{(\ell_2)}[i']$.

(E-1) captures the case that a 3rd round S-box input has been in $\mathcal{Q}'_S$ or a 2nd round S-box output has been in $\mathcal{Q}'_S$, (E-2) captures collisions among the 3rd round S-box inputs for a single construction query or among the 2nd round S-box ouputs for a single construction query.

Proof. Consider (E-1) first. Conditioned on $\neg\Theta^2_{\text{bad}}$ and the values in $V_2^{(1)}$, there exists $i' \in \{w/2+1..w\}$ such that $v_2^{(\ell)}[i'] = \overline{S_2}(u_2^{(\ell)}[i'])$ is unifrom in at least $2^n - p - wq/2$ possibilities. Since

$$u_3^{(\ell)}[w/2+1..w] = \mathrm{T_{BL}} \cdot u_2^{(\ell)}[1..w/2] \oplus \mathrm{T_{BR}} \cdot v_2^{(\ell)}[w/2+1..w] \oplus k_2[w/2+1..w], \tag{10}$$

and since every entry in the $(i' - w/2)$ th column of $\mathrm{T_{BR}}$ is nonzero, for any $i \in \{w/2+1..w\}$ we have

$$\Pr[u_3^{(\ell)}[i] = u_3] \le \frac{p + wq/2}{2^n - p - wq/2}.$$

Similar to the $\Pr[v_2^{(\ell)}[i] = v_2]$. Summing over the $wq/2$ choices of $(\ell, i) \in \{1, \ldots, q\} \times \{w/2+1, \ldots, w\}$, we reach

$$\Pr[(\text{E-1})] \le \frac{wq(p + wq/2)}{2^n - p - wq/2}.$$

Next, consider (E-2). Depending on whether $\ell_1 = \ell_2$, we will divide the discussion into two cases.

For the case of $\ell_1 = \ell_2 \in \{1, \ldots, q\}$, fix distinct $i_1, i_2 \in \{w/2+1, \ldots, w\}$. Consider the condition $u_3^{(\ell_1)}[i_1] = u_3^{(\ell_1)}[i_2]$ first. Conditioned on $\neg\Theta^2_{\text{bad}}$, there exists $i_3 \in \{w/2+1, \ldots, w\}$ such that $v_2^{(\ell)}[i_3]$ is uniform in at least $2^n - p - wq/2$ possibilities. We refer to Eq. (10) for the expression of $u_3^{(\ell)}[w/2+1..w]$. By the 2nd condition in Definition 1, the $(i_1 - w/2, i_3 - w/2)$ th and $(i_2 - w/2, i_3 - w/2)$ th entries of $\mathrm{T_{BR}}$ are not equal. So, the probability to have $u_3^{(\ell_1)}[i_1] = u_3^{(\ell_1)}[i_2]$ is equal to the probability that $v_2^{(\ell_1)}[i_3]$ equals some fixed value,which is at most $1/(2^n - p - wq/2)$.

For the case of $\ell_1 \ne \ell_2$, fix $i_1, i_2 \in \{w/2+1, \ldots, w\}$. By $\neg$(C-1) and $\neg$(C-3), there exists $i_3, i_4 \in \{w/2+1, \ldots, w\}$ such that:

1. $u_2^{(\ell_1)}[i_3] \notin U_2^{(1)}$, $u_2^{(\ell_2)}[i_4] \notin U_2^{(1)}$ and
2. $u_2^{(\ell_1)}[i_3] \ne u_2^{(\ell_2)}[i_3]$ or $u_2^{(\ell_1)}[i_4] \ne u_2^{(\ell_2)}[i_4]$.

Wlog assume $u_2^{(\ell_1)}[i_3] \ne u_2^{(\ell_2)}[i_3]$. Note that, by $\neg$(C-3), $u_2^{(\ell_1)}[i_3] \ne u_2^{(\ell_2)}[i_5]$ for any $i_5 \in \{w/2+1, \ldots, w\} \setminus \{i_3\}$. Since on the $w/2$ values $\{\overline{S_2}(u_2^{(\ell_1)}[i])\}_{i \in \{w/2+1,\ldots,w\}}$ and on the $w/2 - 1$ values $\{\overline{S_2}(u_2^{(\ell_1)}[i])\}_{i \in \{w/2+1,\ldots,w\} \setminus \{i_3\}}$, $\overline{S_2}(u_2^{(\ell_1)}[i_3])$ remains uniform in at least $2^n - p - wq/2$ possibilities. By this, since (the $(i_3 - w/2)$ th column of) $\mathrm{T_{BR}}$ has no zero entry, the probability to have $u_3^{(\ell_1)}[i_1] = u_3^{(\ell_2)}[i_2]$ is equal to the probability that $\overline{S_2}(u_2^{(\ell_1)}[i_3])$ equals some fixed value, which is at most $1/(2^n - p - wq/2)$.

Similar to the $\Pr[v_2^{(\ell)}[i] = v_2]$. By a union bound over the conditions and over all ℓ_1, ℓ_2, i_1, i_2, we reach

$$\Pr[(\text{E-2})] \le \binom{wq/2}{2} \cdot \frac{2}{2^n - p - wq/2}.$$

Using $p + wq/2 \le 2^n/2$, we finally have

$$\Pr[\text{Bad}_2(S_1, S_4)] \le \frac{4wq(p + wq/2) + w^2q^2}{2^{n+1}}.$$

Lemma 6. *For any good extended transcript τ', one has*

$$(2^{wn})_q \cdot \mathrm{p}_{\mathrm{mid}}(\tau') \ge 1 - \frac{4wq(p + wq/2) + w^2q^2}{2^{n+1}}.$$

Proof. Fix any good extended transcript $\tau' = (\mathcal{Q}'_C, \mathcal{Q}_S, \mathcal{Q}'_S, (k_0, k_1, k_2, k_3, k_4))$. Our goal is then to prove that $\mathrm{p}_{\mathrm{mid}}(\tau')$ is close enough to $1/(2^{wn})_q$. In order to do so, we have:

$$\begin{aligned}
\mathrm{p}_{\mathrm{mid}}(\tau') =& \Pr\left[(\mathcal{C}_{\mathbf{k}}^{\mathrm{T}}[\mathcal{PS}] \vdash \mathcal{Q}'_C) \middle| (S_1 = S_1^*) \wedge (S_4 = S_4^*) \wedge (S_2 \vdash \mathcal{Q}_{S_2}^{(1)}) \wedge (S_3 \vdash \mathcal{Q}_{S_3}^{(1)})\right] \\
\ge& \Pr\Big[(\mathcal{C}_{\mathbf{k}}^{\mathrm{T}}[\mathcal{PS}] \vdash \mathcal{Q}'_C) \wedge \neg \text{Bad}_2(S_1, S_4) \Big| (S_1 = S_1^*) \wedge (S_4 = S_4^*) \\
& \qquad \wedge (S_2 \vdash \mathcal{Q}_{S_2}^{(1)}) \wedge (S_3 \vdash \mathcal{Q}_{S_3}^{(1)})\Big] \\
\ge& \Big(1 - \Pr[\text{Bad}_2(S_1, S_4)]\Big) \\
& \cdot \Pr\Big[(\mathcal{C}_{\mathbf{k}}^{\mathrm{T}}[\mathcal{PS}] \vdash \mathcal{Q}'_C) \Big| \neg \text{Bad}_2(S_1, S_4) \wedge (S_1 = S_1^*) \wedge (S_4 = S_4^*) \\
& \qquad \wedge (S_2 \vdash \mathcal{Q}_{S_2}^{(1)}) \wedge (S_3 \vdash \mathcal{Q}_{S_3}^{(1)})\Big] \\
\ge& (1 - \frac{4wq(p + wq/2) + w^2q^2}{2^{n+1}}) \cdot \frac{1}{2^{wnq}}.
\end{aligned}$$

Finally, we get

$$\begin{aligned}
(2^{wn})_q \mathrm{p}_{\mathrm{mid}}(\tau') &\ge (1 - \frac{4wq(p + wq/2) + w^2q^2}{2^{n+1}}) \cdot \frac{(2^{wn})_q}{2^{wnq}} \\
&\ge 1 - \frac{4wq(p + wq/2) + w^2q^2}{2^{n+1}}.
\end{aligned}$$

4 Attack Against 3 Rounds

In this section, we show an attack on 3 rounds HADES. Concretely, let $\mathcal{C}$ be the 3-round HADES using linear transformations T. I.e.,

$$\mathcal{C}_{\mathbf{k}}^{\mathrm{T}}[\mathcal{S}](x) := k_3 \oplus \mathrm{T}\Big(\overline{S_3}\Big(k_2 \oplus \mathrm{T}\big(\overline{\mathcal{PS}^{S_2}}(k_1 \oplus \mathrm{T}(\overline{S_1}(k_0 \oplus x)))\big)\Big)\Big).$$

We show an attacker D, given access to an oracle $\mathcal{O}: \{0,1\}^{wn} \rightarrow \{0,1\}^{wn}$, that distinguishes whether $\mathcal{O}$ is an instance of $\mathcal{C}_{\mathbf{k}}^{\mathrm{T}}[\mathcal{S}]$ using uniform keys or a wn-bit random permutation. The attacker D proceeds as follows:

1. Fix $\Delta_4 = \Delta_5 = 0^{w/2}$. Then $\Delta_2 = \mathrm{T}_{\mathrm{BR}}^{-1} \cdot \mathrm{T}_{\mathrm{BL}} \cdot \Delta_1$. Fix a $wn/2$-bit difference Δ_1 and compute Δ_2 and Δ_3. Note that $\mathrm{T}(\Delta_1 \| \Delta_2) = \Delta_3 \| \Delta_4$.
2. Then for $\mathrm{T}(\Delta_3 \| \Delta_5) = \Delta_6 \| \Delta_7$, compute Δ_6.
3. Choose inputs x, x' such that $x \oplus x' = \Delta_1 \| \Delta_2$, query $\mathcal{O}(x)$ and $\mathcal{O}(x')$ to obtain y and y' respectively, and compute the output difference $\Delta_8 := y \oplus y'$.
4. Set $\hat{y} := y'[1] \| y[2] \| \cdots \| y[w]$ and $\hat{y}' := y[1] \| y'[2] \| \cdots \| y'[w]$. Compute Δ_3'. Then $\Delta_2' = \mathrm{T}_{\mathrm{UR}}^{-1}(\Delta_3' \oplus \mathrm{T}_{\mathrm{UL}} \cdot \Delta_1')$.
5. Query $\mathcal{O}^{-1}(\hat{y})$ and $\mathcal{O}^{-1}(\hat{y}')$ to obtain $\hat{x}$ and $\hat{x}'$ respectively.
6. If $\Delta_2' = \mathrm{T}_{\mathrm{UR}}^{-1}(\Delta_3' \oplus \mathrm{T}_{\mathrm{UL}} \cdot \Delta_1')$, then output 1; otherwise, output 0.

It is not hard to see that if $\mathcal{O}$ is a random permutation on $\{0,1\}^{wn}$ then D outputs 1 with negligible probability. On the other hand, we claim that when $\mathcal{O}$ is an instance of the 3-round HADES then D always outputs 1. To see this, consider the propagation of the input difference $\Delta_1 \| \Delta_2$. By step 1, the 2nd round input difference must be $\Delta_3 \| 0^{w/2}$, the output difference of 2nd round also be $\Delta_3 \| 0^{w/2}$. This means the 3rd round input difference, denoted $\Delta_6 \| \Delta_7$ can be computed by $\Delta_6 = \mathrm{T}_{\mathrm{UL}} \cdot \Delta_3$ and $\Delta_7 = \mathrm{T}_{\mathrm{BL}} \cdot \Delta_3$. Let x_3 and x_3' be the intermediate values of the input of 3rd round during evaluation of $\mathcal{O}(x)$ and $\mathcal{O}(x')$, $\hat{x_3}$ and $\hat{x_3}'$ be the intermediate values of the input of 3rd round during evaluation of $\mathcal{O}(\hat{y})$ and $\mathcal{O}(\hat{y}')$. By step 4, observe first that $\hat{x_3} \oplus \hat{x_3}' = x_3 \oplus x_3'$. Then $\Delta_6 = \Delta_6'$ and $\Delta_7 = \Delta_7'$. That means $\mathrm{T}_{\mathrm{UL}} \cdot \Delta_3 = \mathrm{T}_{\mathrm{UL}} \cdot \Delta_3' \oplus \mathrm{T}_{\mathrm{UR}} \cdot \Delta_5'$ and $\mathrm{T}_{\mathrm{BL}} \cdot \Delta_3 = \mathrm{T}_{\mathrm{BL}} \cdot \Delta_3' \oplus \mathrm{T}_{\mathrm{BR}} \cdot \Delta_5'$. Then we can compute Δ_3' and Δ_5'. Then by $\mathrm{T}_{\mathrm{UL}} \cdot \Delta_1' \oplus \mathrm{T}_{\mathrm{UR}} \cdot \Delta_2' = \Delta_3'$ we can induce $\Delta_2' = \mathrm{T}_{\mathrm{UR}}^{-1}(\Delta_3' \oplus \mathrm{T}_{\mathrm{UL}} \cdot \Delta_1')$. This completes the analysis.

5 Conclusion

We show that, with four rounds and a linear permutation layer, 4-round HADES structure is secure up to n/2 adversarial queries, which ensures the birthday bound security. This provides provable security supports for the real world HADES structures.

It remains open whether our birthday bound on 4 rounds is tight. A similar open question has been left regarding 3-round full SPNs. We believe that beyond-birthday bounds can actually be proven, but new techniques are needed. Another interesting future work is to establish better security for more rounds (and in particular, to characterize the influences of full versus partial SPN rounds on security bounds) for future work.

Acknowledgements. We sincerely thank the reviewers of Cryptology and Network Security 2022 for their invaluable comments that help improving the quality of this paper. This work was partly supported by the Program of Qilu Young Scholars (Grant No. 61580089963177) of Shandong University.

References

1. Selent, D.: Advanced encryption standard. Rivier Acad. J. **6**(2), 1–14 (2010)
2. Gérard, B., Grosso, V., Naya-Plasencia, M., Standaert, F.-X.: Block ciphers that are easier to mask: how far can we go? In: Bertoni, G., Coron, J.-S. (eds.) CHES 2013. LNCS, vol. 8086, pp. 383–399. Springer, Heidelberg (2013). https://doi.org/10.1007/978-3-642-40349-1_22
3. Albrecht, M.R., Rechberger, C., Schneider, T., Tiessen, T., Zohner, M.: Ciphers for MPC and FHE. In: Oswald, E., Fischlin, M. (eds.) EUROCRYPT 2015. LNCS, vol. 9056, pp. 430–454. Springer, Heidelberg (2015). https://doi.org/10.1007/978-3-662-46800-5_17
4. Bar-On, A., Dinur, I., Dunkelman, O., Lallemand, V., Keller, N., Tsaban, B.: Cryptanalysis of sp networks with partial non-linear layers. In: Oswald, E., Fischlin, M. (eds.) EUROCRYPT 2015. LNCS, vol. 9056, pp. 315–342. Springer, Heidelberg (2015). https://doi.org/10.1007/978-3-662-46800-5_13
5. Dinur, I., Liu, Y., Meier, W., Wang, Q.: Optimized interpolation attacks on LowMC. In: Iwata, T., Cheon, J.H. (eds.) ASIACRYPT 2015. LNCS, vol. 9453, pp. 535–560. Springer, Heidelberg (2015). https://doi.org/10.1007/978-3-662-48800-3_22
6. Grassi, L., Lüftenegger, R., Rechberger, C., Rotaru, D., Schofnegger, M.: On a generalization of substitution-permutation networks: the HADES design strategy. In: Canteaut, A., Ishai, Y. (eds.) EUROCRYPT 2020. LNCS, vol. 12106, pp. 674–704. Springer, Cham (2020). https://doi.org/10.1007/978-3-030-45724-2_23
7. Grassi, L., Kales, D., Khovratovich, D., Roy, A., Rechberger, C., Schofnegger, M.: Starkad and poseidon: new hash functions for zero knowledge proof systems. iacr cryptol. eprint arch. 2019, 458 (2019)
8. Grassi, L., Khovratovich, D., Rechberger, C., Roy, A., Schofnegger, M.: Poseidon: a new hash function for Zero-Knowledge proof systems. In: 30th USENIX Security Symposium (USENIX Security 21), pp. 519–535 (2021)
9. Keller, N., Rosemarin, A.: Mind the middle layer: the HADES design strategy revisited. In: Canteaut, A., Standaert, F.-X. (eds.) EUROCRYPT 2021. LNCS, vol. 12697, pp. 35–63. Springer, Cham (2021). https://doi.org/10.1007/978-3-030-77886-6_2
10. Luby, M., Rackoff, C.: How to construct pseudorandom permutations from pseudorandom functions. SIAM J. Comput. **17**(2), 373–386 (1988)
11. Patarin, J.: The "Coefficients H" technique. In: Avanzi, R.M., Keliher, L., Sica, F. (eds.) SAC 2008. LNCS, vol. 5381, pp. 328–345. Springer, Heidelberg (2009). https://doi.org/10.1007/978-3-642-04159-4_21
12. Guo, C., Standaert, F.X., Wang, W., Wang, X., Yu, Y.: Provable security of SP networks with partial non-linear layers. IACR Transactions on Symmetric Cryptology, pp. 353–388 (2021)
13. Dodis, Y., Katz, J., Steinberger, J., Thiruvengadam, A., Zhang, Z.: Provable security of substitution-permutation networks. Cryptology ePrint Archive (2017)
14. Cogliati, B., Lee, J.: Wide tweakable block ciphers based on substitution-permutation networks: security beyond the birthday bound. Cryptology ePrint Archive (2018)
15. Daemen, J., Rijmen, V.: The wide trail design strategy. In: Honary, B. (ed.) Cryptography and Coding 2001. LNCS, vol. 2260, pp. 222–238. Springer, Heidelberg (2001). https://doi.org/10.1007/3-540-45325-3_20

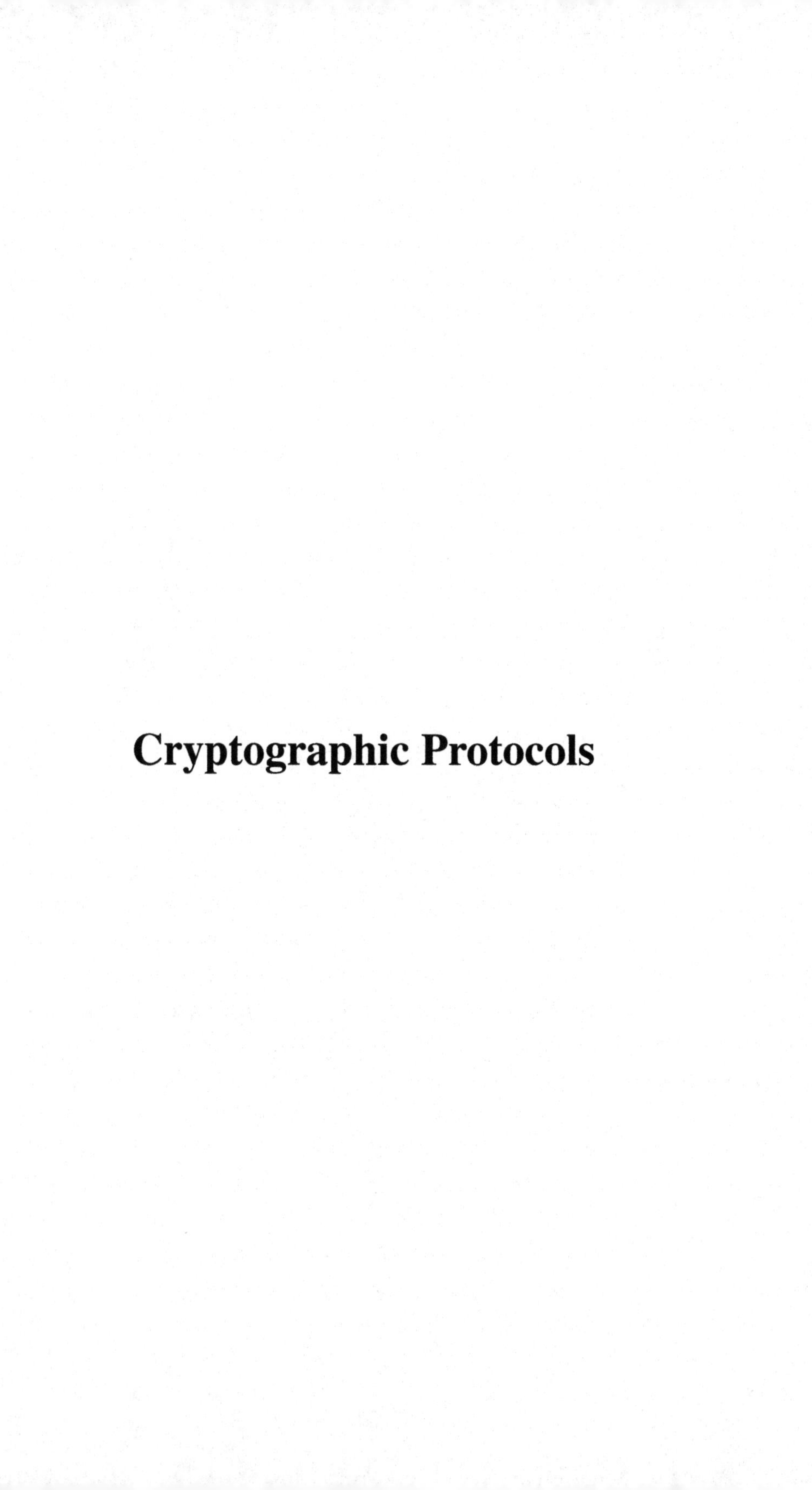

Cryptographic Protocols

Practical Single-Pass Oblivious Aggregation and Billing Computation Protocols for Smart Meters

Kalikinkar Mandal(✉)

Faculty of Computer Science, University of New Brunswick,
Fredericton, NB E3B 5A3, Canada
kmandal@unb.ca

Abstract. In this paper, we first propose the notion of authenticated aggregator-oblivious encryption (AAOE) and then develop a privacy-preserving smart metering protocol based on it. Our protocol enjoys computing aggregated metering data periodically and the time-of-use tariff-based billing of customers simultaneously, without revealing actual metering data to the utility provider. Our protocol construction is based on computationally cheap primitives, namely aggregator-oblivious encryption and message authentication code. We analyze the security of our protocol, and evaluate their performance on a real-world dataset.

Keywords: Secure aggregation · Oblivious billing · Smart metering · AMI

1 Introduction

Smart grid is the modernization of a power grid by utilizing advanced communication, information and computing technologies for better real-time demand-response management, high-quality energy delivery, reliable operation, and automation. Advanced metering infrastructure (AMI) is a key component in a smart grid that has a critical role for secure, reliable, and energy efficient operations of the smart grid. An AMI enables the two-way information flow between smart meters and the utility provider (UP). Through smart metering data, the UP can better understand and estimate the needs for customers in terms of an efficient demand-response management, reduce operational costs and energy losses, and an improved grid efficiency. Moreover, the UP can generate the accurate and real-time bills that can give insights to customers about their usages. Dynamic time-of-use (TOU) tariffs offer different prices at different times of the day (e.g., hourly rates, $ per kWh), which has benefits on having cheaper electricity bills with consuming less electricity during peak periods. These days household energy monitors are installed in houses for ease of monitoring real-time energy consumption [6,9,10]. The deployment of smart meters is a continued-effort taking place worldwide for an energy efficient and sustainable world. For

A. R. Beresford et al. (Eds.): CANS 2022, LNCS 13641, pp. 279–291, 2022.
https://doi.org/10.1007/978-3-031-20974-1_14

instance, there have been 123 million smart meters deployed by 2020, and 223 million smart meters expected to be deployed by 2024 in European Union [2]. In US, there were 115 million smart meters deployed by 2021 [5].

While fine-grain energy consumption data of customers give various benefits such as effective demand-response, forecasting the supply and TOU billing, it poses legitimate privacy threats to customers through analyzing smart metering data. It may reveal sensitive information about power consumption behavior, power-hungry devices in houses, individuals' presence at home, religious beliefs, disabilities and illnesses [26,28,29,41,42,46]. Given the widespread deployment of smart meters worldwide, data protection and privacy regulation authorities such as EU's GDPR [4], UK's DPA 2018 [3] and US Court of Appeals [8] have recognized the importance of protecting smart metering data privacy.

1.1 Related Work

Privacy-Preserving Aggregation Protocols. Secure or privacy-preserving data aggregation is a mechanism to collect data from smart meters in an aggregate-sum form, without having access to individual metering data. Li et al. [36] proposed the first homomorphic encryption (HE) (e.g., Paillier) based secure data aggregation for smart meters against semi-honest adversaries. Secure data aggregation schemes using additive HE were proposed in [25,27]. Private aggregated statistics computation schemes were designed using differential privacy (DP), stream cipher encryption, secret-sharing, Paillier HE scheme or a combination of these techniques [11,14,18,20,31,34,40,43] for smart meters.

Another line of work has aimed to develop techniques for secure aggregation. Shi et al. [47] introduced aggregator-oblivious encryption (AOE) to remove the notion of trusted aggregator, and as an application, they developed a smart metering data aggregation protocol using the DDH-assumption based AOE scheme and DP. Joye and Libert [33] proposed a new AOE scheme (Paillier-style) based on the Decision Composite Residuosity assumption. After that, several schemes have been proposed to design privacy-preserving streaming/time-series data aggregation with untrusted aggregators, e.g., [15,16,24,35]. Mustafa et al. [39] recently proposed a privacy-preserving protocol for smart metering operational data collection using MCP techniques. Another line of work has focuses on anonymous metering data collection, e.g., [12,13,23].

Privacy-Preserving Smart Metering Billing Protocols. A privacy-preserving or oblivious TOU-based bill computation is a mechanism to compute the bill of a customer, without revealing fine-grain metering data to the utility provider. Existing privacy-preserving billing computation techniques use zero-knowledge (ZK) proof techniques (constructed based on cryptographic techniques such as commitment, Camenisch-Lysyanskaya (CL) signature or EC-DSA signature, bilinear pairing, or AES) e.g., [30,38,44,45] to hide metering data while convincing the utility provider that no tampering on the metering data is done. In [19], a billing protocol with improved privacy of [44] is proposed, and their construction is based on differential privacy, signature scheme, commitment scheme, and discrete logarithm based zero-knowledge proof of knowledge. Recently, [45] revisits the work of [44] where the formalization of billing schemes is done, and a private billing scheme is proposed in which a smart meter can send readings to multiple users. The work [37] proposed a system for private billing and load monitoring for smart meters. [17] presented a private smart metering billing mechanism without revealing the billing payment. The reader is referred to [32] for a survey on different privacy-preserving techniques for smart meters.

1.2 Our Contribution

Our goal in this paper is to design lightweight privacy-preserving smart metering protocols that can compute both metering data aggregation and billing, simultaneously, in a single-pass. Our contributions are summarized as follows: We first introduce the notion of authenticated aggregator oblivious encryption (AAOE), which is a hybrid encrypt-then-MAC approach where the encryption is performed by an AOE scheme and the integrity of an AOE ciphertext is assured using a MAC algorithm. The security of the AAOE scheme is under indistinguishability under chosen-plaintext attack (IND-CPA) and integrity of ciphertext (INT-CTXT). Next, we propose an oblivious aggregation and billing protocol (called OABC protocol) based on an AAOE scheme where each smart meter needs to perform one AOE encryption and one MAC on an AOE ciphertext for both aggregation and billing. The security of the protocol is proved against semi-honest adversaries. Finally, we implement our OABC protocol to demonstrate its efficiency on a real-world metering dataset and TOU tariff [1].

2 Preliminaries

2.1 Cryptographic Tools

Aggregator-Oblivious Encryption. Suppose there are n users $\mathcal{U} = \{\mathcal{U}_i\}_{i=1}^n$ involved in an aggregation process where each user has a private input x_i. Aggregator-oblivious encryption (AOE) is a cryptographic scheme that enables computing an aggregate-sum on inputs $\{x_i\}$. See [47] for the definition of an AOE scheme. Several AOE schemes have been proposed in [15,33,47]. The Joye and Libert (JL) AOE scheme is an efficient one which we use as an example to describe our protocols. The security of the JL AOE scheme is based on the Decision Composite Residuosity (DCR) assumption in the random oracle model.

Definition 1. *(Joye-Libert (JL) AOE Scheme). [33] The* JL aggregator-oblivious encryption *(JL AOE) is a tuple of three algorithms which are defined as:*

JLAOE.*Setup*(1^κ)*: On a security parameter κ, the trusted dealer generates two large primes p and q of almost an equal size and computes $N = pq$. It uses a hash function $H : \{0,1\}^* \rightarrow \mathbb{Z}_{N^2}^*$ that is viewed as a random oracle. Denote λ be the bit length of N. A secret key sk_i for each user is sampled from $\pm\{0,1\}^{2\lambda}$ for $i \in [1,n]$, and the secret key for the aggregator sk_0 is computed as $\mathsf{sk}_0 = -\sum_{i=1}^n \mathsf{sk}_i$. The public parameters are $\mathsf{param} = \{N, H\}$.*

$\mathsf{JLAOE}.\mathit{Enc}(\mathsf{param}, \mathsf{sk}_i, x_i)$: *Each user* $\mathcal{U}_i$ *encrypts its private value* x_i *using the secret key* sk_i *to obtain a ciphertext* ct_i *as* $ct_i = \mathit{Enc}(\mathsf{param}, \mathsf{sk}_i, x_i) = (1 + x_i N)H(t)^{\mathsf{sk}_i} \mod N^2$ *where t is a timestamp.*

$\mathsf{JLAOE}.\mathit{AggDec}(\mathsf{param}, \mathsf{sk}_0, ct_1, ct_2, \cdots, ct_n)$: *The aggregator uses its secret key* sk_0 *to compute the aggregate-sum* $X = \sum_{i=1}^{n} x_i$ *as* $X = \mathit{AggDec}(\mathsf{param}, \mathsf{sk}_0, ct_1, ct_2, \cdots, ct_n) = \left(\prod_{i=1}^{n} ct_i\right) \cdot H(t)^{\mathsf{sk}_0} \mod N^2$.

Message Authentication Code. A message authentication code (MAC) is a tuple of two deterministic algorithms $\mathsf{MAC} = (\mathsf{MAC.TGen}, \mathsf{MAC.Verify})$ where the tag generation algorithm $\mathsf{MAC.TGen} : \mathcal{K} \times \mathcal{M} \rightarrow \mathcal{T}$ accepts a key from $\mathcal{K}$ and a message from $\mathcal{M}$ and outputs a tag in $\mathcal{T}$, and the tag verification algorithm $\mathsf{MAC.Verify} : \mathcal{K} \times \mathcal{M} \times \mathcal{T} \rightarrow \{0, 1\}$ accepts a key from $\mathcal{K}$, a message from $\mathcal{M}$ and a tag from $\mathcal{T}$ and outputs either 1 or 0 if the verification succeeds or fails, respectively. For a message $M \in \mathcal{M}$ and $K \in \mathcal{K}$, $\mathsf{MAC.TGen}$ produces a tag, $\mathsf{tag} \leftarrow \mathsf{MAC.TGen}(K, M)$, and the verification algorithm outputs $\{0, 1\} \leftarrow \mathsf{MAC.Verify}(K, M, \mathsf{tag})$.

3 Our Smart Metering System Model

Our system model, that is similar to the ones considered in [31,38,44], consists of three main entities, namely a set of smart meters ($\mathcal{M}_i$), Electricity Monitor (EM)/In-home Display/Plug-in devices connected to smart meters, and an Electricity Utility Provider (UP). Figure 1 shows a high-level overview of the system model. Like in [12,21,44], we assume that each smart meter is tamper-resistant equipped with a hardware security module (HSM). We assume the smart meter and its EM device implement a secure channel for communication.

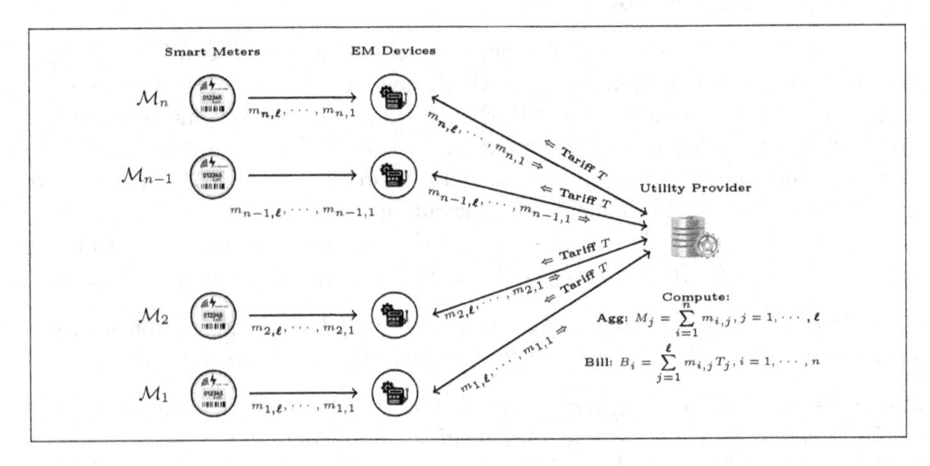

Fig. 1. Our system model for smart metering, without privacy

3.1 Problem Statement

Assume there are n smart meters $\mathcal{M} = \{\mathcal{M}_i, 1 \leq i \leq n\}$ in our system. Let $\mathbf{m}_i = (m_{i,1}, m_{i,2}, \cdots, m_{i,\ell})$ denote the energy consumption of $\mathcal{M}_i$ for ℓ time intervals, where the reading $m_{i,j}$ is the energy consumption in the time interval Δt_j. The TOU-tariff for ℓ time intervals is denoted by $T = (T_1, T_2, \cdots, T_\ell)$, which is the same for all smart meters (for simplicity) and publicly known.

- **Secure metering data aggregation:** The UP wishes to obtain the aggregated meter readings $M_j = \sum_{i=1}^{n} m_{i,j}$ for each time interval Δt_j, without revealing individual meter $\mathcal{M}_i$'s private reading $m_{i,j}$ to the UP.
- **Oblivious billing computation:** In the TOU-tariff based billing, the pricing for each time interval Δt_j may be different. For the meter $\mathcal{M}_i$, the billing for the tariff T is computed as $B_i = \sum_{j=1}^{\ell} m_{i,j} T_j$. The UP and smart meter $\mathcal{M}_i$ wish to compute the bill B_i in an oblivious manner, without revealing private metering data $\mathbf{m}_i$ to the UP, while convincing the UP that no metering data is tempered and the bill B_i is correct. The obliviousness is achieved against the UP.

Our goal is to design a single-pass protocol to perform smart metering data aggregation at each time interval Δt_j and compute billing B_i for each smart meter $\mathcal{M}_i$ while ensuring correctness, privacy of metering data and efficiency.

3.2 Threat Model

We consider semi-honest adversaries in our system in which an adversary follows the prescribed instructions of the protocol and may wish to learn any unintended information from the message flows of the protocol. An adversary may compromise some smart meters in $\mathcal{C}$ or the utility provider. We assume that smart meters are tamper-resistant devices, meaning an adversary cannot tamper the HSM of a smart meter. The goal of the adversary is to learn honest meters' private energy consumption data $\{m_{u,j}\}_{u \in \mathcal{M} \setminus \mathcal{C}}$. When the adversary compromises an EM device attached to a smart meter, its goal is to try to cheat in computing a bill by altering metering data.

4 Authenticated Aggregated Oblivious Encryption

We introduce the notion of *authenticated aggregator-oblivious encryption (AAOE)* by the construction of a hybrid encrypt-then-MAC approach, where the encryption is performed by an AOE scheme, and the ciphertext authentication is provided by a MAC algorithm. We formally define an AAOE scheme in Definition 2.

Definition 2. *An* authenticated aggregator-oblivious encryption *(AAOE) is a tuple of three algorithms which are defined as:*

$\mathsf{AAOE}.\mathit{Setup}(1^\kappa) \rightarrow \{\mathit{sk}_0, (\mathit{sk}_i, \mathsf{K}^i_{\mathsf{mac}})\}$: *On a security parameter* κ, *a trusted dealer generates the system parameters, denoted by* param *and a secret key* sk_i *of each user* $\mathcal{U}_i$, $i \in [1, n]$ *for an* AOE *scheme. It also randomly samples a MAC key* $\mathsf{K}^i_{\mathsf{mac}} \leftarrow \mathcal{K}$ *for each user* $\mathcal{U}_i$. *The key pair* $(\mathit{sk}_i, \mathsf{K}^i_{\mathsf{mac}})$ *is given to user* $\mathcal{U}_i$. *The aggregator is given the decryption key* $\mathit{sk}_0 = \sum_{i=1}^n \mathit{sk}_i$ *and the MAC verification keys* $\{\mathsf{K}^i_{\mathsf{mac}}\}_{i=1}^n$.

$\mathsf{AAOE}.\mathit{Enc}(\mathit{param}, \mathit{sk}_i, \mathsf{K}^i_{\mathsf{mac}}, x_i) \rightarrow (ct_i, \mathit{tag}_i)$: *Each user* $\mathcal{U}_i$ *computes* (ct_i, tag_i) *using* $(\mathit{sk}_i, \mathsf{K}^i_{\mathsf{mac}})$ *where the ciphertext* $ct_i = \mathsf{AOE}.\mathit{Enc}(\mathit{param}, \mathit{sk}_i, x_i)$ *is an AOE ciphertext of private value* x_i *and* $\mathit{tag}_i = \mathit{MAC.TGen}(\mathsf{K}^i_{\mathsf{mac}}, ct_i)$ *is a tag on the ciphertext* ct_i. AOE.*Enc uses different timestamps used as* nonce *for different* x_i.

$\mathsf{AAOE}.\mathit{AggDec}(\mathit{param}, \mathit{sk}_0, \{\mathsf{K}^i_{\mathsf{mac}}\}_{i=1}^n \{(ct_i, \mathit{tag}_i)\}_{i=1}^n) \rightarrow \{X, \perp\}$: *The aggregator first verifies all the tags for all ciphertexts, and accepts the ciphertexts* ct_i *if all tag verifications are successful, i.e.,* $\bigwedge_{i=1}^n \mathit{MAC.Verify}(\mathsf{K}^i_{\mathsf{mac}}, ct_i, \mathit{tag}_i) = 1$. *The aggregator uses the private key* sk_0 *to compute the aggregate-sum* $X = \sum_{i=1}^n x_i$ *as* $X = \mathit{AggDec}(\mathit{param}, \mathit{sk}_0, ct_1, ct_2, \cdots, ct_n)$. *If one of the tag verifications fails, it outputs* $\perp$.

Security. We require the standard security for an AAOE scheme: indistinguishability under chosen-plaintext attack (IND-CPA) is for the encryption and integrity of ciphertext (INT-CTXT) for the MAC. We use the standard security of a MAC, which is the strong unforgeability under chosen message attack (SUF-CMA for short) that is required due to the malleability property of the underlying AOE scheme. In a secure AAOE scheme, any malformed ciphertexts created by the malleability property of the underlying AOE scheme will yield an unsuccessful MAC verification.

Theorem 1. *If the AOE scheme is* IND-CPA *secure and the MAC algorithm is* SUF-CMA *secure, then the above* AAOE *construction is* IND-CPA *and* INT-CTXT *secure, and hence* IND-CCA *secure.*

Proof. The proof is simple and omitted due to the space limit.

5 Our Oblivious Aggregation and Billing Protocol

We now present our oblivious data aggregation and billing computation (OABC) protocol. The construction of the OABC protocol is based on an AAOE scheme that provides the privacy and authentication where the privacy of smart metering data is provided by the underlying AOE scheme and the MAC assures the ciphertext authenticity and integrity of an encrypted meter reading. We employ two different keys: a master AOE key (MK) that is shared between the smart meter and the EM device for the AOE scheme to encrypt meter readings $m_{i,j}$, and a MAC key that is shared between only the smart meter and the utility provider. Figure 2 describes the details of the OABC protocol.

Oblivious Aggregation and Billing Computation (OABC) Protocol
Cryptographic key setup.

- Smart Meter $\mathcal{M}_i$ holds its AOE key sk_i and a MAC key $\mathsf{K}^i_{\mathsf{mac}}$, stored in a HSM.
- EM Device holds the same AOE key sk_i.
- Utility Provider has access to the aggregation key $\mathsf{sk}_0 = \sum_{i=1}^{n} \mathsf{sk}_i$, the billing for each smart meter bk_i, and the MAC key $\mathsf{K}^i_{\mathsf{mac}}$ is shared between meter $\mathcal{M}_i$ and the utility provider.

- KeySetup: Given a security parameter κ (in unary), a trusted party generates two large primes p and q of almost an equal size, and computes $N = pq$. It selects a cryptographic hash function $H : \{0,1\}^* \rightarrow \mathbb{Z}^*_{N^2}$. The public parameter is $\mathsf{param} = (N, H)$. It generates a JL AOE secret key sk_i and a MAC key $\mathsf{K}^i_{\mathsf{mac}}$ for each smart meter $\mathcal{M}_i, i \in [1, n]$. $\{\mathsf{K}^i_{\mathsf{mac}}\}_{i=1}^{n}$ are given to the UP.
- Smart Meter: For each time interval Δt_j, each smart meter $\mathcal{M}_i$ encrypts its reading $m_{i,j}$ using the JL AOE scheme as $C_{i,j} = \mathsf{JLAOE.Enc}(\mathsf{param}, \mathsf{sk}_i, m_{i,j}) = (1 + m_{i,j}N)H(\Delta t_j)^{\mathsf{sk}_i}$ and computes a MAC on $C_{i,j}$ as $\mathsf{tag}_{i,j} = \mathsf{MAC.TGen}(\mathsf{K}^i_{\mathsf{mac}}, C_{i,j})$ and sends the ciphertext and corresponding tag $(C_{i,j}, \mathsf{tag}_{i,j})$ to the UP priodically, $1 \leq j \leq \ell$. It also sends $C_{i,j}$ to the EM device.
- Aggregation by Utility Provider: For each time interval Δt_j, after receiving ciphertexts $\{(C_{i,j}, \mathsf{tag}_{i,j})\}_{i=1}^{n}$ from n smart meters, the utility provider first verifies tags $\mathsf{tag}_{i,j}$ by first running $\{0,1\} \leftarrow \mathsf{MAC.Verify}(\mathsf{K}^i_{\mathsf{mac}}, C_{i,j}, \mathsf{tag}_{i,j})$. If all the tag verifications are successful, the aggregated smart meter reading (M_j) for time interval Δt_j is computed as:

$$C_j = \prod_{i=1}^{n} C_{i,j} = \prod_{i=1}^{n}(1 + m_{i,j}N)H(\Delta t_j)^{\mathsf{sk}_i} = \prod_{i=1}^{n}(1 + m_{i,j}N)H(\Delta t_j)^{\sum_{i=1}^{n}\mathsf{sk}_i}$$
$$= \Big(1 + N\big(\sum_{i=1}^{n} m_{i,j}\big)\Big),$$

followed by computing $M_j = \sum_{i=1}^{n} m_{i,j} = \frac{C_j \cdot H(\Delta t_j)^{-\mathsf{sk}_0} - 1}{N}$.
- Billing Computed by Utility Provider and EM Device: For every ℓ-time interval, the EM device computes a billing key as $\mathsf{bk}_i = U^{\mathsf{sk}_i}$ where $U = \prod_{j=1}^{\ell} H(\Delta t_j)^{T_j}$ and sends bk_i to the utility provider. Upon receiving bk_i for each meter $\mathcal{M}_i$, using $\{(C_{i,j}, \mathsf{tag}_{i,j})\}_{j=1}^{\ell}$, the utility provider computes the bill for the periodic meter reading $\mathbf{m}_i$ and tariff T as:

$$D_i = \prod_{j=1}^{\ell} C_{i,j}^{T_j} = \prod_{j=1}^{\ell} (1 + m_{i,j}N)^{T_j} H(\Delta t_j)^{\mathsf{sk}_i T_j} = \prod_{j=1}^{\ell} \Big(1 + T_j m_{i,j} N\Big)\Big(\prod_{j=1}^{\ell} H(\Delta t_j)^{T_j}\Big)^{\mathsf{sk}_i}$$
$$= \Big(1 + N\sum_{j=1}^{\ell} T_j m_{i,j}\Big)U^{\mathsf{sk}_i},$$

followed by computing the bill B_i for meter $\mathcal{M}_i$ as $B_i = \mathbf{m}_i \cdot T = \frac{D_i \cdot \mathsf{bk}_i^{-1} - 1}{N}$.

Fig. 2. A single-pass oblivious aggregation and billing computation protocol

Efficiency. To compute a bill on ℓ meter readings, the total computational cost for a smart meter is ℓ hash, ℓ JL AOE encryption and ℓ MAC operations. Asymptotically, the computation and communication complexities for the UP are $O(n\ell)$, where n is the number of smart meters and ℓ is the number of time intervals.

Privacy. We consider the security of the OABC protocol against the semi-honest adversaries. We briefly sketch the security arguments, and summarize the security in Theorem 2. We omit the proof due to the space limit. Intuitively, when an adversary compromises the EM device to change a meter reading by altering an AOE ciphertext, the adversary needs to create a valid tag corresponding to the altered ciphertext which is equivalent to breaking the SUF-CMA security of MAC. The adversary, compromising the UP, needs to break the IND-CPA security of the JL AOE scheme or infer any information from the aggregate-sum and billing values $\{M_j, B_i\}_{1\leq j\leq \ell, 1\leq n\leq n}$ to extract information about private meter reading $m_{i,j}$. Thus, the security of the OABC protocol relies on the IND-CPA security of the JL AOE scheme and the SUF-CMA security of MAC. We claim no security when both the EM device and the UP are compromised.

Theorem 2. *Assuming the* JL AOE *scheme is secure under the DCR assumption in the random oracle model and the MAC is SUF-CMA secure, the aggregation and billing computation protocol in Fig. 2 is private in the presence of semi-honest adversaries.*

Adding Robustness/Fault-Tolerance to the OABC Protocol. In the OABC protocol in Fig. 2, the UP cannot compute an aggregate-sum at a time interval if one of smart meters is down or does not participate in the aggregation process. A aggregation protocol is robust or fault-tolerant if the UP can compute aggregate-sums and bills even if some smart meters do not send their data to the UP. In our OABC protocol, the robustness or fault-tolerance property can be enabled by applying the trust relaxation technique of Leontiadis et al. [35] where the users and aggregator can generate their secret keys $\mathsf{sk}_i, \mathsf{sk}_0$ on their own, in the JL AOE scheme, without relying on the trusted dealer (who generates only $N = pq$ and goes offline). We need an additional entity called a collector that is placed in between the EM device and the UP, and there is no collusion between the UP and the collector. Due to the space limit, we omit the details.

6 Experimental Evaluation

Implementation Details. We implement the OABC protocol in Fig. 2 in C++ to evaluate their performance in terms of running time. We instantiate the MAC and hash $H : \mathbb{Z}_N \rightarrow \mathbb{Z}^*_{N^2}$ by the lightweight cipher ASCON [22] and implement parallel instances of ASCON using the bitslice implementation. Note that ASCON can be used for both MAC (called ASCON-MAC) and the hash function. For the hash, we use the eXtendable-Output Function (XOF) mode of ASCON (called

ASCON-XOF) that provides a security level of $\min(2^\kappa, 2^\lambda)$ for an output of 2λ-bit hash value, where κ is the security level [22]. We implement the JL AOE scheme using the GNU GMP library [7]. The experiments were conducted on a desktop with Ubuntu 18.04 OS with Intel i7-9700 CPU 3.00 GHz with 32 GB RAM. We use the fixed-point encoding and decoding technique to deal with floating point numbers. We use the dataset and the time-of-use (TOU) tariffs (cents per kWh) from the Commission for Energy Regulation (CER) in Ireland [1] to evaluate the performance of the OABC protocol.

Experimental Results. We use the parameters of the JL AOE scheme (e.g., a modulus ($N = pq$) of size $\lambda = 3072$ bits) and ASCON that provide a security level of $\kappa = 128$ bits. We benchmark the amount of time required for an authenticated aggregator-oblivious encryption (AAOE) scheme, instantiated by JL AOE and ASCON-MAC. Table 1 presents the time required by the AAOE encryption and decryption functions for different numbers of users. For instance, for $n = 500$ smart meters, the time required by AAOE.Enc and AAOE.Dnc is about 19.43 s, and 47.16 *ms*, respectively.

We report the timing for a smart meter, an EM device, and the utility provider. For the OABC protocol in Fig. 2, we compute the aggregate-sum computation time and billing computation time by the UP. Figure 3 shows the time required by the UP for performing the JL AOE decryption and the tag verification of all ciphertexts using ASCON-MAC. For instance, the time required by the UP to compute the aggregate-sum for 5000 smart meters is 122.08 *ms* where 42.62 *ms* is consumed for all tag verifications and 79.46 *ms* was used for the JL AOE decryption.

Table 1. Timing in millisecond (*ms*) for JL AOE and ASCON-MAC based AAOE encryption and decryption.

# User	AAOE.Enc	AAOE.Dnc
50	1,939	39.89
100	3,915	40.51
200	7,727	42.24
400	15,530	45.47
500	19,436	47.16

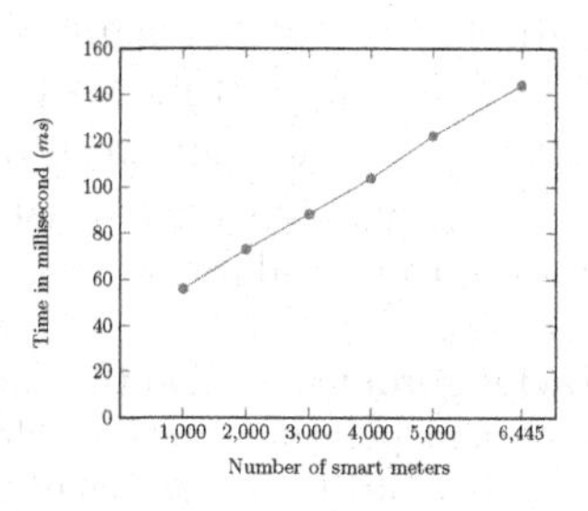

Fig. 3. Timing for computing the aggregate-sum for different numbers of smart meters.

Comparisons. As the implementations of existing protocols are not publicly available, we are unable to provide a comparison on running times w.r.t numerical values with other schemes. However, we provide a comparison with three private billing schemes in [30,38,44] in terms of the number of cryptographic operations performed by smart meters as they are computationally-constrained devices in the system. Table 2 shows a comparison of different billing schemes with ours. Our OABC protocol can be implemented using an AOE scheme and a permutation-based primitive supporting both MAC and hash, where the aggregate-sum computation comes as *free* due to the choice of an AOE scheme, compared to the schemes in [30,38,44]. The size of an AOE ciphertext can also be reduced with the choice of the DDH-based scheme of Shi et al. [47], but that may incur an extra cost for decryption at the UP side.

Table 2. Cryptographic operations and the number of unit crypto operations performed by a smart meter in different schemes.

References	Crypto primitives	# Operations	Functionalities
This work	AOE, MAC, Hash	1 AOE, 1 MAC, 1 Hash	Aggregation & Billing
Rial and Danezis [44]	Sign, Commitment, Hash, NIPK	1 Commitment, 1 Sign, 1 Hash	Billing
Jawurek et al. [30]	Pedersen Commit, PRF, Sign	1 Commit, 1 Sign, 1 PRF	Billing
Molina-Markham et al. [38]	ECC-Pedersen Commit, ECDSA, CL-signature, AES	1 Commit, 1 CL-Sign, 1 ECDSA, 1 AES-Enc, 1 Hash	Billing

7 Conclusion and Future Work

In this work, we introduced the notion of authenticated aggregator-oblivious encryption scheme and presented a privacy-preserving single-pass aggregation and billing protocol where each smart meter needs to perform only one AOE ciphertext computation and a MAC computation for each meter reading. The security of the protocols is analyzed against the semi-honest adversaries. Our OABC protocol is lightweight and can be implemented using *only two* distinct cryptographic primitives namely an AOE scheme and a sponge-permutation based primitive supporting MAC and hash functionalities.

We are extending our work on implementing the proposed protocols on a 32-bit ARM microcontroller used by modern smart meters and making the UP side computation scalable.

Acknowledgement. The author would like to thank the reviewers for their insightful comments and pointing out the reference [17]. This work was supported by the NB Power Cybersecurity research chair grant.

References

1. Commission for energy regulation (cer). (2012). cer smart metering project - electricity customer behaviour trial, 2009–2010 [dataset]. www.ucd.ie/issda/data/commissionforenergyregulationcer/ (2012). Accessed May 2022
2. Benchmarking smart metering deployment in the eu-28. Accessed Aug 2021. https://op.europa.eu/en/publication-detail/-/publication/b397ef73-698f-11ea-b735-01aa75ed71a1/language-en?WT.mc_id=Searchresult&WT.ria_c=37085&WT.ria_f=3608&WT.ria_ev=search (2022). Accessed 10 June 2022

3. Data protection act 2018. www.legislation.gov.uk/ukpga/2018/12/contents/enacted (2022). Accessed 10 June 2022
4. Data protection impact assessment template for smart grid and smart metering systems. https://ec.europa.eu/energy/content/data-protection-impact-assessment-template-smart-grid-and-smart-metering-systems_en?redir=1 (2022). Accessed 10 June 2022
5. The edison foundation. electric company smart meter deployments: Foundation for a smart grid (2021 update), accessed in 2021. www.edisonfoundation.net/-/media/Files/IEI/publications/IEI_Smart_Meter_Report_April_2021.ashx (2022). Accessed 10 June 2022
6. Engage Hub Kit. https://efergy.com/engage/ (2022). Accessed 10 June 2022
7. The gnu multiple precision arithmetic library. https://gmplib.org/ (2022). Accessed 10 June 2022
8. Naperville smart meter awareness v. city of naperville, no. 16–3766 (7th cir. 2018). https://law.justia.com/cases/federal/appellate-courts/ca7/16-3766/16-3766-2018-08-16.html (2022). Accessed 10 June 2022
9. Rainforest Energy Monitoring Gateway for Smart Meters. www.rainforestautomation.com/ (2022). Accessed 10 June 2022
10. Smarter Home Energy Management. www.emporiaenergy.com/ (2022). Accessed 10 June 2022
11. Ács, G., Castelluccia, C.: I have a DREAM! (DiffeRentially privatE smArt Metering). In: Filler, T., Pevný, T., Craver, S., Ker, A. (eds.) IH 2011. LNCS, vol. 6958, pp. 118–132. Springer, Heidelberg (2011). https://doi.org/10.1007/978-3-642-24178-9_9
12. Ambrosin, M., Hosseini, H., Mandal, K., Conti, M., Poovendran, R.: Verifiable and privacy-preserving fine-grained data-collection for smart metering. In: 2015 IEEE Conference on Communications and Network Security (CNS), pp. 655–658 (2015). https://doi.org/10.1109/CNS.2015.7346882
13. Ambrosin, M., Hosseini, H., Mandal, K., Conti, M., Poovendran, R.: Despicable me(ter): Anonymous and fine-grained metering data reporting with dishonest meters. In: 2016 IEEE Conference on Communications and Network Security (CNS), pp. 163–171 (2016). https://doi.org/10.1109/CNS.2016.7860482
14. Barthe, G., Danezis, G., Grégoire, B., Kunz, C., Zanella-Béguelin, S.: Verified computational differential privacy with applications to smart metering. In: 2013 IEEE 26th Computer Security Foundations Symposium, pp. 287–301 (2013). https://doi.org/10.1109/CSF.2013.26
15. Benhamouda, F., Joye, M., Libert, B.: A new framework for privacy-preserving aggregation of time-series data. ACM Trans. Inf. Syst. Secur. **18**(3) (2016). https://doi.org/10.1145/2873069
16. Chan, T.-H.H., Shi, E., Song, D.: Privacy-preserving stream aggregation with fault tolerance. In: Keromytis, A.D. (ed.) FC 2012. LNCS, vol. 7397, pp. 200–214. Springer, Heidelberg (2012). https://doi.org/10.1007/978-3-642-32946-3_15
17. Chow, S.S.M., Li, M., Zhao, Y., Jin, W.: Sipster: settling iou privately and quickly with smart meters. In: Annual Computer Security Applications Conference, pp. 219–234. ACSAC 2021, Association for Computing Machinery, New York, NY, USA (2021). https://doi.org/10.1145/3485832.3488029
18. Danezis, G., Fournet, C., Kohlweiss, M., Zanella-Béguelin, S.: Smart meter aggregation via secret-sharing. In: Proceedings of the First ACM Workshop on Smart Energy Grid Security, pp. 75–80. SEGS 2013, Association for Computing Machinery, New York, NY, USA (2013). https://doi.org/10.1145/2516930.2516944

19. Danezis, G., Kohlweiss, M., Rial, A.: Differentially private billing with rebates. In: Filler, T., Pevný, T., Craver, S., Ker, A. (eds.) IH 2011. LNCS, vol. 6958, pp. 148–162. Springer, Heidelberg (2011). https://doi.org/10.1007/978-3-642-24178-9_11
20. Dimitriou, T., Awad, M.K.: Secure and scalable aggregation in the smart grid resilient against malicious entities. Ad. Hoc. Netw. **50**, 58–67 (2016). https://doi.org/10.1016/j.adhoc.2016.06.014
21. Dimitriou, T., Karame, G.: Privacy-friendly tasking and trading of energy in smart grids. In: Proceedings of the 28th Annual ACM Symposium on Applied Computing, pp. 652–659. SAC 2013, Association for Computing Machinery, New York, NY, USA (2013). https://doi.org/10.1145/2480362.2480488
22. Dobraunig, C., Eichlseder, M., Mendel, F., Schläffer, M.: Ascon PRF, MAC, and short-input MAC. Cryptology ePrint Archive, Paper 2021/1574 (2021). https://eprint.iacr.org/2021/1574
23. Efthymiou, C., Kalogridis, G.: Smart grid privacy via anonymization of smart metering data. In: 2010 first IEEE international conference on smart grid communications, pp. 238–243. IEEE (2010)
24. Emura, K.: Privacy-preserving aggregation of time-series data with public verifiability from simple assumptions. In: Pieprzyk, J., Suriadi, S. (eds.) ACISP 2017. LNCS, vol. 10343, pp. 193–213. Springer, Cham (2017). https://doi.org/10.1007/978-3-319-59870-3_11
25. Erkin, Z., Tsudik, G.: Private computation of spatial and temporal power consumption with smart meters. In: Bao, F., Samarati, P., Zhou, J. (eds.) ACNS 2012. LNCS, vol. 7341, pp. 561–577. Springer, Heidelberg (2012). https://doi.org/10.1007/978-3-642-31284-7_33
26. Farinaccio, L., Zmeureanu, R.: Using a pattern recognition approach to disaggregate the total electricity consumption in a house into the major end-uses. Energy Build. **30**(3), 245–259 (1999). https://doi.org/10.1016/S0378-7788(99)00007-9
27. Garcia, F.D., Jacobs, B.: Privacy-friendly energy-metering via homomorphic encryption. In: Cuellar, J., Lopez, J., Barthe, G., Pretschner, A. (eds.) STM 2010. LNCS, vol. 6710, pp. 226–238. Springer, Heidelberg (2011). https://doi.org/10.1007/978-3-642-22444-7_15
28. Giaconi, G., Gündüz, D., Poor, H.V.: Smart meter data privacy. CoRR abs/2009.01364 (2020). https://arxiv.org/abs/2009.01364
29. Hart, G.: Nonintrusive appliance load monitoring. Proc. IEEE **80**(12), 1870–1891 (1992). https://doi.org/10.1109/5.192069
30. Jawurek, M., Johns, M., Kerschbaum, F.: Plug-in privacy for smart metering billing. In: Fischer-Hübner, S., Hopper, N. (eds.) PETS 2011. LNCS, vol. 6794, pp. 192–210. Springer, Heidelberg (2011). https://doi.org/10.1007/978-3-642-22263-4_11
31. Jawurek, M., Kerschbaum, F.: Fault-tolerant privacy-preserving statistics. In: Fischer-Hübner, S., Wright, M. (eds.) PETS 2012. LNCS, vol. 7384, pp. 221–238. Springer, Heidelberg (2012). https://doi.org/10.1007/978-3-642-31680-7_12
32. Jawurek, M., Kerschbaum, F., Danezis, G.: Sok: privacy technologies for smart grids-a survey of options. Microsoft Res. Cambridge, UK, vol. 1, pp. 1–16 (2012)
33. Joye, M., Libert, B.: A scalable scheme for privacy-preserving aggregation of time-series data. In: Sadeghi, A.-R. (ed.) FC 2013. LNCS, vol. 7859, pp. 111–125. Springer, Heidelberg (2013). https://doi.org/10.1007/978-3-642-39884-1_10

34. Kursawe, K., Danezis, G., Kohlweiss, M.: Privacy-friendly aggregation for the smart-grid. In: Fischer-Hübner, S., Hopper, N. (eds.) PETS 2011. LNCS, vol. 6794, pp. 175–191. Springer, Heidelberg (2011). https://doi.org/10.1007/978-3-642-22263-4_10
35. Leontiadis, I., Elkhiyaoui, K., Molva, R.: Private and dynamic time-series data aggregation with trust relaxation. In: Gritzalis, D., Kiayias, A., Askoxylakis, I. (eds.) Cryptology and Network Security, pp. 305–320. Springer International Publishing, Cham (2014)
36. Li, F., Luo, B., Liu, P.: Secure information aggregation for smart grids using homomorphic encryption. In: 2010 First IEEE International Conference on Smart Grid Communications, pp. 327–332 (2010). https://doi.org/10.1109/SMARTGRID.2010.5622064
37. Lin, H.-Y., Tzeng, W.-G., Shen, S.-T., Lin, B.-S.P.: A practical smart metering system supporting privacy preserving billing and load monitoring. In: Bao, F., Samarati, P., Zhou, J. (eds.) ACNS 2012. LNCS, vol. 7341, pp. 544–560. Springer, Heidelberg (2012). https://doi.org/10.1007/978-3-642-31284-7_32
38. Molina-Markham, A., Danezis, G., Fu, K., Shenoy, P., Irwin, D.: Designing privacy-preserving smart meters with low-cost microcontrollers. In: Keromytis, A.D. (ed.) FC 2012. LNCS, vol. 7397, pp. 239–253. Springer, Heidelberg (2012). https://doi.org/10.1007/978-3-642-32946-3_18
39. Mustafa, M.A., Cleemput, S., Aly, A., Abidin, A.: A secure and privacy-preserving protocol for smart metering operational data collection. IEEE Trans. Smart Grid **10**(6), 6481–6490 (2019). https://doi.org/10.1109/TSG.2019.2906016
40. Ni, J., Zhang, K., Alharbi, K., Lin, X., Zhang, N., Shen, X.S.: Differentially private smart metering with fault tolerance and range-based filtering. IEEE Trans. Smart Grid **8**(5), 2483–2493 (2017). https://doi.org/10.1109/TSG.2017.2673843
41. Prudenzi, A.: A neuron nets based procedure for identifying domestic appliances pattern-of-use from energy recordings at meter panel. In: 2002 IEEE Power Engineering Society Winter Meeting. Conference Proceedings (Cat. No.02CH37309), vol. 2, pp. 941–946 (2002). https://doi.org/10.1109/PESW.2002.985144
42. Quinn, E.L.: Privacy and the new energy infrastructure. Available at SSRN 1370731 (2009)
43. Rastogi, V., Nath, S.: Differentially private aggregation of distributed time-series with transformation and encryption. In: Proceedings of the 2010 ACM SIGMOD International Conference on Management of Data, pp. 735–746. SIGMOD 2010, Association for Computing Machinery, New York, NY, USA (2010). https://doi.org/10.1145/1807167.1807247
44. Rial, A., Danezis, G.: Privacy-preserving smart metering. In: Proceedings of the 10th Annual ACM Workshop on Privacy in the Electronic Society, pp. 49–60. WPES 2011, Association for Computing Machinery, New York, NY, USA (2011). https://doi.org/10.1145/2046556.2046564
45. Rial, A., Danezis, G., Kohlweiss, M.: Privacy-preserving smart metering revisited. Int. J. Inf. Secur. **17**(1), 1–31 (2018)
46. Rouf, I., Mustafa, H., Xu, M., Xu, W., Miller, R., Gruteser, M.: Neighborhood watch: security and privacy analysis of automatic meter reading systems. In: Proceedings of the 2012 ACM Conference on Computer and Communications Security. pp. 462–473. CCS 2012, Association for Computing Machinery, New York, NY, USA (2012). https://doi.org/10.1145/2382196.2382246
47. Shi, E., Chan, T.H., Rieffel, E., Chow, R., Song, D.: Privacy-preserving aggregation of time-series data. In: Proceedings NDSS, vol. 2, pp. 1–17 (2011)

Anonymous Random Allocation and Its Applications

Azam Soleimanian(✉)

ConsenSys, ConsenSys R&D, Paris, France
azam.soleimanian@consensys.net

Abstract. *Random Allocation* -the random assignment of the data to the parties- is a well-studied topic in the analysis of medical or judicial data, and the context of resource distribution. Random allocation reduces the chance of bias or corruption in the relevant applications, which makes the results more reliable. This is done by preventing a special or pre-planned assignment of the data to accommodate the assessment toward the desired results. This paper provides the first formal syntax and security notion of a random allocation scheme. Based on our new security notions of anonymity, confidentiality, and data-integrity, random allocation can cover more applications such as the *distributed audit system* where the confidentiality of data and the anonymity of auditors are of paramount importance. Our protocol allows the parties to stay anonymous during the concurrent executions of the protocol even if they have revealed themselves at a certain execution. The revelation property gives the possibility to the parties to claim certain advantages/faults at the end of a protocol-execution (without breaking the data-privacy or anonymity in other protocol-executions). We instantiate our syntax and prove the security based on simple cryptographic components and assumptions such as the Diffie-Hellman assumption, in the random oracle model.

Keywords: Random allocation · Random assignment · Mix-Net · Single secret election · Anonymity

1 Introduction

Random Allocation is the process of assigning the data to a set of parties based on a one-to-one random map. This concept provides a simple and efficient way for avoiding bias in clinical trials, or for preventing corruption in judicial or evaluation systems [Alt96, FD98]. This is done by preventing a special or pre-planned assignment of the data to accommodate the assessment toward the desired results. The solutions based on random allocations seem very practical, the group of parties agrees on a source of randomness (more precisely, on a random permutation) and respects the allocation.

For example, imagine a clinical trial where there are different research groups, each has its new intervention technique, and they want to know which of these

A. R. Beresford et al. (Eds.): CANS 2022, LNCS 13641, pp. 292–313, 2022.
https://doi.org/10.1007/978-3-031-20974-1_15

techniques is more effective. They assign a random group of participants to each intervention and check the results at the end. This process is known as the Randomized Controlled Trial (RCT).

Similarly, in judicial systems, to reduce the chance of corruption or biased judgment, the cases are randomly assigned to different judges or courts.

Random allocation can be used to address the scalability problem in the large-scale distributed systems where different tasks are assigned to different subsets of the system via a random allocation [GXC+17].

These examples and many others show the importance of random allocation. Despite all these applications [BCKM13], this topic has not been analyzed from a more precise security point of view. This paper puts forth a precise security notion for Random Allocation.

In the rest of the paper, we use the general terms "party" and "data" respectively for interventions and participants' data in our RCT example. We may also use data-owner as a replacement for a participant. When it is clear from the text, we may use data and data-owner interchangeably.

The relevant communities are well aware of minimum security requirements such as"Uniqueness", "Allocation Concealment" and "Blinding" [SG05,SG02].

Uniqueness is a trivial requirement saying that the allocation should be a one-to-one map (more precisely, it is one-group-to-one-party). In our clinical trial example, the Allocation Concealment prevents the researcher groups from influencing the allocation of participants to the interventions. This property is known as the "Fairness" in cryptography.

In a (single)-Blind allocation (again consider RCT example), information that may influence the participants of the experiment is withheld until after the allocation is complete. Unblinding a participant can cause the observer bias or the confirmation bias, which arises from the expectation or the feeling of the participant towards the intervention. To blind the participants, the existing RCT techniques rely on a trusted third party who runs a random allocation and gives the result of the allocation only to the parties. Even though the data-owner may not have a direct interest in unblinding, still this kind of blindness is not realistic for many applications, where the adversary may try to attack the data allocated to a specific party just by colluding with the third party.

We suggest a strong notion of blindness called "Anonymity", which means nobody can identify the party for an allocated pair except the party itself. So, this is the blindness against all except the allocated party. More precisely, if the allocation outputs a pair party-data (i, j) the identity of the party behind the index i is unknown to everybody except the party-itself.

Moreover, we define the notion of "Confidentiality" that preserves the privacy of data against all except its allocated party. Satisfying anonymity and confidentiality, simultaneously, can be challenging since the data-owner needs to encrypt the data with the public key of its allocated party, while the party is anonymous and thus its public key is not known. Our solution allows transferring the data to the allocated parties privately and anonymously.

Note that when the allocation is complete, each party knows with which data it is paired. This may arise more attacks against the *accessibility of data*, where a malicious party tries to replace the legitimate ciphertext with irrelevant data, without being detected. To go around this issue we also present the security notion of "Data-Integrity" which can detect the mentioned attack.

We emphasize that two notions confidentiality and data-integrity have not been studied in the literature of random allocation. Additionally, our definition of anonymity provides a stronger security notion than the mentioned blindness. These properties strengthen random allocation to support more applications such as *distributed audit systems* where auditors should check for the correct executions of different steps in the system. Our security notions allow an auditor to have access only to its allocated part, while the auditor is anonymous and therefore there is less chance for attacks or corruption (meanwhile, the fairness prevents biased judgment).

To summarize, in this paper, we present the first formal cryptographic ground to define and evaluate the security of Random Allocation. We present a protocol that satisfies uniqueness, fairness, and anonymity, and at the same time guarantees data-confidentiality and data-integrity. We call such a protocol as Anonymous Random Allocation (ARA). Our main idea is based on a Single Secret Leader Election (SSLE) scheme [BEHG20, CFG21] which was first motivated by the applications in the proof of stake for the blockchain [BPS16]. The SSLE scheme of [BEHG20] relies on shuffling [Dur64, Hås06, Hås16], re-randomization and commitment. Intuitively, re-randomization and shuffling are mainly used to achieve anonymity, while the commitment is used to reveal the allocations at the end of the protocol. The technique of Rerandomize-and-Shuffle (R&S) is a well-known concept in Mix-Nets [GJJS04, Wik04] which guarantees the anonymity of the senders. The intuition behind this technique is that it inserts the entropy into the relationship between the input and the output of a R&S phase, such that after enough steps of R&S, no one can link the last output to the initial input.

Here, we use a card-based example to explain the intuition behind SSLE and its extension to ARA protocol. Assume that there is a deck of cards and we agree that after shuffling the deck and distributing the cards among the players, the winner is the one who gets the "king of pick". The winner can later prove that he/she is the winner, simply by revealing the target card. Here, there is an attack where one can prepare a copy of the target card in advance and put it in his/her hand. To prevent this attack, the cards should be distributed transparently. More precisely, instead of hiding the cards, we hide the players' identities. First, in an *anonymity phase*, each player chooses a pseudonym, where this pseudonym is the commitment C_s to a selected (unique) secret s, pseudonyms are re-randomized and shuffled among the players such that at the end of this phase each player can link an output to its own pseudonym (while it can not find any link among other outputs and pseudonyms). Then in an *allocation phase*, the cards are shuffled and distributed transparently. The winner of the target card can later reveal itself by revealing its secret (which can be verified against the output of the anonymity phase).

While in SSLE a single data has a distinct value (namely, "king of pick"), in an ARA protocol data is treated equally and the aim is just to distribute the data among the parties (with the same anonymity property of SSLE). On the other hand, the main difference between SSLE and ARA is in the concept of data. While in SSLE data is only an abstraction, in ARA data is based on real-world information. ARA protocol not only extends the idea of SSLE to the distribution of data (rather than single selection), but also allows the existence of real data which can be transferred to the allocated party *privately* and *anonymously*. Such extensions make ARA a proper tool for applications, dealing with real data, demanding privacy of data and anonymity of parties (with revelation at the end) simultaneously. Furthermore, in our security model, we consider parties malicious and the data-owners honest-but-curious.

1.1 Our Technique

The intuition of our ARA protocol is as follows.

Each party P chooses a random secret s, commits to s through the commitment C_s, and adds C_s to the common list L. Then it re-randomizes and shuffles the list, where re-randomization is done as C_s^r for a randomly chosen r. The data-set would be shuffled and assigned to the elements of the list L in order. Intuitively, re-randomizations and shuffles guarantee the anonymity of the parties. While the correct shuffling and the binding property of commitment guarantee uniqueness and fairness. The commitment C_s (to the secret s) is generated such that the party can detect its associated entry in the list L, even after re-randomization. Let the commitment to the secret s be $C_s = (g^r, g^{sr}) = (u, v)$, then the relation $v = u^s$ is preserved through all the re-randomizations. This is important that the commitment is detectable by its owner, as the party needs to reveal itself at the end of the protocol. The above idea - *first commit, then re-randomize and shuffle*- was used in SSLE [BEHG20].[1]

We further extend this protocol to guarantee data-confidentiality and data-integrity. To do so, in the anonymity phase, each party appends its public key to the list L as well. Thus, at the end of this phase, the public key is re-randomized as $\mathsf{apk} = \mathsf{pk}^{r_a}$, where r_a is due to the re-randomization steps during the protocol, and we call it aggregate randomness. The data-owner can encrypt its message $M \in \mathbb{G}$ by a scheme similar to the El-Gamal encryption as $(\mathsf{ct}_0, \mathsf{ct}_1) = (R^r, M \cdot \mathsf{apk}^r)$, where $R = g^{r_a}$ is the (encoding of) aggregate randomness. Thus, to provide access to R, we add the generator g to the list L as well. Namely, in the set L, at first we have $l = (C_s, \mathsf{pk}, g)$ and after re-randomization steps, it changes to $l = (C_s^{r_a}, \mathsf{apk} = \mathsf{pk}^{r_a}, R = g^{r_a})$ which makes the mentioned encryption possible. For the aim of data-integrity, before allocating data to parties, we also add commitments C_m to a data-set DB. After the party has received its ciphertext, it decrypts and compares it against the commitment C_m.

[1] One can say that their protocol has two main phases: anonymity and *random single selection*, while our protocol has a similar anonymity phase pursuing a *random allocation* phase.

Note that unlike the secret s which is refreshed for each allocation, the secret/public key is fixed. Thus, we should make sure the adversary can not link two randomized public keys in two different allocations and break the anonymity. At first glance, the above idea may seem appropriate since the public key is re-randomized as well, and thus by the DDH assumption the re-randomized versions of the public key (in different allocations) all seem random. Unfortunately, the reasoning fails since, by the aim of the protocol, parties have to decrypt their associated ciphertext and check for the data-integrity. This means in the security proof, the simulator needs access to the secret key to simulate concurrent decryption from other allocation queries (while the secret key is not given through the DDH samples). To go around the mentioned issue, we use fresh random encryption keys for each allocation but bind the secret s to the identity of the party through another commitment $H'(\mathsf{pk}, g^s)$ such that after the revelation of s the owner of the pk would be recognized as the allocated party. Thus, the secret s is used for building a detectable-commitment that would be revealed later, the encryption keys $(\mathsf{esk}, \mathsf{epk})$ are used for data-encryption, and pk is used as the unique and fix identity of the party.

Putting together, our technique can be summarized as follows,

1. Each party chooses a fresh secret s and a fresh encryption key pair $(\mathsf{esk}, \mathsf{epk})$, it generates a detectable commitment C_s and appends (C_s, epk, g) to the list L. Then it re-randomizes and shuffles L. It also registers the commitment $H'(\mathsf{pk}, g^s)$.
2. For each data, we add a commitment C_m to the data-set DB. Then the elements of DB are randomly allocated to the element of L. Let us call the allocation as $A_{\mathsf{DB}} = \{(l, C_m) \in L \times \mathsf{DB}\}$.
3. Data is encrypted under its allocated encryption key.
4. The party can reveal its secret and its identity pk to claim an allocated pair.

To achieve confidentiality and data-integrity at the same time, the commitment C_m to the message $M \in \mathbb{G}$ should be hiding (meaning that it does not leak information about the message M). Here we use the hash function H (modeled as the random oracle [BR93,FS87]) to commit to M as $C_m = H(M, D)$ where D is chosen uniformly at random from the appropriate set. Then not only the encryption of M, but also the encryption of D is sent to the party making it possible to compare the received data against the commitment C_m. The opening D must belong to the group $\mathbb{G}$ since we are using the El-Gamal encryption scheme.

1.2 Related Work

Transfer of real data privately and anonymously is not a new problem, and is widely studied in the context of oblivious transfer [Rab05,IPS08], mix-nets [Cha81], onion routing systems [DMS04] and non-interactive anonymous router (NIRA) [SW21].

A 1-out-of-n oblivious transfer is a protocol where the sender holds several messages and the receiver chooses one of them such that the sender transfers the chosen message to the receiver whiteout knowing the choice of the receiver, and mutually the receiver does not get any information about other messages. In an ARA protocol, messages come from different senders and are allocated to different receivers who do not trust each other, this makes ARA a different problem.

Mix-nets and onion routing systems provide a way for anonymous communication where usually the sender of the ciphertext knows with who he/she is communicating and the ciphertext goes through a MPC (i.e., interactive messaging)[2], to hide this information from others. In ARA and non-interactive anonymous router, the assignment (of senders to receivers) is preprocessed which allows separating the (interactive) setup phase from the (non-interactive) messaging phase. Thus, ARA and non-interactive anonymous router are somehow orthogonal concepts to the mix-net and onion routing.

In a non-interactive anonymous router (NIRA), the router can allocate the senders to the receivers while neither the router nor the sender knows the assignment. More detailed, a trusted setup, which is realized by a trusted authority, provides n sender keys, n receiver keys and a token such that the private permutation is encoded inside the token. Each sender can send private messages to its allocated receiver by encrypting its message with its own key, then a router holding the token receives all the ciphertexts and navigates them to the allocated receivers (without knowing the allocation). Finally, the receiver uses its assigned key to decrypt the message.

Unlike NIRA which has an on-the-fly messaging, our ARA protocol has a predefined messaging phase[3] (due to the data-integrity), and the router is replaced with a pool. The ciphertexts are stored in a hash table and each party/receiver can get access to its assigned ciphertext through a flag (where the flag is its randomized public key associated with the ciphertext).

We emphasize that an ARA protocol supports not only anonymity and random allocation but also revelation. This property enables the parties to stay anonymous during the protocol but reveal themselves later, to claim some advantages or to give a proof (for example, to prove the end of the task and so claim their compensation).

Putting together, while ARA shares some similarities with the existing works, it follows a different aim and setting (Random allocation, private and anonymous predefined messaging, and revelation property).

[2] Indeed we are using the mix-net idea as a setup phase.

[3] More precisely, in NIRA a sender chooses its message at the moment, while in ARA the message is the one that was previously committed during the allocation phase.

2 Preliminaries

Notation. In this paper, the security parameter is denoted by κ. We say that a function $\text{negl}(x)$ is negligible if $\text{negl}(\kappa) \leq \kappa^{-\omega(1)}$. For a probabilistic polynomial time (p.p.t) algorithm A, the notation $y \leftarrow A(x)$ means: A receives x as the input and outputs y. The notation $x \xleftarrow{R} X$ stands for sampling the element x uniformly from the set X. We use $\mathcal{A}^{\mathcal{O}(\cdot)}$, to show that $\mathcal{A}$ has the oracle access to the algorithm or interactive protocol $\mathcal{O}$.

Definition 1 (DDH Assumption [DH76]). *For a cyclic group $\mathbb{G}$ of the prime order $p = \text{poly}(\kappa)$ and with the generator g (described by $\mathcal{G} = (\mathbb{G}, p, g)$), we say that the DDH assumption holds in $\mathbb{G}$ if for any p.p.t. adversary $\mathcal{A}$ there is a negligible function* negl *such that for $a, b, c \xleftarrow{R} \mathbb{Z}_p$,*

$$|\Pr[\mathcal{A}(\mathcal{G}, g^a, g^b, g^{ab}) = 1] - \Pr[\mathcal{A}(\mathcal{G}, g^a, g^b, g^c) = 1]| \leq \text{negl}(\kappa)$$

Definition 2 (Shuffle and Random Beacon (RB)). *A random shuffle is a random reordering of the elements of a set. A random beacon is a center or software that generates random values/shuffles. There are different techniques for generating the randomness: randomness from the financial data [BCG15, CH10], or based on cryptographic elements [NP, HMW18, BSL+20, SJK+17] which may provide more features like public verifiability.*

Note that our ARA protocol is already interactive, considering (black-box) interactions with RB improves the efficiency and is pretty realistic since many organizations are using RB for generating their required randomness.

In Appendix A, we also give the definition of other primitives that we will use in ARA, such as hash family, commitment scheme, public key encryption system, and their security notions.

2.1 Syntax and Security of ARA

An ARA protocol is formally defined as follows.

Definition 3 (Anonymous Random Allocation). *An Anonymous Random Allocation is a tuple of six main algorithms/protocols $\Pi = (\mathsf{Setup}, \mathsf{Anonymity}, \mathsf{Alloc}, \mathsf{Enc}, \mathsf{Reveal}, \mathsf{Verif})$ among a set of parties P_i and data-owners D_i as follows (here N is the total number of parties in the system),*

- $\mathsf{Setup}(1^\kappa, N)$*: it generates and returns the public parameters* pp*, a state* st_0*, and public/private keys $(\mathsf{sk}_i, \mathsf{pk}_i)_{i \in [N]}$. All the other algorithms implicitly use* pp *in their inputs.*
- $\mathsf{Anonymity}(\mathsf{st}_c)$*: it is a protocol among a subset of parties (indexed by c), each party who joins, updates the public state* st_c *(set as* st_0 *at the beginning) by adding some public information. Each party keeps track of its corresponding secret information through a private state* pst_c*.*

- $\mathsf{Alloc}(\mathsf{st}_c, \mathsf{DB}, m_1, \ldots, m_n, \mathsf{RB})$: *it is a protocol between parties and data-owners that starts after the anonymity phase. The data-set* DB *is set to the empty at the beginning, and n is the number of parties participating in the allocation c. Assuming n data-owner, each adds its data* C_m *to* DB *where the data corresponds with a message m. Parties receive the data-set* DB*, the random beacon* RB*, and* st_c *as their input, and return an allocation between* st_c *and* DB*. This consequently implies an allocation between the set of parties and the data-set called* $A_{c,\mathsf{DB}}$ *(we can denote the allocation as* $A_{c,\mathsf{DB}} = T \cup \{\mathsf{st}_c, \mathsf{DB}\}$ *where* $T = \{(i,j)\} \subseteq \mathsf{st}_c \times \mathsf{DB}$*). They output the allocation* $A_{c,\mathsf{DB}}$.
- $\mathsf{Enc}(A_{c,\mathsf{DB}}, m)$: *it returns a ciphertext* ct *associated with a public key* $\mathsf{epk} \in \mathsf{st}_c$ *and the message m. Where m and* epk *are an allocated pair through* $A_{c,\mathsf{DB}}$*. The pair* (epk, ct) *is added to a pool.*
- $\mathsf{Reveal}(A_{c,\mathsf{DB}}, \mathsf{pst}_c, c, \mathsf{ct}, \mathsf{pk})$: *Upon receiving* $A_{c,\mathsf{DB}}$*, the party P reveals itself as the owner of* pk *and claims a specific pair party-data* $(i,j) \in A_{c,\mathsf{DB}}$ *by sending a proof* $\pi_{i,j}$*. From the pool, it reads the pair* (epk, ct) *generated by its allocated data-owner j. It runs the decryption over the ciphertext* ct *and may send an invalidity request after (if the decrypted data is not compatible with* DB*). Thus the output is* $(\mathsf{pk}, \pi_{i,j}, (i,j), Result)$ *where* $Result = \mathsf{esk}$ *as an invalidity request, and otherwise* $Result = valid$*.*
- $\mathsf{Verif}(A_{c,\mathsf{DB}}, \mathsf{pk}, \pi_{i,j}, (i,j), c, Result, \mathsf{ct})$: *for the allocation c, it verifies the correctness of a claim (or an invalidity request) that the data j is allocated to the party i who owns the public key* pk.

Note that while we have a fixed setup algorithm, we may have several allocations w.r.t different subsets of parties. Thus, when we say an allocation is indexed by c, it means that all other algorithms are working with the same state st_c (or $A_{c,\mathsf{DB}}$) and are indexed by c.

Security Notion. For all the following security requirements we consider concurrent security which means: several allocations may happen where honest and corrupted parties participate in any number of allocations together. The corruptions are static meaning that at the beginning of each game the adversary declares which parties are corrupted, we denote the set of corrupted parties by $\mathcal{CP}$. We use the term "user" to refer to both parties or data-owners. The threat model assumes that parties are malicious while data-owners are honest-but-curious (HBC).[4]

The uniqueness guarantees that each allocation is a one-to-one map between the set of parties and the data-set (for some applications this might be one group of data to one party[5]). In other words, the adversary tries to find an allocation (indexed by c) such that it is not a one-to-one map.

[4] The definitions of uniqueness, fairness, and anonymity are the generalization of counterpart definitions from the SSLE to the ARA context [BEHG20] (These extend the definitions- from the single selection- to the distribution of data through a 1-to-1 map. Moreover, we also consider malicious parties and HBC data-owners).

[5] For this case, one can randomly distributes the data among n batches and then runs ARA among the parties and batches-of-data.

Definition 4 (Uniqueness). *We say that an ARA protocol Π is unique, if for any p.p.t. adversary $\mathcal{A}$ there is a negligible function* $\text{negl}(\kappa)$ *such that* $\Pr[\mathsf{Unique}_{\mathcal{A}}(1^\kappa) = 1] \leq \text{negl}(\kappa)$, *for the experiment* $\mathsf{Unique}_{\mathcal{A}}(1^\kappa)$ *given in Fig. 1. In this experiment, after many oracle queries to* QARA, *the adversary $\mathcal{A}$ outputs an allocation c allocating two pairs party-data (i, j) and (k, t) (for honest parties) such that they breach the 1-to-1 relation.*

Here $\mathcal{A}^{\mathsf{QARA}}$ *means the adversary has the oracle access to the interactive algorithms* $(\mathsf{QAnonymity}_m, \mathsf{QAlloc}_m, \mathsf{QEnc}_m, \mathsf{QReveal}_m)$ *where $\mathcal{A}$ plays the role of corrupted users and challenger C plays the role of all the honest users. We use the same index m for a set of algorithms to show they are related to the same allocation m. For the index c output by the adversary, we have the condition that the adversary has already queried* $\mathsf{QARA}_c(\cdot)$.

$\mathsf{Unique}_{\mathcal{A}}(1^\kappa)$:
$(\mathsf{pp}, \mathsf{st}_0, \{\mathsf{sk}_i, \mathsf{pk}_i\}_{i\in[N]}) \leftarrow \mathsf{Setup}(1^\kappa, N)$
$in := (\mathsf{pp}, \mathsf{st}_0, \{\mathsf{pk}_i\}_{i\in[N]}, \{\mathsf{sk}_i\}_{i\in\mathcal{CP}})$
$(c; (i, j), (k, t)) \leftarrow \mathcal{A}^{\mathsf{QARA}(\cdot)}(1^\kappa, in)$
such that $(i, j), (k, t) \in A_{c,\mathsf{DB}}$.
output 1 iff
1. $\mathsf{Verif}(A_{c,\mathsf{DB}}, \mathsf{pk}_i, \pi_{i,j}, (i, j), c, Result, \mathsf{ct}_{i,j}) = 1$ and $\mathsf{Verif}(A_{c,\mathsf{DB}}, \mathsf{pk}_k, \pi_{k,t}, (k, t), c, Result, \mathsf{ct}_{i,j}) = 1$.
2. case I. $(i = k \wedge j \neq t)$ for the honest party i or case II. $(i \neq k \wedge j = t)$ for i or k honest.

Fig. 1. The experiment for Uniqueness.

Remark 1. We emphasize that malicious parties always can exchange their claims since they just can share their secrets among themselves and generate proper proofs. This is the reason why in the experiment $\mathsf{Unique}_{\mathcal{A}}(1^\kappa)$ we conditioned the output on honest parties. Though, the mentioned issue can be prevented by the design, where the verification algorithm ignores all the claims deviating from a one-to-one map (which then by the uniqueness, does not include the honest parties, with overwhelming probability).

Fairness is about the uniform distribution of the allocations and the possibility that the honest party can claim its allocated data. By the uniform distribution, the probability that a specific data is allocated to a specific party is equal for all the data and parties. Thus, the adversary aims to decrease the chance that a specific pair happens, for the honest parties, either by changing the distribution or by disturbing the party in the generation of its proof.

Definition 5 (Fairness). *In the experiment* $\mathsf{Fair}_{\mathcal{A}}(1^\kappa)$, *Fig. 2, after many oracle queries to* QARA, *the adversary $\mathcal{A}$ chooses a data-index j hoping that the chosen index would not be allocated to an honest party in the next (i.e., the last) allocation (or no honest party can generate a valid proof to claim otherwise).*

In Fig. 2, let $\mathcal{A}$ play the role of corrupted users and challenger C play the role of honest users. After a challenge request "one more, n", the adversary has *the interactive oracle access just to one allocation indexed by c and including n parties (denoted by* $\mathcal{A}^{\mathsf{QARA}_{c,n}}$*), where* $\perp \leftarrow \mathcal{A}^{\mathsf{QARA}_{c,n}(\cdot)}$ *means* $\mathcal{A}$ *does not have any output apart from the ones in the interactive oracle* $\mathsf{QARA}_{c,n}$*. We say that an ARA protocol is fair if for any p.p.t adversary* $\mathcal{A}$ *there is a negligible function* negl *such that* $\left|\Pr[\mathsf{Fair}_{\mathcal{A}}(1^\kappa) = 1] - \frac{t}{n}\right| \leq \mathrm{negl}(\kappa)$*, where t is the number of the corrupted parties in the challenge allocation c of the game* $\mathsf{Fair}_{\mathcal{A}}(1^\kappa)$*, and n is the total number of parties in this allocation.*

$\mathsf{Fair}_{\mathcal{A}}(1^\kappa)$:
$\mathsf{pp}, \mathsf{st}_0, \{\mathsf{sk}_i\mathsf{pk}_i\}_{i\in[N]} \leftarrow \mathsf{Setup}(1^\kappa, N)$
$in := (\mathsf{pp}, \mathsf{st}_0, \{\mathsf{pk}_i\}_{i\in[N]}, \{\mathsf{sk}_i\}_{i\in\mathcal{CP}})$
$(\text{one more}, n; j) \leftarrow \mathcal{A}^{\mathsf{QARA}(\cdot)}(1^\kappa, in)$
where $\mathcal{A}$ chooses an index $j \leq n$ (a data-owner).
$\perp \leftarrow \mathcal{A}^{\mathsf{QARA}_{c,n}(\cdot)}$
output 1 if for any honest party i in the allocation c:
$\mathsf{Verif}(A_{c,\mathsf{DB}}, \mathsf{pk}_i, \pi_{i,j}, (i,j), c, \mathit{Result}, \mathsf{ct}_{i,j}) = 0$

Fig. 2. The experiment for Fairness.

The anonymity guarantees that for a target data, as long as its allocated party does not reveal itself, no one can predict the allocated party.

Definition 6 (Anonymity). *In the experiment* $\mathsf{Predict}_{\mathcal{A}}(1^\kappa)$*, Fig. 3, after many oracle queries to* QARA*, the adversary* $\mathcal{A}$ *chooses a data-index j hoping that in the next (i.e., last) allocation the chosen index would be allocated to an honest party and the adversary can detect the party (before the parties reveal themselves).*

In Fig. 3, let $\mathcal{A}$ *play the role of corrupted users and challenger C play the role of honest users. After a challenge request "one more, n", the adversary has the interactive oracle access just to one allocation, indexed by c and including n parties, as* $\mathsf{QAnonymity}_{c,n}$*,* $\mathsf{QAlloc}_{c,n}$ *and* $\mathsf{QEnc}(c,n)$ *(but not to* $\mathsf{QReveal}_{c,n}$*). We say an ARA protocol* Π *is Anonymous if for any p.p.t adversary* $\mathcal{A}$ *there is a negligible function* negl *such that* $\Pr[\mathsf{Predict}_{\mathcal{A}}(1^\kappa) = 1] \leq \frac{1}{n-t} + \mathrm{negl}(\kappa)$ *where t is the number of corrupted parties in the allocation c. This means, for the honest parties, the adversary can not guess their allocated data, with the probability of more than* $1/(n-t)$*.*

Confidentiality protects the data against all but the allocated party.

Definition 7 (Confidentiality). *In the experiment* $\mathsf{IND}_{\mathcal{A}}(1^\kappa)$*, Fig. 5, after many oracle queries to* QARA*, the adversary* $\mathcal{A}$ *outputs two messages* (m_0, m_1)*, the challenger chooses one of them randomly and embeds it in the data-set* DB *of the last allocation (for the honest users), they participate in the last allocation with the mentioned* DB*. The adversary wins if it can guess the chosen message.*

In Fig. 5, let $\mathcal{A}$ *play the role of corrupted users and challenger C play the role of honest users. The adversary can send queries to* QAlloc *for messages m (to be embedded in the data-set). It would send a challenge pair* (m_0, m_1) *for a*

$\mathsf{Predict}_{\mathcal{A}}(1^{\kappa})$:
$\mathsf{pp}, \mathsf{st}_0, \{\mathsf{sk}_i, \mathsf{pk}_i\}_{i \in [N]} \leftarrow \mathsf{Setup}(1^{\kappa}, N)$
$in := (\mathsf{pp}, \mathsf{st}_0, \{\mathsf{pk}_i\}_{i \in [N]}, \{\mathsf{sk}_i\}_{i \in \mathcal{CP}})$
$(\text{one more}, n; j) \leftarrow \mathcal{A}^{\mathsf{QARA}(\cdot)}(1^{\kappa}, in)$
where $\mathcal{A}$ chooses an index $j \leq n$ (a data-owner).
$i^* \leftarrow \mathcal{A}^{\mathsf{QAnonymity}_{c,n}(\cdot), \mathsf{QAlloc}_{c,n}(\cdot), \mathsf{QEnc}_{c,m}(\cdot)}$
output 1 if for an honest party i in the allocation c:
$\mathsf{Verif}(A_{c,\mathsf{DB}}, \mathsf{pk}_i, \pi_{i,j}, (i,j), c, Result, \mathsf{ct}_{i,j}) = 1$ and $i^* = i$.
where $\pi_{i,j} \leftarrow \mathsf{Reveal}(A_{c,\mathsf{DB}}, \mathsf{pst}, c, \mathsf{ct}_{i,j})$.

Fig. 3. The experiment for Anonymity.

challenge allocation c (to be used in Alloc_c for the honest data-owners, denoted as $\mathsf{Alloc}(\mathsf{st}_c, \mathsf{DB}(m_b))$). We say that an ARA protocol is confidential if in the experiment $\mathsf{IND}_{\mathcal{A}}(1^{\kappa})$, for any p.p.t adversary $\mathcal{A}$ there is a negligible function $\mathrm{negl}(\kappa)$ *such that* $\Pr[\mathsf{IND}^b_{\mathcal{A}}(1^{\kappa}) = 1,\ b \xleftarrow{R} \{0,1\}] \leq 1/2 + \mathrm{negl}(\kappa)$.

$\mathsf{IND}^b_{\mathcal{A}}(1^{\kappa})$:
$(\mathsf{pp}, \mathsf{st}_0, (\mathsf{sk}_i, \mathsf{pk}_i)_i) \leftarrow \mathsf{Setup}(1^{\kappa}, N)$
$in := (\mathsf{pp}, \mathsf{st}_0, \{\mathsf{pk}_i\}_{i \in [N]}, \{\mathsf{sk}_i\}_{i \in \mathcal{CP}})$
$(\text{one more}) \leftarrow \mathcal{A}^{\mathsf{QARA}(\cdot)}(1^{\kappa}, in)$
$(m_0, m_1) \leftarrow \mathcal{A}^{\mathsf{QAnonymity}_c(\cdot)}$
where for any honest party and data-owner in the allocation c,
$A_{c,\mathsf{DB}} \leftarrow \mathsf{Alloc}(\mathsf{st}_c, DB(m_b))$ and $\mathsf{ct}_b \leftarrow \mathsf{Enc}_c(A_{c,\mathsf{DB}}, m_b)$
$b' \leftarrow \mathcal{A}^{\mathsf{QARA}}(A_{c,\mathsf{DB}}, \{\mathsf{ct}_b\})$
output 1 if $b' = b$.

Fig. 4. The experiment for Confidentiality.

Remark 2. Note that we can not preserve the confidentiality of data that is allocated to the adversary. Simply, because data is revealed to its allocated party, and the adversary already knows the data. That is why the challenger gives ct_b only for honest users.

The Data-integrity guarantees that an honest party would get access to the correct allocated data stored in DB. More precisely, the adversary tries to find a pair party-data (i, j) for an allocation c such that the embedded message m in the data-set is different from the embedded message in the ciphertext, while the verification still passes. Data-integrity can prevent man-in-the-middle attacks where the adversary tries to replace the legitimate ciphertext with a malicious one.

Definition 8 (Data-Integrity). *We say that an ARA protocol Π has Data-Integrity, if for any p.p.t. adversary $\mathcal{A}$ there is a negligible function* negl *such that* $\Pr[\mathsf{Integrity}_{\mathcal{A}}(1^{\kappa}) = 1] \leq \mathrm{negl}(\kappa)$, *where in the experiment* $\mathsf{Integrity}_{\mathcal{A}}(1^{\kappa})$ *the adversary has access to the oracle* QARA, *then it outputs an allocation c which she has already sent a query for that, such that the allocation includes an allocated pair party-data (i, j) and a ciphertext $\mathsf{ct}_{i,j}$ (associated with the allocation c), where the party i is honest and $\mathsf{ct}_{i,j}$ is the corresponding ciphertext from the data-owner j to the party i.*

Integrity$_\mathcal{A}(1^\kappa)$:
$(\mathsf{pp}, \mathsf{st}_0, (\mathsf{sk}_i, \mathsf{pk}_i)_i) \leftarrow \mathsf{Setup}(1^\kappa, N)$
$in := (\mathsf{pp}, \mathsf{st}_0, \{\mathsf{pk}_i\}_{i\in[N]}, \{\mathsf{sk}_i\}_{i\in\mathcal{CP}})$
$(c, (i, j), m_j, \mathsf{ct}_{i,j}) \leftarrow \mathcal{A}^{\mathsf{QARA}(\cdot)}(1^\kappa, in)$
The challenger sets $m'_j = \mathsf{Dec}(\mathsf{pst}_c, ct_{i,j})$ (where pst_c is the private state of party i).
It outputs 1 if $m'_j \neq m_j$ and m'_j and m_j are both compatible with DB.

Fig. 5. The experiment for Data-Integrity.

3 Our ARA Protocol

In this section, we present our ARA scheme based on three main building blocks; R&S, commitment, and encryption system where all are instantiated based on the DDH assumption or collision-resistant hash.

The general idea is that each party, who joins the system, adds its encryption key $(g, g^{\mathsf{esk}}) \in \mathbb{G}^2$ and a detectable-commitment $C_s = (g^{r'}, g^{r's}) \in \mathbb{G}^2$ to the public state and then re-randomizes and shuffles the state. On the other hand, each data-owner generates a hiding commitment C_m to its message m and adds the commitment to DB. Then the elements in the data-set DB are allocated to the elements of the public state.

After the allocation phase, each data owner encrypts its data (message m) and the opening of its commitment. The encryption is done via a randomized public key allocated to its data, via the allocation phase. The allocated party uses its secret key esk to decrypt the ciphertext and if the result is not compatible with the commitment in the DB, it arises an invalidity request. It also outputs the opening of its detectable-commitment C_s, to reveal itself as the allocated party.

There are some details to make the encryption and decryption possible. In particular, we use the El-Gamal encryption. Note that the decryption algorithm of the El-Gamal system only works on messages which are either in the group $\mathbb{G}$ or have a small size (to make the discrete-logarithm operation possible). On the other hand, in our ARA protocol, a data-owner should send the opening (of its committed data) to its allocated party by the El-Gamal encryption. Therefore, we use a commitment scheme where the opening factor belongs to the group $\mathbb{G}$, to be compatible with the decryption of El-Gamal.

As mentioned before, a necessary property is the anonymity which cuts any link between the identity of the party (i.e., its public key) and its inputs to the protocol (through different allocations). For this aim, in each new allocation, parties use fresh inputs (including the secret s for the detectable-commitment and the encryption keys $(\mathsf{esk}, \mathsf{epk})$), while the connection between the inputs and the fixed public key is revealed at the end when the allocation is done. This allows the party to claim an allocation associated with its public key while the anonymity is preserved.

In the following construction $H_1 : \mathbb{G} \rightarrow \{0,1\}^{\mathsf{poly}(\kappa)}$, $H_2 : \mathbb{G} \times \mathbb{G} \rightarrow \{0,1\}^{\mathsf{poly}(\kappa)}$ and $H : \mathbb{G} \times \mathbb{G} \rightarrow \{0,1\}^{\mathsf{poly}(\kappa)}$ are hash functions where H is modeled as the random oracle.

3.1 Construction

Setup: as the input, it receives the security parameters κ and the number of parties N. It creates an empty list L, for the cyclic group $\mathbb{G}$ of prime order p it chooses a generator g, and sets $\mathsf{pp} = (\mathbb{G}, g, p)$ and $\mathsf{st}_0 = L$. It outputs $(\mathsf{pp}, \mathsf{st}_0, \{\mathsf{pk}_i\}_{i \in N})$ where $\mathsf{pk}_i = g^{\mathsf{sk}_i}$ and $\mathsf{sk}_i \xleftarrow{R} \mathbb{Z}_p$ is the secret key of party P_i.

Anonymity Phase: For the allocation c, let the state be $\mathsf{st}_c = (L, t_1, \ldots, t_{i-1})$. Let parties join in order. If P_i is the newly joint party:

- It checks that there are no two same t_j in the state st_c.
- It chooses a secret $s \xleftarrow{R} \mathbb{Z}_p$ and an encryption secret key esk, then it generates an identifiable commitment as $C_s = (u, v) = (g^{r'}, g^{r's})$ for $r' \xleftarrow{R} \mathbb{Z}_p$.
- It appends C_s, the encryption public key $\mathsf{epk} = g^{\mathsf{esk}}$ and the generator g to the list L, i.e., $L \leftarrow L \cup (C_s, \mathsf{epk}, g)$. It stores s and esk in its private state pst_c.
- It re-randomizes and shuffles the elements of L as $l_j^{r_j}$ (where l_j stands for the j-th entry of L) for a randomly chosen $r_j \xleftarrow{R} \mathbb{Z}_p$.
- Finally, it updates the state as $\mathsf{st}_c = (L, t_1, \ldots, t_i)$ where $t_i = (H_1(g^s), H_2(\mathsf{pk}_i, g^s))$ and different from other values t_j. It outputs the updated state st_c.
- **Generating Proof Of R&S**: If P has joined previously (i.e., $P \in \{P_1, \ldots, P_{i-1}\}$): let its identifiable commitment be as $C = (u, u^s)$, P verifies the output of the party P_i by finding the randomized version of C (i.e., it searches for a pair $C' = (u', v')$ from the output such that $v' = u'^s$).

Allocation Phase: This protocol receives the last state st_c and the set $\mathsf{DB} := \emptyset$.

- Each data-owner generates the commitment $C_m = H(M, g^d)$ to its data $M \in \mathbb{G}$, for a unique value $d \xleftarrow{R} \mathbb{Z}_p$ and locally stores $m = (M, g^d)$.
- They add the commitments C_m to the data-set DB.[6]
- Parties receive DB and a public random shuffle (from RB) and apply it over the data-set DB.
- Finally, the elements of the resulting set are allocated one-by-one to the elements of the list L in order, where the resulting allocation is called $A_{c,\mathsf{DB}}$. We will show an allocated pair as $(l, C_m) \in A_{c,\mathsf{DB}}$ where $l = (C_s^{r_a}, \mathsf{aepk} = \mathsf{epk}^{r_a}, R_a = g^{r_a})$ is an element of L and r_a is due to the re-randomization steps (we also can assume that $\mathsf{st}_c, \mathsf{DB} \in A_{c,\mathsf{DB}}$).

Encryption Phase: Upon receiving the allocation $A_{c,\mathsf{DB}}$, such that $(l, C_m) \in A_{c,\mathsf{DB}}$ (and $C_m = H(M, g^d)$ is associated with the data-owner D), the data-owner D encrypts its data $M \in \mathbb{G}$ and its chosen revealing factor g^d by El-Gamal encryption as,

$$\mathsf{ct}_0 = R_a^r, \mathsf{ct}_0' = R_a^{r'}, \ \mathsf{ct}_1 = M \cdot \mathsf{aepk}^r, \ \mathsf{ct}_1' = g^d \cdot \mathsf{aepk}^{r'}$$

where aepk is the anonymous encryption public key of its allocated party, $r, r' \xleftarrow{R} \mathbb{Z}_p$, and R_a is the (encoding of) aggregate randomness (note that $l = (C_s^{r_a}, \mathsf{aepk} =$

---

[6] Since the data-owner is not anonymous, we always can append a unique identifier to C_m to be sure the elements of DB are unique.

$\mathsf{epk}^{r_a}, R_a = g^{r_a}$)). The ciphertext is sent to a pool that can be stored in a key-value hash table (i.e., key$=H(\mathsf{aepk})$, value$= \mathsf{ct} = (\mathsf{ct}_0, \mathsf{ct}_1; \mathsf{ct}'_0, \mathsf{ct}'_1)$).

Reveal: Upon receiving the allocation $A_{c,\mathsf{DB}}$ such that $(l, C_m) \in A_{c,\mathsf{DB}}$ and reading the ciphertext ct (through the pool), the party P as the owner of esk (where esk is the secret key associated with aepk):

- Decrypts $\mathsf{ct} = (\mathsf{ct}_0, \mathsf{ct}_1; \mathsf{ct}'_0, \mathsf{ct}'_1)$ by its encryption secret key esk as $M' = \frac{\mathsf{ct}_1}{\mathsf{ct}_0{}^{\mathsf{esk}}}$ and $g^{d'} = \frac{\mathsf{ct}'_1}{\mathsf{ct}'_0{}^{\mathsf{esk}}}$.
- From its local storage, it recovers its secret s for the commitment C_s (as the proof for the allocated pair $(l, C_m) \in A_{c,\mathsf{DB}}$.
- It sends an invalidity request (for data-integrity) by setting $Result = \mathsf{esk}$ if the decrypted data is not compatible with the commitments C_m in the data-set. More precisely, let $M', g^{d'}$ be the decrypted data:

$$M' = \mathsf{Dec}(\mathsf{esk}, \mathsf{ct}_0, \mathsf{ct}_1),\ g^{d'} = \mathsf{Dec}(\mathsf{esk}, \mathsf{ct}'_0, \mathsf{ct}'_1)$$

  It sends an invalidity request (i.e., $Result = \mathsf{esk}$) if $C_m \neq H(M', g^{d'})$, Otherwise $Result = valid.$
- Finally, it outputs $(\mathsf{pk}, \pi = s, (l, C_m) \in A_{c,\mathsf{DB}}, Result)$.

Verification: upon receiving the allocation $A_{c,\mathsf{DB}}$, the allocated pair $(l, C_m) \in A_{c,\mathsf{DB}}$, the public key pk, the proof $\pi = s$, the request $Result$ and the ciphertext ct (associated with $\mathsf{aepk} \in l$), the verifier:

- Checks if $t = (H_1(g^s), H_2(\mathsf{pk}, g^s)) \in \mathsf{st}_c$.
- For $C_s^{r_a} = (u, v) \in l$, it checks the relation $v = u^s$.
- If the above checks pass, it accepts pk as the owner of the allocated pair $(l, C_m) \in A_{c,\mathsf{DB}}$.
- For $Result = \mathsf{esk}$, first, it checks if $R_a^{\mathsf{esk}} = \mathsf{aepk}$, then it decrypts the associated ct as $(M', g^{d'})$ (through esk), and if $C_m \neq H(M', g^{d'})$, it confirms the invalidity request.

4 Security Analysis

In this section, we analyze the security properties of our ARA protocol.

To prove the uniqueness, we need to show that there is a one-to-one map between the set of registered parties and the data. To do so, first, we show that there is a one-to-one map between the set of registered parties and the set L, from there evidently there is a one-to-one map between L and DB by the construction.

Theorem 1. *If the values t are unique, and H_2 is collision-resistant, then our ARA scheme has the uniqueness property.*

Proof. By the definition of uniqueness (Definition 4), we have,

$$\Pr[\mathsf{Unique}_{\mathcal{A}}(1^\kappa) = 1] \leq \Pr[\mathsf{Unique}_{\mathcal{A}}(1^\kappa) = 1 | \text{ case I}] + \Pr[\mathsf{Unique}_{\mathcal{A}}(1^\kappa) = 1 | \text{ case II}]$$

Since the values t_j are unique, and by the correctness of public shuffle, an honest party would not get assigned to two different data. Thus, case I can not happen. The only situation that case II may happen (i.e., an honest and a malicious party are allocated to the same data) is,

- If $C_s = C_{s'}$ for $s \neq s'$. This is prevented by the binding of $C_s = (g^r, g^{rs})$.[7]
- During the reveal phase the adversary $\mathcal{A}$ can copy the secret s as its own claim. This is prevented by the collision-resistance of hash function H_2 since $H_2(\mathsf{pk}, g^s) \neq H(\mathsf{pk}_{\mathcal{A}}, g^s)$ with overwhelming probability. ■ □

Theorem 2. *If Proofs of R&S are correct and RB outputs uniformly random shuffles, then our ARA protocol satisfies the fairness property.*

Proof. For fairness, two main points help:

- The shuffle on the data-side is uniformly random; this is true since it is a public shuffle generated by RB.
- The pseudonyms of the parties (i.e., C_s) are not removed and are still detectable by the party-itself; this point is guaranteed by the proof of R&S (see the construction, the last step in the anonymity phase or Definitions 13 and 14).

The former guarantees that the probability that a chosen data gets allocated to an honest party is $(n-t)/n + \text{negl}(\kappa)$. The latter guarantees that the honest party can claim its allocated pair successfully (note that in Definition 5, if an honest party can not claim its allocated data, the adversary wins). ■ □

Intuitively, anonymity is guaranteed since, on one hand, the adversary can not detect the randomized version of values associated with honest parties. On the other hand, the honest shuffles are uniform. Putting these two together, the adversary knows which values (after R& S) are associated with the set of honest parties but it can not specifically associate a value to an honest party. Or said in the other words, the adversary faces an entropy $n - t$ out of n (where t is the number of corrupted parties). In the following theorem, we formalized this intuition. We say a shuffle is honest if it is executed by an honest party.

Theorem 3. *If the DDH assumption holds in the group $\mathbb{G}$ and honest shuffles are uniformly random, then our ARA protocol is anonymous.*

Proof. The proof proceeds through a sequence of games.

$\boxed{\mathbf{G}_0}$: is the real game of anonymity (Definition 6).

Let x be the last honest party in the challenge allocation c, and we show the list L with L_x when it reaches x (for the allocation c).

$\boxed{\mathbf{G}_1}$: is similar to $\mathbf{G}_0$, except that, for each honest party, the associate element

[7] It is a binding commitment because for $s \neq s'$ we have $C_s \neq C_{s'}$ (they are different either in the first entry or in the second entry).

$l = ((u, u^s), \mathsf{aepk}, R_a)$ from the list L_x, is replaced with $l = ((u, u^{s'}), \mathsf{aepk}, R_a)$ for $s' \xleftarrow{R} \mathbb{Z}_p$, and from then on s' is used as the secret of the honest user.

$\boxed{\mathbf{G}_2}$: is similar to the game $\mathbf{G}_1$, except that, for each honest party the associated element $l = ((u, u^{s'}), \mathsf{aepk} = R_a^{\mathsf{esk}}, R_a)$ from L_x is replaced with $l = ((u, u^{s'}), R_a^{\mathsf{esk}'}, R_a)$ where $\mathsf{esk}' \leftarrow \mathbb{Z}_p$.

The probability that the adversary wins in the game $\mathbf{G}_2$ is $1/(n-t)$ since s' and esk' are random (and so are not related to any honest party), and particularly that the honest shuffle by x is uniformly random (i.e., neither the values nor the positions do not carry information about the honest parties).

We prove the indistinguishability of adjacent games in Lemmas 1 and 2. ■

□

Lemma 1. *In Theorem 3, two games $\mathbf{G}_0$ and $\mathbf{G}_1$ are computationally indistinguishable under the DDH assumption.*

Proof. The proof proceeds through a hybrid of games as follows (where $\mathbf{G}_{0,0} := \mathbf{G}_0$).

$\boxed{\mathbf{G}_{0,\gamma}}$: is similar to the game $\mathbf{G}_{0,\gamma-1}$, except that, the entry $l_\gamma = ((u, u^s), \mathsf{aepk}, R_a) \in L_x$, as the γ-th element of L_x and associated with an honest party, is replaced with $l_\gamma = ((u, v), \mathsf{aepk}, R_a)$ for $v \xleftarrow{R} \mathbb{G}$.

$\boxed{\mathbf{G}_{0-1}}$: is similar to the game $\mathbf{G}_{0,n}$ (where n is the number of parties in the challenge allocation), except that, each randomness v is replaced with $u^{s'}$ for $s' \xleftarrow{R} \mathbb{Z}_p$.

Note that $\mathbf{G}_{0-1} = \mathbf{G}_1$ and $\mathbf{G}_{0,0} = \mathbf{G}_0$. If l_γ corresponds with a corrupted party, clearly two games $\mathbf{G}_{0,\gamma-1}$ and $\mathbf{G}_{0,\gamma}$ are identical. Thus, in the following, we assume that l_γ is associated with an honest party.

We now are ready to show the indistinguishability of games $\mathbf{G}_{0,\gamma-1}$ and $\mathbf{G}_{0,\gamma}$.

Let $\mathcal{A}$ be the attacker to the DDH problem, and the attacker $\mathcal{B}$ tries to distinguish between $\mathbf{G}_{0,\gamma-1}$ and $\mathbf{G}_{0,\gamma}$. The adversary $\mathcal{A}$ (the simulator) simulates the game for $\mathcal{B}$ as follows:

- $\mathcal{A}$ receives the challenge $(\mathcal{G}, A = g^a, B = g^b, C)$ from its challenger where $C = g^{ab}$ or $C \xleftarrow{R} \mathbb{G}$. It generates the public parameters pp and st_0 via $\mathcal{G}$. It generates the secret/public keys by the real algorithm. Finally, it sends all the public keys, pp, st_0, and the secret keys of the corrupted parties to $\mathcal{B}$. It guesses the index y for the honest party corresponding with l_γ. Where l_γ is the γ-th element of list L_x.
- For the honest party y (its guess), it sets the secret $s_y = a$ and so at the anonymity phase $\mathsf{Anonymity}_c$, the party y inserts the commitment $C_s = (g^r, A^r)$ to the list L.
- When the list L reaches the honest party x (i.e., in L_x), if the simulator knows the secret s, associated with l_γ, it aborts (this means l_γ corresponds with an honest party other than y). Otherwise, l_γ is associated with party y and has

the form $l_\gamma = ((g^{r_a r}, A^{r r_a}), (g^{r_a \mathsf{esk}}, g^{r_a}))$ where g^{r_a} is due to the previous re-randomizations. It re-randomizes l_γ by considering the randomness $r_\gamma = br_a^{-1}$ and so l_γ is replaced with $((B^r, C^r), (B^{\mathsf{esk}}, B))$ while the simulator knows r and esk for the honest party. For the other elements of L_x, it behaves like in the real protocol[8].
- The allocation phase QAlloc_c is done like in the real algorithm.
- When $\mathcal{B}$ outputs its guess for the winner, if the winner is an honest party and $\mathcal{B}$ has guessed it correctly (experiment Predict outputs 1), $\mathcal{A}$ outputs 1. Otherwise, it outputs 0.

In the above simulation, if $C = g^{ab}$, the simulator $\mathcal{A}$ has simulated the game $\mathbf{G}_{0,\gamma-1}$ for $\mathcal{B}$, and if C is random, it has simulated the game $\mathbf{G}_{0,\gamma}$. Thus, if the simulation does not abort and $\mathcal{B}$ distinguishes the games by the probability ϵ, the adversary $\mathcal{A}$ solves the DDH problem with the probability $\frac{1}{n-t} \cdot \epsilon$ (where $(n-t)$ is the number of honest parties in the challenge allocation and is appearing here since y is chosen randomly from the set of honest parties).

For the indistinguishability of $\mathbf{G}_{0,n}$ and $\mathbf{G}_{0-1}$: Note that the game $\mathbf{G}_{0,\gamma}$ was equivalent with the case that the DDH challenge C (used in l_γ) is random. Thus in the game $\mathbf{G}_{0,n}$, the entries associated with honest parties all are replaced with random values C. Consequently, we can replace each (random) challenge C with $B^{s'}$ for $s' \leftarrow \mathbb{Z}_p$ (a fresh s' per each C). Note that all the mentioned changes are possible thanks to the fact that for the challenge allocation c, the adversary does not have access to $\mathsf{QReveal}_c$ (and does not verify the commitments C_s, t). ■ □

Lemma 2. *In Theorem 3, two games $\mathbf{G}_1$ and $\mathbf{G}_2$ are computationally indistinguishable under the DDH assumption.*

Proof. The proof is similar to the proof of Lemma 1, with the difference that, this time the challenge A is used as the encryption secret key esk of the honest party y, and for the re-randomization x uses the randomness $r_\gamma = br_a^{-1}$. This means that before x applies re-randomization, l_γ is $((g^{r r_a}, g^{r s r_a}), (A^{r_a}, g^{r_a}))$ and after it is $l_\gamma = ((B^r, B^{rs}), (C, B))$ (where the simulator knows r and s for the honest parties). All the other steps are similar to the proof of Lemma 1. ■ □

In the following theorem, we discuss the confidentiality of our ARA scheme. We use the hiding property of the commitment $C_m = H(M, g^d)$ where $d \xleftarrow{R} \mathbb{Z}_p$, and also the CPA-security of El-Gamal encryption. The formal proof is more tricky since the randomness d which guarantees the hiding of the commitment is also embedded in the El-Gamal ciphertext. Thus, we should make sure that no information regarding d is leaking through the ciphertexts.

Theorem 4. *If the DDH assumption holds in the group $\mathbb{G}$, our ARA protocol has confidentiality in the random oracle model.*

[8] Note that here is why in the construction of ARA we needed to use separate randomnesses r_j to re-randomize the elements $l_j \in L$ (i.e., $l_j^{r_j}$ rather than l_j^r).

Proof. We proceed through a sequence of games (summarized in Fig. 6).

$\boxed{\mathbf{G}_0}$: is the real game $\mathsf{IND}^0_{\mathcal{A}}(1^\kappa)$ (Definition 7).

$\boxed{\mathbf{G}_1}$: is similar to the game $\mathbf{G}_0$, except that, in the simulation of ct and ct', the anonymous encryption public key aepk is replaced with epk. Two games $\mathbf{G}_0$ and $\mathbf{G}_1$ are indistinguishable since the challenger (having the role of the honest party and honest data-owner) knows the key epk and does not need $R_a = g^{r_a}$ to generate ct (remember that in the ARA construction, the key epk was unknown to the encryptor and so we used R_a to make the encryption possible). On the other hand, two distributions (aepk^r, R_a^r) and $(\mathsf{epk}^{r'}, g^{r'})$ are identical.

$\boxed{\mathbf{G}_2}$: is similar to the game $\mathbf{G}_1$, except that, the message M_0 in the ciphertext is replaced with M_1, for all the honest parties.

This game is indistinguishable from $\mathbf{G}_1$ thanks to the security of El-Gamal encryption. To see this, let $\mathcal{A}$ be the attacker to the CPA-security of El-Gamal encryption and $\mathcal{B}$ be the adversary trying to distinguish two games $\mathbf{G}_1$ and $\mathbf{G}_2$. The adversary $\mathcal{A}$ simulates the game for the adversary $\mathcal{B}$ as follows:

- The adversary $\mathcal{A}$ receives the set of corrupted parties from $\mathcal{B}$. It chooses an honest party P^* randomly, and receives the public key epk^* from its challenger (where it sets epk^* as the encryption public key of its chosen honest party P^* for the challenge allocation c). It runs the real algorithm Setup to generate $(\mathsf{pp}, \mathsf{st}_0, \{\mathsf{pk}_i\}_i)$. Finally, it sends $(\mathsf{pp}, \mathsf{st}_0, \{\mathsf{pk}_i\}_{i \in N})$ and $\{\mathsf{sk}_i\}_{i \in \mathcal{CP}}$ to $\mathcal{B}$.
- For the challenge allocation c, it uses epk^* in $\mathsf{Anonymity}_c$ associated with P^*.
- The adversary $\mathcal{B}$ sends its chosen challenge (M_0, M_1), where $\mathcal{A}$ outputs the challenge M_0, M_1 as well.
- They run $\mathsf{Alloc}(\mathsf{st}_c, \mathsf{DB}(M_0))$, i.e., for the honest data-owners, $\mathcal{A}$ embeds M_0 in the data-set.
- When the adversary $\mathcal{A}$ receives $\mathsf{ct} = \mathsf{Enc}(\mathsf{epk}^*, M_b) = (g^r, M_b \cdot (\mathsf{epk}^*)^r)$ it forwards it to $\mathcal{B}$. It chooses $d \xleftarrow{R} \mathbb{Z}_p$ to simulate $\mathsf{ct}' = \mathsf{Enc}(\mathsf{epk}^*, g^d)$ and $C_m = H(M_0, g^d)$.
- When $\mathcal{B}$ outputs b', the adversary $\mathcal{A}$ also outputs b'.

$\boxed{\mathbf{G}_3}$: is similar to the game $\mathbf{G}_2$, except that, the simulator replaces the randomness d with d' in the ciphertext. The simulation is as before except that the adversary $\mathcal{A}$ sends the challenge $(D_0, D_1) = (g^d, g^{d'})$ for its chosen $d, d' \xleftarrow{R} \mathbb{Z}_p$. It relays $(\mathsf{ct}, \mathsf{ct}') = \mathsf{Enc}(\mathsf{epk}, M_1), \mathsf{Enc}(\mathsf{epk}, D_b)$ and $C_m = H(M_0, D_0)$ to $\mathcal{B}$. The indistinguishability of $\mathbf{G}_3$ and $\mathbf{G}_2$, is similar to the one for $\mathbf{G}_2$ and $\mathbf{G}_1$.

$\boxed{\mathbf{G}_4}$: is similar to the game $\mathbf{G}_3$, except that, for the challenge allocation QAlloc_c, the simulator replaces C_m with $H(M_1, D_0)$. These two games are indistinguishable because D_0 is chosen randomly from a large space and is unknown to $\mathcal{B}$, and thus $\mathcal{B}$ can not efficiently find $H(M_0, D_0)$ or $H(M_1, D_0)$ (through the RO queries).[9]

[9] In fact, this is the hiding property of commitment C_m.

$\boxed{\mathbf{G}_5}$: is similar to the game $\mathbf{G}_4$, except that, we simulate the ciphertext ct' as $\mathsf{Enc}(\mathsf{epk}, D_b)$. These two games are indistinguishable by the security of El-Gamal, similar to games $\mathbf{G}_2$ and $\mathbf{G}_3$.

$\boxed{\mathbf{G}_6}$: is similar to the game $\mathbf{G}_5$, except that, the key epk is replaced with aepk. The proof of indistinguishability is similar to the one for games $\mathbf{G}_0$ and $\mathbf{G}_1$. Note that this is the real game IND^1 (i.e., IND^b for $b = 1$). ■ □

Theorem 5. *If the commitment C_m is binding (or equivalently, H is collision-resistant), then our ARA protocol satisfies data-integrity.*

Proof. In the experiment $\mathsf{Integrity}_{\mathcal{A}}(1^\kappa)$, assume that the adversary outputs an allocated pair $(l, C_m) \in A_{c,\mathsf{DB}}$ and also $(m = (M, d), (\mathsf{ct}, \mathsf{ct}'))$, where $l = (C_s^{r_a}, \mathsf{aepk}, R_a)$ and aepk is associated with esk. From the received ciphertexts we have,

$$M' = \mathsf{Dec}(\mathsf{esk}, \mathsf{ct}_0, \mathsf{ct}_1), \; g^{d'} = \mathsf{Dec}(\mathsf{esk}, \mathsf{ct}'_0, \mathsf{ct}'_1)$$

The adversary wins if $C_m = H(M, g^d)$ while $m \neq m'$ for $m' = (M', g^{d'})$. Which is equivalent to breaking the binding property of the commitment scheme C_m. This completes the proof. ■ □

A Appendix : Missing Materials

Definition 9 (Collision-Resistant Hash Function) $\mathcal{H} = \{H_i : \mathcal{X} \to \mathcal{Y}\}_{i \in \mathcal{I}}$ *is a family of collision-resistant hash functions if:*
Generation. *There is a p.p.t. algorithm* $\mathsf{Gen}(1^\kappa)$ *which outputs* $i \in \mathcal{I}$.
Efficient Evaluation. *Given x and i, one can compute $H_i(x)$ in time polynomial in κ.*
Collision-Resistance (CR). *For every p.p.t. adversary $\mathcal{A}$ there is a negligible function* negl *such that for* $i \leftarrow \mathsf{Gen}(1^\kappa)$

$$\Pr\left[(x, x') \leftarrow \mathcal{A}(1^\kappa, i) \;:\; \begin{matrix} x \neq x' \wedge \\ H_i(x) = H_i(x') \end{matrix}\right] \leq \mathrm{negl}(\kappa).$$

Let $\mathcal{E} = (\mathsf{KeyGen}, \mathsf{Enc}, \mathsf{Dec})$ be an encryption system, in the following definition pp stands for the public parameters (e.g., for the El-Gamal encryption it is the group description).

Definition 10 (IND-CPA encryption [KL14]*). A public key encryption* $\mathcal{E} = (\mathsf{KeyGen}, \mathsf{Enc}, \mathsf{Dec})$ *is IND-CPA, if for any p.p.t adversary $\mathcal{A}$, arbitrary messages m_0, m_1 (such that $|m_0| = |m_1|$), there is a negligible function* negl *such that:*

$$|\Pr[\mathcal{A}(1^\kappa, \mathsf{pp}, \mathsf{pk}, \mathsf{Enc}(\mathsf{pk}, m_0)) = 1] - \Pr[\mathcal{A}(1^\kappa, \mathsf{pp}, \mathsf{pk}, \mathsf{Enc}(\mathsf{pk}, m_1)) = 1]| \leq \mathrm{negl}(\kappa)$$

where $(\mathsf{pp}, \mathsf{pk}) \leftarrow \mathsf{KeyGen}(1^\kappa)$.

Definition 11 (Commitment[KL14]**).** *A commitment scheme is a tuple of four algorithms* $\mathcal{C} = (\mathsf{Setup}, \mathsf{Commit}, \mathsf{Open}, \mathsf{Verif})$ *as follows:*

- $\mathsf{Setup}(1^\kappa)$: *it returns the public parameters* pp, *which is the implicit input of all the following algorithms.*
- $\mathsf{Commit}(m)$: *it returns a commitment* c *to the message* m.
- $\mathsf{Open}(c, m)$: *it returns an opening* π, *for the commitment* c *to the message* m.
- $\mathsf{Verif}(c, m, \pi)$: *it returns* 1, *if the opening* π *and the message* m *are compatible with the commitment* c, *otherwise it returns* 0.

Definition 12 (Security of Commitment: Binding and Hiding).

- **Binding.** *we say that a commitment scheme* $\mathcal{C}$ *is (computationally) binding, if for any p.p.t. adversary* $\mathcal{A}$ *there is a negligible function* negl *such that:*

$$\Pr\left[(c, m, m', \pi, \pi') \leftarrow \mathcal{A}(1^\kappa, \mathsf{pp}) \;:\; \begin{array}{l} \mathsf{pp} \leftarrow \mathsf{Setup}(1^\kappa) \\ m \neq m' \\ \mathsf{Verif}(c, m, \pi) = 1 \\ \mathsf{Verif}(c, m', \pi') = 1 \end{array}\right] \leq \mathrm{negl}(\kappa)$$

- **Hiding.** *We say that a commitment scheme* $\mathcal{C}$ *is (computationally) hiding, if for any p.p.t. adversary* $\mathcal{A}$, *arbitrary messages* m_0, m_1 *(such that* $|m_0| = |m_1|$*), and* $\mathsf{pp} \leftarrow \mathsf{Setup}(1^\kappa)$, *there is a negligible function* negl *such that:*

$$|\Pr[\mathcal{A}(1^\kappa, \mathsf{pp}, \mathsf{Commit}(m_0)) = 1] - |Pr[\mathcal{A}(1^\kappa, \mathsf{pp}, \mathsf{Commit}(m_1)) = 1]| \leq \mathrm{negl}(\kappa)$$

A Randomize-and-shuffle (R& S) scheme is a scheme that receives a list $L = \{\ell_i\}_i$ *and updates it to* L^* *such that* L^* *and* L *are equal up to a randomization and a shuffle.*

Definition 13 ***(a R& S scheme).*** *A R& S scheme associated with the list* L *is a tuple of p.p.t. algorithms as follows,*

Game	Ciphertext & Commitment	Justification
$\mathbf{G}_0$	$\mathsf{ct} = \mathsf{Enc}(\mathsf{aepk}, M_0)$ $\mathsf{ct}' = \mathsf{Enc}(\mathsf{aepk}, g^d; g^{r_a})$ $C_m = H(M_0, g^d)$	Real Game
$\mathbf{G}_1$	$\mathsf{ct} = \mathsf{Enc}(\boxed{\mathsf{epk}}, M_0)$ $\mathsf{ct}' = \mathsf{Enc}(\boxed{\mathsf{epk}}, g^d)$ $C_m = H(M_0, g^d)$	info.the.
$\mathbf{G}_2$	$\mathsf{ct} = \mathsf{Enc}(\mathsf{epk}, \boxed{M_1})$ $\mathsf{ct}' = \mathsf{Enc}(\mathsf{epk}, g^d)$ $C_m = H(M_0, g^d)$	El-Gamal
$\mathbf{G}_3$	$\mathsf{ct} = \mathsf{Enc}(\mathsf{epk}, M_1)$ $\mathsf{ct}' = \mathsf{Enc}(\mathsf{epk}, \boxed{g^{d'}})$ $C_m = H(M_0, g^d)$	El-Gamal
$\mathbf{G}_4$	$\mathsf{ct} = \mathsf{Enc}(\mathsf{epk}, M_1)$ $\mathsf{ct}' = \mathsf{Enc}(\mathsf{epk}, g^{d'})$ $C_m = H(\boxed{M_1}, g^d)$	RO
$\mathbf{G}_5$	$\mathsf{ct} = \mathsf{Enc}(\mathsf{epk}, M_1)$ $\mathsf{ct}' = \mathsf{Enc}(\mathsf{epk}, \boxed{g^d})$ $C_m = H(M_1, g^d)$	El-Gamal
$\mathbf{G}_6$	$\mathsf{ct} = \mathsf{Enc}(\boxed{\mathsf{aepk}}, M_1)$ $\mathsf{ct}' = \mathsf{Enc}(\boxed{\mathsf{aepk}}, g^d)$ $C_m = H(M_1, g^d)$	info.the.

Fig. 6. Overview of games for Confidentiality

- Randomize(L): *it receives the list* $L = \{\ell_i\}_i$, *it chooses the randomnesses* r_i *and randomizes elements of* L *to* $L' = \{\ell'_i\}_i$ *such that* $\ell'_i = \ell_i^{r_i}$, *then it outputs* L'.
- Shuffle(L'): *it received a randomized list* L' *and shuffle its elements. It outputs the result to* L^*. *It outputs* L^*.

Definition 14 ***(Proof of R&S).*** *A proof of R& S guarantees that the R& S has been executed correctly and* L *and* L^* *are equal up to a randomization and a shuffle of their elements. Indeed, it is a simple check comparing* L *with* L^* *as follows,*

- *for each element* $\ell_i \in L$, *there is an element* ℓ_j^* *in* L^* *such that* $\ell_j^* = \ell_i^{r_i}$ *for a randomness* r_i.

References

Alt96. Altman, D.G.: Better reporting of randomised controlled trials: the consort statement. BMJ **313**, 570 (1996)

BCG15. Bonneau, J., Clark, J., Goldfeder, S.: On bitcoin as a public randomness source. IACR Cryptol. ePrint Arch. **2015**, 1015 (2015)

BCKM13. Budish, E., Che, Y.-K., Kojima, F., Milgrom, P.: Designing random allocation mechanisms: theory and applications. Am. Econ. Rev. **103**(2), 585–623 (2013)

BEHG20. Boneh, D., Eskandarian, S., Hanzlik, L., Greco, N.: Single secret leader election. In AFT 2020: 2nd ACM Conference on Advances in Financial Technologies, New York, NY, USA, 21–23 October 2020, pp. 12–24. ACM (2020)

BPS16. Bentov, I., Pass, R., Shi, E.: Snow white: provably secure proofs of stake. IACR Cryptol. ePrint Arch. **2016**, 919 (2016)

BR93. Bellare, M., Rogaway, P.: Random oracles are practical: a paradigm for designing efficient protocols. In: Denning, D.E., Pyle, R., Ganesan, R., Sandhu, R.S., Ashby, V. (eds.) ACM CCS 93, pp. 62–73. ACM Press, November 1993

BSL+20. Bhat, A., Shrestha, N., Luo, Z., Kate, A., Nayak, K.: Randpiper - reconfiguration-friendly random beacons with quadratic communication. IACR Cryptol. ePrint Arch. **2020**, 1590 (2020)

CFG21. Catalano, D., Fiore, D., Giunta, E.: Efficient and universally composable single secret leader election from pairings. IACR Cryptol. ePrint Arch. **2021**, 344 (2021)

CH10. Clark, J., Hengartner, U.: On the use of financial data as a random beacon. In: Jones, D.W., Quisquater, J.-J., Rescorla, E., (eds.) 2010 Electronic Voting Technology Workshop / Workshop on Trustworthy Elections, EVT/WOTE 2010, Washington, D.C., USA, 9–10 August 2010. USENIX Association (2010)

Cha81. Chaum, D.: Untraceable electronic mail, return addresses, and digital pseudonyms. Commun. ACM **24**(2), 84–88 (1981)

DH76. Diffie, W., Hellman, M.E.: New directions in cryptography. IEEE Trans. Inf. Theory **22**(6), 644–654 (1976)

DMS04. Dingledine, R., Mathewson, N., Syverson., P.F.: Tor: the second-generation onion router. In Matt Blaze, editor, Proceedings of the 13th USENIX Security Symposium, 9–13 August 2004, San Diego, CA, USA, pp. 303–320. USENIX (2004)

Dur64. Durstenfeld, R.: Algorithm 235: random permutation. Commun. ACM **7**(7), 420 (1964)

FD98. Featherstone, K., Donovan, J.L.: Random allocation or allocation at random? patients' perspectives of participation in a randomised controlled trial. BMJ **317**, 1177 (1998)

FS87. Fiat, A., Shamir, A.: How to prove yourself: practical solutions to identification and signature problems. In: Odlyzko, A.M. (ed.) CRYPTO 1986. LNCS, vol. 263, pp. 186–194. Springer, Heidelberg (1987). https://doi.org/10.1007/3-540-47721-7_12

GJJS04. Golle, P., Jakobsson, M., Juels, A., Syverson, P.: Universal re-encryption for mixnets. In: Okamoto, T. (ed.) CT-RSA 2004. LNCS, vol. 2964, pp. 163–178. Springer, Heidelberg (2004). https://doi.org/10.1007/978-3-540-24660-2_14

GXC+17. Gao, Z., Xu, L., Chen, L., Shah, N., Lu, Y., Shi, W.: Scalable blockchain based smart contract execution. In: 23rd IEEE International Conference on Parallel and Distributed Systems, ICPADS 2017, Shenzhen, China, 15–17 December 2017, pp. 352–359. IEEE Computer Society (2017)

Hås06. Håstad, J.: The square lattice shuffle. Random Struct. Algorithms **29**(4), 466–474 (2006)

Hås16. Håstad, J.: The square lattice shuffle, correction. Random Struct. Algorithms **48**(1), 213 (2016)

HMW18. Hanke, T., Movahedi, M., Williams, D.: DFINITY technology overview series, consensus system. CoRR, abs/1805.04548 (2018)

IPS08. Ishai, Y., Prabhakaran, M., Sahai, A.: Founding cryptography on oblivious transfer – efficiently. In: Wagner, D. (ed.) CRYPTO 2008. LNCS, vol. 5157, pp. 572–591. Springer, Heidelberg (2008). https://doi.org/10.1007/978-3-540-85174-5_32

KL14. Katz, J., Lindell, Y.: Introduction to Modern Cryptography, Second Edition. CRC Press (2014)

NP. NIST-Project. NIST randomness beacon. https://beacon.nist.gov/home

Rab05. Rabin, M.O.: How to exchange secrets with oblivious transfer. Cryptology ePrint Archive, Report 2005/187 (2005). https://eprint.iacr.org/2005/187

SG02. Schulz, K.F., Grimes, D.A.: Blinding in randomised trials: hiding who got what. Lancet **359**(9307), 696–700 (2002)

SG05. Schulz, K.F., Grimes, D.A.: Allocation concealment in randomised trials: defending against deciphering. Epidemiol. Ser. **359**, 614 (2005)

SJK+17. Syta, E., et al.: Scalable bias-resistant distributed randomness. In: 2017 IEEE Symposium on Security and Privacy, SP 2017, San Jose, CA, USA, 22–26 May 2017, pp. 444–460. IEEE Computer Society (2017)

SW21. Shi, E., Wu, K.: Non-interactive anonymous router. In: Canteaut, A., Standaert, F.-X. (eds.) EUROCRYPT 2021. LNCS, vol. 12698, pp. 489–520. Springer, Cham (2021). https://doi.org/10.1007/978-3-030-77883-5_17

Wik04. Wikström, D.: A universally composable mix-net. In: Naor, M. (ed.) TCC 2004. LNCS, vol. 2951, pp. 317–335. Springer, Heidelberg (2004). https://doi.org/10.1007/978-3-540-24638-1_18

ACDC: Anonymous Crowdsourcing Using Digital Cash

Luis A. Saavedra(✉) and Alastair R. Beresford

Department of Computer Science and Technology, University of Cambridge, Cambridge, UK
{Luis.Saavedra,Alastair.Beresford}@cl.cam.ac.uk

Abstract. Crowdsourcing applications are vulnerable to Sybil attacks where attackers create many accounts to submit bogus or malicious data at scale. The traditional approach to manage Sybil attacks is privacy invasive since it requires contributors to identify themselves when contributing data. In this paper we present a new reporting protocol which supports the anonymous submission of data to crowdsourcing systems by honest contributors, while identifying malicious individuals who attempt to submit multiple reports. Our approach builds on Chaum's digital cash, and we demonstrate its practicality and deployability on mobile devices based on its low storage, network, runtime, and power requirements.

Keywords: Digital cash · Crowdsourcing · Anonymity · Sybil attacks

1 Introduction

Crowdsourcing apps outsource the collection and processing of data to the *crowd*, a loose collection of contributors who support the operation of the app by providing or processing data. Crowdsourcing apps can operate entirely in the virtual domain, and include tasks such as labelling photos, and can also cross the boundary into the real-world, using mobile devices owned by individuals to collect information about our physical environment. Such technologies bring many benefits, including cheap and scaleable ways to monitor road-related events such as congestion, accidents and hazards, showing occupancy of public spaces, transport, and private venues (e.g. Waze and Google Maps) or generating temperature and air quality (AQI) maps [11,39,41].

Crowdsourcing apps authenticate individuals who provide their data via direct personal identifiers obtained during registration, such as name and email address; or indirect identification methods, such as rate limiting by IP address. Authentication is required to prevent Sybil attacks [19] where a malicious contributor overwhelms a crowdsourcing system with enough bogus data that the app no longer functions correctly [32,49]. Once data are collected, many crowdsourcing apps apply anonymisation or privacy-preservation algorithms such as differential privacy to aggregate or summarise data safely before publication.

A. R. Beresford et al. (Eds.): CANS 2022, LNCS 13641, pp. 314–325, 2022.
https://doi.org/10.1007/978-3-031-20974-1_16

This approach requires individuals to trust the app with their data and (where applicable) that the privacy-preserving processing steps are applied correctly.

In this paper we improve the privacy of data contributors in crowdsourcing systems by separating contributor authentication (required to prevent Sybil attacks) from the individual reports submitted by the contributor. Our approach improves the privacy of contributors since reports often contain sensitive information about the person, such as the places they visit in a city.

Our approach builds on Chaum's digital cash [8,10], allowing authenticated contributors to obtain a limited number of digital tokens which can then be attached to reports in a crowdsourcing app, thereby allowing the app to know such reports come from a genuine contributor, but prevent apps from associating particular contributions with specific individuals. The use of Chaum's protocol allows the system to identify malicious contributors who attempt to contribute multiple data items using a single digital token.

The reported data may itself contain information which allows re-identification of the contributor, so we explore the use of k-anonymity to provide data privacy of the report contents too. We illustrate our approach by focusing on location information, which is required in almost all apps in the real world and also has repeatedly been shown to contain sensitive personal information [16,26,51]. We use the running example of crowdsourcing traffic data since the mobility of contributors and frequent reporting requirements make it particularly challenging, however our approach is applicable to a wide range of crowdsourcing scenarios.

Our paper makes the following contributions:

- A new protocol for anonymous data collection that prevents Sybil attacks.
- A method to cryptographically bind data items to digital tokens, allowing data to be shared over untrusted networks, such as peer-to-peer networks.
- Support for client-side k-anonymity, suitable for use in crowdsourcing applications in the physical domain.
- An evaluation of the practicality of our proposal, where we find that one million validated data items can be stored in 3.6 GB; data submission from a smartphone takes less than 34 ms and 6.5 mJ; and signature and verification steps performed by crowdsourcing applications take less than 100 ms.
- An evaluation of our k-anonymity approach to protect the privacy of data items themselves, showing, through traffic simulations, that 20% of cars can always report with k between 22 and 25 in a medium-sized European city.

2 System Overview and Security Goals

Separating the verification of contributor identities and the submission of reports protects contributor privacy. We assume the presence of an identity authority that authenticates contributors but is not involved in the reporting or app data processing. Apps collect valid reports from contributors registered in the system but do not know the identity of contributors. Therefore, there are three different types of entity: the identity authority, the apps, and the contributors who submit reports. In our traffic reporting example, identity authorities might be car manufacturers or smartphone vendors; apps run by city councils or another app developer; and contributors could be car drivers or public transport passengers.

Identity authorities identify contributors based on credentials already used by crowdsourcing systems, and might include personal data such as IP or email addresses, digital attestation by smartphones, hardware tokens, or other methods. Identity authorities then provide contributors with a limited number of digital tokens which can be attached to reports which contributors can share with apps. Apps can then check that the digital tokens are valid (and therefore come from a genuine contributor) without revealing the identity of the contributor either to the app or the identity authority. Thus our approach meets our primary privacy goal: it allows crowdsourcing platforms to prevent Sybil attacks through contributor authentication, without either the identity authority or the app being able to associate a specific report with a particular contributor. In order to protect apps against malicious contributors, our protocol should ensure that digital tokens cannot be forged or attached to more than one report (i.e. prevent double spending). It should prevent multiple, colluding contributors from send more valid reports to an app than they are authorised to submit.

In order to prevent apps from identifying contributors through their network address, we assume reports are submitted to apps via trusted proxies or anonymous communication networks such as Tor, Loopix, or Nym [17,18,42].

3 Authentication Protocol

Our system requirements are similar to Chaum's digital cash [8–10], where the *identity authority* is equivalent to the bank, *apps* to merchants, and *contributors* to customers. The blind token generation in this scheme meets our primary security goal, preventing the apps and identity authority from associating a specific token with a contributor, and also prevents double spending.

However, there is an important difference: in the case of digital cash, the token is the entire piece of information sent by the customer to the merchant. In our scheme, the contributor needs to bind the token with a report in a non-invertible way, preventing any intermediary who might receive the report from altering the contents of the report or extracting the token (see Sect. 4). It also prevents a malicious app from altering the report or extracting the token in the case where we wish to have an external validator to check the work of an app.

To do so, we follow the token generation protocol as presented by Chaum. The identity authority can use different private keys to sign valid tokens for different crowdsourcing reporting periods as well as limit the number of tokens and reports per contributor. Our protocol follows the payment protocol [10, pp.320–321] except for step 3. Instead of simply answering the app's challenge Z, Alice computes a new challenge $Z' = h(Z, R)$ where R is her report and h is a collision-free one-way cryptographic hash function specified by the identity authority. Subsequently, steps 4–6 are adjusted to include verification and forwarding of the variables Z' and R. By answering challenge Z' instead of Z, Alice has bound her report to the token, preventing their undetectable modification.

Our modified version of Chaum's protocol meets our security goals. Chaum's RSA-based blind signature scheme has been proven secure in the random oracle model [4]. Digital cash protocols [9,10] were also proven secure [20], including the inability to forge or alter tokens, link contributors to tokens, and distinguish two tokens submitted by the same contributor.

In the original protocol, banks generate digital cash based on actual Fiat currency deposited. In our use case, the identity authority can decide how many reports each contributor is allowed to submit in a given reporting period. This is a policy question that can be decided via discussion between the identity authority and the apps. For example, the identity authority could issue one token per time period per device; one per contributor; or a different number of tokens for different types of device. Furthermore, the identity authority might have different types of token, or different tokens for different apps, allowing apps to set their own policies. Since the identity authority sees contributor identities, different numbers of tokens can be issued for different types of contributor. These could be made visible to apps by the identity authority by using different private keys for each type, or not. Our protocol therefore supports a range of policy options. The constraint is each app has to decide how many tokens are issued per-identity and how contributors are grouped into different types (if any).

4 *K*-Anonymous Reporting

While our protocol guarantees that reports are submitted anonymously to apps, the contents of those reports may reveal the contributor's identity. One of the biggest risks is a report containing location data, since it is essential in many crowdsourcing scenarios and may also identify individuals uniquely, even when no other information is reported. For example, a sequence of timestamped contributor locations may record a journey from home to work, which has previously been shown to uniquely identify most individuals [30]. In this section we focus on how to protect the privacy of contributors submitting reports which include location data; apps may need to protect other types of potentially identifiable information in a similar way depending on the data collected.

We assume that the electronic devices of contributors can communicate peer-to-peer wirelessly with other devices nearby. This includes smartphones communicating using Bluetooth or WiFi Direct, or vehicles talking with other vehicles and local infrastructure using wireless vehicle communications. Our basic idea is to use the local wireless network to check physical proximity of k contributors who also intend to submit a report to an app. Doing so means that each contributor knows that there will be k reports received by the app from this location, thereby protecting location privacy through k-anonymity. In order to allow contributors to check that $k-1$ others intend to submit reports from their current location, contributors can share their reports via the peer-to-peer network.

Since our protocol in Sect. 3 binds a report to a token, these reports can safely be shared with otherwise untrusted local contributors over the peer-to-peer network as the report cannot be modified and the token cannot be recovered or attached to a new report. The downside of sharing reports in this way is that there may not be k nearby contributors, and if one or more nearby contributors are malicious, then the contents of the reports might be shared with the app or another entity without reaching the required threshold to achieve k-anonymity.

To solve this problem, we introduce a three-phase protocol. In the first phase, each contributor, c, creates a hash of their token, $H_c = h(C_c)$ and broadcasts this to all other local contributors. When a contributor receives k or more distinct hashed token values, they enter the second phase by forming a single challenge, Z_c, which is the concatenation of all the hashed token values received along with a hash of their report ($Z_c = H_1|H_2|...|H_k|R_c$); including the hash of the report in Z_c binds the token to the report. The contributor runs through our reporting protocol (see Sect. 3) using Z_c as the challenge to produce a response, U_c. This way each contributor can only perform the second phase once, otherwise the contributor will reveal their identity to the identity authority and app in the third phase as the token would be double spent. Then, contributors broadcast their token C_c and values of Z_c and U_c to all other contributors on the local network. Note these values are sufficient to validate the token, challenge and report, but not enough for others to generate a new response [10].

In the third phase, contributors check the validity of all tokens C_{c_1} through C_{c_k} using the challenges Z_{c_1} through Z_{c_k} and their responses U_{c_1} to U_{c_k} respectively. If the challenges are valid, then each contributor knows that there are at least k contributors with valid tokens connected to the local network. Each contributor, c, can now submit their report along with Z_c and U_c to the app.

Applying this protocol to the traffic reporting example, vehicles can detect each other's presence over a local network, run through the three-phase protocol initially and then, if the threshold k is reached, submit their reports to the app.

5 Results, Performance and Simulations

This section discusses protocol performance in terms of storage, CPU, time, and power requirements, as well as a brief feasibility assessment. We also estimate values of k for the k-anonymous protocol based on traffic simulations.

Storage: before tokens are used, contributors need to store each signed token of size N, together with 5 parameters of size N (a, c, d, x, and y) [10]. Thus $6N$ storage is required for each token. After reporting, the identity authority will need to store the following values: the token, report R, challenge Z, and $Z' = h(Z, R)$, as well as the response U which requires $3N$ storage. In order to detect double-spending, Z and Z' need to be of length N. The report R can be of any arbitrary size $|R|$, thus each report and token requires $6N + |R|$ of storage. Assuming RSA 4 096 is used as the secure signing algorithm $N = 4\,096$ bit. If $|R| = N$, then each transaction and report requires 3.6 KB of storage; this report size is more than enough to store timestamps, position and traffic condition data in our example. This would scale as 179.2 MB, 1 GB, and 3.6 GB to store 50 000, 279 000, and 1 million validated tokens and reports, respectively.

CPU Performance: we measured the performance of a Python implementation of Chaum's digital cash protocol [37] using random contributor identifiers and token values, resulting in 1 024 bit tokens. The timing data were obtained using a laptop with an Intel Core i7 (I7-9750H) running Python 3.9.2 and macOS 10.15.7. After running warm up operations, the timing results for 100 000 operations are summarised by their mean and standard deviation, since they present normal distributions. The only exception is the signing operation by the identity authority, which presents a binormal distribution, possibly due to occasionally hitting an uncommon (uncached) code path. However, the frequency of the second peak is negligible and of the order of ten times lower than the most frequent values in the histogram. The creation of the token candidates by contributors takes a mean of 30.3 ms with a standard deviation of 4.2 ms (30.3 ± 4.2 ms), and payment takes 183.5 ± 35.1 ms. The identity authority signs each token in 20.2 ± 1.8 ms, verifying each in 92.6 ± 15.8 ms. The verification and its timings depend heavily on the size of the database in the implementation tested. A distributed system or simply reordering tokens could optimise the results.

Power Consumption: we evaluate the feasibility of our approach on mobile devices by measuring the power consumption on a smartphone. We place a power sensor between the battery and the smartphone, similar to previous approaches [35,43]. For the smartphone we use a Motorola Moto E6 Plus (XT2025-2) as it comes with a removable battery. We measure an upper bound of the total power consumed, obtaining readings at a rate of 2 KHz [48]. The device runs on battery power with display and Wi-Fi off during the measurements. Each operation is run 100 times in order to time and measure their power consumption (Table 1).

Table 1. Android operation timings and power consumption

	Mean	Std deviation	Power consumption	Std deviation
SHA-256	1.54 ms	0.21 ms	0.40 mJ	0.05 mJ
SHA-512	1.54 ms	0.21 ms	0.40 mJ	0.06 mJ
Blinding step	16.31 ms	3.20 ms	3.44 mJ	0.78 mJ
Verifying step	33.19 ms	2.41 ms	6.49 mJ	4.52 mJ

These measurements show hashing operations are very fast and have negligible impact on power consumption (<0.5 mJ). The blinding and verifying steps require more computational effort but little power: 3.44 mJ and 6.49 mJ. Furthermore, token generation could be run while connected to power overnight. These numbers are very small: previous research estimates 4G/LTE network transmission to consume 12.8 J to send a single packet [33]. Thus, the network cost necessary for all crowdsourcing applications is going to dominate over any energy consumption associated with the CPU requirements of the protocol.

5.1 *K*-Anonymity

We used Veins, a vehicular network simulation software which combines traffic and network communication simulations, to perform a brief feasibility assessment and estimate realistic values of k in the domain of urban traffic congestion [46]. Our simulations are based on the real road map from the Aarhus (Denmark) city centre, obtained from OpenStreetMap. We simulate traffic volumes by using data from the CityPulse Aarhus traffic dataset [13], together with speed limits, junctions and traffic light simulations in Veins. We assume vehicles can communicate using a peer-to-peer protocol with a broadcasting range of 300 m as proposed by the U.S. Department of Transportation [40].

We measure the number of vehicles that are in range of each other for 5 s, enough time to exchange messages and reports. We run two simulations to cover volumes of traffic representative of peak (5 000 vehicles) and off-peak (2 000 vehicles) periods. The results were plotted and form long-tailed distributions in both scenarios, indicating there are areas where only low values of k are possible. The values of k obtained for indicative percentiles are summarised in the Table 2.

Table 2. Values of k for indicative percentiles

Percentiles	0–40	50	60	65	70	75	80	85	90	95
k for 2,000 vehicles	1	3	5	9	11	14	22	30	38	47
k for 5,000 vehicles	1	2	4	5	6	8	25	50	80	112

With 2 000 vehicles we find that at any time, one in five vehicles has 21 or more vehicles nearby, and one in ten has 37 or more. When simulating 5 000 vehicles our results show one in five vehicles has 24 or more nearby, and one in ten has 79 or more at any time.

In other words, half of all vehicles at any point in time have no anonymity ($k = 1$) and are driving around with no other vehicles within 300 m. Conversely, 20% of the time, vehicles are able to communicate with over 20 other vehicles within 300 m. This is likely to be acceptable for many crowdsourcing applications as occasional reports are all that is required. For example, in the domain of traffic monitoring, sporadic reports are useful, and in particular, reports will be produce in all of the busy areas since these will have high values for k.

6 Related Work

Previous research has proposed addition of noise and homomorphic encryption for privacy-preserving measurement aggregation by untrusted entities [23, 38, 45], and identity-based encryption to allow anonymous crowdsourcing [14, 15]. However, these assume arbitrary, unauthenticated contributors, making it impossible to identify Sybil attacks and penalise dishonest contributors.

Pseudonym-based approaches to location privacy include mix zones [6,7], silent period [34], and some blind signature schemes [1]. However, all of these rely on middleware systems, or have no ability to limit user contributions, thus being vulnerable to Sybil attacks. The SPPEAR approach [29] uses pseudonyms and authorisation tokens, but cannot guarantee contributor privacy when some of its entities collude. It is also very inefficient compared to our approach, requiring more than 20 s to issue 50 pseudonyms, and results in significant CPU use in mobile devices. Blind signature schemes have been proposed for anonymous authentication of vehicles, but require extra trusted infrastructure to be deployed [3,50]. Another approach is k-anonymity, which ensures that any particular record is indistinguishable from at least $(k-1)$ other records [44]. Spatial and temporal cloaking techniques proposed for k-anonymity assume trusted service providers [31], and are vulnerable to subtraction and negation attacks [5].

Differential privacy enables the publication of aggregate statistics of a dataset via the addition of noise by the aggregator [21,22]. However, it is unsuitable for small amounts of data and relies on a trusted third-party data collector to apply the differential privacy algorithms. Local differential privacy approaches like RAPPOR ensure responses sent to aggregators are already differentially private [25], but lose detail quickly and degrade their privacy protection much faster than the central model with periodic reports [24,36,47]. Another approach is shuffle model differential privacy, with results similar to the central model for secure aggregations [2,12,27,28] but combines limitations of central and local approaches: degraded data quality and granularity and requiring trusted entities.

7 Conclusion

In this paper we improved on the privacy of data contributors in a crowdsourcing system by devising a protocol which separates contributor authentication (required to prevent Sybil attacks) from the individual reports submitted to apps. Since crowdsourcing apps operating in the real-world typically gather location data as part of any report, we proposed a protocol to protect the location privacy of all contributors. Our approach does not need a trusted app, trusted middleware systems nor additional infrastructure. Instead, we rely on an identity authority to oversee contributor identification and registration, adapting Chaum's digital cash scheme to blindly sign and limit the number of reports a contributor can submit over a defined period of time.

The protocols have modest implementation requirements: one million validated reports and tokens fit within 3.6 GB; computation time typically takes less than 34 ms; and power consumption in handheld devices is very modest at 6.5 mJ. The practical feasibility of the k-anonymous protocol implementation was shown via simulation of vehicles driving around in a medium-sized European city: we found that 20% of the vehicles could submit reports at any time with a k between 22 and 25 for typical traffic volumes during peak and off-peak times.

Acknowledgements. We thank Daniel Hugenroth for his help in obtaining mobile device power consumption measurements. We are grateful to anonymous reviewers for their feedback. We acknowledge and thank Fundación Mapfre Guanarteme and Nokia Bell Labs for their generous financial support. The views, opinions and findings in this paper are those of the authors and not necessarily those of our funders.

References

1. Aslam, B., Zou, C.C.: One-way-linkable blind signature security architecture for VANET. In: 2011 IEEE Consumer Communications and Networking Conference (CCNC), pp. 745–750 (2011). https://doi.org/10.1109/CCNC.2011.5766590
2. Balle, B., Bell, J., Gascón, A., Nissim, K.: Private summation in the multi-message shuffle model. In: Proceedings of the 2020 ACM SIGSAC Conference on Computer and Communications Security, CCS 2020, pp. 657–676. Association for Computing Machinery, New York (2020). https://doi.org/10.1145/3372297.3417242
3. Baza, M., et al.: Detecting Sybil attacks using proofs of work and location in VANETS. IEEE Trans. Dependable Secure Comput. **19**(1), 39–53 (2022). https://doi.org/10.1109/TDSC.2020.2993769
4. Bellare, M., Namprempre, C., Pointcheval, D., Semanko, M.: The One-More-RSA-inversion problems and the security of Chaum's blind signature scheme. J. Cryptol. **16**(3) (2003). https://doi.org/10.1007/s00145-002-0120-1
5. Beresford, A.R.: Location privacy in ubiquitous computing. Ph.D. thesis, University of Cambridge (2004)
6. Beresford, A., Stajano, F.: Location privacy in pervasive computing. IEEE Pervasive Comput. **2**(1), 46–55 (2003). https://doi.org/10.1109/MPRV.2003.1186725
7. Beresford, A., Stajano, F.: Mix zones: user privacy in location-aware services. In: IEEE Annual Conference on Pervasive Computing and Communications Workshops, Proceedings of the Second, pp. 127–131 (2004). https://doi.org/10.1109/PERCOMW.2004.1276918
8. Chaum, D.: Blind signatures for untraceable payments. In: Chaum, D., Rivest, R.L., Sherman, A.T. (eds.) Advances in Cryptology, pp. 199–203. Springer, Boston, MA (1983). https://doi.org/10.1007/978-1-4757-0602-4_18
9. Chaum, D.: Online cash checks. In: Quisquater, J.-J., Vandewalle, J. (eds.) EUROCRYPT 1989. LNCS, vol. 434, pp. 288–293. Springer, Heidelberg (1990). https://doi.org/10.1007/3-540-46885-4_30
10. Chaum, D., Fiat, A., Naor, M.: Untraceable electronic cash. In: Goldwasser, S. (ed.) CRYPTO 1988. LNCS, vol. 403, pp. 319–327. Springer, New York (1990). https://doi.org/10.1007/0-387-34799-2_25
11. Chen, M., Yang, J., Hu, L., Hossain, M.S., Muhammad, G.: Urban healthcare big data system based on crowdsourced and cloud-based air quality indicators. IEEE Commun. Mag. **56**(11), 14–20 (2018). https://doi.org/10.1109/MCOM.2018.1700571
12. Cheu, A., Smith, A., Ullman, J., Zeber, D., Zhilyaev, M.: Distributed differential privacy via shuffling. In: Ishai, Y., Rijmen, V. (eds.) EUROCRYPT 2019. LNCS, vol. 11476, pp. 375–403. Springer, Cham (2019). https://doi.org/10.1007/978-3-030-17653-2_13
13. CityPulse EU FP7 project: Smart City Datasets (2016). http://iot.ee.surrey.ac.uk:8080/datasets.html
14. De Cristofaro, E., Soriente, C.: Short paper: PEPSI–privacy-enhanced participatory sensing infrastructure. In: WiSec 2011, pp. 23–28. Association for Computing Machinery, New York (2011). https://doi.org/10.1145/1998412.1998418

15. De Cristofaro, E., Soriente, C.: Extended capabilities for a privacy-enhanced participatory sensing infrastructure (PEPSI). IEEE Trans. Inf. Forensics Secur. **8**(12), 2021–2033 (2013). https://doi.org/10.1109/TIFS.2013.2287092
16. De Montjoye, Y.A., Hidalgo, C.A., Verleysen, M., Blondel, V.D.: Unique in the crowd: the privacy bounds of human mobility. Sci. Rep. **3**(1), 1–5 (2013). https://doi.org/10.1038/srep01376
17. Diaz, C., Halpin, H., Kiayias, A.: The Nym Network (2021). https://nymtech.net/whitepaper
18. Dingledine, R., Mathewson, N., Syverson, P.: Tor: the second-generation onion router. Technical report, Naval Research Lab Washington DC (2004)
19. Douceur, J.R.: The Sybil attack. In: Druschel, P., Kaashoek, F., Rowstron, A. (eds.) IPTPS 2002. LNCS, vol. 2429, pp. 251–260. Springer, Heidelberg (2002). https://doi.org/10.1007/3-540-45748-8_24
20. Dreier, J., Kassem, A., Lafourcade, P.: Formal analysis of E-cash protocols. In: 2015 12th International Joint Conference on E-Business and Telecommunications (ICETE), vol. 04, pp. 65–75 (2015)
21. Dwork, C.: Differential privacy: a survey of results. In: Agrawal, M., Du, D., Duan, Z., Li, A. (eds.) TAMC 2008. LNCS, vol. 4978, pp. 1–19. Springer, Heidelberg (2008). https://doi.org/10.1007/978-3-540-79228-4_1
22. Dwork, C., Roth, A.: The algorithmic foundations of differential privacy. Found. Trends Theor. Comput. Sci. **9**(3–4), 211–407 (2014). https://doi.org/10.1561/0400000042
23. Erkin, Z., Troncoso-pastoriza, J.R., Lagendijk, R., Perez-Gonzalez, F.: Privacy-preserving data aggregation in smart metering systems: an overview. IEEE Signal Process. Mag. **30**(2), 75–86 (2013). https://doi.org/10.1109/MSP.2012.2228343
24. Erlingsson, Ú., Feldman, V., Mironov, I., Raghunathan, A., Talwar, K., Thakurta, A.: Amplification by shuffling: from local to central differential privacy via anonymity. In: Proceedings of the Thirtieth Annual ACM-SIAM Symposium on Discrete Algorithms, pp. 2468–2479. SIAM (2019). https://doi.org/10.1137/1.9781611975482.151
25. Erlingsson, U., Pihur, V., Korolova, A.: RAPPOR: randomized aggregatable privacy-preserving ordinal response. In: Proceedings of the 2014 ACM SIGSAC Conference on Computer and Communications Security, CCS 2014, pp. 1054–1067. Association for Computing Machinery, New York (2014). https://doi.org/10.1145/2660267.2660348
26. Gambs, S., Killijian, M.O., Núñez del Prado Cortez, M.: De-anonymization attack on geolocated data. J. Comput. Syst. Sci. **80**(8), 1597–1614 (2014). https://doi.org/10.1016/j.jcss.2014.04.024. Special Issue on Theory and Applications in Parallel and Distributed Computing Systems
27. Ghazi, B., Kumar, R., Manurangsi, P., Pagh, R., Sinha, A.: Differentially private aggregation in the shuffle model: almost central accuracy in almost a single message. In: Meila, M., Zhang, T. (eds.) Proceedings of the 38th International Conference on Machine Learning. Proceedings of Machine Learning Research, vol. 139, pp. 3692–3701. PMLR, 18–24 July 2021. https://proceedings.mlr.press/v139/ghazi21a.html
28. Ghazi, B., Manurangsi, P., Pagh, R., Velingker, A.: Private aggregation from fewer anonymous messages. In: Canteaut, A., Ishai, Y. (eds.) EUROCRYPT 2020. LNCS, vol. 12106, pp. 798–827. Springer, Cham (2020). https://doi.org/10.1007/978-3-030-45724-2_27

29. Gisdakis, S., Giannetsos, T., Papadimitratos, P.: SPPEAR: security & privacy-preserving architecture for participatory-sensing applications. In: Proceedings of the 2014 ACM Conference on Security and Privacy in Wireless & Mobile Networks, WiSec 2014, pp. 39–50. Association for Computing Machinery, New York (2014). https://doi.org/10.1145/2627393.2627402
30. Golle, P., Partridge, K.: On the anonymity of home/work location pairs. In: Tokuda, H., Beigl, M., Friday, A., Brush, A.J.B., Tobe, Y. (eds.) Pervasive 2009. LNCS, vol. 5538, pp. 390–397. Springer, Heidelberg (2009). https://doi.org/10.1007/978-3-642-01516-8_26
31. Gruteser, M., Grunwald, D.: Anonymous usage of location-based services through spatial and temporal cloaking. In: Proceedings of the 1st International Conference on Mobile Systems, Applications and Services, MobiSys 2003, pp. 31–42. Association for Computing Machinery, New York (2003). https://doi.org/10.1145/1066116.1189037
32. Hern, A.: Berlin artist uses 99 phones to trick Google into traffic jam alert. The Guardian (2020). https://www.theguardian.com/technology/2020/feb/03/berlin-artist-uses-99-phones-trick-google-maps-traffic-jam-alert
33. Huang, J., Qian, F., Gerber, A., Mao, Z.M., Sen, S., Spatscheck, O.: A close examination of performance and power characteristics of 4G LTE networks. In: Proceedings of the 10th International Conference on Mobile Systems, Applications, and Services, MobiSys 2012, pp. 225–238. Association for Computing Machinery (2012). https://doi.org/10.1145/2307636.2307658
34. Huang, L., Matsuura, K., Yamane, H., Sezaki, K.: Enhancing wireless location privacy using silent period. In: IEEE Wireless Communications and Networking Conference, vol. 2, pp. 1187–1192 (2005). https://doi.org/10.1109/WCNC.2005.1424677
35. Hugenroth, D.: Measuring energy consumption of privacy-preserving protocols for fun and profit (2021). https://mobiuk.org/2021/abstract/S5-P2_Hugenroth_MeasuringEnergyConsumptionPrivacyPreserving.pdf. mobiUK 2021
36. Joseph, M., Roth, A., Ullman, J., Waggoner, B.: Local differential privacy for evolving data. In: Bengio, S., Wallach, H., Larochelle, H., Grauman, K., Cesa-Bianchi, N., Garnett, R. (eds.) Advances in Neural Information Processing Systems, vol. 31. Curran Associates, Inc. (2018)
37. Kamthe, N.S., Kamala, K.K., Husaini Basha, A.S., Sharma, P.: Project_DigitalCash (2020). https://github.com/koushik-kumar/Project_DigitalCash
38. Liu, Y., Guo, W., Fan, C.I., Chang, L., Cheng, C.: A practical privacy-preserving data aggregation (3PDA) scheme for smart grid. IEEE Trans. Industr. Inf. **15**(3), 1767–1774 (2019). https://doi.org/10.1109/TII.2018.2809672
39. Meier, F., Fenner, D., Grassmann, T., Otto, M., Scherer, D.: Crowdsourcing air temperature from citizen weather stations for urban climate research. Urban Climate **19**, 170–191 (2017). https://doi.org/10.1016/j.uclim.2017.01.006
40. National Highway Traffic Safety Administration: NHTSA: Vehicle-to-Vehicle Communication (2021). https://www.nhtsa.gov/technology-innovation/vehicle-vehicle-communication
41. Overeem, A., Robinson, J.C.R., Leijnse, H., Steeneveld, G.J., Horn, B.K.P, Uijlenhoet, R.: Crowdsourcing urban air temperatures from smartphone battery temperatures. Geophys. Res. Lett. **40**(15), 4081–4085 (2013). https://doi.org/10.1002/grl.50786

42. Piotrowska, A.M., Hayes, J., Elahi, T., Meiser, S., Danezis, G.: The loopix anonymity system. In: 26th USENIX Security Symposium (USENIX Security 17), pp. 1199–1216. USENIX Association, Vancouver, August 2017. https://www.usenix.org/conference/usenixsecurity17/technical-sessions/presentation/piotrowska
43. Rice, A., Hay, S.: Decomposing power measurements for mobile devices. In: 2010 IEEE International Conference on Pervasive Computing and Communications (PerCom), pp. 70–78 (2010). https://doi.org/10.1109/PERCOM.2010.5466991
44. Samarati, P., Sweeney, L.: Protecting privacy when disclosing information: k-anonymity and its enforcement through generalization and suppression. Technical report, SRI International (1998)
45. Shi, E., Chan, T.H., Rieffel, E., Chow, R., Song, D.: Privacy-preserving aggregation of time-series data. In: Proceedings NDSS, vol. 2, pp. 1–17. Citeseer (2011)
46. Sommer, C., German, R., Dressler, F.: Bidirectionally coupled network and road traffic simulation for improved IVC analysis. IEEE Trans. Mob. Comput. **10**(1), 3–15 (2011). https://doi.org/10.1109/TMC.2010.133
47. Tang, J., Korolova, A., Bai, X., Wang, X., Wang, X.: Privacy loss in Apple's implementation of differential privacy on macOS 10.12. arXiv preprint arXiv:1709.02753 (2017)
48. Texas Instruments: INA219 data sheet, product information and support (2021). https://www.ti.com/product/INA219
49. Wang, G., Wang, B., Wang, T., Nika, A., Zheng, H., Zhao, B.Y.: Ghost riders: Sybil attacks on crowdsourced mobile mapping services. IEEE/ACM Trans. Network. **26**(3), 1123–1136 (2018). https://doi.org/10.1109/TNET.2018.2818073
50. Wang, X., Jiang, J., Zhao, S., Bai, L.: A fair blind signature scheme to revoke malicious vehicles in VANETs. Comput. Mater. Continua **58**(1), 249–262 (2019). https://doi.org/10.32604/cmc.2019.04088
51. Zang, H., Bolot, J.: Anonymization of location data does not work: a large-scale measurement study. In: Proceedings of the 17th Annual International Conference on Mobile Computing and Networking, pp. 145–156 (2011). https://doi.org/10.1145/2030613.2030630

Blockchain and Payment Systems

Analyzing Price Deviations in DeFi Oracles

Ankit Gangwal[1(✉)], Rahul Valluri[1], and Mauro Conti[2]

[1] International Institute of Information Technology, Hyderabad, India
gangwal@iiit.ac.in, rahul.valluri@students.iiit.ac.in
[2] University of Padua, Padua, Italy
mauro.conti@unipd.it

Abstract. Decentralized Finance (DeFi) promises to transform the traditional financial systems into fair and transparent protocols that do not require trusted third parties. To circumvent the high volatility of crypto-assets, DeFi protocols advocate collateralizing their assets against conventional financial instruments. To do so, these protocols require access to external or off-chain data, such as asset exchange rates. DeFi protocols rely on oracles to access such information. Importing external data onto the chain via oracles consists of multiple data processing and aggregation stages. Thus, it is critical to minimize errors or deviations while the ground truth data moves through these stages. In this paper, we investigate the degree of price deviations at different levels between the data source and the final output rendered to an on-chain requester. In particular, we focus on Chainlink's oracle network for ETH-USD pricing. Our results show that despite checks and balances, the output rendered to the requester considerably deviates from data reported by the sources.

Keywords: Blockchain · DeFi · Oracle · Price deviations

1 Introduction

Blockchain-based systems, e.g., cryptocurrencies, eliminate the need for trusted intermediaries in transactions and make financial tools universally accessible. Decentralized Finance (DeFi) aims to further extend the concept of open financial systems. DeFi brings traditional as well as novel financial tools to the blockchain via smart contracts. By using blockchain as a building block, DeFi naturally inherits openness, decentralization, and censorship-resistance properties. Such properties are difficult to incorporate in the design of our traditional financial systems. Furthermore, DeFi advocates for interoperability and modular (Lego-like) design that enables component import from other DeFi products [23].

Like any other blockchain-based system, a DeFi protocol does not have direct access to external or off-chain data. In other words, they can only operate over the data that is already available or fed into the blockchain. Any interactions with the external world would require an intermediary. It is critical for DeFi

A. R. Beresford et al. (Eds.): CANS 2022, LNCS 13641, pp. 329–338, 2022.
https://doi.org/10.1007/978-3-031-20974-1_17

protocols to have near real-time access to market prices of both crypto and non-crypto assets. It is so because these assets are used as collateral in DeFi while their value is ever-changing or even volatile. To get access to real-world information, DeFi uses *oracles* [16]. An oracle is a data reporting infrastructure that acts as a bridge between DeFi and assets' off-chain price sources. With the increasing popularity and adaption of DeFi, the role of oracles is becoming more critical [13]. Nowadays, a wide variety of applications use oracles, e.g., synthetic assets [21], automated market maker [25], derivatives [6], non-fungible tokens [8].

The introduction of third-party data feeders, i.e., oracles, in DeFi is orthogonal to the fundamental concepts of blockchain decentralization. By using the services of an oracle, a DeFi protocol puts trust in a third-party intermediary. However, such a loss of decentralization is inevitable for a DeFi protocol that essentially need off-chain data for executing its core functionalities. This dilemma is known as *the oracle problem* [11]. A poorly managed or maliciously reporting oracle can put investors' funds to risk. Oracle-related vulnerabilities [12,22] have enabled a number of DeFi hacks [20]. A recent study [14] highlights that about two-third of DeFi hacks were results of oracle exploitation. By September 2021, the total value locked in DeFi projects was over 100 billion USD [23]. Therefore, it is important to understand and minimize the risks posed by oracles.

DeFi platforms naturally tend to use multiple oracles to minimize centralization and dependence on a single oracle. Different oracles can have dissimilar frequency of data updates. To further complicate the scenario, prices values reported by different oracles may differ from each other due to their distinct data sources. So, an aggregator node is needed to resolve disputes and aggregate price-values from multiple oracles. Building a price-value reporting infrastructure from scratch can be time consuming. Thus, to speed up the development of their core functionalities, several DeFi platforms choose to use pricing services from other platforms, such as Chainlink[1]. Chainlink is an important player in the DeFi ecosystem that offers a variety of services; price feeding is one such service. Chainlink runs a network of decentralized oracles and renders off-chain price-values to on-chain services. A multitude of DeFi projects, including several leading projects (e.g., Aave, Ampleforth), integrate[2] with Chainlink. As far as the projects with a use case of an oracle are concerned, we found that the majority of top-30 [10] DeFi projects by market capitalization rely on Chainlink.

Motivations: Irrespective of the type (i.e., first-party or third-party), any price-value reporting infrastructure in DeFi involves multiple entities (e.g., data source, oracle, aggregator) between the ground truth and a data requester. Thus, there exist different sources of errors in such a reporting infrastructure. Both over-reported and under-reported data have their own adverse effects. Over-reporting may induce customer churn while under-reporting may lead to platform exploitation. One of the key responsibilities of an aggregator in the infrastructure is to minimize the price deviations before rendering the data to the requester. To this end, an aggregator incorporates different measures (e.g., statistical mean, mode, median, time-weighted average) [13,16]. Hence, it is crucial

[1] https://chain.link/.
[2] https://chainlinkecosystem.com/ecosystem.

to understand the effectiveness of such measures. In this study, we focus on Chainlink's oracle network [7] for ETH-USD [9], which is one of the most common price-value pairs in the DeFi as well as the blockchain ecosystem.

Contributions: The major contributions of this paper are as follows: (1) we empirically evaluate the effectiveness of the aggregator node in the process of minimizing price deviations; (2) we investigate the degree of price deviations at different levels between the ground truth and the final output rendered to a requester; and (3) we make our collected data available[3] in the spirit of reproducible research.

Organization: The remainder of this paper is organized as follows. Section 2 presents a summary of the related works. Section 3 elucidates the price deviation issue in DeFi oracles. Section 4 elaborates our evaluation methodology and assessment of the price deviations in Chainlink's oracle network. Finally, Sect. 5 concludes the paper and outlines the directions for future works.

2 Related Works

In this section, we discuss the state of the art directly related to our work. DeFi platforms execute in the on-chain world, and depending on their target applications, such platforms typically require asset data from the off-chain world (e.g., the Internet). An oracle is the bridge between these two worlds. The work in [11] discusses the oracle problem and explains how an oracle can undermine the decentralization of blockchains. The authors in [2,4,26] survey the existing oracle implementations and define different types of interactions that happen between the on-chain and off-chain elements. The works in [18,19] discuss best practices and common design patterns for oracles. Eskandari et al. [13] further classify the existing oracles using a modular framework. The works in [1,12] propose decentralization of blockchain oracles. Similarly, Breidenbach et al. [7] discuss a multilayered approach for oracle's decentralization. Berger et al. [5] present an architecture for secure oracle usage. Lo et al. [17] present an approach to evaluate the reliability of oracles. Their evaluation approach uses the probability of failure rate to rank an oracle. The work in [3] explores the possibilities of using automated market maker projects, such as Uniswap[4], as price-value feeding oracles. Williams et al. [24] use game theory to understand the conditions for generating incentives over valid oracle queries for both cooperative and non-cooperative participants. Kaleem et al. [15] analyze usage trends, oracle pricing, and service quality associated with ChainLink on the Ethereum network. Liu et al. [16] discuss the technical architectures of mainstream DeFi platforms and investigate the deviations between external market prices and price-values retrieved from commonly used oracles. Different from the state of the art, our work explores the degree of price deviations at different levels between the ground truth and the final values provided to a data requester.

[3] https://github.com/CiaoAnkit/DeFiOraclesPriceDeviations.
[4] https://uniswap.org/.

3 Price Deviations in DeFi Oracles

A typical infrastructure that retrieves data from the off-chain world to the on-chain world involves several active entities, where each type of entity performs a specific set of actions. Figure 1 depicts an overview of retrieving the off-chain ground truth data for an on-chain data requester. While some implementations may combine distinct entities in practice (e.g., sources with feeders), we show each entity type separately. To remain in line with the goals of this study, we refrain from diving into the internal mechanics (for instance, polling frequency, selection mechanism, aggregation techniques) of different entities.

Ground truth is the data that DeFi oracles aim to fetch on-chain. *Data sources* reside closer to the ground truth. Sensors, humans, and APIs are some common types of data sources. These sources measure, congregate, and record a representation of the ground truth. Depending on the configuration, a data source may only be capable of storing the observed data momentarily. *Data feeders* interface with the sources to collect observed data. It is worth mentioning that a data feeder may connect with one or more sources to avoid failures, increase reliability, minimize the impact of a faulty/malicious source, etc. On the other side, data feeders provide their accumulated data to an on-chain *data aggregator.* In fact, data feeders are the bridge between off-chain and on-chain world and thus, are called oracles in the DeFi terminology. An aggregator generally selects and contracts with multiple oracles for a reliable data stream. Next, the aggregator aggregates the data (using statistical measures, majority voting, etc.) from multiple oracles and resolves any dispute before presenting the data to *requester.*

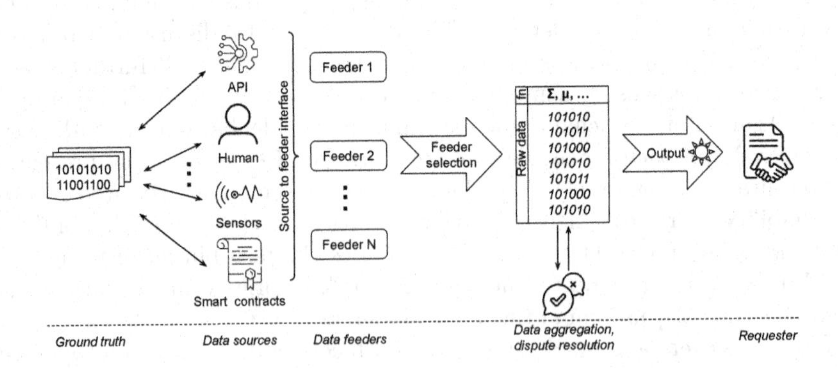

Fig. 1. An abstract view of fetching off-chain data for an on-chain requester.

When the ground truth data is in transit towards the requester, we can observe the data-in-transit at three different spots. The first observable data is reported by the data sources (cf. ① in Fig. 2), the second observable data comes from oracles (cf. ② in Fig. 2), and the third observable data is the final output of the aggregator (cf. ③ in Fig. 2). Ideally, the ground truth data should experience negligible alterations in the transit. However, each data processor (i.e., sources, oracles, and aggregator) processes the data coming from previous stages according to its own logic. More importantly, oracles and aggregators process data coming from multiple sources and multiple oracles, respectively. Consequently, the data-in-transit suffers variations.

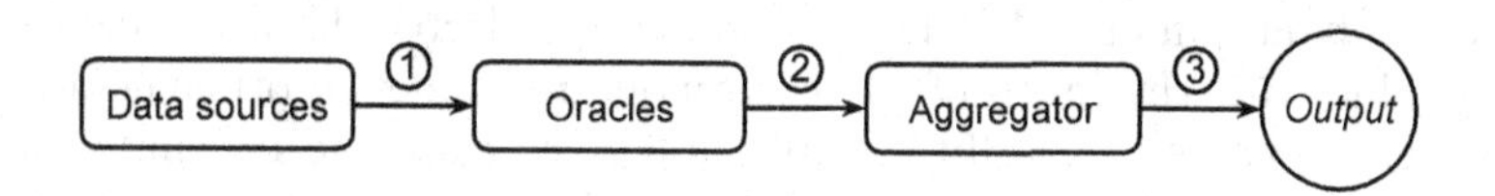

Fig. 2. The typical hierarchy of data reporting stack in DeFi.

Each data processor should intuitively incorporate mechanisms that minimize the price deviations. Nevertheless, it is ultimately the responsibility of an aggregator to choose (many) reliable oracles that use trustworthy data sources. In this paper, we study the price deviations at different stages between the data sources and the output of the aggregator. In particular, we analyze and compare the price-value data reported at stages ①, ②, and ③ indicated in Fig. 2. Furthermore, we want to understand how effective is the aggregator's aggregation of oracle data, i.e., if and by how much the output of the aggregator deviates from the data reported by the sources.

4 Evaluation

In this section, we present our analysis of the price deviations in Chainlink's oracle network. Section 4.1 elaborates our data collection phase. We present our findings from the analysis of the collected data in Sect. 4.2.

4.1 Data Collection

To collect price-value data for our analysis, we first identified the nodes at various levels in Chainlink's oracle network for ETH-USD price feeds. At the time of our study, it consisted[5] of one aggregator node and thirty-one oracle nodes. We also identified the data source nodes used by these oracle nodes. Two (i.e., AmberData[6] and Kaiko[7]) out of the nine data source nodes either required subscription or were not responding consistently. Thus, we continued with AlphaVantage[8], BraveNewCoin[9], CoinCap[10], CoinGecko[11], CoinMarketCap[12], Coin-

[5] https://data.chain.link/ethereum/mainnet/crypto-usd/eth-usd.
[6] https://web3api.io/api/v2/market/prices/eth/latest.
[7] http://us.market-api.kaiko.io/v1/data/trades.v1/spot_direct_exchange_rate/eth/usd.
[8] https://alphavantage.co/query.
[9] http://bravenewcoin.p.rapidapi.com/market-cap.
[10] https://api.coincap.io/v2/rates/ethereum.
[11] https://api.coingecko.com/api/v3/coins/ethereum/market/_chart/range.
[12] https://pro-api.coinmarketcap.com/v2/cryptocurrency/quotes/latest.

Paprika[13], CryptoCompare[14]. The data for the aggregator node and each of the oracle nodes was fetched[15] using a public contract address[16] while the data for source nodes was retrieved via their respective open APIs mentioned above.

We used automated python scripts to collect live data from April 17, 2022, 10:00 AM to May 23, 2022, 07:45 AM. We configured our scripts to execute once every fifteen minutes. While processing the collected data, we replaced any missing value with the mean of the corresponding values of other nodes in the same class. For cases when all the nodes in a given class had missing values, we discarded all the values collected in that round completely. Our final database has a total of 3399 rows of values and 40 columns (i.e., one aggregator node, thirty-one oracle nodes, seven data sources, and one column for timestamps).

4.2 Analysis of Price Deviations

To analyze the price deviations, we process our database of collected values row-by-row. For each row, we compute the average of oracle values (μ^O), maximum of oracle values (max^O), minimum of oracle values (min^O), average of source values (μ^S), maximum of source values (max^S), and minimum of source values (min^S). The aggregator node's values (v^A) are used as-is. Since the oracle nodes depend on the values from source nodes, μ^O should remain between max^S and min^S. Similarly, the aggregator node depends on the values from oracle nodes, v^A should remain between max^O and min^O. However, the true price deviations can be determined by comparing v^A against max^S and min^S. In what follows, we present our findings on the price deviations at different levels.

Figure 3 depicts the instances when μ^O exceeded max^S or fell below min^S. The positive values show μ^O-max^S when μ^O exceeded max^S while the negative values show μ^O-min^S when μ^O fell below min^S. A zero value denotes that μ^O was between max^S and min^S. Our analysis shows that μ^O exceeded max^S or fell below min^S on 35.36% of occasions, and the range of deviations was from –32.15 USD to +9.76 USD per ETH.

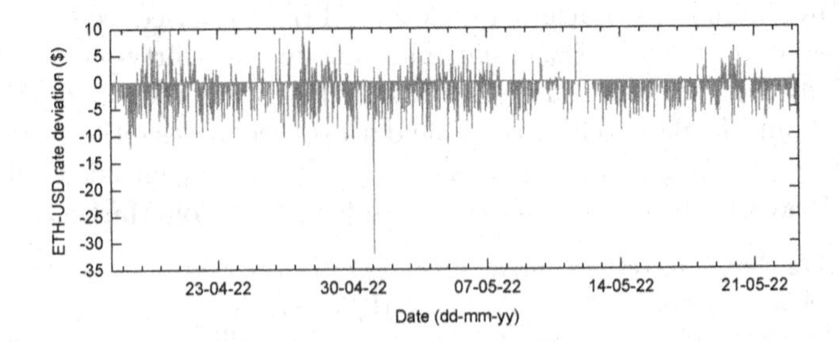

Fig. 3. The instances when μ^O exceeded max^S or fell below min^S. For such cases, positive values show μ^O-max^S while negative values show μ^O-min^S.

[13] https://api.coinpaprika.com/v1/tickers/eth-ethereum.
[14] https://min-api.cryptocompare.com/data/price.
[15] https://api.reputation.link/contract/.
[16] 0x37bc7498f4ff12c19678ee8fe19d713b87f6a9e6.

Next, Fig. 4 shows the instances when v^A exceeded max^O or fell below min^O. The positive values show v^A-max^O when v^A exceeded max^O while the negative values show v^A-min^O when v^A fell below min^O. A zero value denotes that v^A was between max^O and min^O. We find that v^A exceeded max^O or fell below min^O on only 3.09% of occasions. It appears that the aggregator's aggregation mechanism significantly controls the high number of deviations observed in oracles' output against data sources (cf. Fig. 3). However, the range of deviations in v^A further broadened and was from –37.22 USD to +17.36 USD per ETH.

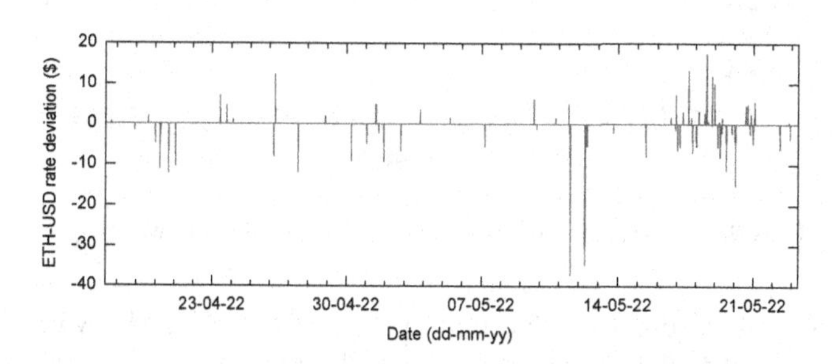

Fig. 4. The instances when v^A exceeded max^O or fell below min^O. For such cases, positive values show v^A-max^O while negative values show v^A-min^O.

To understand the overall impact of the aggregator's aggregation of oracles' output, we compare v^A against max^S and min^S. Figure 5 exhibits the instances when v^A exceeded max^S or fell below min^S. Again, the positive values show v^A-max^S when v^A exceeded max^S while the negative values show v^A-min^S when v^A fell below min^S. A zero value denotes that v^A was between max^S and min^S. Surprisingly, v^A exceeded max^S or fell below min^S on 38.36% of occasions, which is even more than the deviations observed in oracles' output against data sources (cf. Fig. 3). At the same time, the range of deviations was also astonishingly high, i.e., from –75.31 USD to +21.21 USD per ETH.

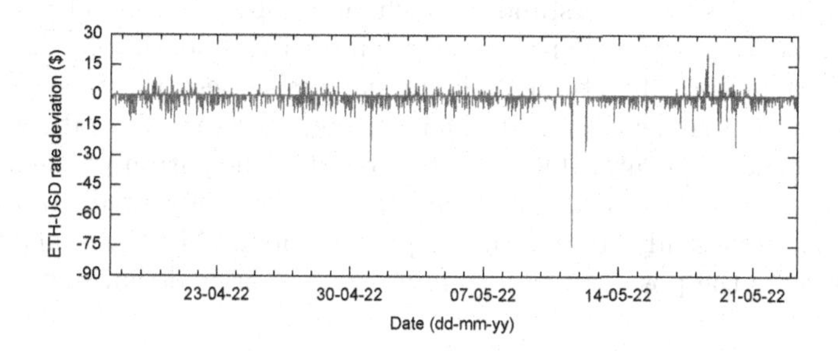

Fig. 5. The instances when v^A exceeded max^S or fell below min^S. For such cases, positive values show v^A-max^S while negative values show v^A-min^S.

As a further analysis, we compare v^A against μ^S. The plot in Fig. 6 illustrates v^A-μ^S. Here, 33.39% of values experienced a deviation of at least ±5 USD per ETH, and about 99% of values deviated within ±20 USD per ETH. Nevertheless, the overall deviation range was from –91.35 USD to +29.12 USD per ETH.

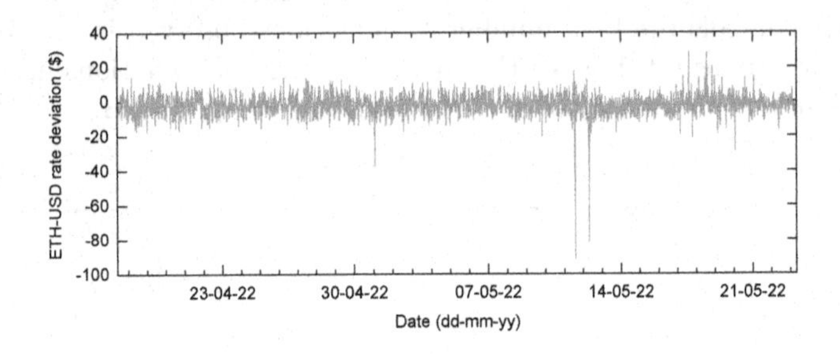

Fig. 6. The deviation of v^A from μ^S, the plot shows v^A-μ^S.

Based on our study, we infer mainly two reasons for the wide deviations between the output of the aggregator and the ground truth data reported by the sources. First, the aggregator is exposed to only oracle nodes. Second, each oracle node may use a distinct set of source nodes. Consequently, even a few faulty/malicious data sources/oracles can significantly affect the aggregator's output. Therefore, the aggregator must select reliable oracles and use robust mechanisms for data aggregation.

5 Conclusion and Future Works

DeFi platforms, like any other blockchain-based system, execute with on-chain data. Any interaction with the off-chain world requires an intermediary. DeFi oracles act as the bridge between these two worlds. However, oracles themselves rely on data sources. Thus, an aggregator is engaged to collect and sanitize data from multiple oracles before rendering it to an on-chain requester. This process of fetching the ground truth data onto the chain can induce variations in data while it is in transit. Understanding such price deviations is crucial because both over-reporting and under-reporting can lead to undesirable situations. In this paper, we empirically studied Chainlink's oracle network. In particular, we investigated the price deviations at different stages between the data sources and the output of the aggregator. Our results show that the output of the aggregator considerably deviates from the data reported by the data sources. In the future, we will extend our study to cover other publicly accessible oracle networks. We will also explore the possibilities to minimize these price deviations.

References

1. Adler, J., Berryhill, R., Veneris, A., Poulos, Z., Veira, N., Kastania, A.: Astraea: a decentralized blockchain oracle. In: IEEE International Conference on iThings, GreenCom, CPSCom, SmartData, pp. 1145–1152 (2018)

2. Al-Breiki, H., Rehman, M.H.U., Salah, K., Svetinovic, D.: Trustworthy blockchain oracles: review, comparison, and open research challenges. IEEE Access **8**, 85675–85685 (2020)
3. Angeris, G., Chitra, T.: Improved price oracles: constant function market makers. In: ACM Conference on Advances in Financial Technologies, pp. 80–91 (2020)
4. Beniiche, A.: A study of blockchain oracles. arXiv preprint:2004.07140 (2020)
5. Berger, B., Huber, S., Pfeifhofer, S.: OraclesLink: an architecture for secure oracle usage. In: IEEE International Conference on Blockchain Computing and Applications, pp. 66–72 (2020)
6. Biryukov, A., Khovratovich, D., Tikhomirov, S.: Findel: secure derivative contracts for ethereum. In: International Conference on Financial Cryptography and Data Security, pp. 453–467 (2017)
7. Breidenbach, L., et al.: Chainlink 2.0: next steps in the evolution of decentralized oracle networks. White Paper, pp. 1–136 (2021)
8. Chainlink: 16 Ways to Create Dynamic Non-Fungible Tokens (NFT) Using Chainlink Oracles (2020). https://blog.chain.link/create-dynamic-nfts-using-chainlink-oracles/
9. Chainlink: ETH-USD data feeds (2022). https://data.chain.link/ethereum/mainnet/crypto-usd/eth-usd
10. CoinMarketCap: Top DeFi Tokens by Market Capitalization (2022). https://coinmarketcap.com/view/defi/
11. Egberts, A.: The Oracle Problem - An Analysis of How Blockchain Oracles Undermine the Advantages of Decentralized Ledger Systems. Available at SSRN 3382343 (2017)
12. Ellis, S., Juels, A., Nazarov, S.: Chainlink: a decentralized oracle network. White Paper, pp. 1–38 (2017)
13. Eskandari, S., Salehi, M., Gu, W.C., Clark, J.: SoK: oracles from the ground truth to market manipulation. In: 3rd ACM Conference on Advances in Financial Technologies, pp. 127–141 (2021)
14. Finance Magnates: DeFi Startup Acala to Restructure Oracle Network - For the Better (2020). https://www.financemagnates.com/thought-leadership/defi-startup-acala-to-restructure-oracle-network-for-the-better/
15. Kaleem, M., Shi, W.: Demystifying pythia: a survey of chainlink oracles usage on ethereum. In: International Conference on Financial Cryptography and Data Security, pp. 115–123 (2021)
16. Liu, B., Szalachowski, P., Zhou, J.: A first look into DeFi oracles. In: IEEE International Conference on Decentralized Applications and Infrastructures, pp. 39–48 (2021)
17. Lo, S.K., Xu, X., Staples, M., Yao, L.: Reliability analysis for blockchain oracles. Comput. Electr. Eng. **83**, 1–10 (2020)
18. Mühlberger, R., et al.: Foundational oracle patterns: connecting blockchain to the off-chain world. In: International Conference on Business Process Management, pp. 35–51 (2020)
19. Pasdar, A., Dong, Z., Lee, Y.C.: Blockchain Oracle Design Patterns. arXiv preprint:2106.09349 (2021)
20. Peaster, W.M.: Biggest DeFi hacks in 2020 (2021). https://defiprime.com/hacks2020
21. Salehi, M., Clark, J., Mannan, M.: Red-black coins: dai without liquidations. In: International Conference on Financial Cryptography and Data Security, pp. 136–145 (2021)

22. samczsun: So You Want to Use a Price Oracle (2020). https://samczsun.com/so-you-want-to-use-a-price-oracle/
23. Werner, S.M., Perez, D., Gudgeon, L., Klages Mundt, A., Harz, D., Knottenbelt, W.J.: SoK: decentralized finance. arXiv preprint:2101.08778 (2021)
24. Williams, A.K., Peterson, J.: Decentralized common knowledge oracles. arXiv preprint:1912.01215 (2019)
25. Zaugust: CoFiX: A Computable Trading System (2020). https://github.com/Computable-Finance/Doc
26. Zhao, Y., Kang, X., Li, T., Chu, C.K., Wang, H.: Towards trustworthy DeFi oracles: past, present, and future. arXiv preprint:2201.02358 (2022)

Redacting Blockchain Without Exposing Chameleon Hash Collisions

Thiago Leucz Astrizi(✉) and Ricardo Custódio

Universidade Federal de Santa Catarina (UFSC), Florianópolis, Brazil
thiago.leucz.astrizi@posgrad.ufsc.br, ricardo.custodio@ufsc.br

Abstract. A new implementation of a redactable blockchain is proposed: a construction where trusted authorities can change past blocks without invalidating the blockchain and without needing a hard fork. Like previous works, it uses a chameleon hash function—a special kind of hash function where it is possible to compute collisions efficiently if a trapdoor is known. One problem with most chameleon hash functions is that collision-resistance and security are invalidated or severely weakened if a collision is publicized. It turns out that redacting a blockchain in existing constructions reveals collisions. Previous works dealt with this using public-key encryption schemes and non-interactive zero-knowledge proofs to achieve what is known as Enhanced or Full Collision-Resistance. Here instead, we propose a simpler and hopefully faster construction. We use a subset of chameleon hash schemes where the trapdoor also allows for first-preimage computation. We build a redactable blockchain using this stronger property where redactions do not expose collisions.

Keywords: Redactable blockchain · Chameleon hash · Post-quantum cryptography

1 Introduction and Previous Works

A blockchain is a linked list of signed elements where each block links the previous one using hash pointers. They can act as a mirrored database where some protocol is used to achieve consensus over its content. The application that popularized this concept was Bitcoin, a digital currency designed for decentralized operation proposed by Satoshi Nakamoto in [20].

The blockchains used in most digital currencies are usually immutable. Once something is registered in the blockchain, it can be removed only using hard forks: changes in the blockchain protocol and software where participants could agree to ignore and remove some undesirable blocks. Doing so invalidates transactions after the removed block and, therefore, is an inviable option when needing to change or remove an old block.

However, a blockchain can be attacked by malicious users who insert illegal content into the blocks. This is not just a hypothetical scenario. This type of attack can be spotted in the wild as malware and child abuse images are stored

A. R. Beresford et al. (Eds.): CANS 2022, LNCS 13641, pp. 339–358, 2022.
https://doi.org/10.1007/978-3-031-20974-1_18

on the Bitcoin blockchain [3]. This can pose legal problems and discourage users from storing local copies of the blockchain. Thus, blockchain immutability, in some contexts, may be undesirable.

A mutable blockchain could provide defenses against such attacks and some additional advantages, like allowing old blocks to be compressed or merged, making the chain smaller. However, such changes should be sporadic and only in exceptional circumstances, following precise rules. Otherwise, this could damage the trust in the chain.

The first paper that proposed a redactable blockchain was [3]. The idea was to use a chameleon hash instead of a usual hash function as part of the hash pointer. Chameleon hash functions were described first at [16]. They are hash functions with a trapdoor that allows a person to compute second-preimages. Manipulating a randomness parameter with the help of the trapdoor, any two messages could be set to collide. However, without the knowledge of the trapdoor, the function behaves exactly like a usual collision-resistant hash function.

However, a redactable blockchain built with a chameleon hash presents some challenges. Most chameleon hash constructions are collision-resistant only if an adversary cannot obtain sample collisions. When a collision is revealed, it could be possible to compute new collisions or even extract the secret trapdoor. The problem is that a naive construction of a redactable blockchain would always reveal a sample collision after each redaction.

To address this challenge, Ateniese proposed two solutions in [3]. First, one could use a chameleon hash from [5] that, under some assumptions, would not have the security compromised by leaked collisions. However, that construction had security proof in the non-standard generic group model and is based on the discrete logarithm assumption, which would not be safe against quantum attackers.

The second solution proposed was using a new primitive called "secret-coin chameleon hash". Such a primitive was built by combining a classical chameleon hash with a public-key encryption scheme (PKE) and a non-interactive zero-knowledge proof (NIZK). In [10], a secret-coin chameleon hash scheme was built directly from a PKE and NIZK scheme without needing another intermediate chameleon hash. This solution is more general than the first solution, but the public-key encryption scheme and zero-knowledge proofs add overhead and usually increase the number of required assumptions.

Other previous solutions for this problem outside the scope of blockchains are the identity-based chameleon hash [5] and labeled chameleon hash [9]. They are alternative constructions that retain security even after collisions are leaked. However, such solutions are less adequate in blockchains, where usually it is not desirable to depend on some central authority to manage user identities and enforce the uniqueness of labels.

Finally, there are also proposals to construct redactable blockchains using primitives other than chameleon hash functions. According to [22], besides redactable blockchains based on chameleon hash functions, we also have:

Consensus-Based Mechanisms: When changes in the blockchain are made following some protocol where some participants can vote and decide how eventual redactions are performed. This mechanism is decentralized and, because of this, cannot use a typical chameleon hash function;

Meta-Transaction-Based Redaction Mechanisms: These mechanisms act on transactions, not on entire blocks. Each transaction can have more than one possible version, but only one of the versions is active at a given time. Special meta-transactions are sent to the chain to add new versions and change the active version of a given transaction. Inactive blocks can be permanently removed or encrypted if one needs to hide them. Their original hash is preserved to ensure that the blockchain can be correctly verified even after redaction;

Pruning-Based Redaction Mechanisms: This method is used on specific blockchains where the entire transaction history is not expected to be permanently stored. Old blocks can be expired and replaced by new blocks containing a snapshot with all information from expired blocks that are still relevant.

The different redaction techniques can also be divided between those that redact entire blocks of the blockchain and those that redact only specific transactions inside the blocks.

Our Proposal. In this article, a new construction for redactable blockchains is proposed based on the chameleon hash function and focused on redacting entire blocks.

Like in the first solution from [3], we use a simple chameleon hash without needing more complex cryptographic primitives. However, while that construction can be seen as a blockchain where a chameleon hash replaces the hash function, we replace the hash function with the composition of a chameleon hash and a hash function. A non-redacted block is chained as expected in typical blockchains, while a redacted block is chained using only the chameleon hash, ignoring the hash function. Allowing two kinds of chaining, we can both identify and distinguish redacted blocks, forbidding secret redactions, and we also can prevent the leaking of collisions in the chameleon hash.

This is done using a special property present in some specific chameleon hash functions, where the trapdoor allows for first-preimage computation, not only for second-preimage computations.

When comparing our work with works like [11] that use consensus-based redacting, our proposal is more difficult to adapt to previously existing blockchains as we need to use it from the beginning of the chain. We also require a trusted central authority to perform redactions. However, we can allow virtually instantaneous and accurate redacting without needing the miners' vote. This could make our scheme more attractive for private blockchains, where we have a degree of centralization anyway, and in scenarios where we want to ensure that those court rulings to remove inappropriate content can be met.

The redactions in our proposal are not meant to change meaningfully the data stored in the blockchain (e.g., undoing monetary transactions in a cryptocurrency) because we do not assume that the changes will necessarily be enforced in all copies of the blockchain. Instead, they are meant to be used in scenarios like compressing old blocks to save space without changing the stored data, or erasing illegal content inserted in the comments inside smart contracts. In such cases, if a bad-behaved user ignores the redaction, it would still agree with other users about the blockchain state.

This work is organized as follows. Section 2 introduces the cryptographic primitives we use in this work. We also present the fundamentals of the bitcoin backbone protocol and existing proposals on how to create redactable blockchains using chameleon hash functions. Section 3 presents our new reducible blockchain construct using chameleon hash functions and compares it to previous constructs. Section 4 discusses the security requirements for the chameleon hash in our proposed editable blockchain. Section 5 describes some existing chameleon hash functions compatible with our reducible blockchain construction. Section 6 presents data about the performance of our build. We also compared the times for other editable blockchains in the literature and a regular non-editable blockchain. Finally, Sect. 7 presents the conclusion summarizing the results and contribution of the article.

2 Preliminaries

2.1 Classical Chameleon Hash Scheme

A classical chameleon hash scheme CH is a tuple of three efficient algorithms (CH.*KeyGen*, CH.*Hash*, CH.*Collision*) defined over three sets: M (the message space), R (the randomness space) and D (digest space). We define the three algorithms as:

- CH.$KeyGen(1^\lambda) \rightarrow (ek, tk)$: Given an input a security parameter 1^λ and outputs a pair of keys: an evaluation key (ek) and trapdoor key (tk);
- CH.$Hash(ek, msg, rnd) \rightarrow dgt$: Given an evaluation key ek, some message $msg \in M$ and a randomness $rnd \in R$, this algorithm returns a $dgt \in D$;
- CH.$Collision(tk, msg, rnd, msg') \rightarrow rnd'$: Given a trapdoor key tk, a message $msg \in M$, a randomness $rnd \in R$ and a second message $msg' \in M$, this algorithm returns a $rnd' \in R$ such that CH.$Hash(ek, msg, rnd)$ = CH.$Hash(ek, msg', rnd')$.

Note that CH.*Collision* computes an arbitrary second-preimage. There is no consensus on how to name this algorithm in the literature. Some authors use the name "*Forge*" [4] because it allows for creating forgeries in signatures using the primitive. Others call it "*Coll*" [7] as the abbreviation of "collision" and some others use H^{-1} [19] meaning that it is the inverse of the hash function H. Here the name "*Coll*" was preferred, but it is used in the non-abbreviated form.

A secure chameleon hash should be collision-resistant, which means that given an evaluation key ek, no adversary should be able to find different inputs for CH.$Hash(ek, \cdot, \cdot)$ that produces the same output. More formally, the collision-resistance means that for all adversaries $\mathcal{A}$, we have this upper bound involving the probability of $\mathcal{A}$ finding a collision following the rules described below:

$$\begin{aligned}
Pr[(ek, tk) \xleftarrow{\$} \text{CH}.KeyGen(1^\lambda);\\
&(msg_1, rnd_1, msg_2, rnd_2) \xleftarrow{\$} \mathcal{A}(1^\lambda, ek):\\
&(msg_1, rnd_1) \neq (msg_2, rnd_2) \text{ and}\\
&\text{CH}.Hash(ek, msg_1, rnd_1) = \text{CH}.Hash(ek, msg_2, rnd_2)] < negl(\lambda),
\end{aligned}$$

where $negl(\lambda)$ denotes some negligible function and λ is the security parameter.

By definition above, the collision-resistance is achieved if no adversary is able to find a collision, except with negligible probability. It models the security in a scenario where $\mathcal{A}$ is not given access to sample collisions. The only information given to it is the security parameter and the evaluation key ek. This security definition is insufficient if we want to use chameleon hash functions in scenarios where sample collisions may be leaked. However, still, we want that no adversary could find new collisions other than the leaked ones.

A stronger version of collision-resistance is the **full collision-resistance**. It requires that an adversary cannot find new collisions in the chameleon hash even if it has access to an oracle that shows him the result of CH.$Collision(tk, \cdot, \cdot, \cdot)$. More formally, this property requires the following upper bound for the probability of $\mathcal{A}$ finding a collision given the new rules below:

$$\begin{aligned}
Pr[(ek, tk) \xleftarrow{\$} \text{CH}.KeyGen(1^\lambda);\\
&(msg_1, rnd_1, msg_2, rnd_2) \xleftarrow{\$} \mathcal{A}^{CH.Collision(tk,\cdot,\cdot,\cdot)}(1^\lambda, ek):\\
&(msg_1, rnd_1) \neq (msg_2, rnd_2) \text{ and}\\
&\text{CH}.Hash(ek, msg_1, rnd_2) = \text{CH}.Hash(ek, msg_2, rnd_2)\\
&\text{and the pair } (msg_2, rnd_2) \text{ was not sent or computed by a query.}] < negl(\lambda),
\end{aligned}$$

where $negl(\lambda)$ denotes some negligible function and λ is the security parameter.

The difference between the above definition and the previous one is that now the adversary can run the $CH.Collision$ algorithm, even without knowing the trapdoor. Therefore, it can compute a polynomial number of sample collisions. However, now we challenge it to find a collision where at least one of the inputs was not obtained running that algorithm.

2.2 Secret-Coin Chameleon-Hash

A secret-coin chameleon hash scheme SCH is a tuple of efficient algorithms (SCH.$KeyGen$, SCH.$Hash$, SCH.$Verify$, SCH.$Collision$) defined over two sets: M (the message space) and D (digest space). We define the four algorithms as:

- SCH.$KeyGen(1^\lambda) \rightarrow (ek, tk)$: On input a security parameter from $\mathbb{N}$, this algorithm outputs an evaluation key ek and a trapdoor key tk;

- SCH.$Hash(ek, msg) \rightarrow (dgt, str)$: Given a evaluation key ek and a message $msg \in M$, this algorithm outputs a digest $dgt \in D$ and a verification string str;
- SCH.$Verify(ek, msg, dgt, str) \rightarrow b$: Given an evaluation key ek, a message $msg \in M$, a digest $dgt \in D$ and a verification string str, this algorithm outputs the $b = 1$ if dgt is a legitimate digest for msg or outputs $b = 0$ otherwise;
- SCH.$Collision(tk, msg_1, dgt, str_1, msg_2) \rightarrow str_2$: Given a trapdoor key tk, messages $msg_1, msg_2 \in M$, a digest $dgt \in D$ and a verification string str_1 this algorithm outputs a second verification string str_2 such that

$$\text{SCH}.Verify(ek, msg_1, dgt, str_1) = 1 \Longrightarrow \text{SCH}.Verify(ek, msg_2, dgt, str_2) = 1.$$

The full collision-resistance for secret-coin chameleon hash also assumes that no adversary is able to find new collisions, except with negligible probability, even if given access to an oracle that provides sample collisions. More formally, the full collision-resistance for secret-coin chameleon hash requires the following upper bound for the probability of any adversary $\mathcal{A}$ finding a collision:

$$\begin{aligned}
&Pr[(ek, tk) \xleftarrow{\$} \text{SCH}.KeyGen(1^\lambda);\\
&\quad (msg_1, dgt, str_1, msg_2, str_2) \xleftarrow{\$} \mathcal{A}^{\text{SCH}.Collision(tk,\cdot,\cdot,\cdot,\cdot)}(1^\lambda, ek):\\
&\quad msg_1 \neq msg_2 \text{ and } \text{SCH}.Verify(ek, msg_1, dgt, str_1) = 1 \text{ and}\\
&\quad \text{SCH}.Verify(ek, msg_2, dgt, str_2) = 1 \text{ and}\\
&\quad (msg_2, dgt) \text{ never was sent in a collision query.}] < negl(\lambda),
\end{aligned}$$

where $negl(\lambda)$ denotes some negligible function and λ is the security parameter.

2.3 Basics on Bitcoin Backbone Protocol

We present here a basic notation to describe a blockchain using the model from [14] that describes the Bitcoin backbone protocol.

The blockchain is described with the help of two hash functions H and G. Both are modeled as random oracles. Each query to the oracle representing H must pass two values: a counter and the data to be hashed. In each round, the parties that participate in the protocol must initialize their counters to zero and increment it after each new query to H. A maximum of q queries is allowed for each party in each round. The query limit is only for new queries: verifying previously computed hashes (even when initially computed by other parties) does not require the counter to be incremented. Therefore, it is not subject to the limit q. This is required to model a limit to the number of hash queries when mining new blocks.

A block is a triple $B = (s, x, ctr)$. The element s is taken from the set of possible digests for the hash function H. The element $x \in \{0,1\}^*$ is the block content. And $ctr \in \mathbb{N}$ is the counter value for H.

We say that a block is valid if:

$$\mathbf{validblock}_q^d(B) := (H(ctr, G(s, x)) < d) \wedge (ctr < q) = 1$$

The value d models how difficult the puzzle is to be solved as proof of work and is updated after each round. The value q models the expected time for mining a block.

A list of blocks is a blockchain:

$$C = ((s_0, x_0, ctr_0), (s_1, x_1, ctr_1), \ldots)$$

The last block of a blockchain is its head, denoted by $Head(C)$. Any blockchain C with a head (s, x, ctr) can be extended to a longer chain $C' := C||B'$ appending a new valid block $B' = (s', x', ctr')$ such that $s' = H(ctr, G(s, x))$. A blockchain is valid if, for all blocks except the first one, we have that $s_i = H(ctr_{i-1}, G(s_{i-1}, x_{i-1}))$.

2.4 Ateniese's Redactable Blockchain

Here we describe the changes in the Bitcoin backbone protocol made by Ateniese in [3] to create a simple redactable blockchain using a classical chameleon hash.

Ateniese's blockchain uses the same hash function H, but replaces the hash function G with a classical chameleon hash CH.$Hash$. A trusted party with authority to redact the blockchain knows the trapdoor key tk. The evaluation key ek is public.

A block is a tuple $B = (s, x, ctr, rnd)$, where rnd is an element from the chameleon hash randomness space in the case of a classical chameleon hash.

A block is valid if:

$$\textbf{validblock}_q^d(B) := (H(ctr, \text{CH}.Hash(ek, (s, x), rnd)) < d) \wedge (ctr < q) = 1$$

It is possible to extend a chain C with $Head(c) = (s, x, ctr, rnd)$ attaching a valid block $B' = (s', x', ctr', rnd')$ such that $s' = H(ctr, \text{CH}.Hash(ek, (s, x), rnd))$.

The party who knows the chameleon hash trapdoor tk can redact a block finding a collision in the chameleon hash. Both s and x can be redacted, keeping the block and the blockchain valid. This construction can be further customized. We could let only x be redacted, replacing the hash computation by $H(ctr, s, \text{CH}.Hash(ek, x, rnd))$. We could separate redactable and non-redactable parts in a block with the same idea. The chameleon hash processes the redactable parts, and the non-redactable part is processed just by H.

Each time a redaction is required, the trusted party who knows the chameleon hash trapdoor, after computing the collision, must broadcast a message requiring all the clients to update and redact a given block or sequence of blocks. Not necessarily all clients will comply with the redaction. Some of them could still store old versions of the blocks in their copies of the blockchain. However, the possibility of redaction allows well-behaved users to comply with the law when illegal content is detected in the block and is redacted by the trusted party.

Notice that when this is done, a sample collision is always revealed. This limits the usage of this simple construction to a single chameleon hash construction from [5] that can be proven to remain secure even if collisions are leaked.

However, that construction has some drawbacks. First, it is not safe against post-quantum adversaries as it bases its security on discrete logarithms. Second, it uses a non-standard model in its security proof, considering only generic attacks to the discrete logarithm problem.

Existing solutions for these problems usually involve replacing the classical chameleon hash with a secret-coin chameleon hash. Then, instead of storing the randomness rnd with each block, we store the pair (dgt, str) composed of the chameleon hash digest and verification string. After this, the protocol can be easily adapted to support this type of chameleon hash.

Ateniese's proposed the first secret-coin chameleon hash to solve this problem in [3], but the security assumptions did not guarantee that attackers could not produce further changes in blocks that were already redacted. The first secret-coin chameleon hash with this guarantee, achieving full collision-resistance, was proposed in [10].

While dealing successfully with the problems of classical chameleon hash functions, using a secret-coin chameleon hash has the disadvantage of being more complex and requiring more cryptographic assumptions. They usually require the usage of public-key encryption schemes and non-interactive zero-knowledge proofs.

3 Redacted Blockchain Based on Preimage Chameleon Hash Functions

Our suggestion to propose an alternative construction to redactable blockchains involves using chameleon hash functions where knowing the trapdoor key tk allows us to compute first preimages, not only second-preimages. Following the naming from [1], we call them "preimage chameleon hash functions".

We can model these more powerful chameleon hash schemes by extending its definition with the following additional algorithm:

- $\text{CH}.Preimage(tk, msg, dgt) \rightarrow rnd.$
  Given the trapdoor tk, some message msg and a digest dgt, this algorithm returns some randomness rnd such that $\text{CH}.Hash(ek, msg, rnd) = dgt.$

We will also require an additional property called **strong uniformity** for these chameleon hash schemes. This property means that there is a distribution $\mathcal{D}_r$ from which we can pick $rnd \in R$ such that for all pair of keys (ek, tk) and for all $msg \in M$, no adversary can distinguish between $(rnd, \text{CH}.Hash(ek, msg, rnd))$ when rnd is chosen from distribution $\mathcal{D}_r$ and $(\text{CH}.Preimage(tk, msg, dgt), dgt)$, when dgt is chosen uniformly at random from digest space D.

A non-redacted block now is a tuple (s, x, ctr, rnd). The elements s, x, and ctr are the same used in a regular blockchain. The element rnd is a chameleon hash randomness, like in Ateniese's redactable blockchain.

Redacted blocks will be different and distinguishable from non-redacted blocks. A redacted block is a tuple $(s', x', ctr, rnd', dgt, rnd)$. The two randomness values rnd' and rnd represent the new randomness, respectively, in the redacted block and the old randomness before the block was redacted. The new value *dgt* represents the old chameleon hash digest in the block before the redaction. These additional elements will ensure that even after redaction, we still could check the validity of the blocks.

A non-redacted block $B = (s, x, ctr, rnd)$ is valid if:

$$\textbf{validblock}_q^d(B) := (H(ctr, rnd, \text{CH}.Hash(ek, (s, x), rnd)) < d) \wedge (ctr < q) = 1$$

A redacted block $B' = (s', x', ctr, rnd', dgt, rnd)$ is valid if:

$$\textbf{validblock}_q^d(B') := (H(ctr, rnd, dgt) < d) \wedge (ctr < q) = 1$$

The rules to append a new non-redacted block in the blockchain are basically the same.

Given a block B=(s, x, ctr, rnd), to create a redacted block B'=(s', x', ctr, rnd', dgt, rnd) to replace it, the party with the trapdoor tk can choose a desired s' and x' and should store in dgt the value $\text{CH}.Hash(ek, (s, x), rnd)$. Next, it should compute the new rnd' with $\text{CH}.Preimage(tk, (s', x'), dgt')$, where $dgt' = H(ctr, t, dgt)$.

This way, a redacted block is chained differently than a non-redacted block. As in a regular blockchain, non-redacted blocks are chained, storing the double computed hash in the next block. Meanwhile, redacted blocks are chained, making the result of a single computed hash match the digest stored in the next block after the block is changed. This can be done because the hash function is a preimage chameleon hash (Figs. 1 and 2).

$$\boxed{(s_0, x_0, ctr_0, rnd_0) \leftarrow (s_1, x_1, ctr_1, rnd_1) \leftarrow (s_2, x_2, ctr_2, rnd_2)}$$

Fig. 1. Before redacting block B_1: The next block is correctly chained when $s_2 = H(ctr_1, rnd_1, CH.Hash(ek, (s_1, x_1), rnd_1))$.

$$\boxed{(s_0, x_0, ctr_0, rnd_0) \leftarrow (s_1', x_1', ctr_1, rnd_1', dgt_1, rnd_1) \leftarrow (s_2, x_2, ctr_2, rnd_2)}$$

Fig. 2. After redacting block B_1: The next block is correctly chained when $s_2 = \text{CH}.Hash(ek, (s_1', x_1'), rnd_1')$. The old values (dgt_1, rnd_1) are still stored in B_1 to allow users to compute the function $\textbf{validblock}_q^d$.

To make a redaction, the authorized party broadcasts the new redacted block to all clients and asks them to change their copy in the blockchain. A proposed redaction should be rejected if the redacted block is not valid, if the values (ctr, rnd_1) are different in the redacted and non-redacted block, or if the dgt stored in the redacted block is not the same value that was computed before the block was redacted.

A redacted block can easily be identified by the different format and also because it is chained differently. This blockchain construction forbids secret changes in the blockchain: all redactions leave a "scar" in the chain. This is done to increase the trust in the blockchain and prevent that redactions are misused. This is also why we use the chameleon hash randomness as input for H when checking the block validity. This ensures that the party with a trapdoor cannot make invisible redactions computing collisions instead of preimages.

4 Security Discussion

The different chaining in redacted and non-redacted blocks prevents redactions from leaking sample collisions for the chameleon hash, provided that we redact each block with the same key at most once. In this case, a collision would be leaked by a redaction only if one could produce and store in the blockchain values (x, rnd) such that:

$$H(ctr, t, rnd, \mathrm{CH}.Hash(ek, (s, x), rnd)) = \mathrm{CH}.Hash(ek, (s, x), rnd)$$

In the Bitcoin backbone protocol, H is modeled as a random oracle, and therefore, computing this is as hard as performing a preimage attack against the chameleon hash. Likewise, finding a collision during normal usage, without using the trapdoor is guaranteed to be infeasible, provided that the chameleon hash has weak collision-resistance.

However, if a block is redacted twice with the same key, a collision is leaked, and our construction is not secure anymore. To prevent this, the central authority that is authorized to make redactions should publish a list of trusted keys for the chameleon hash. If it needs to redact twice a block, it could generate a new pair of keys and append the new evaluation key to the list of trusted keys. This also requires dealing with the possible revocation of keys, a problem that we leave to further work.

It can be argued that while we do not reveal collisions, we reveal preimages after each redaction. Thanks to the chameleon hash's weak collision resistance, the input for H in each block is always distinct, except with negligible probability. Therefore, when considering H as a random oracle, the information revealed by each redaction is always a random digest whose distribution is indistinguishable from the uniform and its respective preimage composed by a specific message (the redacted block) and its randomness rnd.

To ensure that the chameleon hash is secure under this circumstance, we can define a new kind of collision-resistance where we give the adversary access to an oracle that, given any message msg_i chosen by the adversary, returns a digest dgt chosen uniformly at random and the output for $\mathrm{CH}.Preimage(tk, msg_i, dgt)$.

The following theorem shows that all chameleon hash schemes with weak collision-resistance and strong uniformity property keep their collision-resistance even in this scenario where the adversary can communicate with such an oracle.

Theorem 1. *No efficient adversary can find collisions (except with negligible probability) in a chameleon hash with weak collision-resistance and strong uniformity, even if given access to an oracle that outputs* $\mathrm{CH}.Preimage(tk, msg_i, dgt_i)$ *for a random digest* dgt_i *chosen uniformly at random and a message* msg_i *chosen by the adversary.*

Proof. Let's prove by contradiction, assuming that CH is collision-resistant and has strong uniformity, but assuming that we have an efficient adversary $\mathcal{A}$ that, given access to such oracle, can find a collision in CH.

We can then build a new adversary $\mathcal{B}$ that is initialized with an evaluation key ek and then tries to find a collision in CH.

Adversary $\mathcal{B}$ works initializing adversary $\mathcal{A}$ with ek and then waiting for its queries for the oracle.

For each query msg_i, adversary $\mathcal{B}$ chooses a random rnd_i using the standard distribution from CH defined by the strong uniformity property. Then, it computes $dgt_i = \text{CH}.Hash(ek, msg_i, rnd_i)$ and send as response for the query the pair (rnd_i, dgt_i). Note that by the strong uniformity property, the digest dgt_i is indistinguishable from a digest chosen uniformly at random and rnd_i is indistinguishable from a value produced by CH.*Preimage*.

After making a polynomial number of queries, adversary $\mathcal{A}$ outputs a possible collision. Adversary $\mathcal{B}$ outputs the same values and halts.

Note that if $\mathcal{A}$ succeeds with a non-negligible probability of finding a collision, then adversary $\mathcal{B}$ also succeeds with the same probability. Moreover, this contradicts the weak collision-resistance assumption. □

Also, notice that the digest for H and for the chameleon hash CH have the same number of bits. In practice, digests for chameleon hash functions are much larger than digests for SHA256. Therefore, to use our construction, we usually need to use a hash function that allows us to adapt the digest size, like SHAKE256. Depending on the particular hash function and chameleon hash, a conversion function also could be needed to allow us to compare both values.

5 Instantiating Preimage Chameleon Hash Functions

Here we present different constructions of chameleon hash functions from the literature that are compatible with our proposed construction.

5.1 Classical Construction Based on Factoring and Modular Square Root

We will describe here the chameleon hash proposed at Sect. 4.5 from [6]. This chameleon hash is of particular interest because its hash can be computed using only multiplications, and therefore is fast to compute.

The chameleon hash scheme is defined over sets (M, R, D) where $M = \{0, 1\}^k$ and both R and D are the set of quadratic residues modulo n. The value k is a constant. This scheme requires that all hashed messages have the same length. If necessary, this is achieved first by passing the data to a regular hash function like SHA256, and then passing the output to the chameleon hash function. Doing this, we still have a chameleon hash, as the composition of a regular hash function and a chameleon hash function is also a chameleon hash function.

To generate the pair of keys, a user selects a pair of primes (p, q) and set $n = pq$. It also chooses a vector $\mathbf{e}$ with k different prime numbers that are also quadratic residues modulo n. The trapdoor key is $tk = (p, q, \mathbf{e})$. The evaluation key is $ek = (n, \mathbf{e})$.

To compute the chameleon hash, we use the following formula, recalling that the message $\mathbf{m}$ is a binary vector:

$$\text{CH}.Hash(ek, \mathbf{m}, r) = r^2 \cdot \prod_{0 \le i < k} \mathbf{e}[i]^{\mathbf{m}[i]} \pmod n \tag{1}$$

Computing a hash means multiplying at most k different numbers with the square of the randomness r.

Finding the correct $r \in R$ such that any possible message $\mathbf{m} \in M$ results in a target digest $d \in D$ can be done computing:

$$\text{CH}.Preimage(tk, \mathbf{m}, d) = \sqrt{(\prod_{\mathbf{m}[i]=1} \mathbf{e}[i])^{-1} d} \mod n \tag{2}$$

Knowing the trapdoor (p, q) it is possible to compute the modular square root in Eq. 2 using, for example, Tonelli-Shanks algorithm. Computing modular square roots like this is a hard problem, provided that the factoring problem is also hard.

As this chameleon hash produces only quadratic residues as a digest, when adapting it for use in our redactable blockchain, we should accept the blockchain as valid only when the chameleon hash of a redacted block is equal to the square of the value stored in the next block modulo n.

Theorem 2. *The above chameleon hash construction based on multiplication modulo n has weak collision resistance, provided that factoring n is hard.*

Proof. To prove this, first, we show that if we could find collisions in that chameleon hash, we could, with non-negligible probability, find the modular square root of a random integer x modulo n.

To compute this, we first create a vector $\mathbf{e}$ with k primes that are quadratic residues modulo n. We compute them by generating random numbers, squaring them modulo n and then storing the prime results in the vector. By doing this, we will know the modular square root for all primes in $\mathbf{e}$ and we could store them in a separate vector. After this, we randomly choose one of the positions in the vector $\mathbf{e}$ and store x there, overwriting any previous value. This will let us produce a valid evaluation key $ek = (n, \mathbf{e})$.

We pass this evaluation key to the collision-finder and obtain a collision (m, r), (m', r'). If these pairs are a collision, we can obtain an equation in the form below:

$$\mathbf{e}[a_1] \cdot \mathbf{e}[a_2] \ldots \mathbf{e}[a_n] \cdot r^2 \equiv \mathbf{e}[b_1] \cdot \mathbf{e}[b_2] \ldots \mathbf{e}[b_m] \cdot r'^2 \pmod n \tag{3}$$

Depending on the bits of the colliding message, one of the values $\mathbf{e}[i]$ from Eq. 3 could be the value x whose modular square root we want to discover, as we placed it in the evaluation key $\mathbf{e}$.

If, for example, x appears on the left side on Eq. 3, but not on the right side, we can obtain its modular square root solving:

$$\sqrt{x} = \sqrt{\frac{\mathbf{e}[a_1] \cdot \mathbf{e}[a_2] \dots \mathbf{e}[a_n] \cdot r^2}{\mathbf{e}[b_1] \cdot \mathbf{e}[b_2] \dots \mathbf{e}[b_m] \cdot r'^2}} \pmod{n} \quad (4)$$

As we know the square root of all numbers in $\mathbf{e}$ (except x), we can solve the right side of the above equation, and then we obtain the square root of x. The case when x is on the right side, but not the left side of Eq. 3 is analogous.

The probability of having x on one side, but not on the other side of the equation is the probability that m and m' have different bits in the position chosen randomly to store x. If they are part of a valid collision, then necessarily $m \neq m'$. Therefore, in the worst case both messages differ in at least 1 bit. The two messages have k bits. Then the probability that we have x in only one side of the equation is at least $1/k$, provided that our collision-finder found a valid collision.

Given access to an oracle that solves a single modular square root modulo n, it is known that we can factorize n with probability $1/2$. Therefore, being $Adv_{\mathrm{CH}}^{CR}(\lambda)$ the advantage of a given adversary to find a collision in CH, the probability that we will factorize n using this method, and this adversary, represented by Adv_{FACT}, is:

$$Adv_{FACT} \geq \frac{1}{2k} Adv_{\mathrm{CH}}^{CR}(\lambda) \quad (5)$$

Therefore, if we could find collisions in this chameleon hash, then we could factorize n with non-negligible probability, which contradicts our assumption. □

Theorem 3. *The chameleon hash described in this section have strong uniformity.*

Proof. To prove this, it suffices to show that both the set of valid randomness and the set of valid digests have the same number of elements (because they are the same). Therefore, there is a one-to-one correspondence between each possible randomness and possible digest for all messages. If we choose $rnd \in R$ from a uniform distribution, the strong uniformity property is achieved. □

In [6], Bellare noticed that on practice, computing modular square roots modulo composite numbers appears to be a hard problem not only when the numbers are random: it is also unknown how to compute modular square roots for short integers. Therefore, the performance of this construction can be greatly improved if, instead of filling vector $\mathbf{e}$ with random primes, we fill it with short primes that are quadratic residues modulo n at the coast of this stronger assumption.

5.2 Post-Quantum Construction Based on Lattices

Lattice-based chameleon hash functions were first proposed in [8]. The main technique of the construction is using what was presented as "preimage sampleable (trapdoor) functions" (PSF) in [15]. These functions can be implemented in several ways and are denoted by $f_A : X \to Y$, where A is a public parameter that defines the function. The function has the property that, if given a "small" value sampled from a Gaussian distribution (being small usually means being a vector with a small euclidean norm), the output is statistically close to uniform. This property, among others, is required for the security of most constructions using such functions.

The public parameter A usually is generated with a trapdoor T. Using this trapdoor, for any element $y \in Y$, it is possible to sample a preimage $x \in X$ such that $f_A(x) = y$ and that if y was chosen from a uniform distribution, then x is small and produced following a Gaussian distribution. We will denote by SamplePre this algorithm. Computing f_A preimages without the trapdoor must be infeasible.

Let $\mathcal{R}_q = \mathbb{Z}_q[x]/(f(x))$ be a polynomial ring with coefficients modulo q where $f(x)$ is a polynomial with degree n. It is possible to build a preimage sampleable function $f_{\hat{\mathbf{a}}}$ that maps vectors from $\mathcal{R}_q^m$ to $\mathcal{R}_q$ computing the following dot product:

$$f_{\hat{\mathbf{a}}}(\hat{\mathbf{x}}) = \hat{\mathbf{a}} \cdot \hat{\mathbf{x}}, \tag{6}$$

where $\hat{\mathbf{a}}$ is indistinguishable from a vector chosen uniformly at random from $\mathcal{R}_q^m$. Producing a suitable $\hat{\mathbf{a}}$ with a trapdoor can be achieved using the technique from [18] generalized to the ring setting.

The security of this construction can be reduced to the hardness of solving the following problem:

Definition 1. *R-$SIS_{m,q,\beta}$* ***Problem:*** *Given a vector $\hat{\mathbf{a}} \in \mathcal{R}_q^m$ chosen uniformly at random, find $\hat{\mathbf{x}} \in \mathcal{R}_q^m$, such that $\hat{\mathbf{a}} \cdot \hat{\mathbf{x}} = 0$ and such that $||\hat{\mathbf{x}}|| < \beta$.*

Using this ring definition for $f_{\hat{\mathbf{a}}}$, we can build a post-quantum chameleon hash based on the one proposed in [8]. For the key generation, we produce a suitable $\hat{\mathbf{a}}$ indistinguishable from a random vector from $\mathcal{R}_q^m$ and a corresponding trapdoor T. The chameleon hash is computed with the following equation:

$$\text{CH}.Hash(\hat{\mathbf{a}}, msg, \hat{\mathbf{r}}) = H(msg) + \hat{\mathbf{a}} \cdot \hat{\mathbf{r}}, \tag{7}$$

where H is a regular hash function modeled as a random oracle that produces elements from $\mathcal{R}_q$ and $\hat{\mathbf{r}}$ is small and sampled from a discrete Gaussian distribution. To link the security of this construction with the R-$SIS_{m,q,\beta}$ problem, we also require that sampled elements $\hat{\mathbf{r}}$ are sufficiently small, such that if we add four of them, we would still get an element with norm smaller than β with overwhelming probability.

The algorithm to compute the preimage for this chameleon hash can be defined as below:

$$\text{CH}.Preimage(tk, msg, \mathbf{d}) = \text{SamplePre}((\hat{\mathbf{a}}, T), \mathbf{d} - H(msg)) \tag{8}$$

Theorem 4. *The chameleon hash construction presented in Eq. 7 is collision-resistant in the random oracle model, assuming that the R-SIS problem is hard* *for a given set of parameters* (m, q, β) *shared with the chameleon hash construction and that* $f_{\hat{\mathbf{a}}}(\hat{\mathbf{x}}) = \hat{\mathbf{a}} \cdot \hat{\mathbf{x}}$ *is a secure preimage sampleable function.*

Proof. We show how a collision finder for the presented chameleon hash can be used to create an algorithm to solve $R\text{-}SIS_{m,q,\beta}$ with non-negligible probability.

The algorithm simulates the challenger in the following way.

- **Setup:** Our collision-finder algorithm receives the random vector $\hat{\mathbf{a}}$ and the system parameters (m, q, β). The algorithm passes the system parameter to the collision-finder and also the evaluation key $ek = \hat{\mathbf{a}}$.
- **Random Oracle Query:** For each query msg_i, we sample a small vector $\hat{\mathbf{r}}_i$ from a Gaussian distribution in $\mathcal{R}_q$. Next, we compute $f_{\hat{\mathbf{a}}}(\hat{\mathbf{r}}_i) = \hat{\mathbf{a}} \cdot \hat{\mathbf{r}}_i$ and send this as a response to the query. By the properties of the preimage sampleable function, given an adequate standard deviation, the result would be indistinguishable from random and uniform.
- **Output:** Our collision-finder will produce as output $((msg', \hat{\mathbf{r}}'), (msg'', \hat{\mathbf{r}}''))$. Without loss of generality, we will assume that msg' and msg'' were queried in the random oracle query. Therefore, for known values $\hat{\mathbf{r}}_i$ and $\hat{\mathbf{r}}_j$, we have:

$$\hat{\mathbf{a}}\hat{\mathbf{r}}_i + \hat{\mathbf{a}}\hat{\mathbf{r}}' = \hat{\mathbf{a}}\hat{\mathbf{r}}_j + \hat{\mathbf{a}}\hat{\mathbf{r}}'' \tag{9}$$

  And with this equation, we can find a solution to the $R\text{-}SIS$ problem:

$$\hat{\mathbf{a}}(\hat{\mathbf{r}}_i + \hat{\mathbf{r}}' - \hat{\mathbf{r}}_j - \hat{\mathbf{r}}'') = 0 \tag{10}$$

  Therefore, if we successfully could compute collisions, with roughly the same probability, we could obtain a solution to the $R\text{-}SIS$problem.

□

For a construction based on $R\text{-}SIS$ that does not require the random oracle model, see the full version of [12]. Here we opted for this construction because it avoids one additional matrix multiplication and the bitcoin backbone protocol already assumes the random oracle model.

We can also use a construction for a preimage sampleable function that maps $\mathcal{R}_q \times \mathcal{R}_q$ to $\mathcal{R}_q$, which is used by the lattice-based Falcon signature:

$$f_{\mathbf{a}}((\mathbf{x}_0, \mathbf{x}_1)) = \mathbf{x}_0 + \mathbf{a}\mathbf{x}_1, \tag{11}$$

where $\mathbf{a} \in \mathcal{R}_q$.

This preimage sampleable function uses a different technique to obtain $\mathbf{a}$ that requires extra cryptographic assumptions besides the hardness of the $R\text{-}SIS$ problem, namely the NTRU assumption. The first chameleon hash using this function was proposed in Sect. 4.2 from [17]. That chameleon hash equation is:

$$\text{CH}.Hash(ek = (\mathbf{a}, \mathbf{h}), \mathbf{m}, (\mathbf{r}_0, \mathbf{r}_1)) = (\mathbf{r}_0 + \mathbf{a}\mathbf{r}_1) + \mathbf{h}\mathbf{m} \tag{12}$$

, where $\mathbf{h}$ is an element from $\mathcal{R}_q$ chosen uniformly at random, $\mathbf{a}$ is indistinguishable from a randomly chosen element from $\mathcal{R}_q$ and is part of the preimage sampleable function and $\mathbf{m}$ is an element from $\mathcal{R}_q$ with binary coefficients.

Like in the previous scheme, the chameleon hash randomness is processed by the preimage sampleable function and, using the corresponding SamplePre algorithm, it is possible to implement a CH.*Preimage* algorithm.

Theorem 5. *The chameleon hash construction presented in Eq. 12 is collision-resistant, assuming that solving the R-$SIS_{3,q,\beta}$ problem is hard.*

Proof. Here we restate the proof present in [17]. If we had an algorithm that can find collisions in that chameleon hash, we could use it to solve the R-$SIS_{3,q,\beta}$ problem proceeding as below.

Given an instance $(\mathbf{e}_1, \mathbf{e}_2, \mathbf{e}_3)$ of the R-$SIS_{3,q,\beta}$ problem, first we check if one of these polynomials is invertible. This will be true if all its coefficients are different than zero, which will happen with probability $(1 - 1/q)^n$. Let's assume that $\mathbf{e}_1$ is the invertible polynomial chosen.

Next, we produce a valid chameleon hash evaluation key computing $\mathbf{a} = \mathbf{e}_2/\mathbf{e}_1$ and $\mathbf{h} = \mathbf{e}_3/\mathbf{e}_1$. This produces a key $ek = (\mathbf{a}, \mathbf{h})$ with uniform distribution.

We pass this key for our collision-finder, that would return as collision the values $(\mathbf{m}, \mathbf{r}_0, \mathbf{r}_1)$ and $(\mathbf{m}', \mathbf{r}'_0, \mathbf{r}'_1)$. If this is a valid collision, by Eq. 12, we have:

$$(\mathbf{r}_0 - \mathbf{r}'_0) + \mathbf{a}(\mathbf{r}_1 - \mathbf{r}'_1) + \mathbf{h}(\mathbf{m} - \mathbf{m}') = 0 \tag{13}$$

Which, by the way that we produced the keys, is equal:

$$\mathbf{e}_1/\mathbf{e}_1(\mathbf{r}_0 - \mathbf{r}'_0) + \mathbf{e}_2/\mathbf{e}_1(\mathbf{r}_1 - \mathbf{r}'_1) + \mathbf{e}_3/\mathbf{e}_1(\mathbf{m} - \mathbf{m}') = 0 \tag{14}$$

We can rewrite this as $1/\mathbf{e}_1$ multiplied by a sum. As this is a multiplication that results in zero, either $1/\mathbf{e}_1$ or the other multiplicand is zero. As it is impossible for the inverse of a polynomial be zero, this means that the second multiplicand below is zero:

$$\mathbf{e}_1(\mathbf{r}_0 - \mathbf{r}'_0) + \mathbf{e}_2(\mathbf{r}_1 - \mathbf{r}'_1) + \mathbf{e}_3(\mathbf{m} - \mathbf{m}') = 0 \tag{15}$$

Therefore, $(\mathbf{r}_0 - \mathbf{r}'_0, \mathbf{r}_1 - \mathbf{r}'_1, \mathbf{m} - \mathbf{m}')$ is a solution for the R-$SIS_{3,q,\beta}$ problem. □

Theorem 6. *Both post-quantum chameleon hash constructions presented in this Section, based on $f_{\hat{\mathbf{a}}}$ and $f_{\mathbf{a}}$ preimage sampleable functions, have the strong uniformity property.*

Proof. This is ensured by the properties of the preimage sampleable function and the corresponding SamplePre algorithm. Provided that the randomness is chosen following a sufficiently narrow Gaussian distribution, the output of $f_{\hat{\mathbf{a}}}$ or $f_{\mathbf{a}}$ will be statistically close to uniform over its range. In both cases the result is added with another element derived from the message therefore, final result also will be statistically close to uniform. □

6 Experiments

To test the viability and performance of our construction, we implemented it using different preimage chameleon hash schemes known in the literature.

Our tests were run in a Dell notebook with a Quad-Core Intel Core i5-3210M 2.50GHz with 4GB of memory and running Ubuntu 20.04.3. While measuring running time, the tests were performed 1000 times, and the mean was extracted. Given the measured standard deviation, we computed the error margin given an interval of confidence of 95%, assuming a normal distribution. We aimed in all constructions for a security level near to 128 bits. The code used to measure running times and sizes can be checked in [2].

To compare the performance of our construction, first we measured the time needed to perform known blockchain operations from the literature. The first measured value is the time needed to compute the hash for a regular non-redactable blockchain. For this, we generated a random 1MB block and then measured the time to perform the SHA256 function over the random block, and then over the computed digest. The result is given in the first line of Table 1.

Next, we tested the performance of two existing redactable blockchains proposed in the literature. First, we implemented Ateniese's redactable blockchain described in Sect. 2.4 using the chameleon hash described in Sect. 4 from [5] over an elliptic curve group. This construction was chosen because of its simplicity: it is built using a classical chameleon hash instead of requiring the more expensive secret-coin chameleon hash. However, it relies on the non-standard generic group model for its security proof. We used a 384-bit curve to account for the security impact of leaked collisions during redaction.

The second existing construction that we tested was Ateniese's redactable blockchain built using the secret-coin chameleon hash proposed in [10]. That construction was instantiated with the Elgamal signature, as suggested in that article. We choose this construction because it is relatively simple compared with other secret-coin chameleon hash functions. At the same time, it is one of the few that have a security proof for its full collision-resistance.

For these constructions, we measured the hashing time and the redaction time. For the secret-coin chameleon hash construction, we also measured the verification time. To better present the result, we also put between parenthesis how much slower the hashing time is when compared with the hashing of a simple non-redactable blockchain. We also present in bytes the additional data that must be appended to each block of the blockchain in each construction to allow for redactions. The result is presented in Table 1.

Having these previous values for comparison, we then tested our construction using four different preimage chameleon hash functions. The first construction was the one described in Sect. 5.1 based on the Factoring assumption. We aimed to achieve 128 bits of security and choose $k = 256$ and a 2982-bit integer as n to account for the non-tight security proof.

The second preimage chameleon hash was the one described in the same Subsect. 5.1, but having the optimization described in the last paragraph. We used the additional assumption that it is hard to compute the modular square

Table 1. Testing existing constructions proposed in the literature. The confidence interval for the timings is 95%. Time in ms. Size in bytes.

Blockchain type	Hashing time	Verification time	Redaction time	Added data
Regular Non-redactable	3.491 ± 0.023	Equal hashing	-	0
Ateniese's [5]	4.849 ± 0.023 (+38.0%)	Equal hashing	5.488 ± 0.046	64
Ateniese's secret-coin [10]	11.589 ± 0.037 (+232.0%)	10.889 ± 0.019	10.345 ± 0.045	1,272

root of small primes. Other than that, we used exactly the same parameters from the first preimage chameleon hash.

The third preimage chameleon hash was the one described in Subsect. 5.2 in Eq. 7 based solely in the *R-SIS* assumption. We built the chameleon hash using the [21] library and using the same parameters presented in [13] to achieve a security level of about 100 bits.

The last tested implementation was the second construction described in Subsect. 5.2 in Eq. 12, using the *R-SIS* and NTRU assumption. We used the same implementation as [17], with parameters that, according to that article, achieved 114 bits of security against classical attackers and 103 bits of security against quantum attackers.

The results for these tests can be seen in Table 2. We measured the hashing and redaction time and the additional data that need to be stored in each block. Furthermore, as our proposed scheme needs bigger digest sizes, while the other schemes use a SHA256 digest to represent each block, Table 2 also presents the different digest size for each construction. The digest sizes will have the same number of bytes than the chameleon hash digest.

Table 2. Testing our proposed construction with different preimage chameleon hash functions. The confidence interval for the timings is 95%. Time in ms. Size in bytes.

Preimage chameleon hash assumption	Hashing time	Redaction time	Added data	Digest size
Factoring	5.405 ± 0.063 (+54.8%)	16.025 ± 0.031	373	373
Modular Square Root (small primes)	3.964 ± 0.005 (+13.5%)	16.032 ± 0.021	373	373
R-SIS	11.749 ± 0.043 (+236%)	32.208 ± 0.111	128,383	4,191
NTRU and *R-SIS*	4.208 ± 0.036 (+20.5%)	4.514 ± 0.029	8,192	896

It should be noted that in the last two preimage chameleon hash from Table 2, the size of the additional data appended to each block of the blockchain can be reduced if we run a compression algorithm during the hashing. Therefore, there is a possible trade-off between the hashing time and the size of this data.

The results show that our proposed scheme, when combined with the post-quantum chameleon hash from [17] or the classical construction from [6], can create a redactable blockchain with better performance than all other tested proposals. They achieve a performance penalty of respectively just 20.5% and 13.5% when compared with a regular non-redactable blockchain.

By comparison, when using Ateniese's construction with a chameleon hash based on the generic group model from [5], the performance penalty is about 39%. Moreover, our scheme works without needing the generic group model and also can be used with more implementations of chameleon hash functions.

7 Conclusion

This work proposed a new construction of redactable blockchains using chameleon hash functions. The advantage of this construction is that even if redactions are made, it does not reveal sample collisions in the chameleon hash. This opened up the possibility of using different chameleon hash constructs to build redacted blockchains. Since our scheme uses the chameleon hash as a black box and does not require zero-knowledge non-interactive proofs, it is possible to use it with any chameleon hash whose trapdoor allows preimage computations and has the described strong uniformity property.

Noteworthy, using constructs from [17] and [6], it was possible to create a construct with a faster hash time than was possible with previous redactable blockchains. Furthermore, combining our scheme with two different post-quantum constructions of chameleon hash functions allowed it to remain secure even against quantum adversaries.

Acknowledgments. This study was financed in part by the Fundação de Amparo à Pesquisa e Inovação do Estado de Santa Catarina (Fapesc).

References

1. Astrizi, T., Custódio, R., Moura, L.: Post-quantum signature with preimage chameleon hashing. In: XX Simpósio Brasileiro de Segurança da Informação e de Sistemas Computacionais. SBC, Av. Getulio Vargas, 333 (2020)
2. Astrizi, T.L.: Repository with the tests (2022). https://github.com/thiagoharry/blockchain_tests
3. Ateniese, G., Magri, B., Venturi, D., Andrade, E.: Redactable blockchain-or-rewriting history in bitcoin and friends. In: 2017 IEEE European Symposium on Security and Privacy (EuroS&P), pp. 111–126. IEEE (2017)
4. Ateniese, G., de Medeiros, B.: Identity-based chameleon hash and applications. In: Financial Cryptography, LNCS 3110. pp. 164–180. Springer, Berlin, Heidelberg (2004).
5. Ateniese, G., de Medeiros, B.: On the key exposure problem in chameleon hashes. In: International Conference on Security in Communication Networks. pp. 165–179. Springer (2004)

6. Bellare, M., Ristov, T.: A characterization of chameleon hash functions and new, efficient designs. Journal of cryptology 27(4), 799–823 (2014)
7. Blazy, O., Kakvi, S.A., Kiltz, E., Pan, J.: Tightly-secure signatures from chameleon hash functions. In: Public-Key Cryptography - PKC 2015, LNCS 9020. pp. 256–279. Springer, Berlin, Heidelberg (2015).
8. Cash, D., Hofheinz, D., Kiltz, E., Peikert, C.: Bonsai trees, or how to delegate a lattice basis. In: Annual international conference on the theory and applications of cryptographic techniques. pp. 523–552. Springer (2010)
9. Chen, X., Zhang, F., Kim, K.: Chameleon hashing without key exposure. In: International Conference on Information Security. pp. 87–98. Springer (2004)
10. Derler, D., Samelin, K., Slamanig, D.: Bringing order to chaos: the case of collision-resistant chameleon-hashes. In: Public Key Cryptography (1), pp. 462–492 (2020)
11. Deuber, D., Magri, B., Thyagarajan, S.A.K.: Redactable blockchain in the permissionless setting. In: 2019 IEEE Symposium on Security and Privacy (SP), pp. 124–138. IEEE (2019)
12. Ducas, L., Micciancio, D.: Improved short lattice signatures in the standard model. In: Annual Cryptology Conference. pp. 335–352. Springer (2014)
13. El Bansarkhani, R., Buchmann, J.: Improvement and Efficient Implementation of a Lattice-Based Signature Scheme. In: Lange, T., Lauter, K., Lisoněk, P. (eds.) SAC 2013. LNCS, vol. 8282, pp. 48–67. Springer, Heidelberg (2014). https://doi.org/10.1007/978-3-662-43414-7_3
14. Garay, J., Kiayias, A., Leonardos, N.: The bitcoin backbone protocol: Analysis and applications. In: Annual international conference on the theory and applications of cryptographic techniques. pp. 281–310. Springer (2015)
15. Gentry, C., Peikert, C., Vaikuntanathan, V.: Trapdoors for hard lattices and new cryptographic constructions. In: Proceedings of the Fortieth Annual ACM Symposium on Theory of Computing, pp. 197–206 (2008)
16. Krawczyk, H., Rabin, T.: Chameleon hashing and signatures. IACR Cryptol. ePrint Arch. **1998**, 10 (1998)
17. Lu, X., Au, M.H., Zhang, Z.: Raptor: a practical lattice-based (linkable) ring signature. In: International Conference on Applied Cryptography and Network Security. pp. 110–130. Springer (2019)
18. Micciancio, D., Peikert, C.: Trapdoors for lattices: Simpler, tighter, faster, smaller. In: Annual International Conference on the Theory and Applications of Cryptographic Techniques. pp. 700–718. Springer (2012)
19. Mohassel, P.: One-time signatures and chameleon hash functions. In: Selected Areas in Cryptography, LNCS 6544. pp. 302–319. Springer, Berlin, Heidelberg (2011).
20. Nakamoto, S.: Bitcoin: A peer-to-peer electronic cash system. Decentralized Business Review, p. 21260 (2008)
21. Rohloff, K., Cousins, D., Polyakov, Y.: PALISADE Lattice Cryptography Library (release 1.11.7), April 2022. https://palisade-crypto.org/
22. Zhang, D., Le, J., Lei, X., Xiang, T., Liao, X.: Exploring the redaction mechanisms of mutable blockchains: A comprehensive survey. International Journal of Intelligent Systems 36(9), 5051–5084 (2021)

Codes and Post-quantum Cryptography

Efficient Proofs of Retrievability Using Expander Codes

Françoise Levy-dit-Vehel[1] and Maxime Roméas[2](✉)

[1] LIX, ENSTA Paris, INRIA, IPP, 91120 Palaiseau, France
levy@ensta.fr
[2] LIX, École polytechnique, INRIA, IPP, 91120 Palaiseau, France
romeas@lix.polytechnique.fr

Abstract. Proofs of Retrievability (PoR) protocols ensure that a client can fully retrieve a large outsourced file from an untrusted server. Good PoRs should have low communication complexity, small storage overhead and clear security guarantees. We design a good PoR based on a family of graph codes called expander codes. We use expander codes based on graphs derived from point-line incidence relations of finite affine planes. Høholdt *et al.* showed that, when using Reed-Solomon codes as inner codes, these codes have good dimension and minimum distance over a relatively small alphabet. Moreover, expander codes possess very efficient unique decoding algorithms. We take advantage of these results to design a PoR scheme that extracts the outsourced file in quasi-linear time and features better concrete parameters than state-of-the-art schemes w.r.t storage overhead and size of the outsourced file.

Keywords: Proofs of retrievability · Expander codes · Outsourced storage

1 Introduction

1.1 Context and State-of-the-Art

With the continuous increase in data creation, individuals and business entities call upon remote storage providers to outsource their data. This new dependency raises some issues, as storage providers can try to read or modify the client's data. Besides, when a client does not often access his data, service providers can delete it to make room for another client's data. In this context, it appears important to deploy client side protections designed to bring security guarantees like confidentiality and integrity. In this work, we focus on the following problem: given a client who stored a file on a server and erased its local copy, how can he check if he is able to retrieve his file from the server in full? Addressing this issue is the goal of cryptographic protocols called Proofs of Retrievability (PoRs).

The first PoR scheme was proposed in 2007 by Juels and Kaliski [8] and was based on checking the integrity of some sentinel symbols secretly placed by the client before uploading its file. This scheme has low communication but

A. R. Beresford et al. (Eds.): CANS 2022, LNCS 13641, pp. 361–370, 2022.
https://doi.org/10.1007/978-3-031-20974-1_19

its drawback is that it is bounded-use only. Shacham and Waters [15] proposed to correct this drawback by appending some authenticator symbols to the file. Verification consists in checking random linear combinations of file symbols and authenticators. Then comes a few PoR schemes based on codes. Bowers *et al.* [3] proposed a double-layer encoding with the use of an inner code to recover information symbols and an outer code to correct the remaining erasures. Dodis *et al.* [4] formalize the verification process as a request to a code which models the space of possible answers to a challenge. In 2013, Paterson [13] laid the foundation for studying PoR schemes using a coding theoretic framework. Following these ideas, Lavauzelle and Levy-dit-Vehel [9] (2016) used the local structure of the lifted codes introduced by Guo *et al.* [5] to build a PoR scheme, that compares favourably to those presented above w.r.t. storage overhead. In 2022, Levy-dit-Vehel and Roméas [10] proposed a framework for the design of secure and efficient PoR schemes based on Locally Correctable Codes. They also reevaluated the security and the parameters of the [9] PoR scheme.

We design a PoR scheme based on expander codes. In 1996, Sipser and Spielman [16] introduced these codes that are based on expander graphs. Expander codes possess very efficient unique decoding algorithms. We will use an erasure decoding algorithm derived from [16,19] during the extraction phase of our PoR.

The expander codes used for our PoR scheme are based on a family of graphs with excellent expansion. These graphs are derived from point-line incidence relations in the affine plane $\mathbb{F}_q^2$. The expansion of these graphs was studied by Tanner in 1984 [18]. A line of work of Høholdt *et al.* [2,6,7] studied the dimension and minimum distance of expander codes based on the previously mentioned graphs with Reed-Solomon codes as inner code. Finally, we use an audit procedure for generic erasure codes adapted from [8,15] in the Constructive Cryptography (CC) framework of [11] by Badertscher and Maurer [1]. We also prove the security of our PoR scheme using the CC security model for PoRs of [1].

1.2 Contributions

We use an audit procedure from [8,15] translated in the CC framework by Badertscher and Maurer [1] to design a PoR scheme based on expander codes. Recall that an expander code is constructed using a regular expander graph, a so-called inner linear code and, for every vertex v of the graph, an ordering on the edges incident to v. A codeword is a labeling of the edges such that, for every vertex v of the graph, the vector supported by the edges incident to v is a codeword of the inner code. By encoding the client's file with a well-chosen expander code, we manage to design a PoR scheme with storage overhead linear in the size of the outsourced file $|F|$ and communication complexity in $\mathcal{O}(|F|^{1/3} \cdot \log |F| \cdot \sigma)$ for σ bits of statistical security. Furthermore, we give concrete parameters for file sizes ranging from a few MB to hundreds of GB. Our parameters are a lot better than the ones of [9]. When using the same alphabet size and security parameters as other code-based PoRs [8,9,15], our scheme is capable of reaching higher rates and storing larger files. We give parameters and comparisons with other PoRs in Sect. 3.4. We optimize the parameters of our scheme using expander codes based on q-regular graphs derived from point-line incidence relations in finite geometries. The properties of these graphs and of expander codes based on these graphs are studied in [2,6,7,18]. We chose these graphs because they have very good expansion and a good ratio between their regularity q and their number of edges q^3. We show that these two facts when combined permit us to reach lower communication complexity and storage overhead than previous code-based PoRs. Moreover, these graphs exist for every prime power q. By choosing q to be a power of 2 and a Reed-Solomon code of length q as inner code, we can use the erasure decoder for Reed-Solomon codes of [17] with complexity $\mathcal{O}(q \log^2 q)$. Using this decoder along with a fast unique erasure decoding algorithm for expander codes [16,19], we are able to extract the outsourced file in quasi-linear time $\mathcal{O}(q^3 \log^2 q)$ in the input size $Rq^3 \log q$, where $0 < R < 1$ is the rate of the code. For $q = 512$, our PoR stores files of size 124 MB vs 35 MB for the PoR of [9] with storage overhead of 21% vs 319% for [9].

Organization of the Paper. In Sect. 2, we give the required background. In Sect. 3, we describe our audit procedure and we optimize our PoR. Finally, we compare the performance of our PoR against other schemes in Sect. 3.4.

2 Background

2.1 The Constructive Cryptography Model

The CC model, introduced by Maurer [12], aims at asserting the real security of cryptographic primitives. To do so, it redefines them in terms of so-called *resources* and *converters*. Starting from a basic resource (e.g. communication channel, shared key, memory server...), a converter (a cryptographic protocol) aims at constructing an enhanced resource, *i.e.* one with better security guarantees. The starting resource, lacking the desired security guarantees, is often called the *real* resource and the obtained one is often called the *ideal* resource, since it does not exist as is in the real world. An example of ideal resource is a confidential server, where the data stored by a client is readable by this client only. The only information that leaks to other parties is its length. This resource does not exist, but it can be emulated by an insecure server on which the client uses an encryption protocol where the encryption scheme is IND-CPA secure. We say that this *construction* of the confidential server is secure if the real world - namely, the insecure server together with the protocol - is *just as good* as the ideal world - namely, the confidential server. This means that, whatever the adversary can do in the real world, it could as well do in the ideal world.

We recall the constructions of [1,10] that we will use in this work. The first resource is the authenticated server-memory resource denoted by $\mathbf{aSMR}_{\Sigma,n}$ where Σ is the alphabet and n the memory size. The resource allows the client to read and write data blocks that are encoded as elements of a finite alphabet Σ via its interface C. The interface C_0 is the initialization interface used to set up the initial state of the resource. The server can be "honest but curious" by obtaining the entire history of accesses made by the clients (a log file) and reading their data at interface S_H. The server can also be intrusive by deleting or restoring previously deleted data using its interface S_I when the resource is set into a special write mode. A deleted data block is indicated by the special symbol ϵ. Thus, if we store a codeword on the **aSMR**, the adversary can only introduce erasures and not errors. We use the **aSMR** specification of [10] because it is tailored for code-based PoRs with its $\mathcal{O}(\log n)$ communication complexity per read query. Indeed, code-based PoRs require a large number of read queries and only one write query to outsource the encoded file. The **aSMR** resource is described in Fig. 1 and is constructed in [10] using a simple MAC-based protocol. Each symbol is stored alongside a MAC tag, this yields a storage overhead of κn where κ is the length of a MAC tag.

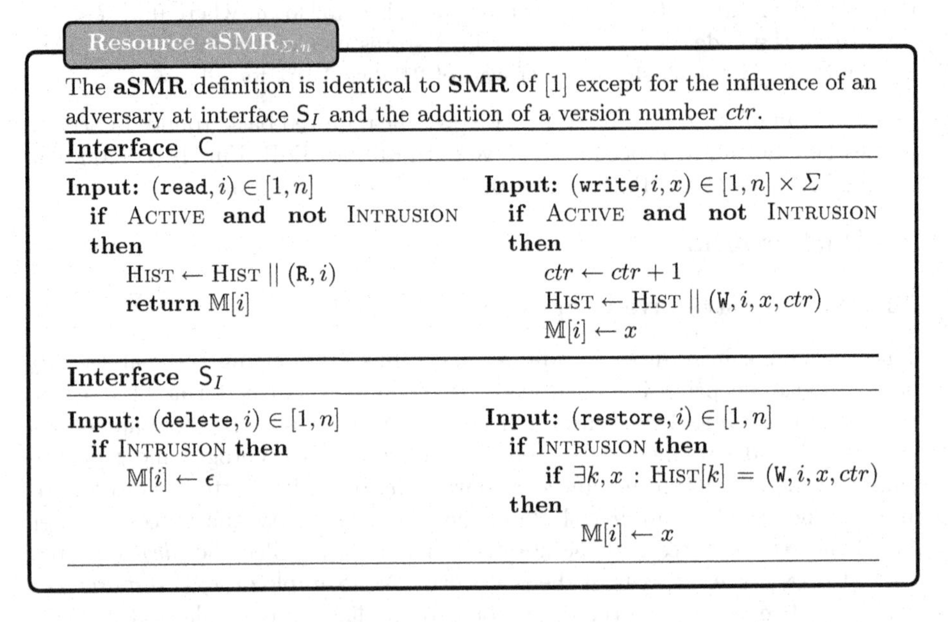

Fig. 1. The authentic SMR of [10] (only interfaces C and S_I are shown)

2.2 Proofs of Retrievability

Proofs of Retrievability (PoR) are cryptographic protocols whose goal is to guarantee that a file stored by a client on a server remains retrievable in full. PoRs thus involve two parties: a client who owns a file F and a server, here modelled as an SMR, on which F is stored. We use the CC based definition of PoR security as presented in [1]. Namely, a PoR scheme is composed of a pair of converters $\mathsf{por} := (\mathsf{por\_init}, \mathsf{por\_audit})$ and works in three phases:

- *An initialization phase.* The client converter init encodes the file F into $\mathbf{Init}(F) = (\tilde{F}, \texttt{data})$. The converter sends `data` (*e.g.* keys, etc.) to the client, then it sends $\tilde{F}$ to the SMR with a `write` query and erases F from the client's memory.

- *An audit phase.* The client converter audit probes some symbols of the server's memory and outputs accept if it believes that the file is retrievable in full and reject otherwise.
- *An extraction phase.* If the client has been convinced by the audit phase, he can send read to recover his whole file with high probability.

A PoR scheme is considered secure if it constructs an ideal abstraction of a PoR (introduced in [1]). This abstraction consists of an ideal SMR $\mathbf{aSMR}_{\Sigma,n}^{\mathsf{audit}}$ that considers the client's interface augmented with an audit mechanism. On an audit request, the resource checks whether the current memory content is indeed the newest version that the client wrote to the storage. If a single data block has changed, the ideal audit will detect this and output reject to the client. In case of a successful audit (returning accept), this guarantee holds until the server gains write-access to the storage, in which case a new audit has to reveal whether modifications have been made.

2.3 Expander Graphs and Expander Codes

We recall the definitions and well known properties of expander graphs and expander codes. We follow the presentation of [14]. Let $G := (V, E)$ be an undirected d-regular graph on n vertices. The *expansion* of G is $\lambda := \max\{\lambda_2, |\lambda_n|\}$, where $\lambda_1 \geq \lambda_2 \geq \ldots \geq \lambda_n$ are the eigenvalues of the adjacency matrix of G. We say that G is a *Ramanujan* graph if $\lambda \leq 2\sqrt{d-1}$. For a vertex $v \in V$, let $\Gamma(v)$ be the set of vertices adjacent to v. Let $\mathcal{C}_0 \subseteq \mathbb{F}_q^d$ be a linear code, called the *inner code.* Fix an order on the edges incident to each vertex of G, and let $\Gamma_i(v)$ be the i-th neighbor of v. Using the graph G and the inner code $\mathcal{C}_0$ we can construct a new code, called an *expander code.* The expander code $\mathcal{C} := \mathcal{C}(G, \mathcal{C}_0)$ is defined as the set of all labelings of the edges of G that respect the inner code $\mathcal{C}_0$. It has length $nd/2$. More precisely, we have the following definition.

Definition 1 (Expander Code). *Let $\mathcal{C}_0 \subseteq \mathbb{F}_q^d$ be a linear code, and let $G = (V, E)$ be a d-regular expander graph on n vertices. The expander code $\mathcal{C}(G, \mathcal{C}_0) \subseteq \mathbb{F}_q^E$ is a linear code of length $nd/2$, so that for $c \in \mathbb{F}_q^E$, $c \in \mathcal{C}$ if and only if, for all $v \in V$, $(c_{(v,\Gamma_1(v))}, \ldots, c_{(v,\Gamma_d(v))}) \in \mathcal{C}_0$.*

If $\mathcal{C}_0$ is a linear code of rate R_0, then $\mathcal{C}(G, \mathcal{C}_0)$ is a linear code of rate at least $2R_0 - 1$. We say that an undirected graph $G = (L \cup R, E)$ is bipartite if, for all vertices $v \in L$, we have $\Gamma(v) \cap L = \emptyset$ and, for all vertices $v \in R$, we have $\Gamma(v) \cap R = \emptyset$. It is known that expander codes constructed from bipartite graphs have good distance [16,19]:

Proposition 1. *Let $\mathcal{C}_0 \subseteq \mathbb{F}_q^d$ be a linear code with relative distance δ, and let $G = (L \cup R, E)$ be a d-regular bipartite expander graph with expansion λ. Then the expander code $\mathcal{C}(G, \mathcal{C}_0)$ has distance at least $\delta(\delta - \lambda/d)$.*

Moreover, $\mathcal{C}$ can be efficiently decoded up to this fraction of erasures [16,19].

Proposition 2. *Let $\mathcal{C}_0 \subseteq \mathbb{F}_q^d$ be a linear code with relative distance δ. Let $\mathcal{D}(d)$ be the time needed to uniquely decode $\mathcal{C}_0$ from $\delta - 1/d$ erasures. Let $G = (L \cup R, E)$ be a d-regular bipartite expander graph on n vertices with expansion λ. Let $\epsilon > 0$ and suppose that $\frac{\lambda}{d} < \frac{\delta}{2}$. Then, the decoder of [14] uniquely decodes the expander code $\mathcal{C}(G, \mathcal{C}_0)$ from up to $(1-\epsilon)\delta(\delta - \lambda/d)$ erasures in time $n \cdot \mathcal{D}(d)/\epsilon$.*

3 PoR with Expander Codes

3.1 Audit

Our scheme will use a generic audit for erasure codes presented in the CC framework by Badertscher and Maurer in [1]. We describe how [1] implemented the ideas of [8,15] to construct an $\mathbf{aSMR}^{\mathsf{audit}}_{\Sigma^k,1}$ from an $\mathbf{aSMR}_{\Sigma,n}$. Let $(\mathsf{enc}, \mathsf{dec})$ be an (n, k, d) erasure code and $F \in \Sigma^k$ be the client's file. We describe the PoR scheme $\mathsf{ecPor} := (\mathsf{ecInit}, \mathsf{ecAudit})$ for erasure codes. On input `init` to ecInit, the converter sends `init` to $\mathbf{aSMR}_{\Sigma,n}$ and computes the encoding $\bar{F} := \mathsf{enc}(F) \in \Sigma^n$. Then, for all $i \in [n]$, the converter sends $(\mathtt{write}, i, \bar{F}_i)$ to $\mathbf{aSMR}_{\Sigma,n}$.

On input $(\mathtt{read})$ to either ecInit or $\mathsf{ecAudit}$, the converter retrieves the whole memory content via $(\mathtt{read}, i)$ requests and obtains for each location, either a symbol $v_i \in \Sigma$ or the erasure symbol $\perp$. If v_i is returned, set $W_i := v_i$, else set $W_i := \perp$. If $|\{i \in [n] \mid W_i = \perp\}| > d - 1$, the converter outputs ϵ at its outside interface, otherwise it computes $F := \mathsf{dec}(W)$, and outputs F.

Finally, on a query `audit`, the converter $\mathsf{ecAudit}$ chooses a random subset $S \subseteq [n]$ of size t and outputs $(\mathtt{read}, i)$ to $\mathbf{aSMR}$ for each $i \in S$. If all read instructions for $i \in S$ returned a non-erased symbol, the converter outputs `accept`. Otherwise, it outputs `reject`. The integer t is chosen according to the security level we want to achieve. The security of the scheme is given by:

Theorem 1. **([1]).** *Let $n, k, d \in \mathbb{N}$. Let $(\mathsf{enc}, \mathsf{dec})$ be an (n, k, d) erasure code for alphabet Σ and erasure symbol $\perp$. Let $\rho := 1 - \frac{d-1}{n}$ be the minimum fraction of symbols needed to recover the file. Then, the above protocol $\mathsf{ecPor} := (\mathsf{ecInit}, \mathsf{ecAudit})$ that chooses a random subset of size t during the audit, constructs the $\mathbf{aSMR}^{\mathtt{audit}}_{\Sigma^k,1}$ from the $\mathbf{aSMR}_{\Sigma,n}$. More specifically, there exists a simulator sim such that for all distinguishers $\mathbf{D}$ performing at most q audits,*

$$\Delta^{\mathbf{D}}(\mathsf{ecInit}_{\mathsf{C}_0}\mathsf{ecAudit}_{\mathsf{C}}\mathbf{aSMR}_{\Sigma,n}, \mathsf{sim}^{\mathsf{S}}\mathbf{aSMR}^{\mathtt{audit}}_{\Sigma^k,1}) \le q \cdot \rho^t$$

3.2 Description of Our PoR with Expander Codes: The General Case

Let $\mathcal{C}_0$ be a linear code of length d, relative distance δ_0 and rate R_0. Using the Singleton bound, we have $\delta_0 \le 1 + \frac{1}{d} - R_0$. Let G be a d-regular bipartite graph on n vertices with expansion λ. We instantiate the PoR scheme $\mathsf{ecPor} := (\mathsf{ecInit}, \mathsf{ecAudit})$ with the expander code $\mathcal{C}(G, \mathcal{C}_0)$.

In the following, we determine the number t of edges probed during the audit needed to reach a given security level. If we suppose that $\frac{\lambda}{d} < \frac{\delta_0}{2}$, using the Singleton bound, we must have $R_0 < 1 + \frac{1}{d} - \frac{2\lambda}{d}$. Moreover, if $\mathcal{C}_0$ is Maximum Distance Separable, this implication becomes an equivalence. This is why, from now on, we will suppose that the inner code $\mathcal{C}_0$ is MDS. We take G to be a bipartite expander graph with expansion λ such that $\frac{\lambda}{d} < \frac{\delta_0}{2}$. Using Proposition 1, the minimum distance $\delta_\mathcal{C}$ of $\mathcal{C}(G, \mathcal{C}_0)$ is at least $\delta_0(\delta_0 - \lambda/d) > 2\lambda^2/d^2$.

Let $\epsilon > 0$. If we want to correct a $(1-\epsilon)\delta_\mathcal{C}$ fraction of erasures, the minimum fraction of valid edges needed to recover our file is

$$\rho = 1 + \frac{1}{nd} - (1-\epsilon)\delta_\mathcal{C} \leq 1 + \frac{1}{nd} - (1-\epsilon)\frac{2\lambda^2}{d^2}$$

Let σ be a statistical security parameter and t be the number of edges probed during the audit. Our scheme is considered secure if $\rho^t \leq 2^{-\sigma}$. We want to choose t such that $t \geq -\sigma/\log \rho$. *Approximation*: If $\frac{1}{nd} - (1-\epsilon)\frac{2\lambda^2}{d^2} \approx 0$, we have

$$\frac{-\sigma}{\log \rho} \approx \frac{nd^2\sigma}{2(1-\epsilon)n\lambda^2 - d} = \frac{d^2\sigma}{2(1-\epsilon)\lambda^2 - \frac{d}{n}}$$

Moreover, if G is Ramanujan, we have $\lambda \leq 2\sqrt{d-1}$ and $\frac{-\sigma}{\log \rho} \approx \frac{d\sigma}{8(1-\epsilon)}$. If G has expansion $\sqrt{d}$ instead, we have $\frac{-\sigma}{\log \rho} \approx \frac{d\sigma}{2(1-\epsilon)}$.

Note that our scheme requires the adversary to only introduce erasures (and not errors). We enforce this using an **aSMR**. After a successful audit, the client can extract its file by running the decoder of Proposition 2 which runs in time $\mathcal{O}(n \cdot \mathcal{D}(d)/\epsilon)$, where $\mathcal{D}(d)$ is the complexity of $\mathcal{C}_0$'s decoder.

3.3 Instantiation with the Point-Line Incidence Graph of the Plane

Let Γ be the point-line incidence graph of the affine plane over $\mathbb{F}_q$ without the vertical lines. This graph is q-regular, has $2q^2$ vertices and expansion $\sqrt{q}$ (see the work of Tanner [18]). We have $\Gamma := (V_1 \cup V_2, E)$ where

$$V_1 := \{(x,y) \mid x, y \in \mathbb{F}_q\}, \quad V_2 := \{(a,b) \mid a, b \in \mathbb{F}_q\}, \text{ and}$$
$$E := \{((x,y),(a,b)) \mid (x,y) \in V_1, (a,b) \in V_2, ax + b - y = 0\}$$

This graph is an excellent choice for our PoR scheme. Recall that the rate of the inner code is upper bounded by $1 + \frac{1}{d} - \frac{2\lambda}{d}$ and the rate of the expander code is lower bounded by $2R_0 - 1$. The graph Γ also has a nice ratio between its regularity q and its number of edges q^3. Since we need to probe a number of edges linear in q, this ensures that our PoR scheme has communication complexity of order cubic root of the size of the outsourced file. This is in line with or even better than other code-based PoR schemes, such as [9] (which has communication complexity of order square root of the file size for $m = 2$). Our inner code $\mathcal{C}_0$ will be a Reed-Solomon code of rate $R_0 < 1 + \frac{1}{d} - \frac{2\lambda}{d}$. This code is MDS, and thus we can use the decoder of Proposition 2 for our extraction phase. Moreover, because our inner code is a Reed-Solomon code, we can use the following result of Beelen *et al.* [2]. Let $\mathbb{F}_q := \{\alpha_1, \alpha_2, \ldots, \alpha_q\}$. We use the following labeling (of [2]) for the edges of Γ : if $(x, y) \in V_1$, $\Phi_{(x,y)}(i) := (x, y, \alpha_i, y - x\alpha_i)$ and, if $(a, b) \in V_2$, $\Phi_{(a,b)}(i) := (\alpha_i, a\alpha_i + b, a, b)$. When q is a power of 2 or a prime, Beelen *et al.* [2] showed that when using this labeling on the graph Γ with a Reed-Solomon code of rate $1/2 < R_0 \leq 1$ as inner code, we obtain an expander code of rate *exactly* $R := R_0^3 + R_0(1 - R_0)(2R_0 - 1)$.

3.4 Parameters

Let σ be the statistical security parameter ($\sigma = 40$) and κ be the computational security parameter[1] ($\kappa = 128$). Set q, a power of 2. Let G be the q-regular point-line incidence graph over $\mathbb{F}_q^2$. This graph has $2q^2$ vertices, q^3 edges and expansion $\lambda := \sqrt{q}$. Let the inner code $\mathcal{C}_0$ be a Reed-Solomon code of length q and rate $R_0 = \max\{\frac{k}{q} \mid k \in \mathbb{N} \text{ and } \frac{k}{q} < 1 + \frac{1}{q} - \frac{2\lambda}{q}\}$. We take R_0 to be as big as possible to reduce the storage overhead of the PoR while still having a quasi-linear time decoder for the expander code. Indeed, since q is a power of 2, $\mathcal{C}_0$ can be erasure decoded in time $\mathcal{O}(q \log^2 q)$ thanks to the decoder of Tang and Lin [17].

Our expander code $\mathcal{C}(G, \mathcal{C}_0)$ has length q^3, rate $R := R_0^3 + R_0(1 - R_0)(2R_0 - 1)$ and alphabet $\mathbb{F}_q$. Let $|F|$ be the size of the outsourced file in bits. It is such that $|F| = Rq^3 \log(q)$. Using Proposition 2, we get a decoder for $\mathcal{C}(G, \mathcal{C}_0)$ (and thus an extraction phase) running in time $\mathcal{O}(2q^3 \log^2 q)$ which is quasi-linear in the input size $q^3 \log q$. The storage overhead is given by $1/R - 1$, which is the redundancy of the code. The parameters of our PoR and their asymptotic behavior are given in Table 1. Even though our PoR has the same asymptotic behavior than the PoR of [9], we show in Table 2 that we get much better parameters in practice.

Table 1. The parameters of our scheme when using the point-line incidence graph over $\mathbb{F}_q^2$ and a Reed-Solomon code as inner code.

	Exact value	Asymptotics ($\lvert F\rvert \to \infty$)
C. storage overhead	κ	$\mathcal{O}(1)$
S. storage overhead	$(\frac{1}{R} - 1)\lvert F\rvert + q^3\kappa$	$\mathcal{O}(\lvert F\rvert)$
comm. C. → S.	$\frac{q\sigma}{2} \log(q^3)$	$\mathcal{O}(\lvert F\rvert^{\frac{1}{3}} \log \lvert F\rvert)$
comm. S. → C.	$\frac{q\sigma}{2}(\kappa + \log q)$	$\mathcal{O}(\lvert F\rvert^{\frac{1}{3}} \log \lvert F\rvert)$

In Table 2, we give concrete parameters of our PoR scheme for different values of q. We compare our scheme with the PoR of [9]. For $q = 512$, [9, Fig. 6] and its new security analysis by [10] gives a PoR with codewords of length q^3 that stores 35.9 MB files with storage overhead of 319%. In Table 2, we see that for $q = 512$ and codeword length q^3, our PoR stores 124 MB files with storage overhead of 21%, the same communication complexity as [9] and a quasi-linear

[1] Of the MAC used to construct the **aSMR**.

Table 2. Effective parameters of our PoR using the point-line incidence graph over $\mathbb{F}_q^2$ for different values of q and Reed-Solomon codes as inner code. The graph is q-regular with $2q^2$ vertices. We choose the largest possible rate yielding a quasi-linear time decoder. The statistical security parameter is 40.

q	R_0	R	$2q^2$	$\|F\|$	$\frac{1}{R}-1$	Comm./$\|F\|$
256	0.878	0.758	131,072	12 MB	0.320	2×10^{-4}
512	0.913	0.827	524,288	124 MB	0.210	6×10^{-5}
1024	0.938	0.876	2,097,152	1.176 GB	0.141	1×10^{-5}
2048	0.956	0.912	8,388,608	10.772 GB	0.096	3×10^{-6}
4096	0.968	0.936	33,554,432	96.485 GB	0.068	8×10^{-7}
8192	0.978	0.956	134,217,728	854.055 GB	0.046	2×10^{-7}

time extraction phase. Do note that using any Ramanujan graph instead of the point-line incidence graph yields substantially worse parameters.

References

1. Badertscher, C., Maurer, U.: Composable and robust outsourced storage. In: Proceedings of Topics in Cryptology - CT-RSA 2018 - The Cryptographers' Track at the RSA Conference 2018, San Francisco, CA, USA, 16–20 April 2018, pp. 354–373 (2018). https://doi.org/10.1007/978-3-319-76953-0_19
2. Beelen, P., Høholdt, T., Piñero, F., Justesen, J.: On the dimension of graph codes with reed-Solomon component codes. In: 2013 IEEE International Symposium on Information Theory, pp. 1227–1231 (2013). https://doi.org/10.1109/ISIT.2013.6620422
3. Bowers, K.D., Juels, A., Oprea, A.: Proofs of retrievability: theory and implementation. In: Proceedings of the 2009 ACM Workshop on Cloud Computing Security, pp. 43–54. CCSW 2009, ACM, New York, NY, USA (2009). https://doi.org/10.1145/1655008.1655015
4. Dodis, Y., Vadhan, S., Wichs, D.: Proofs of retrievability via hardness amplification. In: Reingold, O. (ed.) TCC 2009. LNCS, vol. 5444, pp. 109–127. Springer, Heidelberg (2009). https://doi.org/10.1007/978-3-642-00457-5_8
5. Guo, A., Kopparty, S., Sudan, M.: New affine-invariant codes from lifting. In: Proceedings of the 4th Conference on Innovations in Theoretical Computer Science, ITCS 2013, pp. 529–540. ACM, New York, NY, USA (2013). https://doi.org/10.1145/2422436.2422494
6. Høholdt, T., Justesen, J.: Graph codes with reed-Solomon component codes. In: 2006 IEEE International Symposium on Information Theory, pp. 2022–2026 (2006). https://doi.org/10.1109/ISIT.2006.261904
7. Høholdt, T., Justesen, J.: The minimum distance of graph codes. In: Chee, Y.M., et al. (eds.) IWCC 2011. LNCS, vol. 6639, pp. 201–212. Springer, Heidelberg (2011). https://doi.org/10.1007/978-3-642-20901-7_12
8. Juels, A., Kaliski, Jr., B.S.: PORs: proofs of retrievability for large files. In: Proceedings of the 14th ACM Conference on Computer and Communications Security, CCS 2007, pp. 584–597. ACM, New York, NY, USA (2007). https://doi.org/10.1145/1315245.1315317

9. Lavauzelle, J., Levy-Dit-Vehel, F.: New proofs of retrievability using locally decodable codes. In: International Symposium on Information Theory ISIT 2016, pp. 1809–1813. Barcelona, Spain (2016). https://doi.org/10.1109/ISIT.2016.7541611
10. Levy-Dit-Vehel, F., Roméas, M.: A framework for the design of secure and efficient proofs of retrievability. Cryptology ePrint Archive, report 2022/064 (2022). https://ia.cr/2022/064
11. Maurer, U.: Constructive cryptography – a new paradigm for security definitions and proofs. In: Mödersheim, S., Palamidessi, C. (eds.) TOSCA 2011. LNCS, vol. 6993, pp. 33–56. Springer, Heidelberg (2012). https://doi.org/10.1007/978-3-642-27375-9_3
12. Maurer, U., Renner, R.: Abstract cryptography. In: In Innovations In Computer Science. Tsinghua University Press (2011)
13. Paterson, M., Stinson, D., Upadhyay, J.: A coding theory foundation for the analysis of general unconditionally secure proof-of-retrievability schemes for cloud storage. J. Math. Cryptol. **7**(3), 183–216 (2013). https://doi.org/10.1515/jmc-2013-5002
14. Ron-Zewi, N., Wootters, M., Zémor, G.: Linear-time erasure list-decoding of expander codes. In: 2020 IEEE International Symposium on Information Theory (ISIT), pp. 379–383 (2020). https://doi.org/10.1109/ISIT44484.2020.9174325
15. Shacham, H., Waters, B.: Compact Proofs of Retrievability. In: Pieprzyk, J. (ed.) ASIACRYPT 2008. LNCS, vol. 5350, pp. 90–107. Springer, Heidelberg (2008). https://doi.org/10.1007/978-3-540-89255-7_7
16. Sipser, M., Spielman, D.: Expander codes. IEEE Trans. Inf. Theory **42**(6), 1710–1722 (1996). https://doi.org/10.1109/18.556667
17. Tang, N., Lin, Y.: Fast encoding and decoding algorithms for arbitrary (n, k) Reed-Solomon codes over $\mathbb{F}_{2^m}$. IEEE Commun. Lett. **24**(4), 716–719 (2020). https://doi.org/10.1109/LCOMM.2020.2965453
18. Tanner, R.M.: Explicit concentrators from generalized n-gons. SIAM Journal on Algebraic Discrete Methods **5**(3), 287–293 (1984). https://doi.org/10.1137/0605030
19. Zémor, G.: On expander codes. IEEE Trans. Inf. Theory **47**(2), 835–837 (2001). https://doi.org/10.1109/18.910593

Post-Quantum Electronic Identity: Adapting OpenID Connect and OAuth 2.0 to the Post-Quantum Era

Frederico Schardong[1,2(✉)], Alexandre Augusto Giron[2,3], Fernanda Larisa Müller[2], and Ricardo Custódio[2]

[1] Federal Institute of Rio Grande do Sul, Rolante, Brazil
frederico.schardong@rolante.ifrs.edu.br
[2] Federal University of Santa Catarina, Florianópolis, Brazil
muller.larissa@grad.ufsc.br, ricardo.custodio@ufsc.br
[3] Federal University of Technology-Parana, Toledo, Brazil
alexandregiron@utfpr.edu.br

Abstract. The quantum threat affects a multitude of network protocols, frameworks, and systems that use public-key cryptography. OpenID Connect (OIDC) and OAuth 2.0 are no exception, which means they must transition to Post-Quantum Cryptography (PQC). However, the long lifetime of access tokens necessitates this shift, if we consider the possibility of a *record-now-decrypt-later* attacker retrieving and subsequently impersonating users with these tokens. In this research, we conduct a thorough literature review to identify existing solutions to this problem, suggest modifications to OAuth 2.0 and OIDC and their underlying protocols to make them quantum-safe, then implement and evaluate the effects of PQC on a realistic OIDC study case. Our findings reveal that PQC-based OIDC has the same or better performance in low-latency settings, but the handshake of PQC-based TLS accounts for fifty percent of the overall duration in high-latency scenarios.

Keywords: Post-Quantum Cryptography · PQC · OpenID Connect · OAuth · OAuth 2.0 · Electronic Identity · Identity.

1 Introduction

The OAuth 2.0 protocol introduced standard flows for a client (such as a web application or mobile app) to interact with an Identity Provider (IdP) and obtain *authorization* to access electronic IDentity (eID) attributes or perform actions on behalf of an eID [6]. However, due to its emphasis on authorization rather than authentication, crucial aspects of eID were omitted. For example, there is no regulated method for requesting common eID attributes such as name and

This study was supported by the Federal Institute of Rio Grande do Sul (IFRS) and by the Federal University of Technology - Parana (UTFPR).

A. R. Beresford et al. (Eds.): CANS 2022, LNCS 13641, pp. 371–390, 2022.
https://doi.org/10.1007/978-3-031-20974-1_20

email address, nor for requesting two-factor authentication. The OpenID Connect (OIDC) protocol was developed to address these issues [27]. In practice, it is an extension of OAuth 2.0 that introduces uniformity for common attributes (*e.g.*, name, email, address, phone number, etc.) and permits Service Providers (SPs) to request IdPs to enforce multi-factor authentication, among other features. OAuth 2.0 and OIDC are the current *de facto* standards for working with eIDs. They are utilized daily by billions of users via industry-leading IdPs like Google and Facebook (now Meta).

However, these users are susceptible to quantum attackers disclosing their private information or impersonating them. Although there is no known quantum computer with sufficient processing power to break the cryptographic protocols underlying OAuth 2.0 and OIDC, intercepted communications can be stored for when such devices become available. Specifically, a *record-now-decrypt-later* attack could be used to retrieve access tokens from the past, enabling impersonation in the future. Consequently, these protocols (and their implementations) must be updated immediately to counteract this threat.

Quantum threats target applications and network protocols reliant on classical cryptography. By classical cryptography, we mean public-key schemes based on the Integer Factorization Problem (IFP), the Discrete Logarithm Problem (DLP), and the Elliptic Curve Discrete Logarithm Problem (ECDLP). Several network protocols, including JSON Web Token (JWT) and TLS, employ these schemes, which are vulnerable to Shor's algorithm [31]. Under Grover's algorithm [5], symmetric-key schemes such as AES are also threatened by quantum computing. If their security settings can be increased, they won't need to be replaced once their security is cut in half. Maintaining the initial guarantees only requires doubling the security parameters.

In this context, classical public-key schemes will likely be replaced in the future by Post-Quantum Cryptography (PQC) or quantum-safe cryptography [21]. PQC algorithms are based on a variety of mathematical problems believed to be intractable by both non-quantum and quantum adversaries. The alternative PQC solutions are based on lattice-based cryptography, multivariate cryptography, code-based cryptography, hash-based cryptography, or isogeny-based cryptography. In this context, a global-scale transition to PQC is expected in the coming years, with systems, protocols, and applications in general beginning to use new cryptographic schemes. We anticipate that the same transition will occur for OAuth 2.0 and OIDC. One challenging part of this transition to PQC is the increased size, which can impose delays in the protocol. Besides, they can incur in other performance drawbacks (*e.g.*, increased computational time).

In this research, we analyze the essential components of OAuth 2.0 and OIDC, suggesting and empirically evaluating modifications to protect them from quantum attackers. In conclusion, our contributions are as follows:

- We conduct a rigorous and reproducible systematic literature review to determine the current state of post-quantum OIDC and OAuth 2.0;
- We propose improvements to OAuth 2.0 and OIDC, as well as their underlying protocols TLS and JWT, to make them quantum-safe;

- We provide a post-quantum implementation of OpenID Connect, built with the integration of PQC algorithms in JWT and also TLS, as well increasing parameters in symmetric primitives; and
- We conduct a series of reproducible experiments using a realistic scenario and multiple configurations to evaluate the performance of our proposal.

The rest of this article is structured as follows. Section 2 goes over OAuth 2.0, OIDC, TLS, and PQC. The rigorous systematic literature review conducted to discover and evaluate existing approaches is then presented in Sect. 3. Section 4 proposes changes to these protocols to make them more resistant to quantum attackers, and Sect. 5 introduces our evaluation strategy and the results obtained. Section 6 concludes with closing remarks.

2 Background

2.1 OAuth 2.0

The OAuth 2.0 protocol was introduced in 2012 to allow third-party applications to access data and perform actions on behalf of users [6]. It is based on the distribution of tokens and establishes four roles: (i) the end-user is the *resource owner*; (ii) the *client* is the application that requests the resource owner's data; (iii) the *authorization server*, *i.e.*, the IdP, grants *access tokens* for a client to access the resource owner's data after authenticating the resource owner and obtaining their authorization; and (iv) the *resource server* hosts the protected resources and responds to requests.

The protocol provides three standardized flows for clients to obtain resource owner data, one of which is intended to facilitate the transition from basic and digest authentication schemes, as well as other schemes, to the two major flows. The *authorization code grant*, in which tokens are exchanged between the Relying Party (RP) and the IdP over a secure back channel, and the *implicit grant*, in which all interactions occur through the user's browser, are the two flows in question. Effectively, only the *authorization code grant* should be used, as the *implicit grant* is known to have security flaws, such as the impossibility to detect replay attacks [19]. The *authorization code grant* is depicted in Fig. 1, where red text indicates OAuth's optional parameters that are mandatory on OIDC and bold red text indicates new mandatory values added by OIDC.

First, the user requests a protected resource from the RP via their user agent or attempts to access a restricted area. If there is no cookie or other storage mechanism storing a session identifier proving that the end user has previously authenticated and authorized this client to access their data, the *authorization code grant* process begins. Users are frequently presented with one or more IdPs in which the RP is registered and asked to select one.

Second, the RP directs the unknown user to the TLS-secured authorization endpoint of the selected IdP. The protocol does not specify how the RP finds the authorization endpoint. This usually occurs during the client registration

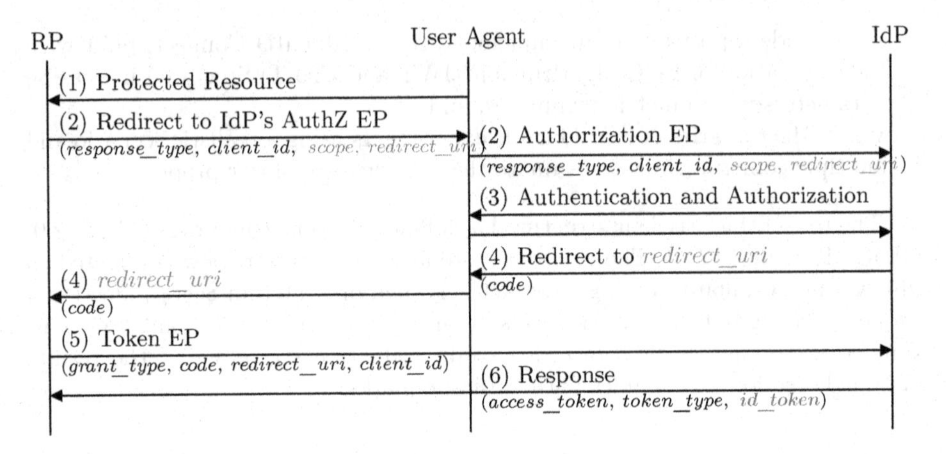

Fig. 1. OAuth 2.0's *authorization code grant* flow. Dark-colored values indicate mandatory parameters, while red-colored values are optional values made mandatory by OIDC. The bold red *id_token* is a new, mandatory OIDC value. (Color figure online)

process in the IdP, which is also out of scope. The user agent performs the redirect, which includes two mandatory parameters: `response_type`, which contains the value `token` indicating that this is the *authorization code grant* flow, and `client_id`, which contains the RP's identification. In OAuth 2.0, the `scope` and `redirect_uri` are optional parameters, whereas they are required in OIDC, as will be explained later. The `scope` parameter specifies which personal information the RP requests from the IdP. For example, the user's e-mail and postal addresses, or permission to perform an action on the user's behalf, such as updating an attribute. The `redirect_uri` parameter specifies the RP-controlled URL to which the user agent will be redirected after authentication and authorization. These parameters are optional, and if they are not specified, the values established during the client registration process are used.

Third, after receiving the request, the IdP authenticates the user and obtains their permission to access the requested resource. The protocol does not specify how users are authenticated or granted authorization. Similarly, available scopes are defined by the IdP and communicated to the RP either during the client registration process or via another mechanism. Authentication can be as simple as a username and password, or as sophisticated and secure as multi-factor authentication. This is not covered by OAuth 2.0.

Fourth, if the user is successfully authenticated and grants authorization, the IdP issues a short lived *authorization code*. The `code` parameter of the redirect response is used to send this to the RP via the user agent. If an error occurs, the IdP notifies the user and uses the `error` parameter instead of `code`.

Fifth, the client makes a TLS-secured token endpoint request. Four parameters are required: (i) `grant_type` is `authorization_code`; (ii) `code` is the authorization code from the previous step; (iii) `redirect_uri` is the same as in the second step or is omitted; and (iv) `client_id` is the same as in the second step if no client authentication is performed. It is important to note that in OAuth 2.0, web applications are considered *confidential clients* and thus require some form of authentication to access the token endpoint. Although the protocol does not specify an authentication mechanism for clients, the OAuth 2.0 Security Best Current Practice [19], an RFC that addresses OAuth 2.0 security, recommends a challenge-response protocol specifically designed to authenticate clients [25].

In the sixth and final step, the IdP verifies that the `authorization_code` received was issued to the authenticated client and that the `redirect_uri` matches what was provided in the second step, if previously informed. An `access_token` is then issued along with a `token_type`, which instructs the RP on how to make requests to the user-authorized protected resources. In OIDC, an `id_token` is also issued. After receiving the `access_token`, the client can use it to request the protected resources from the resource server.

2.2 OpenID Connect

Even though OAuth 2.0 standardizes roles, flows, and messages, practitioners must still fill in numerous gaps. It does not, for example, address client registration, indicate the authentication factors used, or create a mechanism for clients to discover IdP endpoint URIs. OpenID Connect was presented as a solution for these and other issues [27].

OIDC adds an identity layer to OAuth 2.0. This is accomplished in a non-destructive manner by leveraging OAuth 2.0 optional parameters and the requirement to ignore unrecognized request and response parameters to/from the token and authorization endpoints. The modifications to the OAuth 2.0 three-party handshake are depicted in red in Fig. 1 and described below.

First, the `scope` parameter must contain the value `openid`. This is possible due to the fact that OAuth 2.0 permits multiple values separated by spaces for this parameter. OIDC defines four additional scopes that the RP can use to request user-related information: (i) `profile`, which requests the user's `name`, `nickname`, `picture`, `website`, `gender`, `birthdate`, and other personal data; (ii) `email` requests access to `email` address and `email_verified`, a boolean value indicating whether or not it has been verified; (iii) `phone` asks for `phone_number` and `phone_number_verified`; and (iv) `address`.

It is worth noting that in OIDC, user-related data is referred to as claims. A claim is a piece of information asserted about the user by the IdP or other attribute provider. The user claims requested by the client are accessed via the `userinfo_endpoint`, which receives a valid `access_token` and returns the claims this token is authorized to access.

Second, in OIDC, the `redirect_uri` parameter is required and must match the URI specified in the client registration. The *OIDC core* specification, like OAuth 2.0, assumes the RP is registered and knows the IdP's communication endpoints. These two challenges are addressed by two additional specifications: *OpenID Connect Dynamic Client Registration* (OIDC-DCR) [26] and *OpenID Connect Discovery* (OIDC-D) [28]. These two specifications, along with the *OIDC core*, make up what is collectively referred to as the *OIDC dynamic*. In the

OIDC-DCR specification, a client sends one or more `redirect_uri` and other optional parameters and receives a `client_id` and optionally a `client_secret`. The OIDC-D protocol defines the URI `/.well-known/openid-configuration`, which clients use to discover the endpoints and algorithms supported by an IdP.

The final and most significant modification to the OAuth 2.0 three-party handshake occurs in the response of the token request: OIDC adds a required response argument named `id_token`. This token contains information regarding the user's authentication, including the token's issuer, the intended audience (one or more `client_id`), a unique identifier of the end-user in the IdP, the date and time of the authentication, and the token's issued and expiration times. This token may also include optional information such as the *authentication context class*, which indicates the level of assurance of the authentication process [9], and an array of IdP-defined *authentication method reference*, such as password, PIN, and facial recognition.

2.3 OAuth 2.0 and OIDC Security Considerations

Known threats to these two protocols include resource owner password guessing, token fabrication, Cross-Site Request Forgery (CSRF), eavesdropping access tokens, and client impersonation of resource owner [20]. Let us roughly divide the attack surfaces into two categories: communication and stationary. To mitigate communication-related threats, both OAuth 2.0 and OIDC require the use of Transport Layer Security (TLS) [24] to authenticate RP and IdP and to ensure the integrity and confidentiality of exchanged messages [6,27]. Regarding stationary data protection, however, the original OAuth 2.0 specification does not specify how tokens (`refresh_token` and `access_token`) should be constructed; it only states that other parties should be unable to generate, modify, or guess them [6]. The OIDC protocol, on the other hand, requires the use of JWT [13] to implement the `id_token` [27].

The JWT is a JSON-based data structure consisting of a header, content, and signature. The header describes the cryptographic operations performed on the content: none, encryption, signature, or both. The JWT-based `id_token` must be signed. The IdP makes the public keys for signature verification available in a publicly accessible endpoint called `jwks_uri`, the value of which can be found using OIDC-D [28]. This URI returns a *JSON Web Key (JWK)* [11], a JSON structure containing the public key, key id, and other key-related data. It is worth noting that there is an OAuth 2.0 equivalent to the OIDC-D specification, namely the *OAuth 2.0 Authorization Server Metadata* [16], as well as a specification that standardizes the use of JWT for OAuth 2.0, namely the *JSON Web Token (JWT) Profile for OAuth 2.0 Access Tokens* [4].

2.4 Transport Layer Security 1.3

To exchange protocol messages, OpenID Connect and OAuth 2.0 require a secure and authenticated communication channel. Both standards require the use of TLS for communication security. The TLS protocol (version 1.3) is defined on

RFC 8446 [24] and is often used in this scenario. TLS consists of three components: a Handshake protocol, where an Authenticated Key Exchange (AKE) takes place; a Record protocol specifies symmetric encryption for the communication; and an Alert Protocol, which specifies error messages and conditions.

TLS Handshake. An AKE is performed in every TLS 1.3 full handshake. The parties exchange a shared secret that is further derived into a set of traffic keys, later used in the Record Protocol for encrypting application data. During the handshake, the TLS server authenticates itself to the TLS client. A x509 digital certificate is often used, but authentication with Pre-Shared-Key (PSK) is also supported. The server can, optionally, request client authentication. We describe the handshake in three steps:

1. The client send the first handshake message: `ClientHello`, among with optional extensions. Normally it sends a random nonce, protocol versions, list of supported ciphersuites, among other information. For forward secrecy, a `keyshare` is sent composed by the Elliptic-Curve Diffie-Hellman Ephemeral (`ECDHE`) public part. Although optional, at least a keyshare or a Pre-shared-Key message must be sent.
2. The server replies with negotiated parameters, such as the selected ciphersuite, and additional (optional) messages. A certificate and certificate verify message is often present part of TLS server authentication. The first is the digital certificate and the second is a signature for key confirmation. An alternative is the server authentication through the PSK, *e.g.* in a resumption session, where the certificate is not sent by the server. The authentication ends with the `finished` message, where a HMAC is computed from the transcript of the handshake context. At this point, the server can send encrypted application data to the client.
3. Upon reception, the client can complete the `ECDHE` KEX and derive symmetric keys for the communication. The handshake is completed with the client's `finished` message.

TLS Record Protocol. After the authentication and exchange of symmetric keys, the parties then communicate application data using encrypted records. The ciphersuite in use is the one agreed during the handshake; if they do not agree on a ciphersuite they abort the communication (specified in the Alert Protocol). Examples of ciphersuites specified by IANA include [8]: `TLS_AES_128_GCM_SHA256`, `TLS_CHACHA20_POLY1305_SHA256`, among others.

TLS Alert Protocol. It defines error situations and actions that TLS peers have to take. There are two types of alerts: closure or error. Closure alerts are important to avoid the "truncation attack" [3], and they occur voluntarily, whereas an error alert causes both parties to immediately close the connection. All alert messages are encrypted as specified by the current connection state.

2.5 Post-Quantum Cryptography

At the time of writing, algorithms part of Post-Quantum Cryptography (also called Quantum-Safe cryptography) are under scrutiny by the cryptographic community. Designed to be resistant to a Cryptographically Relevant Quantum Computer (CRQC), PQC algorithms can execute in classical computers to protect data against both classical and quantum attackers. The protection is based on mathematical assumptions with no (known) quantum or classical solution.

NIST is conducting a notable PQC standardization process [21], and several international agencies have declared that they will follow the NIST PQC process [7]. The proposals are for Key Exchange (KEX) and digital signatures. Currently at Round 4, NIST selected CRYSTALS-Kyber for KEX, and Dilithium, denoted as the primary choice, Falcon, and SPHINCS+ for digital signatures. Even though some PQC algorithms belong to the same group (or type), their public keys and output sizes are different. This information is presented in Table 1. The sizes are given in bytes, and correspond to NIST security levels 1 through 5. Level 5 increases both security and the size of public keys and outputs.

Table 1. PQC algorithms sizes (NIST's Process Round 4 finalists)

Type	Based on	Algorithm	Public key size	Output size
KEX	*Lattice*	Kyber	800 to 1568	768 to 1568
Signature	*Lattice*	Dilithium	1312 to 2592	2420 to 4595
		Falcon	897 to 1793	690 to 1330
	Hash	SPHINCS+	32 to 64	7856 to 49856

The differences between the algorithms compose some of the important factors to consider when deploying PQC in network protocols. For instance, Sikeridis et al. [32] showed that the increased size of PQC can slowdown network performance due to TCP congestion control mechanisms. In addition to sizes, computational cost is also an important factor, but it can vary significantly on different hardware and specific implementations.

Post-Quantum Adoption in TLS. One of the weaknesses of TLS 1.3 is that it does not prevent from quantum attacks. To address this issue, researchers start to develop and test quantum-safe algorithms integrated in the protocol's handshake. One notorious initiative is the Open-Quantum Safe (OQS) project, which provides PQC libraries and integrates it in a variety of network protocol implementations, such OpenSSL [33]. Using those libraries, literature shows different TLS benchmarks comparing post-quantum and classical implementations [22,32]. In summary, lattice-based algorithms are generally fast but with an increase in terms of size of cryptographic objects (*e.g.*, public keys). Additionally, there are disruptive proposals, which changes the TLS handshake aiming for a better performance. One example is KEMTLS [29] and KEMTLS-PDK

[30], which replaces signature schemes used in TLS handshakes by post-quantum KEMs. Still, PQC adoption in TLS remains challenging in practice, since revocation data in TLS, PKI migration issues and other situations are not yet fully explored by the literature.

3 Related Work

3.1 Method

The review protocol consists of five steps [17]: (i) research questions definition; (ii) search strategy for primary studies; (iii) definition of inclusion criteria; (iv) classification of the papers; and (v) data extraction.

The first step is to establish the scope, which we do by developing two research questions. We want to understand "*How and which PQC algorithms were used to secure OpenID Connect and OAuth 2.0?*" and "*What is the impact of replacing quantum-vulnerable cryptographic primitives with PQC alternatives?*" Our search strategy is based on these research questions and consists of using related PQC terms defined in a search string. The search string is used to query primary study sources (*e.g.*, SpringerLink). We constructed the string in accordance with the Population, Intervention, Comparison, Outcomes, and Context (PICOC) guideline [23], where the *population* consists of OpenID Connect, OAuth 2.0, and JWT; post-quantum cryptography is the *intervention* technique; and the underlying mathematical assumptions and names of PQC algorithms were used for *comparison*. It is worth noting that when we ran the search string, we discovered that the terms referring to the PICOC *outcomes* and *context* significantly reduced the number of papers returned by the search libraries. As a result, we simplified the search string in order to increase the number of papers. Figure 2 depicts the final search string.

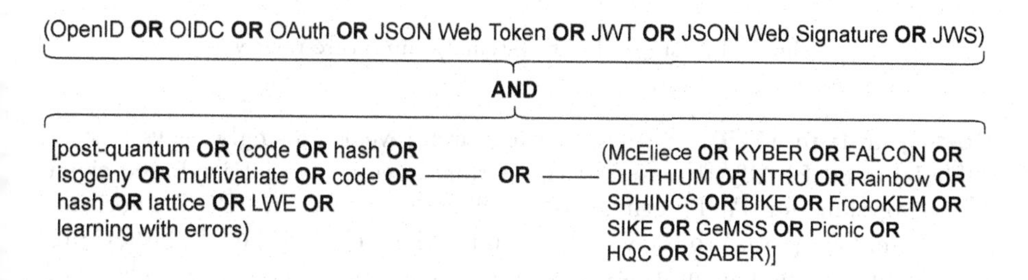

Fig. 2. Search string.

Typically, a systematic study identifies selection criteria for relevant papers, *i.e.*, papers that provide (partial or complete) answers to the research questions. In Table 2, we define one Inclusion Criterion (IC) and two Exclusion Criteria. In summary, ECs exclude papers that are not primary computer science studies, and if the paper satisfies IC-1, it will be included in our results set.

Table 2. Inclusion and exclusion criteria.

Inclusion criteria	
IC-1	The paper investigates or proposes post-quantum OAuth 2.0 or OpenID Connect.
Exclusion criterion	
EC-1	The search result is a book of proceedings.
EC-2	The research work is not in the area of computer science.

3.2 Execution

Figure 3 depicts the search execution method. We queried databases for primary studies and patents on May 4, 2022. Each action outlined eliminates unrelated search results. After applying Inclusion Criteria (IC), the final set of related works consists of a single primary study. This finding suggests that little research has been conducted on this subject to date.

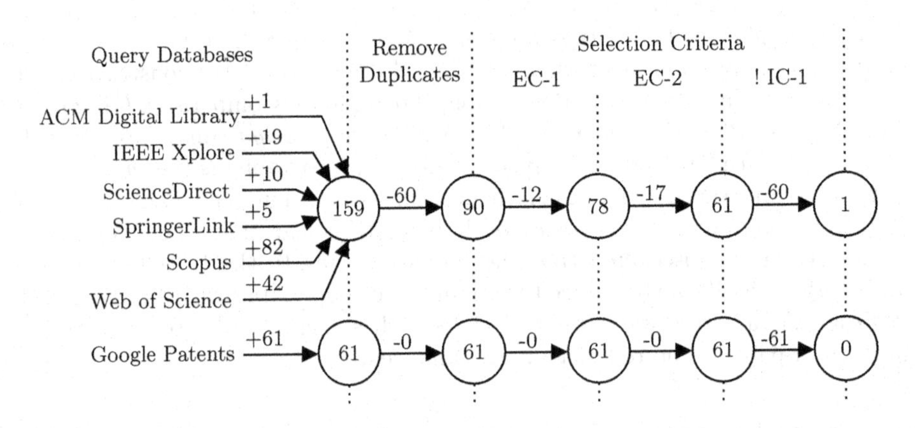

Fig. 3. The steps of our systematic literature review.

Post-Quantum JWT. Our systematic search revealed a single relevant work. Alkhulaifi and El-Alfy [1] assessed the performance of two lattice-based signature algorithms for JWT authentication. They compared two PQC algorithms (Dilithium and qTesla) to RSA in their study. They selected the NIST PQC process (Round 2) implementations using security levels one and three. The JWT body in their implementation is composed of random data. They demonstrated that Dilithium achieves superior performance when deployed in an HTTP client-server implementation, both in terms of requests per second and average response time. The comparison focuses solely on signatures, so the transfer of public keys does not factor into the evaluation. In addition, their research only considered local evaluations, *i.e.*, client and server running on the same machine, thereby excluding network conditions from the analysis.

Open Challenges. After conducting a systematic literature review, we identified open challenges. First, there are no practical OIDC or OAuth 2.0 post-quantum evaluations. A practical evaluation would include network conditions imposed by geographically distant servers and the connections required to complete authentication and authorization processes following these protocols. This void is the primary focus of our efforts. Secondly, the only post-quantum JWT evaluation does not take elliptic-curve signatures into account, resulting in superior performance and smaller sizes compared to RSA [1]. It is crucial to include elliptic curves in the analysis, particularly when comparing to PQC sizes.

4 Post-Quantum OAuth 2.0 and OIDC

OAuth 2.0 and OIDC are application-level protocols that delegate the majority of the security heavy-lifting to TLS and JWT. Aside from mandating the use of these protocols as building blocks and providing implementation guidance to prevent security flaws, few security requirements remain undefined.

OAuth 2.0 includes numerous security considerations for protocol-level messages and parameters. The only other security requirement besides the use of TLS is that the probability of an attacker guessing a token must be less than or equal to 2^{-128} and ideally 2^{-160} [6]. In other words, servers must issue tokens randomly (one token must be independent from others). Consequently, given that: (i) access tokens can have a long lifetime; and (ii) a malicious agent can perform a *record-now-decrypt-later-attack* with a quantum computer using Grover's algorithm [5]; the probability of guessing a token must be reduced to less than 2^{-256} and preferably less than 2^{-320} to account for quantum attackers.

Transporting tokens via OAuth 2.0 and OIDC requires the use of the TLS protocol. At the time of writing, the most recent version of TLS is 1.3, which is also vulnerable to quantum attacks. In the context of TLS, there are three major concerns about quantum attackers. First, the minimum block size for symmetric encryption in AES is 128 bits, which is vulnerable to Grover's algorithm and must be increased to 256 bits in order to maintain the same level of security. Second, TLS authenticates the server and, if mutual authentication is enabled, the client using x509 digital certificates. Since the authenticity of digital certificates is dependent on digital signatures and Shor's algorithm [31] poses a threat to IFP, DLP, and ECDLP-based signature algorithms such as RSA and ECDSA, quantum-safe signature schemes must be utilized instead. Third, TLS employs KEX mechanisms such as DHE and ECDHE to derive symmetric keys and for Forward Secrecy. However, these mechanisms are vulnerable to Shor's algorithm and must therefore be replaced with quantum-safe alternatives.

Quantum attackers also pose a threat to the JWT family of specifications. The JSON Web Encryption (JWE) [15] and JSON Web Signature (JWS) [12] standards describe, respectively, how to encrypt and sign JWTs. Although token encryption is not required by OAuth 2.0 or OIDC, 256-bit AES must be used to achieve 128-bit security against quantum attackers if it is used. JWE implementations must support both 128-bit and 256-bit AES block sizes [10], in general, not a significant issue. Additionally, the same flaws that affect x509 signatures also affect JWT signatures. Consequently, PQ signature algorithms are required.

To successfully communicate, both IdP and RP must support PQ signature algorithms in their TLS and JWT implementations. Unlike TLS, where the handshake is terminated if client and server support different signature algorithms, in OIDC the "signing party MUST select a signature algorithm based on the algorithms supported by the recipient" [27]. Thus, we propose replacing "MUST" with "MAY" to allow the signing party to refrain from signing a JWT with an insecure signature algorithm if the recipient does not support PQ signature.

Finally, it is critical to consider the implications of increasing symmetric encryption block and key sizes, as well as replacing KEX and signature algorithms with quantum-resistant alternatives. At the time of writing, the NIST standardization process was not completed. Nonetheless, the finalists' KEX and signature algorithms have larger key and signature sizes than elliptic curve solutions. As a result, identity architects and implementers must be aware of the additional requirements for storing and transporting PQ-JWTs in PQ-TLS. To that end, we empirically evaluate the NIST's final signature algorithms in a real-world OAuth 2.0 and OIDC implementation with PQ-TLS, as described below.

5 Empirical Evaluation

5.1 Case Study

Although the three-party authorization handshake is emphasized in scientific and non-scientific literature, it represents only a portion of the interactions that occur when a real RP consumes user data from an IdP. Figure 4 depicts the entirety of our scenario, which includes the following interactions.

The first set of interactions is identified by the dotted rectangle with a capital letter A in the upper-right corner. As stated previously, an RP must first determine the URLs of an OIDC provider's endpoints. The OIDC-D [28] specification defines `/.well-known/openid-configuration` for this specific purpose. In response to an HTTP `GET` request to this resource, the IdP returns a JSON containing its endpoints. Figure 4 depicts the endpoints returned by the IdP that are subsequently utilized. The RP then accesses the `jwks_uri` returned in the previous step to obtain the public keys used to sign the tokens.

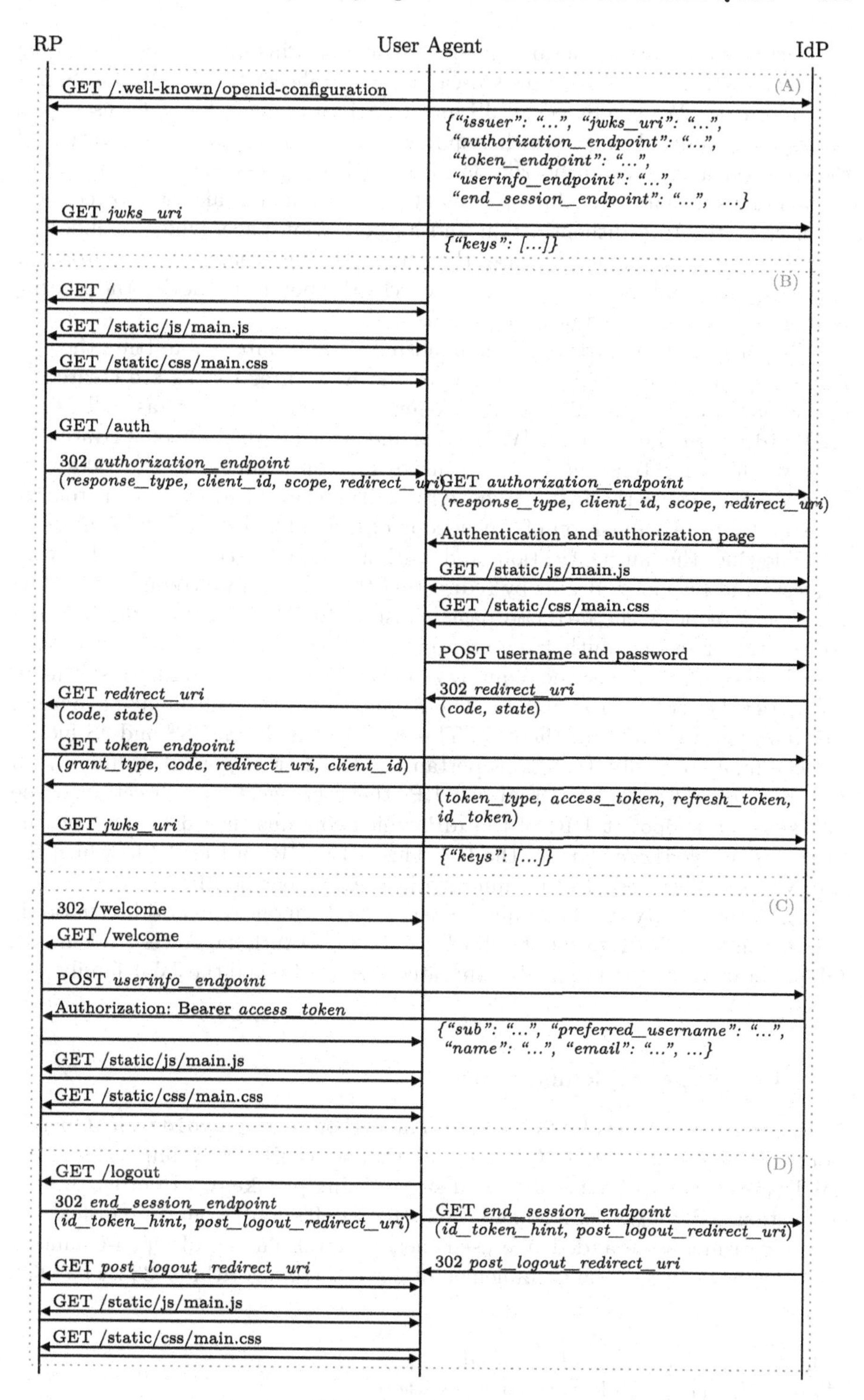

Fig. 4. The realistic evaluation scenario.

The second set of interactions, referred to as B, begins with the user accessing the RP's main page, which uses Cascading Style Sheets (CSS) and JavaScript (JS) resources. We combined all JS and CSS into a single file. The user then accesses a protected page, which requires identification and authentication of the end user as well as authorization for the RP to access their personal information. This initiates the three-party authorization handshake, which redirects the user to the IdP authentication and authorization page, which includes its own CSS and JS resources. The user then enters their username and password for authentication and, on the same page, checks the box to authorize the sharing of their nickname, full name, and e-mail.

The back-channel portion of the handshake begins after submitting the correct information and being redirected to the RP. Three tokens are created in our scenario: the OAuth 2.0 `access_token` and `refresh_token`, as well as the OIDC `id_token`. They are all JWT-based and signed with the same private key. It is worth noting that the RP then makes a second request to the `jwks_uri`. This occurs because the IdP may have rotated the keys used to sign the tokens, necessitating the acquisition of a new copy of the public key currently in use.

Following the authentication and authorization dance, the third set of requests and responses begins by redirecting the user to a welcoming page. The user agent requests the `welcome` page, causing the RP to contact the IdP and request the previously authorized user data. The RP incorporates the previously issued `access_token` into the request, which is validated by the IdP, resulting in the retrieval of the requested data. The RP assembles the welcoming page using this data and returns it to the user. This page also includes CSS and JS files.

The final group of interactions pertains to the user's logout. Beginning with the user requesting logout from the RP, the user agent is redirected to the `end_session_endpoint` URI of the IdP, which contains the `id_token`, and the `post_logout_redirect_uri` of the RP. This is the URI of the RP to which the user will be redirected after terminating her session on the IdP.

There are twenty two GET and POST requests in our real-world scenario. It is build on top of OAuth 2.0 [6], JWT Profile for OAuth 2.0 Access Tokens [4], OIDC core [27], discovery [28], RP-Initiated Logout [14] and the JWT family [10–13,15].

5.2 Prototype Implementation

We implemented the evaluation scenario in Python 3 using `pyoidc`[1], an OpenID Foundation-certified OIDC Core, OIDC-D, and OIDC-DCR implementation. JWTs are assembled, encrypted, and signed using `pyjwkest`[2]. In order to have a functional PQ-OIDC implementation, the NIST's fourt round finalist signature algorithms were added. We used the Python 3 binding of Open-Quantum Safe (OQS) to access the C implementation of these algorithms [33]. The OQS

[1] https://github.com/OpenIDC/pyoidc.
[2] https://github.com/IdentityPython/pyjwkest.

project also provides a modified `libssl` containing the PQ-KEX and PQ signing algorithms, which our Python implementation employs for PQ-TLS. Our implementation and empirical evaluation are embedded within Docker containers, making it simple to reproduce our experiments. The source code for our implementation and experiments is open-source and publicly available[3].

5.3 Experiment Plan

The experiment entails evaluating the size of messages exchanged and the elapsed time for pre-quantum and post-quantum KEX and signature algorithms in the previously described evaluation scenario on servers with increasing geographical distance. Let us concentrate on the impact of size on PQ algorithms. Except for cryptographic objects, the content of messages exchanged in our scenario remains constant, allowing us to create an estimate of the impact of cryptographic objects in pre-quantum and post-quantum OIDC. The overall cost $OIDC^{size}$, in bytes, can be defined as shown in Eq. 1.

$$\begin{aligned} OIDC^{size} = & N_{TLS} * (TLS^{size}_{KEX} + TLS^{size}_{Auth}) + \\ & N_{JWT} * JWT^{size}_{Sig} + \\ & N_{JWK} * JWK^{size}_{PK} \end{aligned} \quad (1)$$

Where N_{TLS} is the number of TLS Handshakes; TLS^{size}_{KEX} refers to the size of the TLS `ClientHello` and `ServerHello` messages; TLS^{size}_{Auth} corresponds to the size of TLS authentication considering handshake signature and certificates; N_{JWT} is the number of JWTs exchanged and JWT^{size}_{Sig} is the size of the signature present in each JWT; N_{JWK} is the number of public keys stored in JWKs exchanged in the scenario, and JWK^{size}_{PK} the size of those keys.

It is important to note that for TLS authentication, we incorporate the Certificate Authority (CA) intermediate and root certificates. Also, to better reflect real-world settings, the server certificate incorporates Signed Certificate Timestamps, a standard for publicly reporting TLS server certificates as they are issued or observed for the sake of auditing CAs' activity [18]. In addition, due to TLS connection resumption across peers, not all TLS handshakes in the real world have identical sizes. To simulate the worst-case scenario, however, we perform a new TLS handshake for each of the $N_{TLS} = 22$ connections. Consequently, this model provides an upper bound for the expected cost (in terms of size) for OIDC scenarios. Furthermore, N_{JWK} is 2 as there are two calls for the `jwks_uri`, and N_{JWT} is 8: the IdP issues one `access_token`, one `refresh_token`, and one `id_token` that are sent to the RP; the RP then sends the `access_token` to consume the `userinfo_endpoint`; and the request to `/logout` and the following redirect results in the exchange of the `id_token` four times.

Table 3 shows configurations used in each experiment, as well as the expected costs, in bytes. The first two rows show the experiments where classical cryptography is in use, while the following rows compose the post-quantum evaluations.

[3] https://github.com/fredericoschardong/post-quantum-oidc-oauth2.

We estimate the costs of the cryptographic objects present in each TLS handshake (second and fourth columns), as well as the JWT and JWK (fifth and sixth columns), which include a digital signature and the public key. Unlike the TLS handshake, which occurs for all twenty-two requests in our scenario, the JWT and JWK parts are present in some messages, as described above.

Table 3. Algorithm configurations with expected costs in terms of size

TLS_{KEX}	TLS_{KEX}^{size}	TLS_{Auth} JWT_{Sign}	TLS_{Auth}^{size}	JWT_{Sig}^{size}	JWK_{PK}^{size}	$OIDC^{size}$
ECDHE	626	ECDSA	1563	64	64	48798
		RSA 2048	3309	256	256	89130
Kyber512	1976	Dilithium 2	19419	2420	1312	492674
		Dilithium 3	26576	3293	1952	658392
		Dilithium 5	36309	4595	2592	884214
		Falcon-512	7541	690	897	216688
		Falcon-1024	13919	1330	1793	363916
		SPHINCS+128	103553	17088	32	2458406
		SPHINCS+192	215166	35664	48	5062532
		SPHINCS+256	316869	49856	64	2458406

We selected ECDHE and Kyber512 for the pre-quantum and post-quantum TLS KEX, respectively. ECDHE p256 is standardized and Kyber is the finalist of the NIST Round 4 standardization process. As we can see in Table 3, TLS authentication have a significant impact, and so we compared two commonly-used classical algorithms (ECDSA p256 and RSA2048) against three post-quantum (Falcon, SPHINCS+, and Dilithium), the latter are going to be standardized by NIST. For simplicity, the same algorithm is used for TLS authentication and JWT Signature. The overall cost is increased in the post-quantum scenarios. Regarding SPHINCS+, we selected SHAKE256 as hash function, due to the overall performance without considering hardware optimizations; and with `fast-simple` parameter set, also focusing on performance (please refer to [2] for additional information).

5.4 Experimental Results

We ran the realistic scenario a thousand times for each algorithm configuration described in Table 3 on Amazon EC2 t2.micro instances with 1 vCPU and 1 GB of RAM in five distinct locations and collected data. We begin by outlining the timings for each algorithm option. Figure 5 depicts the results of all scenarios examined, highlighting the timings of TLS handshakes in relation to the entire OIDC time. When network latencies increase between scenarios, we can see distinct behavior. Post-quantum algorithms benefit from low latencies, achieving similar (or even greater) performance than classical algorithms. When considerable latencies are present (140ms, 225ms, and 320ms scenarios),

RSA and ECDSA perform better. The increased size of PQC algorithms has a severe impact on network performance, frequently requiring additional round trips to convey data, particularly at the TCP level due to congestion management techniques. When post-quantum methods are tested at the same latency, the total duration varies little between Dilithium and Falcon, but significantly with SPHINCS+. We can also see that TLS costs account for a large portion of total time, particularly in PQC configurations.

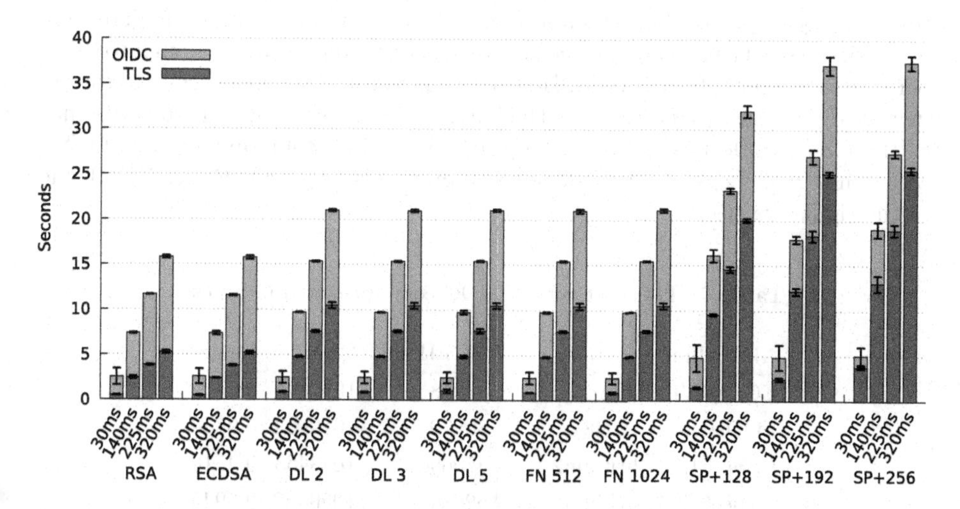

Fig. 5. Average OIDC and TLS timings for various latency settings.

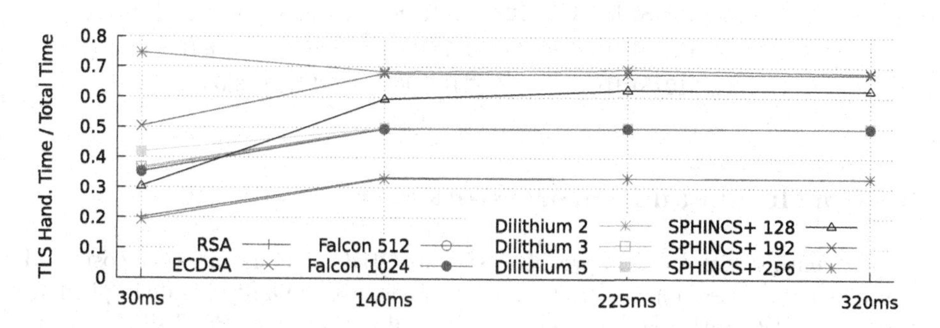

Fig. 6. The ratio between TLS handshake and overall OIDC time.

Figure 6 depicts a new perspective on TLS costs. It displays the average TLS handshake time in relation to the average total time, allowing us to compare the PQC and conventional algorithms. The ratio for Falcon and Dilithium is approximately 50% on the 140ms, 225ms and 320ms scenarios. This finding implies that enhancing TLS handshake may result in improved OIDC overall performance.

Finally, Table 4 compares the costs in terms of bytes of the 22 TLS handshakes (KEX and Authentication) to the application payloads (including HTML, CSS, and JS content, as well as JWT and JWK sizes). It is evident that the larger application size sizes (about 1 MB) contribute to obfuscating the distinctions between PQC instances (with different parameter sets). On the other hand, when these costs are compared to the traditional techniques, the slowdowns are considerably more visible, as seen in Fig. 5. This is an interesting finding: despite increasing security parameters, the cost did not rise considerably enough to cause performance issues (from 1 to 5). However, our SPHINCS+ instances excessively increased the sizes, which explains the longer timings (Fig. 5). This suggests that SPHINCS+ should not be the first option for all TLS components (*e.g.*, OCSP Stappling, SCT Logs) or TLS-dependent protocols (*e.g.* OAuth 2, OIDC) due to the signature size.

Table 4. TLS cost versus OIDC cost, measured in bytes.

Algorithm	TLS Hand.	OIDC	Ratio
ECDHE/ECDSA	48158	1017405	0.0473
ECDHE/RSA2048	86570	1019903	0.0848
Kyber512/Dilithium2	470690	1043463	0.4510
Kyber512/Dilithium3	628144	1056528	0.5945
Kyber512/Dilithium5	842270	1072090	0.7856
Kyber512/Falcon512	209374	1025579	0.2041
Kyber512/Falcon1024	349690	1034530	0.3380
Kyber512/SPHINCS+128	2321638	1857118	1.2501
Kyber512/SPHINCS+192	4777124	2182244	2.1891
Kyber512/SPHINCS+256	7014590	2314753	3.0304

6 Conclusion and Future Works

Experimenting with PQC in protocols such as OIDC demonstrates the costs and consequences of its adoption. In this paper, we assess a Quantum-safe implementation of OIDC with realistic scenarios, including the use of PQC signatures in JWT tokens and post-quantum TLS as the underlying security protocol.

In our study of a realistic scenario, we demonstrated that the quantity and complexity of requests to use OIDC exceeds the three-party handshake established in OAuth 2.0. Nonetheless, we successfully incorporated PQC into the proposed OIDC study case, and the experiments demonstrated that the network has a considerable impact on performance. Our PQC implementation in lower latencies has demonstrated competitive performance against RSA and ECDSA.

Consequently, our empirical evaluation has demonstrated that PQC algorithms do not decrease OIDC performance in such scenarios. However, when latency increases, we discovered substantial performance issues, primarily owing to the increased size of PQC objects exchanged between the parties involved. Surprisingly, we found no significant variations in performance between PQC algorithms of varying security levels when comparing conventional to PQC methods.

We discovered that the TLS cost in OIDC constitutes a considerable portion of the costs, both in terms of time and size, particularly when network latencies are greater. Since we simulated actual setups (*e.g.*, SCTs and OCSP Stappling in certificates), we conclude that our findings provide an upper bound on TLS costs when evaluating it as a drop-in replacement for PQC in OIDC.

The scope of this work allows for several other areas of research to be pursued in the future. For example, we examine a PQC-only deployment, but another option may be hybrid PQC, which employs both PQC and classical algorithms. Using hybrids in OIDC would necessitate their deployment in TLS and JWT, the latter of which will almost certainly encounter compatibility challenges due to its list of authorized methods. Furthermore, certain techniques, such as KEMTLS [29], try to reduce the TLS costs of PQC. If TLS costs are reduced, performance benefits in PQ-OIDC can be expected.

References

1. Alkhulaifi, A., El-Alfy, E.S.M.: Exploring lattice-based post-quantum signature for JWT authentication: review and case study. In: 2020 IEEE 91st Vehicular Technology Conference (VTC2020-Spring), pp. 1–5 (2020). https://doi.org/10.1109/VTC2020-Spring48590.2020.9129505
2. Aumasson, J.P., et al.: Sphincs+: submission to the NIST post-quantum project (2021). https://sphincs.org/data/sphincs+-r3.1-specification.pdf
3. Berbecaru, D., Lioy, A.: On the robustness of applications based on the SSL and TLS security protocols. In: Lopez, J., Samarati, P., Ferrer, J.L. (eds.) EuroPKI 2007. LNCS, vol. 4582, pp. 248–264. Springer, Heidelberg (2007). https://doi.org/10.1007/978-3-540-73408-6_18
4. Bertocci, V.: JSON Web Token (JWT) Profile for OAuth 2.0 Access Tokens. RFC 9068 (2021)
5. Grover, L.K.: A fast quantum mechanical algorithm for database search. In: Proceedings of the 28th ACM Symposium on Theory of Computing, pp. 212–219 (1996)
6. Hardt, D.: The OAuth 2.0 Authorization Framework. RFC 6749 (2012)
7. Howe, J., Prest, T., Apon, D.: Sok: How (not) to design and implement post-quantum cryptography. Cryptology ePrint Archive, report 2021/462 (2021). https://ia.cr/2021/462
8. (IANA), I.A.N.A.: Transport layer security (TLS) parameters (2022)
9. Johansson, L.: An IANA Registry for Level of Assurance (LoA) Profiles. RFC 6711 (2012)
10. Jones, M.: JSON Web Algorithms (JWA). RFC 7518 (2015)
11. Jones, M.: JSON Web Key (JWK). RFC 7517 (2015)
12. Jones, M., Bradley, J., Sakimura, N.: JSON Web Signature (JWS). RFC 7515 (2015)

13. Jones, M., Bradley, J., Sakimura, N.: JSON Web Token (JWT). RFC 7519 (2015)
14. Jones, M., De Medeiros, B., Agarwal, N., Sakimura, N., Bradley, J.: Openid connect RP-initiated logout 1.0. The OpenID Foundation, p. S3 (2022)
15. Jones, M., Hildebrand, J.: JSON Web Encryption (JWE). RFC 7516 (2015)
16. Jones, M., Sakimura, N., Bradley, J.: OAuth 2.0 Authorization Server Metadata. RFC 8414 (2018)
17. Keele, S., et al.: Guidelines for performing systematic literature reviews in software engineering. Technical report (2007)
18. Laurie, B., Langley, A., Kasper, E., Messeri, E., Stradling, R.: Certificate Transparency Version 2.0. RFC 9162 (2021)
19. Lodderstedt, T., Bradley, J., Labunets, A., Fett, D.: OAuth 2.0 Security Best Current Practice. Internet-Draft 20, Internet Engineering Task Force (2022)
20. Lodderstedt, T., McGloin, M., Hunt, P.: OAuth 2.0 Threat Model and Security Considerations. RFC 6819 (2013)
21. NIST: Post-quantum cryptography (2016). https://csrc.nist.gov/Projects/Post-Quantum-Cryptography. Accessed 26 June 2021
22. Paquin, C., Stebila, D., Tamvada, G.: Benchmarking post-quantum cryptography in TLS. In: Ding, J., Tillich, J.-P. (eds.) PQCrypto 2020. LNCS, vol. 12100, pp. 72–91. Springer, Cham (2020). https://doi.org/10.1007/978-3-030-44223-1_5
23. Petersen, K., Vakkalanka, S., Kuzniarz, L.: Guidelines for conducting systematic mapping studies in software engineering: an update. Inf. Softw. Technol. **64**, 1–18 (2015)
24. Rescorla, E.: The Transport Layer Security (TLS) Protocol Version 1.3. RFC 8446, August 2018. https://doi.org/10.17487/RFC8446
25. Sakimura, N., Bradley, J., Agarwal, N.: Proof Key for Code Exchange by OAuth Public Clients. RFC 7636 (2015)
26. Sakimura, N., Bradley, J., Jones, M.: OpenID connect dynamic client registration. The OpenID Foundation, p. S3 (2014)
27. Sakimura, N., Bradley, J., Jones, M., De Medeiros, B., Mortimore, C.: OpenID connect core 1.0. The OpenID Foundation, p. S3 (2014)
28. Sakimura, N., Bradley, J., Jones, M., Jay, E.: OpenID connect discovery. The OpenID Foundation, p. S3 (2014)
29. Schwabe, P., Stebila, D., Wiggers, T.: Post-Quantum TLS Without Handshake Signatures, pp. 1461–1480. Association for Computing Machinery, New York, NY, USA (2020). https://doi.org/10.1145/3372297.3423350
30. Schwabe, P., Stebila, D., Wiggers, T.: More efficient post-quantum KEMTLS with pre-distributed public keys. In: Bertino, E., Shulman, H., Waidner, M. (eds.) ESORICS 2021. LNCS, vol. 12972, pp. 3–22. Springer, Cham (2021). https://doi.org/10.1007/978-3-030-88418-5_1
31. Shor, P.W.: Algorithms for quantum computation: discrete logarithms and factoring. In: Proceedings 35th Annual Symposium on Foundations of Computer Science, pp. 124–134. IEEE, Santa Fe, NM, USA (1994). https://doi.org/10.1109/SFCS.1994.365700
32. Sikeridis, D., Kampanakis, P., Devetsikiotis, M.: Assessing the overhead of post-quantum cryptography in TLS 1.3 and SSH. In: Proceedings of the 16th International Conference on emerging Networking EXperiments and Technologies, pp. 149–156. Association for Computing Machinery, New York, NY, USA (2020)
33. Stebila, D., Mosca, M.: Post-quantum key exchange for the internet and the open quantum safe project. In: Avanzi, R., Heys, H. (eds.) SAC 2016. LNCS, vol. 10532, pp. 14–37. Springer, Cham (2017). https://doi.org/10.1007/978-3-319-69453-5_2

Author Index

Alquié, Didier 245
Aly, Abdelrahaman 44
Astrizi, Thiago Leucz 339

Baghery, Karim 23
Bardeh, Navid Ghaedi 23
Barthoulot, Anaïs 143
Beresford, Alastair R. 314
Blazy, Olivier 143

Canard, Sébastien 143
Chan, Kwan Yin 89
Chassé, Guy 245
Chen, Shaozhen 203
Ciampi, Michele 3
Conti, Mauro 329
Custódio, Ricardo 339, 371

Faonio, Antonio 122

Gangwal, Ankit 329
Gao, Yuan 258
Giron, Alexandre Augusto 371
Guo, Chun 258

Hou, Zezhou 203

Javeed, Arsalan 188

Krzywiecki, Łukasz 225

Levy-dit-Vehel, Françoise 361
Li, Manman 203
Lin, Dongdong 203

Mandal, Kalikinkar 279
Müller, Fernanda Larisa 371
Murthy, Shyam 167

Nawaz, Kashif 44
Neef, Sebastian 71
Nitaj, Abderrahmane 245

Roméas, Maxime 361

Saavedra, Luis A. 314
Salazar, Eugenio 44
Salin, Hannes 225
Savas, Erkay 188
Schardong, Frederico 371
Soleimanian, Azam 292
Soriente, Claudio 122
Sucasas, Victor 44

Truong, Hien Thi Thu 122

Unal, Musa Sadik 188

Valluri, Rahul 329
Vasco, Maria Isabel Gonzalez 122
Visconti, Ivan 3
Vivek, Srinivas 167

Wisiol, Nils 71

Yilmaz, Cemal 188
Yuen, Tsz Hon 89

Printed in the United States
by Baker & Taylor Publisher Services